Dear instructors,

As the authors of this book, we'd like to take a moment to introduce you to *Introduction to Criminal Justice: A Balanced Approach*.

If you're like us, you receive several introductory textbooks to consider at the beginning of each semester. Why did we decide to add one more? We felt students would benefit from a balanced, student-centered learning experience. We also felt providing students with a strong research and theory base that includes the issues currently facing criminal justice professionals would be instrumental in their long-term success.

Let us explain what we mean by balanced. First, we set out to give equal treatment to each of the three components of the criminal justice system: law enforcement, courts, and corrections. Second, within each section we include three chapters. The first chapter introduces students to the component, the second chapter looks at how the process functions, and a final chapter provides a deeper analysis of the issues facing each area. Third, we've made considerable efforts to address controversies and issues in criminal justice from an objective standpoint. Crime and criminals are not defined as inherently bad or evil, nor are traditional responses to crime. Instead, we want students to approach the study of criminal justice with an open mind. In doing so, students will identify the complexities confronting criminal justice professionals.

That leads to the goal of creating a student-centered approach which asks students to see criminal justice as a collection of individuals formally charged with controlling the behavior of others. Their decisions matter. Beyond recognizing criminal justice as a "collection of individuals," we also stress to students that they will someday be one of those individuals given the responsibility for responding to crime. With emphasis in the text and pedagogical tools such as "College Students and Criminal Justice" and "Ethical Decision Making" boxes, we hope to draw students into the importance of choice and action.

We accomplish these goals using our diverse research and professional strengths to our advantage. Will is a former police officer, Nancy studies the courts from a criminal justice and political science background, and Brian, the former president of ACJS, focuses his research on corrections, punishment strategies, and white-collar crime. Together, we offer students a practical and empirical basis for understanding the criminal justice system.

We hope you find our balanced and student-focused orientation to *Introduction to Criminal Justice* useful.

All best,

Brian Payne, Will Oliver, and Nancy Marion

Finding BALANCE

FOUNDATIONS *of* CRIMINAL JUSTICE

BALANCE OF CONTENT

The authors give equal attention to the major topics related to criminal justice instead of privileging one area of the justice process, successfully balancing the foundations with the three parts of the criminal justice system—policing, courts, and corrections.

BALANCE OF ISSUES AND PERSPECTIVES

Alongside the chapters on policing, corrections, and courts, the authors added unique chapters covering Issues in Policing, Corrections, and Courts, which takes students beyond theory and into practice.

BALANCE OF RESEARCH AND THEORY

Strong coverage of both criminal justice research and theory prepares students to think analytically about the causes of crime and how they relate to criminal justice policies and evidence-based solutions.

> **"I appreciate the balanced approach as well as the dilemmas that are present at the end of each section."**
>
> —Mia Green, Bridgewater State University

> **"I feel the writing style is very much in line with that of an introductory course. It is easy to understand and written in a way that students would find interesting. Balanced and articulate."**
>
> —Jennifer Riggs, Eastern New Mexico University

Crime as a Product of Choice	Crime as a Product of Biological Factors	Crime as a Product of Social Factors	Crime as a Product of Social Psychological Factors	Crime as a Product of Cognitive Processes
Classical School of Thought	Positive School of Thought	Social Disorganization Theory	Life Course Theory	Differential Association Theory
Deterrence Theory	Evolutionary Theory	Subcultural Theories	General Strain Theory	Differential Reinforcement Theory
Rational Choice Theory	Biosocial Theory	Conflict Theory	Social Control Theory	Neutralization Theory
Routine Activities Theory	Neurological Theory	Social Strain Theory	Self-Control Theory	Labeling Theory

Making DECISIONS

POLICING
COURTS
CORRECTIONS

Ethical Decision Making boxes present an ethical scenario that criminal justice professionals or students might confront to encourage students to critically think through the potential ramifications of their decisions.

ETHICAL DECISION MAKING

The following case involves the death of a prison nurse. Read the description provided by the Occupational Safety and Health Administration and answer the questions that follow:

On the afternoon of October 25, 2010, Employee#1, a 55-year-old female prison nurse, was treating inmates for alcohol withdrawal at a county detention facility. As medications were being administered, one of the inmates grabbed an unsecured metal desk lamp and violently struck the nurse in the head. The severely injured nurse slumped to the floor and was rushed to a nearby hospital, where she was immediately place on emergency life support. She died from her injuries three days later.

YOU DECIDE

1. Based on the information provided, what are the reasons you would or would not support the death penalty in this case?

2. Should the prison be held liable on any level for the inmate's behavior?

Source: Occupational Safety and Health Administration. (n.d.). Inmate strikes and fatally injures prison nurse. Retrieved from https://www.osha.gov/pls/imis/accidentsearch.accident_detail?id=202507927

"Ethical Decision Making should always be a part of the curriculum, as it helps the students to think outside a 'black and white' world."

—Deborah Woodward,
University of Central Florida

Criminal Justice Pioneer boxes highlight important decisions these pioneers made that led to important contributions to the field.

"[Pioneer Boxes] help provide a special look at an individual who helped shape the criminal justice system. These will encourage students to look at the history and life of this individual."

—Christopher Salvatore, Montclair State University

WILLIAM BRATTON

CRIMINAL JUSTICE PIONEER

William "Bill" Bratton was born on October 6, 1947, and has had a storied career in American policing. After serving briefly in the Military Police during the Vietnam War, Bratton became a police officer in his hometown of Boston, Massachusetts. He rose quickly through the ranks to the police department's second-highest rank before becoming the Boston Metro police chief. Then he took a similar position with the New York City Transit Police before returning home as the superintendent in chief of the Boston Police Department. From there he was hired by the New York City Police Department (NYPD) to be its chief (1994–1996), he then served as the Los Angeles Police Department chief (2002–2009), and finally he was asked to return to the NYPD (2014–). He has been a reform-minded chief, often coming into police departments during troubled times, fixing many of the problems, and leaving them better than when he arrived. He has also been a lightning rod for controversy, especially when he began implementing such programs as broken windows policing or zero-tolerance policing. His implementation of CompStat was and remains quite controversial, and each time he has had to deal with the many issues covered in this chapter, he has been a focus of many hot-button issues in policing. Despite all of that, he has been honored with numerous awards, has been asked to consult with police departments all over the world, and has led three of the most renowned police departments in the United States.

STUDENT Centered

Students have roles in and make decisions about the criminal justice system. **Introduction to Criminal Justice** provides students with those connections and roles.

College Students and Criminal Justice boxes solidify criminal justice concepts by asking students to relate to something about their own lives to criminal justice.

Criminal Justice and the Media boxes look at applications and the interplay of the media, including social media, within the criminal justice system.

CRIMINAL JUSTICE and COLLEGE STUDENTS

CREATING CRIMINAL JUSTICE SURVEYS

On any given day, you likely ask many different questions of those around you. Have you ever realized that you can ask questions in a way that lead individuals to certain answers? For example, imagine asking a friend how much he or she likes your new shirt. Here are three possible ways you could ask the question: (a) Do you like my shirt? (b) How much do you like my shirt? or (c) Don't you like my shirt?

All three questions aim for the same information, but how the [...] results. When asking

questions about criminal justice, crime, and victimization, researchers use caution to make sure that the questions themselves do not lead respondents to specific answers.

With regard to crime, think of three different ways you might ask someone if he or she has ever committed a specific crime. Next, in small groups or as a class, discuss the various ways that you might ask individuals about their criminal behavior. What factors might lead individuals to be dishonest in answering these kinds of questions? Are there things that researchers can do to encourage accurate reporting?

CRIMINAL JUSTICE and the MEDIA:
FACEBOOK AS A CRIMINAL JUSTICE RESEARCH TOOL

Many of you likely have Facebook pages that you use to keep in touch with dozens, if not hundreds, of your friends on a regular basis. It probably does not take a scientist to tell you that some people often post fairly private information on their Facebook pages. Social scientists have, in fact, explored Facebook postings of criminal justice students. In particular, criminologists Jeff Lee and Angela Largess reviewed the Facebook postings of college students enrolled in a criminal justice program. What they found was somewhat surprising and troubling. Pictures of the students

appearing to be inebriated, possibly using drugs, and passed out on their floor were among the postings found. In this case, the researchers were able to ask their research questions and answer them by reviewing publicly available records. What would researchers learn if they reviewed your Facebook page?

Source: Lee, J., & Largess, A. (2010). What were you thinking? Criminal justice students and their social networking sites. Presented at the Georgia Political Science Association annual meeting, November 11.

> "I really liked the **College Students and Criminal Justice** boxed feature. I found it helpful and think the students will really enjoy it."
>
> —Jamie Snyder, John C. Calhoun State Community College

> "Media has always played a role in shaping public opinion, so these boxed features are also important in allowing the student to understand the role of the media in the criminal justice system. "
>
> —James M. Stewart, Calhoun Community College

> "**Criminal Justice and the Media** is also a beneficial section, as the students need to be able to recognize and understand the role that media plays to the benefit (or detriment) to the criminal justice system."
>
> —Deborah Woodward, University of Central Florida

"This textbook bridges empirically based facts born from research with current news and events on issues of crime and justice to make for an accessible, informative resource for students of all levels."

—Nancy G. La Vigne, Director, Justice Policy Center, Urban Institute

Admissible or Inadmissible Evidence pre-tests ask students to read a list of statements at the beginning of each chapter and determine if its "admissible" (true) or "inadmissible" (false) as a strategy for improving the student's understanding of the material. Students are directed to the back of the book for answers.

Beyond a Reasonable Doubt concepts checks assess the student's understanding of relevant concepts.

ADMISSIBLE or INADMISSIBLE Evidence.

Read the statements that follow. If the statement is true, circle *admissible*. If the statement is false, circle *inadmissible*.

1. **Admissible   Inadmissible**   Inmates give up their right to reasonable health care when sentenced to prison.
2. **Admissible   Inadmissible**   Recent data show that the rate of AIDS-related deaths is lower in prisons than in the community.
3. **Admissible   Inadmissible**   Research shows that females on electronic monitoring experience the sanction differently than males do.
4. **Admissible   Inadmissible**   It is believed that corrections officers engage in more corruption than other criminal justice officials.
5. **Admissible   Inadmissible**   Some states still authorize the use of the firing squad as a death penalty method.
6. **Admissible   Inadmissible**   Federal laws require that juveniles be punished in the same way as adults.
7. **Admissible   Inadmissible**   The brutalization perspective suggests that putting violent offenders to death increases victimization for community members.
8. **Admissible   Inadmissible**   According to restorative justice principles, offenders must be punished for the public good.

──── BEYOND A REASONABLE DOUBT 14.1 ────

Which Supreme Court case gave prisoners the right to challenge prison rules, policies, and procedures?

(a) *Cooper v. Pate*, (b) *Miranda v. Arizona*, (c) *Gideon v. Wainwright*, (d) *Escobedo v. Illinois*, (e) none of the above

HELP WANTED: DRUG ABUSE TREATMENT SPECIALIST

DUTIES:

- The incumbent provides individual and group counseling/therapy to inmates with drug abuse problems within the Bureau of Prison's treatment framework. He or she is also responsible for the education of prison staff about drug abuse, drug abuse treatment, and the local prison program.

- The incumbent administers eligibility and psychosocial assessments as the basis for individual treatment planning. The incumbent is responsible for providing residential and/or nonresidential treatment to offenders who volunteer for treatment and are diagnosed with a drug use disorder.

- Along with all other correctional institution employees, the incumbent is charged with responsibility for maintaining security of the institution. The staff's correctional responsibilities precede all others required by this position and are performed on a regular and recurring basis.

REQUIREMENTS: Bachelor's degree

ANNUAL SALARY: $52,830–$80,414

Source: Adapted from USAJOBS.gov. Retrieved from https://www.usajobs.gov/GetJob/ViewDetails/367347200

Help Wanted boxes in each chapter highlight a specific job related to the topic addressed to demonstrate the connection the chapter discussion has with careers in criminal justice.

"I think it is incredibly important to give students a basic understanding of what they can do with their degree. We need all the help we can get in this arena. Setting expectations is incredibly important."

—David Khey,
Loyola University New Orleans

LEARNING Solutions

Interactive eBook also available—**FREE** when bundled with the print version!

This dynamic Interactive eBook goes way beyond highlighting and note-taking! Your students can read their mobile-friendly eBook anywhere, anytime with **easy access across desktop, smartphone, and tablet devices.** Using the VitalSource Bookshelf® platform, students can **download the book to a personal computer** and read it offline, **share notes and highlights with instructors and classmates** who are using the same eBook, and **"follow" friends and instructors as they make their own notes and highlights.** By simply clicking on icons in the eBook, your students can experience a broad array of integrated multimedia resources.

VIDEO
Hot Spot Policing

JOURNALS
Capturing Crime

AUTHOR VIDEO
The Importance of Theory

CAREER VIDEO
Jail Adminsrator

FEATURE VIDEO
Death Row Exonerees Discuss Time in Prison

Video–Relevant interviews, lectures, personal stories, inquiries, animated graphics, and other clips bring deeper learning and understanding as you explore key topics.

Journal–Access to articles from SAGE's influential journals, such as *Crime and Delinquency, Theoretical Criminology, Criminal Justice Review*, and more, offer important background and exposure to seminal work in your field of study.

Author Video–Original videos showcase authors Brian K. Payne, Willard M. Oliver, and Nancy E. Marion, introducing each chapter and giving students insight into tough concepts.

Career Video–Interviews with criminal justice professionals discussing their day-to-day work and current issues related to technology, diversity, and cutting-edge developments in their field are available.

Feature Video–Exclusive interviews with three death row exonerees sharing their experiences regarding the trial process, prison, and reentry.

"Witness to Innocence" exonerees share their story in exclusive SAGE video.

BUNDLE OPTION

Instructors: Bundle the **Interactive eBook** for Payne's *Introduction to Criminal Justice* with the print book at no additional cost to your students. Learn more about this bundle by visiting **sagepub.com** or calling **1.800.818.7243**.

ISBN: 978-1-5063-1577-5

TEACHING Solutions

SAGE edge select for Instructors supports teaching with quality content and a rich learning environment for students, featuring:

- ➡ Course Management System integration to make it easy for student test results to seamlessly flow into instructor gradebooks.

- ➡ Test banks built on Bloom's Taxonomy to provide a diverse range of test items with Respondus test generation.

- ➡ Sample course syllabi with suggested models for structuring one's course.

- ➡ Editable, chapter-specific PowerPoint® slides that offer flexibility when creating multimedia lectures.

- ➡ EXCLUSIVE access to full-text SAGE journal articles to expose students to important research and scholarship tied to chapter concepts.

- ➡ Video and multimedia content that enhance student engagement and appeal to different learning styles.

- ➡ All instructor material and tools which are easily integrated through a Course cartridge.

SAGE edgeselect™

BUNDLE OPTION

Instructors: Bundle **SAGE edge select** for Payne's *Introduction to Criminal Justice* with the print book at no additional cost to your students. Learn more about this bundle by visiting **sagepub.com** or calling **1.800.818.7243**.

ISBN: 978-15063-1699-4

Instructors,

Sign in at **edge.sagepub.com/payne** or contact your sales representative to access your password-protected account.

INTRODUCTION TO CRIMINAL JUSTICE

To my family—Kathleen (my best friend), Chloe (my ballerina), Charles (my mini me),
and Claire (my constant reminder of what really matters in this life)—B.K.P.

To Ilaria Fellers, forever "Nonna."—W.M.O.

SAGE was founded in 1965 by Sara Miller McCune to support
the dissemination of usable knowledge by publishing innovative
and high-quality research and teaching content. Today, we
publish more than 850 journals, including those of more than
300 learned societies, more than 800 new books per year, and
a growing range of library products including archives, data,
case studies, reports, and video. SAGE remains majority-owned
by our founder, and after Sara's lifetime will become owned by
a charitable trust that secures our continued independence.

Los Angeles | London | New Delhi | Singapore | Washington DC

INTRODUCTION TO
CRIMINAL JUSTICE

a balanced approach

Brian K. Payne
Old Dominion University

Willard M. Oliver
Sam Houston State University

Nancy E. Marion
University of Akron

Los Angeles | London | New Delhi
Singapore | Washington DC

Los Angeles | London | New Delhi
Singapore | Washington DC

FOR INFORMATION:

SAGE Publications, Inc.
2455 Teller Road
Thousand Oaks, California 91320
E-mail: order@sagepub.com

SAGE Publications Ltd.
1 Oliver's Yard
55 City Road
London EC1Y 1SP
United Kingdom

SAGE Publications India Pvt. Ltd.
B 1/I 1 Mohan Cooperative Industrial Area
Mathura Road, New Delhi 110 044
India

SAGE Publications Asia-Pacific Pte. Ltd.
3 Church Street
#10-04 Samsung Hub
Singapore 049483

Printed in Canada

ISBN 978-1-4522-5892-8

Publisher: Jerry Westby
Associate Editor: Jessica Miller
Editorial Assistant: Laura Kirkhuff
eLearning Editors: Allison Hughes, Nick Pachelli
Production Editor: David C. Felts
Copy Editor: Amy Marks
Typesetter: C&M Digitals (P) Ltd.
Proofreaders: Ellen Brink, Ellen Howard,
                Victoria Reed-Castro
Indexer: Scott Smiley
Cover Designer: Gail Buschman
Marketing Manager: Terra Schultz

This book is printed on acid-free paper.

15 16 17 18 19 10 9 8 7 6 5 4 3 2 1

BRIEF CONTENTS

CONTENTS

PART I. FOUNDATIONS OF CRIMINAL JUSTICE   xxiv

©istockphoto.com/david franklin

CHAPTER 1. INTRODUCTION TO CRIMINAL JUSTICE   2

CHAPTER 2. PERSPECTIVES ON CRIME AND CRIMINAL JUSTICE RESEARCH   32

CHAPTER 3. AN INTRODUCTION TO MEASURING CRIME AND CRIME PATTERNS   64

CHAPTER 4. AN INTRODUCTION TO CRIME TYPOLOGIES 100

CHAPTER 5. AN INTRODUCTION TO CRIMINOLOGICAL THEORY 140

PART III. THE COURTS 270

CHAPTER 9. AN INTRODUCTION TO THE COURTS: HISTORY, STRUCTURE, AND ACTORS 272

CHAPTER 10. THE JUDICIAL PROCESS 306

CHAPTER 11. ISSUES IN THE COURTS 342

PART IV. CORRECTIONS 380

CHAPTER 12. AN INTRODUCTION TO CORRECTIONS: HISTORY, STRUCTURE, AND ACTORS 382

CHAPTER 13. PUNISHING OFFENDERS IN PRISONS, JAILS, AND THE COMMUNITY 416

CHAPTER 14. ISSUES IN CORRECTIONS

PART V. CONTEMPORARY CHALLENGES 491

© iStockphoto.com/colnihko

CHAPTER 15. CURRENT AND FUTURE CRIMINAL JUSTICE ISSUES 492

PREFACE

*I*ntroduction to Criminal Justice: A Balanced Approach explores criminal justice from a student-centered perspective by introducing students in introductory criminal justice courses to the multifaceted nature of criminal justice. By exploring criminal justice from a broad and balanced perspective, students will understand how decision making is critical to the criminal justice process. In particular, students will come to appreciate how their own future careers will be shaped by decisions they make, as well as by the decisions that others make.

➡ A Balanced Approach

In this context, the notion of a "balanced approach" refers to eight characteristics of this book. First, the book gives balanced attention to the major topics related to criminal justice. Some texts give more attention to one area of the justice process at the expense of other topics. In this book, the amount of attention given to criminal justice topics is balanced across law enforcement, the courts, and corrections. Also, it is recognized that, for students to understand these three areas, they must have a solid foundation in (or a broad understanding of) general topics related to criminal justice and criminology. As a result, the first section of the book, which represents about a third of the material in the book, is designed to provide the foundation needed to deliver a balanced discussion about law enforcement, the courts, and corrections.

Second, the notion of a balanced approach refers to our efforts to address both sides of controversial issues from an objective standpoint. Crime and criminals are not defined as inherently bad or evil, nor are traditional responses to crime. Instead, we approach the study of criminal justice with an open mind. This approach enables students to identify with the complexities that often confront criminal justice professionals. These complexities represent the ethical issues that criminal justice professionals face, and alternative viewpoints must be considered in addressing these issues.

Third, we use various strategies to promote critical thinking throughout the text. Our efforts are especially devoted to encouraging students to place themselves into specific situations to decide how they would respond to the situation with a balanced (and effective) criminal justice response. Chapters include topics specifically relevant to college students, and boxes (described below) are used in a way that incorporates the book's study site. We see this part of our balanced approach as particularly useful in introducing modern criminal justice students to the topic. Consider that most criminal justice programs identify critical thinking as a learning outcome for their introductory criminal justice courses.

Fourth, the balanced perspective also allows us to explore how justice can be achieved. Few symbols better capture the ideals of justice than the scales of justice. In reality, efforts to control crime sometimes fall short of achieving or meting out justice. To promote our balanced approach, in addition to discussing obstacles to achieving justice, we also address strategies to overcome those obstacles as well as activities criminal justice majors can engage in to promote justice.

Fifth, the balanced approach we take also reflects the multiple dimensions of criminal justice. Attention is given to the multiple ways that criminal justice is defined. On one level, the phrase *criminal justice* refers to the system our society uses to respond to criminal behaviors. On another level, *criminal justice* refers to practical actions carried out by those professionals given the duty of protecting us from wrongdoing. On yet another level, *criminal justice* refers to the process that offenders and victims go through when their cases are brought into the justice system. On still another level, *criminal justice* refers to a scientific discipline that uses research and evidence-based practices to understand the criminal justice system; the processes used to define crime; the experiences of victims, offenders, and criminal justice officials; as well as a number of other topics. Our book conceptualizes criminal justice in a way that balances each of these aspects of the topic.

Sixth, based on the multifaceted nature of criminal justice, we balance the practical aspects of criminal justice with the evidence-based research that has helped to shape current criminal justice practices. Criminal justice concepts are frequently oversimplified for students on the grounds that they would not understand the research that guides criminal justice practices. From our perspective, such an assumption is not simply wrong, it is insulting to criminal justice students. By balancing criminal justice practice with criminal justice research, we provide students a broad and balanced introduction to criminal justice: the system, the practice, the process, and the discipline. As Frank Hagan points out in his research methods book, we would be appalled if medical professionals did not understand how the research that guides their practices was conducted or if they did not fully understand the potential causes of disease. In a similar way, we should be equally appalled if criminal justice professionals (and students) do not understand the way that research and theory influences criminal justice practices. We believe that it is best to create the foundation for this understanding among criminal justice students as early as possible in their academic lives.

Seventh, we also balance the topics covered in the text in a way that is responsive to the recommendations of criminal justice scholars. As an illustration, about a decade ago the Academy of Criminal Justice Sciences (ACJS) developed certification standards for academic criminal justice programs. The standards were the result of long discussions among criminal justice professors teaching in all types of criminal justice programs—from two-year programs to doctoral programs. In the end, the standards pointed to specific topics that ACJS believes should be a part of academic criminal justice programs. One of the certification standards (B-5) includes the following language: "The broad scope of the field of criminal justice/criminology is reflected in the undergraduate curriculum and is a *balanced presentation* of the issues of the field" (emphasis added).

Table P1 shows how these standards guided the development of our book. Although we are illustrating how our book relates to these standards, it must be stressed that this book is not endorsed or certified by ACJS as the association is not in the business of endorsing or certifying books. However, the three authors' active affiliation with the academy cannot be separated from our lives as professors and authors. Hence, we used the academy's recommendations to guide our thinking. By design, the certification standards promote a balanced approach to understanding

TABLE P1	Parallels Between *Introduction to Criminal Justice: A Balanced Approach* and ACJS Certification Standards	
CONTENT AREA	**RELATED TOPICS INCLUDE BUT ARE NOT LIMITED TO ...**	**CHAPTERS WHERE THE TOPICS ARE COVERED**
Administration of Justice	Contemporary criminal justice/criminology system	Chapters 1–15
	Major systems of social control and their policies and practices	
	Victimology	
	Juvenile justice	
	Comparative criminal justice	
Corrections	History, theory, practice, and legal environment	Chapters 12–14
	Development of correctional philosophy	
	Incarceration, diversions, and community-based corrections	
	Treatment of offenders	
Criminological Theory	Nature and causes of crime	Chapters 4–5
	Typologies	
	Offenders	
	Victims	
Law Adjudication	Criminal law	Chapters 2, 9–11
	Criminal procedures	
	Prosecution	
	Defense	
	Court procedures and decision making	
Law Enforcement	History, theory, practice, and legal environment	Chapters 6–8
	Police organization, discretion, and subculture	
Research and Analytic Methods	Quantitative—including statistics—and qualitative methods for conducting and analyzing criminal justice/criminology research in a manner appropriate for undergraduate students	Chapters 2–3

ACJS website

criminal justice. Demonstrating how our book parallels these standards further shows how this book is grounded in a balanced approach. More information about the ACJS certification process is available online at www.acjs.org.

Finally, the balanced approach we take also reflects the multiple dimensions of criminal justice. Attention is given to criminal justice as (a) a system, (b) a process, (c) a career, (d) a major, (e) an institution of social control, (f) a social science, (g) a center of many controversial issues, and (h) a collection of individuals charged with formally controlling the behaviors of others through a complex decision-making process while responding to structural and societal influences and demands. Beyond recognizing that criminal justice is a "collection of individuals," we also stress that many criminal justice students will someday become part of the "collection of individuals" given the responsibility of responding to crime.

Our diverse research and professional backgrounds allow us to provide both academic and practical insight into various phases of the justice process. One of us (Oliver) has expertise in policing and, as a former police officer, is able to describe police issues through this balanced perspective. Another one of us (Marion) has expertise in studying and writing about the courts from criminal justice and political science perspectives. This background results in a description of the judicial process that is academically grounded while focused on the political realities that drive the court system. And yet another one of us (Payne) has focused much of his research on corrections and various punishment strategies. As a teenager, in a manner of speaking, he even "served time" in a juvenile facility. Collectively, we have the academic training in areas of criminal justice, criminology, political science, and sociology. We bring together our experiences and our training in a way that offers students a practical and empirical basis for understanding criminal justice.

➡ An Emphasis on Critical Thinking

As an illustration of the way that criminal justice can be viewed as a collection of individuals charged with making decisions, consider that the activities of professionals in the criminal justice system are guided by a series of decisions made by the professionals themselves as well as decisions made by those outside of the system. On one level, the decisions are influenced by broader structural and political influences. On another level, the decisions made in specific criminal cases have consequences for those involved in the specific cases. The following decisions highlight the types of decisions that are relevant to the criminal justice system's response to crimes:

- ➡ An offender decides whether to commit a crime. That decision is influenced by a number of factors and has consequences for the victim of the crime.

- ➡ The victim or a witness decides whether or not to report the crime to the police. That decision is influenced by different factors, and the degree to which the victim or witness participates with the justice system has consequences for the justice system.

- The police officer responding to the reported crime decides whether a crime has been committed, whether an arrest is warranted, and how to initiate the justice system's response to the crime.

- The police officer's supervisor, and the supervisor's superiors, decide the degree of resources that will be devoted to investigating a reported crime.

- The investigator decides whether enough evidence exists to clear the offense and whether to turn the case over to the prosecution.

- The prosecutor decides whether the offender should be charged and what those charges should be.

- A magistrate or judge decides whether bail should be granted to the offender or whether the offender should be held in jail pending trial.

- The prosecutor and defense attorney decide whether a plea bargain is warranted.

- The judge decides whether to accept a negotiated plea.

- The prosecutor decides whether the case should proceed to trial and what evidence to use in the case.

- The prosecutor, defense attorney, and judge decide who will be jurors in cases that go to trial.

- The prosecutor and defense attorney decide which witnesses they will ask to testify and what questions to ask those witnesses.

- The judge decides whether to dismiss criminal cases.

- The jury decides whether or not the offender is guilty.

- The judge decides whether to accept the jury's decision.

- A probation officer decides what information to provide the judge to help the judge decide what sentence should be given to the offender.

- The judge decides how to sentence the offender, typically within guidelines provided by statutes.

- Corrections professionals decide where incarcerated offenders will be imprisoned and the degree of supervision to give offenders sentenced to probation.

- Probation and parole officials decide whether offenders are abiding by their conditions of probation or parole.

This brief list highlights some of the common decisions made in the criminal justice system. The list could go on and on. The point is that the criminal justice system can be viewed as a living system influenced by the decisions made by individuals inside the system and outside the system. Their decisions will influence how cases proceed through the justice process. The decisions have extraordinarily significant implications for other peoples' lives. Deciding to arrest a suspect will change the course of the suspect's life, as well as the lives of the suspect's loved ones. Decisions made by others in the justice process will have equal, if not greater, consequences for suspects.

➡ Distinctive Chapter Content

This book includes several features that enhance its usefulness for students and professors alike. These features include the following:

- ➡ Learning objectives for each chapter are listed at the beginning of the chapter. Instructors can select from these objectives as they develop syllabi for their introductory criminal justice courses, and the objectives can be used to assess learning in these courses.

- ➡ Following the learning objectives, each chapter has a feature called "Admissible or Inadmissible Evidence." This feature includes eight statements related to the information provided in the chapter. Some of the statements are true and some are false. Students are asked to identify the statement as "Admissible" if it is true or as "Inadmissible" if it is false. Some of these questions could easily be included on quizzes or exams.

- ➡ The major sections of each chapter include features called "Beyond a Reasonable Doubt." These are multiple-choice questions that assess students' knowledge about a specific concept in that section. Some of these questions could also be easily included on quizzes or exams.

- ➡ Each chapter includes a feature called "Criminal Justice and College Students." This feature gives students a brief introduction and asks them to relate something about their own lives to criminal justice. Are their parts of their community that have "broken windows" and might result in crime? How might they study certain criminal justice issues? How are college campuses similar to prisons? These, and other questions, are included in these features. Also, whether in person or online, students are encouraged to complete these features along with other students from their class. After all, criminal justice professionals address problems as teams. Criminal justice students can do likewise.

- ➡ Several of the chapters include "Criminal Justice Pioneer" boxes. Using the expertise of one of the authors, Will Oliver, who happens to be the historian for the Academy of Criminal Justice Sciences, the boxes from background information about select criminal justice professionals who had a long-lasting, if not permanent, influence on the criminal justice system.

- ➡ Each chapter includes "Ethical Decision Making" boxes. These boxes present an ethical scenario that criminal justice professionals or students might confront. Critical thinking questions are included to encourage students to think through the potential ramifications of their decisions.

- "Help Wanted" boxes are included in each chapter. Each box focuses on a specific job related to the specific chapter in which the feature is found. The details (which include duties, educational requirements, and salaries) come from actual job advertisements.

- "Criminal Justice and the Media" boxes are included in each chapter. These boxes provide an overview of the way that various media issues relate to criminal justice topics. The boxes focus on both traditional media and social media.

- The "Just the Facts" feature in each chapter summarizes the highpoints of the chapter. Students may find it useful to read these *before* reading the chapter to gain an overview of the concepts to be covered.

- "Critical Thinking Questions" are included at the end of each chapter. These questions are intended to promote discussion related to the topics addressed in the chapter.

- "Key Terms" lists the terms highlighted in boldface and with margin definitions throughout the text. Students who are able to grasp these terms will have a full understanding of the chapters.

- The comprehensive glossary at the end of the book provides definitions for all of the key terms highlighted throughout the text.

➡ Resources for Instructors and Students

Many electronic features are also included with *Introduction to Criminal Justice: A Balanced Approach*, including SAGE edge select.

⑤SAGE edgeselect™

SAGE edge select is a robust online environment designed to customize and enhance each student's learning experience. Carefully crafted tools and resources encourage review, practice, and critical thinking, giving students the edge they need to master course content.

SAGE edge select for Instructors supports teaching with quality content and a rich learning environment for students, featuring:

- **Course Management System integration** to make it easy for student test results and graded assignments to seamlessly flow into instructor gradebooks

- **Test banks built on Bloom's Taxonomy** to provide a diverse range of test items with Respondus test generation

- **Sample course syllabi** with suggested models for structuring one's course

- Editable, chapter-specific **PowerPoint®️ slides** that offer flexibility

- **Video and multimedia content** that enhance student engagement and appeal to different learning styles

- All instructor material and tools which are easily integrated through a **Course cartridge**

SAGE edge select for Students helps students accomplish their coursework goals in an easy-to-use learning environment that offers:

- **Diagnostic pre-tests** to identify opportunities for improvement, tying individual learning needs to chapter learning objectives

- **Personalized study plans** with focused recommendations to address specific knowledge gaps and additional learning needs

- **Post-tests** to track student progress and ensure mastery of key learning objectives

- Mobile-friendly **eFlashcards** which strengthen understanding of key concepts

- Mobile-friendly practice **quizzes** to encourage self-guided assessment and practice

- Carefully selected **video** and **multimedia content** that enhance exploration of key topics

- EXCLUSIVE access to full-text **SAGE journal articles**, which support and expand on chapter concepts

ACKNOWLEDGMENTS

Many different individuals helped us get this book to completion. Thanks to Old Dominion University graduate assistants Lora Ilieva and Brandon Foster for helping to coordinate parts of the glossary, locate photos, and create various maps and figures. Thanks also to Georgia State doctoral student Susannah Tapp for her help in locating and verifying references throughout the book. Craig Hemmens provided language early on to assist in developing the legal themes integrated throughout the book. Jessica Miller's editorial feedback and guidance helped to frame our thoughts in each chapter. Many of the positive comments from reviewers were a direct result of Jessica's efforts. Amy Marks did an outstanding job as copy editor, and we are grateful for her expertise. Nick Pachelli reminded us of Martin Scorsese while he was filming us for the electronic materials . . . he was patient, insightful, and entertaining. Terra Schultz and Christina Fohl developed an incredible marketing plan that highlights all that this book has to offer. Finally, we appreciate Jerry Westby's guidance and patience as we made our way through the justice system. We cannot thank the entire SAGE team enough for all of the time they put into this book.

In addition, reviewers provided feedback on many different versions of the manuscript. We are indebted to the following reviewers for their insight:

Ken Ayres, Kentucky Wesleyan College

Wayne L. Babish, University of Pittsburgh

Robert L. Bing III, University of Texas at Arlington

Heidi S. Bonner, East Carolina University

Christine Capps Broeker, Seminole State College of Florida

Chris Chaney, Modesto Institute of Technology

Mary Beth Finn, Herzing University

Natalie W. Goulette, University of Western Florida

Mia Green, Bridgewater State University

Ralph Grunewald, University of Wisconsin -Madison

Engin Gulen, Sam Houston State University

Marilyn Horace-Moore, Eastern Michigan University

Polly A. Johnson, Austin Community College

Coy Johnston, Arizona State University

Shawn Keller, Florida Gulf Coast University

Rebecca Loftus, Arizona State University

Dennis W. McLean, Keiser University

Robert J. Mellin, University of Maryland University College

John Michaud, Husson University

Mia Ortiz, Bridgewater State University

James Kane Record, California University of Pennsylvania

Jennifer Riggs, Eastern New Mexico University

Christopher Salvatore, Montclair State University

Jo Ann Short, Northern Virginia Community College-Annandale Campus

Shel Silver, Ashford University

Jamie Snyder, Calhoun Community College

James M. Stewart, Calhoun Community College

Jerry Stinson, Southwest Virginia Community College

Katie L. Swope, Stevenson University

William T. Valenta, Jr., University of Pittsburgh

Deborah Woodward, University of Central Florida

Yuning Wu, Wayne State University

Jay Zumbrun, Community College of Baltimore County

We would also like to extend our gratitude to the individuals who participated in the filming for this text:

Dennis Bachman, Kansas Racing and Gaming

Cathy Bates, Academy of Criminal Justice Sciences

Ray Bynum, University of Phoenix

Lori Coppenrath, DLR Group

Gary Drinkard, Witness to Innocence

Paul Elam, Public Policy Associates

Ashley Fundack, Morris Hardwick Schneider

Craig Hemmens, Washington State University

Dave Keaton, Witness to Innocence

Nancy La Vigne, The Urban Institute

Mitch Lucas, Charleston County

Juan Melendez, Witness to Innocence

Ruth Moyer, Gerald A. Stein, P.C.

Kathy Spillman, Witness to Innocence

Terry Stokes, City of Charlotte

Mike Verro, Excelsior College

ABOUT THE AUTHORS

Brian K. Payne received his doctorate in criminology from Indiana University of Pennsylvania in 1993. He is currently the vice provost for graduate and undergraduate academic programs at Old Dominion University, where he is tenured in the Department of Sociology and Criminal Justice. He is a former editor of the *American Journal of Criminal Justice,* past president of the Academy of Criminal Justice Sciences and past president of the Southern Criminal Justice Association. Payne is the author or coauthor of more than 160 journal articles and seven books including *White-Collar Crime: The Essentials* (Sage), *Family Violence and Criminal Justice* (Elsevier, with Randy Gainey), and *Crime and Elder Abuse: An Integrated Perspective* (Charles C Thomas). He won the local Pinewood Derby when he was in the fourth grade.

Willard M. Oliver is a professor of criminal justice at Sam Houston State University in Huntsville, Texas. He holds a doctorate and a master of arts degree in political science from West Virginia University and master of science and bachelor of science degrees from Radford University. He has taught criminal justice for over 20 years, primarily in the area of policing, crime policy, and criminal justice history. He is the author of numerous textbooks, including *Community-Oriented Policing, Homeland Security, Homeland Security for Policing,* and *A History of Crime and Criminal Justice in America.* He has published over 50 peer-reviewed journal articles and numerous articles for professional publications. Oliver serves as the editor for the *Journal of Qualitative Criminal Justice & Criminology* and is the official historian for the Academy of Criminal Justice Sciences. He is a retired military police officer with the U.S. Army Reserves and a former police officer. Oliver is an avid runner and has completed 10 marathons. He is married and has three children.

Nancy E. Marion is a professor of political science at the University of Akron. She holds a doctorate and a master of arts degree in political science from the State University of New York, a master of science degree in criminal justice from American University, and a bachelor of science degree in administration of justice from the Pennsylvania State University. She is the author of numerous peer-reviewed journal articles and books. Her research interests center around the interplay of politics and criminal justice.

PART I

FOUNDATIONS OF CRIMINAL JUSTICE

© istockphoto.com/david franklin

FOUNDATIONS *of* CRIMINAL JUSTICE

CRIME

Crime Theories

Crime as a product of social factors

Crime as a product of social psychological factors

Crime as a product of biological factors

Crime as a product of cognitive processes

Crime as a product of choice

Crime Typologies

Violent Crime

Property Crime

Public Order Crime

Crime Within Complex Organizations

Criminal Justice Research

Survey Research

Experiments

Archival Research

Field Studies

Case Studies

Measuring Crime

Uniform Crime Reporting (UCR)

National Crime Victimization Survey (NCVS)

National Incident–Based Reporting System (NIBRS)

Crime Prevention

Situational Crime Prevention

Crime Prevention Through Environmental Design (CPTED)

Routine Activities Theory

Evidence-Based Policies

1

INTRODUCTION TO CRIMINAL JUSTICE

© iStockphoto/Terraxplorer

BRIAN WAS 15 THE FIRST NIGHT HE SPENT IN A JUVENILE HOME. The 10-bed dormitory room was half-full with five other boys—Harry, Dale, David, Wayne, and John (Brian's bunkmate). Brian was similar to the other boys in many ways. They ate a lot of food, hated doing their homework, and thought they knew everything about the world. Brian was different in one important way: He was there because his parents had become house parents in the juvenile home. The other boys were there because the courts had labeled them "in need of supervision" and sent them to the home.

During his first week in the home, Brian quickly learned about the "house rules." Wayne told him to sleep with his socks on or else Harry might "have sex with his feet" while he was trying to sleep. John showed him how to finish his daily chores each morning in time to have a few extra minutes before the bus came. David showed him that being nice to the other boys would keep him safe, an important point for Brian since he didn't want to get beaten up.

About six months after arriving at the juvenile home, Brian's parents announced that they were leaving their jobs there and returning to the town where Brian grew up. Brian later realized how much those six months had affected his life. Unfortunately, he lost touch with the boys who lived in the home and he never returned.

Brian enrolled in a juvenile justice class as a junior in college, thinking it might help him better understand his own experiences in the juvenile home. That class, and his experiences in the home, led Brian to decide that he wanted to learn even more about crime and criminal justice. Later, Brian got his master's and doctoral degrees in criminology. He eventually found his passion as a criminal justice scholar. In addition to teaching many different classes, Brian has authored or coauthored many research articles and books. In fact, he is a coauthor of this book.

—Brian K. Payne

©alessandro0770/Veer

LEARNING OBJECTIVES

After reading this chapter, students will be able to:

1.1 Identify the three main components of the criminal justice system

1.2 Determine whether cases reported in the media adequately reflect the bulk of cases processed through the justice system

1.3 Describe the relationship between the criminal justice system and the juvenile justice system

1.4 Explain how criminal justice is a social science

1.5 Describe the history of criminal justice as a field of study

1.6 Compare and contrast criminal justice and criminology

1.7 Explain the role that criminal justice has in your life

1.8 Describe the process of ethical decision making in the criminal justice system

ADMISSIBLE or INADMISSIBLE Evidence

Read the statements that follow. If the statement is true, circle *admissible*. If the statement is false, circle *inadmissible*. Answers can be found on page 517.

1. **Admissible Inadmissible** The overarching goal of the criminal justice system is to punish offenders.

2. **Admissible Inadmissible** If a juvenile is the offender, a different type of police officer is called to respond to the crime scene.

3. **Admissible Inadmissible** The initial appearance is the first stage of the criminal justice process.

4. **Admissible Inadmissible** Most criminologists agree that criminal justice is a practice, not a science.

5. **Admissible Inadmissible** Academic criminal justice programs are a relatively new type of college program, beginning in the past 10 years or so.

6. **Admissible Inadmissible** *Determinism* means that behavior is caused by preceding events.

7. **Admissible Inadmissible** Criminal justice and criminology are distinct areas of study.

8. **Admissible Inadmissible** Male college students have victimization rates lower than males who are not college students.

Stories about criminal justice are all around us. From controversy surrounding a situation in which the leader of a neighborhood watch group shot an unarmed African American male to a case where a woman suspected of killing her two-year-old daughter was found not guilty, we are inundated with criminal justice stories. The stories we hear are often just that—superficial, and sometimes inaccurate, descriptions of actual events. To fully understand these "stories," it is helpful to have a basic understanding of criminal justice. Figure 1.1 depicts how different groups view criminal justice. As an introduction to criminal justice, this chapter focuses on the criminal justice system, the juvenile justice system, the criminal justice process, and the roles of criminal justice.

AUTHOR VIDEO
Define Criminal Justice

criminal justice system: A phrase used to describe the three main components of criminal justice: the police, the courts, and corrections.

The Criminal Justice System

The phrase **criminal justice system** is used to describe the three main components of criminal justice: the police, the courts, and corrections. In

FIGURE 1.1 The Many Dimensions of Criminal Justice

Criminal justice can be viewed as . . .
A system responding to crimes by adults
Distinct from the juvenile justice system
A process
An academic discipline
A social science
The center of many controversial issues
Distinct from criminology, or the study of crime
A collection of individuals charged with responding to crime
A major for many college students

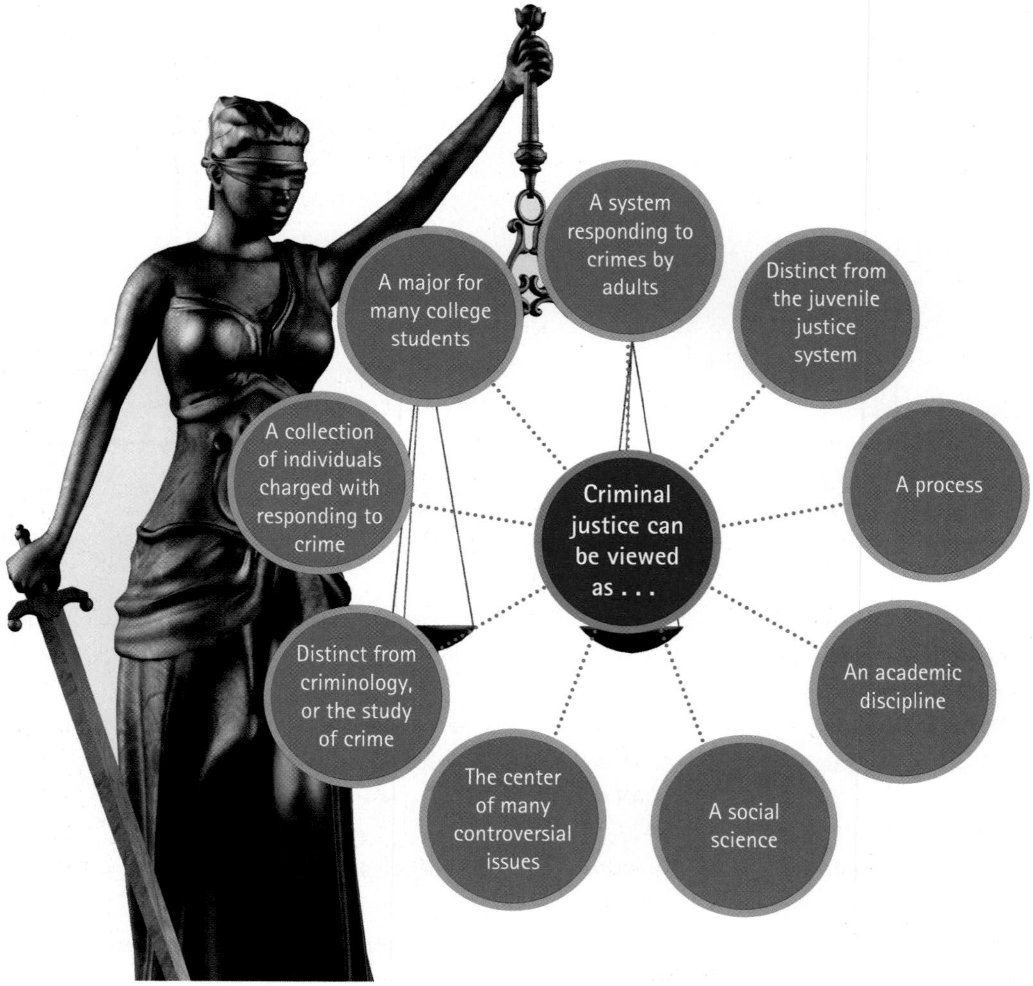

some ways, these three components can be seen as subsystems of the broader criminal justice system. Each subsystem has specific roles and responsibilities that are designed to further the aims of the criminal justice system. Of course, it is the individuals who work in these subsystems who carry out the activities required to meet these duties.

Stories about criminal justice often unfold in the media, as was the case for Casey Anthony and Aaron Hernandez.

REUTERS/Red Huber/Pool; © Don Kelly Photo/Corbis

A great deal of discussion has centered on whether the criminal justice system is actually a system. Those who argue that the three subsystems come together to form a system point to at least four different facets of criminal justice to suggest that a criminal justice *system* does, in fact, exist. First, it can be argued that the three components of the justice process have one overarching goal: public safety. Much more is written later in this text about the way that the agencies involved in each of these components promote public safety. As an introduction, the components of the justice system work toward the public safety goal in the following way:

- Actors in the police subsystem enforce the law, maintain order, and provide services to protect members of the community.

- Actors in the courts determine whether suspects are guilty of criminal behavior to determine whether they should be punished for their alleged transgressions. Prosecutors are charged with representing the state in criminal trials. Judges oversee the court process and, among other things, sentence offenders in an effort to promote public safety.

- Actors in the corrections subsystem supervise and counsel convicted offenders in an effort to prevent future crime and protect the public.

Whether the justice system meets the goal of public safety is debatable. Still, the fact that the three components share a similar goal lends credence to the idea that a criminal justice system exists.

Second, one can point to the way that offenders enter one part of the system and exit another part of the system as an indication of how the three components operate in a systemic way. That offenders move from one component of the system to another suggests that the components are working together as a system. Consider Lindsay Lohan's case. Initially arrested by police in May 2007 for drunk driving, Lohan subsequently had numerous contacts with other parts of the justice system as her case progressed. In fact, she was in court twenty times, on probation for more than five

Linsday Lohan made more than 20 court appearances. The criminal justice process routinely requires multiple court appearances. This photo shows the actress leaving after her final court appearance.

© Ted Soqui/Corbis

years, and spent 250 days in rehab and nearly two weeks in jail.[1] In other words, Lohan moved from one part of the justice system to the next.

Third, experts have pointed to the interdependent nature of the components of the justice process to illustrate the systemic nature of criminal justice. In short, what happens in one part of the system has implications for what happens in other parts of the system.[2] If a police department begins to arrest more offenders for drunk driving, for example, more offenders will be sent to the courts for prosecution. The higher number of offenders in the courts, in turn, will have implications for the corrections subsystem.

Finally, to some observers the criminal law is structured in such a way that it guides the behavior of all individuals operating in the criminal justice system. The police enforce the criminal law, the courts adjudicate the criminal law, and the corrections subsystem applies penalties that are prescribed in the criminal law. In many ways, the criminal law is the glue that binds together the components of the criminal justice system.

BEYOND A REASONABLE DOUBT 1.1

Which of the following is *not* one of the main components of the criminal justice system?

(a) Police, (b) The courts, (c) Corrections, (d) The legislature, (e) All are major components of the criminal justice system.

The answer can be found on page 521.

➡ The Juvenile Justice System

Some individuals refer to what they call a **juvenile justice system**. In theory, the juvenile justice system is the system through which cases involving juvenile offenders are processed. In reality, the juvenile justice system differs little in appearance from the criminal justice system. For the most part, police officers charged with enforcing the law make no distinction between adult criminals and juvenile offenders in terms of the specific practices they engage in to apprehend them. Of course, what officers do with different types of offenders may be influenced by juvenile status. For example, a police officer who catches a young person engaging in illegal acts might choose to take that young person home to his or her parents. If a police officer catches one of the authors doing something illegal, the officer is unlikely to take us home to our aging parents. But, the simple fact remains that, when reacting to crime, there are no "juvenile police officers" and "adult offender police officers."

Although a case can be made that the juvenile justice system is a mere reflection of the criminal justice system, it is important to note that "juvenile court" and "juvenile corrections agencies" do exist. However, juvenile courts are typically in the same courthouse as "adult courts," the employees work for the same agency in both types of courts, and the types of individuals working in juvenile and adult courts have similar

juvenile justice system: The system through which cases involving juvenile offenders are processed.

qualifications. The same can be said of corrections agencies: They are typically adjoined to adult corrections agencies, and the employees are similar in both settings.

To be sure, police, judges, corrections officials, and other criminal justice officials respond differently to younger offenders than they do to older offenders. However, this response occurs in the same broader justice system. Much more is written about juvenile offending, juvenile policing, juvenile courts, and juvenile corrections throughout this book in conjunction with discussion of the broader areas of policing, courts, and corrections.

> **BEYOND A REASONABLE DOUBT 1.2**
>
> Which of the following is *not* a part of the juvenile justice system?
>
> (a) Juvenile police officers, (b) Juvenile courts, (c) Juvenile detention, (d) Juvenile corrections, (e) All are components of the juvenile justice system.

The answer can be found on page 521.

arrest: When a suspect is taken into custody by law enforcement officers under suspicion that he or she violated a law.

booking: The process of formally recording the charges against a person into police records; often includes a mugshot, fingerprints, and other personal information.

initial appearance: When the suspect first appears before a judicial official to be formally notified of the charges, advised of his or her rights, and notified of bail decisions (in some jurisdictions).

➡ The Justice Process

The President's Commission on Law Enforcement and Administration of Justice offered one of the most comprehensive and earliest depictions of the justice process (see Figure 1.2). More attention is given to the stages of the justice process later in this book. For now, a summary of the stages of the criminal justice process is warranted:

- ➡ *Investigation.* The police investigate suspected offenses after citizens report the offense or authorities identify possible offending through their own proactive efforts. The investigation will focus on whether a crime was committed, who is suspected of committing the crime, whether an arrest is warranted, and when an arrest should occur.

- ➡ *Arrest.* As an initial step in the formal processing of a case, an **arrest** entails formally taking a suspect into custody.

- ➡ *Booking.* To formally record the arrest, **booking** of a suspect involves procedures such as fingerprinting, taking mug shots, completing arrest records, and so on.

- ➡ *Initial appearance.* During the **initial appearance**, the suspect appears before a magistrate or similar official and is formally notified of the

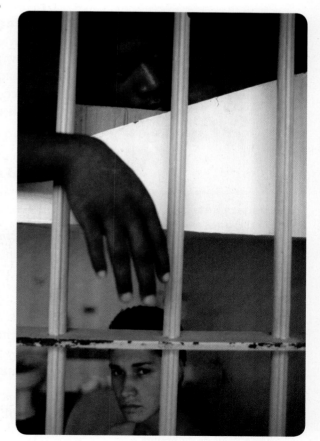

Juvenile offenders frequently serve their sanctions in facilities connected to adult prisons.

© Andrew Lichtenstein/Corbis/APImages

charges, advised of his or her rights, and notified of bail decisions (in some jurisdictions). In minor cases, summary trials may be held before the judge at this juncture, with the judge determining guilt or innocence and sentencing cases in which guilt is determined.

- *Preliminary hearing.* Some jurisdictions hold a **preliminary hearing** in which a judge determines if probable cause exists to suggest the suspect committed a crime in the judge's jurisdiction. *Probable cause* refers to facts that would lead a reasonable person to conclude that the suspect committed a crime. The judge decides if the evidence reasonably shows that (a) a crime was committed within his or her jurisdiction and (b) the suspect committed the crime.

- *Grand jury or information.* In more serious cases, the prosecutor may present the case to a *grand jury* in an effort to seek an indictment against the suspect. The purpose of the grand jury hearing is to determine whether sufficient evidence exists to suggest that the case should proceed to trial. An indictment is a written statement describing the charges and the evidence in the case. In less serious cases, the prosecutor moves the case forward by issuing to the court an *information* (a formal charging document detailing the case).

- *Arraignment.* After the indictment or information is filed, the **arraignment** is held. The suspect is formally notified of the charges; advised of his or her legal rights; and asked whether he or she wants to plead guilty, not guilty, or no contest. If the defendant pleads guilty, the sentencing process occurs next, assuming the judge accepts the plea. If the defendant pleads not guilty, the case proceeds to trial.

- *Trial.* It is commonly estimated that less than 10% of cases go to trial because the vast majority of defendants plead guilty. During the **trial** the prosecution is expected to prove beyond a reasonable doubt that the defendant committed the offense or offenses with which he or she is charged.

- *Sentencing.* For a defendant found guilty, a hearing will be held in which the judge will sentence the offender. Possible sentences include incarceration, probation, fines, restitution, or the death penalty (for capital offenses in states that allow the death penalty).

- *Appeals.* A defendant may appeal the court's ruling to an appellate court. The appellate court will decide whether to hear the appeal or reject it without a hearing. Death penalty convictions are automatically granted appellate review.

- *Sanction.* Those who are sentenced to a year or more of incarceration will be sent to prison, whereas those sentenced to less than a year of incarceration will be sent to jail. Offenders on probation will be supervised in the community for the duration of their sanction. Those released from prison on parole will be supervised in the community by parole officers for the length of their sanction.

preliminary hearing: The stage in the criminal justice process (in some jurisdictions) when a judge determines if probable cause exists to suggest that the suspect committed a crime.

arraignment: The first stage of the trial process; a defendant appears before the judge to respond to charges by pleading guilty, not guilty, or nolo contendere (no contest).

trial: A legal proceeding in which evidence is presented to a jury or a judge to determine the guilt or innocence of a defendant.

➧ *Release.* Offenders are released from the justice process by completing their sanctions, being pardoned or paroled, or successfully appealing their conviction.[3]

A few points about the criminal justice process are worth highlighting. First, cases do not always flow smoothly from one point to the next. Second, officials may decide to drop a case from the justice process. Third, specific jurisdictions have rules and guidelines stipulating how cases will be processed through the justice system. Fourth, the juvenile justice process flows differently than the adult justice process, depending on the nature of the juvenile case entering the system. Finally, the seriousness of various types of cases influences how they are processed through the justice system. In other words, the notion of process should not lead one to assume that all cases are treated similarly.

Crime Control and Due Process Models

Scholars have described the criminal justice process in different ways. In *The Limits of the Criminal Sanction*, Herbert Packer described two models to characterize the justice process: the **crime control model** and the **due process model**.[4] The crime control model refers to situations in which cases are processed with a primary focus given to the need to protect the public. In this model, the police are charged with enforcing the law in an effort to maintain public safety and keep criminals from spiraling out of control. Emphasis is placed on processing cases efficiently in ways that maximizes resources, while recognizing that budgetary

crime control model:
A model characterizing the criminal justice system, in which cases are processed with a primary focus given to the need to protect the public.

due process model:
A model characterizing the criminal justice system that emphasizes the protection of defendants' rights and is driven by respect for the "formal structure of the law."

The criminal justice process includes various professionals working in vastly different settings . . . from the street, to the courtroom, to prisons and jails.

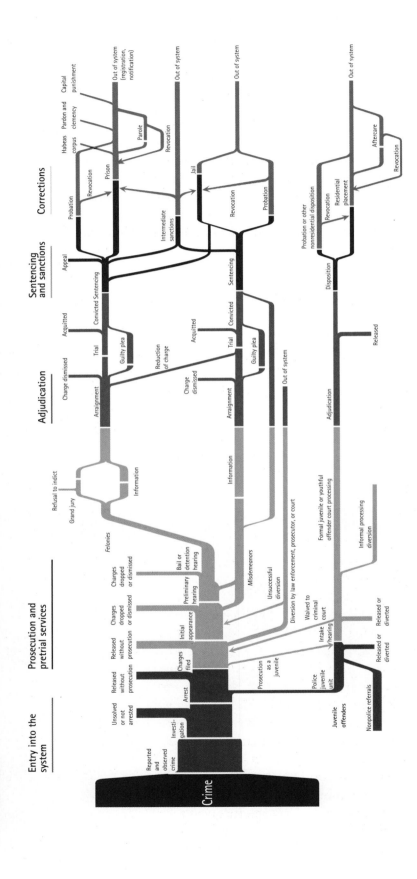

FIGURE 1.2   The Criminal Justice Process

Note: This chart gives a simplified view of caseflow through the criminal justice system. Procedures vary among jurisdictions. The weights of the lines are not intended to show actual size of caseloads.

The U.S. Department of Justice, Office of Justice Programs, Bureau of Justice Statistics

constraints limit long, drawn-out processes. Packer notes that a "premium [is placed] on time and finality" in the crime control model. He adds that under this model the justice process "is seen as a screening process in which each successive state—prearrest investigation, arrest, postarrest investigation, preparation for trial, trial or entry of plea, conviction, disposition—involves a series of routinized operations whose success is gauged primarily by their tendency to pass the case along to a successful conclusion."[5]

In contrast, the due process model emphasizes the protection of defendants' rights and is driven by respect for the "formal structure of the law." In the due process model, "each successive stage is designed to present formidable impediments to carrying the accused any further along in the process."[6] As you learn more about the criminal justice process later in this book, for example, you will see that it takes less evidence to arrest suspects than it takes to convict them. Whereas the crime control model views the justice process as an assembly line, the due process model views the process as an obstacle course. Packer summarizes the two models suggesting that "the due process model insists on the prevention and elimination of mistakes to the extent possible; the crime control model accepts the probability of mistakes up to the level at which they interfere with the goal of repossessing crime."[7]

These two models are particularly useful in that they highlight how cases are potentially processed when different values drive the justice process, and these different values depend on the type of case and the actors involved in the process.

> **wedding cake model:**
> An analogy used to describe the types of cases that flow through the criminal justice system.

Wedding Cake Model of Justice

Other scholars have also highlighted the differential processing of cases throughout the justice process. Building on the work of legal scholars Lawrence Friedman and Robert Percival, Samuel Walker discussed what is widely known as the **wedding cake model** of criminal justice (see Figure 1.3). Imagine a wedding cake that has multiple layers. Layers at the top of the cake are smaller, and layers at the bottom are much larger. Using this analogy, Walker describes four layers of cases that flow through the criminal justice process. The top layer of cases are celebrated cases that receive a great deal of attention from the media. Examples include cases involving O. J. Simpson (the former Hall of Fame football player who was accused of killing his ex-wife, Nicole, and her friend Ron Goldman), Richard Zimmerman (a neighborhood watch volunteer accused of murdering an unarmed teen, Treyvon Martin), and Bernard Madoff (the former Wall Street executive who duped investors out of billions). The public is inundated with such cases, which is problematic given that they do not represent how the majority of cases are processed through the justice system. Indeed, these cases represent a

FIGURE 1.3   Wedding Cake Model of Justice

Celebrated Cases

Heavy-Duty Felonies

Lightweight Felonies

Misdemeanors

© iStockphoto.com/azshooter

Treyvon Martin's case is an example of what Samuel Walker means by layer one cases: the case went through the entire justice process, it received a great deal of publicity, and it did not represent most criminal justice cases.

Photos Released to Public by Family of Trayvon Martin

VIDEO

O. J. Simpson's Acquittal

small fraction of all the cases that make their way through the justice system (just as the top layer of the wedding cake is the smallest part of the cake). In short, Walker points out that cases in the top layer are different from other cases because (a) they go through the full criminal justice process, (b) they receive a great deal of publicity, and (c) they paint a distorted picture of the justice process because they receive so much publicity.

Walker used the example of O. J. Simpson's acquittal to illustrate this layer. One could also consider Casey Anthony's case, which a reporter from *Time* magazine dubbed as "the social media trial of the century,"[8] as another example of a celebrated case. Anthony, a single mom, was accused of killing her two-year-old daughter, Caylee. The case received a tremendous amount of attention from the national media, with national television news programs covering the case as it made its way through the entire criminal justice process. In the end, a jury found Anthony not guilty of the charges. Members of the public might have assumed from this case that most trials fail to result in convictions, which is not at all true. Other distortions may have surfaced from this case as well. Here are just a few facts to refute the distortions:

- Most murder defendants are not young single mothers.
- Most murder victims are not two-year-old children.
- Most defense attorneys do not reach star status from homicide cases.
- Most cases do not go to trial.

The second layer of cases in the justice process, according to Walker, includes "heavy-duty felonies," or cases that criminal justice officials decide warrant more attention and resources. A felony is a crime that can result in a penalty of incarceration for a year or more in prison or the death penalty. According to Walker's model, with regard to heavy-duty felonies, the decision to classify certain types of cases is informal, with officials asking questions such as "How much is this case worth?" and "How bad is this offender?"[9] By deciding which cases are serious, officials can more efficiently process less serious cases through the justice system. As Walker writes, "The shared definition of seriousness facilitates rapid disposition of a high volume of cases"[10] In other words, officials can give less time, attention, and resources to cases in lower parts of the wedding cake.

Cases in the third layer include "lightweight" felonies. These would include felony offenses that do not seem to involve serious offenders or may not seem to be "worth" a great deal to prosecutors or law enforcement. Walker suggests that officials will consider the defendant's prior record and the relationship between the victim and the suspect when making these decisions. Suspects with no history of crime would be more likely to have their offenses defined as "lightweight felonies" (assuming they are not local celebrities). In addition, if the victim and the suspect know one another, the case is more likely to be defined as less serious.

At the bottom of the wedding cake are the vast majority of cases processed through the justice system: misdemeanors. Misdemeanors are crimes for which the most serious penalty would be one year in jail; these cases are typically heard in what are referred to as lower courts. In reality, most misdemeanor convictions result in less serious penalties, including fines, probation, restitution, or a very short jail sentence. According to Walker, "Because of the huge volume of cases and their relative lack of seriousness, relatively little concern is shown for the formalities of the felony process" in the processing of misdemeanor cases through the justice process.[11] Walker concludes his discussion of the wedding cake model with two points: "(1) the lower courts are very different from the upper courts and (2) there are significant differences between courts in different jurisdictions."[12]

BEYOND A REASONABLE DOUBT 1.3

The _____ model refers to situations in which cases are processed with a primary focus given to the need to protect the public.

(a) crime control, (b) due process, (c) wedding cake, (d) substantive, (e) legal

---

The answer can be found on page 521.

➡ The Roles of Criminal Justice

Although criminal justice can be seen as both a system and a process, in reality the phrase *criminal justice* refers to much more than a system or a process. Generally speaking, the various roles of criminal justice include the following:

AUTHOR VIDEO
Definition of a System

- ➡ Criminal justice as an academic discipline
- ➡ Criminal justice as a social science
- ➡ Criminal justice as a setting for controversial issues
- ➡ Criminal justice versus criminology
- ➡ Criminal justice as a collection of individuals
- ➡ Criminal justice and college students

Criminal Justice as an Academic Discipline

At your college, there are likely several disciplines that offer degree programs. Many of those disciplines have likely been around for a long time. Criminal justice, by contrast, has a rather short history. The first criminology major was offered in 1937 and the first School of Criminology was created in 1950 at the University of California at Berkeley. August Vollmer, a professor of police administration in Berkeley's Department of Political Science and former police chief, is credited with leading the development of criminology at his university.[13] Vollmer worked for years trying to develop coursework for police officers at Berkeley. After World War I, he produced a report titled *The Police* for the Wickersham Commission. This report prompted the Rockefeller Foundation to fund police education initiatives at Berkeley in the early 1930s.[14] These initiatives led to the development of the criminology major a few years later. The "Criminal Justice Pioneer" box in this chapter provides additional insight into August Vollmer's life.

The "modern emergence of [criminal justice]" is traced to President Lyndon Johnson's Commission of Law Enforcement and Administration of Justice, which called for the education of criminal justice professionals and improved criminal justice research efforts as strategies to address the crime problem.[15] Among the recommendations the commission made in its several-hundred-page report, *The Challenge of Crime in a Free Society*, were the following:[16]

- Creation of research units in criminal justice agencies
- Dedication of funds to develop criminal justice research institutes across the United States
- Expansion of criminal justice programs in colleges and universities
- Federal support to develop new education and training programs

The commission was particularly focused on the need to offer criminal justice programs in higher education:

Higher education has played an uneven part in criminal justice. A few law schools have engaged for years in research, and in representation of indigent defenders; their professors have been responsible for a major share of modern criminal legislation and much of the informed criticism of the criminal process. On the other hand, until recently little emphasis was given to preparing students to practice criminal law. Universities like the University of California at Berkeley and Michigan State University have had police science departments for several decades, but they have existed too much in isolation from the rest of the academic community. The same thing is to a large extent true of teaching and research in the corrections field. All operating agencies of justice urgently need the close contact with academic thought that could be achieved through use of faculty consultants; seminars and institutes to analyze current problems and innovations; advanced training programs for judges,

AUGUST VOLLMER

August Vollmer was born on March 7, 1876, in New Orleans, Louisiana, to parents who had immigrated recently from Germany. In 1905, he stopped a runaway railcar from hitting a passenger train, and the editor of the local newspaper encouraged him to run for town marshal. He did and won by a landslide against the corrupt incumbent. He ran again in 1907 and won, and then in 1909, Berkeley converted the position and Vollmer was appointed police chief, a position in which he would serve until 1932.

Vollmer was an innovative chief. He was the first to put all of his officers on bicycles in 1910, and he adopted motorcycles and patrol cars early. Through his leadership and the assistance of many of his officers, he contributed to creating the first crime lab, the modern polygraph, and the two-way radio in patrol cars. Vollmer was also very progressive; he did not believe in police brutality, he opposed

capital punishment, and he favored the decriminalization of drugs. This was all in the 1920s and 1930s!

Vollmer's greatest contribution to American policing, however, was in the area of education. He started a program of in-service training for his

Library of Congress Prints and Photographs Division Washington, D.C.

officers (1906) and a police academy (1907), and he developed the first criminal justice degree at the University of California at Berkeley (1916). Although the degree was known as criminology, it was largely police science, and in later years developed into criminal justice. Therefore, in 2016, criminal justice education will celebrate its 100th anniversary, and you are reading this book most likely because of the pioneering work of August Vollmer.

W. M. Oliver. *August Vollmer: The father of American policing* (forthcoming). Durham, NC: Carolina Academic Press.

police administrators, and correctional officers; and more operational research projects and surveys conducted in conjunction with agencies of justice.[17]

After Johnson's commission published its report, the Law Enforcement Assistance Administration (LEAA) was created as part of the Omnibus Crime Control and Safe Streets Act of 1968. The LEAA was charged with revolutionizing criminal justice. Among the accomplishments of the agency were the following:[18]

- Encouraged for the first time state-level planning in criminal justice by spurring the formation of criminal justice state planning agencies.

- Contributed to law enforcement professionalism by providing higher education opportunities. The Law Enforcement Education Program (LEEP) enabled 100,000 students to attend more than 1,000 colleges and universities. A significant majority of current criminal justice leaders around the country are LEEP alumni.

- Laid the foundation for the development of standards for police, court, and correctional agencies.

➡ Encouraged the use of targeted strategies (for example, the establishment of career criminal units in prosecutors' offices).

➡ Launched the victim witness movement, encouraging prosecutors and other parts of the criminal justice system to undertake victim-witness initiatives.

➡ Enabled technological advances, including the development of bulletproof vests and forensic applications of DNA technology.

LEEP doled out more than $300 million to higher education institutions in an effort to support the development of criminal justice programs.[19] Criminal justice programs changed significantly after LEEP. In the 1970s, attention was given to training criminal justice professionals, but little attention was given to who was serving as educators. In the 1980s, more attention was given to educating (rather than training) in criminal justice programs, and a greater emphasis was placed on using highly qualified instructors (much like the instructors you now have in your criminal justice classes).[20]

In 1982, the LEAA was disbanded after facing a great deal of criticism, much of which was politically motivated. In 1984, the Justice Assistance Act led to the development of federal agencies that carried out functions similar to the LEAA.[21] Today, federal agencies such as the Bureau of Justice Assistance, National Institute of Justice, Office on Violence Against Women, and Office for Victims of Crime are among the major federal agencies supporting criminal justice training and research.

JOURNAL
Criminal Justice
Graduate Programs

To be sure, criminal justice has gone through various stages as an area of study. In its early stages, the academic area of study was viewed very much as a "cop shop." Initially, scholars from other disciplines questioned whether topics of interest to criminal justice professors "belonged in the academic community."[22] Such questions were followed by "questions about academic quality because of faculty credentials and the general ability to conduct research on par with the social, managerial, and behavioral sciences."[23] Through a concerted effort by leaders in the field, and the growth of the programs in colleges and universities across the world, criminal justice has garnered respect as a discipline. Describing this respect, James Finckenhauer,[24] former president of the Academy of Criminal Justice Sciences, made the following comments: "Criminal justice is clearly an accepted academic discipline, at least in most places and is an enormously popular one everywhere."[25] He highlighted three accomplishments of criminal justice higher education: (a) the professionalization of criminal justice practices, (b) the education of thousands of students in the area of criminal justice, and (c) the development of new careers such as security specialists, crime analysts, forensic scientists, and criminal justice planners. Several professional associations now exist that promote and support criminal justice scholarship and educational efforts.

As evidence of the increased popularity of criminal justice programs, in 1975 there were 55 criminal justice programs offered in colleges and universities across the United States. By 1990, there were 687 such programs.[26] More recent estimates suggest that there are roughly

1,000[27] or 2,000[28] college programs offering criminal justice coursework. The popularity of the criminal justice major stems from two factors: (a) Criminal justice is incredibly interesting, and (b) the demand for criminal justice professionals is growing.

Table 1.1 shows some of the careers available to criminal justice majors. Currently, more than three million individuals are employed in criminal justice careers, and each of these careers is expected to grow in the future. Even if crime and violence decreases, the need for criminal justice professionals will remain. Although many of these careers are in public agencies, private companies also hire professionals to do "criminal justice"–related work, including security work, forensics, audits, and investigations. You will read much more about these careers in later chapters, when the specific occupations are addressed. For now, make a note to update your resume so that you are prepared for the criminal justice adventures that await you. The "Help Wanted" box in this chapter describes the job duties and salary for one job that may be of interest to some of you.

Criminal justice conferences are held throughout the year so researchers and professionals can discuss the most effective criminal justice practices.

Department of Justice

BEYOND A REASONABLE DOUBT 1.4

_____ created the first criminology program at the University of California at Berkeley.

(a) Jerry Westby, (b) Dean Dabney, (c) Robert Mutchnick, (d) August Vollmer, (e) Emile Durkheim

---

The answer can be found on page 521.

Criminal Justice as a Social Science

As noted earlier, criminal justice has not always been held in high regard. When colleges and universities first developed criminal justice programs, questions surfaced about whether the area of study was actually a science. Other social science disciplines have faced similar questions. In 1970, Robert Bierstedt addressed concerns about whether sociology was a science in *The Social Order*.[29] To demonstrate his belief that sociology was a science, he outlined the way that the discipline adhered to specific principles of science that guide other disciplines and "harder" sciences such as physics, biology, and chemistry. Later, researchers Jack Fitzgerald and Steven Cox described the way that these principles relate to criminal justice

TABLE 1.1	**Common Careers in Criminal Justice**			
JOB TITLE	**JOB DESCRIPTION FROM BUREAU OF LABOR STATISTICS**	**ANNUAL MEAN WAGE IN 2014**	**EXPERIENCE NEEDED**	**NUMBER OF JOBS IN 2014**
Correctional Officer	Oversee those awaiting trial or sentenced to serve time in jail or prison.	$44,910	No	395,000
Court Reporter	Attend legal proceedings and create transcripts.	$55,000	No	18,330
Criminal Justice or Law Enforcement Teacher, Postsecondary	Teach courses in criminal justice, corrections, or law enforcement administration.	$61,750	No	14,890
Lawyer	Advise and represent individuals, businesses, or government agencies on legal issues or disputes.	$133,470	J.D. required	1,132,000
Paralegal or Legal Assistant	Perform tasks to support lawyers, including maintaining and organizing files, conducting legal research, and drafting documents.	$51,840	No	417,000
Police Officer or Detective	Enforce laws to protect people and their property.	$59,560–$80,540	Recruit training for entry; experience for higher level	844,000
Private Detective or Investigator	Find facts and analyze information about legal, financial, and personal matters. May offer services such as verifying people's backgrounds, tracing missing persons, investigating computer crimes, or protecting celebrities.	$52,880	Some	98,000
Probation Officer or Correctional Treatment Specialist	Work with and monitor offenders to prevent them from reoffending.	$53,360	No	100,000
Security Guards and Gaming and Surveillance Officers	Patrol and inspect property against fire, theft, vandalism, terrorism, and illegal activity. They monitor people and buildings in an effort to prevent crime	$28,080	No	899,000
Substance Abuse and Behavior Disorder Counselor	Advise people who have alcoholism or other types of addiction, eating disorders, or other behavioral problems. Provide treatment and support to help clients recover from addiction or modify problem behaviors.	$41,870	No	85,180

Bureau of Labor Statistics

research. Using these works as a foundation, one can also demonstrate how modern criminal justice researchers and criminal justice practitioners are guided by the principles of science. These principles include objectivity, parsimony, ethical neutrality, determinism, and skepticism.

Objectivity as a principle of science means that criminal justice scholars must not let their values drive their research endeavors. Criminal justice scholars will examine many controversial issues. To study these topics effectively, criminal justice researchers must set aside their own values and beliefs. Researchers who study sex offenders, for example, must approach the topic without letting their values influence the research endeavor. In a similar way, criminal justice professionals must approach criminal cases in an objective

objectivity: A principle of science suggesting that scientists must not let their values drive their research endeavors.

HELP WANTED: CRIMINAL INVESTIGATOR

DUTIES:

- Serve as a journeyman investigator responsible for independently planning, developing, and conducting criminal investigations involving highly technical computer programs and other advanced technology issues requiring exceptional levels of expertise and knowledge.

- Lead a joint investigative task force or serve as a member of a joint task force concerning network intrusions investigations, computer crime vulnerability assessments, or other investigations requiring the knowledge of a criminal investigator with advanced technology training and experience.

- Independently execute planning and coordination with other federal criminal investigators and worldwide law enforcement agencies such as the Defense Criminal Investigative Service (DCIS); Federal Bureau of Investigation (FBI); Air Force Office of Special Investigations (AFOSI); Naval Investigative Service (NIS); allied and other foreign countries' national police forces; and other federal, state, and local police agencies.

- Share vital criminal intelligence to plan and conduct large-scale raids, or searches, and conduct extensive, and often dangerous, undercover or surveillance operations with worldwide law enforcement agencies.

- Lead and conduct intricate or delicate criminal/computer investigations involving senior public officials or multinational corporations having continuing political or media interest.

REQUIREMENTS: Bachelor's degree

ANNUAL SALARY: $50,540

Adapted from USAJOBS.gov. Retrieved from https://www.usajobs.gov/GetJob/ViewDetails/363412600

---

way—with an open mind. It is our hope that readers will also approach the topics addressed in this book with an open mind.

Parsimony means that scientists must create the simplest explanations possible in examining the topics under study. This is much easier in the hard sciences, where topics such as energy can be reduced to rather simple formulas (for example, $E = mc^2$). Describing criminal behavior and criminal justice activities is not quite so simple. Still, as you will read about later in this text, criminal justice researchers have developed a number of rather simple explanations for crime and criminal justice actions. Just as researchers must develop simple explanations for the topics they study, criminal justice professionals must develop simple descriptions of offenses they are investigating. When presenting cases to judges and juries, for instance, prosecutors must make sure that their cases are easily understood.

Ethical neutrality suggests that criminal justice researchers should not allow their own ethical beliefs (or ideas about right and wrong) to guide their research efforts. Also, researchers have an ethical duty to respect the rights of their research subjects. Criminal justice researchers, like researchers from other disciplines, must ensure that the research subjects involved in their projects are not harmed. Colleges and universities require all research involving human subjects to be approved by a human subjects review board, which is typically called the college's institutional review board. According to federal

parsimony: A principle of science suggesting that scientists must create the simplest explanation possible in examining the topics under study.

ethical neutrality: A principle of science that states researchers should not allow their own ethical beliefs to guide their research efforts.

policy, when college institutional review boards review proposals involving prisoners, "at least one member of the Board shall be a prisoner, or a prisoner representative with appropriate background and experience to serve in that capacity."[30] The prisoner representative could be someone (practitioner or scholar) who is familiar with prison life. The board reviews research proposals to ensure that studies will not violate the rights of research subjects or otherwise harm them. Just as criminal justice researchers exercise great caution to protect the rights of research subjects, criminal justice professionals must go to great lengths to ensure that they do not violate suspects' constitutional rights. Bear in mind—especially in the interests of objectivity—that these rights are not "offenders' rights." They are individuals' rights: Each of us have rights that protect us against certain behaviors of criminal justice professionals. You will read more about these rights throughout this book.

Determinism means that behavior is caused or influenced by preceding events. On one level, criminal justice researchers point to a number of external factors that might contribute to criminal behavior. On another level, researchers may examine those factors within an individual that lead to criminal behavior. In some ways, the ideal of determinism is in contrast to "free will," which minimizes the relevance of external factors and suggests that individuals make a conscious decision to engage in specific activities. In an effort to balance deterministic and free-will perspectives, one might ask what leads individuals to make these decisions. It is insufficient to suggest that they simply make choices without delving deeper into the decision-making process. Indeed, the criminal justice process is—in many ways—based on a balancing of deterministic and free-will assumptions. In particular, criminal justice professionals will engage in activities designed to keep individuals from offending (for example, in an ideal system, the behaviors of criminal justice professionals should "cause" individuals to "choose" not to commit a crime).

Skepticism means that scientists must question and re-question everything. Criminal justice researchers must not accept the findings from prior research studies as fact. By questioning prior findings, the accuracy of prior research is either confirmed or new ways for approaching criminal justice topics will follow. In a similar way, criminal justice professionals must question and re-question (a) whether specific cases belong in the justice system, (b) whether prior agencies made the right decisions on specific cases, and (c) whether specific policies are appropriate in the criminal justice process.

Criminal Justice as a Setting for Controversial Issues

determinism:
A principle of science suggesting that behavior is caused or influenced by preceding events.

skepticism: A principle of science that states scientists must question everything.

Criminal justice is at the center of many controversial issues. These issues are frequently depicted on television shows and in the press. Issues such as the death penalty, appropriate handling of sex offenders, police corruption, racial profiling, drug legalization, prostitution, whether abortion is tied to the crime rate, torture, prison overcrowding, and drunk driving are just a handful of the hundreds of types of controversial issues that arise in discussions about criminal justice. Let's review three controversial criminal justice cases to demonstrate the complexity of these issues.

On April 29, 2014, the state of Oklahoma attempted to execute convicted murderer Clayton Lockett by lethal injection. Typically, inmates are unconscious from the injection in about 30 seconds or so and pronounced dead within a few minutes. In Lockett's case, he was still awake 16 minutes after receiving the injection. Laying on the gurney, he was flailing around violently. Lockett tried to sit up and said one word: "Man." The warden ordered the curtains to the viewing rooms closed. The injection had not killed him, and the prison doctor indicated that no lethal drugs remained. Corrections department director Robert Patton was preparing to halt the execution when Lockett died of a massive heart attack. Figure 1.4 provides a timeline of the execution. Critics of the death penalty vocally demonstrated their disdain for the sanction. The parents of the woman who Lockett murdered released this statement shortly after the botched execution:

> God blessed us with our precious daughter, Stephanie for 19 years. Stephanie loved children. She worked in Vacation Bible School and always helped with our Church nativity scenes. She was the joy of our life. We are thankful this day has finally arrived and justice will finally be served.—Susie and Steve Neiman, 4-29-14[31]

In another case, a university student reported that while she was on spring break in Florida, she was sexually assaulted by three fellow students. The attackers reportedly shared video depicting the incident around their campus. The victim reported the incident to campus authorities. After an investigation and a hearing, the three men were found responsible for sexual assault and harassment. As a penalty, they were not allowed to walk at commencement and they were to be expelled after their graduation. The victim dropped out of the university. She told a reporter, "This is my family's worst nightmare. They aren't here to protect me. And they're really upset that something happened. It really took a toll on us and has been hard on all of us."[32]

In a third case, Weldon Angelos was convicted in 2004 of selling small amounts of marijuana to undercover law enforcement officers on multiple occasions. Because he had a gun concealed under his clothes, he was sentenced to 55 years in prison. This was the equivalent of a life sentence for Angelos. The long sentence

FIGURE 1.4   Timeline of Clayton Lockett's Execution

5:19 pm
Lockett taken to the execution chamber.

5:22
Lockett restrained on execution table.

5:27
Phlebotomist enters chamber to identify best place for the IV.

6:18
IV is placed in Lockett's groin area, determined to be the only viable insertion point.

6:20
Phleblotomist leaves the execution chamber.

6:23
Execution chamber shades opened. Lockett declines opportunity to make a final statement.

6:23
Lethal injection begins to be administered through the IV.

6:30
Doctor reports that Lockett is still awake.

6:33
Doctor reports that Lockett is unconcious, and additional combination of drugs is administered through the IV.

6:38
Lockett tries to sit up and starts writhing on the gurney. He mumbles. The only word individuals hear is, "Man." Reporters later said that Lockett appeared to be experiencing pain.

6:42
Shades to execution chamber closed.

6:44 to 6:56
Doctor examines Lockett. Announces that he still has heartbeat.

6:56
Director of Corrections calls off the execution.

7:06
Lockett declared dead from massive heart attack.

was the result not of an irrational judge, but of a sentencing system that determined this was the appropriate sentence. In fact, in his written opinion, sentencing judge Paul Cassell wrote that he viewed the sentence as "unjust, cruel, and irrational." He added that because the case was "one of those rare cases where the system has malfunctioned, the President [should] commute this unjust sentence." In 2013, a group of current and former judges, prosecutors, defense attorneys, scholars, political officials, and others familiar with the case sent President Barack Obama a letter requesting that the sentence be commuted. Angelos remains in prison, serving a sentence longer than would be served by kidnappers, rapists, and aircraft hijackers.

These three cases only begin to introduce you to the range of issues that surface in criminal justice discussions. Oftentimes it is believed that clear lines exist between what is "right" and "wrong." In reality, most issues cannot be dissected so simply. Did the convicted murderer deserve to die? Should the next execution have been halted because of the botched execution? Should universities punish students for actions they commit while on spring break? What sanctions should have been given in the sexual assault case? Is a 55-year sentence for selling marijuana while possessing a handgun appropriate?

In this text, you will read about numerous controversial issues surfacing in policing, the courts, and corrections. In discussing these criminal justice issues, we will use a balanced approach to demonstrate all sides of the issues. It is our hope that, in doing so, we will give you a foundation from which you can think more scientifically about these issues.

Criminal Justice Versus Criminology

Thus far, our discussion has focused on what we have called the discipline of criminal justice. In our field, the area of study focusing on criminal justice topics has several different names. Each name tends to connote a slightly different focus. *Criminal justice* focuses primarily on the justice process,

Criminal justice covers a range of controversial issues, and it's important to approach them from a balanced perspective.

© Mark Jenkinson/CORBIS; © istockphoto/Bob Ingelhart; © istockphoto/e_rasmus

with a particular emphasis given to the agencies and officials involved in the process. **Criminology**, in turn, focuses primarily on crime and criminals in an effort to understand and explain behavior. Some scholars might identify with one of the areas more than the other area. Even so, scholars from both areas seem to appreciate the need to understand both. For instance, it is impossible to understand and explain crime without also understanding the criminal justice process.

Academic departments often select between the two names to identify the nature of the curriculum offered in the department. Other departments or colleges label themselves "Criminology and Criminal Justice" or "Criminal Justice and Criminology" because it is truly impossible to separate crime, criminals, and the criminal justice process in our scholarly pursuits. Combining the two areas also offers a balanced foundation from which students will gain a full understanding about crime and criminal justice. Also, joining the two names strengthens our area of study by limiting unnecessary debates about the relative importance of the two areas. Note, too, that some programs are called "Justice Studies," others are called "Administration of Justice," and others are called "Crime, Law, and Society" or some variation. Regardless of what the academic program is called, all of the programs recognize the need for students to adequately understand the criminal justice process.

Criminal Justice as a Collection of Individuals

Criminal justice can also be defined by the actions of those individuals engaged in the criminal justice process. In particular, criminal justice can be viewed as a collection of individuals charged with making decisions as part of a formal effort to control human behavior. These decisions will ultimately affect how a case is processed through the justice system. It is important to recognize that the activities of professionals in the criminal justice system are guided by a series of decisions made by the professionals as well as by those outside of the system. On one level, the decisions are influenced by broader structural and political influences. On another level, the decisions made in specific criminal cases have consequences for those involved with those specific cases. Figure 1.5 shows the various types of decisions made in the criminal justice process.

The criminal justice system can be viewed as a living system influenced by the decisions made by individuals inside the system and outside the system. Their decisions will influence how cases proceed through the justice system. The decisions have extraordinarily significant implications for other peoples' lives. Deciding to arrest a suspect will change the course of the suspect's life, as well as the lives of the suspect's loved ones. Decisions made by others in the justice process will have equal, if not greater, consequences for suspects.

Because of the ramifications of these decisions, criminal justice professionals must approach their professions in an ethical way. *Ethical decision making* refers to the process of considering multiple options; deciding the appropriateness of each option; and assessing the conse-

criminology: The academic study of crimes and the circumstances surrounding them.

FIGURE 1.5   **Decisions Made in the Criminal Justice Process**

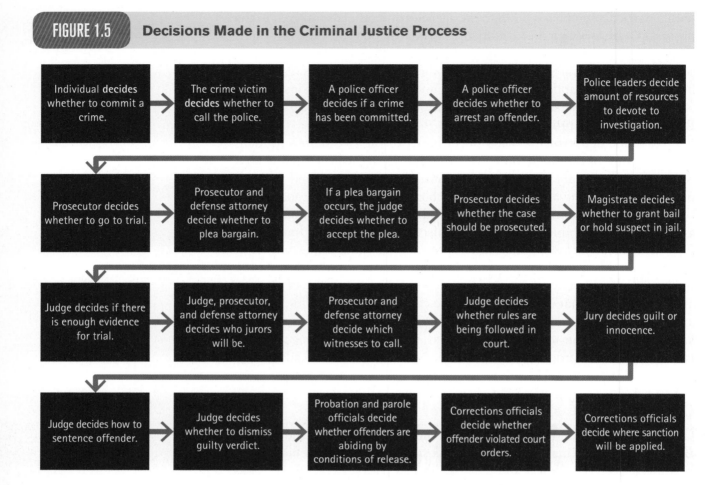

quences of each option for the suspect, the criminal justice official, the criminal justice agency, and the broader community. Throughout this book, we include boxed features that ask you to read a criminal justice scenario and engage in the ethical decision-making process. The "Ethical

One of the most powerful decisions made in the criminal justice process occurs during the sentencing hearing.

Decision Making" box in this chapter includes a scenario that we hope never happens to you.

Criminal Justice and College Students

Just as criminal justice professionals make decisions that influence case processing, college students make decisions that are relevant to criminal justice. Consider the following decisions that college students might need to make:

AUTHOR VIDEO
Levels of Student
Involvement

- Whether to declare criminal justice as a major
- Whether to attend every criminal justice class
- Whether to do an internship with a criminal justice agency
- Whether to go to graduate school in criminal justice
- Which criminal justice agency they want to work for

College students also might find themselves playing one or more of several roles that are relevant to the criminal justice process. These roles include

ETHICAL DECISION MAKING

THE CHOICE TO ENFORCE THE LAW (OR NOT)

Randy Rainey is a 42-year-old single father who returned to school in hopes of completing a double major in criminal justice and management. He is employed as a loss prevention officer at a retail store and wants to become a regional director of loss prevention. He knows that he will need to work his way up through the loss prevention ranks but that he also needs to have the requisite education to meet his career goals.

His favorite professor is his advisor, Dr. Jame. Randy enjoys taking Dr. Jame's classes and talking with the professor about his career goals.

One Wednesday evening, Randy is working his loss prevention job. He is watching the cameras when he sees his favorite professor enter the store. Curious about the shopping habits of his mentor, Randy decides to "follow" Dr. Jame through the store by watching the security cameras. He is stunned at what he subsequently sees: Dr. Jame steals more than $200 worth of infant formula by putting items in his infant

son's oversized diaper bag. Randy has several decisions to make:

YOU DECIDE

1. Should Randy confront Dr. Jame? Why or why not?

2. Should he ask his supervisor to handle the case? What would the supervisor think about Randy's decision not to handle the case himself?

3. If he stopped Dr. Jame, should he call the police? Why or why not?

4. What are some possible reasons that Dr. Jame stole the formula? Should those factors affect Randy's decision to bust Dr. Jame? Should those factors affect decisions to better secure formula in the future? Explain.

5. Should Randy continue to take classes offered by Dr. Jame? Explain.

6. What if Dr. Jame stole something cheaper, like a package of diapers that costs $10? Would this change any of your answers to the preceding questions?

(a) victims, (b) offenders, (c) current or future practitioners, (d) research subjects, (e) future policy makers, and (f) future researchers.[33]

College Students as Victims

College students are not isolated from the crime problem. A review of victimization experiences between 1995 and 2002, comparing college students and non–college students, found similar violent victimization rates in male college students and male nonstudents, whereas victimization rates were lower in female college students than in female nonstudents.[34] However, compared to male students, female students are more frequently the target of certain types of victimization, such as sexual assault, and authorities often give these offenses inadequate attention.[35]

College Students as Offenders

Some college students may be offenders, in the past, currently, or in the future. Offenses committed during the college years appear to be tied to the lifestyles of college students.[36] In particular, offenses frequently attributed to college students include public drunkenness, minor drug offenses, simple assault, sexual assault, and computer crimes such as piracy. As a note of warning, these offenses can be particularly devastating to a criminal justice student's future career. Some college criminal justice programs require their majors to report any arrests to the program administrators. The guidelines for one program, for example, state:

> A Criminal Justice student arrested for any criminal offense, for driving under the influence of alcohol or drugs, or for fleeing a police officer, is expected to file a written report with the CJ program coordinator. The report will include (a) date of arrest, (b) date of court appearances, and (c) final disposition. The initial report is expected to be filed no later than 72 hours following the arrest. Failure to comply with this expectation may result in disciplinary probation and/or dismissal from the program.[37]

Far too many criminal justice majors have likely been forced to change their career choice as a result of misdeeds they committed while in college. In a related vein, see the "Criminal Justice and the Media" box in this chapter for some advice related to your Facebook posts.

College Students as Criminal Justice Practitioners

College students often fulfill the role of criminal justice practitioner. In some cases, criminal justice majors in particular might be current criminal justice professionals. For some jobs in criminal justice, a college degree may not be necessary to enter the profession, but a degree is typically necessary to advance in a criminal justice career. As a result, professionals who began their criminal justice careers without a degree frequently enter college as nontraditional college students. The presence of such students in criminal justice courses makes for lively discussions as the professionals are able to bring insight to courses that otherwise would not be present.

[CRIMINAL JUSTICE and the **MEDIA:**

FACEBOOK AND FUTURE CAREERS IN CRIMINAL JUSTICE]

Do you have a Facebook page? Are you cautious with what you post on Facebook? To some observers, Facebook postings may seem to be nothing more than a way for college students to share evidence of the "good time" they had over the weekend. However, the postings can have a long-lasting impact on students' abilities to secure future employment. It is quite common now for employers, particularly criminal justice agencies, to search the Internet for content related to future employees. Searching Facebook pages is, in fact, now a routine part of background checks in some criminal justice professions.

Some of you may feel comforted by the fact that your Facebook pages are private. After all, you can select "privacy" settings so that only your "friends" can see what you post on your page. A few things are worth considering in response to this belief about privacy. For example, if your friends can view content on your Facebook page, *their* friends might also be able to view parts of your page if they tag your page or save any content from your page. Although most Facebook users are probably already aware of this, many were surprised to learn from an Associated Press article that Facebook users are sometimes required by potential employers to turn over their Facebook passwords, or at least to log in to their Facebook pages during job interviews, so that the employers can review the Facebook postings, regardless of the user's privacy settings (McFarland, 2012). According to McFarland, some employers ask potential employees to "friend" background investigators as part of their background check.

Of course, you can refuse to log in to your Facebook page during a job interview or deny the friend request made by the investigator, but as one chief deputy told McFarland, allowing employers to access their Facebook pages "speaks well of the people we have apply." By implication, refusing to open up your Facebook page to interviewers does not speak so well.

As a result of the Associated Press article, legislators across the United States proposed laws prohibiting employers from requesting password information from potential employees, and Maryland was the first state to pass such legislation in June 2012 (Bennett-Smith, 2012). Other states may follow suit, but employers are still able to review Facebook postings available through public settings.

Bennett-Smith, M. (2012, June 11). Job interviewer asks for Facebook password. *Christian Science Monitor.* Retrieved from http://www.csmonitor.com/Business/2012/0611/Job-interviewer-asks-for-Facebook-password.-Should-you-give-it; McFarland, S. (2012, March 21). "Job seekers getting asked for Facebook passwords." *USA Today.* Retrieved from http://usatoday30.usatoday.com/tech/news/story/2012-03-20/job-applicants-facebook/53665606/1

Of course, many criminal justice majors are not employed as criminal justice professionals while they are college students. These students may have the goal of entering a criminal justice career after receiving their degree. Indeed, many criminal justice careers require at least an associate degree, if not a bachelor's degree, for employment. Interestingly, research shows that the better education that students receive, the more satisfied they will be with their careers later in life.[38] See the "Criminal Justice and College Students" box in this chapter for some points to ponder about your own future in criminal justice.

College Students as Research Subjects

College students are frequently research subjects in criminal justice studies. The benefits of using college students in criminal justice research studies include the following:[39]

CRIMINAL JUSTICE and **COLLEGE STUDENTS**

YOUR FUTURE IN CRIMINAL JUSTICE

You chose this criminal justice course for a reason. Reflect for a moment on that reason. For those of you who are not criminal justice majors, you may have selected the course because it seemed interesting. For others of you who are criminal justice majors, you may aspire to work in criminal justice at some point in the future. A few of you may have chosen the class for practical reasons: It may have been the only class open when you registered for classes.

Regardless of why you chose this class, look to your future and consider how criminal justice will affect your life. Take out a note card, draw a line down the middle of the card, and in the right-hand column, write the

following words (as a list): *victims, offenders, current or future practitioners, research subjects, future policy makers,* and *future researchers.*

Next, beside each word or phrase, indicate whether you anticipate playing that role in criminal justice in the future. For the roles in criminal justice that you expect to play, briefly explain how (for example, for "current or future practitioner," write down the career you might be interested in).

Finally, use the notecard as a bookmark as you read the rest of the text. This will help you to remember the important roles you might play in criminal justice in the future.

- ➡ Students are easily accessible.

- ➡ Student samples are cost- and time-efficient.

- ➡ Researchers can measure change fairly easily with students.

- ➡ Students are people, too.

- ➡ Students reflect culture.

- ➡ Students tend to be close to the age category most often involved in crime or deviance.

- ➡ Students can learn from the research process.

Studies using college students as a sample tend to focus on the behaviors of college students, their victimization experiences, tests of theory, and attitudes of students. Although a number of limitations exist with using college students as research subjects, the discipline of criminal justice has learned a great deal from our college student research subjects.

College Students as Future Policy Makers

Some college students have a role as future policy makers. Think about that . . . you, or your study partner, might be a future legislator. Just for fun, put the word *Governor* or *Senator* in front of your name. Sounds good, doesn't it? Although we are making light of this suggestion, the real fact is that most legislators have a college education. Learning about criminal justice from a balanced perspective as college students will provide future policy makers the foundation they need to begin to formulate effective criminal justice policies. We hope you hang on to this book to be on the safe side, so that when you become governor you will have a handy resource to remind yourself about criminal justice issues.

JOURNAL
Attitudes About
Criminal Justice

College Students as Future Researchers

Some college students will go on to become criminal justice researchers. Your professors were once students themselves. Something got them excited about criminal justice. For our field to grow, current college students must also get excited about the discipline. It is our hope that some of you will become so excited about criminal justice that you will consider a future career as a criminal justice scholar. At the very least, we hope we don't scare you off!

In this text, we view criminal justice as (a) a system, (b) a process, (c) a career, (d) a social science, (e) the center of many controversial issues, and (f) a collection of individuals charged with formally controlling the behaviors of others through a complex decision-making process while responding to structural and societal influences and demands. Beyond recognizing that criminal justice is a "collection of individuals," bear in mind that many of you will someday become part of that collection of individuals who are responsible for responding to crime. Whether as police officers, professionals in the courts, corrections officials, policy makers, or officials in private security careers, the individuals in these careers make decisions about other peoples' lives, and these decisions have very real ramifications for the way that the justice process unfolds. (Good luck, governor!)

Just the Facts: Chapter Summary

- The phrase *criminal justice system* is used to describe the three main components of criminal justice: the police, the courts, and corrections.

- The stages of the criminal justice process include the following: investigation, arrest, booking, initial appearance, preliminary hearing, grand jury or information, arraignment, trial, sentencing, appeals, sanction, and release.

- Walker's wedding cake model of criminal justice describes four layers of cases that flow through the criminal justice process: celebrated cases, heavy-duty felonies, lightweight felonies, and misdemeanors.

- The "modern emergence of [criminal justice]" is traced to the President Lyndon Johnson's Commission of Law Enforcement and Administration of Justice, whose report *The Challenge of Crime in a Free Society*

called for the education of criminal justice professionals and improved criminal justice research efforts as strategies to address the crime problem.

- Criminal justice researchers and practitioners parallel the principles of sciences described by Bierstedt: objectivity, parsimony, ethical neutrality, determinism, and skepticism.

- As professionals in a social science discipline, criminal justice researchers and criminologists have recently become more instrumental in helping to determine the efficacy of criminal justice policies.

- Criminal justice focuses primarily on the justice process, with particular emphasis given to the agencies and officials involved in the process. Criminology, in turn, focuses primarily on crime and criminals in an effort to understand and explain behavior.

2

PERSPECTIVES ON CRIME AND CRIMINAL JUSTICE RESEARCH

© iStockphoto/AnderAguirre

© alessandro0770/Veer

PROFESSOR MARTIN SANCHEZ-JANKOWSKI STUDIED GANGS over a 10-year timeframe by observing and participating in the activities of gangs (37 in all) in three different cities: Boston, Los Angeles, and New York. As Sanchez-Jankowski noted, he was not able to simply show up and say, "I am a professor and I want to study you."[1] Instead, he had to earn the trust of the gang members before they would agree to be part of the study. Beyond reading the gang members consent forms, Sanchez-Jankowski noted that the gang members would monitor their own behavior to see if arrests occurred after they committed illegal acts in front of the researcher. Many of the gangs he studied would also pick fights with Sanchez-Jankowski as part of their efforts to decide whether to trust him. Sanchez-Jankowski observed that "it was considered acceptable to fight and lose, but it was unacceptable to refuse to fight."[2]

After gaining access to the gangs, Sanchez-Jankowski immersed himself into their cultures. He wrote:

> I participated in nearly all things they did. I ate where they ate, I slept where they slept, I stayed with their families, I traveled where they went, and in certain situations where I could not remain neutral, I fought with them. The only things that I did not participate in were those activities that were illegal. As part of our mutual understanding, it was agreed that I did not have to participate in any activity (including taking drugs) that was illegal.[3]

In many ways, Sanchez-Jankowski became a gang member for 10 years of his life. He fought with other gangs and was "held up at least 20 times, stabbed more than once—a wound to the wrist required 50 stitches—shot in the leg in a drive-by attack and clubbed by a cop during a gang bust in 1983."[4]

LEARNING OBJECTIVES

After reading this chapter, students will be able to:

2.1 Discuss the legal perspective of crime

2.2 Define how crime is a violation of the criminal law

2.3 Discuss the social perspective of crime

2.4 Compare and contrast norm violations and ethical violations

2.5 Discuss the behavioral perspective of crime

2.6 Determine the types of research methods used in scholarly criminal justice studies

2.7 Evaluate the strengths and weaknesses of common criminal justice research strategies

ADMISSIBLE or INADMISSIBLE Evidence

Read the statements that follow. If the statement is true, circle *admissible.* If the statement is false, circle *inadmissible.* Answers can be found on page 517.

1. **Admissible   Inadmissible**   The phrase *actus reus* refers to the principle of guilty mind.

2. **Admissible   Inadmissible**   From a legal perspective, harm occurs in all types of crimes, including victimless crimes.

3. **Admissible   Inadmissible**   Affirmative defenses are legal strategies in which the defendant admits to committing the crime but provides either a justification or an excuse.

4. **Admissible   Inadmissible**   *Status offenses* refers to a class of offenses that are illegal for juveniles but not adults.

5. **Admissible   Inadmissible**   The concept of *mores* describes norms that are based on moral beliefs.

6. **Admissible   Inadmissible**   Most criminal justice studies are experiments.

7. **Admissible   Inadmissible**   Researchers rarely use police records to study criminal justice topics.

8. **Admissible   Inadmissible**   Findings from criminal justice research studies are not facts or proof of any kind; rather, findings should be seen as part of a broader effort to enhance understanding about criminal justice.

Studying gangs is not an easy task. One researcher actually joined multiple gangs in his efforts to study them.

© Iain McKell/Getty Images

rofessor Sanchez-Jankowski certainly went beyond the call of duty. Still, his immersion in the gang culture provided insightful and useful information about gangs. For our purposes, his study provided insight into the criminal law, how we define crime, and how researchers study criminal justice. We discuss these areas throughout this chapter. Indeed, a balanced understanding of criminal justice requires students to understand the different ways that crime is defined, how crime is a violation of the criminal law, and the types of research methods criminal justice scholars use to study crime and criminal justice topics. Understanding these topics gives criminal justice students the foundation they need to explore how we measure the extent of crime, crime trends and patterns, crime types, the causes of crime, and the processing of criminal cases through the criminal justice system.

How one defines crime is particularly important. After all, one's definition of crime will influence (a) how individuals react to behaviors defined as crime, (b) who is defined as a criminal, (c) estimates about the extent of behaviors defined as crime, (d) explanations of different behaviors defined as crime, and (e) how and whether cases are processed through the justice system. In our view, crime can be examined from legal, behavioral, and social perspectives. Figure 2.1 summarizes these three perspectives.

➡ Legal Perspectives of Crime

When we think about crime, the images that come to mind usually involve the law in some way. One might say that crime is a violation of legal codes.

FIGURE 2.1   **Perspectives on Crime**

Legal Perspective
- Crime is a violation of the criminal law.

Social Perspective
- Crime is defined by members of society.

Behavioral Perspective
- Crime is defined by specific actions and their consequencs.

© istockphoto.com/DNY59; © istockphoto.com/MaestroBooks; © istockphoto.com/KatarzynaBialasiewicz

However, many different types of legal codes exist, and not everyone would agree that violations of those legal codes are necessarily crimes. Your university, for example, has legal codes that your professors are expected to follow as well as codes that you are expected to follow. A violation of one of these codes (for example, cheating on a test) would not be defined as a crime. To fully define crime from a legal perspective, it is important to consider that (a) crime is an illegal act according to the criminal law, (b) crime is an illegal act committed without defense, and (c) juveniles who violate the criminal law are defined as juvenile delinquents.

Crime as an Illegal Act According to the Criminal Law

The **criminal law** is the branch of law that proscribes formal punishment for the violation of society's rules, or offenses against the state, in contrast to *civil law*, which proscribes punishment for violations against the individual. In other words, the criminal law defines those behaviors that are illegal, or "crimes." One of the most popular legal definitions of *crime* was offered in 1960 by Paul Tappan, who wrote, "Crime is an intentional act or omission in violation of criminal law committed without defense or justification and sanctioned by the state as a felony or misdemeanor."[5] The criminal law can be distinguished from other forms of law because it proscribes specific punishments for offenders who are convicted of violating the criminal law. Tappan asserted that crime is restricted to offenses that are defined as *felonies* or *misdemeanors* in the criminal law. As noted in Chapter 1, felonies are more serious offenses that could result in a sanction of a year or more in prison or the death penalty. Misdemeanors are less serious offenses that proscribe punishments no greater than a year in jail. In reality, most misdemeanors never result in incarceration.

By limiting his definition of crime to felonies and misdemeanors, Tappan excluded from his classification a number of behaviors that are technically illegal and are treated by the justice system as illegal. In particular, **summary offenses** are minor offenses that "are defined as such to allow the justice system to dispense with them readily."[6] You may know someone who has been arrested for disorderly conduct. This would be a summary offense. Other examples of summary offenses include public drunkenness, loitering, many traffic offenses, and underage drinking. While not technically crimes, according to Tappan, those charged with and convicted of these offenses will still be punished. The maximum punishment, however, is less than the maximum punishment that would be possible for a misdemeanor.

Increasingly, the federal criminal law is being used to govern individual behavior. In the past, law enforcement was traditionally done at the state level. As offenders' crimes changed and grew across state and country borders, federal law enforcement has expanded its reach. Congress has passed criminal laws against offenses such as selling drugs, kidnapping, gun crimes, and terrorism. Of course, state laws also regulate these offenses, adding to the complexity involved in understanding the criminal law. A key point about the criminal law is that criminal law statutes are

VIDEO
How I Defend the Rule of Law

criminal law: The branch of law that prescribes formal punishment for the violation of society's rules, or offenses against the state.

summary offenses: Minor offenses that the justice system is able to handle fairly quickly.

more specific in defining the various elements (or parts) of a crime than was the case under common law (which refers to law derived from customs or precedents rather than statutory law).

BEYOND A REASONABLE DOUBT 2.1

_____ is the branch of law that proscribes formal punishment for the violation of offenses against the state.

(a) State law, (b) Criminal law, (c) Civil law, (d) Tort law, (e) Procedural law

---

The answer can be found on page 521.

Legal Elements of Criminality

Legal scholars have recognized five elements of criminality. At different stages of the criminal justice process, criminal justice officials decide the degree to which these elements are present in the suspect's actions. As the case proceeds through the justice system, the standards of proof for establishing each of these elements increase. These five elements are as follows:[7]

- *Commission of an act.* A criminal act (*actus reus*) must be committed, though failure to act may be a crime in some situations. Examples of failure to act include the failure to perform a legal duty (such as failing to register a handgun when the law requires it, failing to pay income taxes, or failing to report child abuse if one has a legal duty to do so) or the failure to intervene to prevent serious harm when a special relationship exists between the parties (as in the case of parents and their children).

- *Criminal intent.* The offender must have intended to commit the crime.

- *Concurrence.* The act and the intent must be joined together.

- *Causation.* The action must be a direct cause of harm.

- *Harm.* The term *harm* refers to the injury to another. Harm occurs in all crimes, even in so-called victimless crimes.

The notion of criminal intent warrants further discussion. *Intent* is a complicated legal concept. At the simplest level, for an act to be considered a crime under the criminal law, the offender must have intended to commit the action. The phrase *mens rea* refers to an offender's criminal intent, or guilty mind. If an individual did not intend to commit the action, or if intent cannot be inferred to exist, then a basic element of the legal definition of crime is not present. Legal scholars have described four different types of intent:[8]

- **General intent** is present when the suspect intended to commit the crime but may not have intended the specific consequences. For example, if someone is killed during a robbery, but the robber only intended to steal, it can be suggested that the suspect had "general intent" for the killing.

general intent: The suspect intended to commit the crime but may not have intended the specific consequences.

- **Specific intent** is present when the suspect intended to commit the crime, and the specific consequences from the crime can be linked "specifically" to the criminal act. For example, in an assault in which one individual hits another, the offender specifically intended to hurt the victim.

- **Transferred intent** involves an individual's being held liable for the behavior of others if the individual's behavior contributed to the crime. For example, in some jurisdictions, in a drive-by shooting the driver can be charged with murder even though the driver did not perform the killing.

- **Criminal negligence** involves an individual's being held liable if his or her failure to act in a reasonable way can be connected to harmful results. For example, if someone drives erratically and causes an accident that kills another person, the driver could be charged with negligent homicide, even though he or she did not "intend" to kill someone.

> **specific intent:** A suspect intended to commit an act, and specific consequences can be associated with that act.
>
> **transferred intent:** An individual may be held liable for the behavior of others on the assumption that the individual's behavior contributed to the crime.
>
> **criminal negligence:** Individuals fail to act in a reasonable way and this failure to act can be connected to harmful results.
>
> **defense:** A legal strategy that defendants use to establish that they should not be found guilty of a specific crime.

Occasionally, individuals can be charged with and convicted of an offense without direct proof of criminal intent. For example, the concept of *strict liability* provides that suspects can be held accountable regardless of whether criminal intent is proven when the state or governing authority believes it is appropriate to establish laws waiving the intent requirement. Statutory rape laws are an example. An individual over the age of consent could have sex with someone under the legal age of consent under the mistaken belief that the sex partner was of legal age. In this case, the individual did not intend to commit a crime. Still, that person can be held criminally liable because statutory rape laws follow the principle of strict liability. In addition, in some cases employers can be held accountable for their employees' behaviors under the legal principle of *vicarious liability*. Note, however, that civil penalties (such as fines) would be applied in these situations rather than criminal penalties such as incarceration. If, for example, a restaurant is found liable because one of its workers served someone too much alcohol, the owner of the restaurant would be fined under the civil law, but he or she would not be sentenced in criminal court to sanctions such as incarceration or probation.

Crime as an Illegal Act Without Defense

When suspects are charged with a crime, the law provides them several possible legal defenses. Generally speaking, a **defense** is a legal strategy that defendants use to establish that they should not be found guilty of a specific crime. If the defendant's attorney successfully argues the defense, the defendant will be found not guilty of the crime. A common defense is an *alibi defense*, in which a particular defendant provides evidence that he or she was not present at the crime. In a rather famous instance, Juan

Larry David's *Curb Your Enthusiasm* filming at the Dodgers ballpark provided an alibi for an offender who was charged with murder. Incidentally, the episode that was being filmed was one where David hired a prostitute to ride in his car with him so he could use the HOV lane and get to the baseball game on time. The prostitute later smoked a marijuana joint with David's father. They didn't need an alibi because their behavior was fiction.

Catalan, a defendant accused of murder, used Larry David's popular HBO series *Curb Your Enthusiasm* as an alibi. The defendant stated that he could not have committed the crime in question because at the time the crime was taking place he was at a Los Angeles Dodgers baseball game, where it so happened that David's crew was filming scenes for an episode of the show. A review of the video outtakes showed that Catalan really was at the baseball game. Charges were subsequently dropped. Unfortunately, the man spent almost five months in jail before his defense attorney was able to locate the outtakes and establish the alibi.

Affirmative defenses are legal strategies in which the defendant admits to committing the crime but provides either a justification or an excuse. Note that these legal concepts have different connotations than what typically comes to mind when one thinks of justifications and excuses. In a justification defense, the defendant admits responsibility for the action but argues that given the specific dynamics of the action, the behavior was not criminal. For example, we can consider self-defense, consent, and execution of legal duties as types of justification defenses. Table 2.1 provides an overview of various defenses. They are discussed in more detail in Chapter 10.

TABLE 2.1	**Common Legal Defenses for Criminal Law**
DEFENSE	**EXPLANATION**
Self-Defense	Self-defense may be successfully claimed if the defendant can demonstrate that he or she used force to repel an imminent, unprovoked attack, in the reasonable belief that he or she was about to be seriously injured. The defendant may only use as much force as is necessary to repel the attack. There are a number of limitations and exceptions to the general rules of self-defense. These include the retreat doctrine, which states that a person must retreat rather than use deadly force if doing so is possible without endangering the person's life. The castle doctrine, on the other hand, states that persons attacked in their home need not retreat from a potentially deadly invasion and/or attack. Self-defense also may apply to the defense of others, and in some limited circumstances to the defense of property.
Consent	Consent is a defense to some crimes, albeit a controversial one. Most jurisdictions provide that persons may consent to suffer what otherwise would be an actionable injury. What acts a person can consent to suffer are quite limited, however, and it must be demonstrated that the consent was voluntary, knowing, and intelligent. As we have seen, the "consent" of a minor to have sex with an adult is not considered voluntary, knowing, and intelligent and would therefore not be a legally permissible consent defense. An example of voluntary, knowing, and intelligent consent is that of the professional athlete who chooses to engage in activity where injury similar to an assault may occur.
Execution of Public Duties	Agents of the state, such as police officers or soldiers, are permitted to use reasonable force in the lawful execution of their duties. This defense allows the use of deadly force under the proper circumstances and allows police to engage in activities that are otherwise criminal if they are doing so as part of their law enforcement efforts, such as posing as a drug dealer. The most controversial element of this defense is police killings, since officers are limited to the circumstances under which deadly force can be used.
Intoxication	There are two forms of intoxication, voluntary and involuntary. Voluntary intoxication never provides a complete defense but in some states may negate the mens rea component for an offense requiring the specific intent by reducing the degree of the crime charged in some states. In other states, the rule is that the voluntary act of drinking establishes voluntariness and thus cannot be used as any kind of mitigation. It also may be used to argue for a lesser penalty. Involuntary intoxication may provide a defense if it can be shown that the actor was unaware that he or she was being drugged. In such cases, the actor is excused because he or she is not responsible for becoming intoxicated; consequently, it would be unfair to hold him or her liable for the resulting uncontrollable action. The Supreme Court has held that due process does not require that states allow the defense of intoxication (*Montana v. Egelhoff*, 1996).
Age	Historically, youth has been treated as a defense to criminal liability on the ground that persons below a certain age lack the requisite mental capability to form mens rea. Under the common law, there was a presumption that children under the age of seven years were incompetent. Today, the various jurisdictions define the age of majority (when one becomes an adult) at varying ages. Those classified as juveniles are dealt with not in the criminal justice system but rather in the juvenile justice system.

Reprinted from Hemmens, C., Brody, D., & Spohn, C. (2009). *Criminal courts*. Newbury Park, CA: Sage.

The decision to label a behavior as crime will determine whether the case continues in the justice process. The "Ethical Decision Making" box in this chapter illustrates how decisions are potentially shaped by factors beyond legal ones.

Crime as Juvenile Delinquency

Conceptually, different sets of laws exist for adults and juveniles. Most states define juveniles as individuals under the age of 18. If an individual is over age 18 when he or she commits an illegal act, the act is called a crime. If the individual is under age 18, the behavior is labeled **juvenile delinquency** (and the offender is called a *juvenile delinquent*, as opposed to a criminal). **Status offenses** refers to a class of offenses that are illegal for juveniles but not adults. Running away, drinking alcohol, smoking tobacco, and skipping school are examples. If one of the authors wanted to run away, for instance, there is nothing to stop us from doing so (except mortgages and spouses that would . . . well, never mind). If we wanted to skip our classes, we'd get in trouble with our bosses, but the police would, we hope, not be called. For juveniles, different labels are used to describe their illegal behavior and different standards are in place for their conduct. As we discuss in later chapters, these different labels and standards are also applied through a different set of procedures in the justice process.

➡ Social Perspectives of Crime

Whereas some individuals define crime as violations of the criminal law, others focus on how society creates definitions of appropriate and inappropriate behavior. From this perspective, crime can be defined as a

VIDEO
What I Learned as a Kid in Jail

juvenile delinquency: Illegal behaviors committed by individuals under age 18.

status offenses: A class of offenses that are illegal for juveniles but not adults.

ETHICAL DECISION MAKING

THE PROCESS OF LABELING BEHAVIOR AS CRIME

As a college student, you have been hired as a part-time security specialist for the campus police department. The experience will help you as you think about possible careers in criminal justice. Part of your responsibilities include walking in the dorms to ensure that residents are not breaking laws or dorm policies. One Saturday evening, you are walking through the newest dorm on campus when you smell smoke coming from one of the rooms. You knock on the door and everything gets quiet in the room. About a half-minute later a student opens the door. You recognize the student immediately as Pat, who you sit by in your favorite criminal justice class, but

you don't know Pat's age for certain. You've always felt a special connection to Pat, although the two of you have never talked. As you look in the room, you see what appears to be an empty 40-ounce can that once contained beer and you smell alcohol on Pat's breath.

YOU DECIDE

1. Has a crime been committed? Explain.
2. Should you report the case to the campus police? Why or why not?
3. What are the ramifications of calling the behavior a crime in this situation?

Setting determines whether behavior is defined as normal, deviant, or criminal. Hitting another person in most settings would be considered a crime. In a boxing ring, this behavior is normal.

REUTERS/Yuya Shino

JOURNAL
Tolerance for Law Violations and Social Projection Among Offenders and Nonoffenders

violation of norms, an ethical violation, a social construction, and a social justice issue.

Crime as a Violation of Norms

Norms are accepted standards for behavior and conduct. The term *deviance* is used to refer to the violation of norms, whereas the term *deviants* describes individuals who break the norms. Sociologists use the concept of *mores* to refer to norms based on moral beliefs. Norms that prohibit incest, for instance, would be mores. The label *folkways* refers to norms based on rituals or customs.[9] When you go to class, you are dressed in clothing that represents your culture's customs. Of course, if you go to class without any clothes at all, then you are violating mores (and the law). Similarly, if you wear a Halloween costume to class in February, you would be violating folkways.

Whether norm violations are defined as criminal depends on the setting, relationships, justifications, and time. Consider the behavior of hitting another person. In some settings, hitting is not simply normal behavior, it is expected behavior. In a boxing match or mixed martial arts competition, we expect parties to beat on one another. In other settings, we view hitting as inappropriate and criminal.

With regard to relationships, the ties between two individuals will play a role in determining whether behavior is defined as appropriate or criminal. In September 2009, many people were stunned when they heard about a man who slapped a stranger's child in a Walmart. Apparently the girl was crying and the man told the girl's mother that he was going to hit the child if the mother didn't get her to calm down. Then he allegedly hit the two-year-old girl four times. Public outrage ensued. How could a stranger hit someone else's child? Had the mother hit her child herself, no one would have heard of the incident. Because of the relationship between the "hitter" and the "hittee" in this case, the story made national news and was defined as a crime by most commentators. The man was subsequently charged with felony cruelty to children.

In terms of justifications, there are some situations where behavior, such as hitting, is defined as appropriate behavior rather than criminal. If we use the Walmart case as an example, as part of the outrage, many bloggers commented that if someone ever hit their child, they would hit the aggressor themselves. In this context, hitting someone who, in the eyes of the masses, deserves to be harmed is not always defined as criminal.

With regard to timing, it is significant to note that standards of conduct (or norms) have varied over time. Using hitting as an illustration, at one point in time ancient philosophers used to "beat their pupils unmercifully."[10] This was acceptable behavior. Imagine if one of your professors hit students as part of his or her pedagogical efforts. Beyond leading to interesting comments on ratemyprofessors.com, such behavior would undoubtedly be defined as criminal nowadays. Similarly, in the past, violence by husbands toward their wives was condoned and even promoted. Today, such behavior is widely agreed to be unacceptable.

BEYOND A REASONABLE DOUBT 2.2

_____ refers to the violation of societal norms.

(a) Crime, (b) Law, (c) Folkways, (d) Deviance, (e) Mores

The answer can be found on page 521.

Crime as an Ethical Violation

Crime can also be defined as an ethical violation. Ethics are essentially moral principles that are used to determine right from wrong. When individuals talk about a "code of ethics," they are referring to morally derived principles that guide individuals in specific situations. To some individuals, violations of ethical codes are crimes. This does not necessarily mean that individuals have broken the law or done anything illegal when they violate ethical codes. For instance, physicians have a set of demanding ethical principles that guide their activities. Violating those ethical principles would not necessarily mean they have violated the law, but some observers would argue that such violations nonetheless are criminal in nature. The American Medical Association offers the following distinction between ethical principles and legal ideals:

> Ethical values and legal principles are usually closely related, but ethical obligations typically exceed legal duties. In some cases, the law mandates unethical conduct. In general, when physicians believe a law is unjust, they should work to change the law. In exceptional circumstances of unjust laws, ethical responsibilities should supersede legal obligations. The fact that a physician charged with allegedly illegal conduct is acquitted or exonerated in civil or criminal proceedings does not necessarily mean that the physician acted ethically.[11]

The notion that ethical principles "exceed" the law suggests a moral connotation to ethical principles; consequently, violations of ethical codes would be deemed immoral. The phrase *natural law* is used to refer to moral law. Natural crimes, then, are violations that virtually everyone agrees are inappropriate. Murder, rape, and incest are cited as natural crimes. Scholars often refer to natural crimes as inherently evil crimes (or **mala in se offenses**), in contrast to crimes that are simply illegal because a particular government chooses to make the behavior illegal (known as **mala prohibita offenses**).

Crime as a Social Construction

Another way to define crime is to consider how society decides to label certain behaviors as crime. Some sociologists and criminologists have

mala in se offenses: Crimes considered to be inherently evil.

mala prohibita offenses: Crimes that are illegal simply because a particular government chooses to make the behaviors illegal.

asserted that society constructs crime through decisions to label certain behaviors as crime, referred to as the *social construction* of crime. Why is it, for example, illegal to engage in prostitution in most places in the United States, except for a few counties in Nevada? Why is it that cocaine and heroin were legal to use in the United States until the early 1900s, but now they are illegal? Why is it illegal to sell alcohol on Sundays in some U.S. communities but not in others? The answer to each of these questions, according to Howard Becker, is found in his classic book, *Outsiders,* in which he wrote, "Social groups create deviance by making the rules whose infraction constitutes deviance."[12]

Erich Goode offers an insightful discussion about defining the concept of drug from a social constructionist perspective. Goode notes that some people define the concept based on the effects of different substances and offer definitions such as "substances that affect individuals either physically or psychologically." As Goode notes, however, many substances affect individuals. Food has physical and psychological effects, but food is not labeled a drug. Herbs and vitamins affect individuals, but these too are not labeled as drugs. Goode concludes, then, that a drug is whatever society chooses to label a drug. Why is marijuana labeled a drug, but other herbs are not? According to Goode, marijuana is a drug because society chooses to label it a drug and some herbs are not drugs because society chooses not to label those as drugs.[13]

Social constructionists argue that a number of political and social factors influence societal decisions to attach the label of crime to certain behaviors. Consider alcohol laws. Alcohol was made illegal under Prohibition in 1919 under the Volstead Act, which was the 18th Amendment of the U.S. Constitution, after a group of powerful advocates convinced legislators that the substance (like cocaine and heroin at the time) should be illegal. The act was repealed in the early 1930s, partly because the drug was more socially accepted then, but also because of economic reasons. In particular, with the Great Depression's toll on individuals, it was believed that the funds spent enforcing Prohibition could be better spent in other areas, and it was recognized that a tax on alcohol could raise government funds needed to provide public services.[14] Today, laws governing alcohol crimes vary across the states, suggesting that states "socially construct" their laws based on certain political and social factors (see Figure 2.2).

Social constructionists focus primarily on the process of defining acts as deviant or illegal. They have been criticized for not trying to change the political and social structure that creates definitions of crime.[15] They are viewed as passive participants in the understanding of law, rather than active contributors to the changing of law. Still, those writing from this perspective have provided a great

Why is marijuana use illegal in most states? Some would argue that marijuana use is harmful and may lead to additional drug abuse. Social constructionists might simply say that marijuana use is illegal for one simple reason: because society has chosen to call marijuana use illegal.

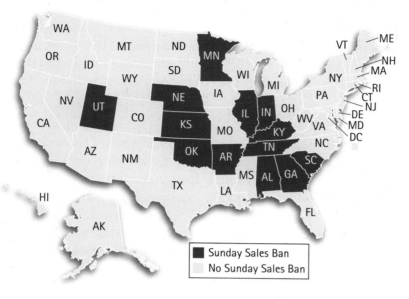

FIGURE 2.2 **Laws Banning or Restricting Sunday Alcohol Sales for Off-Premises Consumption as of 2014**

■ Sunday Sales Ban
□ No Sunday Sales Ban

Alcohol Policy Information System

deal of insight into the way that laws are shaped, developed, implemented, and enforced.

Crime as a Social Justice Issue

Increasingly, some scholars are beginning to describe crime as a social justice issue. *Social justice* has been described as a "contentious concept" because it is interpreted so many different ways.[16] At the heart of most definitions of social justice is a belief in fairness and equality among all human beings. According to the Center for Economic and Social Justice, social justice "imposes on each of us a personal responsibility to work with others."[17] In terms of criminal justice and an approach that views crime as a social justice issue, some scholars have noted that certain social problems are tied intrinsically to crime problems. Consider social problems such as homelessness, poverty, and mental health issues. To advocates of a social justice orientation, these social issues must be addressed in order to address the crime problem. Bear in mind that criminal justice officials spend a great deal of their time and effort responding to situations that arise as a result of homelessness, poverty, and mental health problems. Rather than treating individuals as criminals in these situations, advocates would argue that efforts should be directed toward eradicating issues such as poverty and homelessness. Through these sorts of efforts, it is believed that social justice can promote what is referred to as "sustainable justice," or a type of justice that does not result in offenders reoffending and victims being revictimized—a justice that lasts.[18]

VIDEO
Crime as a Social Justice Issue

➡ Behavioral Perspectives of Crime

Whereas legal definitions of crime focus on how crime is defined in the criminal law and social definitions of crime focus on how members of society define crime, behavioral perspectives of crime focus on an individual's specific actions, the harm caused by those actions or behaviors, and whether those behaviors can be captured within a broader conceptualization of crime. In addition, researchers use behavioral perspectives to measure crime.

Crime as Harmful Conduct

Crime can be defined according to the level or types of harm caused by particular behaviors. From this perspective, acts do not have to be illegal to be considered crime; rather, they simply have to cause harm. Criminologists use the phrase *environmental crime*, for example, to refer to a range of harmful behaviors that are perpetrated against the environment. These behaviors are not necessarily illegal, but they are arguably harmful. Some observers have also referred to *political crime* or *state crime* as categories of crime. These crimes refer to situations in which government bodies harm individuals, groups, or other government bodies through unnecessary and unwarranted actions.[19] Human rights violations, torture, the supporting of dictators, and environmental destruction are but a few examples. Many of these behaviors are not criminally illegal, but they have the potential to be quite harmful.

Another way to think about crime as harmful conduct is to think about times when something unwanted happened to you and you thought, I've been robbed. Maybe you made a purchase that turned out to be worth less than what you paid, your so-called friend never paid back the money you loaned him or her, or your high school teacher rigged the voting process so that you would not be elected to the homecoming court. Unless an offender used force to take something from you, you were not technically robbed. Still, if you were harmed, the behavior causing the harm can be defined as crime from this orientation. The fact that we use the concept of being robbed to describe these situations suggests that on some level we do, in fact, define such behaviors as criminal.

Crime as Research Definitions

Criminal justice scholars also develop definitions of crime in the research studies they conduct. When researchers study and gather data about crime, they must develop procedures and definitions that allow them to reliably and validly measure the behaviors they are defining as crime. Imagine a survey in which one of the questions asks, "Have you ever been victimized?" or "Have you ever committed a felony?" The responses to the items would not be reliable or valid because respondents could interpret the questions in different ways. Researchers take great care to

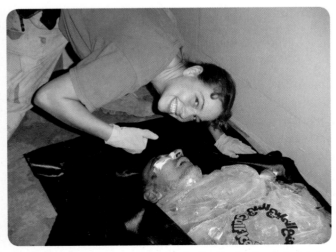

The human rights violations committed at the Abu Ghraib prison in Baghdad, Iraq is an example of crime as harmful conduct.

ensure that they have developed definitions and measures that accurately represent the behavior they are studying. The way that researchers define crime will have implications for the observations they make about the behavior.[20]

➡ Research in Criminal Justice

Criminal justice researchers use a variety of strategies to study crime and criminal justice. Generally speaking, these strategies include surveys, archival research, experiments, field studies, and case studies. Many criminal justice studies include a combination of these research methods. We discuss these methods separately here simply to introduce you to the way that criminal justice scholars use these methods in their research endeavors. Table 2.2 summarizes the research methodologies.

Survey Research and Criminal Justice

Surveys involve researchers asking respondents a series of questions about the topic under study and drawing conclusions from the responses. You

TABLE 2.2	Criminal Justice Research Strategies	
RESEARCH STRATEGY	**TYPES**	**ISSUES**
Surveys	Face-to-face	Not everyone wants to participate
	Telephone	Levels of comprehension vary among respondents
	On-site administration	Rapport needs to be developed
	Mail	Some respondents may not be honest
	Electronic	
Archival Research	Police records	Records are not flexible
	Prosecutor's records	Methods of record maintenance change over time
	Judicial records	Records may be missing
	Trial transcripts	Cannot probe deeper than records allow
	Social services records	
	Newspaper articles	
	Websites	
	Television shows	
	Music lyrics	
	Textbooks and other publications	
Experiments	Classic experiment	Criminal justice scholars are not always well-trained to do experiments
	Natural experiment	Some studies are seen as artificial because of researcher manipulation
	Field experiment	
	Quasi-experiment	
Field Studies	Complete observer	These studies are time consuming
	Participant as observer	Respondents react to being observed
	Complete participant	Gaining access to the field is difficult
Case Studies	Focus on famous criminal	These studies lack explanatory power
	Focus on typical criminal	They are difficult to conduct without proper training
	Focus on criminal event	Multiple methods are used in case studies
	Focus on criminal justice process	

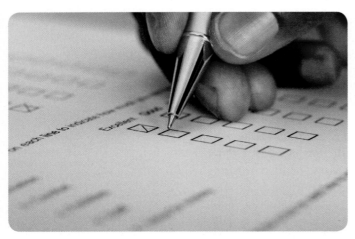

Surveys are routinely conducted by criminal justice researchers in an effort to better understand crime and how the criminal justice system operates.

©iStockphoto.com/AndreyPopov

have probably done informal surveys for as long as you could talk. The very nature of communication requires that individuals ask one another questions. Perhaps you can remember either conducting or responding to your first survey when you were in elementary school. Maybe you wrote or received a note such as this one:

Dear Pat,

Do u LIKE me? Yes No Mabee

Cirkle 1

Kim

You have come a long way in your ability to do surveys, and so have criminal justice scholars! Indeed, researchers are very careful about how they word questions on their surveys (see the "Criminal Justice and College Students" box in this chapter).

What Types of Surveys Are Used in Criminal Justice Research?

Generally speaking, five types of surveys are conducted in criminal justice:

- *Face-to-face surveys* involve researchers asking the questions in person. This process is particularly useful when research subjects have varying reading levels because respondents do not have to read the survey. Also, being able to see the research subject allows the researcher to observe respondents' nonverbal cues and follow up with probing questions if a respondent reacts a certain way to a specific question.

- *Telephone surveys* involve scholars (or research assistants) calling research subjects on the telephone and asking them questions to gather their responses to a questionnaire. With changes in technology, and increases in the use of cell phones, it has become more difficult to conduct telephone surveys.

- *Mail surveys* involve researchers mailing questionnaires to respondents' home or business addresses. These surveys involve no direct personal contact between the researcher and the respondent.

- *Electronic surveys* are similar to mail surveys, except they use electronic-based technologies to correspond with research subjects. Researchers are able to reach a large number of potential respondents in the time it takes to hit the "send" button or post a link on a website. Disadvantages include that many individuals may not complete online surveys or that surveys sent to individuals' email addresses may get caught in spam filters or ignored altogether by the email recipients. Still, such surveys have become tremendously popular in criminal justice research.

CRIMINAL JUSTICE
and COLLEGE STUDENTS

CREATING CRIMINAL JUSTICE SURVEYS

On any given day, you likely ask many different questions of those around you. Have you ever realized that you can ask questions in a way that leads individuals to certain answers? For example, imagine asking a friend how much he or she likes your new shirt. Here are three possible ways you could ask the question: (a) Do you like my shirt? (b) How much do you like my shirt? or (c) Don't you like my shirt?

All three questions aim for the same information, but how the questions are asked may influence the results. When asking questions about criminal justice, crime, and victimization, researchers use caution to make sure that the questions themselves do not lead respondents to specific answers.

With regard to crime, think of three different ways you might ask someone if he or she has ever committed a specific crime. Next, in small groups or as a class, discuss the various ways that you might ask individuals about their criminal behavior. What factors might lead individuals to be dishonest in answering these kinds of questions? Are there things that researchers can do to encourage accurate reporting?

➡ *On-site administration surveys* involve researchers asking a group of respondents who happen to be at the same place at the same time to complete a survey. This process is quick, easy to administer, and cost effective.

Who Is Surveyed in Criminal Justice Research?

Criminal justice scholars certainly have a range of survey methodologies at their disposal. In addition to choosing which methodology to use, scholars also select whom to survey. Common research subjects include active offenders, incarcerated offenders, victims, criminal justice practitioners, members of the public, and criminal justice officials. With regard to active offenders, some criminal justice scholars have devoted their careers to studying these individuals. These researchers often rely on recruiters to identify research subjects and spend a great deal of time developing relationships with the communities where active offenders live. Interviewing robbers,[21] gang members,[22] drug dealers,[23] and shoplifters[24] has led to better understanding about the decision-making process that offenders used in engaging in these crimes.

Some researchers select incarcerated offenders rather than active offenders as their research subjects. Heith Copes and Lynne Vieraitis interviewed incarcerated identify thieves in an effort to shed some light on the offenders' motivations for offending, the patterns surrounding identity theft, and offenders' assessments of risk.[25] According to the authors, because the offenders had already been convicted, they really had no incentive to lie about or downplay their offending. In another research project, David May and Peter Wood surveyed incarcerated offenders in an effort to

Some researchers prefer to interview gang members in their natural setting so they can acquire information that has not been influenced by the criminal justice process.

© George Steinmetz/Corbis

JOURNAL
Offender Perceptions of Graduated Sanctions

get the offenders to compare incarceration as a punishment with other forms of punishment.[26] Among other things, their research found that sanctions that are often viewed as lenient by the public are viewed as punitive by offenders.

A great deal of debate in criminal justice has centered on which survey methodology is more effective: interviews with incarcerated offenders or interviews with active offenders. Interviews with active offenders can be conducted shortly after the offense, which makes it easier for the offenders to recall aspects of their offenses. Also, active offenders can be paid for their participation, which enhances the likelihood that they will participate, although members of the public may question whether it is appropriate to pay offenders for their participation. On the flip side, there is a possibility that active offenders may be less truthful than convicted offenders.[27] In addition, convicted offenders can provide insight about the incarceration experience, and they are easier to locate than active offenders. Even in the face of such debate, it is clear that both types of interviews have significant value for the discipline.

Some criminal justice researchers focus their efforts on surveying victims of crime. These studies may focus on either current or past victims. The studies are particularly useful in that they provide insight into the consequences of victimization, factors that may have prevented victimization, reasons for reporting or not reporting the victimization, and information about the victims' experiences with the justice process. Researchers must be careful not to revictimize individuals by asking them inappropriate questions about their victimization experience. Large-scale victimization surveys are discussed further in Chapter 3.

Criminal justice researchers also frequently survey different types of criminal justice professionals as part of their scholarly pursuits. Such studies provide a bird's-eye view into the way criminal justice officials carry out their duties and perceive issues related to their careers. In one study, Kathleen Fox and Jodi Lane interviewed 30 prosecutors in Florida to determine how the officials perceived gangs in a city that was seen as being in the early stages of developing a gang problem.[28] The authors noted that interviewing prosecutors provided an "insider's perspective of gang members."[29] Their interviews provided insight into effective policies that have real potential to reduce gang crimes. These included "parenting assistance, prevention and early intervention programs for youth, education, and law enforcement/sanctions."[30] Without these interviews, it might have been assumed that prosecutors would have advocated a pure law enforcement response. The interviews showed that they supported more holistic responses.

Many criminal justice scholars have conducted surveys of members of the public. These surveys often focus on one of three topics: opinions about the criminal justice system, offending behaviors, and victimization experiences. Brandon Applegate, Frank Cullen, and their coauthors have conducted a number of attitudinal surveys focusing on how members of the public perceive punishment. Such research is instrumental in that it demonstrates that the public does not appear to be as punitive as is typically assumed.

Surveys on offending behaviors, referred to as self-report surveys, ask respondents to indicate how often they have engaged in different behaviors and frequently aim to explain, or at least identify, those factors that potentially contribute to offending. These surveys can be distinguished from active offender and incarcerated offender surveys in that the respondents include a range of citizens, and researchers do not know respondents' offender status prior to surveying them. Criminal justice scholars have demonstrated that self-report studies of juveniles are particularly useful for measuring and understanding delinquent behavior by juveniles.[31] These studies typically show that crime occurs much more frequently than one would expect in comparison to crime statistics released by police agencies.

In a similar way, criminal justice scholars have conducted surveys of the general public to identify and explain victimization experiences of citizens. The National Violence Against Women Survey, for example, was a telephone survey of 16,000 respondents (8,000 males and 8,000 females) funded by the National Institute of Justice and the Centers for Disease Control and Prevention. Respondents were asked about their experiences with rape, assault, and stalking. The findings from the survey showed that nearly one in five women reported being raped at some point in their life, slightly more than half reported being assaulted as a child, and 8% reported being stalked.[32] A number of scholars have used the data gathered from this study to write scholarly articles about violence and victimization.

As mentioned earlier, students are also sometimes subjects in criminal justice surveys. The benefits and drawbacks of using students in such surveys were highlighted in Chapter 1. At this juncture, it seems appropriate to note that students are sometimes active researchers on research projects they conduct with their professors. For professors, writing with students can be a rewarding experience. For students, writing with professors can be a significant part of their growth in their collegiate years.

BEYOND A REASONABLE DOUBT 2.3

_____ surveys involve researchers asking a group of respondents who happen to be at the same place at the same time to complete a survey.

(a) Mail, (b) Electronic, (c) Telephone, (d) On-site administration, (e) All of the above

---

The answer can be found on page 521.

Archival Research and Criminal Justice

Archival research refers to the use of archives, or records, to conduct scientific endeavors. These records can be written, videotaped, audiotaped,

archival research: The use of archives to conduct scientific endeavors.

or recorded in some other manner. Criminal justice scholars routinely use archives to study criminal justice issues. Typically, researchers develop a coding schedule that they use to gather information from a particular record. In some ways, the coding schedule is similar to a survey that one might use as part of a survey study. Instead of surveying the respondents, criminal justice researchers will "interview" the records with the coding instrument as a guide.

Criminal justice researchers have conducted archival studies using a variety of different types of archives, including criminal justice records and popular media records.

Criminal Justice Records

Criminal justice researchers use a variety of criminal justice records in conducting archival research. These records include police records, prosecutor's records, judicial decisions, and court records. Police records are commonly used to examine different criminal justice topics, but researchers cannot simply show up to a police department and ask to review their files. Typically, researchers will develop a rapport with the police administration before the police department trusts the researchers enough to grant them access to police files. Jessina Pizzaro and her coauthors reviewed the police records of 513 homicides that were investigated by the Newark Police Department's homicide unit.[33] The author team examined the criminal lifestyles of victims and offenders involved in the homicides. Although they found that both victims and offenders were frequently involved in criminal lifestyles, two types of homicide victims existed: those who were "heavily enmeshed" in a criminal lifestyle and those who were "less enmeshed."[34] Clearly, it would have been impossible for the research team to interview homicide victims.

Prosecutor's records have also been used in archival research studies. Here again, researchers need to develop a rapport with prosecutors before gaining access to prosecutors' files. Prosecutors' records include more complete information about the criminal justice process than police records do, simply because cases are further along in the process when prosecutors are involved in the case. In one study, for example, researchers examined prosecutors' records to examine the factors that influenced prosecutors' decisions to file charges in sexual assault cases and found that victim characteristics were more likely to influence decision making than were legal factors related to the evidence.[35] In particular, victims who were younger and were viewed as having issues with their character were less likely to have their cases prosecuted. To be sure, had the researchers asked prosecutors directly about the factors that influenced decision making, prosecutors might have pointed to evidentiary strength before victim characteristics.

Researchers have also examined judicial decisions. All individuals have access to judicial decisions and court opinions as written public records. The use of judicial decisions as a sampling frame is more common among legal scholars, and the research questions—not surprisingly—frequently focus on issues directly related to the law. One author team, for example, reviewed judicial decisions about bail bonds agents and bounty hunters in an effort to shed light on the legal framework that has given these individuals the legal authority to make arrests and search suspects' homes without warrants.[36]

Court records, including indictments and trial transcripts, have also been examined in archival criminal justice studies. Transcripts are not quite as accessible as judicial decisions or indictments, but they are still public records that researchers can access. In one study, for example, Carolyn Hartley reviewed trial transcripts in 40 domestic violence cases involving males who were accused of abusing their female partners.[37] Twenty-one of the cases were homicides, and 19 were physical assaults. Hartley was able to identify common defense strategies (self-defense claims, character assassination toward the victim, claims of innocence, pleas for lenience, and painting positive portrayals of the suspect). She also illustrated how defense attorneys used misinformation as part of the process to defend clients. By using archives in her study, Hartley was able to access 40 victims, 40 offenders, 40 defense attorneys, and 40 prosecutors. No other research method would have given her this access.

Popular Media

Criminal justice researchers have also used various forms of popular media as records in their archival research. These media sources include newspaper articles, websites, television shows, music lyrics, and textbooks. With regard to newspaper articles and criminal justice research, Greg Barak developed the phrase "newsmaking criminology" to refer to the "processes whereby criminologists use mass communication for the purposes of interpreting, informing and altering the images of crime and justice, crime and punishment, and criminals and victims."[38] One way that criminal justice scholars use mass communication to interpret images of crime is through archival studies focusing on newspaper articles. Often, the use of newspaper articles in criminal justice studies can be helpful in demonstrating how criminal justice problems are defined and framed in the popular media. The articles can also serve as a source of specific information that can be used to study a criminal justice problem. For example, Philip Stinson examined 2,119 cases of police misconduct committed by 1,746 police officers that were reported in the national media between 2005 and 2007. By using newspaper articles as his database, Stinson gained access to a significant number of police misconduct cases, many more than he would have accessed through other methods. In fact, Stinson is continuing to collect newspaper articles on police misconduct for a broader study he is conducting that is funded by the National Institute of Justice.[39]

In a similar way, television shows have been used as records in criminal justice archival research studies. In one study, for example, Sarah Britto and Dean

Facebook and other social media sites are increasingly become popular sources for criminal justice researchers.

© George Steinmetz/Corbis

justice trends and crime patterns over time. Third, when archives are accessible, researchers can develop a large sample with relative ease (it is much easier to collect 100 case files than it is to conduct 100 interviews). Finally, through archival research, researchers are able to gain access to inaccessible subjects.[48] As with other research strategies, a number of limitations surface when using archives in criminal justice research studies: the archives are inflexible, data-recording strategies change over time, missing data may create problems, and researchers cannot probe as they might in face-to-face interviews.

Surveys and archival research are the most popular types of criminal justice studies. Research strategies used less frequently, but providing important information nonetheless, include experiments, field studies, and case studies.

Experiments and Criminal Justice

Experiments are studies in which the researcher introduces a manipulation (known as a treatment) in order to observe the consequences of that manipulation. The aim is to decide whether the manipulation causes or influences specific outcomes. In criminal justice experiments, phenomena that are manipulated include criminal justice policies, criminal justice practices, survey questions, roles of research subjects, and the environmental setting. In the classic experiment, researchers have two groups that are randomly selected: an experimental group and a control group. The experimental group is manipulated, but the control group is not (the experimental group receives the treatment but the control group does not). Pretest and posttest observations are performed on both the experimental and control groups and differences between the two groups in the posttest that are beyond those differences found in the pretest are attributed to the manipulation. Classic experiments are rare in criminal justice and more common in other sciences such as psychology, biology, and medicine.

Different types of experiments exist. A laboratory experiment refers to an experiment that occurs in a scientific laboratory, whereas a field experiment occurs outside of the laboratory but the researcher still manipulates phenomena being studied. A quasi-experiment is a study that mimics an experiment, but it does not possess all of the qualities of the classic experiment. A natural experiment is a study that observes natural changes in an environment and assesses the consequences of those changes (for example, researchers have examined the changes in crime patterns before and after Hurricane Katrina in New Orleans).

One of the most popular experiments involving a criminal justice topic, but a study that was conducted by a psychologist in 1971, is Philip Zimbardo's Stanford Prison Experiment. In this experiment, Zimbardo created a prison in the basement of the Psychology Department at his university and asked students to take on the roles of either prisoners or guards. The prisoners were treated just as regular prisoners would be treated: They were stripped upon entry, searched, and controlled. The guards took on the role of guards very quickly and seemingly with ease. Initially, the study was to last for two weeks, but it was stopped in less than a week because the students serving as prisoners were experiencing trauma and the students serving as guards were exploiting their power. The study demonstrated the psychological pressures that inmates experience and the adaptations that guards make in their efforts to control inmates. For our purposes, the study demonstrated that experiments have significant utility in criminal justice studies.

Criminal justice experiments have been conducted on policing practices, court processes, treatment programs, and punishment alternatives. The Kansas City Preventive Patrol Experiment, conducted between 1972 and 1973, is one of the most well-known policing experiments. It called into question traditional understanding about the ability of patrol efforts to control crime. The resulting 910-page report changed our understanding about policing. This experiment is discussed in detail in Chapter 7.

Another significant policing experiment was the Minneapolis Domestic Violence Arrest Experiment. In this experiment, led by researchers Larry Sherman and Richard Berk, the Minneapolis Police Department tested the effectiveness of three strategies for responding to domestic violence: arresting the abuser, ordering the suspect away for eight hours, and attempting to restore order through advice and mediation.[49] Domestic violence calls were randomly assigned to the three intervention strategies; that is, police officers would respond with whichever strategy the specific call was assigned to receive. The researchers tracked the offender's behaviors for six months after their police contact. Results showed that arrested suspects were less likely than subjects receiving the other strategies to engage in subsequent violence. In terms of policy implications, the authors suggested, "We favor a presumption of arrest; an arrest should be made unless there are good, clear reasons why an arrest would be counterproductive. We do not, however, favor requiring arrests in all misdemeanor domestic assault cases."[50]

This study changed the way that police departments began to respond to domestic violence calls. Although the authors did not call for mandatory arrest policies, departments across the United States began to develop such policies in response to this study as well as political and social factors calling for a stern response to domestic violence. In an interesting twist, less than 10 years after the study was published, the lead investigator wrote that "mandatory arrest may make as much sense as fighting fire with gasoline."[51] Evidence about the effectiveness of mandatory arrest has been lacking, and the possibility remains that such policies may create more harm than good.

Experiments are advantageous in that they are viewed as the "gold standard" for testing criminal justice policies and practices.[52] A number of disadvantages limit their use. First, they can be time consuming to conduct. Second, criminal justice scholars do not always receive a great deal of training in their graduate coursework on how to conduct and evaluate experiments. Also, some observers have argued that the importance or value of experiments in criminal justice is overstated.

CAREER VIDEO
Director of the
Urban Institute

The answer can be found on page 521.

JOURNAL

Managing Fieldwork Dilemmas in Criminal Justice

Field Research and Criminal Justice

Field research studies involve researchers entering a particular setting in the "real world" in order to study the topic of interest. Stages of field research studies in criminal justice include the following:[53]

- *Getting in.* Researchers must gain access to the setting they select for study.

- *Becoming invisible.* Researchers try to ensure that subjects are not "performing" for them.

- *Watching, learning, and listening.* Researchers observe and watch for patterns.

- *Note taking.* At available times, researchers write down their observations.

- *Departure.* Researchers leave the field.

- *Analysis.* Researchers study their field notes and observations.

- *Writing.* Researchers write about their field study.

Researchers will fulfill one of three roles in criminal justice field studies: **complete observer, participant as observer,** or **complete participant.**

Some criminal justice scholars have conducted field studies serving as complete observers. In these cases, researchers do not participate in the activity they are studying; they focus all of their efforts on observing the activity. In one recent study, for example, Dean Dabney spent four months in the field observing the practices of homicide detectives with an aim toward identifying the coping strategies of the detectives. In the beginning months of the study, Dabney observed entire shifts that the detectives worked. During down time, dinner, and breaks, he would interview them about their coping strategies. For each homicide that was reported, he accompanied the detectives to the homicide scenes to observe their behaviors. Toward the end of the study, Dabney spent his time visiting homicide scenes. Detectives telephoned him whenever a homicide occurred and he met them at the scene of the crime. As a complete observer, he did not participate with the research subjects; he observed them.

In field studies where the researcher's role is participant as observer, the researcher actually participates in the activities, but the research subjects know that the participant is observing them. Recall the description of Sanchez-Jankowski's research from the beginning of this chapter. The advantage of this strategy is that the researcher can ask "research-type"

complete observer: A role for researchers in which they do not participate with the research subjects; they only observe.

participant as observer: A role for researchers in which they participate in the activities, but the research subjects know that they are being observed.

complete participant: A role for researchers in which they participate in activities with the research subjects but do not identify themselves as researchers.

questions and not worry about being identified as a researcher.

Some field researchers enter the field they are studying in the role of complete participant. In these cases, the researcher participates in activities with the research subjects but does not identify himself or herself as a researcher. In one of the more well-known studies involving this role, eight research assistants had themselves admitted to mental hospitals without letting the staff know they were researchers.[54] The stays in the mental hospitals ranged from 7 to 52 days, with the departure date determined by the time at which staff believed it was appropriate to release the "pseudopatient." The observations of the research assistants highlighted the way that patients were treated in depersonalized ways. All of the research assistants were released with labels of "schizophrenia in remission." David Rosenhan stressed that his finding demonstrates

Demonstrating the value of studying "famous" offenders, various criminal justice researchers have studied Bernie Madoff's white-collar crime case in an effort to better understand various dynamics related to white-collar crime.

© Orjan F. Ellingvag/Dagens Naringsliv/Corbis

how "sticky" diagnostic labels are once they are attached to individuals. These findings could not have been obtained had the staff known the true identity of the "pseudopatients." One can't help but wonder whether the label of "criminal" has a similar strength. In many ways, participant observer studies using the complete participant strategy are similar to undercover police strategies.

Field studies allow researchers access to the research subjects' "real lives." At least two drawbacks surface in these studies. First, the studies are extremely time consuming to conduct. Your professors typically cannot just drop everything to spend a great deal of time in the field. Second, for participant observer and complete observer projects, there is a possibility that individuals act a certain way because researchers are watching them. This effect is called the Hawthorne effect, in reference to a classic study of worker productivity that found that all workers in the Hawthorne Works plant increased their productivity, even though researchers provided better work environments for only some of the workers. The conclusion was that being watched makes people behave differently.

Case Studies and Criminal Justice

Case studies are research efforts that are "in-depth and detailed explorations of single examples (an event, process, organization, group, or individual) . . . [that] seek to understand [a] larger phenomenon."[55] Features of criminal justice case studies include, but are not limited to, the following:

- They use a sample size of one.
- Some focus on a specific celebrated criminal.
- Some focus on a specific "typical" criminal.
- Some focus on a specific criminal event.
- Some focus on a specific process.
- Most are multimethod in nature.

In terms of sample size, case studies typically have just one "subject" involved in the study. A well-known criminal justice case study, for example, examined what was referred to as the "Ford Pinto Case." In particular, Frank Cullen and his colleagues examined the controversies surrounding the Ford Pinto in the mid-1970s after the Ford Motor Company came under scrutiny for a series of high-profile accidents.[56] The automobile giant was eventually charged criminally by prosecutor Michael Cosentino, who asserted that the company was responsible for the deaths of three girls (Judy, Lin, and Donna Ulrich) who were killed in a Pinto crash in 1978. Using just a sample size of "one" by focusing on this specific case, the authors were able to identify those factors that contributed to the prosecutor's decision to file criminal charges against the company.

Some criminal justice case studies have focused on celebrated criminals. Focusing on celebrated offenders is seen as advantageous for two reasons. First, because many individuals are familiar with the infamous offenders, their cases can be used to highlight accurate and inaccurate portrayals of justice that surfaced when the offender was processed in the justice system. Second, the cases tend to generate interest in criminal justice, which provides a forum for researchers to educate the public about crime and justice issues. Bernard Madoff's crimes and the justice system's response to his case are illustrative. Various researchers have examined different aspects of the case to generate understanding about criminal justice issues. In addition, the public's interest in criminal justice issues appeared to increase during and after Madoff's criminal trials. Researchers were able to focus on the Madoff case in order to generate understanding about white-collar crime.

Some criminal justice scholars have conducted case studies on "typical" offenders, or offenders who are not well known. One of the most cited criminal justice case studies is Edwin Sutherland's The Professional Thief.[57] This work describes the criminal career of Chic Conwell. Sutherland demonstrated that crime was, in fact, a profession in this work, which begins with the following statement: "the professional thief is one who steals professionally."[58] Sutherland, using insight from Conwell, provided an extremely interesting depiction of the life of the professional thief, with comparisons made to amateurs and other types of criminals included. The study led other criminal justice scholars to focus on single offenders in their efforts to understand and explain specific types of crime. For example, researchers have conducted case studies on burglars,[59] those who sell stolen goods,[60] and appliance repairmen who rip off customers.[61]

According to one scholar, "The application of the case study approach to an analysis of the operation of the justice process is particularly useful in that it requires the researcher to be sensitive to the complex pattern of relationships between and among several variables."[62] In particular, case studies on criminal justice processes tend to demonstrate the interactions

Studying the massacre perpetrated by Eric Harris and Dylan Klebold provided useful information about the criminal justice system.

occurring between criminal justice subsystems and broader systems including the political, social, technological, and educational systems.

Some criminal justice case studies focus on specific criminal events. In these situations, rather than focusing on the criminal actor, the researchers examine the criminal behavior or the reaction to criminal behavior. In one study, Matt DeLisi studied the changes in the activities occurring in a pretrial services unit after the Columbine High School massacre, which resulted in the deaths of 13 people at the hands of two students—Eric Harris and Dylan Klebold. DeLisi found that the massacre appeared to have a direct impact on the functioning of the pretrial services unit in the week after the massacre.[63] Fewer cases were sent to jail for intake, but a higher number of violent offenders were detained in jail, suggesting officials from the unit were less likely to release violent offenders back into the community after Columbine. DeLisi concluded, "A sensational current event like the Columbine High School Massacre affected criminal justice system response."[64] Studying this one criminal event provided useful information about the criminal justice system.

Another feature of criminal justice case studies is that they are frequently multimethod research projects. This means that researchers will use more than one research method to conduct their studies. For example, Kitty Calavita, Henry Pontell, and Robert Tillmann examined the crime-related factors that contributed to the collapse of the savings and loans industry in the 1980s and 1990s.[65] Calavita and her research team reviewed public records, analyzed media reports, watched congressional testimony, and conducted interviews with key informants as part of their case study. Although they used these other methods, their research would be classified as a case rather than as one of the other methodologies because their focus was on just one event or phenomenon.

A final feature of criminal justice studies is that they are incredibly interesting and typically easy to read and comprehend. Similar to a John Grisham novel, case studies often read like well-thought-out stories. Unlike a good Grisham novel, however, case studies are nonfiction rather than fiction. The fact that the stories are full of facts (pun intended) makes case studies all the more interesting. Consider a case study titled "Sipping Coffee With a Serial Killer," by James C. Oleson.[66] As part of his dissertation research, which focused on criminals who were geniuses, Oleson conducted six separate interviews with a self-reported serial killer. Oleson presented the dilemmas he faced in deciding how to schedule time with the serial killer, how to develop rapport with him, and how to ensure his own safety. He took the findings from his coffee excursions and developed a reasoned and solid case study that provides theoretical and practical insight into our understanding of serial killers.

A few weaknesses of case studies limit their use in criminal justice. First, it is well accepted that case studies, because they focus on a single phenomenon, cannot be assumed to reflect all types of phenomena related to the studied topic. Second, case studies can be extremely time consuming to complete, causing some researchers to select other methods to study criminal justice issues. Third, most scholarly journals prefer to publish shorter articles. Depending on the topic, it is sometimes difficult to present a case study adequately in a short article. As a result, many case studies are published in book format, as book chapters, or in the few journals that publish longer articles. Finally, because case studies are used relatively infrequently, criminal justice scholars are often not adequately trained on how to conduct studies using this methodology.[67] Figure 2.3 shows how often case studies, and other research methods, were used in six criminal justice journals over a three-year timeframe.

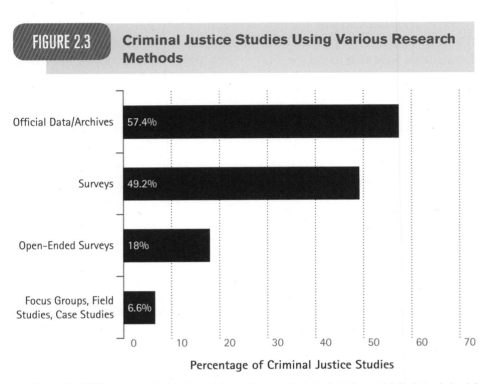

FIGURE 2.3 **Criminal Justice Studies Using Various Research Methods**

Percentage of Criminal Justice Studies

- Official Data/Archives: 57.4%
- Surveys: 49.2%
- Open-Ended Surveys: 18%
- Focus Groups, Field Studies, Case Studies: 6.6%

Crow, M.S., & Smykla, J. (2013). A mixed methods analysis of methodological orientation in national and regional criminology and criminal justice journals. *Journal of Criminal Justice Education, 24,* 536–555.

➡ Summarizing Criminal Justice Research

AUTHOR VIDEO
Future of Criminal Justice

In concluding our discussion of criminal justice and research, we must stress a few points. First, although we described these research methods separately, a number of them involve multiple research methods. Indeed, mixed methods are often viewed as the ideal strategy for conducting research. The use of mixed methods is also known as triangulation, in reference to the idea that the researchers are "triangulating" their results with multiple methods (see Figure 2.4).

Second, findings from research studies—in any discipline, not just criminal justice—are not facts or proof of any kind. Rather, findings should be seen as part of a broader effort to enhance our understanding about criminal justice. A research finding showing that drugs are related to crime, for instance, cannot be interpreted as proof that drugs cause crime. Instead, such a finding only means that a particular study found

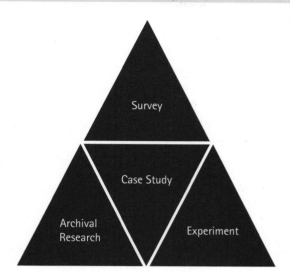

FIGURE 2.4   **Triangulating Research Means Using Multiple Research Methods in One Study**

this relationship. Building one study's findings with other studies' findings helps to generalize our understanding about criminal justice.

Third, the notion of decision making extends beyond criminal justice officials to researchers and research subjects: Research studies are conducted by individuals who make decisions about their research efforts, and they are conducted about individuals who make decisions about their own behaviors as well. At the risk of oversimplifying this, researchers are people, too!

Finally, it bears repeating that criminal justice is a science. Its scholars use scientific research methods to study criminal justice issues and its scholars are scientists, just as biologists, chemists, and physicists are scientists. Indeed, your professor is one of the scientists working to generate understanding about criminal justice. And just like Professor Sanchez-Jankowski(the researcher who joined gangs in his effort to study them), your professor works very hard at generating understanding about criminal justice.

Certainly, the definitions that researchers use to define crime and the types of research methodology and crime data-gathering techniques they use will influence a study's findings. However, for criminal justice students, the more they know about criminal justice research, the more job opportunities that will be open to them. The "Help Wanted" box in this chapter describes one such position.

Just the Facts: Chapter Summary

- One's definition of crime will influence (a) how individuals react to behaviors defined as crime, (b) who is defined as a criminal, (c) estimates about the extent of behaviors defined as crime, (d) explanations of different behaviors defined as crime, and

(e) how and whether cases are processed through the justice system.

- Legal scholars have described four different types of intent: general intent, specific intent, transferred intent, and criminal negligence.

- Norms are accepted standards for behavior and conduct. *Deviance* refers to the violation of norms, and *deviants* describes individuals who break the norms.

- Two overlapping factors determine whether norm violations are crimes: how the audience defines the norm violation and the context surrounding the norm violation.

- Ethics are essentially moral principles that are used to determine right from wrong.

- The *social construction of crime* refers to the assertion of some sociologists and criminologists that society constructs crime through decisions to label certain behaviors as crime.

- Conceptually, different sets of laws exist for adults and juveniles. The concept of *juvenile delinquency* refers to situations when individuals under the age of 18 break the law.

- Criminal justice is a science: Its scholars (including your professor) are scientists, just as biologists, chemists, and physicists are scientists, and they use scientific research methods to study and generate understanding of criminal justice issues.

- In their efforts to research crime and criminal justice, criminal justice scholars use the same types of research methods that other social scientists use.

- The methods used include surveys, archival research, experiments, field studies, and case studies.

- Surveys involve researchers asking respondents a series of questions and drawing conclusions from the responses about the topic under study.

- Common research subjects in surveys include active offenders, incarcerated offenders, victims, criminal justice practitioners, members of the public, and criminal justice officials.

- The types of archives that criminologists have used to study criminal justice topics include police records, prosecutor's records, judicial records/judicial decisions, trial transcripts, social services records, newspaper articles, websites, television shows, music lyrics, textbooks, and other publications.

- Experiments are studies in which the researcher introduces a manipulation (known as a treatment) in order to observe the consequences of that manipulation. The aim is to decide whether the manipulation causes or influences specific outcomes.

- Field research studies involve researchers entering a particular setting in the "real world" in order to study the topic of interest.

- Researchers fulfill one of three roles in criminal justice field studies: complete observer, participant as observer, and complete participant.

Critical Thinking Questions

1. Select three songs—one by Johnny Cash, one by Eminem, and one by the Dixie Chicks—and perform empirical lyricism by identifying themes in the lyrics related to crime and criminal justice.

2. What are the components of an experiment?

3. Would you be interested in performing a study similar to the one conducted by Sanchez-Jankowski? Why or why not?

4. Which type of survey would you most prefer to use as a researcher? Explain.

5. Write a case study describing your experience as a criminal justice student.

6. Why does it matter how crime is defined?

7. Compare and contrast legal definitions of crime with socially constructed definitions.

8. What is meant by "crime as social justice"?

9. How do you define crime?

10. How is the criminal law related to crime? Explain.

Key Terms

archival research (49)

complete observer (56)

complete participant (56)

criminal law (35)

criminal negligence (37)

defense (37)

general intent (36)

juvenile delinquency (39)

mala in se offenses (41)

mala prohibita offenses (41)

participant as observer (56)

specific intent (37)

status offenses (39)

summary offenses (35)

transferred intent (37)

$SAGE edgeselect™

edge.sagepub.com/payne

Sharpen your skills with SAGE edge select!

With carefully crafted tools and resources to encourage review, practice, and critical thinking, SAGE edge select gives you the edge needed to master course content. Take full advantage of open-access key term flashcards, practice quizzes, and video content. Diagnostic pre-tests, a personalized study plan, and post-tests are available with an access code.

3

AN INTRODUCTION TO MEASURING CRIME AND CRIME PATTERNS

© alessandro0770/Veer

NOT LONG AGO, POLICE IN WINDSOR, MASSACHUSETTS, were investigating a case known as the "puffy coat" robbery case. The suspects in the case were 16-year-old and 23-year-old males. The robbers wore puffy coats while robbing a series of convenience stores located near one another. They even robbed the same gas station twice: once 11 days before Christmas and once the day after Christmas. This case is relevant for our purposes because it highlights several issues that we discuss in this chapter. First, a company that rates the safety of cities across the United States has rated Windsor as the safest city in the country. But this rating does not mean that crime does not occur there. Further, strategies for counting and measuring crime make it difficult to identify cities as "safe" or as "more dangerous" in comparison to one another. Second, the offenders were in an age group that commits the bulk of offenses. Third, the crimes occurred at a time of year when certain types of crimes are known to escalate. Finally, the offenders concentrated their crimes around certain locations, a common occurrence, according to criminal justice experts.

LEARNING OBJECTIVES

After reading this chapter, students will be able to:

3.1   Describe the main strategies used to measure the amount of crime occurring in the United States

3.2   Compare and contrast the various crime measurement strategies

3.3   Identify three crime patterns that characterize the distribution of various offenses

3.4   Explain why crime varies across time and space

3.5   Describe juvenile offending trends and the aging-out phenomenon

3.6   Discuss three reasons why it is believed that men commit more crime than do women

Of course, not all offenders are younger, nor do they all concentrate their offending at certain time periods or in certain locations. Still, it is important that we understand how crime is measured and distributed. This chapter focuses on how we measure crime and victimization and how we use that information to shed some light on various crime

ADMISSIBLE or INADMISSIBLE Evidence

Read the statements that follow. If the statement is true, circle *admissible.* If the statement is false, circle *inadmissible.* Answers can be found on page 517.

1.   **Admissible   Inadmissible**   The National Incident-Based Reporting System uses information from more than 90% of police departments to describe how much crime occurs in the United States.

2.   **Admissible   Inadmissible**   In the Uniform Crime Reports, Part I offenses include murder, robbery, arson, larceny, motor vehicle theft, rape, aggravated assault, and burglary.

3.   **Admissible   Inadmissible**   Data from the Uniform Crime Reports and National Crime Victimization Survey show the same figures for the amount of crime occurring in the United States.

4.   **Admissible   Inadmissible**   One of the disadvantages of the Uniform Crime Reports is that the crime data were not collected until the advent of the Internet.

5.   **Admissible   Inadmissible**   The South has the highest rates of both violent and property crime, whereas the Northeast has the lowest rates.

6.   **Admissible   Inadmissible**   When females are involved in criminal groups, they tend to be involved as accomplices to powerful males.

7.   **Admissible   Inadmissible**   Home burglaries occur most often at night when residents are sleeping at home.

8.   **Admissible   Inadmissible**   Violent crime rates are higher during summer months than during other times of year.

Research shows that the bulk of crimes are committed by individuals who are younger.

© istockphoto/Bob Ingelhart

AUTHOR VIDEO
Measuring Crime

patterns. Understanding these topics has significant utility for promoting community safety.

➡ Measuring the Extent of Crime

Criminologists have long grappled with effective ways to measure the extent of crime and to provide accurate crime data for policy makers, researchers, and citizens. An accurate awareness about the extent of crime serves several purposes: explaining crime and demographic trends, understanding cultures and subcultures, measuring quality of life, promoting evidence-based prevention strategies, and developing evidence-based policies.[1]

Explaining Crime and Demographic Trends

To develop appropriate and accurate explanations of crime, we must first know how much crime is occurring in particular areas. Trying to explain crime without knowing how much crime occurs would be like ordering off a menu when you don't know the price of the food you are ordering: It would be a foolish exercise that could result in nothing but confusion. In addition, information about the extent of crime committed across various demographic groups (particularly by age category, gender, and racial category) sheds light on potential causes of crime and criminal justice enforcement patterns. Much more is written about the causes of crime in Chapter 5. For now, it is sufficient to say that we need to know about the extent of crime in order to explain crime.

Understanding Cultures and Subcultures

If a particular culture has no violent crime, then certain assumptions could be made about that culture. Conversely, if violence appears to be alarmingly common, then a different set of assumptions could be made. The same can be said of specific subcultures within different neighborhoods and communities: The extent of crime and types of crime committed by members of different subcultures tells us about those subcultures. In making this suggestion, however, we must be sure that assumptions about cultures and subcultures are based on empirical data rather than preconceived opinions.

Measuring Quality of Life

The formula is simple: The more crime that a particular area has, the lower the quality of life in that area. Similarly, the less crime, the higher the quality of life. Interestingly, a recent study found that quality of life (for example, happiness) was tied more to signs of social disorder than to signs of physical disorder.[2] *Social disorder* refers to types of relationships in a community, whereas *physical disorder* includes the types of disorder you can actually see (such as litter, graffiti, burglar bars, and the like). Perhaps your own selection of a home or an apartment was informed by your community's crime rate. In effect, you used crime data to determine how to best maintain your own quality of life given your own life circumstances.

Promoting Evidence-Based Crime Prevention Strategies

If certain types of crime are rare or infrequent in a particular area, then specific crime prevention strategies may do little to prevent crime in that area. Consider a gated community. If crime data demonstrate that homes are virtually never burglarized, then residents could forego the decision to purchase home security systems. In the rural town where one of the authors grew up, nobody locked their doors. Why? Because the crime data showed us that nobody ever broke into our homes. By contrast, in the home where his family lived a few years ago, they had an assortment of locks on the doors and windows in response to the published crime data that seemed to indicate the neighborhood was a haven for drug offenders, prostitution, and burglaries. (If only he had kept the garage rather than converting it, his car would not have been broken into so many times.)

Developing Evidence-Based Policies

By identifying the extent of crime and crime trends, practitioners and policy makers are able to develop policies informed by actual trends rather than feelings, emotions, or opinions about crime. As one author team noted, "Crime reduction is a major purpose of criminal justice policy."[3] To determine whether criminal justice policies are reducing crime, we must first know how much crime is occurring.

— BEYOND A REASONABLE DOUBT 3.1 —

Which of the following is not a reason we measure the amount of crime?

(a) To identify crime trends, (b) To understand cultures and subcultures, (c) To determine where hospitals should be placed, (d) To develop evidence-based policies, (e) To measure quality of life

---

The answer can be found on page 521.

➡ Strategies Used to Measure the Amount of Crime

All localities and states report the extent of crime through different publications and venues. Most colleges and universities, except for online colleges, are required by law to maintain and report to the public data about crime reported to the police. These data are particularly useful in helping to develop specific crime prevention and intervention strategies, but localized information is not useful in helping to understand societal crime trends and patterns. The three main strategies for measuring the extent of crime across the United States are the Federal Bureau of Investigation's Uniform Crime Reports reporting program, the Bureau of Justice Statistics'

AUTHOR VIDEO
Crime Trends

National Crime Victimization Survey, and the National Incident-Based Reporting System.

Uniform Crime Reports

The Federal Bureau of Investigation (FBI) administers the **Uniform Crime Reports** (UCR) program as a strategy to collect data about crimes that are reported to the police. More than 18,000 police departments across the United States report information to the FBI about crimes occurring in their jurisdictions. Chances are that even your campus police department, if your college has one, reports data to the FBI as part of the UCR program. The data are informative in that they provide an indicator of the amount of crime reported to the police each year. Policy makers and researchers have used the data to better understand various dynamics related to crime.

The creation of the UCR program in 1930 was hailed as "one of the most important events in the history of criminal statistics in the U.S."[4] The International Association of Chiefs of Police (IACP) called for the creation of such a program in response to concerns that the media were misrepresenting the true nature of crime across the United States. At the time, law enforcement leaders and social scientists, particularly social science statisticians, were interested in developing a national crime reporting system. Law enforcement leaders, including August Vollmer (see Chapter 1), wanted a system that would accurately portray crime in their communities.[5] Prior to the development of the UCR program, Vollmer said:

> Before energy is expended to improve police procedure, it will first be necessary to collect reliable statistical data. We hear on all sides that crime of one type or another has increased; that cities are overrun with gunmen; that juvenile delinquency has reached such enormous proportions that national safety is endangered. These statements have been repeated so often that even conservative police officials now believe it to be true, although they are the sole possessors of such facts as are available concerning crime conditions in this country, and these facts have never been compiled, compared, evaluated, or interpreted. . . . I conclude that statistics furnish a powerful means of discovering the causes of crime, provided they are used critically and carefully.[6]

Law enforcement leaders agreed with Vollmer's assessment. Famed FBI director J. Edgar Hoover was on the advisory group discussing the creation of the crime reporting program (see the "Criminal Justice Pioneer"

Uniform Crime Reports: A program administered by the FBI as a strategy to collect data about crimes that are reported to the police.

The UCR provides information on crimes reported to the police.

J. EDGAR HOOVER

On May 10, 1924, Attorney General Harlan Fiske Stone appointed 29-year-old J. Edgar Hoover as acting director of the Federal Bureau of Investigation, and by the end of the year Hoover was named director.

As director, Hoover put into effect a number of institutional changes to correct criticisms made by his predecessor's administration. Hoover fired a number of agents whom he considered to be political appointees and/or unqualified to be special agents. He ordered background checks, interviews, and physical testing for new agent applicants, and he revived the earlier FBI policies of requiring legal or accounting training.

Under Hoover, the FBI grew in responsibility and importance, becoming an integral part of the national government and an icon in American popular culture. In the 1930s, the FBI attacked the violent crime by gangsters and implemented programs to professionalize U.S. law enforcement through training and forensic assistance.

During the 1940s and 1950s, the FBI garnered headlines for its staunch efforts against Nazi and communist espionage. During World War II, the bureau took the lead in domestic counterintelligence, counterespionage, and countersabotage investigations. President Franklin Roosevelt also tasked the bureau with running a foreign intelligence service in the Western Hemisphere. This operation was called the Special Intelligence Service, or SIS. In the early years of the Cold War, the Bureau took on the added responsibility of investigating the backgrounds of government employees to ensure that foreign agents did not infiltrate the government. More traditional criminal investigations, including car thefts, bank robberies, and kidnappings, also remained important.

In the 1960s and early 1970s, the FBI took on investigations in the field of civil rights and organized crime. The threat of political violence occupied many of the bureau's resources, as did the threat of foreign espionage. In spite of Hoover's age and length of service, presidents of both parties kept him at the helm of the bureau. When Hoover died in his sleep on May 2, 1972, he had led the FBI for 48 years.

National Photo Company Collection (Library of Congress)

Adapted from Federal Bureau of Investigation, http://www.fbi.gov/about-us/history/directors/hoover

box in this chapter). The IACP published the first edition of the UCR in early 1930. Later that same year, in July, the FBI assumed responsibility for administering the UCR program. Since then, the program has been an extraordinarily valuable resource for policy makers, criminal justice practitioners, and criminologists.

The findings from the UCR program are released each year in a publication titled *Crime in the United States*. The UCR program categorizes crimes as Part I and Part II offenses. Generally speaking, **Part I offenses** are viewed as more serious offenses. These offenses, and the way the FBI defines them, are as follows:[7]

- *Criminal homicide*: (a) Murder and nonnegligent manslaughter: the willful (nonnegligent) killing of one human being by another. Deaths caused by negligence, attempts to kill, assaults to kill, suicides, and accidental deaths are excluded. The program classifies justifiable homicides separately and limits the definition to (1) the

Part I offenses: Criminal homicide, forcible rape, robbery, aggravated assault, burglary, larceny–theft, motor vehicle theft, and arson.

killing of a felon by a law enforcement officer in the line of duty; or (2) the killing of a felon, during the commission of a felony, by a private citizen. (b) Manslaughter by negligence: the killing of another person through gross negligence. Deaths of persons due to their own negligence, accidental deaths not resulting from gross negligence, and traffic fatalities are not included in the category manslaughter by negligence.

➡ *Forcible rape*: The penetration, no matter how slight, of the vagina or anus with any body part or object, or oral penetration by a sex organ of another person, without the consent of the victim.

➡ *Robbery:* The taking or attempting to take anything of value from the care, custody, or control of a person or persons by force or threat of force or violence and/or by putting the victim in fear.

➡ *Aggravated assault:* An unlawful attack by one person upon another for the purpose of inflicting severe or aggravated bodily injury. This type of assault usually is accompanied by the use of a weapon or by means likely to produce death or great bodily harm. Simple assaults are excluded.

➡ *Burglary:* The unlawful entry of a structure to commit a felony or a theft. Attempted forcible entry is included (also known as breaking and entering).

➡ *Larceny-theft:* The unlawful taking, carrying, leading, or riding away of property from the possession or constructive possession of another. Examples are thefts of bicycles, motor vehicle parts and accessories, shoplifting, pocket-picking, or the stealing of any property or article that is not taken by force and violence or by fraud. Attempted larcenies are included. Embezzlement, confidence games, forgery, check fraud, and the like, are excluded.

➡ *Motor vehicle theft:* The theft or attempted theft of a motor vehicle. A motor vehicle is self-propelled and runs on land surface and not on rails. Motorboats, construction equipment, airplanes, and farming equipment are specifically excluded from this category.

➡ *Arson* (added in 1979 to the Part I offenses): Any willful or malicious burning or attempt to burn, with or without intent to defraud, a dwelling house, public building, motor vehicle or aircraft, personal property of another, or the like.

Part I offenses have also been labeled *index offenses* in reference to the reporting program's past efforts to develop a crime index. The *crime index* referred to the total number of Part I offenses (excluding arson), whereas the *modified crime index* referred to the total number of all Part I offenses. Because a high number of larcenies drove up the crime index, and the larcenies are not as serious as other Part I offenses, the UCR program stopped reporting the crime index and modified crime index in 2004.[8]

Part II offenses are technically less serious offenses, though most criminologists agree that such a statement is misleading given the breadth of offenses included as Part II offenses. Table 3.1 lists Part II offenses and their definitions. The UCR includes arrest data about these offenses. Although only arrest data are provided, a great deal of information can be derived from the UCR each year. Perhaps the most important finding from the reports is that arrest rates have decreased over the past two decades, and the most recent UCR shows that crime dropped between 2012 and 2013.

> **Part II offenses:** Offenses that are technically less serious than Part I offenses.

TABLE 3.1	Definitions of Part II Offenses
OFFENSE	**DEFINITION**
Curfew Loitering Violations	Violations by juveniles of local curfew or loitering ordinances.
Disorderly conduct	Any behavior that tends to disturb the public peace or decorum, scandalize the community, or shock the public sense of morality.
Driving Under the Influence (DUI)	Driving or operating a motor vehicle or common carrier while mentally or physically impaired as the result of consuming an alcoholic beverage or using a drug or narcotic.
Drug Abuse Violations	The violation of laws prohibiting the production, distribution, and/or use of certain controlled substances. The unlawful cultivation, manufacture, distribution, sale, purchase, use, possession, transportation, or importation of any controlled drug or narcotic substance. Arrests for violations of state and local laws, specifically those relating to the unlawful possession, sale, use, growing, manufacturing, and making of narcotic drugs. The following drug categories are specified: opium or cocaine and their derivatives (morphine, heroin, codeine); marijuana; synthetic narcotics—manufactured narcotics that can cause true addiction (Demerol, methadone); and dangerous nonnarcotic drugs (barbiturates, Benzedrine).
Drunkenness	To drink alcoholic beverages to the extent that one's mental faculties and physical coordination are substantially impaired. Driving under the influence is excluded.
Embezzlement	The unlawful misappropriation or misapplication by an offender to his/her own use or purpose of money, property, or some other thing of value entrusted to his/her care, custody, or control.
Forgery and Counterfeiting	The altering, copying, or imitating of something, without authority or right, with the intent to deceive or defraud by passing the copy or thing altered or imitated as that which is original or genuine; or the selling, buying, or possession of an altered, copied, or imitated thing with the intent to deceive or defraud. Attempts are included.
Fraud	The intentional perversion of the truth for the purpose of inducing another person or other entity in reliance upon it to part with something of value or to surrender a legal right. Fraudulent conversion and obtaining of money or property by false pretenses. Confidence games and bad checks, except forgeries and counterfeiting, are included.
Gambling	To unlawfully bet or wager money or something else of value; assist, promote, or operate a game of chance for money or some other stake; possess or transmit wagering information; manufacture, sell, purchase, possess, or transport gambling equipment, devices, or goods; or tamper with the outcome of a sporting event or contest to gain a gambling advantage.
Liquor Laws	The violation of state or local laws or ordinances prohibiting the manufacture, sale, purchase, transportation, possession, or use of alcoholic beverages, not including driving under the influence and drunkenness. Federal violations are excluded.
Offenses Against Family and Children	Unlawful nonviolent acts by a family member (or legal guardian) that threaten the physical, mental, or economic well-being or morals of another family member and that are not classifiable as other offenses, such as assault or sex offenses. Attempts are included.
Other Assaults	Assaults and attempted assaults where no weapon was used or no serious or aggravated injury resulted to the victim. Stalking, intimidation, coercion, and hazing are included.

(Continued)

TABLE 3.1	Definitions of Part II Offenses (Continued)
OFFENSE	**DEFINITION**
Prostitution and Commercialized Vice	The unlawful promotion of or participation in sexual activities for profit, including attempts. To solicit customers or transport persons for prostitution purposes; to own, manage, or operate a dwelling or other establishment for the purpose of providing a place where prostitution is performed; or to otherwise assist or promote prostitution.
Sex Offenses	Offenses against chastity, common decency, morals, and the like. Incest, indecent exposure, and statutory rape are included. Attempts are included. (excludes forcible rape, prostitution, and commercialized sex).
Stolen Property (e.g., buying)	Buying, receiving, possessing, selling, concealing, or transporting any property with the knowledge that it has been unlawfully taken, as by burglary, embezzlement, fraud, larceny, robbery, etc. Attempts are included.
Suspicion	Arrested for no specific offense and released without formal charges being placed.
Vagrancy	The violation of a court order, regulation, ordinance, or law requiring the withdrawal of persons from the streets or other specified areas; prohibiting persons from remaining in an area or place in an idle or aimless manner; or prohibiting persons from going from place to place without visible means of support.
Vandalism	To willfully or maliciously destroy, injure, disfigure, or deface any public or private property, real or personal, without the consent of the owner or person having custody or control by cutting, tearing, breaking, marking, painting, drawing, covering with filth, or any other such means as may be specified by local law. Attempts are included.
Weapons: Carrying, Possessing, etc.	The violation of laws or ordinances prohibiting the manufacture, sale, purchase, transportation, possession, concealment, or use of firearms, cutting instruments, explosives, incendiary devices, or other deadly weapons. Attempts are included.
All Other Offenses	All violations of state or local laws not specifically identified as Part I or Part II offenses, except traffic violations.

Federal Bureau of Investigation

crime clock: Data reported in *Crime in the United States,* providing a general breakdown of how frequently crime occurs.

For the Part I offenses, the UCR's *Crime in the United States* publication includes a wealth of data about specific crime rates, demographic characteristics of suspects, and crime trends. Crime rates refers to the number of Part I offenses that occur per 100,000 residents. Figure 3.1 shows crime rates for Part I offenses. Property crime rates (for burglary, larceny-theft, and motor vehicle theft) are considerably higher than violent crime rates (for murder, forcible rape, robbery, and aggravated assault). In 2013, approximately 8,630,000 property crimes were reported to the police. This compares to fewer than 1.2 million violent crimes being reported the same year. Larceny-theft is always the most frequently reported crime, and murders are the least frequent Part I offense. As shown in Figure 3.1, each of the offense types dropped dramatically between 1993 and 2013.

The UCR's *Crime in the United States* also reports what is known as the **crime clock** (see Figure 3.2). The crime clock provides a general breakdown of how frequently crime occurs, assuming that crime happens with the same frequency every day of the year, at each time of day. Such an assumption is misleading, however, because crime varies each hour of the day, each day of the week, each day of the month, and each month of the year. As a result, most experts caution against making statements such as, "A violent crime occurs every 25 seconds in the United States." The statement is inaccurate for at least two reasons. First, the UCR collects information about crimes known to the police. A large number of crimes are not reported to the police. Second, no type of crime occurs regularly over time. Some crimes occur more frequently at certain times of the day, on

FIGURE 3.1   Property and Violent Crime Rates, 1993–2013

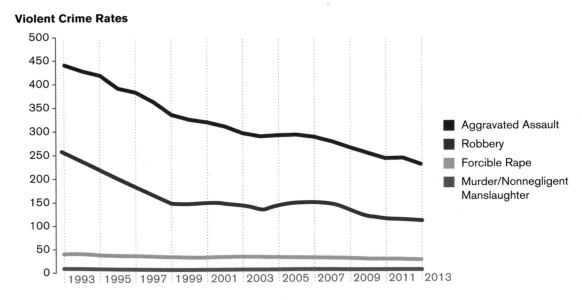

Violent Crime Rates

Legend:
- Aggravated Assault
- Robbery
- Forcible Rape
- Murder/Nonnegligent Manslaughter

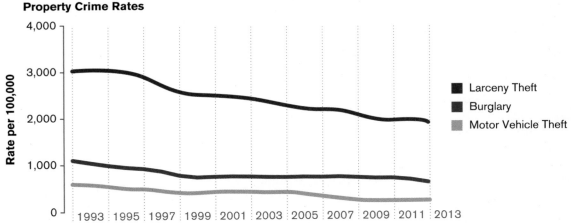

Property Crime Rates

Rate per 100,000

Legend:
- Larceny Theft
- Burglary
- Motor Vehicle Theft

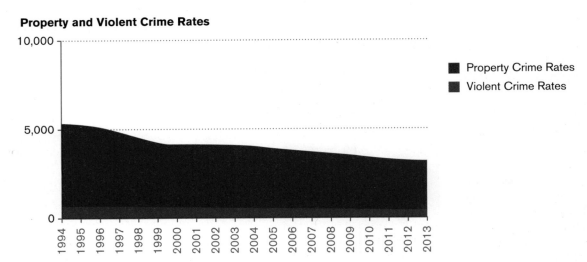

Property and Violent Crime Rates

Legend:
- Property Crime Rates
- Violent Crime Rates

The U.S. Department of Justice, Office of Justice Programs, Bureau of Justice Statistics

certain days of the week, and in certain months. Saying that crime occurs regularly would be like saying that the weather is the same every place in the United States, every hour of the day, every day of the week, and every month of the year.

The UCR also provides information about the clearance rate for the Part I offenses. **Clearance rate** refers to the percentage of crimes that were "solved" either by arrest or exceptional means. The UCR considers a crime cleared by arrest if one of three conditions is met: (a) A suspect is arrested, (b) a suspect is charged with an offense, and (c) a suspect's case is sent to the court for prosecution. In some situations, an arrest or charges may not be immediately possible. In these situations, the crime can be cleared by "exceptional means" if each of the following conditions is met:[9]

- The suspect has been identified.

- The agency has gathered enough evidence that would support an arrest.

- The suspect's exact location is identified.

- The agency confronted a situation outside of its control that prevented the suspect from being arrested.

Typically, violent crimes have higher clearance rates, and property crimes have lower clearance rates. In particular, murder usually has the highest clearance rate and motor vehicle theft and burglaries generally have the lowest clearance rates. In 2013, nearly two-thirds of murders and nonnegligent manslaughters were cleared, whereas just 14.2% of motor vehicle thefts and 13.1% of burglaries were cleared. What this means is that if your home is broken into, more likely than not the offender will not be caught. A similar situation arises for larceny-theft: In 2013 about one in five larcenies was cleared.

clearance rate: The percentage of crimes that were "solved," either by arrest or exceptional means.

FIGURE 3.2   Crime Clock

2013 CRIME CLOCK STATISTICS

A Violent Crime occurred every	27.1 seconds
One Murder every	37.0 minutes
One Rape every	6.6 minutes
One Robbery every	1.5 minutes
One Aggravated Assault every	43.5 minutes
A Property Crime occurred every	3.7 seconds
One Burglary every	16.4 seconds
One Larceny-Theft every	5.3 seconds
One Motor Vehicle Theft every	45.1 seconds

Federal Bureau of Investigation

The FBI releases the preliminary crime reports in June and annual reports in September each year. Typically, a great deal of media attention follows the release of the reports. How do you think the data can be incorrectly used?

© AP Photo/Rick Bowmer

The UCR also reports information about *crime trends* over time and between years. Although the UCR is published each year, in the middle of the year, the FBI typically releases preliminary data that compare crimes between the current year and prior year. Whereas the preliminary reports highlight between-year trends, the annual reports highlight long-term trends across each of the offense types.

With regard to annual changes over time, a review of the annual crime reports shows that crime increased significantly between 1960 and the early 1990s, and has dropped precipitously since then. Criminologists have suggested several reasons for this crime drop, and these reasons are addressed later in this chapter. For now, note that we would not even know about this crime drop if national databases on crime did not exist. Figure 3.3 shows the change in crime rates between 2012 and 2013. As you can see, rates of all types of crime decreased between the two years.

A wealth of information is available in the crime reports. For many students, you can even learn about how much crime was reported to the police at your college or university (see the "Criminal Justice and College Students" box in this chapter).

Criticisms of the UCR

Several criticisms have been leveled against the UCR program. One of the most common criticisms is that the database does not include crimes that are not reported to the police. An assortment of factors influence victims' decisions to report their victimization to the police. Among other things, decisions to contact the police are influenced by (a) the victim's perceptions of the seriousness of the offense, (b) prior experiences with the justice system, (c) whether an insurance agency requires the victim to contact the police, (d) whether the victim is a stranger or an acquaintance (victims are less likely to report the crime if they know the offender), (e) concerns about retaliation, (f) whether the victim has cognitive impairments that prohibit them from contacting the police, and (g) fear of revictimization by the

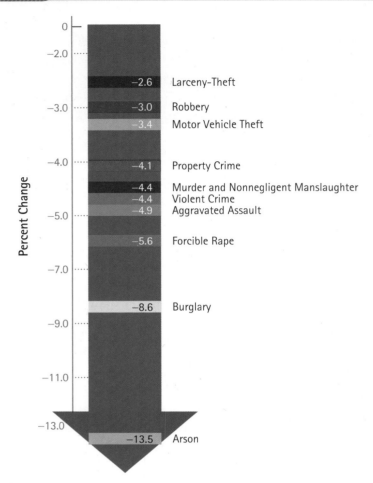

FIGURE 3.3   Changes in Crime Rates, From 2012 to 2013

Federal Bureau of Investigation.

CRIMINAL JUSTICE
and COLLEGE STUDENTS

CRIME ON YOUR CAMPUS

Think about your college or a college near you. Next, think about how many crimes you believe were reported by campus police to the FBI's UCR program. In particular, how many larcenies, robberies, and assaults do you think were reported? Discuss your answers with a few classmates. Then, go to the UCR's website and find out for yourselves how much crime was reported. You can access the university reports by going to the UCR website (http://www.fbi.gov/about-us/cjis/ucr/), clicking on the Crime in the United States link, clicking on the year you are interested in, and clicking on Table 9. In a small group, discuss whether your estimates were above or below what was reported to the FBI. What do you think accounts for the differences?

justice system.[10] The phrase **dark figure of crime** is used to describe the amount of crime that is not reported to the police.

Other authors have criticized the UCR program for mischaracterizing the crime problem. In particular, some experts argue that the eight Part I, or index, offenses are not necessarily more serious than Part II offenses. Consider the difference between larceny and embezzlement. If your professor steals your book bag, this would be a larceny: a Part I offense. In contrast, if your professor embezzled $100,000 from the workplace, this would be a Part II offense. Most observers would agree that stealing $100,000 is worse than stealing a book bag (unless you are the one who lost the book bag and you are really attached to that book bag). Still, the embezzlement would not be captured as a Part I offense. As an illustration, Bernard Madoff's arrest for embezzling billions of dollars would be coded as a Part II offense, whereas Winona Ryder's arrest for shoplifting a few thousand dollars' worth of goods from a Beverly Hills Saks Fifth Avenue Store would be coded as a Part I offense.

Incidentally, although the Part I and Part II offense dichotomy may misrepresent the actual seriousness of offenses, the distinction captures more accurately perceptions of seriousness, which are important given that perceived seriousness affects decisions to contact the police.[11] Offenses defined as serious tend to be those that result in bodily injury, involve property of significant value, are committed by strangers, or involve actions of breaking and entering. Gove and his coauthors conclude that Part I offenses "are valid indicators of serious crimes as defined by the citizenry."[12] In other words, most individuals would perceive situations in which their professor committed burglary (for example, breaking into an apartment to steal a book bag) to be more serious than embezzlement (for example, stealing from the workplace).

Another criticism of the UCR is that law enforcement agencies routinely underreport or overreport crime when completing the monthly crime reports (see the "Ethical Decision Making" box in this chapter). In some

> **dark figure of crime:**
> A phrase used to describe the amount of crime that is not reported to police.

Whose offense was more serious? Bernard Madoff's Ponzi scheme or Winona Ryder's shoplifting incident? The UCR categorization would imply that Ryder's was more serious, but in reality, Madoff's offenses created untold damage.

cases, departments classify more serious crimes, such as aggravated assault, as less serious offenses, such as simple assault, in an effort to lower the "official" crime rate.[13] One city official disparaged such practices stating, "We have a right to hear precisely what's going on. If we aren't given the unvarnished truth, it makes it rather difficult to do what's right for our community."[14]

Some criminologists have criticized the UCR for failing to provide data in a timely fashion. As of January 2015, for example, the FBI had published data for 2013, but not 2014. According to Richard Rosenfeld, the inability to provide timely crime data has serious consequences, including (a) negatively influencing policy development, (b) prohibiting effective planning, (c) making it more difficult to distribute financial resources, and (d) misinforming the public about crime.[15] Rosenfeld argued that the Bureau of Justice Statistics, rather than the FBI, should administer the UCR program. After all, a program specializing in data collection and statistical analyses should be able to gather data more efficiently. As part of his argument, Rosenfeld quoted former FBI director Robert Mueller, who said of the UCR program: "We collect, we announce, we pass on. We do not analyze."[16]

Criminologists have also criticized the UCR for being limited in the amount of data that is collected from police agencies. For instance, little information is collected about the specific incident, the victim, and the dynamics surrounding the offense. As is discussed in the next two sections, the FBI has developed other strategies to address this concern.

BEYOND A REASONABLE DOUBT 3.2

Which agency administers the Uniform Crime Reports?

(a) The Federal Bureau of Investigation, (b) The National Institute of Justice, (c) The Bureau of Justice Statistics, (d) The Central Intelligence Agency, (e) The Office of Inspector General

---

The answer can be found on page 521.

VIDEO
Janet Lauritson and the NCVS

National Crime Victimization Survey

Whereas the UCR program collects information about crimes reported to the police, the **National Crime Victimization Survey** (NCVS) collects information directly from residents of the United States to assess their victimization experiences. Initially called the National Crime Survey, the NCVS was created in 1972 after President Johnson's Commission on Crime and the Administration of Justice called for national data collection strategies to increase understanding about the dark figure of crime. The NCVS has changed significantly since it was created roughly a half-century ago. The crime incident report part of the survey instrument was initially a four-page survey with 20 questions and subquestions; the current version includes a 24-page survey with questions and subquestions.[17] Other changes

National Crime Victimization Survey: Survey that collects information directly from residents of the United States to assess their victimization experiences.

ETHICAL DECISION MAKING

CRIME DATA REPORTING

As part of your undergraduate criminal justice internship, you are hired to work in the campus police department. Your job is to fill out the forms used to report crimes known to your department to the FBI each month. After reviewing the FBI's UCR handbook and participating in a training session, you learn that the prior intern who had your job routinely underreported the amount of crime when filling out the monthly reports. Your supervisor explains that the underreporting is justified because the guidelines for reporting crime are somewhat vague and many crimes reported to the police probably did not occur. You learn that the bulk of police calls seem to be for stolen books and book bags, which are occasionally located (suggesting they were just lost and not stolen).

After inquiring about this underreporting, you learn that police administrators do not want to see higher crime rates in the monthly reports.

YOU DECIDE

1. Should you underreport crime in the same way that it has been underreported in the past? Why or why not?

2. Under what circumstances would it be appropriate to underreport crime to the FBI? How does discretion play into such decisions?

3. What are the implications of your decision for the campus community? What are the implications of your decision for your future career?

include that the initial NCVS program surveyed businesses and included face-to-face interviews for all contacts with respondents. The business surveys stopped in the mid-1970s, and phone interviews were implemented for follow-up interviews in the early 1980s.[18]

The NCVS collects information about household and personal victimization and asks respondents about the costs of victimization and whether they reported their victimization to the police. The survey is funded by the Bureau of Justice Statistics, and data are collected by the U.S. Census Bureau. Once individuals are selected to be a part of the sample, respondents are interviewed every six months for three years and are asked during each interview whether they have experienced specific types of victimization in the past six months.[19] The findings from the survey provide estimates of threatened, completed, and attempted rapes, aggravated assaults, simple assaults, burglary, person theft, burglary theft, property theft, and motor vehicle theft.[20]

The practice of asking about victimization within a specific amount of time is known as **bounding**, which is important because researchers do not want to double-count a specific victimization type. The label **telescoping** is used to refer to situations in which respondents "indirectly identify the timing of past events."[21] Interviewers for the NCVS review each respondent's prior responses to determine if it appears that the respondent has reported the same victimization multiple times. The interviewer will follow up with the respondent to determine whether the most recently reported victimization is the same victimization reported in the earlier survey. NORC at the University of Chicago was recently called

bounding: The process of asking about victimization within a specific amount of time in order to reduce the likelihood of double-counting a specific instance of victimization.

telescoping: Situations in which respondents indirectly identify the timing of past events.

upon by the Bureau of Justice Statistics to explore the feasibility of changing the NCVS to a 12-month bounding period, which would cut down on the costs of doing the survey every six months.[22] The research is examining whether telescoping may increase with a longer time period and whether interviewers can use certain cues to reduce telescoping. Preliminary results suggest that "telescoping will be more important" with the longer reference period.[23]

The most recent NCVS found that, between 2012 and 2013, violent crime rates decreased from 26.1 to 23.2 per 1,000 persons and property crime rates decreased from 155.8 to 131.4 per 1,000 persons.

An ongoing question in criminal justice centers on which database is more accurate: the UCR or the NCVS. It can be particularly confusing when the two strategies show different crime trends. One author team quoted a state criminal justice agency head who once asked, "Did crime go up in 1986?" because the UCR showed that crime increased by 10% and the NCVS showed no change.[24]

A cursory review of NCVS and UCR data over time shows that the UCR portrays a smaller decline in crime over time. Figure 3.4 shows the UCR and NCVS trends in aggravated assault rates over recent years. Eric Baumer and Janet Lauritsen scrutinized data from the two sources and found that the NCVS showed that robbery, rape, and aggravated assault decreased by

FIGURE 3.4   UCR and NCVS Aggravated Assault Trends, 1993–2013

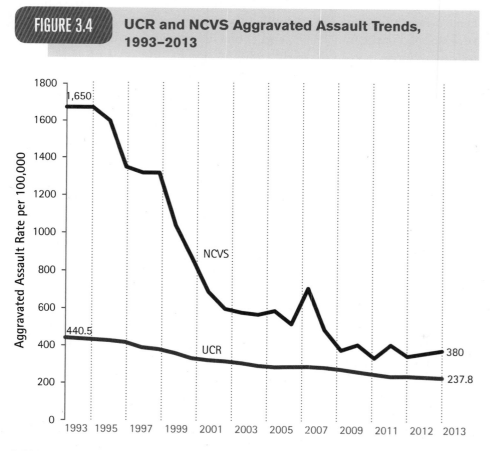

The U.S. Department of Justice, Office of Justice Programs, Bureau of Justice Statistics, Federal Bureau of Investigation

51% in the 1990s, whereas the UCR showed that crime decreased by 27% in the same timeframe.[25] Baumer and Lauritsen concluded that changes in decisions to report crime to the police account for much of the difference in the way crime trends are portrayed over time.[26] Drawing attention to the fact that the UCR gathers data from reports to the police and the NCVS collects information directly from victims, the authors noted that several factors have potentially resulted in victims being more willing to call the police: (a) Police were more involved in their communities in the 1990s than they were before, (b) members of the public held more favorable attitudes about the police in the 1990s than they did before, (c) members of the public became more punitive, (d) victims have been given a more central role in the criminal justice process over time, (e) technological shifts have made it easier to report crime, and (f) individuals have become less trustworthy and more prone to contacting formal agencies for assistance. According to the author team, the findings demonstrate "the need to corroborate findings about crime trends from multiple data sources."[27]

National Incident-Based Reporting System

A recognition of the limitations of the UCR to provide contextual information about incidents of crime, and appreciation for the detailed information provided by the NCVS, has led to the development of a third national crime reporting system: the **National Incident-Based Reporting System** (NIBRS).

Also administered by the FBI, the NIBRS was created in the late 1980s in an effort to provide more detail about crime incidents. By 2010, 43% of law enforcement agencies were certified to participate in the NIBRS program, though less than 30% of state programs provided all of their crime data through the NIBRS. Because of the low participation rate by agencies, the amount of crime reported in the NIBRS is about one-fourth of the amount reported in the UCR.[28]

One of the reasons for the lower agency participation rate is that the NIBRS is so detailed. The system captures 57 data elements related to the offense, offender, victim, property, and arrestee. This means that, in comparison to the UCR program, it would take the law enforcement agency much longer to compile the data required for the NIBRS program. Table 3.2 highlights differences between the UCR and NIBRS programs. For example, the UCR provides aggregate counts of offenses, whereas the NIBRS provides detailed information about individual incidents. Also, the UCR does not distinguish between attempted and completed offenses, whereas the NIBRS does. This means that the NIBRS provides a much more detailed portrait of crime.

The NIBRS also captures information on a broader range of offenses (see Table 3.3). The application of the *hierarchy rule* also varies between the two sources of crime data. The hierarchy rule refers to the UCR's practice of counting only the most serious offense if an offender is arrested for committing several offenses in the same incident. Kal Penn (Kumar of *Harold and Kumar* fame) had a frightening experience that exemplifies this rule. In April 2010, he was robbed at gunpoint by an offender who stole Penn's wallet and

National Incident-Based Reporting System: A national crime reporting system developed in the late 1980s in an effort to provide more detail about crime incidents.

two cell phones. The offender was caught and charged with robbery and assault with a deadly weapon. With respect to crime data reporting, only the robbery would be counted in the UCR program, whereas both offenses would be captured in the NIBRS program.

Other differences between the NIBRS and the UCR are that (a) the NIBRS includes information about all rapes, whereas until 2013 the UCR collected information only about rapes of females, (b) the NIBRS distinguishes between completed and attempted offenses, whereas the UCR does not, (c) the NIBRS collects information about weapons for all offenses, whereas the UCR provides weapons information for murder, robbery, and aggravated assault, and (d) the NIBRS provides details on incidents of 57 offenses (eight index offenses and 49 other offenses), whereas the UCR provides information about 29 offenses (eight index offenses and 21 other offenses).[29]

Additional advantages of the NIBRS cited in the literature include the following:[30]

- The program captures different types of victims (businesses and communities) and victimless crimes.

- It provides additional data about victims of all ages with more precision.

- It provides better and more reliable data about violence against women.

- It allows researchers to examine links between victimization and arrests.

Most experts agree that, when all agencies eventually participate in the NIBRS program, it should be more useful than the UCR and the NCVS

TABLE 3.2	Differences Between the UCR and the NIBRS	
ITEM	**UCR**	**NIBRS**
Crime count	Consists of monthly aggregate crime counts for eight index offenses	Consists of individual incident records for eight index crimes and 38 other offenses with details on offense, offender, victim, and property
Incidents reported	Records one offense per incident as determined by hierarchy rule	Records each offense occurring in the incident
Hierarchy rule effect	Suppresses count of lesser offenses in multiple offense incidents	No effect, given that all offenses in the incident are counted
Completed versus attempted	Does not distinguish between completed and attempted offenses	Does distinguish between completed and attempted offenses
Rape counting	Records rape of females only	Records rape of males and females
Weapon information	Collected for murder, robbery, and aggravated assault	Collected for all violent offenses
Arrest counts	Provides counts of arrests for eight Part I offenses and 21 other offenses	Provides details on arrests for eight Part 1 offenses and 49 other offenses

TABLE 3.3   Offenses Included in the NIBRS

GROUP A OFFENSES (REPORTS EXTENSIVE DATA)		GROUP B OFFENSES (ARRESTEE DATA ONLY)
Arson	Kidnapping/abduction	Bad checks
Assault offenses	Larceny/theft offenses	Curfew/loitering/vagrancy violations
o Aggravated assault	o Pocket-picking	Disorderly conduct
o Simple assault	o Purse-snatching	Driving under the influence
o Intimidation	o Shoplifting	Drunkenness
Bribery	o Theft from building	Family offenses, nonviolent
Burglary/breaking and entering	o Theft from coin-operated machine or device	Liquor law violations
Counterfeiting/forgery	o Theft from motor vehicle	Peeping tom
Destruction/damage/vandalism of property	o Theft of motor vehicle parts or accessories	Runaway
Drug/narcotic offenses	o All other larceny	Trespass of real property
o Drug/narcotic violations	Motor vehicle theft	All other offenses
o Drug equipment violations	Pornography/obscene material	
Embezzlement	Prostitution offenses	
Extortion/blackmail	o Prostitution	
Fraud offenses	o Assisting or promoting prostitution	
o False pretenses/swindle/confidence game	Robbery	
o Credit card/automatic teller machine fraud	Sex offenses, forcible	
o Impersonation	o Forcible rape	
o Welfare fraud	o Forcible sodomy	
o Wire fraud	o Sexual assault with an object	
Gambling offenses	o Forcible fondling	
o Betting/wagering	Sex offenses, nonforcible	
o Operating/promoting/assisting gambling	o Incest	
o Gambling equipment violations	o Statutory rape	
o Sports tampering	Stolen property offenses (receiving, etc.)	
Homicide offenses	Weapon law violations	
o Murder and nonnegligent manslaughter		
o Negligent manslaughter		
o Justifiable homicide		

National Archive of Criminal Justice Data

in painting a picture of local indicators of crime.[31] In other words, local law enforcement agencies and communities should be able to make more effective use of NIBRS data than other forms of nationally collected data. Shortly after the NIBRS program was created, Michael Maxfield described the program as "a new approach to measuring crime, one that is simultaneously ambitious, revolutionary, evolutionary, cumbersome, little-known, and disappointingly slow to be adopted."[32] More than a decade later, one could probably make the same statement today: The NIBRS has been "disappointingly slow to be adopted."

Learning from Kumar: Kal Penn was robbed at gunpoint and his offender was charged with robbery and assault. The UCR program would only count the most serious offense, while NIBRS would provide information about both offenses.

© Xavier Collin/Celebrity Monitor/Splash News/Corbis

Regardless of the strategy used to measure crime, criminal justice statisticians use the data they gather to examine crime patterns. The "Help Wanted" box in this chapter includes an overview of the duties assigned to these officials. As discussed in the next section, a number of patterns have been identified from the crime and victimization data.

➡ Crime Patterns

Criminologists have identified a number of different crime patterns based on data gathered from research studies and data from the official sources of crime and victimization surveys. In particular, criminologists have demonstrated how crime varies across the following dimensions: age, region, race/ethnicity, gender, community, time, and social class. Each of these dimensions is addressed in the sections that follow.

Age and Crime

Criminologists agree that crime is, for the most part, a young person's game. This does not mean that older individuals do not commit crime or experience victimization. Instead, it can simply be suggested that the bulk of offenses are committed by younger individuals and the majority of crime victims are also younger individuals. Figure 3.5 shows what is often called the **age-crime curve**. As shown in the figure, the bulk of crimes are committed by individuals between the ages of 15 and 24. The phrases *aging out* and *maturation hypothesis* have been used to describe the way that young offenders eventually come to a point in their lives when they choose to stop committing offenses.

Some researchers have identified offenders who have apparently chosen to continue to commit crime throughout their lives. Terri Moffit developed a taxonomy of two types of offenders: **adolescence-limited offenders**, who do, in fact, age out of crime, and **life-course-persistent offenders**, who continue to engage in crime throughout their lives.[33] The concepts of *career criminal* and *criminal careers* are related. *Criminal career* refers to situations in which offenders engage in offending over a specified period of time (for example, the period of time is their career). In contrast, **career criminal** refers to a member of the small group of offenders who appear to commit the vast majority of offenses. The career criminal concept is traced to research by Marvin Wolfgang and his colleagues, who examined the offending behaviors of a sample of 9,945 juvenile delinquents in the now-classic study *Delinquency in a Birth Cohort*.[34] The authors found that 6% of the juveniles accounted for more than half of the crimes and nearly three-fourths of all the homicides committed by the cohort.

In another classic study, titled *Unraveling Juvenile Delinquency*, Sheldon and Eleanor Glueck examined delinquency by 500 male juvenile offenders at different stages of their lives.[35] Their research team interviewed subjects at average ages of 14, 25, and 32 over a 25-year timeframe. Follow-up

age-crime curve: A line graph that illustrates the percentage of crimes committed by members of different age groups.

adolescence-limited offenders: Offenders whose antisocial behavior is temporary and does not extend beyond adolescence.

life-course-persistent offenders: Offenders who continue to engage in crime throughout their life.

career criminal: A member of the small group of offenders who appear to commit the vast majority of offenses.

FIGURE 3.5   Age-Crime Curve, 2013

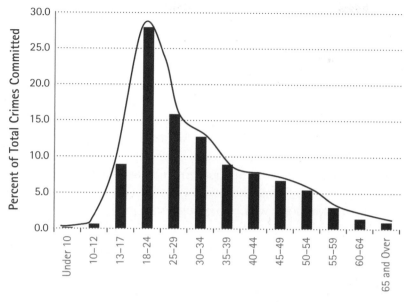

Federal Bureau of Investigation

analyses by John Laub and Robert Sampson on these 500 offenders found that they accounted for 10,000 crimes over their lives (between the ages of 7 and 70).[36] However, the authors found that, even among those actively involved in offending early in their lives, most offenders eventually stopped committing crime. They concluded: "Aging out of crime is thus the norm—even the most serious delinquents desist."[37]

This aging-out phenomenon has been used to explain the crime drop in the 1990s. In particular, in a rather controversial article, John Donohue and Steven Levitt argued that the crime drop was attributed to the passing of *Roe v. Wade* in 1973.[38] The authors contended that legalizing abortion prevented the births of hundreds of thousands of children who would have been born into potentially bad parenting situations. Presumably, 19 years later, there were fewer individuals in the age group that commits the most crime because of the abortions that occurred in the aftermath of *Roe*. Hence, according to Donohue and Levitt, fewer crimes were committed because of the decrease in the number of potential offenders living in bad parenting environments. Their findings have been widely criticized and debated.[39]

Region and Crime

Figures 3.6a shows the distribution of crime across regions according to Uniform Crime Reports data. The South has the highest rates of both violent and property crime, whereas the Northeast has the lowest rates. In 2013, 37.4% of U.S. residents lived in the South, but 43% of

VIDEO
Raising Adam Lanza

Most criminologists agree that the vast majority of crimes are committed by younger persons. Were there things you did as a younger person that you would not do now?

© istockphoto/debichambers

reported aggravated assaults, 44% of murders, and 45% of all the burglaries committed in the United States were committed in that region. Also, 42% of the property crimes were committed in the South.[40] Figures 3.6b and 3.6c show snapshots of the way crime trends were distributed across the United States in 2012.

The phrase **southern subculture of violence** has been used to characterize the higher crime rates found in the South. Those describing the southern subculture of violence suggest that southerners are socialized to accept, and use, violence in certain types of situations, particularly when the violence is perceived to help protect one's honor. This explanation is potentially useful to help explain the higher rates of violence, but it seems to do little to explain the higher rates of property crime in the South.

An interesting study on the southern culture of violence was conducted by Richard Nisbett and Dov Cohen, who examined the topic from the perspective of a "culture of honor," which they suggested prevailed in the South.[41] Their research was rather innovative. In addition to surveying male research subjects to see how they would respond to different insulting behaviors, including

> **southern subculture of violence:** A phrase used to characterize the higher crime rate in the South, suggesting that southerners are socialized to accept, and use, violence in certain situations.

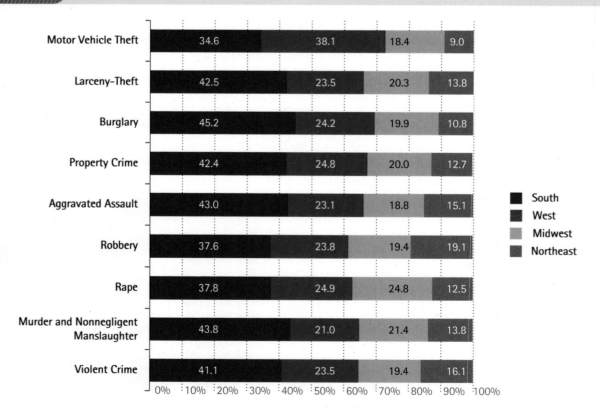

FIGURE 3.6a   Regional Crime Patterns, 2013

Crime	South	West	Midwest	Northeast
Motor Vehicle Theft	34.6	38.1	18.4	9.0
Larceny-Theft	42.5	23.5	20.3	13.8
Burglary	45.2	24.2	19.9	10.8
Property Crime	42.4	24.8	20.0	12.7
Aggravated Assault	43.0	23.1	18.8	15.1
Robbery	37.6	23.8	19.4	19.1
Rape	37.8	24.9	24.8	12.5
Murder and Nonnegligent Manslaughter	43.8	21.0	21.4	13.8
Violent Crime	41.1	23.5	19.4	16.1

Percent Distribution by Region

| FIGURE 3.6b | **Snapshot of Violent Crime, 2013** |

42.5 Percent of Robberies Occurred on Streets or Highways (Only 1.9% at Banks).

225,227
5.9%
Midwest

Northeast
4.3%
187,464

272,815
4.1%
West

South
3.9%
477,640

Firearms Were Used in 69% of the Murders Reported.

The South Accounted for 41.1% of all Reported Violent Crimes.

Aggravated Assaults Accounted for 62.3% of Reported Violent Crimes.

Federal Bureau of Investigation

| FIGURE 3.6c | **Snapshot of Property Crime, 2013** |

Larceny–Theft
6,004,453 Nationwide

Property Crime Resulted in Losses Estimated at $16.6 Billion.

Arson*
44,245 Nationwide

73.9% of Burglaries Occurred at Residences.

Larceny-Theft Accounted for 69.6% of All Reported Property Crimes.

8.6%
Burglary
1,928,465
Nationwide

42.4% of the Estimated Property Crimes Reported Were in the South.

3.3%
Motor Vehicle Theft
699,594
Nationwide

Only Limited Data is Available for Arson Because of Limited Participation and Varying Collection Procedures By Law Enforcement Agencies.

Federal Bureau of Investigation

someone trying to kiss their girlfriend, the researchers hired research assistants to actually insult the research subjects, with the subjects not knowing that the "insulter" was a part of the study. When the subjects arrived to participate in the study, they were told to fill out a survey, take the completed survey to the end of a long narrow hallway, and then return to the lab. While taking the survey down the hall, they passed by the research assistant, who was forced to close an open file cabinet drawer so that the subject could get to the end of the hallway. When the subject passed back by the research assistant, the assistant slammed the file cabinet door shut, bumped into the subject, called him an "asshole," and went into a different room. Other research assistants were stationed in the hallway to observe the research subject's reactions. The subject went into the lab and researchers gathered additional data, including cortisol samples, from the subject. In addition to this experiment, the researchers conducted two others as part of the same project. Here is how they summarized their findings:[42]

- Southerners were made more upset by the insult, as indicated by their rise in cortisol levels and the pattern of emotional responses they displayed as rated by observers (though the finding about emotional reactions must be considered tentative because of the failure to replicate it in Experiments 2 and 3, in which emotional expression may have been inhibited).

- Southerners were more likely to believe the insult damaged their masculine reputation or status in front of others.

- Southerners were more likely to be cognitively primed for future aggression in insult situations, as indicated by their violent completions of the "attempted kiss script" in Experiment 1. Southerners were more likely to show physiological preparedness for dominance or aggressive behaviors, as indicated by their rise in testosterone levels.

- Southerners were more likely to actually behave in aggressive ways during subsequent challenge situations . . . .

- Southerners were more likely to actually behave in domineering ways during interpersonal encounters, as shown in the meeting with the evaluator.

Nisbett and Cohen suggested that the southern subculture of honor is traced to the region's past herding economy that required southerners to fight off those who tried to steal their livestock.[43] This claim has been disputed, with one author suggesting that the higher rates of violence in the South are tied to "childhood experiences, poverty, and religiosity."[44] Others have suggested that the types of values attributed to the South are actually rural values, rather than southern values, and that similar types of value-driven violence would be found in rural communities, regardless of the region in which the community is located.[45] Perhaps the most important question to ask right now is how you would react if someone bumped into you and called you an "asshole." Would the values you have learned influence your response?

Race/Ethnicity and Crime

Data from the Uniform Crime Reports show that Blacks/African Americans are overrepresented in each offense type. In 2013, roughly 13% of the American population was Black, in comparison to nearly a third

VIDEO

Law Enforcement and Race

of arrestees for all offense types. For robberies, 68.6% of arrestees were Blacks and roughly half of all murders involved Black suspects. Figure 3.7 shows the distribution in arrests for Whites and Blacks in 2013. Blacks were overrepresented for each category of crime.

Violent victimization rates also vary by race in data from the 2013 National Crime Victimization Survey. Whites and Asians had the lowest violent victimization rates, whereas Blacks, American Indians, and those of two or more races had victimization rates that far exceeded their representation in the general population. Similar findings are uncovered when

 Arrest by Race, Percentage Distribution, 2013

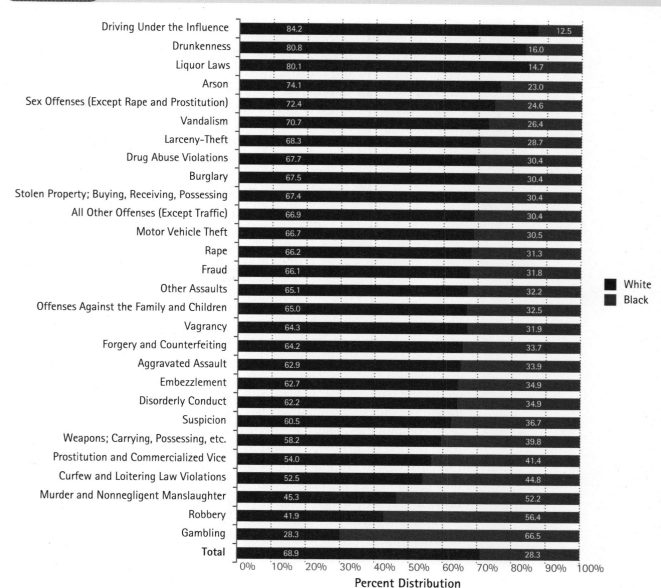

Federal Bureau of Investigation

examining the homicide offending and victimization data provided in the FBI's Supplemental Homicide Reports.

These stark racial disparities in offending and victimization have led some observers to suggest that race causes crime and victimization. Indeed, some conservatives on the far right have intimated that such statistics are evidence that crime is potentially caused by the color of one's skin.[46] As one author team has noted, the overrepresentation of minorities in crime data "has led to misperceptions about race and crime."[47] Criminal justice scholars have urged commentators to look more closely at the data in an effort to understand why crime and victimization rates are higher among various racial/ethnic groups. It is not enough to say simply that crime or victimization is higher among a particular group. Instead, it is necessary to examine what it is about particular groups that elevates crime and victimization rates. For minorities, potential explanations of these higher crime rates include inequality, differential parenting, and systemic discrimination.

With regard to inequality, some observers have argued that a long history of discrimination and prejudicial attitudes toward Blacks has fostered oppression and created a situation in which impoverished minorities turn to crime in order to adapt to the pressures from the oppression. Somewhat related, it has been noted that the many minority offenders reside in disadvantaged communities that were created, in part, by "urban renewal."[48] Robert Sampson and William Julius Wilson suggested that "the profound changes in the urban structure of minority communities in the 1970s may hold the key to understand . . . increases in violence."[49] They also wrote: "In structurally disadvantaged slum communities it appears that a system of values emerges in which crime, disorder, and drug use are less than severely condemned and hence expected as part of everyday life."[50]

Some scholars have suggested that racial offending patterns are potentially explained by different types of parenting and child-rearing strategies by different races.[51] According to Michael Gottfredson and Travis Hirschi, Blacks are more likely than Whites to have a lower self-control as a result of minimal "levels of direct supervision by family." In turn, this lower self-control increases the likelihood of criminal behavior. From this perspective, it is believed that Black parents are more prone than White parents to use ineffective parenting strategies. Also, a higher number of single-parent families in the minority community has been attributed to higher crime rates in these communities. This higher rate of single-parent families is, according to some observers, attributed in part to the strict sentencing laws we have in the United States. According to this framework, by removing Black males from their communities and placing them in prison, neighborhoods become weaker because they have a higher number of single-parent families.[52]

Systemic inequality is another potential explanation for the difference in offending and victimization rates between minorities and Whites. This perspective suggests that Blacks and Whites are treated differently by criminal justice professionals, and this differential treatment may result in higher arrest and incarceration rates for Blacks. On one level, this

HELP WANTED: CRIMINAL JUSTICE STATISTICIAN

DUTIES:

- Consults and collaborates with governmental officials, professional associations, and others to advise on the application of statistics to criminal justice issues, policies, and programs.

- Provides technical guidance to contractors or grantees on documentation requirements including problem reports and troubleshooting plans. Ensures the contractor/grantee performs in accordance with established procedures and that statistical research conforms to established specifications and requirements.

- Performs statistical data collection requirements activities, such as preparing, processing, and coordinating ad hoc and standing collection requirements. Ensures the collection of statistical data and use of collection systems to satisfy immediate, mid-range, and long-term statistical data collection requirements.

- Provides administrative and technical supervision necessary for accomplishing the work of the unit.

- Performs the administrative and human resource management functions relative to the staff supervised. Plans, schedules, and assigns work to subordinates.

- Establishes guidelines and performance expectations for staff members; provides feedback and periodically evaluates employee performance. Provides advice, counsel, and/or instruction to staff members. Recommends or approves appointments, selections, or reassignments to positions appropriate to the selection authority delegated. Effects disciplinary measures as appropriate to the authority delegated in this area. Carries out Equal Employment Opportunity (EEO) policies and program activities.

- Manages, leads, or performs scientific work in applying statistical theories, techniques, and methods for gathering, studying, analyzing, interpreting, and reporting on statistically quantified information.

REQUIREMENTS: Bachelor's degree; master's degree preferred

ANNUAL SALARY: $106,263–$157,100

Adapted from USAJOBS.gov. Retrieved from https://www.usajobs.gov/GetJob/ViewDetails/364825000

---

differential treatment may be the result of prejudicial attitudes of some criminal justice officials. The phrase **driving while Black** refers to the belief that Black drivers are more likely than White drivers to be stopped by police. Some research supports the suggestion that Black drivers are more likely to be stopped,[53] whereas other studies have identified the vast methodological difficulties that arise in trying to study this topic.[54] Incidentally, demonstrating that college campuses are a part of the "real world," a study of more than 10,000 traffic stops on a college campus found that Black drivers were more likely than White drivers to be searched, but they were less likely to receive a legal sanction.[55] According to the authors:

> A possible explanation of these contradictory findings is that police officers may use a minor traffic violation as a pretext to stop and search Black male drivers/vehicles for further investigation, because

driving while Black: The belief that Black drivers are more likely than White drivers to be stopped by police.

of the suspicion of illegal activities such as drug trafficking. When illegal contrabands were not found, officers might terminate interactions by issuing only verbal warnings, because initial primary reasons for traffic stops would not assure any legal sanctions.[56]

On another level, the differential treatment may be built in to laws created by politicians. Crack cocaine laws are illustrative. In the 1980s and 1990s, states began to pass severe laws for possession of crack cocaine, which has been referred to as "poor man's cocaine." Experts note that crack cocaine use is higher among Blacks, whereas cocaine use is higher among Whites. Although the effects of the two drugs are similar, penalties for crack cocaine violations are far more severe than are the penalties for cocaine use. Research by Allison Chappell and Scott Maggard shows that Blacks and Hispanics receive longer sentences than Whites for drug law violations and that "crack is treated much more harshly than powder cocaine in the court system in New York."[57] The authors suggest that a combination of institutional racism and decision-making practices by criminal justice officials may contribute to these inequalities.

Gender and Crime

Year after year, the vast majority of crimes are committed by males, but the trends over time show female arrests increased between 2003 and 2013, whereas male arrests decreased. The number of larceny arrests increased approximately 30% for females. Despite these increases, males were still arrested for nearly three times as many crimes as females in 2013.

A number of suggestions have been put forth to explain the different offending patterns observed between males and females. These hypotheses include the chivalry hypothesis, the parenting hypothesis, biological explanations, socialization hypotheses/gender roles explanations, and the accomplice hypothesis. The **chivalry hypothesis** refers to the possibility that females and males are treated differently by criminal justice officials and this differential treatment may, in fact, insulate females from future offending. In particular, it has been argued that female delinquents are treated more leniently by the police, and this lenient treatment may reduce the negative consequences of being labeled as an offender.

The **parenting hypothesis** suggests that differences in offending patterns in males and females result from different ways that boys and girls are treated by their parents. Just as the criminal justice system is seen as treating females more leniently, some observers have posited that parents use more positive child-rearing practices with their daughters than they use with their sons. Research shows that when negative

chivalry hypothesis:
A hypothesis explaining gender differences in crime that suggests that females and males may be treated differently by criminal justice officials, insulating females from future offending.

parenting hypothesis:
A hypothesis explaining gender differences in crime that suggests that differences in males and females result from different ways that boys and girls are treated by their parents.

Criminologists have suggested different explanations for why females engage in criminal behavior. Which of those explanations do you think are most plausible?

© Blend Images/Getty Images

parenting practices (such as abuse) are employed, boys react by externalizing their feelings through aggressive/criminal behavior whereas girls react by internalizing their behavior through self-harmful behaviors (for example, depression, eating disorders).[58]

Biological explanations (discussed in more detail in Chapter 5) point to biological differences between males and females to explain differences in aggression and offending. Research shows that males' and females' brains develop differently as a result of biological and environmental forces and these differences in brain development have been linked to the higher rates of crime by males.[59] Wright and his coauthors conclude, "There are important physiological and sociological factors that go a long way towards toward understanding why males and females think differently and, thus, act accordingly (i.e., criminal or not, respectively)."[60]

Socialization explanations, or the **gender role hypothesis**, point to the differences in the way that boys and girls are treated by all members of society and suggest that these differences help to explain why boys and girls behave differently. For instance, boys and girls are expected to adhere to different set of norms. One author highlights the importance of gender roles in the following way: "Our entire society is organized around gender roles. Females are socialized to be 'feminine' (passive, dependent, nurturant) and then urged to pair with males, who are socialized to be 'masculine' (active, independent, macho)."[61] From this perspective, males are socialized to use power and violence in certain situations, whereas females are socialized to avoid violence. One study exploring video games found that 41% of the video games had no female characters and that when females were included they were depicted as sex objects in 27% of the games and as "damsels in distress" in 21% of the games.[62] From these results, Tracy Dietz concluded:

> These depictions of women are detrimental to both girls and boys inasmuch as both may internalize these expectations and accept the idea that women are to be viewed as weak, as victims, and as sex objects. Furthermore, both girls and boys may come to believe that the contributions of women in everyday life are less important than those of men. Indeed, the effects of the internalization of this ideology may be most prominent upon the socialization of boys because they may be more likely to play the games more frequently.[63]

The **accomplice hypothesis** suggests that females' involvement in crime is often in the role of an accomplice. Researchers have noted that females are less likely than males to lead criminal groups.[64] Jennifer Schwartz and Darrell Steffensmeier point out that when females are involved in criminal groups, they tend to be involved as accomplices to powerful males. They conclude, "the saying 'she did it all for love' is sometimes overplayed in reference to female offending, but the role of men in initiating women into crime—especially serious crime—is a consistent finding across research."[65]

gender role hypothesis: A hypothesis that explains gender differences in crime that suggests that different norms for the behavior of boys and girls may lead to differences in criminal behavior.

accomplice hypothesis: A hypothesis explaining gender differences in crime that suggests that female involvement in crime is often in the role of an accomplice.

Communities and Crime

Researchers have also demonstrated that certain types of crime are more likely to occur in certain communities than in others. For example, drunk driving is more likely to occur in rural communities perhaps because public transportation options don't exist and drinking establishments may be located farther away from the drinker's residence.[66] Also, in rural communities, police officers will be called upon to address much different types of crimes than they would in urban communities. Below is a sampling of the offenses reported in the local newspaper's "crime report" from the small town where one of the authors grew up:[67]

- Three different people complained about three different dogs Friday; all three dogs were picked up.

- Police picked up a loose dog at Katherine and Keating Monday; the owner came to the station to claim it.

- A calico cat was reported lost on Pine Street Sunday.

- A Smith Avenue resident told police that his cat was outside Sunday evening, and when it returned, it had a bullet wound in its jaw.

- There was a complaint about a dog at the ambulance barn Saturday.

- A yellow Labrador reported missing last week was located up Skinner Creek, and a different dog was returned to its Katherine Street owner.

- A man came into the Port Allegany Police Station last Saturday night to complain that he had been headbutted by another man in a bar. The log noted that the butter will be charged.

Crime rates vary across rural and urban communities, and the types of crimes committed in the two types of community also vary. Does this necessarily mean that rural communities are safer?

© Lawrence Sawyer/Getty Images

A review of these crime reports showed that animal cases were the most frequently identified crimes in the small town, with 13% of the offenses involving animals.[68] Although problems with animals, such as stray dogs and cats, are likely to occur in urban communities as well, these cases are unlikely to be the most commonly reported offenses in those communities.

For victims, the dynamics of victimization are different across communities as well. Being victimized in a rural community, for example, may create more stigma for victims. Consider a case in which an offender was prosecuted for marital rape in a small town. By the very nature of the offense, and the fact that everyone in the rural community knew about the offense, the victim's identity became known to members of the community.[69] Although most media outlets protect the identity of rape victims, in this case the victim was not afforded this protection.

Time and Crime

Research also shows that crime tends to vary across time, in terms of time of day, day of the week, month, and time of year. In terms of time of day, one author team suggested that "Crime varies greatly by hour of day—more than by any other variable."[70] Some offenses occur more frequently during the day whereas others occur more frequently in the evening. Burglaries of homes occur more frequently in the daytime, when homes are vacant, whereas burglaries of businesses occur more frequently in the evening, when businesses are vacant.[71] Juvenile offending tends to peak when juveniles get out of school on school days, and between 7 and 9 p.m. on other days.[72] Murders more frequently occur on weekends during evening or early morning hours.[73] These temporal patterns reflect the types of activities that individuals engage in on a daily basis, given that individuals' behaviors will influence opportunities for crime and victimization.

Some practitioners claim that a full moon means more crime. To date, no studies have demonstrated such a relationship.

© Thinkstock/Jupiterimages

JOURNAL
Crime and Time

A similar point can be made about day of the week and month of the year. The types of social activities in which individuals engage are related to types of victimization. Violence, including murder, peaks on the weekends and during summer months, primarily because individuals engage in more social activities during those times. Increases in temperature have also been linked to violence.[74] One study found that, for robberies, the temperature effect is "stronger in higher SES communities" and for locations near commercial zones and subway stations.[75] This finding also makes sense when considering the increased amount of social activities individuals engage in around businesses and subways when the weather is warmer.

With regard to time of year, some research has found that certain types of crimes increase around holidays. One research study, for example, found that thefts in nursing homes increased at Christmas and on birthdays when residents presumably were receiving gifts from their loved ones.[76] Another study examined calls to police in one city over a three-year period and found that "major holidays primarily were associated with an increase in expressive crimes and a decrease in instrumental crimes."[77] *Expressive crimes* refers to those offenses that are conducted in order to express an emotion (for example, interpersonal violence), whereas instrumental crimes are those conducted with a specific purpose in mind (for example, theft, burglary). The authors conclude that holidays bring people together, many of whom consume too much alcohol but stay at home, which would make interpersonal violence more likely but burglary less likely.

These time patterns, combined with location patterns known to exist, are used by criminal justice officials to decide how to allocate resources. If you are in a major city on New Year's Eve, for example, you will notice an increase in the number of police officers working in certain parts of the city. In a rather innovative use of Twitter, one researcher showed how tweeting can be used to predict crimes. The "Criminal Justice and the Media" box in this chapter provides insight into this study.

Some practitioners claim that crime increases when there is a full moon. This relationship is attributed to an increase in opportunities for crime because of the increased lighting from the full moon and a belief that the lunar cycle influences individuals' moods and behaviors. In one of the few studies to examine the link between full moons and crime rates, a team of researchers examined police data, weather data, and astronomical data in one city and found that a relationship did not exist between moon cycle and crime rates.[78]

BEYOND A REASONABLE DOUBT 3.3

In which month would we expect to find the most violence?

(a) March, (b) July, (c) October, (d) December, (e) It depends on the state in which you live

---

The answer can be found on page 521.

Social Class and Crime

Many early research studies suggested a relationship between social class and crime, with members of the lower class overrepresented as offenders. Criminologists have cited at least six possible reasons to explain apparent ties between class and crime: stress from poverty, lower-class values, violence leading to lower social class, inequality breeding crime, inequality breeding differential treatment from the justice system, and methodological limitations. With regard to stress from poverty, some criminologists point to the way that poverty produces pressures that may lead individuals to engage in offending behaviors. Incidents of child abuse, for example, that stem from poverty have been tied to the stress that poverty creates in lower-class families.[79]

Those who see lower-class values as contributing to crime suggest that a differential value system between the classes leads to behaviors that foster criminal behavior. Members of the lower class might have values that are more supportive of violence/offending than other classes. Researchers, for example, have suggested that lower-class values such as the following may foster crime, particularly when these values conflict with middle-class values:[80]

- Less of a focus on ambition in comparison to middle class youth

- Less emphasis on classroom success in comparison to middle-class youth

- Support for short-term gratification rather than long-term gratification

- Attitudes supportive of violence to solve problems

- Lower levels of respect for property

CRIMINAL JUSTICE and the MEDIA:
TWEETING ABOUT CRIME

Based on the long history of research that showed consistent temporal and geographic patterns surrounding crime, Matthew Gerber, a researcher at the University of Virginia, examined whether Twitter feeds could be used to predict crimes that occurred in Chicago over a three-month timeframe. Reviewing tweets and crimes reported to the police over this period, and using "Twitter-specific linguistic analysis and statistical topic modeling to automatically identify discussion topics," (p. 115), Gerber found that his program was able to predict 19 of 25 crimes at a better rate than standard prediction strategies. In particular,

this strategy was able to predict the crimes of drug offenses, stalking, and criminal damage. It makes sense when you think about it. Tweets have a time stamp and the location from which tweets were sent can be determined through GPS. Given that both time and location are tied to crime patterns, Twitter might be a valuable tool for predicting future crime. Gerber recommended, in particular, that this might be a viable strategy for allocating police resources.

Gerber, M. (2014). Predicting crime using Twitter and kernel density estimation. *Decision Support Systems, 61*, 115–125.

Some observers have also recognized that violence itself, either experiencing it or witnessing it, can create situations in which individuals' social class status is decreased. For example, victims of domestic violence will have problems finding and maintaining employment, which could reduce their social status. According to some estimates, domestic violence "causes U.S. women to miss about 8 million days of work and lose about $727 million in wages each year."[81] In addition, being exposed to violence reduces academic achievement, which will affect one's social status, and experiencing violence potentially leads to posttraumatic stress disorder (PTSD), which is linked with unemployment.[82]

Inequality has also been seen as perpetuating crime. From this perspective, individuals with less power have fewer resources, and these limited resources potentially create situations in which members of the lower class turn to crime in an effort to level the playing field. Consider those who have no opportunity to go to college or find a career. Offending may be an adaptation to the inequality.

Differential treatment from the justice system may also result from inequality. In this context, many observers have suggested that the higher arrest rates among the poor reflect the power that the upper class has over the lower class in the creation and application of the law. In effect, some criminologists argue that the powerful use the criminal law to exert and maintain their power over the lower class.[83] Moreover, some criminologists point out that a range of harmful behaviors by the powerful (for example, discrimination and pollution) are not defined nor treated as violations of the criminal law.

Somewhat related, methodological limitations have also been used to explain the apparent link between social class and offending. In particular, researchers have noted that arrest data and self-report data yield different conclusions about the presence and strength of a relationship between social class and crime. Arrest data might suggest a relationship between class and crime, but self-report data, where individuals are asked to report their own offending, show no relationship.[84] Some criminologists have suggested that evidence for a link between class and crime is "weak at best."[85]

As noted in the beginning of this chapter, measuring crime accurately is important in order to identify effective ways to respond to crime. Inaccurate crime measures may result in overzealous responses to certain classes of offenders. Alternatively, accurate crime measures should provide information needed to develop effective evidence-based responses to crime.

Just the Facts: Chapter Summary

- An accurate awareness about the extent of crime serves several purposes, including explaining crime, understanding cultures and subcultures, measuring quality of life, promoting evidence-based prevention strategies, and developing evidence-based policies.

- The Uniform Crime Reports (UCR) program categorizes crimes as Part I and Part II offenses. Part I offenses include criminal homicide, forcible rape, robbery, aggravated assault, burglary, larceny-theft, motor vehicle theft, and arson.

- Part II offenses are technically less serious offenses, though most criminologists agree that such a statement is misleading given the breadth of offenses included as Part II offenses.

- With regard to annual changes over time, a review of the annual crime reports shows that crime increased significantly between 1960 and the early 1990s, and has dropped precipitously since then.

- The National Crime Victimization Survey (NCVS) collects information directly from residents of the United States to assess their victimization experiences.

- The practice of asking about victimization within a specific amount of time is known as bounding, which is important because researchers do not want to double-count a specific victimization type.

- A cursory review of NCVS and UCR data over time shows that the UCR portrays a smaller decline in crime over time.

- A recognition of the limitations of the UCR to provide contextual information about individual incidents, and appreciation for the detailed information provided about incidents from the NCVS, has led to the development

of a third national crime reporting system: the National Incident-Based Reporting System (NIBRS).

- The bulk of offenses are committed by younger individuals, and the majority of crime victims are in the same stage in the life course.

- The phrase "southern subculture of violence" has been used to characterize the higher crime rate found in the South.

- Blacks/African Americans were overrepresented in each offense type in terms of offending and victimization in recent crime data.

- For minorities, potential explanations of these higher crime rates include inequality, differential parenting, and systemic discrimination.

- Suggestions for the different offending patterns observed between males and females include the chivalry hypothesis, the parenting hypothesis, biological explanations, the gender role hypothesis, and the accomplice hypothesis.

- Researchers have also demonstrated that certain types of crime are more likely to occur in certain communities than in others.

- Research also shows that crime tends to vary across time, in terms of time of day, day of the week, month, and time of year.

- Criminologists have cited at least six possible reasons to explain apparent ties between class and crime: stress from poverty, lower-class values, violence leading to lower social class, inequality breeding crime, inequality breeding differential treatment from the justice system, and methodological limitations.

Critical Thinking Questions

1. Do age, race, and gender "cause" crime? Explain.

2. Access the UCR online. Compare your region's crime rate with another region's crime rate. Why do you think those differences exist?

3. Which system provides better estimates: the UCR or the NCVS? Explain.

4. Why is it important to gather information about the extent of crime?

5. What are the advantages of the NIBRS program?

6. Should the government devote more resources to collecting crime data? Explain.

7. Why is crime higher at certain times of day and during certain times of the year?

8. Discuss three reasons why minorities have higher crime and victimization rates.

9. Compare and contrast the concepts of *aging out* and the *accomplice hypothesis*.

Key Terms

accomplice hypothesis (93)

adolescence-limited offenders (84)

age-crime curve (84)

bounding (79)

career criminal (84)

chivalry hypothesis (92)

clearance rate (74)

crime clock (72)

dark figure of crime (77)

driving while Black (91)

gender role hypothesis (93)

life-course-persistent offenders (84)

National Crime Victimization Survey (78)

National Incident-Based Reporting System (81)

parenting hypothesis (92)

Part I offenses (69)

Part II offenses (71)

southern subculture of violence (86)

telescoping (79)

Uniform Crime Reports (68)

$SAGE edgeselect™

edge.sagepub.com/payne

Sharpen your skills with SAGE edge select!

With carefully crafted tools and resources to encourage review, practice, and critical thinking, SAGE edge select gives you the edge needed to master course content. Take full advantage of open-access key term flashcards, practice quizzes, and video content. Diagnostic pre-tests, a personalized study plan, and post-tests are available with an access code.

Thousands of different types of crime exist. Criminal justice scholars use crime typologies to more succinctly categorize these crime varieties. In looking at this crime scene, how might you categorize the crime that occurred?

© Mikael Karlsson / Alamy

AUTHOR VIDEO
Crime Typologies

▶ Why Study Crime Typologies?

A *crime typology* is a framework for understanding the thousands of types of crime that exist. It is important to focus on crime typologies for at least five reasons. First, by focusing on crime types, criminal justice scholars are able to focus their research on specific causes of specific types of crime. The causes of drug offenses, for instance, are potentially different from the causes of terrorism. By focusing on separate types of crime, criminal justice scholars can identify those differences.

Second, policy makers can make better use of information from scholars who address specific categories of crime. To be sure, different policies are needed for different categories of crime. A policy that works to control sex offenses, for example, will not necessarily work to control other types of offending. Only by categorizing crimes into different types are we able to inform policy makers about appropriate responses.

Third, and somewhat related, criminal justice decision makers categorize their responses to crime based on crime types. In larger jurisdictions, for example, police departments, prosecutorial agencies, probation departments, and so on might have specific units to address different types of crime (for example, a sex offender unit, a gang unit, a white-collar crime unit). Even if smaller departments do not have specific units, the way officials respond to different categories of crime will be informed by crime type.

Fourth, by necessity, laws are designed to categorize crimes. A murder is different from a theft, and within each crime type, specific categories of the crime type exist. As you will see, legally speaking, there are different types of murders, thefts, drug offenses, and the like. By recognizing crime types, we can better understand legal responses to crime.

Finally, the sheer number of different types of crime specified in legal codes means that criminal justice scholars must focus on crime categories in order to make sense of those offenses. Although the criminal law describes thousands of different types of crime, criminologists have categorized crime in an effort to help shape our understanding of crime types and crime patterns. It would be impossible to discuss all the types of crime that exist. Criminologist Dean Dabney has offered a "manageable and meaningful list of crime types" to help simplify our understanding about the numerous types of crime that exist.[2] A modified version of his typology includes a focus on four broad categories, each of which has multiple subcategories. These broader categories include violent crime, property crime, public order crime, and crime within complex organizations.

FIGURE 4.1	**Types of Violent Crime**

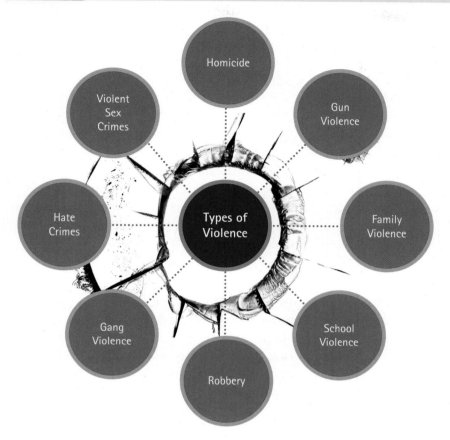

National Institute of Justice; © iStockphoto.com/Christopher Badzioch

---

BEYOND A REASONABLE DOUBT 4.1

A _____ is a framework for understanding the many different types of crime that exist.

(a) perspective, (b) law, (c) method, (d) crime typology, (e) none of the above

---

The answer can be found on page 521.

➡ Violent Crime

Violent crime is crime that causes victims direct physical harm or threat of physical harm. Although thousands of laws govern against various types of violent actions, in general one can point to the following types of violent crime: homicide, assault, violent sex crime, and robbery. Within each of these broader categories, several specific varieties of violence exist (see Figure 4.1).

Homicide

Homicide refers to the killing of one human being by another. Not all homicides are necessarily criminal. Criminal homicides include murder,

homicide: The killing of one human being by another; may be criminal or justifiable.

manslaughter, and negligent homicide. The classification of criminal homicides once cases enter the justice system is determined by decisions made by justice officials at different stages of the justice process. As cases proceed through the justice system, the way that a criminal homicide is defined might, in fact, change from one degree of murder to another, or from one type of homicide to another.

Murder

Most states classify **murder** according to different degrees, with *first-degree murder* describing homicides that are premeditated and deliberate and *second-degree murder* describing homicides that are not planned but are intentional. Across the states, different definitions of premeditation and planning exist. In some states, premeditation must involve careful planning, whereas in others, premeditation occurs as soon as someone forms the intent to kill another person. In all states, first-degree penalties are the most severe and second-degree penalties are less severe.

Manslaughter

Manslaughter is typically classified as voluntary or involuntary manslaughter. **Voluntary manslaughter** refers to killings that are intentional but in response to some form of provocation, or perceived provocation, though words alone are not enough to be considered provocation. Voluntary manslaughter cases are often referred to as "heat of passion" killings. **Involuntary manslaughter** refers to situations in which reckless acts lead to unintentional killings. Consider Michael Jackson's death as an illustration. Conrad Murray, Jackson's personal doctor, was found guilty of involuntary manslaughter for Jackson's death after he gave the pop star a fatal dose of sedatives. Murray did not intend to or mean to kill Jackson. But his actions were defined as reckless enough to warrant an involuntary manslaughter conviction.

Negligent Homicide

Negligent homicide refers to accidental (or unintentional) killings in which the offender should have reasonably known that his or her behavior could lead to someone's death. Negligent driving is frequently offered as an example. Cases involving neglect of children or older adults are other examples. In these situations, the suspect had a duty to act in a certain way and his or her negligence, or failure to act accordingly, can be held against the suspect if someone dies as a result of those actions. Consider, for example, a case in which a nursing assistant leaves a nursing home, allowing patients to be unattended. If one of the patients dies while the assistant is away, he or she could be charged with negligent homicide. Countless other examples could be provided. The key is that someone's reckless behavior or inaction led to another person's death.

Specific Types of Homicide

Many different types of homicide exist. Albert Roberts and his coauthors have identified the following types of homicides: (a) homicides precipitated

---

VIDEO
Conrad Murray
Sentenced

murder: Certain classifications of homicide; *first-degree murder* typically describes premeditated and deliberate homicides and *second-degree murder* typically describes unplanned but intentional homicides.

manslaughter: Killings under circumstances that do not amount to murder.

voluntary manslaughter: Killings that are intentional but in response to some form of provocation, or perceived provocation.

involuntary manslaughter: Situations in which reckless acts lead to unintentional killings.

negligent homicide: Accidental (or unintentional) killings in which the offender should have reasonably known that his or her behavior could lead to someone's death.

by an altercation or argument, (b) homicide committed during the commission of a felony, (c) domestic-violence-related homicides, and (d) homicides after an accident.[3] The authors found those offenders most likely to commit additional drug crimes and violent crimes were offenders involved in felony homicides and those involved in precipitated homicides, with domestic-violence-homicide offenders being least likely to reoffend. Related to family violence homicides, the concepts of infanticide, parricide, and eldercide are used by criminal justice scholars to describe homicides between relatives. *Infanticide* refers to instances in which infants are killed, *parricide* refers to killing one's parents, and *eldercide* refers to killing older relatives or care recipients.

Note that legal scholars refer to the "felony murder rule" to reflect laws that stipulate that all individuals involved in the commission of a felony can be convicted of a murder if the murder occurred during the felony. Several years ago, one of the authors had a student who was involved in a felony murder. The student was driving a car in which the occupants wanted to frighten another group of people with whom they had experienced run-ins. They drove by the home of this other group and fired a weapon toward the home. The shots killed someone in the home. Ironically, the police officer who drove the student to jail was another one of the author's students, and his seat in class was right next to the other student's. The author asked the police officer student what he said to the other student when he was driving him to jail. He responded, "I asked him if he wanted me to take notes for him."

Other types of homicide include serial killings, mass murders, and justifiable homicide.

Serial Killings **Serial killings** refers to crimes committed by an individual who kills several victims over a period of time. In general, serial killers generate great public interest, but they commit few murders in comparison to the total number of murders. Public fascination with serial killers is traced to Jack the Ripper, a serial killer who in the 1880s murdered prostitutes in London and sent letters to the police about his acts. In general, the public is quite fascinated with serial killers.

Serial killers frequently target certain types of victims or commit specific types of offenses. Danny Rollings, known as the Gainesville Ripper, targeted college females at the University of Florida and committed a series of crimes there that almost paralyzed the university. Ted Bundy confessed to murdering 30 women in the mid-1970s. He raped many of his victims and had sex with some of the decomposed bodies. He also decapitated some of his victims and kept their heads as souvenirs. Orville Majors, a licensed practical nurse from Indiana, allegedly killed approximately 130 patients in the early to mid-1990s. He reportedly killed those patients who he felt required too much care. Jeffrey Dahmer murdered 17 males between the late 1970s and early 1990s, raping, dismembering, mutilating, and cannibalizing many of his victims. In 2002, Lee Malvo and John Muhammad used a high-powered rifle to shoot and kill victims at various Washington, D.C., and northern Maryland locations, including gas stations and retail outlets. While some scholars have developed typologies to describe the typical serial offender, experts agree that there are no universal causes of these behaviors, that there are no clear distinguishing features between serial killers and

serial killings: Crimes committed by individuals who kill several victims over a period of time.

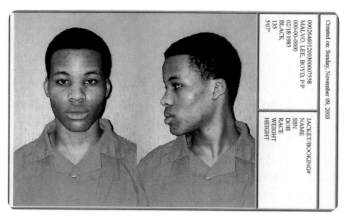

Lee Boyd Malvo's murders can be characterized as serial killings because multiple victims were killed at different points in time.

© CNP/Corbis

other violent offenders, and that there is no clear "generic template" to characterize serial killers.[4]

Mass Murders **Mass murders** refers to crimes committed by individuals who kill a large number of victims all at once. For instance, James Holmes was accused of murdering 12 individuals and injuring another 58 in a July 2012 shooting at a Colorado theater on the opening night of the Hollywood blockbuster *The Dark Knight*. Some observers use the phrase *spree killing* to refer to situations in which the killings are spread over multiple locations. Consider the case of Seung-Hui Cho, an English major at Virginia Tech, who killed 28 students and four professors, on campus on April 16, 2007. Cho began his killing spree by shooting to death two students in a dormitory around 7:15 a.m. and then killing 30 additional victims two hours later in a classroom building on campus. The university was faulted by many for not warning students after the first two killings occurred. Since then, universities across the United States have revised their notification and security processes in an effort to prevent similar acts.

Justifiable Homicide **Justifiable homicide** refers to a homicide in which the killing is justified in the eyes of the law. In these cases, a police officer or a citizen kills another person who is in the process of committing a felony. One author compared justified homicides by police and citizen-initiated homicides and found that (a) police were slightly more likely to use weapons, (b) females were more likely to kill acquaintances and males and police officers were more likely to kill strangers, (c) citizens were more likely to kill African Americans, and (d) police more frequently committed their justified homicides when responding to attacks or offenders resisting arrests, whereas citizens more frequently committed justifiable homicides in response to burglaries and larcenies.[5]

Homicide Over Time

Homicide rates have dropped significantly since 1993, when 25,426 individuals were murdered and the homicide rate was 9.5 per 100,000 residents. In 2013, 11,230 fewer individuals were murdered in the United States, which was roughly half the 1993 rate, at 4.5 per 100,000 residents.

Criminologists have offered different explanations for the drop in homicides, which was accompanied by a drop in other types of offending as well. Law enforcement leaders and politicians attributed the crime drop to "smart and aggressive policing."[6] The "Boston Miracle" refers to the 80% drop in Boston's homicide rate in the 1990s and the belief that the reduction was the result of a partnership between African American ministers and law enforcement.[7] Graham Ousey and Matthew Lee pointed to changes in drug market activity, including a "kinder and gentler" drug market, potentially influencing the reductions in violence.[8]

mass murders: Crimes committed by individuals who kill a large number of victims all at once.

justifiable homicide: Homicides in which the killing is justified in the eyes of the law.

Researchers have highlighted other possible factors, including an improved economy, incapacitation effects (more offenders in prison), increases in community-wide efforts to resolve disputes, and changes in the drug market giving fewer criminal opportunities for young people.[9] In terms of the economy, Al Blumstein and Richard Rosenfeld hypothesized that downturns in the economy will produce an increase in homicides.[10] Interestingly, with the most recent economic downturn, the homicide rate continued to decrease. In his efforts to explain this unexpected relationship, Rosenfeld told a reporter, "I am surprised by the overall decline in both violent and property crime during and since the recent recession. I've studied crime trends in relation to economic conditions for some time, and the 2008–09 recession is the first time since WW II that crime rates have not risen during a substantial downturn in the economy."[11] In the same article, Frank Zimring, another well-regarded criminologist, characterized the ingredients causing the unexpected decrease in homicides as "the mystery meat in the recipe of recent years."

Assault

Under common law, the phrase "assault and battery" made a clear distinction between **assault** (the attempt or threat to inflict harm on another) and **battery** (the actual completed assault). In many states today, legal definitions no longer distinguish between the two, with "assault and battery" merged into the offense of assault. Degrees of assault (first, second, and so on) are assigned based on the seriousness of harm, whether a weapon is used, and the potential for harm. In state laws, categories are often referred to as aggravated (more serious) and simple assaults.

Dabney's classification of assault refers to nonsexual violent crimes. Types of violence are defined in many different ways. Some classifications define violence by the type of weapon used (gun violence), some define violence by the relationship between victims and offenders (family violence) or by where it occurs (school violence), others define violence by the intent of the offender (hate crimes), and still others define violence by who is committing the violence (gang violence). To shed some light on these classifications, we focus here on gun violence, family violence, school violence, hate crimes, and gang violence.

Gun Violence

Guns are routinely used in many types of violent crime and property crime. Figure 4.2 shows the types of weapons used in homicides reported to the police in 2013. Handguns were used in approximately two-thirds of the homicides.

Anthony Braga cites estimates suggesting that gun violence costs $80 billion each year in the United States. He also notes that guns are more often used by younger offenders against other young offenders and that guns are used especially frequently in gang feuds.[12] In addition, the vast majority of young offenders and young victims have had multiple prior contacts with the criminal justice system for a variety of offenses. The

assault: The attempt or threat to inflict harm on another person.

battery: An actual completed assault.

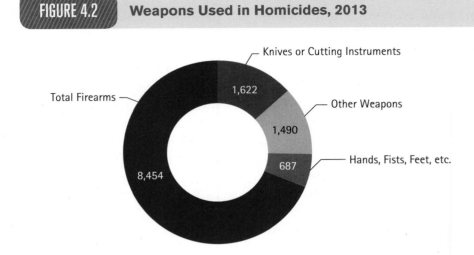

FIGURE 4.2 **Weapons Used in Homicides, 2013**

Knives or Cutting Instruments

1,622

Other Weapons

1,490

Hands, Fists, Feet, etc.

687

Total Firearms

8,454

Federal Bureau of Investigation

phrase "cafeteria-style offenders" refers to the wide assortment of crimes committed by this group of offenders.[13]

Family Violence

Many crimes happen in families. In fact, available data suggest that we are more likely to be harmed by someone we know than by a stranger. Many of these *acquaintance victimizations* are cases of family violence. In general, three types of family violence exist: child abuse, intimate partner violence, and elder abuse.

Child abuse (or child maltreatment) refers to crimes of violence perpetrated against a child by someone who has power over the child. The varieties of child abuse typically cited by researchers include physical abuse, neglect, sexual abuse, and emotional/verbal abuse. In 2012, 3.4 million reports of child abuse were made to social services.[14] Of those reported cases, approximately 2.1 million were investigated and 686,000 were substantiated. The fact that the others were not substantiated does not mean abuse did not occur; it simply means that abuse could not be substantiated. Intentionally false reports of child abuse are rarely made to authorities.

Although all types of abuse are devastating, the consequence of *child neglect* can be especially serious in terms of the child's health, long-term development, and emotional well-being. Neglect involves situations in which parents fail to provide children the level of physical and emotional care they need. Research shows that neglected children are more likely than abused children to commit criminal acts, though all types of maltreated children are at a higher risk to enter lives of crime than are nonmaltreated children. Child abuse victims also have a higher risk of future victimization than do children who are not abused. In particular, boys who experience abuse are more prone to become partner abusers, whereas girls who experience abuse are more likely to be victims of partner abuse.[15]

child abuse: Also known as child maltreatment; crimes of violence perpetrated against a child by someone who has power over the child.

Intimate partner violence describes abusive behaviors between partners. A variety of terms have been used to describe these behaviors, including *domestic violence, spousal abuse, partner violence,* and *couple violence.* Although many researchers have argued that males are more frequently abusers and females are more often victims, research by Murray Straus and Richard Gelles suggests that males and females have somewhat equivalent offending and victimization rates in these cases.[16] Those who call into question these findings suggest that the forms of violence by females are typically done to protect themselves from aggressive males, and the seriousness of the violence by females is not comparable to that used by males (males hit harder and cause more damage).

The consequences of child abuse can have long-lasting effects on victims.
© istockphoto/Imgorthand

Domestic violence scholar Michael Johnson has described two types of violence that happen in these families: patriarchal terrorism and common couple violence.[17] **Common couple violence** refers to occasional "outbursts" of violence that either males or females may perpetrate against their spouses. **Patriarchal terrorism** refers to "systematic male violence" over time.[18] Johnson argues that the distinction is important because the two types of spousal violence would warrant different responses and treatments for victims and offenders.

Not all forms of spousal abuse are necessarily physical. Emotional abuse is frequently used to control the victim of spousal abuse. Also, violence does not typically happen every day of the marriage. Lenore Walker has discussed the cycle of violence to illustrate how violence occurs throughout a marriage.[19] The first part of the cycle is the honeymoon stage. The two partners enjoy their time with one another and violence is not even on their radar, at least initially. Next, the tension-building stage occurs over time, with different tensions arising in the relationship. Third, the abuse episode occurs. In many cases, victims will seek shelter and leave the abusive relationship after the abusive episode. Many domestic violence victims return to their abusers, and the cycle begins again. The abuser uses his or her charm to convince the victim to return to the relationship.

Stalking is one type of intimate partner violence. *Stalking* refers to "repeated and unwanted attention, harassment, contact, or any other behavior directed at a specific person that would cause a reasonable person to feel fear."[20] Types of stalkers include the rejected stalked, the intimacy seeker, the incompetent stalker, the resentful stalker, and the predator.[21] More recently, patterns of stalking have expanded to include *cyber stalking,* which refers to situations in which stalkers use electronic technology to harass or stalk the victim.

Elder abuse is another type of family violence. Only since the 1990s have criminal justice officials begun to play a role in responding to elder abuse. Although elder abuse can be defined many different ways, the following definition offers a criminological definition of the offense type:

common couple violence: Occasional "outbursts" of violence that either males or females may perpetrate against their spouses.

patriarchal terrorism: "Systematic male violence" over time within a family unit.

elder abuse: Violence targeted at an elderly person; it can include emotional, financial, physical, or sexual abuse, and neglect.

Schools are supposed to be safe havens. Violence, however, occurs frequently in some schools across the United States.

Wikimedia Commons

"any criminal, physical, or emotional harm or unethical undertaking advantage that negatively affects the physical, financial, or general well being of an elderly person."[22]

School Violence

School violence refers to violence that occurs in the school setting. Members of the public frequently refer to the Columbine High School massacre in which two students murdered a dozen fellow students and a teacher before committing suicide. School shootings, although they receive a great deal of public attention, are extraordinarily rare. Other types of violence, however, occur with great regularity in schools across the United States. According to the National Center for Education Statistics, in 2011, 52 victimizations per 1,000 students occurred, 28% of students between the ages of 12 and 18 reported being bullied during the school year, and 9% reported experiencing cyberbullying.[23]

Cyberbullying refers to the use of technology to harass or harm the victim. These offenses could be done through text messages, Internet posts, Facebook, Instagram, tweets, or other computer-driven mechanisms. The damage to victims can be especially harmful and long lasting. Consider that communications done through cyberspace exist forever. As with other forms of bullying, some forms of cyberbullying have been tied to suicides by victims. In a recent case, two girls were arrested after their Facebook post reportedly led another girl to kill herself.[24] Somewhat boldly, one of the girls who was arrested posted the following on her Facebook page just days before her arrest: "Yes IK I bullied REBECCA nd she killed her self but IDGAF." The charges were later dropped after the juveniles agreed to go to counseling.

Based on existing bullying estimates, some observers have argued that bullying is even more problematic than serious forms of violence in schools. *Bullying* refers to repeated harmful behaviors targeting an individual or a group. Such actions can be verbal, emotional, or physically abusive. It has been suggested that a "culture of bullying" exists in some schools.[25] What this suggests is that values, beliefs, and norms may foster bullying in some places. The consequences of bullying can be devastating and have long-term effects on its victims. Victims will skip school, have problems learning the material in their courses, and may experience severe forms of depression as a result of bullying victimization.

Just as different communities will develop their own crime prevention strategies, it has been argued that different schools may need to use different school violence prevention and intervention measures. Some schools, for example, might have policies prohibiting the wearing of gang colors or baggy clothes, whereas others may have bag, desk, or locker checks on a routine basis. Installing security equipment such as metal detectors, fences, and special locks on windows and doors may also be part of a school's violence prevention measures.[26]

Hate Crimes

Hate crimes refers to situations in which a person is targeted for victimization because of his or her demographic characteristics (including gender, race, religion, health status, or sexuality). It is not illegal to "hate" people, but it is illegal to victimize people because of that hatred. According to the Federal Bureau of Investigation, in 2012, 5,796 hate crime incidents were reported "as a result of bias toward a particular race, religion, sexual orientation, ethnicity/national origin, or physical or mental disability." Just under half of these cases were racially motivated, and about one-fifth were motivated by either sexual orientation or religious biases. Data from the National Crime Victimization Survey suggest a higher frequency of hate crimes than is revealed through police reports. In particular, analysis of the victimization data found that an average of 195,000 hate crimes occurred per year between 2003 and 2009, and most of those incidents (90%) were motivated by racial or ethnic bias.[27] The same study showed that the hate crime rate decreased from 0.8 per 1,000 individuals to 0.5 per 1,000 in the same timeframe.

Much debate exists regarding whether a separate category of crimes governing against hatred-oriented behaviors is needed. Critics of such proposals note that traditional laws can be used to sanction the offensive behaviors, regardless of offenders' motivations. Supporters of hate crime laws note, among other things, that such laws promote acceptance and send a message that discriminatory and prejudicial actions are wrong. Indeed, many past crimes that were handled as traditional crimes would likely now be considered hate crimes.

Gang Violence

One of the earliest definitions of a "gang" was offered by Frederic Thrasher, who is regarded as the father of gang research:

> The gang is an interstitial group originally formed spontaneously, and then integrated through conflict. It is characterized by the following types of behavior: meeting face to face, milling, movement through space as a unit, conflict, and planning. The result of this collective behavior is the development of tradition, unreflective internal structure, esprit de corps, solidarity, morale, group awareness, and attachment to a local territory.[28]

Thrasher identified the following types of gangs, based on research he conducted in Chicago in the 1920s:

- *The diffuse gang.* A short-lived gang that has very little focus and purpose
- *The solidified gang.* A gang that lasts longer and is involved in more conflict
- *The conventional gang.* A group whose members are involved in conventional activities (like the athletic club)
- *The criminal gang.* A group that is involved in criminal activities

hate crimes: Situations in which one is targeted for victimization because of demographic characteristics (including gender, race, religion, health status, or sexuality).

Since then, criminologists have examined other types of gangs and developed more modern typologies to describe gang activity. The term *gang* most likely conjures images of the Crips, Bloods, Hell's Angels, M13, or some other violent gang. In reality, it is estimated that more than 33,000 gangs are criminally active in the United States. The FBI estimates that more than 1.4 million individuals are members of the gangs believed to exist in the United States. A 2011 assessment by the National Gang Intelligence Center suggested that "gangs are responsible for an average of 48 percent of violent crime in most jurisdictions and up to 90 percent in several others."[29]

Concern about gang violence has spread across the United States. Research suggests that, among juveniles, gang members have higher rates of delinquency than non–gang members.[30] No state is immune from gang activity. In terms of gang violence, gang members tend to target their violence toward other gang members, and common forms of violence include assault, intimidation, and gun violence.

Violent Sex Crime

Under common law, sex crimes were defined as a man's having *carnal knowledge* (that is, sexual contact) through force with a woman to whom he was not married. States have changed their laws to reflect that both men and women can be victims of rape. Also, the elements of "threat of force" and "without the victim's consent" have been added to statutes, so that **rape** now is typically defined as "having carnal knowledge through force or threat of force and without consent." It was not until the past three decades or so that laws were changed to prohibit men from raping their wives. Also, different degrees of rape exist across states, and the degrees are often based on the amount of force and whether a weapon was used.

Violent sex crime refers to the various types of rape that are committed. In 2013, 79,770 rapes were reported to the police, which was down about 10% from the number reported in 2006.[31] However, it is believed that many rapes are not reported to law enforcement for a variety of reasons. Victims are often embarrassed about their victimization and fear they will be blamed for their experiences. Also, some rape victims believe that going through the justice system will do more harm than good for their own well-being. Most jurisdictions employ victim advocates to help sexual assault victims navigate the justice process. The "Help Wanted" box in this chapter describes one such position.

Many criminologists have suggested that sex offenders are "not like other offenders." According to Lawrence Greenfeld, a review of data from various sources "point[s] to a sex offender who is older than other violent offenders, generally in his early thirties, and more likely to be white than other violent offenders."[32] Nicholas Groth described three types of rape offenders.[33] First, the *power rapist* does not necessarily want to harm the victim but wants to possess the victim sexually. Second, the *sadistic rapist* gains pleasure from harming victims. Third, the *anger rapist* gets little sexual satisfaction from the rape but uses the sexual assault to verbally and physically express anger and rage. Today, most experts note that rape is more often about power and control and less about sexual behavior.

rape: Sexual intercourse by force, threat of force, or deception.

HELP WANTED: VICTIM ADVOCATE COORDINATOR

DUTIES:

- Ensure overall local management of sexual assault awareness, prevention, training, and victim advocacy (VA).

- Work with the Joint Force Headquarters Sexual Assault Response Coordinator to support state National Guard units in the completion of required training and may conduct training as needed.

- Ensure victims of sexual assault receive all needed guidance and emotional support during administrative, medical, investigative, and legal procedures.

- Serve as the point of contact in coordination of victim care from initial report to resolution of victim's health and well-being.

REQUIREMENTS: Master's degree

ANNUAL SALARY: $47,923–$62,297

Adapted from USAJOBS.gov. Retrieved from https://www.usajobs.gov/GetJob/ViewDetails/375676700

Another way to classify sex offenses is to categorize the behavior based on when it occurs in the victim's life course. From this orientation, types of sex abuse include child sexual abuse, date rape, marital rape, and elder sexual abuse.

BEYOND A REASONABLE DOUBT 4.2

_____ is a legal phrase that means sexual contact.

(a) Carnal knowledge, (b) Serial rape, (c) Familial relations, (d) Negligent violence, (e) None of the above

---

The answer can be found on page 521.

Child Sexual Abuse

Child sexual abuse refers to sexual abuse committed against children. Commonly cited estimates suggest that one in four females and one in seven males are sexually abused before the age of 18. Also, a significant proportion of all sexual abuse victims are under the age of 12, with early estimates suggesting that one-third of all sexual abuse cases involve children as victims.[34]

Research shows that offenders use a variety of techniques to justify their sexually abusive activities. In these situations, the relationship begins as a nonsexual relationship, and the offender does things to slowly turn the relationship into a sexual one. Once the activity becomes sexual, offenders frequently "silence" their victims with either promises of gifts or threats of harm. It is widely agreed that the typical sexual abuser is a "father figure" (including stepfathers and grandfathers) rather than a mother, although women are occasionally implicated in these cases.

Over the past decade, the Catholic Church has faced numerous accusations related to sexual abuse perpetrated by priests and other church

child sexual abuse: Sexual abuse committed against a child.

officials toward young members of the church. The John Jay College of Criminal Justice of the City University of New York was hired by a National Review Board, which was formed by the United States Conference of Catholic Bishops, to study child sexual abuse in the Catholic Church. The researchers found that 4% of active priests "between 1950 and 2002 had allegations of abuse" and that most of the incidents occurred in the 1970s and 1980s.[35] In a separate study, a researcher found that victims abused by a priest were more distrustful of religion than those victimized by someone other than a priest.[36]

Date Rape

Date rape is perhaps a misnomer in that it seems to suggest that the rape occurs as part of a date. In reality, date rape is in many ways synonymous with acquaintance rape. In these cases, victims and offenders know one another, are not married, and are not related. Drugs and alcohol are often involved in the offenses. It has long been believed that some rapists use drugs such as Rohypnol (known as roofies or GHB) to incapacitate their victims by spiking their drinks, although one study on urine samples found that alcohol, marijuana, cocaine, benzodiazepines, and amphetamines were more frequently found in the urine samples. Of the 1,179 urine samples tested, the researchers found GHB in only 48 of the samples.[37] Alcohol is the drug implicated most often in date rapes. It could certainly be the case that those victimized through GHB either do not know they were sexually assaulted or are less likely to report the victimization to the police. Or, it could be that GHB is not used nearly as often as some people believe. This does not mean that date rape does not happen frequently, because it does.

Date rape is of particular concern on college campuses. Estimates suggest that the annual sexual assault rate on college campuses is 35 per 1,000 students, meaning that for every 10,000 students a college has, there may be about 350 sexual assaults each year.[38] Research suggests that structural features of colleges and universities fail to prevent and, in some situations, may even contribute to sexual assault on college campuses.[39] Among the potential risk factors for sexual abuse on campus are the age of college students, the sexualized culture of the college campus, and the easy availability of drugs and alcohol and their overuse on college campuses. Another risk factor has to do with the transient nature of the student population. For instance, victims may leave college after experiencing abuse, and offenders may leave their own college campus to find victims. Finally, because sexual assault occurs in the broader community as well as on college campuses, campus advocates need to compete with members of the broader community to fund campus-based sexual assault programs.

Marital Rape

Marital rape refers to instances in which spouses (typically husbands) sexually assault their wives. As noted earlier, marital rape was not criminalized in any state until the 1970s. Estimates suggest that 7.7 million

date rape: Synonymous with acquaintance rape, in which victims and offenders know one another, are not married, and are not related.

marital rape: Instances in which a husband or wife sexually assault their spouse; some state laws require the use of force in order for the act to be classified as rape.

women have been raped by an intimate partner at some point during their lives.[40] In most cases, marital rape victims will not report their victimization to the police. Marital rape laws in some states indicate that, for an act to be rape, the husband must use force against his wife, meaning that threat of force would not be enough for the act to be rape in those states.

Elder Sexual Abuse

Elder sexual abuse refers to a range of sexually oriented behaviors that target older victims. Elder sexual abuse is the least reported type of sexual abuse and the least reported type of elder abuse. Some experts have suggested that sexual assault victims are more likely to be older than younger. A review of elder sexual abuse cases in nursing homes found that residents of long-term-care settings with impairments appeared to be more susceptible to sexual abuse than physical abuse and that these cases rarely have any witnesses.[41] The study also suggested that sexual assaults of nursing home residents frequently involved controlling or degrading the older person. Consider the following examples described in the study:

- The sexual assault involved inserting a banana into the rectum of a patient who suffered from left side paralysis and mental confusion. [They] put the soiled banana into another patient's mouth. Not only did the defendants commit these acts while laughing with amusement, but they bragged and laughed about the assault to their friends.

- [He] is accused of hitting a 78-year-old patient in the face with a diaper and pretending to kiss and simulate sexual intercourse with a 92-year-old resident.

Robbery

State and federal laws typically define **robbery** as taking another person's property by force or threat of force. Because force or threat of force is used, the behavior is typically defined as a violent crime, even though property is stolen in the offense. States will define different degrees of robbery based on whether a weapon is used, the type of weapon used, and the amount of force used. Threat of force is enough to define a theft as a robbery. If someone says, "Give me your money, or I will punch you," and you give your money, this would be defined as robbery.

Across the United States, $404 million was lost to robbery in 2013. Figure 4.3 shows the losses across locations where the robberies occurred. The average loss per robbery was just under $1,170, with banks losing the highest average amount and convenience stores losing the lowest average amount. Figure 4.4 shows the type of force used in the robberies. Guns were used in about 40% of the robberies, "strong-arm" tactics were used just as often, and knives and other forms of threats were used in the remaining robberies.[42] An early study categorized the force used in robberies as threats, prodding force (limited to shoving and pushing),

elder sexual abuse:
Situations in which individuals perform illegal and inappropriate sexual activities targeted against older persons.

robbery: The taking of another person's property by force or threat of force; typically defined as a violent crime.

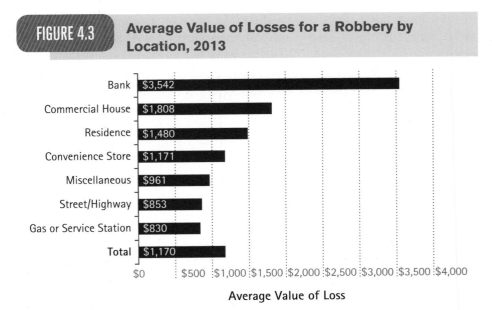

FIGURE 4.3   **Average Value of Losses for a Robbery by Location, 2013**

Federal Bureau of Investigation

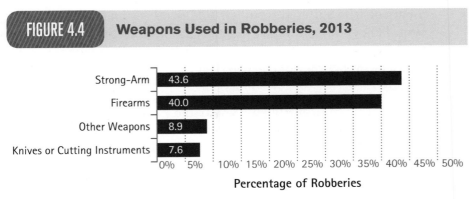

FIGURE 4.4   **Weapons Used in Robberies, 2013**

Federal Bureau of Investigation

and incapacitating force (knocking someone unconscious).[43] Others have described the following methods used by robbers:[44]

- *Confrontation.* Making a demand
- *Blitzes.* Using force first to gain control
- *Cons.* Distracting the victim and then robbing him or her (asking the time, for example)
- *Snatch-theft.* Grabbing an item out of the victim's hands

The vast majority of robberies are committed by younger offenders. Robbers are believed to target individuals who they think have a lot of money or who appear lost.[45] In addition, it has been suggested that although most robberies occur at night, robberies involving older victims happen more frequently in the morning and robberies of teenagers occur after school between 3 p.m. and 6 p.m. In addition, estimates suggest that urban residents are two times as likely as suburban residents to be robbed and that 44% of robberies occur within one mile of one's home.[46]

Some street robbers (as opposed to business robbers) report targeting others involved in criminal activity because they are reasonably certain that the victim (such as a drug dealer) won't contact the police about the victimization.[47] Other robbers, however, told Richard Wright and Scott Decker, in their ethnographic study of robbers, that they prefer noncriminal victims because, as one robber commented, "You don't want to pick somebody dangerous. They might have a gun themselves."[48]

Some robberies are well planned, whereas others are given virtually no thought. When robberies are planned, "planning the escape appears to be the most critical factor."[49] Willis distinguishes between professional robbers and amateur robbers, with the former offenders more likely to work in groups and plan their offenses and the latter offenders working alone and targeting whomever they happen to encounter.[50]

A recent study by Bruce Jacobs and Richard Wright suggests that some robberies are committed in order to send a message.[51] Referred to as *moralistic robberies*, the researchers describe the following three types of robberies done in order to send a message:

> *Market-related* violations emerge from disputes involving partners in trade, rivals, or generalized predators. *Status-based* violations involve encounters in which the grievant's essential character or normative sensibilities have been challenged. *Personalistic* violations flow from incidents in which the grievant's autonomy or belief in a just world have been jeopardized.[52]

Jacobs and Wright's findings are particularly useful because they remind us that robbery, as a violent crime, can be a crime of power and not simply a crime of financial gain. In such cases, items are taken not for their financial value, but rather so that the offender can gain power over the victim.

➡ Property Crime

Whereas violent crime can result in untold harm for crime victims, property crime occurs far more often. This is not to suggest that one type of crime is worse than the other. It is simply a fact that the bulk of crimes that come to the attention of criminal justice authorities are property crimes. As the label suggests, property crime targets an individual's property rather than the individual's physical person. For victims, property crime can be just as harmful as violent crime. Types of property crime include common property crime, burglary, motor vehicle theft, and arson (see Figure 4.5).

FIGURE 4.5	Types of Property Crime

COMMON PROPERTY CRIME	BURGLARY	MOTOR VEHICLE THEFT	ARSON
• Larceny • Shoplifting • Identity theft • Plagiarism	• Novice burglary • Middle-range burglary • Professional burglary	• Carjacking • Joyriding	• Accidental • Intentional • Crisis oriented • Revenge motivated

Common Property Crime

Common property crime refers to a number of different crimes, many of which are relatively minor compared to violent crimes that involve stealing property from other individuals. State laws define hundreds, if not thousands, of different types of property crime. For our purposes, we focus on the property crimes most common and most relevant to readers, including larceny, shoplifting, identity theft, and plagiarism.

Larceny

Generally speaking, legal scholars define **larceny** as taking someone's else's property with intent to keep the property. This definition covers four key elements of larceny:

➥ *The offender must physically move the property*; it is not enough to simply touch someone else's property.

➥ *The property must belong to another person*; that is, individuals cannot steal their own property.

➥ *The offender must have formed mental intent to take the property.*

➥ *The offender must intend to keep the property.*

Most states identify different degrees of larceny (first, second, and so on), and some states distinguish between *grand larceny* and *petty larceny* based on the property's value. The distinction is important because petty larceny tends to be a misdemeanor, which would carry a lesser penalty, and grand larceny would be a felony, which would carry a stiffer penalty. In one case, an offender who was charged with grand larceny for stealing something worth just over $500 (which was the limit this particular state set for grand larceny) argued that because he had a coupon for 10% off any item in the store, he should have been charged with petty larceny. The defense was not successful, but the defendant was later able to plead guilty to the lesser charge.

Larceny-theft is the most common Part I crime reported to the police. In 2013, 6,004,453 larcenies were reported to the police, which represents a 13.4% decrease from the 2004 rate. Just under one-fourth

larceny: The taking of someone's else's property with intent to keep the property.

of those larcenies involved items taken from automobiles, and the average value of the stolen items was $1,259.[53] Research suggests that larceny victimization risks are predicted by "where one goes and what one does."[54] In particular, focusing on a sample of college students, Elizabeth Mustaine and Richard Tewksbury found that a student's risk of being the victim of minor thefts was related to whether the student had a dog. For more on this finding, see the "Criminal Justice and College Students" box in this chapter.

Shoplifting

Shoplifting involves larceny-thefts in which individuals steal from a store. In 2013, 1,074,188 shoplifting incidents were reported to the police and the property stolen had an average value of $207. The true number of shoplifting incidents is much higher given that offenders are able to get away with the offense with some ease and many storeowners, even when they catch shoplifters, may choose not to call the police. It has been suggested that, along with employees' thefts from stores, shoplifting may cost retailers more than $14 billion a year.[55]

Types of shoplifters include (a) *amateur shoplifters*, who rarely shoplift but, when they do, they steal items they will use themselves, (b) *kleptomaniacs*, who steal because of what is believed to be a compulsion, (c) *juvenile shoplifters*, who steal for the excitement they get and the items they steal, (d) *homeless shoplifters*, who steal to survive, (e) *addict shoplifters*, who steal to support a drug problem, and (f) *professional shoplifters*, who steal a significant amount of goods in order to sell them.[56] Professional shoplifters frequently are part of a broader criminal network that buys and sells stolen goods. Many professional shoplifters may sell their stolen goods to individuals known as *fences*, who sell stolen goods. The goods are typically sold at a really low price. Keep in mind that possessing stolen goods is also a crime. Establishing intent can be problematic, but if you buy a $10,000 item for $1,000 from a person wearing an "I am a fence" t-shirt, it would be difficult to argue that you did not know you were purchasing stolen goods.

CRIMINAL JUSTICE and **COLLEGE STUDENTS**

WHO LET THE DOGS OUT? (PREDICTORS OF MINOR THEFT VICTIMIZATION)

Researchers Elizabeth Mustaine and Richard Tewksbury surveyed roughly 1,500 college students to identify predictors of minor theft. Dogs, in particular, were among those factors that reduced the likelihood of victimization for college students. Mustaine and Tewksbury note that students living in off-campus housing would rarely purchase security measures such as locks, exterior lights, or security systems on their own for rental units. Do you own a dog? If so, did you get your pet in order to feel safer or for another reason? List three things that make dogs useful as a security strategy. Compare your answers with what your classmates said.

VIDEO
Identity Theft on Rise

Identity Theft

Simply speaking, **identity theft** means stealing someone else's background. Criminalized under the Identity Theft and Assumption Deterrence Act, identify theft is perpetrated through other crimes including "forgery, counterfeiting, check and credit card fraud, computer fraud, impersonation, pickpocketing, and even terrorism."[57] Historically, identity theft victims were not regarded as true victims. This changed in recent years as the crimes escalated and individuals increasingly experienced enormous losses and consequences to the offense.[58] Of all the complaints received by the Federal Trade Commission (FTC) in 2013, 14% were for identity theft. In fact, identity theft was the most frequent complaint that consumers made to the FTC for 14 years in a row, with 290,056 identity theft complaints made in 2013.[59] In many cases, victims may not know they have had their identity stolen until long after the offender has committed the offense.[60]

Plagiarism

Plagiarism, which refers to stealing the intellectual property of another, is a crime in many states. Plagiarism exists on a continuum. At one end of the continuum are situations in which an author flat out uses another author's words verbatim without citing the original author. At the other end are situations in which an author might cite the original author, but the words and ideas used are not paraphrased adequately or cited appropriately. For students, the penalty is typically a lower grade in a class, a zero on an assignment, or even suspension from college. Some authors have been sued successfully by the victims of plagiarism. Chances are that your professor will not call the police if a student in your class is caught plagiarizing; however, careers of students and faculty have been damaged because of the decision to steal another person's intellectual property (see the "Ethical Decision Making" box in this chapter).

Burglary

VIDEO
Burglary Ringleader Arrested

Under common law, **burglary** was defined as "the breaking and entering the house of another in the night-time, with intent to commit a felony therein, whether the felony be actually committed or not." Over time this definition evolved in state laws to also criminalize breaking and entering during the daytime and breaking and entering into places other than a "house." For example, rental properties, businesses, warehouses, barns, and other structures are now covered under state burglary statutes. Instances in which offenders break or enter into a home without the intention of committing a crime are known as *criminal trespass*. For criminologists studying the behavior, attention is given to those who break into peoples' homes, businesses, or other structures in order to commit a crime.

In 2013, more than 1.9 million burglaries were reported to the police. Combined, those burglaries cost victims a total of $4.5 billion and the average loss per burglary was $2,322. Almost three-fourths of

identity theft: Stealing someone else's background; can be perpetrated through other crimes such as forgery, credit card fraud, and the like.

plagiarism: Stealing the intellectual property of another.

burglary: Unlawful entry into a structure with the intent to commit a felony.

ETHICAL DECISION MAKING

RESPONDING TO PLAGIARISM IN A POLICE LEADERSHIP COURSE

Johan Johnson is a lieutenant in the local police department. He has his hopes set on becoming a deputy chief. Along with 10 other officers, he is selected to participate in a leadership institute administered through a local university. He is honored to be in the program.

As part of the program, the officers are given assignments similar to those given in college courses. As a college graduate, he finds these assignments to be both challenging and rewarding. His current assignment requires him to identify two top police leaders and compare and contrast their backgrounds with their leadership styles. He works for days on end after his shift to complete the assignment.

When he is getting ready to turn in his assignment, one of Johan's fellow officers asks him to turn in her assignment for her because she has a meeting with the chief scheduled. Johan places her folder in his briefcase and leaves for the training site.

After arriving at the training site, Johan reaches in to grab his fellow officer's assignment when two papers fall out of the folder she has given him. In looking at the papers, Johan realizes that his fellow student has plagiarized her assignment.

YOU DECIDE

1. Should Johan turn in his colleague for plagiarism? If so, should he tell the chief or just the instructor of the class?

2. What might be the consequences if Johan turns her in?

3. What might be the consequences if Johan does not turn her in?

---

the burglaries targeted homes; the rest targeted stores, businesses, and other nonresident structures. Among burglaries in which victims knew when the burglary occurred, about two-thirds of residential burglaries occurred during the day, presumably when victims were not home.[61] Among all offenses, burglary has one of the lowest arrest rates, and the vast majority of these crimes are never solved. This means that if your home or apartment is broken into, chances are you won't get your stolen property back.

Deborah Weisel has identified three types of burglars: The *novice burglar* is younger and experienced, and easily deterred by security measures; the *middle-range burglar* is a little more experienced and tends to work alone; and the *professional burglar* is highly skilled, may drive farther to the crime scene, is not deterred by security measures, and has connections with fellow criminals to whom the stolen goods can be sold.[62] Compared to other types of offenses, burglary may be more likely to occur in certain locations than in others. Location is believed to be related to burglary in the following ways:[63]

- Offenders select residences close to them.

- Homes located close to major thoroughfares are more at risk for burglary.

- Displaying signs of wealth increases risk of burglary.

➤ Homes on streets with poor lighting are at a higher risk of being burglarized.

➤ Houses that have been broken into in the past have a higher likelihood of being burglarized again.

➤ Vacant homes are at higher risk for being broken into.

➤ Homes on street corners are at a higher risk for burglary victimization.

Interviews with burglars by Paul Cromwell and his coauthors revealed that many of the burglars selected locations to burglarize based on opportunities.[64] The authors highlighted three types of opportunities: (a) Burglars just happened to be in the "right spot at the right time," for example, they happened to be somewhere when they noticed an open window; (b) the site was a location that the burglar had visited as part of a legitimate role, perhaps as a worker, a delivery person, or a guest; or (c) the offender cruised a neighborhood and identified particular cues about a home that made it attractive for a burglary. Some burglaries likely occur because offenders know that the homes are vacant.

The "Criminal Justice and the Media" box in this chapter describes a case in which a victim's tweets were believed to play a role in a burglary. Perhaps as evidence that opportunistic burglars "think alike," one study found that approximately 1% of all residences in the jurisdiction studied "suffered from 29 percent of the burglaries reported to the police" over a two-year timeframe.[65] The same study found that one-half of the subsequent revictimizations occurred within 30 days of the initial victimization. Another study also found that "the elevated risk of repeat burglary does not last over long time periods."[66]

CRIMINAL JUSTICE and the **MEDIA:**
ONLINE COMMUNICATIONS MAY LEAD TO VICTIMIZATION

Israel Hyman returned home from a trip to visit relatives one spring day and found that his home had been broken into and his computer, two displays, and a printer had been stolen. After thinking about how a burglar would know that his home was empty, he realized that a tweet he had made, which automatically changed his Facebook status, announced to the world that he was not at home. Some observers may be tempted to blame Hyman for his misfortunes, but many social media users regularly post their location status and updates. In the past, it was reported that burglars would search obituaries to learn when homes were vacant. Today, they don't even have to buy newspapers to find out this information. Be sure to check your Facebook status so that you aren't announcing your home or apartment is empty!

We made it to Kansas City in one piece. We're visiting @noellhyman's family. Can't wait to get some good video while we're here. :-)

7:19 PM May 24th from web

 **izzyvideo**
Israel Hyman

https://twitter.com/izzyvideo/status/1908399195

BEYOND A REASONABLE DOUBT 4.3

If an offender breaks into your home and steals your computer, which type of crime has been committed?

(a) Larceny, (b) Burglary, (c) Robbery, (d) All of the above, (e) None of the above

---

The answer can be found on page 521.

Motor Vehicle Theft

Motor vehicle theft refers to instances in which individuals steal automobiles, not when thieves steal items from automobiles. The movie *Fast and Furious* and its sequels glorify motor vehicle theft in their efforts to portray an auto theft ring. Although auto theft rings exist, they are not nearly as violent as portrayed in the movies. Most motor vehicle thefts occur at night, injuries are rare, and most are reported to the police.[67] People may be willing to tolerate some types of theft, but when a car is stolen, people turn to the police out of hopes that the car will be found or at least that auto insurance will cover the theft because it was reported to the police.

Motor vehicle theft has been called the "most under researched Part I crime."[68] One study found that community-level factors that affected motor vehicle theft included racial heterogeneity and being "surrounded by higher motor vehicle theft rate locations initially."[69] The authors suggested that motor vehicle theft expands into surrounding communities because residents in communities where cars are stolen will take additional measures to protect their own cars (known as *target hardening*) and fewer cars will be identified as attractive for theft (*target density*).

Experts suggest that three-fourths of motor vehicle thefts occur within one mile of the victim's home.[70] Hot spots (that is, locations where crimes are more likely) for motor vehicle theft include shopping centers, commuter parking lots, car dealerships, bars, and movie theaters.[71] Describing what is called the "near-repeat pattern," or the likelihood that a crime will occur near geographic locations where similar crimes have occurred recently, Brian Lockwood also suggested that there is a 96% higher chance that a motor vehicle theft will occur "between one and two blocks and within two weeks of an earlier motor vehicle theft beyond what [is expected]."[72]

Different types of motor vehicle theft exist. *Carjacking* refers to instances when the offender steals the car directly from the car owner. This type of crime occurs more often in urban areas than rural areas, and three-fourths of carjackings involved a weapon, with nearly half involving a gun.[73] Penalties for carjacking, particularly when a weapon is used, are higher than are the penalties in other types of motor vehicle thefts. *Victim-absent car thefts* describe situations when the car is stolen while the victim is not near the car. *Joyriding* refers to instances when offenders don't intend to keep the car but are using it simply to get around for a short period of time. Juveniles are more likely to be offenders in joyriding cases. In contrast, professional car thieves are a part of the organized professional crime groups that steal automobiles and resell them.

motor vehicle theft: Instances in which individuals steal automobiles (as opposed to thieves stealing items *from* automobiles).

TABLE 4.1   The Most Stolen Cars, 2013

TYPE OF CAR	NUMBER OF CARS STOLEN
Honda Accord	53,995
Honda Civic	45,001
Chevrolet Pickup (Full Size)	27,809
Ford Pickup (Full Size)	26,494
Toyota Camry	14,420
Dodge Pickup (Full Size)	11,347
Dodge Caravan	10,911
Jeep Cherokee/Grand Cherokee	9,272[1]

National Insurance Crime Bureau

In 2013, Honda Accords were stolen more often than any other automobile.

Wikimedia Commons

In 2013, just under 700,000 motor vehicle thefts were reported to the police. This was down more than 43% from the 2004 level. More than $4.1 billion was lost to motor vehicle theft in 2013, and the average loss per theft was $5,971.[74] Table 4.1 lists the most frequently stolen cars in 2013. Note that the kinds of cars that Vin Diesel steals in *Fast and Furious* are not included in the table, not because those cars are not attractive targets, but because not nearly as many of those high-end cars are available, compared to the types of automobiles listed in the table. Interestingly, according to the National Insurance Crime Bureau, the theft of electronic access codes for automobiles is becoming increasingly problematic.

Arson

Arson occurs when individuals intentionally set a structure on fire. Common law definitions of arson suggested that it was only a crime if the structure was someone else's dwelling place (that is, burning your own property was not arson). State laws expanded to define arson as intentional burning of any structure or property, including the offender's own property and nonresidential structures. In many states, degrees of arson are set based on whether a victim is in the structure (first-degree arson) or not (second-degree arson). Accidental fires are not technically arson, unless the fire was caused by reckless conduct.

Juveniles committed the vast majority of all arsons between 2007 and 2011. Arsons by juveniles have been classified as *accidental arsons* from playing with fire, *intentional arsons* from playing with fire, and *crisis-motivated arsons.* Juveniles committed 80% of the intentional arsons and 99% of the accidental arsons.[75] Motives cited for arson include excitement, vandalism, profit, extremist behaviors, to cover up a crime, and revenge.[76] A revenge-oriented arson that received a great deal of public attention involved Lisa Lopes, the former TLC star who later died in a car crash. Lopes burned down boyfriend Andre Rison's house after setting his shoes on fire in a bathtub. She told officials that she set the shoes on fire as revenge for abuse she said Rison had directed toward her.

Arsonists typically start with small fires (in garbage cans, dumpsters, and so on) and gradually begin to select other targets to prey upon.[77] A number of misguided perceptions about arson exist. Some people mistakenly believe that firefighters are frequently arsonists; in reality, arsons by firefighters are rare. John Hall has cited three myths about arson:[78]

- Arson is the fastest growing crime in the United States. *(They are actually becoming less common.)*

arson: A crime in which an individual intentionally sets a structure on fire.

- Arson is hard to solve because the fires destroy all the evidence. *(All crimes are hard to solve.)*

- Arson becomes more frequent in difficult economic times. *(No such relationship exists.)*

If you have a burning desire to learn more about arson (pun intended), you should visit the National Fire Protection Association's website (http://www.nfpa.org/).

➡ Public Order Crime

Public order crime refers to a class of crimes that appear to be victimless but are classified as crimes because of the belief that they harm the public order in some way. These would also include "crimes of moral turpitude," or crimes defined as illegal because members of the community believe the offenses violate society's morals. Examples of public order crime include alcohol-related crime, prostitution, and status offenses (see Figure 4.6).

Alcohol-Related Crime

In the United States, many alcohol-related crimes exist, including public drunkenness offenses, underage-drinking crimes, and drunk driving. Public drunkenness laws specify that individuals are prohibited from being drunk in a public setting. Such laws give police officers a great deal of discretion. Some state laws specify that individuals may be sentenced to

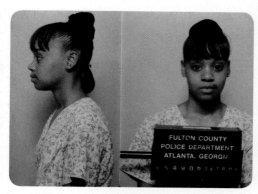

Former TLC singer Lisa Lopes was arrested after burning down her boyfriend's mansion.

© ZUMA Press, Inc. / Alamy

Author Video
Victimless Crimes

FIGURE 4.6   **Types of Public Order Crime**

© iStockphoto.com/mphillips007; © iStockphoto.com/pixhook

public order crime: A class of crimes that appear to be victimless but are classified as crimes because of the belief that they harm the public order in some way.

Streetwalkers are but one of the many types of prostitutes.

Tomas Castelazo

jail for six months for public intoxication. Rarely does this happen, however. The phrase *drunk and disorderly* is frequently used to refer to what it is about being "drunk in public" (known as DIP to police officers) that might get people in trouble with the law. If a group of students are drunk on their walk back to the dorm, they likely will not be confronted by law enforcement unless someone in the group becomes disorderly. In this context, disorderly means being loud, belligerent, and otherwise annoying to the general public. But again, police have tremendous discretion in deciding when to enforce these laws. Some police officers have confessed to goading inebriated disrespectful homeowners or residents into a public setting so that they can arrest them for being drunk in public.

Underage-drinking laws in the United States make it illegal to consume alcohol until the age of 21. It is believed that young people are drinking at an earlier age and engaging in more "extreme" forms of drinking than was the case in the past. Perhaps due to their inexperience with alcohol and overall lower levels of maturity, younger people who consume excessive alcohol are more prone to exhibit a loss of control and aggression. Such reactions have been referred to as "beer muscles." Whatever they are called, these reactions increase the risk of criminal justice contacts. Among college students, underage drinking has been connected to peer pressure, the lack of guardians to keep young people from drinking, and environmental factors such as bars being located close to campus.[79] In the 1970s and early 1980s, the drinking age was 18 in some states and 19 in some others. Advocates from various groups, including Mothers Against Drunk Driving, were instrumental in getting the drinking age raised. In the years after the drinking age was raised, the number of deaths from drunk driving dropped precipitously, from more than 26,000 fatalities in 1982 to about 10,322 in 2012.[80]

Prostitution

Prostitution refers to individuals providing sexual behaviors in exchange for money. Prostitution is illegal everywhere in the United States except for a few counties in Nevada, where prostitution is legal as long as the services occur in a licensed brothel. The term *john* refers to the individual purchasing the sexual activity. Although purchasing and selling sexual favors is illegal, it is believed that more criminal justice attention is given to prostitutes than johns.

Researchers have identified several different types of prostitutes based on the way they organize their services. One author has cited the following types:[81]

➤ *Streetwalkers.* Prostitutes who walk in particular parts of the community where they believe they will be able to ply their trade

➤ *Call girls.* Prostitutes who have regular clients who are willing to pay the high fees charged

➤ *Madams.* Those who manage the prostitutes, providing connections and opportunities with new clients

prostitution: Situations in which individuals provide sexual behaviors in exchange for money; illegal in all states except for Nevada.

- *In-house prostitutes.* Those who are employed in a legal business such as in a modeling agency or a massage parlor, but provide sexual favors to clients

- *Indentured sex slaves.* Trafficked individuals who are forced to prostitute themselves

- *Escort service prostitutes.* Those who provide services at a relatively high fee after advertising "escort services" either in the phone book or online

- *Drug-addicted prostitutes.* Those who provide sexual activity in exchange for drugs or money to buy drugs

- *Homeless prostitutes.* Those who turn to prostitution to survive because they have nowhere to live

- *Part-time prostitutes.* Those who engage in prostitution on an irregular basis

Some jurisdictions have tried innovative strategies to respond to prostitution. "John school" has been used to punish those soliciting prostitutes. In these cases, the offenders must get together with other convicted johns and attend a training where they learn about the problems that arise from prostitution. Community members and former prostitutes confront the johns in an effort to shame them into avoiding future offending. In another jurisdiction, postcards were mailed to the homes of men arrested for prostitution with a notice telling them they should go to the health clinic to be tested for sexually transmitted diseases. The postcards were used so that the johns' spouses would know about the offense. The police department reportedly stopped doing this when a family member of someone in city government received one of the postcards.

In 2008, debate about prostitution hit the national media when Natalie Dylan reportedly offered to sell her virginity at the Moonlite Bunny Ranch, one of Nevada's more famous brothels, because, she said, "Her older sister earned good money working as a prostitute at the Bunny Ranch, and also to change public perceptions of virginity."[82] Reportedly in an effort to raise money for graduate school, she offered her virginity in an online auction, and it has been widely reported that she was offered $3.8 million for her virginity. Eventually the deal fell through when the highest bidder's wife put a stop to it.[83]

Some people have called for the legalization of prostitution on the grounds that the behavior is, to them, a victimless offense. A number of laws on the books regulate against such sexual activity, and supporters of legalization contend that these laws reflect conservative morals rather than actual harm from the offenses. These other "moral turpitude" laws make it illegal, in some states, for men and women to have sexual intercourse unless they are married (to each other). In some states, adultery is criminally illegal. Supporters of the legalization of prostitution contend that just as these other laws are not enforced, even though they too are based on morality, prostitution laws should be relaxed as well. Opponents of prostitution

In some places, such as in a few counties in Nevada, prostitution is legal. The Moonlite Bunny Ranch is a legal brothel in Nevada.

© SANDEE PAWAN/SIPA/Newscom

VIDEO
Juvenile Status
Offenders

legalization point to negative consequences of prostitution, including sexually transmitted diseases, the risk of victimization for prostitutes and johns, emotional consequences for prostitutes and johns, and the negative impact that these activities (like streetwalking) have on the community.

Status Offenses

As noted in Chapter 2, *status offenses* are behaviors that are illegal for juveniles but legal for adults. Most status offenses have no direct victim, unless you consider the juvenile a victim of himself or herself. Part of the current effort to control juveniles has to do with efforts to maintain public order. For example, truancy laws ensure that juveniles are in school and not in the community causing problems. Curfew laws ensure that juveniles are at home and not out late getting into trouble. Runaway laws have a similar purpose: to keep youth at home so that they are not on the streets getting hurt or harming others. These status offenses would be processed through juvenile courts rather than adult courts.

Decriminalization Debates

A great deal of debate has centered on whether public order crimes should be decriminalized. The debate often points to the victimless nature of these offenses and suggests that law enforcement officers, and other criminal justice officials, are spending a great deal of resources responding to these offenses. In *The Honest Politician's Guide to Crime Control* (published in 1972), Norval Morris and Gordon Hawkins called for the decriminalization of several victimless crimes that were illegal, in the authors' opinion, because of morals rather than actual harm.[84] In their own words, Morris and Hawkins recommended the following changes:[85]

1. *Drunkenness.* Public drunkenness shall cease to be a criminal offense.

2. *Narcotics and drug abuse.* Neither the acquisition, purchase, possession, nor the use of any drug will be a criminal offense. The sale of some drugs other than by a licensed chemist (druggist) and on prescription will be criminally proscribed; proof of possession of excessive quantities may be evidence of a sale or of intent to sell.

3. *Gambling.* No form of gambling will be prohibited by the criminal law; certain fraudulent and cheating gambling practices will remain criminal.

4. *Disorderly conduct and vagrancy.* Disorderly conduct and vagrancy laws will be replaced by laws precisely stipulating the conduct proscribed and defining the circumstances in which the police should intervene.

5. *Abortion.* Abortion performed by a qualified medical practitioner in a registered hospital shall cease to be a criminal offense.

6. *Sexual behavior*. Sexual activities between consenting adults in private will not be subject to the criminal law. Adultery, fornication, illicit cohabitation, statutory rape and carnal knowledge, bigamy, incest, sodomy, bestiality, homosexuality, prostitution, pornography, and obscenity; in all of these the role of the criminal law is excessive.

7. *Juvenile delinquency*. The juvenile court should retain jurisdiction only over conduct by children which would be criminal were they adult.

By defining seriousness of crime based on the harm that actions created, rather than the morals attached to behavior, Morris and Hawkins believed more time, effort, and resources could be spent addressing serious crimes. Experts have disagreed about whether public order crimes and moral turpitude crimes should be decriminalized. George Kelling and James Q. Wilson have argued that minor crimes and minor signs of disorder lead to more serious crime and more serious disorder:

This wish to "decriminalize" disreputable behavior that "harms no one"—and thus remove the ultimate sanction the police can employ to maintain neighborhood order—is, we think, a mistake. Arresting a single drunk or a single vagrant who has harmed no identifiable person seems unjust, and in a sense it is. But failing to do anything about a score of drunks or a hundred vagrants may destroy an entire community.[86]

From Kelling and Wilson's perspective, doing nothing about public order crimes like drunkenness, drug use, and prostitution would send a message to the community that these crimes are acceptable, and such a message would then suggest that other crimes are also acceptable. Note that some of the behaviors that Morris and Hawkins wanted decriminalized have, in fact, been legalized, whereas some of the other behaviors have been increasingly criminalized through new laws and stiffer penalties.[87]

BEYOND A REASONABLE DOUBT 4.4

Behaviors legal for adults but illegal for juveniles are known as _____.

(a) juvenile delinquent acts, (b) crimes of moral turpitude, (c) victimless crimes, (d) status offenses, (e) none of the above

---

The answer can be found on page 521.

➡ Crime Within Complex Organizations

Dabney uses the phrase "crime within complex organizations" to describe "any physical or nonphysical illegal act (violent or property offense) that is committed within an organizational context and seeks to further individual or organizational goals, regardless of the social status of that individual or organization."[88] In this context, these offenses include white-collar crime, corporate crime, state crime, and organized crime (see Figure 4.7).

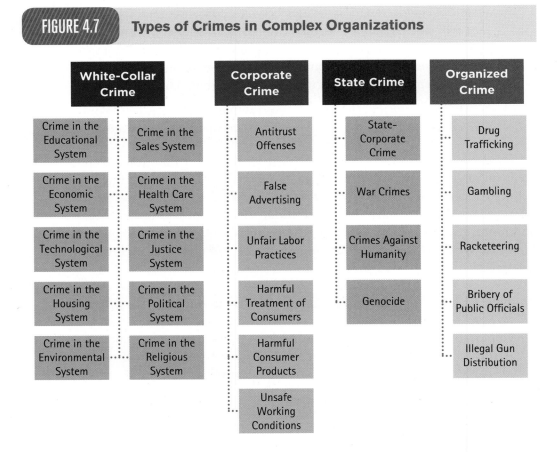

FIGURE 4.7   **Types of Crimes in Complex Organizations**

White-Collar Crime		Corporate Crime	State Crime	Organized Crime
Crime in the Educational System	Crime in the Sales System	Antitrust Offenses	State-Corporate Crime	Drug Trafficking
Crime in the Economic System	Crime in the Health Care System	False Advertising	War Crimes	Gambling
Crime in the Technological System	Crime in the Justice System	Unfair Labor Practices	Crimes Against Humanity	Racketeering
Crime in the Housing System	Crime in the Political System	Harmful Treatment of Consumers	Genocide	Bribery of Public Officials
Crime in the Environmental System	Crime in the Religious System	Harmful Consumer Products		Illegal Gun Distribution
		Unsafe Working Conditions		

White-Collar Crime

The term **white-collar crime** was coined by Edwin Sutherland in a speech he made to the American Sociological Association in 1939. Drawing attention to the fact that individuals with wealth also committed crime, a decade later Sutherland defined white-collar crimes as "crime committed by a person of respectability and high social status in the course of his occupation"[89]

Sutherland's concept generated a great deal of debate. He was criticized by legal scholars for defining as crime behaviors that would not always be defined as illegal in the criminal law, and social scientists criticized him for the vagueness of his concept. Although he alluded to crime by persons of high status, his own research focused either on crimes by corporations or crimes by individuals employed in lower status professions. In fact, he used the example of shoe salespersons to illustrate the concept of white-collar crime and pointed to research he conducted when a shoe salesperson told Sutherland he was taught by his boss to sell shoes to customers even if the shoes did not fit. No one would ever imagine, however, calling the police on shoe salespersons for selling poor-fitting shoes, but the behavior is still deviant. Sutherland's definition of white-collar crime views crime as workplace behavior that is deviant and harmful.

white-collar crime: A crime committed by individuals as a part of their legitimate occupation.

To clear up confusion surrounding the white-collar concept, Marshall Clinard and Richard Quinney divided white-collar crime into two categories: occupational crime and corporate crime.[90] *Occupational crime* refers to instances when individuals commit crime to benefit themselves while at work. Examples include hospital workers stealing drugs, accountants embezzling money for themselves, politicians accepting bribes, retail employees stealing from their jobs, and so on. *Corporate crime* refers to instances when employees break rules in order to benefit the corporation. Examples include when companies illegally pollute the environment, gouge prices, create unsafe products, and so on. The distinction is clear: Occupational crime is done by the worker for his or her own benefit, whereas corporate crime benefits the corporation.

Criminologists have categorized white-collar crime in different ways. For example, white-collar crime can be divided into the following categories:[91]

- *Crimes by workers in sales-oriented occupations.* Includes crimes by retail workers, restaurant employees, automobile mechanics, insurance sales people, and so on. The employee's job centers around selling goods or services, and although offenses may center around the act of selling items and ripping off consumers, in other instances the offenses include crimes against the employer (for example, retail theft, stealing food in restaurants).

- *Crimes in the health care system.* Includes crimes by doctors, nurses, pharmacists, employees of hospitals, nursing home employees, and other employees in the health care industry. Whereas some of these offenses target patients receiving care (for example, theft from patients and patient abuse), others target the insurance system (Medicaid and Medicare fraud and insurance fraud).

- *Crimes in the criminal justice system.* Includes crimes by police officers, prosecutors, judges, defense attorneys, and corrections employees. Examples include corruption, bribery, collusion with offenders, theft from offenders, and so on. These are discussed separately later in the text.

- *Crimes in the political system.* Includes crimes by local, state, and federal government officials such as bribery, corruption, and engaging in unethical activities. Researchers have also discussed khaki-collar crime (crimes by members of the military that are handled as military crimes) and state crime (crimes by governments) as examples of crime in the political system.

- *Crimes in the religious system.* Includes both financial and physical offenses perpetrated by church officials against members of their church. Not all criminologists agree that crimes by priests, such as the widespread child sexual abuse scandal in the Catholic Church, should be categorized as white-collar crime.

Environmental crime refers to crimes that harm the environment. In April 2010, BPs Deepwater Horizon exploded, killing 11 workers and dumping millions of gallons of oil into the Gulf of Mexico.

National Science Foundation

- *Crimes in the educational system.* Includes crimes by professors, college employees, and college students that are committed as part of their college duties. Examples include plagiarism, sexual harassment, financial offenses, and academic dishonesty.

- *Crimes in the economic system.* Includes crimes by stockbrokers, financial advisors, investors, and others working in the economic system. Examples include insider trading, manipulating the stock market, and Ponzi/pyramid schemes. These crimes can damage the faith that members of the society have in our economic system.

- *Crimes in the technological system.* Includes computer crimes and other technological crimes not included in the other categories. Examples include computer embezzlement, unauthorized access to different servers, virus introductions, software crimes, and Internet crimes.

- *Crimes in the housing system.* Includes crimes by those in the banking system and those who rent houses/apartments to renters. Examples include mortgage fraud and slumlord offenses. These crimes can have a serious effect on the community, with consequences including health consequences, financial consequences, decreased property values, and dehumanization of those exposed to shoddy living conditions.

- *Corporate crime.* Includes crimes by corporations. This category is discussed in more detail later in this chapter.

- *Environmental crime.* Includes instances when workers or businesses engage in illegal behaviors that harm the environment or animals in the environment. Examples include air pollution, water pollution, illegal disposal of hazardous waste, and crimes at zoos. Environmental crime can lead to serious physical harms for humans and animals exposed to the harmful practices.

In comparison to street crime, white-collar crime probably causes far more damage than conventional offenses. The average robbery, for example, typically nets about $1,000, whereas the average embezzlement by an employee nets about $100,000.[92] Beyond these monetary losses, victims can experience untold financial and physical harm. Bernard Madoff's Ponzi scheme and Enron's fraudulent actions wiped out thousands of individuals' retirement accounts. Unnecessary surgery, exposure to harmful products, food poisoning, and illegal environmental pollution also cause serious harms to the community. The ability to identify and quantify these harms is difficult, but white-collar crime experts agree that these harms are serious.

The criminal justice system processes white-collar crime cases aggressively once the cases enter the justice system. Criminal sentences given to white-collar crime do not appear to be more lenient than those given to property offenders with similar criminal histories. In fact, some observers have argued that by the time white-collar offenders make it to the sentencing stage, they may be sentenced more severely than lower-class offenders.[93] Jurg Gerber has explained this apparent discrepancy by suggesting that "the apparent harshness of sentencing of white-collar offenders proves to be the result of a diversion of less serious offenders from the criminal court."[94] As noted elsewhere, a white-collar offender who finds himself or herself in a criminal court about to be sentenced by a judge must "have done something 'really really bad.'"[95]

Many of you are likely familiar with the celebrated white-collar crime cases of Martha Stewart and Bernard Madoff. Recall the wedding cake model discussed in Chapter 1. These cases are found in the top layer of cases. They are not your typical white-collar crime cases. The vast majority of white-collar crimes never receive media attention and most do not enter the criminal justice system, but instead are processed through the civil or regulatory justice systems. The *regulatory justice system* refers to the government agency that has authority to regulate behavior in specific occupations; these vary across each occupation. As well, many careers are available for those interested in battling white-collar crime in the justice process.

Andrew Fastow, Enron's former chief financial officer, was sentenced to 10 years in prison after being convicted of various types of white-collar crime.

© RICHARD CARSON/Reuters/Corbis

VIDEO
Martha Stewart Insider Trading

Corporate Crime

Corporate crime, a type of white-collar crime, can also be categorized as a variety of crime occurring in complex organizations. Some authors have used phrases such as "organizational offending," "corporate deviance," "organizational misconduct," and "crime by organizations" to describe instances in which businesses commit crimes against consumers, their own workers, or other businesses.

Corporations have been described as "collections of replaceable people." What this means is that those who work in corporations must work hard in order to keep their jobs. Some people may feel pressured to engage in questionable behavior in order to help the corporation succeed. The line is not always clear in terms of what is appropriate and inappropriate behavior. Employees often feel they have to make a choice: commit questionable actions that benefit the corporation or get fired and have the corporation find another employee who will, in fact, engage in those actions.

corporate crime: Instances when employees break rules in order to benefit the corporation.

Several varieties of corporate crime exist. These include[96]

- *Antitrust offenses.* Refers to crimes that violate laws promoting competition in our economic market. Examples include price fixing, price discrimination, and price gouging.

- *False advertising.* Refers to businesses lying to consumers in order to get them to purchase products. Such actions are criminalized under the Federal Trade Commission Act, but the FTC focuses more on advertisements that target health and safety and those that make promises that consumers would not be able to assess on their own. For example, SAGE could advertise this book as "One of the best introductory criminal justice books available," but they would not be able to say "Payne, Oliver, and Marion's *Introduction to Criminal Justice* is guaranteed to add years to your life."

- *Unfair labor practices.* Refers to situations in which employees are subjected to biased and prejudicial behaviors. Examples include exploitation (being forced to work without pay) and systemic discrimination (in hiring, promotions, and the like).

- *Unsafe work environments.* Refers to situations in which businesses create work environments that are not safe for workers. These environments can lead to acute (immediate) or chronic (long-term) injuries. Workplace injuries decreased between 2003 and 2009, potentially because of the downturn in the economy and higher unemployment rates.

- *Harmful treatment of consumers.* Refers to situations in which a business harms its consumers while the consumers are receiving services from the business.

- *Harmful consumer products.* Refers to companies creating products that harm those who use them. Toys are cited as among the most dangerous types of products; other potentially dangerous products include certain types of automobiles, types of food, and specific types of construction material.

Individuals could be victims of corporate offending without even knowing it, or without defining the behaviors as criminal. Public awareness about corporate offending is relatively new, partly because these cases rarely generate a great deal of media scrutiny and also because many of the cases are so complex that they are difficult to understand.

State Crime

State crime is a variety of crime occurring in complex organizations that occurs in government organizations, in particular. Some authors use the phrase "state corporate crime" (a label created by Ronald Kramer) to draw attention to the way that governments are comparable to corporations, and like corporations, governments occasionally engage in criminal behaviors. State crime has been defined as "any action that violates international public

state crime:
A crime occurring in a government organization.

law and/or a state's own domestic law when the actions are committed by individual actors acting on behalf of, or in the name of the state, even when such acts are motivated by their own personal, economical, political, and ideological interests."[97]

Criminologists point to a number of harms occurring from state crime. In her book *State Criminality: The Crime of All Crimes*, criminal justice scholar Dawn Rothe wrote:

> *State crimes are historically* and contemporarily ever-present with atrocious results leading to more injury and death than all traditional street crimes put together. Consider that genocide and/or crimes against humanity during the 20th century . . . claimed the lives of tens of millions and rendered many more homeless, imprisoned, and psychologically and physically damaged.[98]

Despite this harm, criminal justice researchers have conducted relatively little research on state crime, compared to other criminal justice topics, though the area of study is growing and some scholars have suggested that an entire field of study focusing just on this topic may evolve in the future.[99]

Organized Crime

Organized crime refers to offenses committed by networks or organizations formed for the sole purpose of engaging in illegal practices. Some people confuse the concepts of white-collar, corporate, and organized crime. White-collar and corporate offenses are committed by individuals as a part of their legitimate occupations. Organized crime offenses are committed by individuals as a part of their illegitimate criminal business. According to the FBI, organized crime can be described in the following way:

> [Organized crime refers to] any group having some manner of a formalized structure and whose primary objective is to obtain money through illegal activities. Such groups maintain their position through the use of actual or threatened violence, corrupt public officials, graft, or extortion, and generally have a significant impact on the people in their locales, region, or the country as a whole.[100]

The criminal groups formed to conduct these illegal activities are sometimes referred to as organized crime families or organized crime networks. The terms *mob* and *Mafia* are used to describe organized crime families. The concept of the Mafia is traced to the Sicilian Mafia. It is incorrectly assumed that organized crime primarily involves crime networks from Italy. According to the FBI, the current concerns about organized crime include the following:[101]

- Russian mobsters who fled to the United States in the wake of the Soviet Union's collapse

organized crime: Offenses committed by networks or organizations formed for the sole purpose of engaging in illegal practices.

The Sopranos was one of the most popular television shows about organized crime.

© AF archive / Alamy

- Groups from African countries like Nigeria that engage in drug trafficking and financial scams

- Chinese tongs, Japanese boryokudan, and other Asian crime rings

- Enterprises based in Eastern European nations like Hungary and Romania

Organized crime networks are involved in a range of illegitimate activities including drug trafficking, gambling, fraud, prostitution, racketeering, extortion, bribery of public officials, gun distribution, and other related offenses. The networks frequently hide behind the façade of a legitimate business whose "employees" might look no different from employees in a legitimate business. Competition between the crime networks and efforts to hide their illegal operations from the justice system dramatically increase the risk of violence in organized crime activities. Whereas in the past the reach of these groups tended to be within specific cities such as New York, Chicago, Las Vegas, Baltimore, and Philadelphia, just as legitimate businesses have "globalized," so too have organized crime businesses. The prevalence of international offenses (like frauds and scams originating in other countries) has skyrocketed. Combining all types of organized crime, the FBI estimates that organized crime businesses worldwide illegally profit by about $1 trillion each year.[102]

Compared to interest in offenses such as corporate crime and state crime, the public seems to have considerable interest in organized crime. Consider Hollywood's portrayal of organized crime. *The Sopranos* was one of HBO's most popular shows. *The Godfather*, and each of its sequels, told the story of the fictional crime family the Corleones. Quentin Tarantino's *Pulp Fiction* depicted the laughable, yet violent, experiences of an assortment of organized crime families. The Internet Movie Database (IMDb) maintains a list of the top 250 movies ever made, as voted on by those who visit the site.[103] Three of the five top movies are movies about organized crime: *The Godfather*, *The Godfather II*, and *Pulp Fiction* are ranked second, third, and fifth, respectively.

— BEYOND A REASONABLE DOUBT 4.5 —

_____ refers to offenses committed by networks or organizations formed for the sole purpose of engaging in illegal practices.

(a) Organized crime, (b) Corporate crime, (C) Environmental crime, (d) White-collar crime, (e) None of the above

---

The answer can be found on page 521.

Just the Facts: Chapter Summary

- *Homicide* refers to the killing of one human being by another. Not all homicides are necessarily criminal. Criminal homicides include murder, manslaughter, and negligent homicide.

- Manslaughter is typically classified as voluntary or involuntary manslaughter.

- According to the "felony murder rule," all individuals involved in a felony can be convicted of a murder if a murder occurs during commission of the felony.

- *Serial killings* refers to crimes committed by individuals who kill several victims over a period of time. Mass murders refers to crimes committed by individuals who kill a large number of victims all at once.

- Under common law, the phrase "assault and battery" distinguished between assaults (the attempt or threat to inflict harm on another) and battery (the completed assault).

- All available data suggest that we are more likely to be harmed by someone we know than by a stranger.

- Thrasher identified four types of gangs including the diffuse gang, the solidified gang, the conventional gang, and the criminal gang.

- The common law definition of rape defined it as when a man had carnal knowledge (that is, sexual contact) through force with a woman to whom he was not married.

- According to marital rape laws in some states, for an act to be rape, the husband must use force against his wife, meaning that threat of force would not be enough for the act to be rape in those states.

- A review of elder sexual abuse cases in nursing homes found that victims with impairments appeared to be more susceptible to sexual abuse than physical abuse and these cases rarely have any witnesses.

- Robbers are believed to target individuals who they think have a lot of money or who appear lost. Some robberies are committed in order to send a message.

- *Public order crime* refers to a class of crimes that appear to be victimless but are classified as crimes because of the belief that they harm the public order in some way. Examples of public order crimes include alcohol-related crime, prostitution, and status offenses.

- Crimes within complex organizations include white-collar crime, corporate crime, and state crime.

- Sutherland defined white-collar crimes as "crime committed by a person of respectability and high social status in course of his occupation." In comparison to street crime, white-collar crime probably causes far more damage than conventional offenses.

- *Corporate crime* refers to crimes committed on behalf of, or for the good of, the corporation.

- State crime has been defined as "any action that violates international public law and/or a state's own domestic law when the actions are committed by individual actors acting on behalf of, or in the name of the state, even when such acts are motivated by their own personal, economical, political, and ideological interests."

- Organized crime refers to offenses committed by networks or organizations formed for the sole purpose of engaging in illegal practices.

Critical Thinking Questions

1. How do the patterns of burglary, robbery, and motor vehicle theft vary?

2. Describe the different types of violence and why typologies are used to categorize these forms of violence.

3. Are victimless crimes serious? Explain.

4. Explain how public order crimes are harmful.

5. Is white-collar crime always illegal? Explain.

6. What are the differences between white-collar crime and organized crime?

7. What are the similarities and differences between burglary and robbery?

Key Terms

arson (124)
assault (107)
battery (107)
burglary (120)
child abuse (108)
child sexual abuse (113)
common couple
     violence (109)
corporate crime (133)
date rape (114)

elder abuse (109)
elder sexual abuse (115)
hate crimes (111)
homicide (103)
identity theft (120)
involuntary
     manslaughter (104)
justifiable
     homicide (106)
larceny (118)

manslaughter (104)
marital rape (114)
mass murders (106)
motor vehicle theft (123)
murder (104)
negligent homicide (105)
organized crime (130)
patriarchal terrorism (109)
plagiarism (120)
prostitution (126)

public order crime (125)
rape (112)
robbery (115)
serial killings (105)
state crime (134)
voluntary
     manslaughter (104)
white-collar crime (130)

5

AN INTRODUCTION TO CRIMINOLOGICAL THEORY

© Getty/photofusion

© alessandro0770/Veer

IN JUNE 2014, JEREMY MEEKS BECAME AN INTERNET SENSATION after his mug shot was posted on a police department's website. The mug shot featured a stunningly handsome 30-year-old man with piercing blue eyes who had been arrested and charged with several felonies. In virtually no time at all, 89,000 Facebook users shared the photo. Popular websites such as TMZ, Perezhilton.com, drudgereport.com, and yahoo.com ran updates about the attention Meeks was receiving. He was even offered a modeling contract from a modeling agent (never mind that it was the same agent who represented the Octomom).

Jeremy Meeks became an Internet sensation after his mugshot was posted on a police department's website.
© SPD/Splash News/Corbis

While many observers were focusing on Meeks's good looks, some were drawing attention to his history of offending. Meeks had been incarcerated on two prior occasions for robbery, corporal injury, identity theft, and resisting arrest. He was also reportedly a former member of the Northside Gangster Crips in California. Various commentators were asking why the public found Meeks so attractive, given his past. Alternatively, criminal justice scholars were likely asking about those factors that led Meeks into a life of crime.

LEARNING OBJECTIVES

After reading this chapter, students will be able to:

5.1 Discuss why criminal justice scholars study the causes of crime

5.2 Describe the five theoretical frameworks that criminological theories use to explain crime

5.3 Identify crime prevention strategies that reduce offenders' desires and opportunities for criminal behavior

5.4 Discuss the role of biology on crime

5.5 Explain how social factors might contribute to criminal behavior

5.6 Compare and contrast three different social psychological explanations of crime

5.7 Demonstrate how cognitive processes contribute to criminal behavior

ADMISSIBLE or INADMISSIBLE Evidence

Read the statements that follow. If the statement is true, circle *admissible*. If the statement is false, circle *inadmissible*. Answers can be found on page 517.

1. **Admissible   Inadmissible**   Deterrence theory suggests that future criminal behavior will be deterred if offenders receive the appropriate rehabilitation.

2. **Admissible   Inadmissible**   Criminal justice scholars generally support the notion that biological factors are related to crime.

3. **Admissible   Inadmissible**   Situational crime prevention ideals are based on the principles of routine activities theory.

4. **Admissible   Inadmissible**   Broken windows theory suggests that homes with broken windows are less likely to be burglarized because burglars would not expect to find valuable goods in those homes.

5. **Admissible   Inadmissible**   Life course theory is an interdisciplinary developmental theory that explains human behavior by examining how past events, including turning points, put individuals on certain trajectories for future behaviors.

6. **Admissible   Inadmissible**   Learning theory suggests that criminals have different learning styles than others.

7. **Admissible   Inadmissible**   *Denial of injury* refers to situations in which juveniles convince themselves that their actions will hurt no one and subsequently engage in those actions.

8. **Admissible   Inadmissible**   The notion of a self-fulfilling prophecy suggests that individuals' expectations, whether positive or negative, may lead individuals to meet those expectations.

➡ Why Study the Causes of Crime?

To understand why individuals commit crime, it is helpful to have a basic understanding of prominent theories of crime. This chapter focuses on these theories. Many criminal justice students approach such discussions somewhat tentatively and apprehensively. There is a widespread belief that theory should be left to those in the ivory tower, and assumptions are made implying that theory has little utility. Indeed, some individuals assume that crime occurs simply because offenders *choose* to commit crime. Criminal justice scholars would not necessarily disagree with this suggestion. Most would, however, encourage us to take it a step further and examine what factors might have influenced individuals to choose to commit crime.

Efforts to explain criminal behavior, whether by examining crime patterns or using criminological theories, are useful for four overlapping reasons. First, explaining crime helps to prevent crime. The simplicity of this statement is stunning. How can we stop crime if we don't know what causes crime? Sometimes individuals have inaccurate perceptions about the causes of crime, and these inaccurate perceptions could actually cause more crime rather than stop it.

Second, crime explanations help criminologists to understand their research findings. In one study, for example, a researcher found that homes located in neighborhoods with "throughways" were more likely to be burglarized than homes located in neighborhoods that had fewer entrances into the neighborhood, or were less "permeable."[1] Researchers can use prior crime explanations to make sense of this finding (for example, perhaps criminals make rational decisions based on the likelihood of being able to get away with the crime, which in this case would include the opportunity to leave the neighborhood).

Third, crime explanations guide criminal justice researchers who are testing specific theories. In one study, for example, a research team applied criminological theory to college students' behavior in order to study the factors that contributed to students' decisions to download computer software illegally.[2] Another study applied a criminological theory to students' experiences with theft.[3] In effect, criminological theory is the subject of many criminal justice studies.

Finally, beliefs about the causes of crime influence individual behaviors in the criminal justice system. As a result, criminal justice officials must have the information they need to understand the causes of crime. Criminologist Frank Hagan has asked whether you would go to a doctor who did not understand medical research. He posed this question to demonstrate that we too should expect criminal justice professionals to understand criminal justice research. A similar question could be asked related to causality. Would you go to a doctor who did not know what causes different diseases? Again, just as we expect medical professionals to know the causes of disease, we must expect criminal justice professionals to be able to identify the causes of crime.

In an effort to introduce you to the study of the causes of crime, this chapter focuses on criminological theories. This discussion is meant to be an introduction to these topics. If we have done our job, you will question the accuracy of many of these patterns and theories and consider exploring the topic further through additional readings or coursework.

➡ Explaining Crime Using Criminological Theories

Chapter 3 addressed patterns surrounding crime, and Chapter 4 provided insight into specific types of crimes. These patterns are based on crime data provided by official statistics and criminal justice studies. Beyond these patterns, it is also important to examine how different criminological theories explain crime. Simply put, a *theory* is a potential explanation of reality that is testable and supported by research. All disciplines have theories at the core of their areas of study. A few comments about theory will be helpful here in understanding the role of theory in the field of criminal justice and criminology.

First, criminological theories are *potential* explanations of crime and criminal justice behaviors. The theories are not facts, nor should they be presented as facts. No theory has "proven" why crime exists or why criminal justice officials behave the way they do. If you hear someone say, "It's a fact that people commit crime because . . ." or "Criminological theory has proven that . . . ," you should automatically question the veracity of the comments.

Second, the best criminological theories are those that are testable and adhere to the principle of *parsimony*: They attempt to explain crime and criminal justice behaviors with as few variables as possible. The more complex that theories become, the less useful they are for academics and practitioners alike.

Third, various criminological theories strive to explain crime at different units of analysis. For example, some theories, referred to as *macro-level theories*, examine the way that structural features of society contribute to overall crime rates. Other theories, referred to as *micro-level theories*, examine the way that individual-level factors influence decisions to commit crime. Also, whereas some theories focus on the behaviors of offenders, others focus on the behaviors of criminal justice professionals.

Fourth, criminological theories were developed by criminologists who, like you, were once college students studying different topics, including criminal justice. As such, most criminological theories are similar to theories you might find in other social sciences, including sociology and psychology, and some are related to "harder" sciences such as biology. One difference is that the other disciplines tend to focus on explaining all types of behavior, whereas criminological theories focus on explaining crime. The point here is that the theories were developed by individuals open to interdisciplinary strategies to explain crime. Perhaps one of you will develop the next great criminological theory.

Finally, criminological theories are most useful when public officials use them to develop crime prevention and intervention measures. One author quoted an anonymous individual who said, "Theories are like

JOURNAL
Capturing Crime

FIGURE 5.1   Theories of Criminal Behavior

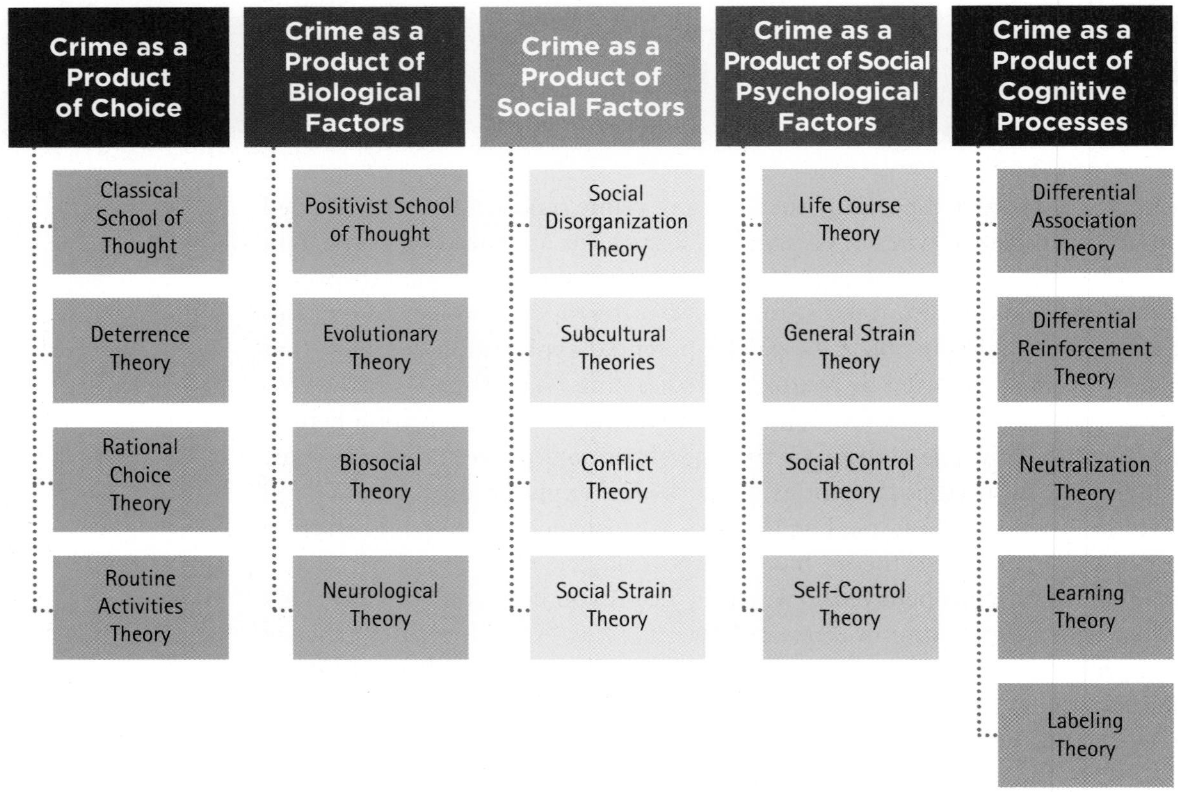

Crime as a Product of Choice	Crime as a Product of Biological Factors	Crime as a Product of Social Factors	Crime as a Product of Social Psychological Factors	Crime as a Product of Cognitive Processes
Classical School of Thought	Positivist School of Thought	Social Disorganization Theory	Life Course Theory	Differential Association Theory
Deterrence Theory	Evolutionary Theory	Subcultural Theories	General Strain Theory	Differential Reinforcement Theory
Rational Choice Theory	Biosocial Theory	Conflict Theory	Social Control Theory	Neutralization Theory
Routine Activities Theory	Neurological Theory	Social Strain Theory	Self-Control Theory	Learning Theory
				Labeling Theory

toothbrushes . . . everyone has one—and nobody wants to use anyone else's."[4] The quote is a little inaccurate in that some criminological theories have widespread appeal: They are simply stated, testable, verified in at least some research, and have at least some practical utility.

Although many criminological theories have widespread appeal, and entire college courses are devoted to different types of criminological theory, this text addresses only a handful of theoretical frameworks and criminological theories. This introduction to theory demonstrates the breadth of these theories and their potential to make a difference in responding to crime. In general, the theoretical frameworks look at (a) crime as a product of choice, (b) crime as a product of biological factors, (c) crime as a product of social factors, (d) crime as a product of social psychological factors, and (e) crime as a product of cognitive processes. Many specific criminological theories can be classified within each of these theoretical frameworks (see Figure 5.1).

➡ Crime as a Product of Choice

rational choice theory: The theory that offenders decide to commit crimes for specific purposes.

Some theories explain crime by focusing on the decisions, or choices, that offenders make and the factors that seem to influence those choices. Theories that view crime as a product of choice include deterrence theory, **rational choice theory**, and routine activities theory.

Deterrence Theory and Rational Choice Theory

Deterrence theory is traced to Cesare Beccaria, a philosopher who has been labeled the father of the **Classical School** of criminology. The central tenet of this school of thought is that offenders choose to commit crime as a result of their free will. In 1775, Beccaria published *An Essay on Crime and Punishment*, which was a relatively short book describing Beccaria's theory of punishment. According to Beccaria, for punishment to be effective, it must meet three criteria: (a) It must be swift, (b) it must be certain, and (c) it must outweigh the pleasure that the offender would get from committing the crime. Beccaria suggested that the closer that "crime" and "punishment" are linked in offenders' minds, the more likely they would choose *not* to commit crime. To Beccaria, two types of deterrence fulfill distinct purposes: *Specific deterrence* focuses on preventing the individual (or specific) offender from committing future offenses, and *general deterrence* focuses on preventing the "general" public from committing future offenses.

Beccaria's theory revolutionized the way punishment was administered and understood. Reviewing the way laws are currently made, it certainly makes sense that recommended punishments must be more severe than the benefits derived from the crime. Beccaria did not support overly punitive sanctions and was opposed to the death penalty. He was in favor of sanctions that are just punitive enough to convince potential offenders not to break the law.

In terms of severity, modern criminologists have discussed what is known as the *brutalization argument*. This argument suggests that punishment that is too severe may lead to more crime rather than prevent future crime. If offenders believe they are being treated unjustly, they may engage in future crime rather than choosing to avoid crime. One of the authors always shares an example from his childhood when he talks about this concept with his students. When he was a teenager, his dad slapped his sister in the face at a rest stop after he saw her stick her tongue out at his mom. After she got slapped, and they were driving away in the family car, he saw his sister give his dad the finger. Rather than preventing rude behavior to one's parents, the "sanction" by the author's father actually seemed to cause additional inappropriate behavior!

Some researchers have examined what they call "perceptual deterrence," which refers to offenders' perceptions of certainty, swiftness, and severity. From this perspective, it matters more how offenders perceive sanctions than whether those sanctions are, in reality, certain, swift, or even severe. From this line of research, researchers have examined which element of the three criteria is most important: certainty, swiftness, or severity. On one level, if an offender is certain he or she can get away with misconduct, it is reasonable to assume that the offender will be particularly likely to engage in crime. Indeed, research shows that certainty is a stronger predictor of deterrence than are severity and swiftness.[5] Also, informal sanctions (losing a job, losing one's family, shame, and so on) have been found to have a deterrent effect. These informal sanctions have been called "the threat of social censure."[6] In fact, these informal sanctions may have a stronger deterrent effect than formal sanctions like incarceration.

deterrence theory: Based on the classical school, the theory that offenders choose to commit crime as a result of their free will.

Classical School: Adherents of the theory that crime is the result of free choice on the part of the individuals.

Cohen and Felson attributed the increase in burglaries in the 1960s to an increase in the number of televisions available to steal and a decrease in the number of women staying at home. How might the Internet be related to this argument today?

© Spaces Images/Getty Images

Rational choice theory, developed by Ronald Clarke and Derek Cornish, is a type of deterrence theory.[7] Rational choice theory posits that, for offenders, the "decision to commit a crime served a specific purpose for the offender."[8] Rational choice theory assumes that behavior is always instrumental and purposeful, and the theory has been criticized for making this assumption.[9] The theory is useful in explaining why some offenders are specialists who concentrate on specific types of offenses. Although rational choice theory focuses on the specific choice to commit a crime, some authors have argued that more attention must be given to decisions to be criminally involved in an assortment of acts (or why some offenders are generalists).[10]

Routine Activities Theory

Routine activities theory was developed by Lawrence Cohen and Marcus Felson in 1979.[11] The researchers used the theory, as a macro-level theory, to explain why burglaries increased in the 1960s. In particular, they demonstrated how in the 1960s more "attractive" targets such as televisions and other consumer goods were left unguarded in homes in the daytime after women started entering the workforce in higher numbers. From these patterns, they suggested that crime occurs when three things occur at the same time and in the same location: (a) A motivated offender is present, (b) capable guardians are absent, and (c) vulnerable targets are present.

Cohen and Felson's theory has been useful to explain societal crime trends such as the link between age and the crime rate, why certain types of crime occur more in the summer, and why crime is distributed differently throughout the day. Some observers have noted that crimes in the workplace increase when unemployment is higher, on the assumption that fewer workers in the workplace means fewer guardians to catch people stealing.[12] The theory has also guided research studies on topics such as larceny, elder abuse, burglary, motor vehicle thefts, and many other specific offense types.

Although Cohen and Felson developed their theory to explain societal crime trends, it also has utility at the individual level. From this perspective, note that all three elements must be present for crime to occur. Let's say your professor leaves his or her office door wide open and the exams for your class are on top of the professor's desk. There could even be a sign on the door that says, "Please come in and steal the exams on top of my desk." The simple fact is that the exams will not be stolen if a "motivated offender" does not come by the office.

JOURNAL
Online Activity and Fraud

routine activities theory: The theory that crime occurs when three things occur at the same time and in the same location: a motivated offender is present, capable guardians are absent, and vulnerable targets are present.

the assumption that by limiting offenders' access to guns, gun violence will be reduced.

Routine activities theory is related to *lifestyle theory*, a theory that explains why victims are victimized rather than why offenders commit crime. The premise of lifestyle theory is that individuals who frequently engage in a higher proportion of risky activities (for example, drug and alcohol use, frequent sexual activity with multiple partners, soliciting prostitutes, visiting dangerous places) are at a higher risk of victimization. Conversely, the less often that individuals engage in risky activities, the lower their victimization rates. Among other things, this theory potentially explains why those who are victimized once have a higher risk of subsequent victimization[19] and also helps to explain the lower victimization rates among older individuals. In particular, older individuals are less likely to engage in the types of activities that would make them targets for certain types of offenses such as robbery, murder, and sexual assault. However, their choice of activities might increase their risk of other types of victimization, such as fraud.[20]

Keep in mind that routine activities theory is not meant to blame victims for their victimization. Instead, the theory's premise is that the routine activities in which individuals engage will predict the types of experiences individuals confront in their lives. For example, research shows that college students are at a much higher risk of sexual assault when they consume too much alcohol.[21] We would not blame those victims for being victimized because the victimization was done by the offender, not the victim. Still, recognizing lifestyle factors that contribute to victimization is helpful in that the information can be used to develop victimization prevention programs.

Some individuals think that security cameras are capable guardians that will reduce the likelihood that individuals will engage in criminal behavior.

Wikimedia Commons. Creator: Dmitry G.

JOURNAL
Electronic Monitoring Sex Offenders

BEYOND A REASONABLE DOUBT 5.1

Which theory suggests that crime occurs as a result of motivated offenders, the absence of capable guardians, and the presence of suitable targets?

(a) Deterrence theory, (b) Rational choice theory, (c) Motivation theory, (d) Guardianship theory, (e) Routine activities theory

The answer can be found on page 521.

➡ Crime as a Product of Biological Factors

Whereas some theories focus on individual choices, other criminological theories consider the influence of biological factors on criminal activity. Biological theories suggest that factors related to an individual's biological makeup contribute to crime. Some of the earliest criminological theories pointed to biological factors as a source of crime. Cesare Lombroso, an Italian physician, was the founder of the **Positivist School** of criminology,

Positivist School: Adherents of the theory that crime is caused by factors beyond choice.

which adhered to the principle of determinism to explain crime. Whereas the Classical School argued that crime was a matter of free choice, the Positivist School argued that crime was caused by factors beyond choice. In *The Criminal Man*, Lombroso identified different types of criminals that were categorized according to his belief about the causes of the criminal's behavior, which were biological and sociological in nature.

One of the types of criminals identified by Lombroso was the born criminal, or the *atavistic throwback*, a term that referred to individuals who, in Lombroso's view, had not evolved completely. They had certain body types and accounted for about one-third of all offenders, according to Lombroso. Lombroso's students continued his work in this area and his daughter, Gina Lombroso, even wrote about the subject.

Further examining the impact of body types on crime, William Sheldon (1940) developed the process of somatotyping as a strategy to show how body type might be related to behavior. Sheldon was a physician by training, and his criminological work showed a medical slant. He identified three body types: *mesomorphs*, who are extremely muscular individuals; *ectomorphs*, who are slender and not muscular; and *endomorphs*, who are overweight. Criminal populations tend to comprise mesomorphs.[22]

Although Sheldon's work has been criticized, it has been noted that "no research specifically refuted" the assumptions of his work.[23] Still, criminal justice and criminology scholars tend to ignore the underlying tenets of Sheldon's propositions. A recent study by Sean Maddan and his colleagues compared the body types of prisoners from Arkansas and found that body type was tied to offense type. Reviewing the body mass indexes (BMIs) of 5,000 male prisoners, the authors found that mesomorphs were more likely than endomorphs to be violent offenders. Of course, finding a relationship between two variables does not necessarily mean that one causes the other. The author team pointed out that "physique is not the cause of crime . . . physique may be an intervening explanatory variable."[24]

Would you characterize these individuals as an endomorph or ectomorph? What is their likelihood of committing crime according to Shelden's theory?

Biological explanations were central to the development of the field of criminology, but they fell out of favor with criminologists for several decades. Edwin Sutherland's sociological approach to explaining crime was credited with "virtually obliterating biological thinking from mainstream criminology."[25] The biological perspective has made a comeback since the 1980s, with some experts predicting that "biological explanations are again gaining credibility and are joining forces with sociological explanations in ways that may soon make them equal partners."[26] Some observers have attributed the renewed focus on biological explanations to James Q. Wilson and Richard Herrnstein's *Crime and Human Nature*, in which the authors argued that human rationality is influenced by biological factors such as genetic predispositions to aggressiveness, impulsiveness, and low intelligence. The authors suggested that the ability to make choices is influenced by genetics and that these genetic predispositions increase the likelihood of bad decision making.

Currently, several different biological theories are used to explain crime (see Table 5.1). Consider the following:

- *Evolutionary theory* views natural selection as producing aggression and points to the way that all animals are capable of being aggressive.[27]

- *Obstetrics explanations* center on the impact of physical anomalies, prenatal health issues such as exposure to nicotine before birth, and birth complications.[28]

- *Biosocial arguments* have been set forth suggesting that those with autonomic nervous system deficits who live in disadvantaged environments are "at the highest risk for antisocial behavior."[29] A review of 34 studies examining biological influences on antisocial behavior concluded that the joint presence of biological and social risk factors "exponentially increases the risk of antisocial and violent behavior."[30]

- *Neurological theories* are supported by research showing that individuals with frontal lobe cortex damage in their brains are more prone to be aggressive and impulsive.[31] Neurological deficits have been identified as "a reasonably well-established" predictor of antisocial behavior.[32]

- Lee Ellis proposed *evolutionary androgenic theory* to explain crimes against persons. The theory proposes that (a) aggressive/criminal behavior "evolved as an aspect of human reproduction" and (b) sex hormones influence brain functions in males in a way that promotes what Ellis refers to as competitive/victimizing behavior.[33]

- *Hormonal theory* points to differences in hormone levels, such as testosterone, and the influence of hormones on behavior. One study found that inmates with higher testosterone levels were more likely to be convicted of violent crimes and that they violated more rules while they were incarcerated.[34]

VIDEO
Anatomy and Violence

TABLE 5.1	Biosocial Explanations of Crime
THEORY	**EXPLANATION**
Eysenck's Biosocial Theory	"Certain biologically-based personality features increase the risk for antisocial outcome, given a particular social upbringing. Individuals are theorized to inherit particular personality features, along with associated autonomic and central nervous system characteristics . . . [Extroverts] are theorized to have a central nervous system that dampens the effect of environmental stimuli. Therefore, punishment does not impact extraverts as much as it does other individuals" (p. 590).
Mednick's Biosocial Theory	"Deficits in the autonomic nervous system of some individuals result in poor avoidance conditioning and an inability to learn law abiding behavior. Children with these autonomic nervous system deficits who are raised in inadequate social environments are considered to be at the highest risk for antisocial outcome" (p. 591).
Buikhuisen's Biosocial Theory of Chronic Juvenile Delinquency	Those prone to antisocial behavior have (a) neurological and cognitive deficits that make it difficult for them to learn avoidance behavior, (b) deficits in their autonomic nervous system that affect socialization, and (c) personalities that "facilitate avoidance learning" (p. 592).
Moffitt's Life Course Persistent Offender Theory	Offenders are characterized as adolescence-limited offenders and life-course-persistent offenders. Adolescence-limited offenders stop offending prior to entering adulthood, whereas life-course-persistent offenders offend throughout their adolescence and adulthood. This theory suggests that "the biological roots of antisocial outcome are present before or soon after birth . . . [and] theorizes that congenital factors—heredity and perinatal complications—produce neuropsychological deficits in the infant's nervous system. . . . Children who are unfortunate enough to have both biological and social deficits are theorized to be at the highest risk for persistent antisocial behavior" (p. 593).

Brennan, P. A., & Raine, A. (1997). Biosocial bases of antisocial behavior: Psychophysiological, neurological, and cognitive factors. *Clinical Psychology Review, 17*(6), 589–604.

Although biological theory is returning in a strong way to criminal justice and criminology, criminal justice graduate students receive little training in this area, which has led John Wright and his coauthors to state the following in an article they subtitled the *miseducation of criminologists*: "an entire body of knowledge . . . has been systematically excluded from the discipline."[35] The authors quote Matthew Robinson, who claimed, "The biological sciences have made more progress in understanding crime over the last 10 years than the social sciences have in the last 50."[36]

One research team has suggested that a fear of "radical medical interventions" leads some people to resist biological explanations of crime.[37] Wright and his colleagues point to three reasons why criminal justice and criminology scholars are resistant to biological theories:[38]

- Many criminologists hold liberal views about the causes of crime, which stands in stark contrast to attributing the cause of crime to the specific offender's characteristics.

- Biological theory historically was tied to racist practices, including fascism and eugenics, which by default places the biological approach in a negative light.

- Biological theory is viewed as a "dangerous" theory because of a concern that such an approach would lead to aggressive efforts to control individuals at the expense of constitutional rights.

Elsewhere, in *Criminals in the Making*, John Wright, Steven Tibbetts, and Leah Daigle set forth specific policy recommendations that could be implemented to address biosocial risk factors for crime. These recommendations include the following:[39]

- Remove environmental toxins

- Share information across service providers

- Provide parenting classes for all serious felons

- Improve training and education of justice professionals

- Continue research into pharmaceutical therapies for behavioral disorder

- Improve access to health care, including mental health care, for pregnant women and infants

- Legally mandate intervention for pregnant women with drug addiction

- Flag at-risk kids in doctors' offices

- Institute universal preschool with full developmental evaluations

➡ Crime as a Product of Social Factors

Other theories consider how social factors (or factors outside of the individual) contribute to crime. These theories include social disorganization theory, subcultural theory, conflict theory, and social strain theory.

Social Disorganization Theory

The general premise of **social disorganization theory** is that communities vary in their ability to regulate residents or people who come into the community. That is, communities vary in terms of their ability to control crime and deviance. Disorganized communities are ones that are less able to control criminal behavior, especially the behavior of youth. Modern social disorganization theory can be traced to **concentric zone theory**, which was developed by Robert Park and Ernest Burgess.[40] Sociologists at the University of Chicago, Park and Burgess examined the layout of the city of Chicago and concluded that the city could be divided into five zones (see Figure 5.3). Zone 1, at the center of the city, was the business district. Zone 2 was labeled the zone of transition. In this zone, businesses and factories were moving into the zone and residents who could afford to do so were

social disorganization theory: The theory that a community's or neighborhood's level of disorganization contributes to the crime rate in that community or neighborhood.

concentric zone theory: A theory developed by Park and Burgess that divided the city into a series of concentric zones with the assumption that crime is more likely to occur in the zones with more disorder.

FIGURE 5.3   **Concentric Zone Map**

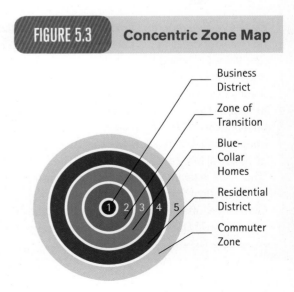

Business District

Zone of Transition

Blue-Collar Homes

Residential District

Commuter Zone

moving out. Those who could not afford to move were stuck in Zone 2. Zone 3 was the "working men's homes," where blue-collar workers lived. Zone 4 was the residential district, which was home to those who were more affluent than the blue-collar workers. Zone 5 was the commuter zone.

Clifford Shaw and Henry McKay tested the concentric zone theory by examining official juvenile delinquency data across the city. Their analysis suggested that offending appeared to be distributed more so in the zone of transition (Zone 2), regardless of who lived in that zone over time.[41] This zone was characterized by high levels in turnover, poverty, and racial heterogeneity (meaning a mixture of different racial groups). The authors suggested that residents in the zone of transition did not have the resources to control crime because of their poverty or the desire to form strong bonds with their neighbors because of the racial heterogeneity and population turnover. They referred to the lack of community in these areas as "social disorganization."

Interestingly, Shaw and McKay's work had a practical and immediate impact on the criminal justice system: It led to the Chicago Area Project, a citywide violence prevention initiative that developed several programs and demonstrated the connections among theory, research, and practice. The theory's impact on the discipline of criminal justice and criminology was relatively insignificant until the 1980s and 1990s, when criminologists revisited social disorganization extensively. The "Criminal Justice and the Media" box in this chapter describes one way in which the media have portrayed social disorganization theory.

As part of this rebirth of social disorganization theory, Robert Sampson and Byron Groves identified three dimensions of social disorganization that

VIDEO
YAR at the Chicago Area Project

CRIMINAL JUSTICE and the MEDIA:
THE WIRE

Baltimore Sun reporter David Simon gained national notoriety for creating the critically acclaimed HBO show *The Wire*. Depicting the lives of those working in the drug trade in the west end of Baltimore, as well as the sometimes-questionable efforts of law enforcement to respond to illicit drugs, the television show bore an uncanny resemblance to reality. In testimony before a congressional committee, Michael Steele, the lieutenant governor of Maryland, commented, "The HBO cable drama 'The Wire' is tantamount to a reality television program in certain parts of our cities." A Maryland congressman, Elijah Cummings, offered a similar observation, stating, "Witness intimidation in Baltimore City is not dreamt up by producers of HBO's critically acclaimed drama 'The Wire.' The threat is real—and the reality is horrific."

The Wire became a part of the political landscape and brought to light discussions about poverty, disorganization, and safety. In terms of concentric zone theory, the neighborhood featured in *The Wire* is most comparable to the zone of transition. Comparing the neighborhood in *The Wire* to more recent versions of social disorganization theory, one would note that the lack of informal social control efforts, the weak social ties, and the high degree of poverty found in the neighborhood contribute to offending.

they believed would promote or inhibit crime: (a) a community's ability to control teenagers, (b) the existence of local friendship networks, and (c) the degree to which residents participate in formal and voluntary community groups.[42] A key assumption of social disorganization theory is that informal social control strategies by residents reduce neighborhood crime rates. It is believed that these strategies potentially mediate (or reduce) the impact that poverty, racial heterogeneity, and population turnover have on crime.[43]

Broken windows theory is often discussed in conjunction with social disorganization theory, though it is actually a separate theory that explains crime by suggesting that minor forms of disorder will lead to additional disorder. The theory was introduced by James Q. Wilson and George Kelling in an article published in *Atlantic Monthly*.[44] The authors cited a 1969 experiment by Stanford psychologist Philip Zimbardo as evidence of their belief that minor problems lead to larger community problems. In particular, Zimbardo placed two abandoned cars with their hoods up in two different locations: one in the Bronx (New York City) and one in Palo Alto, California. The car in the Bronx was vandalized within 10 minutes after it was abandoned, with a small family being the first to steal from the car. In just one day, the Bronx car was virtually stripped all the way down. In contrast, the car in Palo Alto was not touched for a week. Zimbardo then broke one of the windows in the Palo Alto car. It did not take more than a few hours until the car was reportedly "utterly destroyed" by those passing by the car.

According to Wilson and Kelling, "One unrepaired broken window is a signal that no one cares, and so breaking more windows costs nothing."[45] The idea is that signs of disorder breed additional disorder. Their article had a powerful impact on policing, particularly in terms of efforts to reduce serious crime by responding to minor forms of crime (discussed later in Chapter 7). For now, it can simply be suggested that broken windows theory, unlike social disorganization theory, does not view the relationships between community members as contributing to crime; instead, the theory views physical and social disorder as leading to crime.

> **broken windows theory:** The theory that minor crimes and disorder send a signal to people that a community does not care, thus inviting an unwanted element that engages in more serious crime.
>
> **subcultural theory:** The theory that subcultural factors contribute to criminal and delinquent behavior.
>
> **middle-class measuring rod:** The types of values that school children are expected to demonstrate and adhere to in their scholastic endeavors.

Subcultural Theory

Subcultural theory points to the way that subcultural factors contribute to criminal and delinquent behavior. Albert Cohen's middle-class measuring rod is an early example of a subcultural theory.[46] Cohen argued that our schools judge children according to middle-class values and expectations. The phrase **middle-class measuring rod**

Wilson and Kelling believed that one broken window unrepaired sends a message that the community does not care about their community; hence, one broken window leads to many broken windows.

refers to the types of values that school children are expected to demonstrate and adhere to in their scholastic endeavors. Lower-class subcultures, however, teach their children a different set of values and behaviors. By the time they get to school, Cohen argued, lower-class children have the cards stacked against them because they will be judged by a set of standards they have never been taught. This initial setback is seen by many as providing an impetus for misconduct.

Walter Miller suggested that juveniles engage in behaviors to achieve a particular end, and these behaviors are guided by lower-class focal concerns.[47] To Miller, the lower-class culture is not simply a culture that directly contrasts with the middle-class culture. Instead, he views lower-class culture as a culture that is rooted in centuries of change.

Richard Cloward and Lloyd Ohlin also developed a subcultural theory known as *differential opportunity theory*.[48] Their theory recognizes that those who commit delinquent and criminal acts need the opportunity and skills to commit those acts. The theory asserts that "both legitimate and illegitimate opportunities vary across people and places."[49] Imagine if you wanted to be a drug dealer. Would you be able to do it? Differential opportunity theory recognizes that opportunities for certain types of crime vary across subcultures. While the opportunity to go to college may have been blocked for many offenders, the reverse may be true for many college students: Your ability to commit crimes may be blocked by the lack of opportunities to do so.

Marvin Wolfgang and Franco Ferracuti developed their subculture of violence theory to explain why higher rates of violence are found among males, members of the lower class, and minorities.[50] They suggested that cultural norms promote violence more for these subcultures. Although tangential evidence suggests that a "subculture of violence" may exist, it has been "an extremely difficult task" to identify the presence of such a culture.[51]

Elijah Anderson is a strong proponent of subcultural explanations of crime. In *Code of the Street*, Anderson characterized a street culture that is markedly different from the middle-class culture.[52] Anderson suggested that two types of families or orientations exist in urban communities: "decent" and "street" orientations/families. The decent families are committed to middle-class values, whereas the street orientations reject middle-class culture and replace those values with their own values. Still, those in the "decent" families must recognize and adhere to the "street" values in order to coexist in these communities. Indeed, youth from these families "must be able to handle themselves in a street-oriented environment."[53] Anderson's *"code of the street"* is summarized here:

> The code of the street . . . amounts to a set of informal rules governing interpersonal public behavior, including violence. The rules prescribe both a proper comportment and the proper way to respond if challenged. They regulate the use of violence and so supply a rationale that allows those who are inclined to aggression to precipitate violent encounters in an approved way.

The rules have been established and are enforced mainly by the street oriented, but on the streets the distinction between street and decent is often irrelevant; everybody knows that if the rules are violated, there are penalties. Knowledge of the code is thus largely defensive; it is literally necessary for operating in public. Therefore, even though families with a decency orientation are usually opposed to the values of the code, they often reluctantly encourage their children's familiarity with it to enable them to negotiate the inner-city environment.[54]

In essence, those in urban areas learn rules on the street. Early on they learn that behaving certain ways will help to maintain safety. At the same time, they learn that violence is both necessary and justified in certain situations. According to Anderson, "The code of the streets is actually a cultural adaptation to a profound lack of faith in the police and the judicial system."[55]

More recently, criminologists Scott Jacques and Richard Wright have described the "*code of the suburb.*"[56] Such an approach helps to distinguish values between urban and suburban cultures and how those subcultural values may insulate, to a certain degree, members of the suburban culture from victimization. Whereas the "code of the street" promotes violence to solve disputes, the "code of the suburb" promotes peaceful resolution to disputes. According to the authors, "Conflict resolution in middle-class suburban drug markets is a mirror opposite of what occurs on urban street corners," leading them to point out that suburban residents take more precautionary measures to avoid crime. They argue that "because it promotes peace, the code of the suburb is able to shed light on the prevalence and magnitude of violence in drug markets."

> **conflict theory:** The theory that crime is caused or influenced by the actions and decisions of those with power.

Conflict Theory

Recognizing that jails and prisons tend to be filled with lower-class individuals and minorities, **conflict theory** suggests that crime is caused or influenced by the actions and decisions of those with power. Several varieties of conflict theory exist. The general connection between the theories is the recognition that a power imbalance exists between the upper and lower classes and the belief that this imbalance is perpetuated by using crime as a tool to weaken the lower class.

Richard Quinney is one of the most revered conflict theorists. In his seminal work *The Social Reality of Crime*, he argued that policy makers define crime and develop strategies to respond

Some researchers believe that those living communities such as those depicted in this photo learn rules that help them survive. These rules are called the "code of the street."

REUTERS/Shannon Stapleton SS

Jacques and Wright argue that a code of the suburb inhibits crime in suburbs. You probably don't see the same types of activities in front of this house that you would find in front of an urban house.

© Thomas Northcut/Getty Images

to crime in a way that advances the interests of the powerful and weakens the interests of the poor. His theory is outlined in the following six propositions:[57]

Proposition 1: Definition of crime. Crime is a definition of human conduct that is created by authorized agents in a politically organized society.

Proposition 2: Formulation of criminal definitions. Criminal definitions describe behaviors that conflict with the interests of the segments of society that have the power to shape public policy.

Proposition 3: Application of criminal definitions. Criminal definitions are applied by the segments of society that have the power to shape the enforcement and administration of criminal law.

Proposition 4: Development of behavior patterns in relation to criminal definitions. Behavior patterns are structured in segmentally organized society in relation to criminal definitions, and with this context persons engage in actions that have relative probabilities of being defined as criminal.

Proposition 5: Construction of criminal conceptions. Conceptions of crime are constructed and diffused in the segments of society by various means of communication.

Proposition 6: The social reality of crime. The social reality of crime is constructed by the formulation and application of criminal definitions, the development of behavior patterns related to criminal definitions, and the construction of criminal conceptions.

As evidence of this line of thinking, research shows that cities with "more blacks had stronger law enforcement agencies" (in terms of the number of law enforcement personnel).[58] The same study found that the more inequality a city had, the higher the number of police officers the city employed. Various researchers have demonstrated how conflict theory applies to specific types of offending. Also, conflict theory is frequently used to explain why white-collar offenders appear to be treated differently than conventional offenders, particularly when focusing on why some harmful behaviors of white-collar professionals are not defined or treated as crime, but the behaviors of minorities are. The financial meltdown of 2007–2008 is illustrative. Some commentators have pointed to a number of harmful decisions and behaviors by banking officials that led to the meltdown, but to date not one individual has been prosecuted for his or her actions that contributed to the collapse of our economy.

Some conflict theories suggest that governmental actions and policies either directly or indirectly breed crime. Also, as noted in Chapter 3, the decision to incarcerate so many offenders, with minorities overrepresented in the incarceration rate, weakens minority communities and potentially results in more crime.[59] As well, "urban renewal" projects have been seen as weakening stable minority communities by destroying the communities and weakening the connections between residents from those communities.[60]

Social Strain Theory

Strain theory is traced to Emile Durkheim, a sociologist who wrote extensively about various topics, including suicide, crime, and religion. In his research on suicide, Durkheim described the concept of anomie, which refers to the presence of normlessness or confusion. He suggested that normlessness (or anomie) was one source of suicide.

Durkheim's concept of anomie was later understood to be synonymous with strain. In fact, some criminal justice scholars use the phrase **anomie theory** in reference to what others mean by "social strain theory." Following the framework developed by Durkheim, other prominent strain/anomie theories have been developed. The two most prominent strain theories are Merton's social strain theory, and Messner and Rosenfeld's institutional anomie theory.

Merton's Social Strain Theory

Robert Merton's "Social Structure and Anomie" article framed modern versions of strain theory.[61] Merton argued that our capitalist society shapes certain goals for members of our society, while also socializing us about the acceptable strategies to attain those goals. For most individuals, economic success is a goal. Very few individuals strive to be poor and desire poverty. On the contrary, many people want as much money as they can get. Consider the long lines at the convenience store counter for people buying lottery tickets. Although winning the lottery is an acceptable way to get rich, our culture suggests that the most appropriate way to succeed is to work hard, engage in conventional measures such as going to college, and stay out of trouble.

While we learn "conventional goals" and "legitimate means" to attain those goals, and in some instances individuals are able to engage in legitimate means to attain monetary success, in other situations a disconnect exists between goals and means. This disconnect, referred to as anomie or strain, means that some individuals have their opportunities for success blocked.

Merton described five modes of adaptation that characterize how individuals react to strain (see Table 5.2). First, *conformists* accept the goals of society and the legitimate means to attain success. They want economic success and play by the rules to reach that ideal. Second, *innovators* also accept the goals of society, but because of blocked opportunities (that is, strain/anomie), they turn to illegitimate means to attain economic success. Drug dealing, robbery, burglary, white-collar crime, and other economic offenses are examples. Third, *ritualists* accept the legitimate means and do what is expected of them, but they do not have economic success as a

anomie theory: A theory that suggests that crime is produced by normlessness or confusion.

TABLE 5.2	Merton's Modes of Adaptation		
MODE OF ADAPTATION	**RESPONSE TO SOCIETAL GOALS**	**RESPONSE TO SOCIETAL MEANS**	**EXAMPLE**
Conformist	Accepts	Accepts	Individual who works hard in college and strives for economic success
Innovator	Accepts	Rejects	Individual who wants economic success but turns to crime for that success
Ritualist	Rejects	Accepts	Individual who has no goals but does everything he or she is expected to do
Retreatist	Rejects	Rejects	Individual who retreats into drugs or alcohol for escape
Rebel	Rejects/Replaces	Rejects/Replaces	Individual who has goals inconsistent with societal goals and uses illegitimate means to reach those goals (e.g., terrorists)

Merton, R. K. (1938). Social structure and anomie. *American Sociological Review. 3*(5), 672–682.

driving goal. Fourth, *retreatists* reject both the goals and the legitimate means of society. Merton placed homeless individuals and people with alcoholism or drug addiction in this category. Finally, *rebels* refers to individuals who reject the goals and means of society, but replace those goals and means with their own goals and means. Terrorists would be an example. They have replaced the goal of economic success with the goal of creating fear, and they have replaced legitimate means with harmful behaviors.

Some authors have argued that there are additional modes of adaptation. One research team added an adaptation known as the "maximizer," which is defined as "someone who simultaneously uses and incorporates legitimate and illegitimate means of opportunity in the pursuit of profit and/ or monetary gain."[62] Consider as an example individuals who maintain successful jobs, yet still engage in various types of offending to gain additional economic success.

Messner and Rosenfeld's Institutional Anomie Theory

In *Crime and the American Dream*, Steven Messner and Richard Rosenfeld outlined their version of a strain theory by exploring how structural factors related to strain/anomie contribute to overall crime rates in a society.[63] According to the authors, our culture promotes the "American dream," but does not promote values that would help to achieve financial success by legitimate means to the same degree. **Institutional anomie theory** suggests that individuals are socialized to succeed to any cost, but individuals are not provided equal opportunities for success or socialized in how to attain financial success through legitimate efforts. They suggest that anomie exists at the institutional level between the proscription of societal goals and legitimate means. This anomie leads to chaotic and illegitimate efforts to "get rich."

institutional anomie theory: The theory that structural factors related to strain or anomie contribute to overall crime rates in a society.

The authors highlight four values promoted in American society that may promote crime. First, in terms of achievement, we are socialized to always want more. The quotation "second place is the first loser" comes to mind. Next, the ideal of universalism points to the assumption that everyone should want material success, even though it is impossible for everyone to "be rich." Third, the notion of individualism suggests that we should be able to attain our financial goals on our own, without help from others, which again is not plausible. Finally, materialism demonstrates how we are socialized to want material goods and the best new products. *Materialism* refers to the way that our society encourages us to be enamored with material goods and the acquisition of the best new products. Research has shown that institutional anomie theory explains some types of offending, including, but not limited to, homicide,[64] fraud victimization,[65] and embezzlement.[66]

Institutional anomie theory suggests that members of society are socialized to want to get rich, but not everyone can get rich. Many individuals might want to live somewhere like this home, but few actually are able to. Aspiring to unreachable goals creates anomie in the cultural groups.

© Tom Knibbs/Getty Images

BEYOND A REASONABLE DOUBT 5.2

_____ theory suggests that powerful individuals create laws as a way to control lower-class populations.

(a) Conflict, (b) Subcultural, (c) Disorganization, (d) Labeling, (e) None of the above

---

The answer can be found on page 521.

➡ Crime as a Product of Social Psychological Factors

Some theories view crime as caused by interactions between social factors and psychological factors. Theories that consider social psychological factors as the source of crime include life course theory, general strain theory, social control theory, and self-control theory.

Life Course Theory

Life course theory is an interdisciplinary developmental theory that explains human behavior by examining how past events, including turning points, put individuals on certain trajectories for future behaviors. Robert

> **life course theory:** An interdisciplinary developmental theory that explains human behavior by examining how past events put individuals on certain trajectories for future behaviors.

Sampson and Laub view marriage as a turning point that will place individuals on different trajectories.

© Hill Street Studios/Getty Images

Sampson and John Laub made the case for using life course theory to explain crime in their seminal work *Crime in the Making: Pathways and Turning Points Through Life.* Sampson and Laub viewed trajectories, transitions, and transitional events as helping to understand criminal behavior. *Trajectories* refers to "pathways or lines of development throughout life."[67] *Transitions* are "short-term events embedded in trajectories which may include starting a new job, getting married, having a child, or being sentenced to prison."[68] *Transitional events* could result in turning points that alter the trajectories of individuals' lives. For instance, some observers have argued that childhood victimization may be transitional events that place individuals on trajectories for either future victimization or future offending.[69] See the "Ethical Decision Making" box in this chapter for an example of how this issue surfaces in criminal justice responses.

According to Sampson and Laub, social bonds such as marriage and employment are turning points that may lead some offenders to stop committing crime. As age-graded social bonds, this suggestion explains the age-crime curve addressed in Chapter 3. Individuals typically get married and begin their careers later in the life course. Marriage and employment create social bonds for individuals. In the absence of such bonds, there is little to stop the offending. The authors quote the ever-popular Bob Dylan to drive home this point: "When you got nothing, you've got nothing to lose."[70]

In *Shared Beginnings, Divergent Lives: Delinquent Boys to Age 70*, Sampson and Laub revised their life course theory to capture the importance of routine activities and human agency (or decision making) and to explain why some individuals desist from criminal behavior and others begin criminal careers regardless of histories of crime. The current version of their theory now suggests that individuals' structured routine activities are tied to opportunities and "behavioral choices" to engage in offending.[71] The more structured activities that individuals are engaged in, the less likely they will commit crime, and the fewer structured activities they engage in, the more likely they will engage in offending. Focusing on human agency (the ability to make purposeful and reasoned choices), Sampson and Laub also call attention to the importance of "situated choice," or the influence of structural factors on decision making. In some cases, a decision might lead to offenders ending their criminal careers, while in other cases, structural constraints may make decisions to desist pointless. As an analogy, you may decide that you are going to get an

ETHICAL DECISION MAKING

LIFE COURSE VICTIMIZATION AND CRIME

Community college student Rae Kim is doing her internship in the prosecutor's office. She is very much looking forward to the time when she herself will be able to help put criminals behind bars. Having grown up in the inner city, she has seen too many lives ruined as a result of crime.

One afternoon she is reviewing legal cases for her supervisor when she is asked to help review a pre-sentencing investigation report. Her boss wants her to recommend whether a plea bargain should be accepted in a recent domestic violence case. She can't wait to read the file.

It does not take long for Rae's excitement to dissipate. As she reads the file, she sees that both the offender and the victim have long histories of both crime and victimization. Both of them were victimized as young children by their parents. They appear to have histories

of physical neglect and the offender's and victim's upbringing seem amazingly similar, even though they grew up miles apart. Rae reads in the file that two years before this incident, the victim had actually been arrested for beating up the individual who is now the offender.

Rae is suddenly not as eager to make a recommendation to her boss. Who is the offender? Who is the victim? Do their histories of childhood maltreatment influence their current experiences?

YOU DECIDE

1. Should the offender be handled leniently in this case?

2. Based on your response to question 1, what are the consequences for the community?

3. How can the cycle of violence be broken in a way that respects current victims' rights?

A+ in your criminal justice class, but your decision may be influenced by broader factors over which you have no control, such as getting sick and missing class, or the like. The following summarizes Sampson and Laub's modified life course theory:

> Weak informal social controls, minimal structured routine activities, and human agency explain persistence in criminal behavior, independent of earlier patterns of offending. On the flip side, strong informal social control, highly structured routine activities, and human agency explain desistance in adulthood, independent of a history of antisocial behavior.[72]

General Strain Theory

Robert Agnew expanded on Merton's strain theory by addressing strain from a social psychological orientation and examining the sources of strain from an individual level rather than a societal level.[73] In his **general strain theory**, Agnew pointed to three sources of strain: the failure to achieve positively valued goals, the removal or expected removal of positively valued stimuli, and the exposure to and anticipated exposure to negative stimuli. He described two types of strain: objective and subjective strains. *Objective strains* are those that virtually all individuals would agree are negative experiences or stressors. In contrast, *subjective strains* are strains "that are disliked by the people who are experiencing (or have experienced) them."[74]

general strain theory: The theory that crime is caused by the way individuals respond to frustrations they encounter.

FIGURE 5.4   **Elements of the Bond in Hirschi's Social Control Theory**

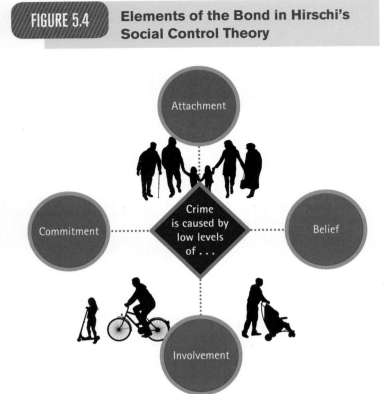

VIDEO

Travis Hirschi Panel

social control theory:
A theory that asserts that individuals commit crime because of weak bonds to societal institutions.

It is from this perspective that Agnew suggests that although virtually everyone experiences strain at some point in their lives, it is the reaction to strain, rather than the mere presence of strain, that leads to crime.[75] For example, he noted that getting angry as a result of strain may help to explain why strain is tied to offending.[76] Broidy and Agnew have also suggested that males and females react to anger differently and that these varied reactions may help to explain differences between the genders in offending patterns.[77] Males tend to turn anger outward and females tend to turn their anger inward, resulting in males directing their behaviors more toward violent crimes and property offenses and females' strain being "conducive to family violence, to escape attempts like running away, and to more self-directed forms of crime, like drug use."[78]

Social Control Theory

Rather than asking why offenders commit crime, **social control theory** begins with the question of why most people don't commit crime. The answer, according to Travis Hirschi, is that most individuals do not commit crime because they have strong bonds to society. Hirschi outlined and tested his social control theory in the classic book *Causes of Delinquency*.[79] According to Hirschi, individuals are bonded to society through four elements: attachment, belief, involvement, and commitment. *Attachment* refers to the degree to which individuals are attached to their parents and positive role models such as teachers. *Belief* refers to whether individuals believe in the rules of society. *Involvement* refers to whether individuals are involved in productive activities so that they don't have time to commit offenses. *Commitment* refers to whether individuals are committed to societal goals (see Figure 5.4).

Hirschi tested his theory by surveying high school students. His study found support for the suggestion that stronger bonds reduced the likelihood of offending, though he noted that he overestimated the importance of involvement. Clearly, it does not take too long to commit an offense, so

FIGURE 5.5   **Characteristics of Low Self-Control and Their Relationship to Crime**

whether juveniles are involved in extracurricular activities may not prevent delinquency. Although involvement was not significant, Hirschi's research suggested that individuals who are strongly invested in their families, jobs, and societal goals are not as likely to commit crime. Research showing that married individuals and employed individuals are less likely to commit crime has been used to illustrate support for social control theory. The assumption is that individuals who are married are attached to their spouses and do not want to weaken that bond by offending, whereas those who are employed are attached to their jobs and have too much to lose by offending.

Various criminal justice practices are designed to strengthen bonds between individuals and their communities; the idea is that these bonds will prevent crime. Requiring probationers to maintain jobs, allowing community-based offenders to live with their families, and trying to teach offenders why they should abide by the law are but a few examples of these practices.

Self-Control Theory

In *A General Theory of Crime,* Michael Gottfredson and Travis Hirschi outlined what is known as **self-control theory**.[80] Based on the assumption that crime and all human behavior are the result of "the self-interested pursuit of pleasure or the avoidance of pain,"[81] the theorists suggested that self-control influences criminal behavior and defined self-control as "the individual characteristic relevant to the commission of criminal acts."[82] According to Gottfredson and Hirschi, those with low self-control are more likely "impulsive, insensitive, physical (as opposed to mental), risk-taking, short-sighted, and non-verbal."[83] They suggest that self-control levels stem from parenting practices and that bad parenting strategies lead to low levels of self-control, whereas appropriate parenting practices lead to higher levels of self-control. They also suggested what is now known as the *stability hypothesis*: Levels of self-control are stable throughout one's life after early childhood. The theorists do not technically see lower self-control as always leading to crime. They wrote, "The link between self-control and crime is not deterministic, but probabilistic, affected by opportunities and other constraints"[84] (see Figure 5.5).

Numerous studies have demonstrated at least some support for the premise that self-control is tied to criminal behavior and other negative social consequences.[85] Research shows that males tend to exhibit lower levels of self-control than do females.[86] Recall that research shows that males have higher offending rates. In line with Gottfredson and Hirschi's recognition of the importance of opportunity,[87] Teresa Lagrange and Robert Silverman

self-control theory: The theory that a lack of self-control is the main factor behind deviant behavior.

CRIMINAL JUSTICE and **COLLEGE STUDENTS**

DO YOU HAVE ENOUGH SELF-CONTROL TO COMPLETE A SELF-CONTROL SCALE?

Below are the items from Grasmick and colleagues' self-control scale. Read each item, and give yourself a 3 if you strongly disagree with the statement, a 2 if you disagree, a 1 if you agree, and 0 if you strongly agree.

1. I often act on the spur of the moment. _____

2. I devote much thought and effort to preparing for the future. _____

3. I often do what brings me pleasure here and now. _____

4. I am more concerned with what happens to me in the long run. _____

5. I frequently try to seek out projects that I know will be difficult. _____

6. When things get complicated, I tend to quit or withdraw. _____

7. The things in life that are easiest bring me the most pleasure. _____

8. I like really hard tasks that stretch my abilities to the limit. _____

9. I feel little need to test myself by doing something a little risky. _____

10. Sometimes I will take a risk just for the fun of it. ___ _____

11. I find no excitement in doing things I might get in trouble for. _____

12. Excitement and adventure are more important than security. _____

13. I would almost always rather do something mental than physical. _____

14. I feel better when I am on the move rather than sitting and thinking. _____

15. I like to read or contemplate ideas more than I like to get out and do things. _____

16. I have more energy and greater need for activities than most people my age. _____

17. I try to look out for others first, even if it means making things difficult for myself. _____

18. I'm very sympathetic to other people when they are having problems. _____

19. If things I do upset people, it's their problem not mine. _____

20. I will try to get things I want even when it's causing problems for others. _____

21. I don't lose my temper very easily. _____

22. When I'm angry I feel more like hurting than talking about why I'm angry. _____

23. When I'm really angry, other people better stay away from me. _____

24. When I have a serious disagreement with someone, I can usually talk calmly about it without getting upset. _____

After you are done, change your scores for these items so that 3 = 0, 2 = 1, 1 = 2, and 0 = 3: 2, 4, 5, 8, 13, 15, 17, 18, 21, 24. Then, sum your scores. Lower scores indicate a lower self-control.

Do you think your score adequately reflects your level of self-control? What factors from your past do you think contribute to your level of self-control? How might your level of self-control contribute to your engagement in different types of behavior such as speeding, smoking, and illegally downloading music?

Grasmick, H G., Tittle, C. R., Bursik, R. J., & Arneklev, B. J. (1993). Testing the core empirical implications of Gottfredson and Hirschi's general theory of crime. *Journal of Research in Crime and Delinquency, 30*, 5–29.

found that the impact of gender on offending was reduced when considering interactions between self-control and opportunity.[88] This finding suggests that self-control is important only when opportunities to engage in crime are present. Even a psychopath is unlikely to engage in a crime if a police officer is in plain sight. And even an alcoholic individual with low self-control will not drink if he or she doesn't have access to alcohol.

One of the strengths of self-control theory is that it is relatively easy to assess. Researchers simply need to measure individuals' levels of self-control and measure whether they commit criminal or deviant behaviors, and then examine whether a relationship appears in their analyses. Of course, we make this sound easier than it really is, but studying whether self-control causes crime is much easier than studying whether labels or values cause crime. Because of the ease of testing the theory, self-control theory is one of the most tested theories in criminal justice and criminology.

Harold Grasmick and colleagues developed a widely used survey to measure self-control.[89] In fact, nearly 800 researchers have referenced the article that first described this scale, and dozens, if not hundreds, of researchers have used the scale in their own research. The survey is included in the "Criminal Justice and College Students" box in this chapter. Hirschi and Gottfredson warned that surveys about self-control must be approached with a degree of caution, given that individuals with low levels of self-control may not have the self-control needed to validly complete surveys. They might rush through answers, give little thought to the questions, and may even be dishonest on some of the questions. Because those with a low level of self-control may not be the "best" types of survey respondents, the theorists conclude that "apparently modest results may in fact be highly supportive of the validity of the theory."[90]

> ## BEYOND A REASONABLE DOUBT 5.3
>
> Which of the following theories suggests that levels of attachment to one's parents are tied to crime?
>
> (a) Life course theory, (b) General strain theory, (c) Social control theory, (d) Self-control theory

The answer can be found on page 521.

➡ Crime as a Product of Cognitive Processes

Another set of crime theories attribute crime to cognitive or psychological processes. The basic premise at the foundation of these theories is that crime is produced, at least in part, by how we think, what we learn, or how we react to the way others see us. These theories include neutralization theory, learning theory, and labeling theory.

Neutralization Theory

Neutralization theory was developed by Gresham Sykes and David Matza, who posited that juveniles tend to know right from wrong, but they engage in delinquent acts after rationalizing (or neutralizing) their

> **neutralization theory:** The theory that juveniles tend to know right from wrong, but they engage in delinquent acts after rationalizing (or neutralizing) their behavior as appropriate in specific situations.

behavior as appropriate in specific situations.[91] They described five types of neutralizations (or rationalizations). First, *denial of injury* refers to situations in which juveniles convince themselves that no one will be hurt from their actions and subsequently engage in those actions. Second, *denial of victim* refers to situations in which juveniles rationalize that the victim deserves the harm that he or she will experience from the victimization. Third, *denial of responsibility* occurs when offenders rationalize that they are not responsible for their behavior and engage in the offending on the basis of that belief. Fourth, *condemnation of condemners* refers to instances when offenders convince themselves that it is okay to commit the offense because those with power commit similar offenses. Finally, *appeal to higher loyalties* includes instances when juveniles justify their behavior by suggesting that they need to commit the offense in order to help a group to which they are extremely loyal (such as their family or gang).

Sykes and Matza's theory has generated a great deal of discussion. Other researchers have suggested additional neutralizations, including the following:

- *Denial of law.* Offenders justify their behaviors on the grounds that the law is unfair.[92]

- *Defense of necessity.* Offenders convince themselves that their behavior is necessary.[93]

- *Claims of entitlement.* Offenders come to believe that they are entitled to certain goods and steal them.[94]

- *Metaphor of the ledger.* Offenders believe that occasional criminal acts are okay.[95]

- *Claims that everyone does it.* Offenders justify behavior by suggesting that the behavior is common.[96]

Researchers continue to explore how different types of offenders use neutralizations to commit their offenses. In one recent study, researchers found that veterinarians who committed deviant acts frequently used neutralizations to justify their behavior.[97] Referencing appeal to higher loyalties, the author described situations in which veterinarians billed owners for putting pets to sleep, when they actually put the pets up for adoption (the pet's life was the higher loyalty). In a more recent study, authors found "modest support" that neutralizations influenced college students' decisions to engage in digital piracy acts, including pirating software, illegally downloading music, and illegally downloading movies.[98] Reviewing the neutralizations described in this section, are there any that you think you might use to justify digital piracy?

Learning Theory

learning theory: A theory that suggests that criminal behavior is learned just as other behavior is learned.

Learning theory suggests that criminal behavior is learned the same way that other behaviors are learned. Edwin Sutherland's *differential association* *theory* is one of the two most popular learning theories. Sutherland outlined his theory in the following nine propositions:[99]

- Criminal behavior is learned.

- Criminal behavior is learned in interaction with other persons in a process of communication.

- The principal part of the learning of criminal behavior occurs within intimate personal groups.

- When criminal behavior is learned, the learning includes techniques of committing the crime, which are sometimes very simple, and the specific direction of motives, drives, rationalizations, and attitudes.

- The specific direction of the motives and drives is learned from definitions of the legal codes as favorable or unfavorable.

- A person becomes delinquent because of an excess of definitions favorable to violation of law over definitions unfavorable to violation of law.

- Differential association may vary in frequency, duration, priority, and intensity.

- The process of learning criminal behavior by association with criminal and anticriminal patterns involves all of the mechanisms that are involved in any other learning.

- While criminal behavior is an expression of general needs and values, it is not explained by those general needs and values since noncriminal behavior is an expression of the same needs and values.

A few points about differential association theory are worth highlighting. First, according to the theory, individuals must know how to commit crime in order to be able to commit crime. Second, knowledge alone is not enough. Offenders must also believe that it is appropriate to commit crime, and they learn values and motivations to justify these crimes.

Ronald Akers developed the other most popular learning theory in criminal justice, initially called *differential association-reinforcement theory* (see Figure 5.6). Akers's theory includes four dimensions:[100]

- *Differential association.* Recognizes that interaction with others is an element of learning.

- *Definitions.* Refers to attitudes, beliefs, and justifications about the appropriateness of actions.

- *Differential reinforcement.* Addresses perceptions of rewards and punishments: When individuals are rewarded for behavior, they continue that behavior; when punished, that behavior should decrease.

- *Imitation.* Individuals tend to perform behaviors after seeing others engage in those behaviors. This is particularly important in the early stages of behavior, and not as important after the offenders has learned how to perform the behavior.

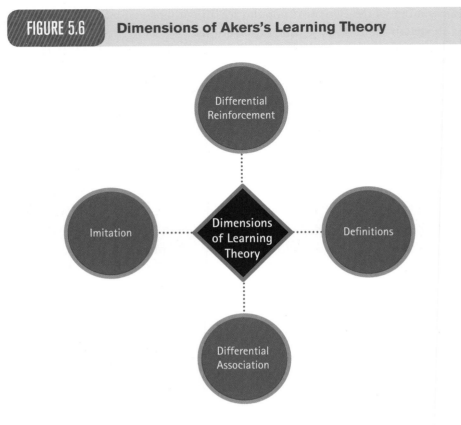

FIGURE 5.6   Dimensions of Akers's Learning Theory

Akers asserted that we tend to spend more time with individuals who reward our behavior. Delinquents and criminals, then, would spend more time with other offenders, who would be more prone to reinforce their behaviors. The more offenders are rewarded for their offending, the more they will continue to engage in those behaviors.

Learning theory has been criticized for being hard to test.[101] Also, authors have suggested that although the theory is useful in explaining group offending when offenses require a great deal of interaction with others (like drug use), it does very little to explain individualistic offending (like violence).[102]

Labeling Theory

Labeling theory calls attention to the way that labeling individuals contributes to future offending. The notion of the *self-fulfilling prophecy* suggests that expectations of individuals, whether positive or negative, may lead individuals to meet those expectations. In a similar way, labeling theorists suggest that labels assigned to individuals may lead individuals to internalize those labels.

Edwin Lemert has discussed two types of deviance: primary deviance and secondary deviance.[103] *Primary deviance* refers to acts of deviance when no public labeling results from the deviance. Imagine a situation in which someone steals an item but does not get caught. In contrast, *secondary deviance* recognizes the effect that being labeled has on self-perceptions and refers to behavior that occurs because an individual has already been labeled

VIDEO
The Wire and
Labeling Theory

labeling theory: The theory that labeling individuals contributes to future offending and that expectations of individuals, whether positive or negative, may lead individuals to meet those expectations.

as deviant. Situations in which individuals assume the label of "thief" because they have been labeled a thief would be illustrative.

Labeling theorists point to two separate ways in which labels promote offending.[104] First, the *deviance amplification hypothesis* posits that labeling individuals as offenders increases the likelihood that those individuals will become offenders. Second, *the differential enforcement/ status characteristics hypothesis* suggests that decisions to label individuals as criminal are influenced by extralegal characteristics such as gender, race, class, and so on. Criminologist Ruth Triplett noted that the first hypothesis is derived from symbolic interactionists' assumptions that draw attention to the way that interactions produce labels, whereas the second hypothesis comes from conflict theory. Triplett suggested further that a combination of the two hypotheses recognizes "the possibility of power differentials in the creation of stereotypes."[105] Stressing that individuals can be labeled by both formal (for example, criminal justice officials) and informal networks (family members, peers, and the like), Triplett suggested that informal labels may have more of an impact on the individual labeled because our relationships with these informal networks mean much more to us.

The power of labels cannot be understated. Jön Gunnar Bernburg and Marvin Krohn asserted that labeling young people as offenders produces a structural disadvantage in that the "offender label" makes it harder for young people to finish school and find a job. It has also been suggested that labeling young people as offenders may lead them to become more attached to, or embedded in, deviant groups such as gangs because "deviant groups provide social shelter from stigma as well as collective rationalizations, definitions, peer pressure, and opportunities that encourage and facilitate deviant behavior."[106]

BEYOND A REASONABLE DOUBT 5.4

_____ is a technique of neutralization described by Sykes and Matza.

(a) Denial of injury, (b) Denial of victim, (c) Appeal to higher loyalties,
(d) Denial of responsibility, (e) All of the above

The answer can be found on page 521.

➡ Concluding Remarks

In concluding this discussion about theory, a few "truisms" about theory are warranted:

- ➡ [Criminal] behavior is a complex set of action.

- ➡ [Criminal] behavior has a complex set of causes.

- ➡ No single cause of [criminal] behavior accounts for the majority of [criminal acts].[107]

AUTHOR VIDEO
Crimes on Campus That Later Become Crime Theory

Rather than addressing "causes" of crime, some observers have argued that it is more appropriate to focus on the "risks" or propensity for offending. Richard Herrnstein suggested,

> Criminal behavior is behavior. It is not necessary to prove that human behavior is multiply determined, for it is obvious. Nothing we do, not even coughing or sneezing, has just one governing antecedent condition. The more complex the set of antecedent conditions, the less sense it makes to frame questions about behavior in terms of cause.[108]

Just as a bunch of things might make someone sneeze, a bunch of things might cause crime. It doesn't get much simpler than that.

Just the Facts: Chapter Summary

- Just as we expect medical professionals to know the causes of disease, we must expect criminal justice professionals to be able to identify the causes of crime.

- According to various theories, crime is a product of choice, biological factors, social factors, social psychological factors, or cognitive processes.

- The central tenet of deterrence theory is free will, and an assumption is made that offenders choose to commit crime as a result of their free will. According to Cesare Beccaria, punishment must meet three criteria in order to be effective: (a) It must be swift, (b) it must be certain, and (c) it must outweigh the pleasure that the offender would get from committing the crime.

- Routine activities theory suggests that crime occurs when three things occur at the same time and in the same location: (a) A motivated offender is present, (b) capable guardians are absent, and (c) vulnerable targets are present.

- Cesare Lombroso, an Italian physician, was the founder of the Positivist School of criminology, which adhered to the principle of determinism to explain crime. One of the types of criminals identified by Lombroso was the atavistic throwback, or the born criminal.

- The general premise of social disorganization theory is that a community's or neighborhood's level of disorganization contributes to the crime rate in that community or neighborhood.

- Broken windows theory explains crime by suggesting that minor forms of disorder will lead to additional disorder.

- Subcultural theory attributes crime to the values and norms that are part of the socialization process.

- Social conflict theory points to the power that majority groups have over others and asserts that crime is caused by abuses of that power.

- Social strain theory suggests that crime occurs because of an inability to attain societal goals.

- Social control theory posits that most individuals do not commit crime because they have strong bonds to society.

- In *A General Theory of Crime*, Michael Gottfredson and Travis Hirschi argue that self-control influences criminal behavior, and they define self-control as "the individual characteristic relevant to the commission of criminal acts."

- Robert Agnew's general strain theory suggests that crime is caused by the way individuals respond to frustrations they encounter.

- Life course theory is an interdisciplinary developmental theory that explains human behavior by examining how past events, including turning points, put individuals on certain trajectories for future behaviors.

- According to neutralization theory, juveniles tend to know right from wrong, but they engage in delinquent acts after rationalizing (or neutralizing) their behavior as appropriate in specific situations.

- Learning theory suggests that criminal behavior is learned just the same way that other behaviors are learned. Edwin Sutherland's differential association theory is one of the most popular learning theories.

- Labeling theory calls attention to the way that labeling individuals contributes to future offending.

Critical Thinking Questions

1. Why do you think individuals commit crime?

2. Find a group of five students to complete the self-control scale in the "Criminal Justice and College Students" box. What patterns do you see?

3. Select two criminological theories and explain how criminal justice professionals use those theories in their jobs.

4. Describe how strain theory might explain academic dishonesty.

5. Compare and contrast Beccaria's and Lombroso's theories.

6. Watch a crime show on television and identify the criminological theories that come to mind when watching the show.

7. Why do we need to know the causes of crime?

8. How is criminological theory related to policy?

Key Terms

anomie theory (159)

broken windows theory (155)

Classical School (145)

concentric zone theory (153)

conflict theory (157)

deterrence theory (145)

general strain theory (163)

institutional anomie theory (160)

labeling theory (170)

learning theory (168)

life course theory (161)

middle-class measuring rod (155)

neutralization theory (167)

Positivist School (149)

rational choice theory (144)

routine activities theory (146)

self-control theory (165)

social control theory (164)

social disorganization theory (153)

subcultural theory (155)

$SAGE edgeselect™

edge.sagepub.com/payne

Sharpen your skills with SAGE edge select!

With carefully crafted tools and resources to encourage review, practice, and critical thinking, SAGE edge select gives you the edge needed to master course content. Take full advantage of open-access key term flashcards, practice quizzes, and video content. Diagnostic pre-tests, a personalized study plan, and post-tests are available with an access code.

PART II

POLICING

©istockphoto.com/101cats

POLICING

BOOKING

Released

ARREST

INVESTIGATION

UNSOLVED/ NOT ARRESTED

?

Policing Strategies

Community Policing

Problem-Oriented Policing

Targeted Policing

Evidence-Based Policing

Predictive Policing

Broken Windows Policing

Hot Spot Policing

Compstat

Zero-Tolerance Policing

Intelligence Led Policing

Influence on Police

Politics

Legislation

Society

Economics

Technology

Police Subculture

6

AN INTRODUCTION TO POLICING

HISTORY AND STRUCTURE

WHEN I ATTENDED COLLEGE and was working on my degree in criminal justice, I already knew I wanted to be a police officer, so I paid special attention to everything my policing professors taught me. I did not think much about policing jurisdiction and the numerous police agencies in the United States, only that I was considering applying for a federal law enforcement position. But after working as a summer cop in New Jersey, I was open to working as a local police officer as well.

When I became a police officer in the Washington, D.C., area, the concept of "jurisdiction" (the area, designated by law, where the police have authority) became very real for me. The county in which I served as a police officer had more than 32 law enforcement agencies, including a county police department, a sheriff's department, a college campus police force, and military police. If you counted the neighboring jurisdictions and Washington, D.C., that number reached close to 100. This raised an interesting issue when it came to jurisdiction.

A number of federal law enforcement agencies also worked in our county, which added to some of the confusion, especially when it came to certain crimes. The worst was bank robbery. The county had jurisdiction, and we were the first to respond to the call; however, we knew that the FBI would arrive within 30 minutes to take over the case. They typically conducted their own investigation, but we, as county police, had to conduct our own. So, we knew we had 30 minutes to get our investigation done before the FBI took over.

Certain calls raised questions of jurisdiction. For instance, our county bordered Washington, D.C., but the Potomac River is situated between the two jurisdictions. When people committed suicide by jumping off of the 14th Street bridge, the question became, Who had jurisdiction to investigate the case when the body was found? It turned out that anything in the water was Washington, D.C.'s, whereas anything on our shore was our responsibility. I had always heard rumors that some fellow police officers, upon finding a body on the shore, would gently push it back into the water and call Washington, D.C., authorities.

—Willard Oliver

LEARNING OBJECTIVES

After reading this chapter, students will be able to:

6.1 Identify the influence of early societal development on the emergence of policing

6.2 Evaluate the influence of the English system of policing on the American system

6.3 Explain the developments in policing during the four main eras

6.4 Distinguish among municipal, county, state, and federal police

6.5 Identify four types of special jurisdiction police agencies

6.6 Describe five different federal police agencies

6.7 Explain how police departments are structured

ADMISSIBLE or INADMISSIBLE Evidence

Read the statements that follow. If the statement is true, circle *admissible*. If the statement is false, circle *inadmissible*. Answers can be found on page 517.

1. **Admissible** **Inadmissible** Every type of society around the world has always had a formal police force.
2. **Admissible** **Inadmissible** The constable and night watch were fictitious characters created by Shakespeare.
3. **Admissible** **Inadmissible** The first formal police department was created in London, England.
4. **Admissible** **Inadmissible** The first formal police department in the United States was created in New York City.
5. **Admissible** **Inadmissible** There are approximately 18,000 police agencies in the United States.
6. **Admissible** **Inadmissible** There are more federal law enforcement officers than any other type of police officer.
7. **Admissible** **Inadmissible** Police departments are a military organization.
8. **Admissible** **Inadmissible** The Department of Homeland Security was created after the terrorist attacks on September 11, 2001.

177

Most countries in the world have one police department, and they don't face these issues. So, how did the United States end up with almost 18,000 police agencies and the thorny issue of determining jurisdiction? The answer to this question has much to do with both the development of U.S. society in general and the development of policing in the United States more specifically. The majority of countries around the world have a very centralized form of government and, as a result, have only one police department, with various branches or field offices in towns and cities throughout the country.[1] Police officers are hired and employed by the national government, they all wear the same uniform of their nation's police, and they all have vehicles marking them as the nation's police force. In the United States, however, because we have a more decentralized form of government and because policing from its inception was seen as a local responsibility, we have no national police force. So, rather than having one police department serving the entire country, we have over 18,000 police agencies serving the American people today.

The different types of police agencies range from small town police departments to large metropolitan police departments like the New York City Police Department, with its more than 34,000 police officers. There are county police agencies—typically sheriff's departments—and special police agencies such as those serving school districts, airports, and universities. In addition, 49 states have their own police agencies, and the federal government has special investigative agencies such as the Drug Enforcement Administration (DEA) and Immigration and Customs Enforcement (ICE), as well as a number of its own police agencies, such as the U.S. Capitol Police and the Smithsonian Office of Protection Services (which polices many of the museums in Washington, D.C.). Each of these agencies has a specific area that they police by law, which is known as their **jurisdiction**, and this is how each agency knows when a particular criminal complaint falls under their responsibility and authority.[2] The word *jurisdiction* means "to speak the law," and in the case of the police, it refers to the right and authority granted to a police agency, a legal body, to administer justice in a defined area of responsibility, often defined by a type of crime or by geographic boundaries. This is how in a university town—where there is

jurisdiction: The geographic area and boundaries where police have the authority of office to enforce the law.

In the United States, over 18,000 police agencies employ police officers across the local, state, and federal governments.

a sheriff's office, a city police department, and a university police department—officers and deputies know who has both the authority and the responsibility to respond to a crime.

To help you understand why there are so many police agencies, in this chapter we explore the development of societies, especially in the United States, and how this development has affected the law, the police, and the concept of jurisdiction. We then present a short history to help you understand how the United States ended up with more than 18,000 police agencies. We explore the various types of agencies you will find when you leave the classroom so that you may better understand not only the different uniforms and patrol vehicles you see, but also the job opportunities available to you in the policing field. Finally, we detail who these police officers are, what they do, and how they organize to perform their duties.

➡ Types of Societies and Policing

According to anthropologists, all societies move through four stages before they become modern societies like the United States: bands, tribes, chiefdoms, and states.[3] *Bands* tend to be small, family based, and nomadic, whereas *tribes* develop more fixed societies, settling in villages, but they remain kin based. In either case, because of their small numbers, the people can generally solve disputes or problems that arise, so a formal police force is not needed. Anthropologist Jared Diamond defines tribes as consisting mostly of extended family, stating that everyone is "related to everyone else, by blood, marriage, or both."[4] It is because of these family ties that Diamond notes, "Those ties of relationship binding all tribal members make *police* [emphasis added], laws, and other conflict-resolving institutions of larger societies unnecessary, since any two villagers getting into an argument will share many kin, who apply pressure on them to keep it from becoming violent."[5] The English historian Charles Reith called this type of policing **kin policing**, which he described as a "force exercised indirectly by the people, from below, upwards."[6] Despite the name *kin policing*, however, as Diamond (1997) explains, "like bands, tribes lack a . . . *police force* [emphasis added]."[7]

Once the tribes grow larger and begin to number in the thousands, these bonds of family begin to break down and other institutions have to step in to control people and deal with conflict resolution. One of these institutions, religion, "helps solve the problem of how unrelated individuals are to live together without killing each other—by providing them with a bond not based on kinship."[8] The other mechanism that can be employed is the formalization of the informal means of social control. The best example of this is the **frankpledge system**, which was put into place in England after the Norman conquest of 1066.[9] In this system, small communities (read: *bands*) were placed into a *tithing*—a collection of 10 men and their families—who would be responsible for conflict resolution within their group. The leader was called the *tithingman*. The tithings were then collected into groups of 10 called the *hundred* (read: *tribes*), and the head of the hundred was—you

kin policing: An early form of policing that relied on family and clans to be responsible for the behaviors of their people.

frankpledge system: The early English system for kin policing that organized 10 families into tithings and 10 tithings into hundreds in order to police their own.

guessed it!—the *hundredman*, who was responsible for dealing with conflicts between tithings. The collection of hundreds was then the *chiefdom*. The frankpledge system is a great example of a chiefdom taking the informal means of control that had existed in the bands and tribes and formalizing them for purposes of social control.

The development of a society into a *state* represents the final movement into modern society, in which populations grow into the multiple thousands, all living in towns and cities and tending to become more *non*egalitarian all the time. The government becomes highly formalized through a centralized hierarchy, with leaders who are generally elected, and through the development of bureaucracies that specialize in particular services (such as the police). In the case of conflict resolution, laws are created, judges appointed, and a police force established. This is the modern government that surrounds all of us, all of the time, at all levels: local (the approximately 20,000 cities and just over 3,000 counties in the United States), state (all 50), and national (our federal government or, more accurately, our national government).

These police forces do not, however, develop instantly overnight as societies transition from chiefdoms to states; rather, they take time to develop and grow. The police system in the United States originated in the British colonies in 1607 with the settling of Jamestown in Virginia. To understand the system of policing in America, we must begin with the English system of policing the modern state, because that is where our system got its start.

BEYOND A REASONABLE DOUBT 6.1

Formal police departments first appeared in what type of society?

(a) Bands, (b) Tribes, (c) Chiefdoms, (d) States, (e) None of the above

---

The answer can be found on page 521.

➡ The English System of Policing

The English system of rudimentary policing began with the previously mentioned Norman Conquest of 1066. In the aftermath of the invasion, as the Normans increased the power of the state, they added to the frankpledge system over the next 200 years and formalized the changes with the Statute of Winchester in 1285.[10] They first established a **night watch** to protect the interests of the cities. This involved watching for enemy attacks and for fires that threatened the towns and cities, which were made entirely of wood; if needed, they alerted the populace by raising the **hue and cry**.[11] This amounted to shouting for help when trouble was at hand, but the people still took care of the problems. The night watch also performed mundane tasks such as lighting streetlamps at night. Soon after, a day watch was added, known as the **ward**, and it was responsible for similar activities during the daytime but also picked up the duties of clearing refuse from the city, as well as taking the bodies of those who died overnight outside

night watch: In the early English system of policing, a semiformal guard for nighttime.

hue and cry: The requirement for good people to shout and come to the aid of people in distress from a crime.

ward: In the early English system of policing, a semiformal guard for daytime.

the city walls to burn them—something made rather famous in the movie *Monty Python and the Holy Grail* ("I'm not dead yet!").

The members of the watch and ward were typically the dregs of society, people who today would be called *indigent*. They were paid very poorly, had no skills or desires to perform their functions, and tended to be derelict in their duties, if not downright corrupt. To supervise those in the watch and ward, the most capable of them was appointed to the role of **constable**, who was paid only slightly better. Constables were typically assigned to very large districts, and it was not unheard of for a constable to supervise upward of 100 watchmen, meaning they too were ineffective in their jobs. Shakespeare's play *Much Ado About Nothing* depicts the incompetence of the constable and the watchman, whose characters were the forerunners of the silent era's Keystone Cops, the recruits in the *Police Academy* movies of the late 20th century, and the hapless law enforcement officers depicted in the more recent *Super Trooper* or *Reno 911!*

The Sheriff

Although the constable and the watch-and-ward system provided some means of protection within the towns and cities, and the frankpledge system provided a mechanism for handling disputes among the people, one position was added to protect the king's interests throughout England and that was the appointment of the *shire-reeve*, more commonly known as the **sheriff**. Since the early 1200s, the story of Robin Hood robbing from the rich and giving to the poor made famous the Sheriff of Nottingham, who pursued Robin Hood. Numerous films have depicted Robin Hood, ranging from the Errol Flynn movie *The Adventures of Robin Hood*; the more modern and gritty *Robin Hood,* starring Russell Crowe, not to mention everyone's favorite cartoon version, Walt Disney's *Robin Hood*. In all of these films, the Sheriff of Nottingham character is portrayed quite accurately, for the shire-reeve was appointed by the king and responsible for protecting the king's interest in his assigned county. The sheriff collected taxes, held court for minor crimes, and was responsible for investigating cases, including those brought to him by the constable. The sheriff typically did not become involved in crimes unless they affected the crown in some manner, such as dereliction of paying taxes or poaching on the king's property, two crimes Robin Hood was said to have committed frequently.

> **constable:** In the early English system of policing, the individual selected to oversee the watch and ward; today, law enforcement officers who work for the courts and may have arrest powers.
>
> **sheriff:** In the early English system of policing, the king's representative of law and order; later adopted in the United States, developing into the county sheriff.

The Thief-Takers

The sheriff, the constable, and the watch-and-ward system were fully implemented by the late 1200s and would remain the primary means for dealing with crime and disorder in England from the 14th to the 18th century. Little changed during this 500-year period, but by the late 1700s, England had industrialized, the population of the cities increased rapidly,

The story of Robin Hood focuses on a hero who stole from the rich to give to the poor. The Sheriff of Nottingham was famous for his efforts to stop Robin Hood from stealing from the king.

and the problems of crime and disorder skyrocketed. Even still, few changes emerged. One attempt at dealing with crime, known as the *parliamentary reward system*, or more informally as the **thief-taker system**, was implemented in 1693.[12] The system drew on the old adage that "it takes a thief to catch a thief," thus if any thief was willing to "rat out" another thief, the government would pay the individual for the information. Although the system worked well to some degree, it did not alleviate the problems of crime and quickly fell into disuse.

Bow Street Runners

The English writer Henry Fielding was not altogether successful as a writer and so he studied to become a lawyer. He was appointed in 1748 as the magistrate for the Bow Street District in London. Fielding then did something unusual. Rather than wait for cases to be brought before him, Fielding hired six constables to act as a quasi–police force and investigation unit. Initially called Mr. Fielding's People, they later became known as the **Bow Street Runners**.[13] Although Fielding died in 1754, his half-brother John succeeded him as magistrate and continued the practice of paying informants, conducting investigations, carrying out criminal raids, posting wanted flyers, registering criminals, carrying firearms and handcuffs, and patrolling Bow Street on horse and foot, all practices of a modern police force.

The London Metropolitan Police

In 1797, another magistrate, Patrick Colquhoun, who was inspired by the work of Henry and John Fielding, attempted to resolve a serious crime problem in London's East End. Merchants were losing money from thieves located along the wharfs of the River Thames, so Colquhoun received permission to create his own police force with 50 officers policing over 30,000 men working on the river trade. The police were not well received, and numerous skirmishes resulted, including one that cost an officer his life, but in the end, Colquhoun's police drove down the level of theft and from a cost-benefit standpoint he was successful. The amount of merchandise recovered far outweighed the cost of the police. Colquhoun's Marine Police Force (also known as the Thames River Police) was even more successful in the long term in that it gave Colquhoun the ability to think about crime, crime prevention, and how best to organize a police force in order to address the problem of crime. He wrote several books, including a *Treatise on the Police of the Metropolis*, which two decades later was read by one member of the British Parliament and would be put into action in order to create what is generally considered the first police department in history.[14]

In 1822, England's home secretary (analogous to the modern-day minister of justice) Robert Peel was faced with the problem of rising crime, particularly in London. Drawing on the works of Fielding and Colquhoun, Peel created a proposal for a professional police force. Although not well received initially, Peel continued to refine his proposal, which ultimately resulted in the passage of the **Metropolitan Police Act of 1829**.[15] Many previous entities had resembled police departments, but the London

thief-taker system: In the early English system of policing, the government's practice of paying criminals to turn in other criminals.

Bow Street Runners: Served as an early police force, patrolling the Bow Street District and investigating crimes.

Metropolitan Police Act of 1829: The act that created the first formally recognized police department in the world in London, England.

Metropolitan Police is generally considered the first modern police department in the world. Peel was then charged with supervising the creation of the new police department, and he hired two men to lead the newly formed organization: Charles Rowan and Richard Mayne. Although atypical to place two people in charge of such an organization, it worked. Rowan brought in his military experience to discipline the new police force, and Mayne had served as a barrister (lawyer) and understood the complexities of both organization and management. They hired over 1,000 new officers from outside of the city in order to avoid political corruption, and soon after being deployed, they became known affectionately as "Bobbies," named for the first police department's founder, Robert Peel, later *Sir Robert Peel* (see the "Criminal Justice Pioneer" box in this chapter).

The impact of England's form of policing on America was profound. At least until 1776, America was an extension of England, as a collection of British colonies. As a result, the 13 original colonies emulated the style of policing found in England. Among the colonies could be found the sheriff, constables, and the watch-and-ward system in various towns and cities. After the colonies declared their independence from England, not much changed, at least not in the 13 new states. Through the Judiciary Act of 1789, the office of the federal U.S. Marshals was created, but the marshals' primary function was to serve the courts in the territorial possessions, land owned by the United States of America, but not yet formed into states. It was not until 1838, in Boston, Massachusetts, that America would form its first modern police department. (See Figure 6.1.)

JOURNAL
Evolving Strategies

SIR ROBERT PEEL

Highly educated, Robert Peel entered politics like his father at a young age (21) and was eventually appointed as the chief secretary in Dublin, Ireland. There, drawing on Patrick Colquhoun's writings, he established the Royal Irish Constabulary, men who were later called "Peelers." He served through a series of other positions before being name home secretary in 1822. It was in this position that Peel helped to establish the London Metropolitan Police Force in 1829, thus earning recognition as the "father of policing." Although the police were not well received at first, they did help to reduce crime and, in time, earned a positive reputation. In 1834, Peel became the prime minister of England and then served a second term from 1841 to 1846. He continued in politics and was knighted with the title of "Sir" for his service to the Crown, which is why he is generally referred to as Sir Robert Peel. (Officially he was known as Sir Robert Peel, Second Baronet, and his son was dubbed Sir Robert Peel, Third Baronet.) Peel was thrown from his horse on June 29, 1850, and died from his injuries three days later.

Sir Robert Peel has been credited with creating the first modern police department. The police officers were called "bobbies" in reference to their service to Sir "Robert."

© Bettmann/CORBIS

FIGURE 6.1   Early History of Policing: A Timeline

1066
Frankpledge system created;
An example of chiefdom

1285
English created night watch system;
Members of the watch shouted if trouble
was at hand

Late 1200s
Sheriff, constable, and watch-and-ward
system fully implemented;
Sheriff also collected taxes

1693
Thief-taker system created;
Thiefs paid for catching other thiefs

1748
Bow Street Runners created by Henry
Fielding;
Fielding hired constables to patrol Bow
Street District in London

1797
Patrick Colquhoun created Marine Police
Force to respond to crime near the River
Thames

1829
Under leadership of Sir Robert Peel, the
Metropolitan Police Act of 1829 was
passed;
London Metropolitan Police Department
was the first modern police department

1845
First police department in the United
States created in New York City

➡ The American System of Policing

Very much like in London, Boston was facing a serious problem of crime and disorder. Between 1834 and 1838, three large-scale riots took place throughout the city, highlighting the need for order. The constables, the watch, and the ward were simply ineffective against the chaos. The answer to their problem was found in the London Metropolitan Police template, although the creation of the first modern police department looked vastly different in Boston than it did in London. In 1838, a bill was passed to create a new police department and to appoint police officers. The Boston Police Department was much smaller than the one in England, officers did not wear uniforms, and they were not issued identifying badges.[16] Their presence was felt less than their counterpart's in England, and they were not very successful in reducing crime. In fact, the police department was not created officially until 1854, when both the watch and the ward were disbanded. This is why many people argue that the New York City Police Department is the first official police department in the United States, as it formed in 1845.

Regardless of which department was first (although typically the credit is given to Boston), the United States slowly began to see several cities adopt the police department model, including New Orleans (1852), Baltimore (1853), Chicago (1855), and Philadelphia (1855). It was not until after the Civil War (1861–1865), however, that the United States witnessed a rapid expansion of police departments across the country.[17] Policing in America at that time did not resemble the modern policing of today. American politics were very different in the late 1800s and early 1900s, and police departments were created and used by politicians very differently than the civil service and "protect and serve" focus of today. This is why two leading police scholars, George L. Kelling and Mark H. Moore, have explained that policing, like any profession, is constantly evolving and changing.[18] They identify three distinct eras that policing has moved through in American history: the political era, the reform era, and the community era. In addition, because Kelling and Moore's research was published in 1988 and they could not have foreseen future changes, another author has argued that in the aftermath of the September 11, 2001, terrorist attacks on the United States, the police have entered a new era of policing, that of homeland security (see Table 6.1).[19] These four eras of policing are discussed more fully in the sections that follow (see Figure 6.2).

TABLE 6.1	The Four Eras of Policing			
ELEMENTS	**POLITICAL ERA**	**REFORM ERA**	**COMMUNITY ERA**	**HOMELAND SECURITY ERA**
Authorization	Politics and law	Law and professionalism	Community support (political), law, professionalism	National/international threats (politics), law (intergovernmental), professionalism
Function	Broad social services	Crime control	Broad, provision of service	Crime control, antiterrorism/counterterrorism, intelligence gathering
Organizational Design	Decentralized	Centralized, classical	Decentralized, task forces, matrices	Centralized decision making, decentralized execution
Relationship to Environment	Intimate	Professionally remote	Intimate	Professional
Demand	Decentralized, to patrol and politicians	Centralized	Decentralized	Centralized
Tactics and Technology	Foot patrol	Preventive patrol and rapid response to calls for service	Foot patrol, problem solving, and the like	Risk assessment, police operations centers, information systems
Desired Outcome	Citizen political satisfaction	Crime control	Quality of life and citizen satisfaction	Citizen safety, crime control, antiterrorism

National Institute of Justice

The Political Era (1830s–1920s)

The political era of policing in the United States is considered to range from the 1830s through the 1920s. Despite lasting for nearly 100 years, this time period saw little change in the political orientation of policing. According to Kelling and Moore, the era began in 1838, with the creation of the Boston Police Department, the first modern police force in the United States.[20]

During the political era, the police did many of the things that are common for police to do today, such as patrolling a beat, responding to crimes, and making arrests. In addition, the police also performed functions that would be rather alien to modern-day police departments, such as dealing with stray animals, providing a crude form of counseling, and running soup kitchens. In addition, many police agencies, such as Boston's, housed the homeless in their police barracks on winter nights when the temperatures dropped below freezing. The police performed these functions primarily because they were the only service organizations operating 24 hours a day that could perform these duties. Eventually animal control, social workers, and charitable organizations (for example, the Red Cross) came into existence and took over many of the responsibilities the police performed during this era. Regardless of the services provided by the police of the time, they were not truly organized to protect and serve the public. Instead, they were organized to protect and serve the *political machine*, a political organization with a boss and known for buying elections, corruption, graft, and brutality, especially in preventing certain groups from voting for the opposition.

American politics in the late 1800s was run largely by the political machine. It was a very corrupt system that did anything and everything to

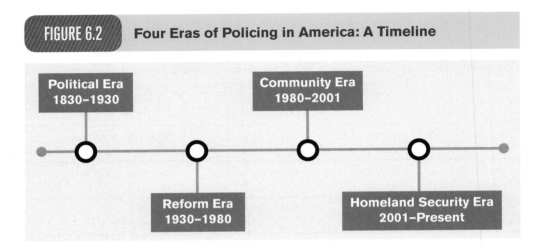

FIGURE 6.2 **Four Eras of Policing in America: A Timeline**

Political Era
1830–1930

Community Era
1980–2001

Reform Era
1930–1980

Homeland Security Era
2001–Present

gain power and, once in power, to keep that power. Elections were far more vicious than they are today, with politicians bribing voters with money, liquor, and other forms of vice, and using strong-men and gangs to prevent certain groups from voting—all depending on which party was currently in power. There was also a strong relationship between politicians and businesses, as well as vice lords. Politicians accepted money from businesses in order to get elected, and once elected, they continued to accept money to prevent any laws from being passed that might hurt those businesses. For instance, if workers wanted to organize into labor unions, businesses would pay politicians to prevent the passage of laws that would allow such organizations to exist, thus remaining in power by pleasing the businesses. The vice lords, who ran illegal operations such as gambling casinos and brothels and kept saloons open on the Sabbath, also had to pay off the politicians in order to keep their corrupt businesses running so that they could remain open and profitable. At the center of all of this, as an extension of the political machine, were the police.

The police during the political era were simply doing the bidding of the political machine. If, for instance, workers wanted to organize a strike or protest against some business, the business owners merely had to notify the politicians, who would dispatch the police to arrest the strikers, beat them into submission, or both, thus protecting the business's interests and keeping the political machine in power. The political machine also needed a means by which to receive payoffs from the vice lords in order for them to continue operating. The police became extortionists for the political machines by telling owners of brothels, gambling halls, and saloons that they had to pay the police weekly for protection. If they did not, the police would close them down. This money was then funneled up to the political machine, with each layer taking a cut. This form of bribery was known as the **spoils system.** For instance, in Chicago it was learned that there was a price list for paying off the police. A massage parlor had to pay the police $25 weekly, a brothel paid between $50 and $100, a gambling hall had to pay $25 per week per gaming table, and for a saloon to open on Sunday the "price" was $50 per month.[21]

spoils system: A politically corrupt system in the 19th century, by which those in political power shared in extortion and bribery money.

Another system, closely related to the spoils system, was the **patronage system**. In 1894 and 1895, the Lexow Committee probed the problems of police corruption in New York City. Testimony collected by the committee exceeded 10,000 pages, and the level of extortion by the police was extensive, including bribery, counterfeiting, voter intimidation, scams, election fraud, and brutality. An important discovery by the committee was the realization that, not only was there a price list for keeping vice establishments open in New York City, but there was also a price list for becoming a police officer and later for being promoted within the department. The political patronage system allowed for the mayor to appoint all government officials, including every police officer, but there was a price to pay to the political machine before that could happen. If someone wanted to be a police officer, he first had to pay a $300–$500 bribe. If a police officer wanted to be promoted to sergeant, he had to pay $1,500–$1,600, and to be promoted to captain, the cost was $12,000–$15,000. This is how the famous New York City Police Department detective, Thomas Byrnes, managed to accumulate $600,000 in savings by the end of his career—on a $5,000 annual salary. By the way, in today's dollars, Byrnes's savings would be the equivalent of over $16 million!

In addition to the patronage and spoils systems, police brutality was a common practice. Police often used force on people rather than making an arrest, or they applied force to carry out some demand by the political machine, such as busting up a strike, or they used brutal means to ensure that various vice lords coughed up the weekly or monthly payoffs. One rather famous police officer in the New York City Police Department was Inspector Alexander "Clubber" Williams, who on his first day as a police officer sent the two biggest toughs to the hospital in order to gain control of his new beat. "There is more law in a policeman's nightstick," Clubber, who was aptly named, liked to say, "than in a decision of the Supreme Court."[22] Another means by which the police employed brutality was known as the **third degree**, in which police commonly beat suspects with their fists, blackjacks, or a section of a rubber hose in order to elicit a confession, regardless of whether the person was guilty of the crime.[23]

The Reform Era (1930–1980)

In response to the corruption and brutality that went with the political era of policing, there were many calls for reform in the early 20th century.[24] It was, however, America's move to Prohibition that would ultimately be the catalyst for reform. As Americans engaged in the "great experiment" of making the import, export, manufacture, and sales of intoxicating liquors illegal, a black market quickly sprang up and the American Mafia rose to power. Instead of curtailing the consumption of illegal alcohol, it appeared to aggravate it,

patronage system: A politically corrupt system in the 19th century, by which government positions (including as police officers) were handed out for political gain.

third degree: A 19th-century police practice that involved using force to keep people in line and beating confessions out of people.

Inspector Alexander "Clubber" Williams was known for his use of brute force to deal with suspects.

Wikimedia Commons

and the police became ever more corrupt and brutal. A national crime commission, known as the Wickersham Commission, was formed in 1928 by President Herbert Hoover and named for its chair, former U.S. attorney general George Wickersham.[25] The commission's reports confirmed what most Americans already knew: The police in the United States were corrupt and brutal, and reforms were badly needed.

The first of the successful reformers, introduced in Chapter 1, was August Vollmer, the police chief from Berkeley, California.[26] There was nothing in Vollmer's past to suggest he would come to be known as the "father of American policing." He had operated a feed store, served in the Philippines during the Spanish-American War, and was a postal carrier from 1900 to 1905. He was asked to run for the position of town marshal in 1905 and won the election by a landslide. Vollmer's predecessor was corrupt, like many cops in the political era, and was on the take from illegal gambling establishments. Everyone wanted Vollmer to clean up the town, and once elected, he did something very strange for policing at the time: He closed down those gambling establishments.

Vollmer believed that police should enforce the law, but he was also kind and compassionate and believed that the police existed to help the citizens of the community (he once babysat a young boy for a month so that his mother could take a job and get on her feet). He was against the political corruption that was common during that time period, and he was vehemently against police use of the third degree. He was truly a progressive police chief, adopting all kinds of reforms. He was the first to give bicycles to all of his officers; he created an early police academy; and he developed in-service training for his officers, the first crime lab in the United States, and the first program for police higher education at the University of California at Berkeley.

Vollmer was also instrumental in educating many of America's future police chiefs, and he influenced them to develop policing as a profession, what has become known as the *professional model of policing*.[27] Vollmer believed that just like doctors, dentists, and lawyers, police officers should be educated in order to do their job and that they should have professional standards and a code of ethics. The other individual responsible for the professionalization of the police was a contemporary of August Vollmer's, J. Edgar Hoover, who was the director of the FBI from 1924 until his death in 1972 (see the "Criminal Justice Pioneer" box in Chapter 3).[28] Hoover also believed that his agents should be professional, well trained, disciplined, and neither corrupt nor brutal. Hoover was instrumental in the creation of the Uniform Crime Reports (see Chapter 3) and the FBI's "Ten Most Wanted List"; he also emphasized crime fighting over all other police duties.

As a result of changes that took place during the reform era, the police became more focused on crime control through the application of the law. To prevent corruption and brutality, the organization of the police became more centralized. As the emphasis was on crime fighting, using the police for preventive patrol became common, and there was a strong emphasis on applying technology to ensure a rapid response by the police.[29] Police communications moved from one-way radios and callboxes, to two-way radios, and eventually the 9-1-1 system. Police also began purchasing "police package" vehicles such as the Ford Crown Vic, Dodge Dart, and Chevy Caprice, which had enhanced features that allowed them to drive fast and run continuously. Further, the use of technology for police detection became commonplace as crime labs became the norm, fingerprinting technology was applied to police work, and criminal investigation became more specialized, focusing on specific crimes. The notion was that the police were the experts and all they needed were the facts of a case to be able to solve it. It turns out that the professionalization of the police had some serious drawbacks, one of them being that it alienated the police from the community.

Community Era (1980–2001)

Police and community relations began to fall apart in the 1960s, fueled by the baby boom—the largest birth cohort the nation has ever known—and issues such as the Vietnam War, women's rights, civil rights, and campus unrest (in which baby boom college students rebelled against college administrators' traditional ways). The police resorted to old tactics to deal with new problems, and the use of police clubs on

J. Edgar Hoover led the FBI for nearly 50 years, from 1924 to 1972.

Wikimedia Commons

college students, water cannons on protestors, and police dogs on civil rights marchers created more animosity between the police and the public. The police, who were now focused primarily on crime fighting, found that crime was rising uncontrollably, riots were breaking out all over the country, and the protests continued. The fact that crime was rising and police-community relations were at an all-time low caused many observers to realize that something had to change; the answer was to find some way to reestablish police and community relations.[30]

The first solution was to train police officers to understand the various populations they served, known more formally as **police-community relations**.[31] Although this helped to foster some communication between police and the community, it was not until two new concepts came along— *community policing* and *problem-oriented policing*—that policing would fundamentally change. The former concept suggested that police should work with the community in partnerships in order to address issues at the local neighborhood level. The latter concept referred to police officers using problem-solving methods to address repetitive problems they encountered while on the beat. Taken together, these two concepts revolutionized policing at the end of the 20th century. They are discussed further in Chapter 7.

Homeland Security Era (2001–Present)

On September 11, 2001, 19 members of Al-Qaeda hijacked four airplanes and crashed two into the twin towers of the World Trade Center in New York City; one into the Pentagon in Arlington, Virginia (where

VIDEO
Houston PD Homeless Outreach

police-community relations: Developed in 1955 and implemented throughout the 1960s, the program that educated police officers on the varying needs of the populations they serve.

the Arlington County Police were the first to respond); and the fourth into the fields near Shanksville, Pennsylvania, because of the bravery of those onboard (the plane was believed to have been heading for the U.S. Capitol or the White House). The United States and its police thus entered the era of **homeland security**. Ever since those tragic events, which may be only vague memories for many of you, the United States has been vigilant against further terrorist attacks. Although many people think of *homeland security* as referring to the U.S. Department of Homeland Security created in 2002, the term also refers to the entire network and infrastructure of federal, state, and local assets that are focused on protecting America's homeland.[32] That includes the police.

Since 9/11, the police have experienced many changes in adapting to their role in homeland security. Police departments across the country have developed homeland security bureaus or units, and states have created Offices of Homeland Security, with roles usually assigned to the state police. All police agencies are learning how to respond better to both terrorist attacks and natural disasters through what is known as the National Response Framework—a set of guiding principles for coordinating the response of all agencies—and through the National Incident Management System—a structured framework for all federal, state, and local government agencies that will respond to such attacks or disasters.[33] The most important aspect of the latter system is the Incident Command System, through which police and other emergency response agencies such as fire departments and emergency medical teams organize their responses.[34] The Incident Command System consists of a management staff to handle large-scale incidents and includes such positions as the incident commander and staff members in charge of personnel, operations, logistics, and finances.

In addition to being prepared for terrorist attacks and natural disasters, the police have also been developing new ways for sharing information and conducting investigations. One way in which the police share information regarding potential threats is through *fusion centers* (see Chapter 7).[35] Located throughout the United States, these fusion centers enable agencies to share and obtain information related to various terrorist threats. A congressional investigation of the fusion centers published in 2012, however, found that there was no evidence of any fusion center uncovering a terrorist threat or plot and that most of the reports they issued were focused on criminal activity, mostly pertaining to drugs and human smuggling.[36] The police have also been involved in *joint terrorism task forces*.[37] These task forces generally consist of federal, state, and local police agencies conducting investigations into potential terror threats. They are almost always comprised of the FBI, which is the lead agency in the United States for investigating terror threats, and the local police agency where the investigation is being

homeland security: The mechanisms put into place after the terrorist attacks of 9/11 in order to better respond not only to terrorist attacks, but also to natural disasters.

Some police departments have created counterterrorism units that are specifically designed to respond to terroristic threats.

Official U.S. Navy Imagery

conducted. The benefit of the joint terrorism task force is that it enhances communication between the agencies and overcomes the problems of jurisdiction. Finally, although many police departments have created *counterterrorism units*, many of these units tend to be minimally staffed and often serve as a point of contact for receiving threat information and coordinating with the fusion centers.[38] In few cases do the counterterrorism units consist of a tactical unit that could respond to terror threats and attacks, such as the New York City Police Department's Counterterrorism Unit.

BEYOND A REASONABLE DOUBT 6.2

Which of the following police eras was motivated primarily by Police Chief August Vollmer?

(a) Political era, (b) Reform era, (c) Community era, (d) Homeland security era, (e) None of the above

---

The answer can be found on page 521.

➡ Policing in America Today

Municipal Police

There are approximately 18,000 police agencies in the United States today. These agencies come in different varieties and sizes (see Figure 6.3). The majority of these agencies are local police departments, which are more officially referred to as **municipal police** agencies, since all towns and cities that are incorporated and have a specific jurisdiction are known as municipalities. These agencies can have anywhere from zero officers (when the police chief quits or retires), to well over 1,000 police officers, and they are located in towns and cities across the United States. The largest municipal police departments in the United States tend to be located in the largest

AUTHOR VIDEO
Policing in America Today

municipal police: The predominant type of law enforcement agency in the United States, representing a municipal government such as a town or city.

FIGURE 6.3   **Types of Police Agencies**

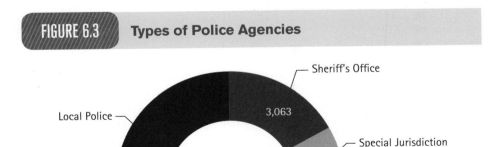

Local Police — 12,501

Sheriff's Office — 3,063

Special Jurisdiction — 1,733

Constable/Marshal — 638

Primary State — 50

Agencies
Total = 17,985

cities, such as New York, Chicago, Los Angeles, Philadelphia, and Houston (see Figure 6.4). The majority of police departments in the United States, however, tend to be much smaller, with an average of 25 officers. The head of the municipal police department is typically a police chief, or sometimes the police commissioner, and this is almost always an appointed position.

Sheriff's Department/Office

The next most common police agency in the United States is the **sheriff's department** or **sheriff's office**.[39] There is a distinction between these

sheriff's department/ office: The highest law enforcement position in a county, providing police services to county residents.

FIGURE 6.4   City Police Departments With 1,000 or More Officers, 2013

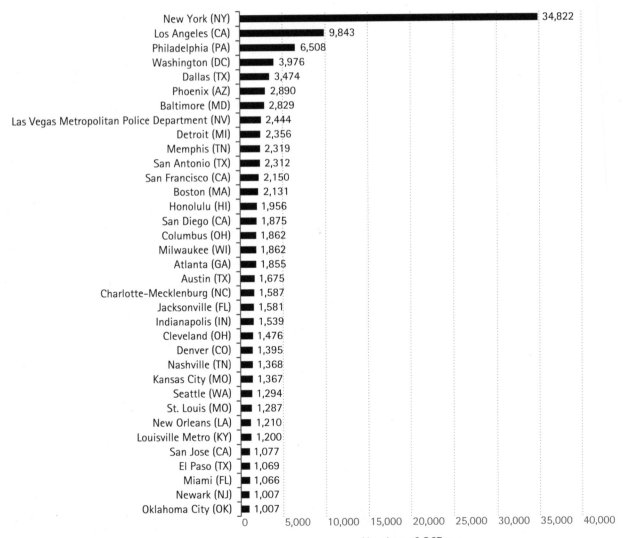

City	Number of Officers
New York (NY)	34,822
Los Angeles (CA)	9,843
Philadelphia (PA)	6,508
Washington (DC)	3,976
Dallas (TX)	3,474
Phoenix (AZ)	2,890
Baltimore (MD)	2,829
Las Vegas Metropolitan Police Department (NV)	2,444
Detroit (MI)	2,356
Memphis (TN)	2,319
San Antonio (TX)	2,312
San Francisco (CA)	2,150
Boston (MA)	2,131
Honolulu (HI)	1,956
San Diego (CA)	1,875
Columbus (OH)	1,862
Milwaukee (WI)	1,862
Atlanta (GA)	1,855
Austin (TX)	1,675
Charlotte-Mecklenburg (NC)	1,587
Jacksonville (FL)	1,581
Indianapolis (IN)	1,539
Cleveland (OH)	1,476
Denver (CO)	1,395
Nashville (TN)	1,368
Kansas City (MO)	1,367
Seattle (WA)	1,294
St. Louis (MO)	1,287
New Orleans (LA)	1,210
Louisville Metro (KY)	1,200
San Jose (CA)	1,077
El Paso (TX)	1,069
Miami (FL)	1,066
Newark (NJ)	1,007
Oklahoma City (OK)	1,007

Number of Officers

Federal Bureau of Investigation

terms. The sheriff's department is subordinate to the county administrator and the sheriff reports to that individual. The sheriff's office is typically an independent government entity, and in this case the sheriff does not report to another public official, only to the people. The United States has just over 3,000 counties, and nearly all of these counties have a sheriff's department or office. These agencies can be very small, like the municipal police, numbering only one or two deputies, or they could have more than 9,000 deputies, as found in the largest county police agency—the Los Angeles County Sheriff's Department. In most cases, the sheriff is an elected official and subordinates are deputy sheriffs rather than police officers.

State Police

Another category of law enforcement agency is the **state police** agency.[40] There are really only 49 state police agencies in the United States, as Hawaii does not have a state police agency, but rather a department of public safety (see the "Criminal Justice and the Media" box in this chapter). Among these 49 state police agencies, there are two different models: the state police model and the highway patrol model. The former represents a police force like any municipal police agency, only the jurisdiction is the entire state, and these officers are generally referred to as the *state police*. The latter is focused on traffic safety along the major highways and interstates, and these officers are generally referred to as *state troopers* or the *state highway patrol*. Most of the state police agencies also patrol the highways and generally maintain a state-level investigation unit. The highway patrol model, however, will typically have a separate bureau of investigation. In Texas, the famous Texas Rangers still exist, and although historically they were their own separate state investigation agency, today they are part of the Texas Department of Public Safety (the official title for the Texas state police). The state police agencies range in size from the Vermont state police department, which has fewer than 1,700 employees, to the California Highway Patrol, which has nearly 120,000 law enforcement employees. State police agencies are typically headed by either a commissioner or a superintendent. Historically, state police agencies are a 20th-century creation: The first was the Pennsylvania State Police, created in 1905, and most other states adopted their agencies by the 1920s or 1930s. Figure 6.5 shows the total numbers of full-time employees in each state's law enforcement agencies.

Constable

A unique category of law enforcement agency in the United States is that of constable.[41] Some states, like Texas and Pennsylvania, have these types of agencies, but they are not widespread elsewhere in the United States. In Texas, constables are elected, and they serve papers and provide courtroom security, but in some cases they perform the same functions as local police in a specific area. In Pennsylvania, they most often protect the election polls and work for the courts, often serving papers and collecting fines. Constables are fully sworn law enforcement officers with full powers of arrest.

state police: A law enforcement agency that represents the state government, often through state-level criminal investigations and the highway patrol.

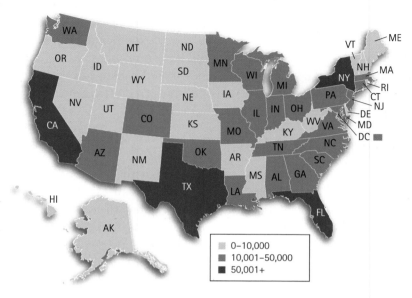

FIGURE 6.5   Full-Time Law Enforcement Employees by State, 2013

- 0–10,000
- 10,001–50,000
- 50,001+

Federal Bureau of Investigation

special jurisdiction police: Police agencies that do not represent a city, county, or state, but rather have a unique jurisdiction or law enforcement responsibility.

Special Jurisdiction Police

Another category of police agencies in the United States is the **special jurisdiction police**. These agencies typically have a specific jurisdiction, and the agency can serve at either the state or the local level. These agencies

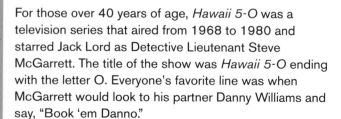

CRIMINAL JUSTICE and the **MEDIA:**
HAWAII 5-O VS. HAWAII 5-0 VS. REALITY

For those over 40 years of age, *Hawaii 5-O* was a television series that aired from 1968 to 1980 and starred Jack Lord as Detective Lieutenant Steve McGarrett. The title of the show was *Hawaii 5-O* ending with the letter O. Everyone's favorite line was when McGarrett would look to his partner Danny Williams and say, "Book 'em Danno."

For all other ages, CBS created a re-imagined *Hawaii 5-0* in 2010, this time with the title ending with a zero (although everyone still pronounces it like the letter O). In this new series, Steve McGarrett, played by Australian

actor Alex O'Loughlin, is a lieutenant commander in the Naval Reserve who teams with Honolulu detective Danny "Danno" Williams.

The concept for the original show is believed to have been based on a special unit that a one-time governor of Hawaii had proposed, but the reality is that Hawaii 5-O, or 5-0, does not exist. Hawaii has a Department of Public Safety, which includes a law enforcement division that oversees the Sheriff Division and the Narcotics Enforcement Division. Otherwise, all policing falls under local (island) responsibility.

can be divided into five general categories (see Table 6.2). The first category is the special jurisdiction of a building or facility, such as public housing, a hospital, public schools, or universities (see the "Criminal Justice and College Students" box in this chapter). The second category includes natural resource officers, often known as game wardens. These officers typically have statewide jurisdiction but are assigned to a specific county or state park. A third category is transportation system and facility police. These are police departments that serve airports, mass transit systems, or ports. The fourth category includes criminal investigation agencies that have a specific focus, such as fraud investigators; fire marshals who conduct arson investigations; or revenue enforcement, which enforces the laws against tax violations. The fifth category covers special enforcement police agencies that enforce very specific laws, such as alcohol laws, gaming laws, or agricultural laws.

Tribal Police

Another category of police in the United States that does not fit neatly into any of the other categories is that of **tribal police**.[42] Many of the Native American tribes in the United States have their own sovereign land,

> **AUTHOR VIDEO**
> Policing and Students on Campuses

> **tribal police:** Police agencies that oversee law enforcement on Native American reservations.

TABLE 6.2	Types of Special Jurisdiction Law Enforcement Agencies, by Number and Full-Time Sworn Personnel	
TYPE	**NUMBER OF AGENCIES**	**FULL-TIME SWORN PERSONNEL**
Public Buildings/Facility	1,126	21,418
Natural Resources	246	14,571
Transportation Systems/Facilities	167	11,508
Criminal Investigation	140	7,310
Special Enforcement	54	2,161
Total	1,733	56,968

CRIMINAL JUSTICE and COLLEGE STUDENTS

CAMPUS POLICE OFFICERS

Select a college or university that you know something about (it could be one you attend or another one). Write down how many officers you think work in that college or university's police department. Do you believe that this is a small, medium, or large department? Next, find the campus police department on the college's website. Is the department organized in a way that you expected it to be organized? Discuss what you found with your classmates.

Tribal police enforce tribal laws, which are different from local, state, and federal laws.

© AP Photo/Ted S. Warren

VIDEO
Small, Rural, Tribal, and Border Regional Center

typically known as reservations. These lands follow the laws of the tribe, not those of the state or the United States, so law enforcement is handled by tribal police. For instance, the Acoma Tribe, located in New Mexico, maintains the Pueblo of Acoma Law Enforcement Services, a tribal police agency serving the people of the famed "Sky City." If a tribe does not have its own police department, then typically the Bureau of Indian Affairs Police (a federal law enforcement agency) performs these duties.

Federal Law Enforcement

The United States does not have a national police force. Our federal government does, however, maintain a number of special jurisdiction police agencies that serve specific functions (see Figure 6.6).[43] These range from small police agencies such as the one located at the

FIGURE 6.6   **Top Ten Federal Law Enforcement Agencies, 2008***

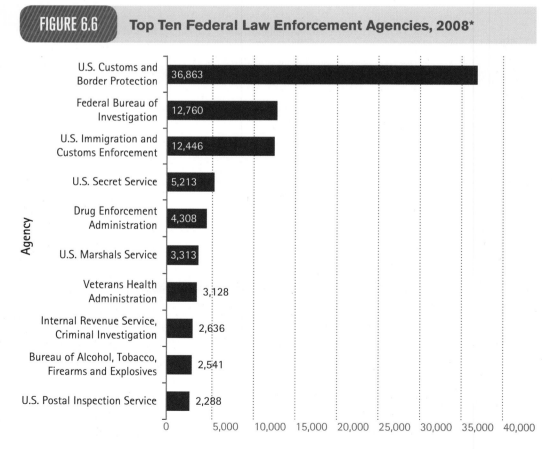

Agency	Number of Full-time Sworn Personnel
U.S. Customs and Border Protection	36,863
Federal Bureau of Investigation	12,760
U.S. Immigration and Customs Enforcement	12,446
U.S. Secret Service	5,213
Drug Enforcement Administration	4,308
U.S. Marshals Service	3,313
Veterans Health Administration	3,128
Internal Revenue Service, Criminal Investigation	2,636
Bureau of Alcohol, Tobacco, Firearms and Explosives	2,541
U.S. Postal Inspection Service	2,288

*Most recent data available.

U.S. Department of Justice

National Zoo in Washington, D.C., or the small police department located at the Hoover Dam, to the U.S. Customs and Border Protection (CBP), which has nearly 37,000 full-time officers. The majority of the federal law enforcement agencies in the United States fall under either the Department of Justice or the Department of Homeland Security. The Department of Justice (DOJ), managed by the U.S. attorney general, oversees the Federal Bureau of Investigation (FBI), the Drug Enforcement Administration (DEA), the Bureau of Alcohol, Tobacco, Firearms and Explosives (ATF), and the U.S. Marshals Service (USMS). Each of these agencies performs specific duties. For example, the FBI is the lead agency for investigating all acts of terrorism in the United States, and the USMS hunts down fugitives from federal justice.

The Department of Homeland Security (DHS), created in 2002 as a response to the terrorist attacks on September 11, 2001, oversees a number of federal law enforcement agencies. These include the CBP, the U.S. Immigration and Customs Enforcement (ICE), the Transportation Security Administration (TSA), the U.S. Coast Guard, and the U.S. Secret Service. The DHS also oversees the Federal Law Enforcement Training Centers, which train nearly all federal law enforcement officers (except for FBI agents, who are trained at the FBI's training center at the Marine Corps Base in Quantico, Virginia). (See the "Help Wanted" box in this chapter.) Each of these agencies also has a specific function, such as the CBP, which works at the United States' borders and other points of entry (for example, at airports); TSA, which provides security at airports throughout the United States; and the Secret Service, which has the dual role of investigating counterfeiting and protecting the president, the vice president, and their families.

The Department of Defense (DOD) maintains a number of federal, or in this case military, police agencies. The DOD itself has a police department, the Department of Defense Police, as does the Pentagon (the headquarters of the U.S. military), known as the Pentagon Force Protection Agency. In addition, each branch of the U.S. military maintains its own police. The U.S. Army has the Military Police and its investigative branch, the Criminal Investigation Division (CID). The U.S. Navy has the Shore Patrol and its investigative branch, the Naval Criminal Investigative Service (NCIS). The Air Force has the Security Forces and the Air Force Office of Special Investigation, and the U.S. Marine Corps maintains its own Military Police. Each of these police forces provides traditional policing in peacetime on military bases or wherever soldiers are deployed. In wartime they serve on the battlefield, providing a variety of functions, including law enforcement, area security, battlefield circulation, prisoner of war camps (for the enemy), and military prisons (for soldiers accused of crimes).

International Policing

Over the past several decades, U.S. police agencies have become more involved in international policing.[44] This typically includes U.S. police officers serving overseas in order to train local police officers or to assist in the

The Naval Criminal Investigative Service, better known as the NCIS, is the investigative branch of the U.S. Navy.

© Joseph Hendricks UPI Photo Service/Newscom

HELP WANTED: FBI SPECIAL AGENT

DUTIES:

- Adhere to strict standards of conduct, foremost being honesty and integrity.

- Endure a rigorous background investigation, credit checks, and a polygraph in order to obtain a Top Secret Security Clearance.

- Pass a Physical Fitness Test (PFT) at least twice during the application process. Upon graduation, agents will also be expected to maintain a level of fitness necessary to effectively respond to life-threatening situations on the job.

- Pass a medical exam, which includes, but is not limited to, meeting visual and hearing standards.

- Successfully complete approximately 18 weeks of employment as a Special Agent trainee, while housed at the FBI Academy in Quantico, VA.

- Upon graduation from the FBI Academy, be available to transfer to one of the FBI's 56 field offices, including San Juan, Puerto Rico, or remote resident agencies (satellite offices) to meet the needs of the FBI. Special Agents rarely return to their processing office. Applicants should ensure that their families are prepared for and support this move.

- Throughout your career, be available for temporary duty assignments, anywhere in the world, on either a temporary or a long-term basis.

- Work a minimum of a 50-hr workweek, which may include odd hours, and be on-call 24/7, including holidays and weekends.

- Carry a firearm and be willing to use deadly force if necessary.

- Be willing and able to participate in arrests, search warrants, raids, and other dangerous assignments, all of which may pose the risk of personal bodily harm.

REQUIREMENTS: Bachelor's degree

ANNUAL SALARY: $59,340–$76,568

Adapted from USAJOBS.gov. Retrieved from https://www.usajobs .gov/GetJob/ViewDetails/377191800

CAREER VIDEO
Former Drug Investigator

policing of the local populace. One entity that does this is the Civilian Police International, known as CivPol, which recruits active police officers to serve as civilian peacekeepers around the world. There is also the United Nations, of which the United States is a member, which maintains a police force known as UNPOL (United Nations Police). These are the so-called "blue hats," for the blue helmets and berets they wear in the areas they police. These police officers also perform peacekeeping operations around the world, and although one can apply directly to UNPOL, the agency tends to hire those with previous police experience. Finally, INTERPOL, the International Police organization, is not really a police force unto itself, but rather an international police organization with 190 member countries that share information and attempt to assist when crimes cross international boundaries.

➡ The Structure of Modern Police Departments

Since the early 20th century, most police departments in the United States have come to be organized in a very similar fashion. Because policing is a paramilitary organization, police departments tend to organize along both a bureaucratic and a military orientation. For instance, they have a *chain of command* that moves from the chief of police at the head of the organization, down through the ranks (often using terms from the military ranks, such as captain, lieutenant, sergeant, corporal, and the like) to the police officers that work the streets. The rank levels tend to follow four categories: (a) command staff, (b) mid-level managers, (c) field supervisors, and (d) line officers. The organizational chart of the Houston Police Department is a good example of a typical police department in the United States. The chief of police is located at the top of the chain of command. He has a staff of personnel who work for him, and these are the command staff (in the figure, the first line of positions under the chief). The next level consists of the mid-level managers, which are the rest of the positions shown in the organizational chart. For instance, near the bottom right is the Traffic Enforcement section. The captain in charge of this function has sergeants under him who serve as field supervisors, who oversee the line officers on the street while they are engaged in traffic enforcement. Other departments follow similar charts. Figure 6.7 shows how the Plymouth Police Department is organized.

For the chief to be able to run the entire police department, he or she has to have these other officers working for him or her. Since one person cannot direct all 5,000 sworn officers, the command staff follows the

FIGURE 6.7   Plymouth Police Department Organizational Chart

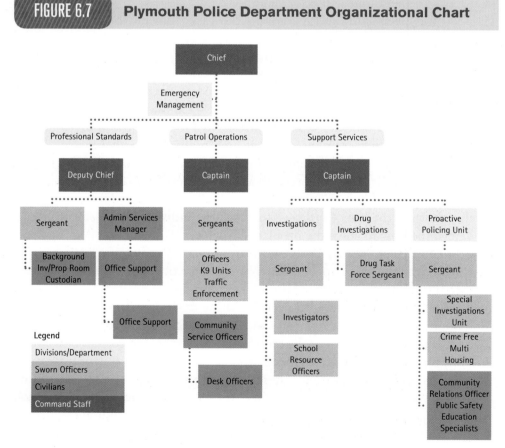

Plymouth Police Department

chief's leadership and direction and then supervises the officers who work for them. Research into organizations and management has shown that most people can effectively manage between five and seven personnel. This is known as the *span of control*. In Houston, for example, the chief has eight people reporting directly to him, so this is still within reason. These personnel have the title of either assistant chiefs or deputy directors, and they oversee specific areas of the police department. Three of them oversee the primary functions of the police department: field operations, or the police officers on the street; investigations, or the detectives; and strategic operations, or the special units such as intelligence, records, and emergency communications. Each of these positions divide the responsibilities of the department, known as the *division of labor*. Nearly every police department, regardless of size, organizes in this fashion: patrol, investigations, and administration. Although the names may be different, the division of labor is the same.

This division of labor also allows for specialization to occur, which is important in any organization, but especially for the police. There are times when the police need a specialized team to respond, such as in a hostage situation. The Houston Police Department can call on the Special Operations section. In other cases, there may be a gang problem, so officers who specialize in gang problems will work for the gang unit. Similarly, in the case of a specific traffic issue, say, a funeral escort, the specialized traffic enforcement unit will be called upon.

It has been said, and it remains the case, that patrol operations (or field operations, as it is called in the Houston Police Department) is the backbone of policing. These officers work 24/7, usually in three shifts: days, evenings, and midnights. In some police departments, these shifts rotate, so that all officers will rotate through days, evenings, and midnights. In other departments, the shifts are fixed and officers always work the same shift. Some departments also have a fourth shift, often called the power shift, which overlaps evenings and midnights, as that is usually the patrol division's busiest time for calls-for-service. These police officers then respond to calls, both emergency and nonemergency, and they work to address the problems of crime, disorder, and traffic-related issues. They do this through the use of *police discretion*, the individual officer's ability to determine how to solve the problems to which he or she is called. Officers may simply deal with a problem informally, they may issue some type of warning, or they may apply the law by issuing a ticket or making an arrest. (See the "Ethical Decision Making" box in this chapter.)

The police officers who perform these duties are first and foremost human beings who for a variety of reasons decide to become police officers. If they can pass all of the required tests, which can consist of written, oral, physical, background, medical, psychological, and polygraph examinations, they may be hired. These individuals will then undergo training at a police academy and then field training on the street, both of which they must pass in order to remain police officers. Although many people apply, not everyone is successful in becoming a police officer. Those who become police officers tend to be males. In the United States, just under

ETHICAL DECISION MAKING

TO ARREST OR NOT?

Officer Marion is a campus police officer at Hypothetical University. Officer Marion loves his job but sometimes gets a little tired of dealing with complaints about students partying in the dorms. One night, as his shift is about to end, he is driving back to the police station when he sees a student drinking what appears to be a beer. Initially he remembers how he occasionally drank beer when he was a college student. The student is not creating any disturbances, but he looks like he is underage. Officer Marion really wants to get home so that he can spend time with his son, who is celebrating his 10th birthday.

YOU DECIDE

1. Should Officer Marion stop the student? What factors might influence this decision?

2. What are some things that could go wrong if the officer decides not to stop the student?

3. Do you think a campus police officer would handle this situation differently than a local police officer? Explain.

12% (or 1 in 8) of police officers are female (see Figure 6.8). Larger cities tend to hire more female police officers and more females as civilian workers. This trend has remained stable over time despite efforts to increase the proportion of female police officers.

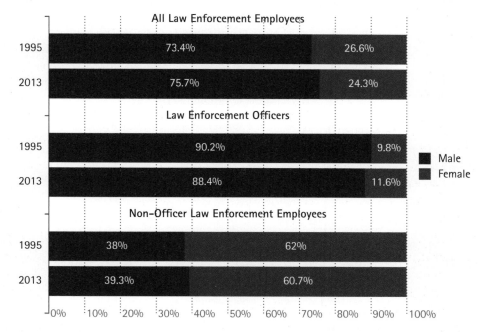

FIGURE 6.8 Law Enforcement Employees, by Sex, 1995 and 2013

National Crime Justice Reference Service

Approximately 25% of the police officers in the United States, or about 1 in 4, are racial or ethnic minorities.[45] The majority tend to be Black/African American (11.9%) and Hispanic/Latino (10.3%). Although the percentages remain relatively low, police departments across the country have been actively recruiting for minority police officers since the mid to late 1990s.

BEYOND A REASONABLE DOUBT 6.3

There are approximately how many police departments in the United States?

(a) 180, (b) 1,800, (c) 18,000, (d) 180,000

The answer can be found on page 521.

Just the Facts: Chapter Summary

- Jurisdiction determines the area of responsibility and authority granted to the police.

- Human societies advance from bands to tribes to chiefdoms and, finally, states.

- The frankpledge system was a formal system of organizing people to informally police themselves.

- England developed sheriffs, constables, and the watch-and-ward system, which served as its rudimentary form of policing for 500 years.

- Sir Robert Peel drew on the work of Henry Fielding and Patrick Colquhoun to create the first bona fide police department through the passage of the London Metropolitan Police Act of 1829.

- The first police department in the United States was the Boston Police Department, formed in 1838.

- Policing in the United States has moved through four eras: the political era (1830s–1920s), the reform era (1930–1980), the community era (1980–2001), and the homeland security era (2001–present).

- The patronage system was a corrupt means of appointing police officers, who then engaged in the spoils system to fund themselves and the political machine.

- The Wickersham Commission revealed widespread use of the third degree and police brutality in the 1920s and called for reform.

- August Vollmer, America's first police reformer, developed the professional model of policing.

- The community era entailed bringing the police and public closer together through problem solving and community policing.

- The homeland security era came about as a response to the 9/11 terrorist attacks. It involves incident command, fusion centers, joint terrorism task forces, and counterterrorism units.

- There are approximately 18,000 police agencies today, including municipal police, sheriffs, state police, constable, marshals, special jurisdiction police, tribal police, federal law enforcement, and, to a limited degree, international police.

- Police organize with a chain of command, span of control, division of labor, and specialization, typically in three areas: patrol, investigations, and administration.

- Police officers in the United States are, on average, 88% male and 12% female, and 25% of officers have a racial or ethnic minority background.

Critical Thinking Questions

1. What does the word *jurisdiction* mean, and how does it apply to the police?

2. Anthropologists talk about four types of societies. Describe each type and how they relate to each other.

3. Explain the English system of rudimentary policing that existed for 500 years.

4. Henry Fielding and Patrick Colquhoun were early experimenters in developing the police. Who were they, and how did they experiment with their ideas?

5. Who is considered the father of policing, and why?

6. There are said to be four eras in American policing. Describe each one in detail.

7. Who is considered the father of *American* policing, and why?

8. How many police agencies exist in the United States, and what do they look like?

9. Describe how the typical police department in the United States is organized.

Key Terms

Bow Street
   Runners (182)
constable (181)
frankpledge
   system (179)
homeland security (190)
hue and cry (180)

jurisdiction (178)
kin policing (179)
Metropolitan Police Act
   of 1829 (182)
municipal police (191)
night watch (180)
patronage system (187)

police-community
   relations (189)
sheriff (181)
sheriff's
   department/office (192)
special jurisdiction
   police (194)

spoils system (186)
state police (193)
thief-taker system (182)
third degree (187)
tribal police (195)
ward (180)

⑧SAGE edgeselect™

edge.sagepub.com/payne

Sharpen your skills with SAGE edge select!

With carefully crafted tools and resources to encourage review, practice, and critical thinking, SAGE edge select gives you the edge needed to master course content. Take full advantage of open-access key term flashcards, practice quizzes, and video content. Diagnostic pre-tests, a personalized study plan, and post-tests are available with an access code.

POLICE STRATEGIES

©alessandro0770/Veer

WHEN I FIRST ENTERED POLICING AS A SUMMER COP in 1986, there was never any talk about police strategies, just good policing. Veteran police officers taught me how to respond to calls-for-service, how to spot criminal activity, and how to conduct investigations and write reports. When I returned to my undergraduate studies in criminal justice, I learned of several new and "cutting-edge" ideas in policing, including broken windows theory, community policing, and problem-oriented policing. Although people were talking and writing about these new police strategies, few agencies were implementing them.

By the early 1990s, when I became a full-time police officer, the agency I worked for decided to test the concepts of community policing in a single neighborhood. I was sent to a community policing training session, but still being a rookie, I was never assigned to the community policing unit. Prior to my leaving the department to enter a career in academia, the agency had expanded the community policing program to two neighborhoods. It was a slow and tentative implementation.

By the mid-1990s, however, the community policing strategy was becoming popular with police departments across the nation because of federal government dollars that were associated with the program. In addition, problem-oriented policing was more widespread and was made popular by its ties to both community policing and the ever-popular annual problem-oriented policing conference. Since that time, new police strategies have been implemented, with names like *zero-tolerance policing*, *pulling-levers policing*, *hot spots policing*, *intelligence-led policing*, and a whole host of other new names. All of this has happened in just 30 years.

The concept of doing "good policing" still exists. It is what police officers do on a daily basis when working patrol. But the student of policing must become familiar with all of the varying police strategies, because most police departments today implement at least one, if not multiple strategies. Being familiar with and understanding these many strategies is important to understanding policing today.

—Willard M. Oliver

LEARNING OBJECTIVES

After reading this chapter, students will be able to:

7.1 Describe the findings from classic police strategy studies

7.2 Explain why police departments conduct patrols

7.3 Describe how the broken windows theory influenced policing

7.4 Compare and contrast police patrol with community policing

7.5 Explain the basics of problem-oriented policing

7.6 Describe at least five types of targeted policing

7.7 Explain how CompStat is applied as a police management strategy

7.8 Evaluate the influence of homeland security and terrorism on policing

ADMISSIBLE or INADMISSIBLE Evidence

Read the statements that follow. If the statement is true, circle *admissible*. If the statement is false, circle *inadmissible*. Answers can be found on page 518.

1. **Admissible Inadmissible** The Kansas City Preventive Patrol Experiment found that police officers on routine patrol prevent crime.
2. **Admissible Inadmissible** The Kansas City Rapid Response Study found that the faster that police officers arrive at a crime scene, the more likely they are to solve the crime.
3. **Admissible Inadmissible** The RAND Corporation Criminal Investigation Study found that what solves most crimes is good old-fashioned criminal investigations conducted by detectives.
4. **Admissible Inadmissible** A *split patrol* refers to half of the officers on patrol being committed to responding to calls-for-service, while the other half are free to conduct their own investigations.

(Continued)

(Continued)

5.   **Admissible   Inadmissible**   Broken windows theory suggest that run-down neighborhoods, where things like broken windows are left unrepaired, communicate that no cares about the neighborhood, thus inviting criminals to commit their crimes in that community.

6.   **Admissible   Inadmissible**   Community policing is a form of targeted policing aimed solely at crime reduction.

7.   **Admissible   Inadmissible**   The SARA model was created as a means of teaching police officers how to implement problem-oriented policing.

8.   **Admissible   Inadmissible**   CompStat was designed to be first and foremost a management tool.

For starters, a *strategy* refers to both a broad set of ideas and a detailed set of plans for achieving a specific goal, usually over an extended period of time. **Police strategies**, then, refers to a broad set of ideas and a set of plans for achieving the primary goal of the police: reducing crime and disorder. Not all police strategies are equal, however, and it is certainly not the case that one strategy fits all. In fact, policing scholar Larry Hoover cautions us to understand that each of these strategies is not an either-or proposition; agencies often employ many different police strategies in order to address the problems of crime and disorder in their jurisdictions.[1] Further, police strategies often overlap one another, they may sound very similar to each other, and multiple strategies may be implemented at the same time. For instance, the community policing strategy may be deployed in tandem with the problem-oriented policing strategy.

To help you gain a better understanding of the strategies that police use for crime control, in this chapter we first discuss the development of policing in the 20th century and the strong belief that the police deter crime. At least that was until studies conducted on policing challenged this belief. We then explain how the many different police strategies came to be, something that is largely a late-20th-century phenomenon. Next, we discuss strategies for deploying officers on the street and the most commonly used police strategies today, including community policing, problem-oriented policing, and CompStat, in addition to some of the newer strategies such as pulling-levers policing, evidence-based policing, and intelligence-led policing. Finally, we address police strategies as they relate to police detectives and criminal investigations.

police strategies: Broad concepts for how best to deploy the police in order to effectively reduce crime and disorder.

Planning meetings are a routine part of the daily operations of most police departments.

© AP Photo/Damian Dovarganes

➡ Police Strategy Studies

As policing was professionalized and reformed in the early 20th century, policing in America developed with the intent of addressing the problems of crime through both deterrence and the solving of crimes. Over time, the following notions built up related to policing: (a) Police officers deter crime through random patrols; (b) the faster that police officers arrive on the scene, the more likely they are to solve the crime; and (c) given the facts of a case and all the latest technology, the police can solve crimes through their expertise. All of this turned out to be wrong.

In the 1960s, with protests against the Vietnam War, demonstrations over civil rights and women's rights, campus unrest, and riots in the street, crime was on the rise and many of the old police tactics were simply not working. President Lyndon Johnson created a crime commission to look at the problems of crime in America and asked for recommendations for change. When the President's Commission on Law Enforcement and Administration of Justice issued its report, *The Challenge of Crime in a Free Society*, many of its recommendations found their way into the **Omnibus Crime Control and Safe Streets Act of 1968.**[2] This bill added or changed numerous laws and allowed for the expenditure of federal funds to improve local policing. The bill created criminal justice programs in colleges and universities across the United States, and it helped to fund police officers earning degrees through what were known as LEEP (Law Enforcement Education Program) funds. The bill also set aside money for police research and highlighted the need for empirical studies in the policing field. For too long, policing had operated on widely held beliefs and not on empirical evidence; therefore, policing research was highly encouraged and money was made available to support it.

In 1970 the Ford Foundation created a police development fund in order to support scholarly police research. The fund was soon renamed the Police Foundation, and it still exists today. The Police Foundation commissioned what would become one of the first empirical studies in policing that attempted to assess the question of police deterrence: Do police officers driving around the neighborhood deter crime through their mere presence? George L. Kelling was the lead researcher, and the study, which took place between 1972 and 1973, was published in 1974.[3] Kelling's study focused on four questions: (a) Would the public notice changes in the level of police patrols? (b) Would the different levels have an impact on crime? (c) Would citizens' fear of crime change with different levels of police patrols? and (d) Would citizen satisfaction change with the various levels of police patrols?

The Kansas City Preventive Patrol Experiment

The Kansas City Preventive Patrol Experiment divided Kansas City into a number of areas and assigned each area one of three treatments (see Figure 7.1). The first set of treatment areas received no routine patrol, and officers were told to stay out of those areas unless they received a call from a citizen. For the second set of treatment areas, police deployment was left unchanged. The police conducted police patrols at the same level of staffing that they always had. The third set of treatment areas, however, would receive two to

AUTHOR VIDEO
Police on Campus

Omnibus Crime Control and Safe Streets Act of 1968: A federal law that provided funding for state and local police.

President Lyndon B. Johnson's Commission on Law Enforcement and Administration of Justice revolutionized the criminal justice process by promoting new laws, funding, and education programs.

© Bettmann/CORBIS

JOURNAL
Another Word on
KCPPE

FIGURE 7.1   **Results of Kansas City Preventive Patrol Experiment**

Treatment Area 2: Police Deployment Remained the Same

Treatment Area 1: Police Enter Areas Only When Called

Treatment Area 3: Police Patrol Doubled or Tripled

No Impact on Crime Rate

Policefoundation.org; © iStockphoto.com/nuranvectorgirl; © iStockphoto.com/AlonzoDesign

three times as many police officers as normal. The researchers anticipated that in the areas where the police presence was all but removed, citizens would notice the change, crime and fear of crime would increase, and citizen satisfaction with the police would decrease; in the areas that received the usual treatment, citizens would see no change in crime or fear of crime, and citizen satisfaction would remain unchanged; and finally, in the areas in which two to three times as many officers were patrolling, citizens would notice the change, crime and fear of crime would decrease, and citizen satisfaction would increase. After running this quasi-experiment and analyzing their findings, the researchers were stunned to find absolutely no changes. Citizens had not noticed the changes in police levels. Crime rates remained stable in all three areas. Fear of crime and citizen satisfaction with the police did not vary. The impact of this landmark study had police professionals rethinking police deployment, and it solidified for the next 30 years the notion that police do not deter crime.

Kansas City Rapid Response Study

A police study conducted in 1976 by the Kansas City Police Department assessed another long-held belief in policing circles: the notion that the faster the police respond to a crime, the more likely the crime will be solved.[4] Findings from the study, known as the Rapid Response Study, were reminiscent of what Kelling had found in the other Kansas City study. Other than for crimes that were in progress, faster police response times had no effect on the resolution of crimes. It did not seem to matter whether the

Police officers spend much of their time patrolling their communities. Research is mixed on the effectiveness of patrol.

© Bob Daemmrich / Alamy

police responded to a call within a few minutes or 20 minutes or 30 minutes. Their chances for eventually solving the crime remained the same. The researchers explored more deeply why this was the case and found that citizens waited, on average, 40 minutes to call the police. It didn't matter whether the police showed up at the crime scene 41 minutes after the crime had been committed or 60 minutes after. The issue was not to get police to the crime scene faster; it was to get citizens to call the police immediately after a crime had occurred. Once again, another long-held belief in policing circles was contradicted by empirical evidence.

The Rapid Response Study found that the amount of time it took officers to respond to a crime scene was not related to solving the crime.

© UpperCut Images/Getty Images

RAND Criminal Investigation Study

Finally, the RAND Corporation conducted a study on police detectives in 1977.[5] The researchers wanted to know how successful police detectives were when it came to solving crimes. It was believed that police detectives, through technology and skill, solved crimes. This idea had taken root because, throughout the 20th century, the police had learned to adapt technology to crime scene investigations, to use crime labs, autopsy reports, fingerprints, and eventually laser technology to find trace evidence. Then, above and beyond the technology, there was the number of personnel assigned to the detective bureaus and the amount of training and education given to these personnel. In other words, detectives, like patrol officers, took up a large share of a police department's resources. The RAND Corporation was asked by the National Institute of Law Enforcement and Criminal Justice to find out how successful detectives were at their jobs. After all, the Kansas City studies found that random patrol and rapid response, long held to be effective, were not.

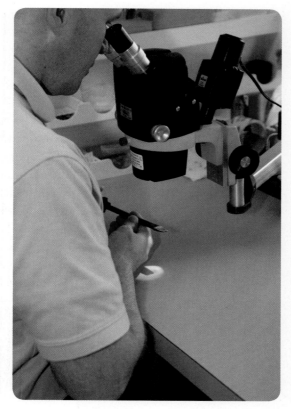

You have probably already figured out what the RAND Criminal Investigation Study showed. Simply put, detective work was found to be superficial, routine, and nonproductive. More specifically, of all the cases that the detectives investigated, only 2.7% of them were cleared through techniques employed by the investigators. In other words, 97.3% of all cases investigated by detectives were solved by the victim, by witnesses, or (less frequently) by the police officers arriving on the scene, *not* by the detectives. All of the personnel and technology put into enhancing criminal investigations simply served as a means for moving cases through the system or were used primarily to corroborate what victims, witnesses, and police officers had already told detectives. Only very rarely (well, 2.7% of the time) did a detective actually solve the crime! Figure 7.2 shows recent clearance rates for a variety of offenses reported to the police.

Technology does not typically solve crimes, but it may help to move cases through the justice process.

© Mikael Karlsson/Alamy

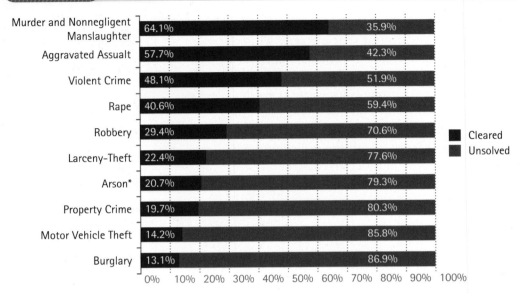

FIGURE 7.2   Offenses Cleared by Arrest or Exceptional Means, 2013

*Not all agencies submit reports for arson to the FBI. As a result, the number of reports the FBI uses to compute the percent of offenses cleared for arson is less than the number it uses to compute the percent of offenses cleared for all other offenses.

Federal Bureau of Investigation

Based on the Kansas City research, it is reasonable to conclude that these offenses were cleared by information that victims, witnesses, and police officers gave to detectives.

Think about this. In just three years, from 1974 to 1977, three of the main pillars of policing were knocked down. Police driving around in random patrols did not deter crime. Police officers responding rapidly to calls did not increase their chance of solving crimes. Finally, throwing more personnel and technology into criminal investigations did not solve most crimes; people coming forward to tell the police what they saw or knew led to crimes being solved. As you can imagine, the late 1970s became a time of upheaval for the police. If the long-held assumptions of policing did not work, what did? Criticism, challenges, and ideas followed, generally in that order. Policing was deemed ineffective and inefficient. The police must change. But how? When that question was asked, the ideas came—new innovations, new ways of policing: the police strategies.

BEYOND A REASONABLE DOUBT 7.1

Which of the following 1970s police studies led to the conclusion that the police do not deter crime?

(a) Kansas City Preventive Patrol Experiment, (b) Kansas City Rapid Response Study, (c) RAND Criminal Investigation Study, (d) The Newark Foot Patrol Study

---

The answer can be found on page 521.

➡ Police Patrol Deployment

From the inception of policing in the United States, even as far back as the days of sheriffs and the watch-and-ward system, the traditional method for police patrol was either by foot or by horse. Policing conducted in the towns and cities primarily saw officers walking a beat; in the more rural parts of America, police patrol was on horseback. In the 1890s, there was a sudden craze over the bicycle, and police officers from New York to St. Louis to Berkeley, California, began riding patrol on bicycles. This stage was short-lived, however, for when Henry Ford's mass production of the automobile began in earnest in the early 20th century, police officers quickly adopted the new form of transportation, and motor vehicles became the primary means for police patrol. So, when O. W. Wilson said that police patrol was the backbone of policing, he assuredly meant police motor vehicle patrols.[6] Police officers almost always rode in tandem in the first 40 years, but Wilson became a strong advocate for the single-officer patrol car, which became the norm.

Many additional forms of transportation have since become common in policing. In addition to automobile patrols, police today often use everything from golf carts and ATVs (all-terrain vehicles) to mopeds and motorcycles. Water patrols use various-sized boats, from small, sleek speed boats to pontoon boats to large search-and-rescue watercraft. Larger metropolitan and state police agencies often employ aircraft in their patrols, mostly helicopters, but some have small airplanes, and more recently many have begun adopting drones (unmanned aerial vehicles). When policing moved into the community era, many police departments returned to having their officers conduct foot, mounted, and bicycle patrols, as it made them more accessible to the public. One of the more interesting means of police patrol today, seen mostly in densely populated areas, parks, and tourist areas in cities, is by Segway.

JOURNAL
Police Foot Patrol

Then and now: One of the first forms of police patrol was bike patrol. Today, officers also patrol on Segways.

© iStockphoto/HultonArchive; © Reuters/CORBIS

These forms of police patrol are focused on several key goals that date as far back as Sir Robert Peel and the creation of the first police department in London, England, in 1829. The police patrol was created to deter crime and maintain public order. In the event that crimes or disorder occurred, the police were then able to respond to these calls-for-service. Research has shown that routine patrols have four primary functions: preventive patrol, calls-for-service, officer-initiated contacts, and administrative duties.[7] **Preventive patrol** is focused on maintaining a visible presence in the community in order to deter criminal behavior and disorderly conduct. As we learned earlier, police driving around in random patrols do not prevent crime, but crime deterrence remains an element of the reason for police patrols. **Calls-for-service** refers to emergency (9-1-1) and nonemergency calls that citizens place to the police, or they may simply involve citizens flagging down the police. In these cases, citizens are making the request for assistance. By contrast, **officer-initiated contacts** occur when officers see some type of traffic infraction or when a misdemeanor or felony is committed in their presence. Finally, *administrative duties* involve filling out patrol vehicle inspections, updating policy manuals, and all of the paperwork that documents officers' actions and the actions of others. See the "Ethical Decision Making" box in this chapter for a look at the kinds of decisions officers confront on patrol.

The police response to calls-for-service has always been one of the four functions of police patrols. Since the creation of the 9-1-1 system, calls-for-service have come to take up a majority of police officers' time. Started in Baltimore, Maryland, in 1968 with an Omnibus Crime Control and Safe Streets Act grant, the 9-1-1 system was well received and began to spread rapidly across the nation. Interestingly, it became a common feature of policing in the late 1970s at the same time that police departments were

preventive patrol: The police strategy by which police officers patrol their beats with the intention that their presence would deter crime.

calls-for-service: The phone calls placed to the police for which a police officer is dispatched.

officer-initiated contacts: The police function by which police officers initiate investigations rather than waiting for calls-for-service.

ETHICAL DECISION MAKING

A POLICE RIDE ALONG

Claire, a student taking an Introduction to Policing class online, has arranged to do a police "ride along" for extra credit. Very excited the night before the ride along, she barely gets any sleep. She arrives for the ride along 15 minutes early and is greeted by Officer Johnson, a patrol officer who has been in the department for four years.

Officer Johnson and Claire ride around for two hours before the officer decides to pull over a car for speeding. After the car stops, Claire walks with the officer so that she can watch as the officer and the driver discuss the speeding violation. Claire is surprised

when she looks in the car and sees that the driver is her friend, Chloe.

After Officer Johnson learns that Claire and Chloe know each other, the officer asks the policing student, "Do you believe I should give Chloe a ticket?"

YOU DECIDE

1. If you were Claire, would you recommend giving Chloe a ticket?

2. Should the officer have asked Claire to make a recommendation?

not rehiring officers because of the Kansas City Preventive Patrol Experiment. It had been reasoned that if police officers do not deter crime, police departments only needed officers to respond to calls. Yet, as the 9-1-1 system took off, there were more calls-for-service, and when someone calls the 9-1-1 emergency system, unless it can be verified that the call is a mistake, a police officer must respond. By the late 1980s, police departments were overwhelmed with 9-1-1 calls, and police officers going on patrol could often expect to run from one call to the next with no time left for their other duties. Combined with nonemergency calls, the whole system was becoming unmanageable.[8]

Broken windows contribute to the level of disorder in a neighborhood and can increase the perception that an area has a problem with crime.

© iStockphoto.com/NoDerog

Police departments began exploring possible responses to the problem by changing how they deployed their officers. Many departments opted to go with a **differential police response** (DPR) system.[9] DPR was a strategy that was very similar to medical triage. When the police receive calls-for-service, many are clear emergencies in which a police response is needed immediately (for example, robbery in progress, rape, carjacking), whereas others may not even need a police officer to respond because the problem can be handled over the phone (for example, minor traffic accidents, lost valuables). Classifying the calls into different categories allowed for the police to respond differently to the calls they received, thus better managing one of their greatest resources: a police officer's time. The pitfall of using a DPR system, however, is that citizens often do not agree with the classification of their call. When they find themselves involved in an accident or the victim of a crime, for them it is the most important problem in the world, and when the police do not respond quickly or at all, no matter how much they are educated on the reasons for the DPR system, they may still develop a negative attitude toward the police.

Another response to the problem came to be known as **split patrols**.[10] To manage the need to perform all of the functions of policing, police departments would split their patrol forces into two groups: one to respond to calls-for-service, the other to conduct routine patrol. The two groups would rotate, each taking their turn at the calls-for-service, which usually entailed running from call to call. A study conducted in Wilmington, Delaware, found that the split patrol (sometimes called split force) system improved both police call-handling and patrol productivity, while at the same time enhancing police professionalism and police accountability.[11] The downside to this system is that the officers who are conducting patrols or other duties are not obligated to respond to calls unless they are "officer needs assistance" calls or for a felony in progress, while the other officers are responding to call after call and seeing the number of calls pending backing up. As one police officer said about the use of split patrols, "The regular officers were really upset while the other guys weren't doing anything."[12]

differential police response: The use of different types of responses for different types of calls in order to deal with a high call volume versus low number of police resources.

split patrols: The policing strategy that involves splitting the police patrol into two groups; one is responsible for calls-for-service, and the other conducts police patrols and investigations.

Broken Windows Theory and Policing

In March 1982, George L. Kelling and James Q. Wilson, a political scientist actively involved in crime policy research, coauthored a paper that woud contribute greatly to changes in American policing.[13] The ideas they shared were both widely and well received, ultimately coming to be known as the broken windows theory.

In their article, Wilson and Kelling talked about how Newark, New Jersey, had started a foot patrol program in order to reduce crime, but although citizen satisfaction with the police increased, crime did not decrease. They argued that each neighborhood is different, but each neighborhood faces two problems: crime itself and fear of crime. They stated that sometimes fear of crime is not necessarily derived from actual crime, but from the perceptions of crime, and that how people perceive crime can also vary. They also articulated that people's fear of crime is often based on the level of disorder they see in their neighborhoods, based on so-called *environmental cues* or *social signaling* (see the "Criminal Justice and College Students" box in this chapter). For instance, if a home has a broken window and that window is not fixed, not only does it send a signal to criminals that no one cares about the neighborhood, but also it tells the people who live there or visit that no one cares. If no one cares and the window does not get fixed, it creates a sense of fear in the community, and it may also invite criminal behavior. Thus was born the *broken windows theory*.

Recognizing how a community decays and generates both fear and crime also tells us how to reverse this downward spiral. The goal is to demonstrate that people care about their communities and that they will not tolerate the crime and disorder. Citizens who live in a neighborhood

CRIMINAL JUSTICE and **COLLEGE STUDENTS**

BROKEN WINDOWS IN OUR LIVES

Have you ever driven or walked into a neighborhood and said to yourself "I shouldn't be here. This is not a safe neighborhood"? Assuming you have, as most of us have had this experience, what was it about the neighborhood that made you come to that realization? List as many reasons as you can.

Now, have you ever driven or walked into a neighborhood and said to yourself "Wow, this is a really nice neighborhood!"? Again, assuming you have, what was it about this neighborhood that made you think that? List as many reasons as you can.

Next, compare your answers for the two neighborhoods. Are there things in common that just had different states of being? For instance, say that you noticed the streets in both neighborhoods. In the not-so-nice neighborhood, you saw potholes and trash, whereas in the nicer neighborhood, there were no potholes and no trash.

Finally, in a small group or as a class, discuss your answers to both questions. Do others share your views on what makes an unsafe versus a safe neighborhood?

have to show they care about their community by using informal control mechanisms, such as fixing broken windows right away, covering over graffiti, or calling public works or the police when a problem first arises. It is important here to understand the difference between formal social control (the police) and informal social control (the community). A leading police scholar describes this difference to large gatherings of police officers by asking them to raise their hands if they were afraid of the police when they were growing up. He says a few hands always go up. He then asks how many people were afraid of their mothers. He says every hand in the room goes up, including his. That, he explains, is informal social control![14]

The police role in all of this, according to Wilson and Kelling, "is to reinforce the informal control mechanisms of the community itself."[15] They realized this could not be done by the police alone, that it would require citizens to become involved in order to reassert their authority over their neighborhoods. However, the police could participate by first cleaning up the criminal problem through arrest and then by asserting their visible authority to deter future crimes, as long as citizens cleaned up their neighborhoods and reasserted their own authority. This strategy requires a police-community partnership, and thus became one of the motivating factors for the adoption of community policing as the United States moved in to the community era of policing.

➡ Community Policing

The concept of **community policing** developed in response to a number of factors that merged together to create what became the predominant method of policing in the 1980s and 1990s.[16] The first factor had to do with police and community relations. In early policing there was little to no concern for developing and maintaining community relations. In the early 20th century, there was a realization that the public needed to be informed, so police departments began developing public relations offices, usually working out of the police chief's office. This type of relationship, however, was simply a one-way communication. The police told the community what they felt was necessary for the public to know. As the civil rights movement developed in the 1950s, a new program developed out of Michigan State University, called police-community relations. In this case, the idea was to teach police officers about the various populations they police and to recognize that each population may perceive the police differently and may have different needs. This involved educating the police on the unique perspectives of women, minorities, juveniles, the elderly, the handicapped, and the mentally ill. The information gathered was helpful, but these programs became a reverse one-way communication, with the community (or at least the instructors) telling the police what they should know and do.

In the early 1970s, **team policing** developed as a better method of improving relations. The idea was to assign certain officers to specific neighborhoods, so that they might better develop police and community relationships. Unfortunately, the police officers assigned to team policing were often

community policing:
A philosophy and strategy of policing aimed at bringing the police and community together in partnerships to address the problems specific to their neighborhoods.

team policing: An early 1970s program that assigned officers permanently to neighborhoods to work with citizens; a forerunner to community policing.

those who did not perform well on the street or were close to retirement. When the teams were staffed adequately with those who performed well, they were typically hampered by having little authority and almost nothing in the way of additional resources. The next evolution of these concepts was to develop a program that would be a two-way communication between the police and citizens and to make team policing the norm throughout the police department so that officers were always assigned to specific neighborhoods and worked with them to address the problems of crime and disorder.

The second factor involved in the development of community policing was the findings of the empirical studies conducted in the 1970s—the Kansas City Preventive Patrol Experiment, the Kansas City Rapid Response Study, and the RAND study—which demonstrated that the police need the assistance of the citizenry to solve crimes and that for too long the police had distanced themselves from the citizens all in the name of professionalism. The so-called **blue wall** that had been built between the police and the people needed to be broken down.

The third factor was the broken windows theory, which demonstrated that if the police and the community work together to stop the decay of a neighborhood and reestablish a sense of community, they can alleviate many of the problems of crime and disorder.

Community policing began to develop in earnest in the early 1980s. It became the most talked about method of policing by the late 1980s, and the 1990s came to be known as the decade of community policing. Yet, one author noted that the community policing of the early 1980s and that of the mid-1990s were assuredly different. He explained that the community era of policing went through **three generations** (see Figure 7.3).[17] First was the *innovation generation*, which ran from 1979 to about 1986. During this time, community policing was more of a local phenomenon among innovative police departments testing out ideas for enhancing police-community partnerships. Some of the early innovators included Madison, Wisconsin; Flint, Michigan; and Newark, New Jersey. In some cases these experiments or demonstration projects involved adopting foot patrols to enhance police-public contacts or establishing police community centers in specific neighborhoods. The primary goal of these programs, which were soon referred to as community policing programs, was to bring the police and the community together to work in partnership to improve the quality of life in the neighborhood.

The second generation was the *diffusion generation*, which ran from 1987 to 1994. During this time, successful programs began to spread across the United States to other police departments. Police agencies began adopting various elements to create their own community policing programs. Many of these came with different names, such as the COPPS (Community Oriented Policing and Problem Solving) program in Hayward, California, or the COPE (Citizen Oriented Police Enforcement) program in Baltimore County, Maryland. The agencies that were adopting community policing tended to be medium- to large-sized agencies, and although community policing was believed by many to be a department-wide initiative, most of the agencies typically implemented a special unit or designated certain neighborhoods as recipients of the community policing program.

blue wall of silence: The concept that police officers protect their own and will not divulge any wrongdoing on the part of another officer.

three generations: The breakdown of the era of community policing into three generations of development, consisting of innovation, diffusion, and institutionalization.

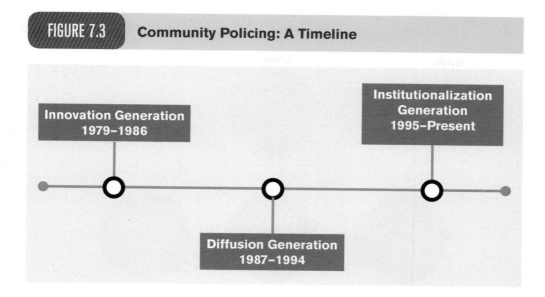

FIGURE 7.3   **Community Policing: A Timeline**

Innovation Generation
1979–1986

Institutionalization
Generation
1995–Present

Diffusion Generation
1987–1994

The third generation of community policing is the *institutionalization generation*, which runs from 1995 onward. In this generation, community policing fast became the most common method of policing that agencies were adopting or at least said they were adopting. In addition, community policing was supported by passage of the Violent Crime Control and Law Enforcement Act of 1994, which put $8.8 billion into funding 100,000 police officers, who were to be used to implement community policing in police departments across the country. As a result of this funding, even the smallest of agencies in the United States could receive funding for their adoption of community policing, so it became a common, institutionalized, program.

Despite the widespread popularity of community policing, it suffered from a definitional problem because it was not based on a specific program or style of policing—the concept had no sole author or architect. In other words, no one could agree on a common definition. This became evident when police departments called their programs by all kinds of names and when what they implemented as community policing differed from agency to agency. One agency might have police-citizen neighborhood patrols, while another might adopt foot patrols for its officers, yet both were doing community policing. One agency might define community policing as a way of thinking about quality-of-life issues that is demonstrated by the agency's commitment to developing police-community partnerships, while another might define it as a special unit, working in a specific neighborhood, to develop communal ties by having officers pay house visits, conducting community meetings, and setting up a police-youth basketball program. The first definition is both vague and visionary, while the latter is very specific and program oriented. Both, though, could have been said to be community policing.

A leading police scholar, Gary Cordner, explained that community policing had come to mean so many things to so many different people that it was important to reach a consensus on the main themes of community policing.[18] Cordner identified the **four dimensions of community policing**: philosophical, strategic, tactical, and organizational (see Figure 7.4). The *philosophical dimension* focuses on community policing

four dimensions of community policing: An interpretation of community policing that includes a philosophy of policing, a strategy for policing, a method of tactical deployment, and a means by which to best organize a department.

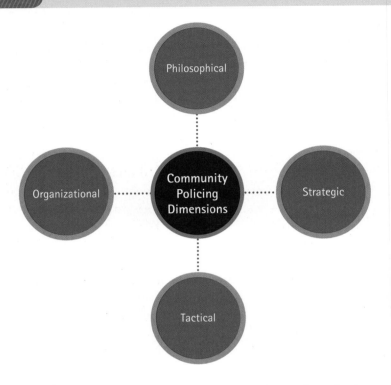

FIGURE 7.4   **Dimensions of Community Policing**

primarily as a new philosophy or way of thinking about policing. It is oriented on the broader functions of the police, such as community service, which then bases itself on the concept of citizen input into the policing process. Whenever the police discuss things such as the values and principles of community policing, the development of partnerships, and the goal of reducing crime and disorder to improve the quality of life, these are the philosophical aspects of community policing that underlie this police initiative.

The *strategic dimension* is an attempt to translate the philosophy into action. Cordner noted that it is often focused on geography, taking community policing to the neighborhood level, assigning police officers to those neighborhoods permanently, and having them work toward taking ownership of their communities and becoming representatives of the police department to the people who live there. This action is based on the philosophy that community policing is about police-citizen partnerships at the neighborhood level. In addition, the prevention of crime and disorder is a primary focus of the community policing strategy, so this dimension may include establishing programs that target crime problems in a neighborhood, working with citizens to have them take more responsibility for the safety of their communities, and bringing in additional social services to improve quality of life. Finally, focusing on the substantive issues is another strategic element of community policing in that police and members of the community work to resolve the problems in their neighborhoods.

The *programmatic dimension* refers to the specific programs that come to encapsulate the community policing philosophy and strategy. These include such things as foot patrols and bike patrols, police-community meetings, and problem-solving approaches to crime and disorder (see the next section, on problem-oriented policing). Programs aimed at implementing community policing reorient the police to focus on specific problems in the neighborhoods they police; they are about solving problems and engaging the community. In short, these are the programs that are implemented under the community policing umbrella.

The *organizational dimension* is focused on how police departments can best organize in order to carry out community policing. An aspect of this dimension involves having officers permanently assigned (at least for extended periods of one to three years) to a neighborhood so that they come to know the community and the issues the neighborhood faces. Another aspect of the organizational dimension is focused on the department's ability to support the community policing officers working in these neighborhoods. The officers who are permanently assigned to neighborhoods come to know what the community wants and needs; thus, they are in the best position to decide what police resources are needed. But as line officers, they are often not in a position to authorize the use of police resources. Thus, decentralizing the police department, which allows for community policing officers to have more authority, is part of the organizational dimension.

The many dimensions and complexities of community policing that developed over the past 30 years beg one question: How successful has community policing been? Since the police are all about reducing crime, if we look at the success of various types of community policing programs at reducing crime, we find mixed results.[19] A few studies claim that it has reduced crime, whereas others have found no evidence to support this effect. Yet many of those studies were not necessarily looking at community policing but rather at other policing methods still to be discussed in this chapter. In sum, there is not a strong foundation of research that has shown community policing to reduce crime. However, when the focus changes to community policing reducing the fear of crime, a strong consensus says that it does reduce the fear.[20] As police develop stronger ties with communities, citizens feel safer about their neighborhoods and so, independent of crime itself, community policing reduces the fear of crime. The moral imperative here is to question whether reducing the fear of crime while not reducing actual crime creates a false sense of security within the community.

➡ Problem-Oriented Policing

Law professor Herman Goldstein from the University of Wisconsin Law School wrote a book in 1977 detailing many of the issues related to long-held assumptions about policing that had no empirical basis. In his book, *Policing a Free Society,* Goldstein reflected on the state of American policing and set himself on a course to think about how policing could be improved.[21] Two years later, he argued in the journal *Crime & Delinquency* that the police focused too much on the means and not on the ends, meaning that

VIDEO
Interview with
Herman Goldstein

police focused on handling calls-for-service without necessarily focusing on the desired outcome or end product: solving problems.[22] If the police could define problems with greater specificity; research the magnitude of those problems; and explore alternatives such as physical changes, developing new skills, and creating new forms of authority, by implementing the process, it may have an effect on the organization. The problem, of course, was the complexity of Goldstein's ideas. Police professionals supported the concept, but they needed to know how to communicate it to line officers.

In reality, what Goldstein was advocating was something we all do every day: solve problems. He was just advocating that we apply it more formally to policing. When your car breaks down, when you have two exams next week that you need to study for, or when a friend asks for your help, you have problems to solve. Let's take something simple. Where are you going to eat lunch? It is a problem. The problem is you are hungry and you want to eat. When faced with this problem, you have to think about your options. You could eat in the cafeteria (it's already paid for), you could eat fast food in the student center (which will cost you money), or you could go home for a peanut butter and jelly sandwich (but it is a long walk back to your dorm or apartment). You then have to think of the constraints you face, such as how much time you have to eat lunch or how much money you have. You then have to analyze and choose the best course of action. If you have only 45 minutes and $2 in your pocket, walking back home would take too long and you can't buy much for $2. The best course of action in this case is probably to eat in the cafeteria. You made a decision, implemented it, and now, after eating in the cafeteria, you can decide whether or not it was a good idea. You might have saved time and money, but was the meal any good?

In policing, police officers have always responded to calls-for-service and then arrived on the scene to solve problems. The issue, as Goldstein saw it, was that the police officer often treats the call as an isolated incident. The location, people, and problem have no past and no future. If the police have responded to that location for the same problem with the same people, it has been forgotten or ignored, and the police try to resolve the issue so that they can leave without thinking about the future and the fact that they, or a fellow officer, will one day have to come back to the same location, for the same problem, to deal with the same people. In this case, the officer is solving the symptoms, not the underlying problem itself. Think about when you get sick on campus and you have a runny nose, headache, and sore throat. So that you can sleep at night, you take that green medicine that knocks you out. In that case, you are dealing with the symptoms of a cold but not the underlying problem causing the symptoms. Goldstein was advocating that the police solve the problem, not the symptoms, in order to improve policing. This strategy would have a positive effect on the police organization as it would reduce calls-for-service to the same address, with the same problem, caused by the same people (see Figure 7.5).

It sounded good, police chiefs admitted, but what they wanted to know was how to teach their officers to do problem solving, or **problem-oriented policing**. Then along came two researchers, John Eck and

problem-oriented policing: A concept for police response widely implemented using the SARA model; it applied problem-solving methods to police work.

FIGURE 7.5   Problem Analysis Triangle

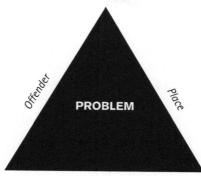

Center for Problem-Oriented Policing

William Spelman, working on a grant in Newport News, Virginia. They consulted with Herman Goldstein to develop a method of teaching police officers how to problem solve, and what they came up with is the **SARA model**, which stands for scanning, analysis, response, and assessment (see Figure 7.6). In the *scanning phase*, police officers are taught to look for problems on their beats and to make connections among the many crimes they face. They are also taught that much of the crime is driven by three factors that are most often connected like a triangle: the offender, the location, and the target or victim. If the police can identify a problem at a specific location, often at a specific time, with the same offenders and/or the same victims, then they will have identified a problem in which the problem-solving model might work.

In the *analysis phase*, police officers begin to analyze the problem in more depth. They draw upon as much data as they can obtain, such as GIS (Geographic Information Systems) software, to see how many and what kinds of crime occur at a particular location, running checks on past police calls-for-service at the location, and conducting background checks on the

SARA model: The four-step model created to instruct police officers on problem-oriented policing; the four steps are scanning, analysis, response, and assessment.

FIGURE 7.6   SARA Model

Scanning   Analysis   Response   Assessment

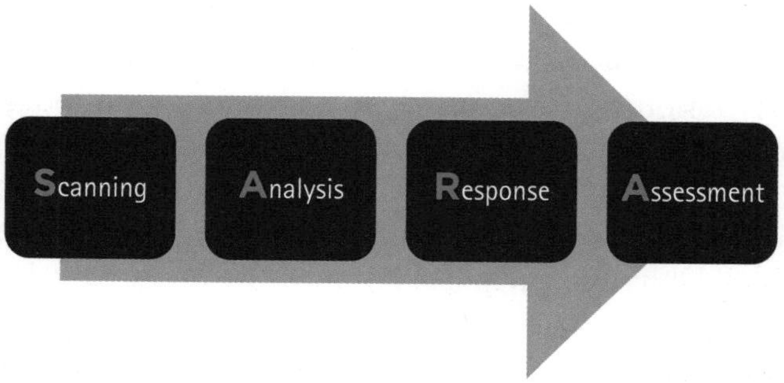

individuals involved to see what kinds of arrests and convictions they may have had—all to get a better understanding of the true nature of the problem. Officers can also go to other government services to see if they have had problems with the same location or people, and they may also go to citizens or citizen groups to collect information. At this stage, the officer also has to determine the desired outcome of the intervention. If the problem is drug dealing and violence on a particular street corner, are the officers after total elimination of drug dealing and violence (which may not be realistic)? Are they intending to substantially reduce the problem (far less violence and drug dealing than in the past)? Are they wanting a reduction in harm (getting the violence to stop but not necessarily the drug dealing)? Or are they trying to find a way of dealing with the problem more effectively (no more street-corner raids but finding a less confrontational way of dealing with the problem)?

In the *response phase*, police officers must develop possible responses to the problem, much like developing a list of places to eat for lunch, and then weight them against the limitations and constraints each faces. The response must address the underlying problem, by dealing with the offender, victims, and locations, and ensure that the response will not cause further problems or harm. Then the officers set about implementing the best course of action from the list of possible solutions to the problem. During the response phase, officers must also monitor the impact that the course of action has on the problem and collect data in order to move into the last phase of the SARA model.

In the *assessment phase*, the officers determine whether the chosen course of action was successful, based on their definition of success (for example, reduction of harm, elimination of the problem). Depending on the outcome, the assessment will tell officers what they need to do next. If the course of action they selected was unsuccessful, then they should consider moving back to the response phase to select and implement another response. If the assessment was positive, then the officers must determine whether they should continue the response, alter the response, or stop the response altogether.

The SARA model has been used widely since the mid-1980s, primarily because it is a problem-solving model that can be taught easily; it is used to address a wide array of problems; and it works well because it concentrates police resources on a specific problem, at a specific time, in a specific location, that often involves the same specific people (offenders and/or victims). It also became widely used because of its natural association with community policing. Most police departments that have adopted community policing have also adopted problem-oriented policing as part of their community policing programs. Many agencies did not adopt community policing, however, but rather problem-oriented policing as a standalone program, such as one of the earliest adopters of problem-oriented policing, the San Diego Police Department. Since those early days, many advances have been made in improving police officers' problem-solving capabilities, and the SARA model is widely used.

Overall, problem-oriented policing has been considered to be an effective police strategy, with only two cautions. First, most of the responses to problems tend to be police-centric, meaning that most police officers do not tend to come up with or implement solutions that are outside of police control, and there is much concern that, in the assessment phase, police officers rarely evaluate the **displacement effect**, in which their responses simply push crime into other areas.[23]

▶ Targeted Policing

During the 1990s, additional programs began to spring up in police departments across the nation. These programs went by many different names but had commonalities in how they were implemented, and eventually specific names were given to them. All of the programs draw on aspects of the broken windows theory and problem-oriented policing concepts. Specifically, broken windows theory articulates that certain neighborhoods have problems of crime and disorder. The problem-oriented policing literature takes it a step further and says that there are often specific locations that have crime and disorder problems often caused by the same offenders and sometimes including the same victims. We know that high levels of crime and disorder tend to be concentrated in specific locations and times, and acts tend to be committed by the same offenders. The key then is for the police to target their resources to these specific problems in order to deter crime. Having police officers drive around neighborhoods does not deter crime (Kansas City Preventive Patrol Experiment), but police officers concentrating their resources on specific targets can have an impact. Several varieties of **targeted policing** exist (see Figure 7.7).

One of the early methods of targeted policing was simply called **directed patrol**. Police officers were often assigned specific crime- or traffic-directed patrols, or they were told to select a specific directed patrol in their beat. Officers were then responsible for monitoring the specific location for crime and disorder by conducting patrols in the area and enforcing the law. One of the authors (Oliver) was a police officer who selected a small park in his beat as his directed patrol. He would often sit in the parking lot while writing reports, and he would frequently drive by or walk through the park during his shift. As a result, he made multiple arrests for illicit activity such as drug use, drug dealing, and prostitution, as well as several arrests for felonious assault and domestic violence. Studies regarding these types of patrols have demonstrated that directed patrols in high crime locations can have a significant effect on crime, disorder, and traffic issues.[24] Specific types of patrol are typically determined by community needs.

This led police to make a more concerted effort at targeting crime problems by implementing what came to be known as **aggressive patrols.** The term *aggressive* means that police officers used the law to intensively target known crime locations. For instance, a well-known house for dealing drugs in a neighborhood could be dealt with through surveillance or undercover investigations as one means to close the house. Another option is to

displacement effect: The movement of the criminal element out of one area and into another when police conduct aggressive policing or crackdowns.

targeted policing: Police target their resources to specific areas, times, and targets in order to deter crime.

directed patrols: Police officers select a specific problem area for crime and/ or disorder and spend shift downtime in that location.

aggressive patrols: The use of the law to investigate potential crimes by way of officers' presence, through heavy enforcement of the law, and stop and frisks.

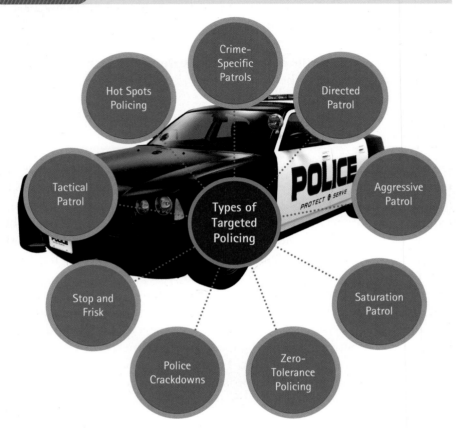

FIGURE 7.7   **Types of Targeted Policing**

Crime-Specific Patrols

Hot Spots Policing

Directed Patrol

Tactical Patrol

Types of Targeted Policing

Aggressive Patrol

Stop and Frisk

Saturation Patrol

Police Crackdowns

Zero-Tolerance Policing

© iStockphoto.com/Nerthuz

have officers aggressively monitor the block around the house for any criminal activity or traffic infractions. At any sign of potential criminal activity, officers would investigate and either make arrests or issue tickets when warranted. The idea is to aggressively target the illegal behavior to force the drug dealing at the house to cease. Research has found this strategy to be very effective, but it can create animosity between the police and citizens.[25]

The use of aggressive patrols led to several other strategies for the police as well. One of these was the use of **saturation patrols**. In this case, rather than having only one officer or a few officers deal with a specific location, the police department would deploy multiple officers. Imagine the block on which a house is known to be the site of drug dealing. All of a sudden there are 15 to 20 police officers on patrol on just that one block. Officers on foot, on bicycles, and in police cars might patrol that one block every day for weeks on end. It would not take long for the word to get out and the drug-dealing establishment to close. This police strategy, as one can imagine, is highly effective and makes an impression, but it also can create animosity between the police and the law-abiding public.

Another aggressive policing strategy, based primarily on the broken windows theory, has come to be known as **zero-tolerance policing**, or sometimes **police crackdowns**. People used to think that police should not focus

saturation patrol: The use of a high number of officers as a show of force to deal with crime at a specific location, at a specific time, and involving specific people.

zero-tolerance policing: This strategy enforces the law on petty crimes and disorder through a no-tolerance policy.

police crackdowns: Shows of force by the police to concentrate on specific crime problems, locations, or persons.

on the little things but rather spend their time and resources enforcing the law related to major felonious crime. Drawing on the broken windows theory, zero-tolerance policing reverses that and says that police should spend time on the minor infractions so that they do not lead to more serious crime. Thus, the police begin focusing their patrols on things that might send a signal that no one cares about the community, such as graffiti, panhandlers, and loitering. By not tolerating these types of minor nuisances, the police send the signal that they will not tolerate serious crime. Although zero-tolerance policing has been found to be effective in dealing with the minor problems, it often comes across as too heavy-handed, and people often feel it is an abuse of police power.[26]

Stop-and-frisk policies have been upheld by the Supreme Court, though these practices create animosity with members of the public.

© Michael Matthews - Police Images / Alamy

Another strategy that developed from the aggressive policing concept was the use of **stop and frisk**. In the landmark case of *Terry v. Ohio* (1968), the Supreme Court ruled that police officers had the right to stop and frisk someone if they had a reasonable suspicion to believe the person had committed, was committing, or was about to commit a crime. A veteran officer by the name of McFadden saw two men acting suspiciously on a street corner in downtown Cleveland, Ohio. He had never seen them before; they were looking about nervously; they retraced their steps repeatedly to look into the same store window; and in between they were talking to each other, when a third man joined them. The officer walked up to them and asked them their names, which they were reluctant to provide. McFadden then grabbed Terry, spun him around, and patted him down for weapons. In the end, he pulled a pistol off of each of the men. The lawyers in this case challenged the arrest as an illegal search and seizure because McFadden did not have probable cause, which he readily admitted. He did, however, have a suspicion, which proved to be quite accurate.

The Supreme Court decided that the police officer had a reasonable suspicion and that the reason for the stop was for the safety of both the officer and the public. In addition, because McFadden simply patted down the men for weapons, only seizing them when feeling something that felt like a gun, it was a limited intrusion and it was reasonable in scope. In its ruling, the Supreme Court created what became known as the stop and frisk, which allows police officers, if they have a reasonable suspicion, for their safety and the safety of the community, to frisk or pat down individuals for weapons. *Terry v. Ohio* has been the basis for numerous other cases, including *Michigan v. Long* (1983), which essentially applied the stop and frisk to an automobile stop, allowing the police to pat down the driver and search the vehicle for weapons based on a reasonable suspicion. Although some evidence suggests that stop and frisk has been effective, it also has created an enormous amount of animosity toward the police, especially in New York City, where it has been used for more than 20 years.[27]

stop and frisk: Allows officers, based on a reasonable suspicion, to stop and detain a person for purposes of a field investigation.

VIDEO
Hot Spots Policing

AUTHOR VIDEO
Hot Spots

Another variation on targeted policing comes from the split patrol concept detailed earlier, in which officers were becoming so tied to 9-1-1 calls that police departments created two patrol forces, one to respond to calls and the other to conduct patrols and perform other police functions. The deployment of a **tactical patrol**, often called *targeted response teams* or *crime response units*, is similar to the split force concept, but in this case one group of police officers conducts routine patrols and responds to 9-1-1 calls, while the other—the tactical patrol—is freed from calls-for-service to target problem locations through multiple means. These officers may be deployed in a saturation patrol, as described earlier, or, for instance, if there was a rash of bank robberies located at major crossroads, these officers might be assigned to all of the banks meeting this criterion with the idea of stopping a bank robbery in progress. Overall, the use of tactical patrols has been demonstrated to reduce both crime and disorder.[28]

Another development in the area of targeted policing is the strategy known as **hot spots policing.** Though similar to many of the other targeted strategies, in this case the emphasis is more on geography and crime. The hot spots are geographic locations that may be a city block, a building, a home, or a cluster of homes. Hot spots could include micro locations, such as a specific street corner, an alley, or the end of a dead-end street. The concentration of crime in these locations may be specific and may be tied to certain individuals, or maybe even one person, but the key is to concentrate police resources on the specific location. The justification here is that the majority of crime in a city can often be traced to just a handful of locations, so if police concentrate their resources in these locations, they stand a good chance of reducing the overall crime figures for the entire city. Overall, hot spots policing has been considered to be highly effective in most cases, not only for reducing crime, but also for dealing with disorder and reducing the number of police calls-for-service.[29]

Just as hot spots policing focuses primarily on geographic location, **crime-specific policing** focuses primarily on, well, crimes. In other words, rather than looking to specific locations for crimes, the police look at specific crimes, such as rapes, burglaries, or robberies. By plotting the locations of specific crimes on a map, they can see trends within the city for those crimes and concentrate their efforts on where those crimes may be occurring. For instance, rapes may be located throughout the city but especially in areas that link high-traffic locations. The police can then develop a specific response to that crime problem to target offenders or protect potential victims.[30]

Finally, **Operation Ceasefire,** or just Ceasefire, is a police strategy that originated in Boston, Massachusetts, in the 1990s. Operation Ceasefire used many different approaches to resolve the problem of youth gun violence. The larger program is discussed in the next section, but the key element related to the reduction of gun violence in Boston was believed to be one particular focus. Based on the notion that a very few people cause most of the problems, Operation Ceasefire figured out who were the perpetrators, or the instigators, of most of the violence, and went to them and told them to stop. The police essentially said that if they continued the

tactical patrol: The use of patrol officers, often in plainclothes, to respond to potential threats of crime and disorder.

hot spots policing: The concentration of police forces on a specific geographic location known to have a high incidence of crime and disorder.

crime-specific policing: A police strategy for targeting specific offenses committed by particular offenders at specific places and times.

Operation Ceasefire: A program in Boston that was aimed specifically at reducing youth gun violence by targeting the few offenders who caused most of the problems.

violence, then every police officer and every police resource the department had would be used to target them to ensure that they would no longer live the way they were used to. If they stopped the violence, they would not be the sole focus of the police and would instead be left mostly to their own devices. The interesting thing is, it worked. The serious offenders who caused most of the problems did not want to lose the lifestyle to which they had become accustomed, and so they stopped short of committing the gun violence that would have made them the sole target of police authority. Taken to other cities, this strategy has proven highly successful.[31] In the same way that hot spots policing focuses on the location and crime-specific policing focuses on the crime, Ceasefire focuses on the most egregious offenders.

In looking at all of the targeted police strategies, a couple of things become clear. First, all of these methods are based on what the Kansas City Preventive Patrol Experiment told us—that police officers on random patrol do not deter crime but that concentrating police resources can, in fact, have an impact on crime. Second, although each of these strategies has a slightly different focus, they are all inherently the same. When the police focus on a specific crime, at a specific location, at a specific time, with specific offenders, and often with specific victims, the police are effective at dealing with crime, and they can deter crime. Note, however, that some police officers—particularly those in smaller agencies—are expected to conduct various types of activities and multiple types of patrol (see the "Help Wanted" box in this chapter).

AUTHOR VIDEO
Issues Raised by Hot Spots Policing

BEYOND A REASONABLE DOUBT 7.2

Which of the following police strategies concentrates police resources on specific locations, at specific times, and often specific individuals?

(a) Problem-oriented policing, (b) Community policing, (c) Targeted policing, (d) Police-community relations

---

The answer can be found on page 521.

➡ Four Related Strategies

Highly related to many of the strategies covered so far are four other strategies. One of these strategies, Crime Prevention Through Environmental Design, developed independently but became part of the community policing movement; another, pulling-levers policing, was associated with Operation Ceasefire; and the other two, evidence-based policing and predictive policing, came out of much of the research that has developed over the years into what works in policing.

Crime Prevention Through Environmental Design

Crime Prevention Through Environmental Design (CPTED) was created by criminologist C. Ray Jeffery and over time has been advanced

Crime Prevention Through Environmental Design: The reshaping of the environment to control the problems of crime and disorder.

HELP WANTED: POLICE OFFICER

DUTIES:

- Prevent, detect, and investigate violations of laws, rules, and regulations involving accidents, crimes, and misconduct involving misdemeanors and felonies

- Make arrests of violators caught in the act or who readily admit to guilt

- Assist in the prosecution of criminals

- Issue citations for personally observed violations of the law, rules, and regulations

- Serve as a source of assistance to persons in emergency situations

- Inform individuals about their rights as suspects and/or witnesses

- Obtain statements from persons involved in or witnessing accidents where the facts appear to be clear and are undisputed by those involved

- Enforce a wide variety of federal, state, county, and agency rules and regulations relating to law enforcement

- Be cognizant of the rights of suspects, the laws of search and seizure, and constraints on the use of force

- Complete, in a timely manner, written reports in a neat, clear, complete, and understandable manner using appropriate forms

- Direct traffic during rush hours

- Perform foot and/or vehicle patrol

- Respond to violation and duress alarms, assisting employees, visitors, or passers-by

- Develop informants and/or informant networks

- Coordinate with other law enforcement agencies to gather facts or evidence for use in assigned cases when necessary

- Write uniform offense reports covering incidents on his/her shift containing pertinent factual information

- Respond to domestic disturbance calls and similar activities requiring police control or action

- Assist assigned investigators, and adjust security measures to prevent a recurrence of crime

- Relieve or rotate through the police operations center to include receiving telephone calls, dispatching personnel, operating all surveillance and security equipment, issuing and controlling of police equipment, preparing the shift journal, and the like

REQUIREMENTS: Bachelor's degree; must hold a current valid unrestricted driver's license; must qualify for, obtain, and maintain firearms certification

ANNUAL SALARY: $35,256–$45,828

Adapted from USAJOBS.gov. Retrieved from https://www.usajobs.gov/GetJob/ViewDetails/379040700

through other contributions regarding urban design and what has been called *defensible space*.[32] In the 1980s, it took on a renewed emphasis because of its close relationship to the broken windows theory and the development of community policing. CPTED is a method for analyzing how the physical environment impacts crime and criminal behavior and then how altering the physical environment deters crime. For instance, college campuses are often designed with pathways, landscaping, and lighting to attract people to follow certain pathways and to congregate in certain areas. Having commonly used areas like these, with high foot traffic, prevents the types of crimes that occur down dark alleys, on hidden pathways, and in isolated areas. Another example is something simple like a parking lot. Although we all like hardtop parking lots, they are less safe than gravel parking lots. It is hard for someone to approach a person getting in or out of a car silently on crunching gravel. Changing the environment makes people more aware. Similarly, we know from research that one of the best places to live is on a cul-de-sac, because people typically enter such streets only if they have a purpose there and because it creates a mini-community where everyone knows who belongs there and who does not. Cul-de-sacs are defensible spaces. Living in an apartment or a home located on a cross street or grid pattern is the least safe because of the open access to those locations; they are not as defensible.[33]

Pulling-Levers Policing

Pulling-levers policing developed out of Operation Ceasefire in Boston in the 1990s.[34] Between 1991 and 1995, Boston experienced 44 youth homicides that were directly related to gangs. Instead of creating a program that focused on just one aspect of the problem, Operation Ceasefire was intent on creating multiple programs to deter youth violence and homicides. Some of the programs focused on the offenders, some on the victims, others were aimed at the schools, some on the teachers, others on the problem of youths bringing guns to school, and still others were gang oriented. In addition to these types of programs, many of the "levers" that were pulled were the use of the law by police officers, school resource officers, and the prosecutor's office. By pulling every lever possible, Operation Ceasefire put pressure on those few people who were perpetrating the crimes to deter them from committing future crimes. If a perpetrator committed another crime, then every possible method available to the police and community was used to target the perpetrator and to make others think twice before committing similar crimes. Operation Ceasefire was intended to tell the few gang members who were perpetrating most of the crime to stop the violence, in addition to pulling all of those other levers. The concept of Ceasefire has focused on the former, whereas *pulling levers* refers to the original program's goal of using multiple methods to deal with a problem.

Evidence-Based Policing

The concept of **evidence-based policing** was more of an evolution in police research.[35] Starting with the research in the 1970s that tested long-held assumptions about policing, to the use of evaluations as part of the assessment phase of the SARA model (as part of problem-oriented policing), research into what works in policing has developed over the past 40 years so that now data are used to determine the best strategies for policing. *Evidence-based policing* refers to the use of data about offenders, victims, and crimes, as well as the geographic nature of all three, to help guide police interventions through the use of empirical studies. In other words, police interventions are assessed for how well they reduce crime and disorder; they must be results oriented. If empirical research shows that an intervention does not reduce crime or disorder, then it is either discontinued or modified until the intervention has been shown to work.

pulling-levers policing: A strategy for the implementation of multiple programs at the same time or in succession in order to address a specific problem of crime or disorder.

evidence-based policing: The use of data and facts (that is, the evidence) to guide the deployment of police in order to resolve crime and disorder in a community.

Predictive Policing

Evidence-based policing involves using empirical data to guide police toward implementing successful interventions and avoiding those that fail to obtain results. **Predictive policing** takes the use of empirical data even further and attempts to make predictions about what crimes are likely to occur, where, and when. Specifically, it refers to the "application of analytical techniques—particularly quantitative techniques—to identify likely targets for police intervention and prevent crime or solve past crimes by making statistical predictions."[36] In light of the power of information technology these days, the analysis of large databases of information can often yield relationships that were not apparent and can then be exploited for purposes of crime prevention and crime control. For example, police in Richmond, Virginia, were faced with the problem of random gunshots being fired to celebrate New Year's Eve. Police consulted databases for the locations, times, and nature of past incidents to predict where the next celebration's guns were most likely to be fired so that officers could be in position when gunshots sounded.[37]

predictive policing: A police strategy that uses empirical data and attempts to make predictions about what crimes are likely to occur, where, and when.

CompStat: A managerial method for holding police managers accountable for the crimes and disorder that occur in their jurisdictions.

> ### BEYOND A REASONABLE DOUBT 7.3
>
> Which of the following police strategies is focused on crime reduction by focusing its attention on location, landscaping, and the use of fencing?
>
> (a) Crime Prevention Through Environmental Design, (b) Pulling-levers policing, (c) Evidence-based policing, (d) Predictive policing

The answer can be found on page 521.

NYPD Police Commissions William Bratton led the development of Compstat, a police supervisory strategy that encourage police supervisors to use real-time evidence to make strategic decisions.

© AP Photo/Seth Wenig

➡ CompStat

Most of this chapter has talked about police strategies. Another strategy was actually developed in New York City as a management tool. In the early 1990s, William C. Bratton (see the "Criminal Justice Pioneer" box in this chapter) was hired as the New York City police commissioner. He assembled a team that wanted to hold precinct commanders accountable for the crime in their jurisdictions with the idea that they should be working to implement the types of strategies discussed earlier in this chapter. What developed was a strategy, a method, and a police management mechanism that came to be known as **CompStat**. There has always been a debate over what CompStat stood for, but

WILLIAM BRATTON

William "Bill" Bratton was born on October 6, 1947, and has had a storied career in American policing. After serving briefly in the Military Police during the Vietnam War, Bratton became a police officer in his hometown of Boston, Massachusetts. He rose quickly through the ranks to the police department's second-highest rank before becoming the Boston Metro police chief. Then he took a similar position with the New York City Transit Police before returning home as the superintendent in chief of the Boston Police Department. From there he was hired by the New York City Police Department (NYPD) to be its chief (1994–1996), he then served as the Los Angeles Police Department chief (2002–2009), and finally he was asked to return to the NYPD (2014–). He has been a reform-minded chief, often coming into police departments during troubled times, fixing many of the problems, and leaving them better than when he arrived. He has also been a lightning rod for controversy, especially when he began implementing such programs as broken windows policing or zero-tolerance policing. His implementation of CompStat was and remains quite controversial, and each time he has had to deal with the many issues covered in this chapter, he has been a focus of many hot-button issues in policing. Despite all of that, he has been honored with numerous awards, has been asked to consult with police departments all over the world, and has led three of the most renowned police departments in the United States.

most observers have agreed that it was a combination of the words *computer* and *statistics*. This was because one of the program's innovators was Jack Maple, who believed that real-time crime analysis was critical to precinct commanders' reducing crime.[38]

To know how to reduce crime in neighborhoods, one has to know what kinds of crime problems exist there. CompStat works through command-level meetings at which the police commissioner and his or her staff meet with precinct commanders and their staffs to ask about the major problems in their areas of responsibility. In these meetings, the commissioner already knows what the problems are, based on a crime analysis. But this approach helps to determine whether the commanders know what is going. If they don't know, they are told to come to the next meeting prepared to discuss the problems. If they do know, they are asked what they are doing to address those problems. Again, if they are not doing anything in particular, at the next meeting they have to let the command staff know what they are doing. Then they are told that they have to reduce the problems within six months to a year. If they cannot achieve a reduction in crime or disorder, they are fired and replaced. Thus, CompStat started out as a managerial tool, but it also found use as a policing strategy. This process was depicted in the HBO hit *The Wire* (see the "Criminal Justice and the Media" box in this chapter).

CompStat has long been held by the NYPD and many of those enthralled by its methods as having been successful. The only problem is that crime began falling in New York City two years before CompStat was implemented and continued to fall for the next 20 years, as it has all

CRIMINAL JUSTICE and the MEDIA:

COMSTAT EMULATES COMPSTAT ON *THE WIRE*

The HBO television series *The Wire*, which ran from 2002 to 2008, was a crime drama that depicted the Baltimore Police Department. One element of the show was the use of ComStat, a slightly altered version of CompStat. Although the depictions of CompStat are assuredly all Hollywood, they do touch on some aspects of how CompStat has been used and some of the strategies discussed in this chapter. For instance, an episode in the third season depicted a ComStat meeting in which a police commander describes how he dealt with street-corner drug dealers. He describes how he used elements of Ceasefire to move drug dealers off street corners and into three areas of the city where they would not be harassed for dealing drugs. The episode depicts the CompStat managerial meetings and how commanders are held responsible for the crime in their jurisdictions, albeit with a fictitious scenario.

HBO. *The Wire*. Retrieved from http://www.hbo.com/#/the-wire/episodes

across the United States. So it begs the question: Did CompStat contribute to the decline in crime, or was it simply good timing? CompStat had been shown to be successful in other cities, but it has been problematic on the management side to hold the command staff accountable. In fact, what many observers believe is the best aspect of CompStat is the fact that it helps police focus on specific problems, similar to many of the other targeted police strategies detailed in this chapter.[39] Table 7.1 shows the number of police agencies using computers for specific tasks across populations. For the most part, these practices appear to be more common in larger police departments.

➡ Homeland Security and Policing

Although the emphasis of homeland security and policing has been on the tragedy of 9/11 and the development of the Department of Homeland Security in its aftermath, some elements of policing have not always tracked with the more common methods of policing. Several events in the 1960s raised awareness that the police often were outgunned and not well prepared tactically to take down a well-armed target. What developed initially was the first **Special Weapons and Tactics (SWAT)** unit by the Los Angeles Police Department. Over time, the adoption of SWAT teams or **special response teams** became common in U.S. police departments. These units were typically reserved, however, for major confrontations, such as hostage situations.

In 1990, when Saddam Hussein invaded Kuwait, the United States went to war and kicked Hussein out of Kuwait. In the aftermath of what was called Operation Desert Storm, there was a military drawdown and excess supplies were available for police departments. Throughout the 1990s, police departments began acquiring various assault gear, protective

Special Weapons and Tactics (SWAT): Police paramilitary units.

special response teams: A variety of special units designed to respond to high-risk situations needing special skills, weapons, and tactics.

TABLE 7.1	Police Agencies Using Computers for Specific Tasks, by Population Served			
POPULATION SERVED	**CRIME ANALYSIS**	**CRIME MAPPING**	**HOTSPOT IDENTIFICATION**	**PROVIDING CRIME MAPS TO OFFICERS IN-FIELD**
1,000,000+	100	100	92	31
500,000–999,999	100	100	100	29
250,000–499,999	100	100	80	48
100,000–249,999	96	94	66	32
50,000–99,999	88	82	56	31
25,000–49,999	69	60	31	16
10,000–24,999	53	41	19	11
2,500–9,999	37	23	9	9
Less than 2,500	21	11	5	8
All Sizes	38	27	13	11

Bureau of Justice Statistics

vests, gas masks, and other assorted military supplies. Because these items were free, police departments began using them for their SWAT teams as a means to save money. Then two things happened. The police SWAT teams began to look and dress more like the military, and with the wide adoption of SWAT teams in the United States, there was a growing use of them by police departments, no longer for the most serious events, but for situations that *might* be serious, such as carrying out search warrants for known drug dealers. This led one researcher to observe the phenomenon he called the militarization of the police in America.[40] The increased use of what are often called **police paramilitary units** (PPUs) came, ironically, at a time when policing in America was embracing community policing. Yet the use of military-style tactics seemed to be at odds with the opening up of relations with the community and sent mixed messages about policing as it entered the 21st century.

> **police paramilitary units:** Specially trained and outfitted police units for use in high-risk situations; commonly called SWAT (Special Weapon and Tactics) teams.

In addition to the PPUs and SWAT teams, many police departments around the nation began entering into agreements with federal law enforcement agencies, through which they would work alongside other state and local agencies to address specific problems by sharing resources. These became known as joint operations and task forces, so that what developed were *joint terrorism task forces* and *joint drug task forces*. These task forces were usually led by the federal law enforcement agencies, often the Federal Bureau of Investigation

SWAT teams are called on to respond to particularly dangerous scenarios.

© iStockphoto/ Vesna Andjic

and the Drug Enforcement Agency, and would be composed of state and local police, as well as other criminal justice representatives, such as the district attorney and the local prosecutor's office. By sharing resources and using police officers from one city to go undercover in another city, their anonymity was almost assured. These task forces have proven successful for enforcement purposes, but they tend to be operationally oriented and often employ military tactics, which are not necessarily in keeping with the overarching philosophy of community policing that was so prominent during the 1990s.

On September 11, 2001, much of the focus of American policing changed from community policing to homeland security. The federal government created the Department of Homeland Security (DHS) and implemented the National Incident Management System (NIMS), a template for future responses to terrorist attacks and natural disasters for all levels of responders: federal, state, and local.[41] As mentioned in Chapter 6, part of the NIMS included implementation of the Incident Command System (ICS), a management structure that would allow multiple agencies to handle the response to terrorist bombings and hurricanes, for example. Most of the initial focus was on ensuring that first responders were well trained, well equipped, and well prepared for similar events in the future. Given that the police are among the first responders, much of the funding, training, and equipment for homeland security was directed toward them.

Being prepared for threats is critical to future responses, but there was also the strong desire to implement methods to *prevent* future terrorist attacks. As a result, homeland security for policing began to develop many new programs that would assist the police in the area of prevention.[42] The concept of **counterterrorism**, which had long been the focus of the military, suddenly became applied to the police. *Counterterrorism* refers to operational methods that work to prevent or stop future terrorist attacks, as well

counterterrorism:
The strategy, tactics, and techniques used by police departments (and others) to stop terrorist threats and acts.

Local police are often first responders in addressing terroristic acts.

REUTERS/Dan Lampariello

as the strategy, operations, and tactics used to respond to terrorist threats. These include not just federal law enforcement response teams, but local response teams as well, and may include SWAT, hostage rescue teams, and bomb squads.

In addition, the collection of intelligence, as well as its analysis, became necessary for the police to be able to conduct counterterrorism operations. Police began creating intelligence collection and analysis centers within their police departments, which led to the creation of **intelligence-led policing**. This model of policing is built around the collection of information, the analysis of threats, and the use of risk assessments to determine potential threats and to create actionable intelligence for police to respond to potential threats. Because only the largest police agencies could afford the creation of intelligence-led policing units, the DHS helped to fund the creation of what became known as **fusion centers**, regional information-sharing centers that would act as focal points for information that may give police departments the actionable intelligence they need to respond. Although the concept has its merits, the execution has not been so successful. A two-year Senate investigation into the success of fusion centers found that they "often produced irrelevant, useless or inappropriate intelligence reporting to DHS, and many produced no intelligence reporting whatsoever."[43]

VIDEO
Policing Fusion Centers

intelligence-led policing: A policing model based on assessment and management of risk by collecting data and converting it into actionable intelligence for the police.

fusion centers: Federally funded and locally staffed shared centers that collect data and share it in real time with the intent of assisting in police investigations.

BEYOND A REASONABLE DOUBT 7.4

Which of the following police strategies demands crime reduction by holding police managers accountable for the areas they police?

(a) Police paramilitary units, (b) Incident Command System, (c) Intelligence-led policing, (d) CompStat

---

The answer can be found on page 521.

Just the Facts: Chapter Summary

- Police strategies are a broad set of ideas and a set of plans for achieving the primary goals of policing: reducing crime and disorder.

- Early studies of police practices, funded by the Omnibus Crime Control and Safe Streets Act of 1968, evaluated long-held police assumptions.

- The three major studies found that police on random patrols do not deter crime (Kansas City Preventive Patrol Experiment), that rapid response to crime scenes does not increase the likelihood that a case will be solved (Kansas City Rapid Response Study), and that more technology for detectives is not what solves most cases (RAND Criminal Investigation Study).

- Police calls-for-service rose dramatically in the 1970s due to implementation of the 9-1-1 system, which prevented officers from being able to conduct other duties, including investigations. Many agencies began implementing differential police response to triage calls, whereas others used split patrols, in which half of patrol officers respond to calls-for-service while the rest perform other duties.

- According to the broken windows theory, when a community allows broken windows to remain broken, it sends a signal that no one cares about the community and invites more crime. This policing model meant that officers should focus on minor crime and disorder as well as work to restore a sense of community to crime-ridden neighborhoods. This led to community policing.

- Community policing developed in the 1980s as a result of the realization that old police methods were not effective, that the police had alienated themselves from the community in the name of professionalism, and that the broken windows theory was a promising approach.

- Community policing went through three generations: innovation (1979–1986), in which ideas were being tested on a small scale; diffusion (1987–1994), in which the concepts began to spread across the country to other police departments; and institutionalization (1995–present), in which the federal government began to fund community policing.

- Community policing consists of four dimensions: philosophical, strategic, programmatic, and organizational.

- Problem-oriented policing, created by Herman Goldstein, acknowledges that police officers often treat calls as isolated incidents, yet they all have a past and a future. If the underlying problem of repeat calls and offenders is solved, then the police will use fewer resources over time.

- John Eck and William Spelman, working with Herman Goldstein, developed the SARA model (scanning, analysis, response, and assessment) to teach police officers problem-solving methods.

- Targeted policing has developed over time and consists of many police programs that are focused on specific problems, in specific locations, at specific times, often dealing with the same offenders and victims. When the police target their resources, they can, in fact, deter crime.

- Targeted policing includes the use of directed patrols, aggressive patrols, saturation patrols, zero-tolerance policing, police crackdowns, stop and frisk, tactical patrols, hot spots policing, crime-specific policing, and Operation Ceasefire.

- Four other related strategies that have developed alongside or out of targeted policing are Crime Prevention Through Environmental Design, pulling-levers policing, evidence-based policing, and predictive policing.

- CompStat was a managerial tool that developed into a police strategy highly related to targeted policing. The managerial aspect involves holding police commanders accountable for the level of crime and disorder in their jurisdictions and demanding reductions over time.

- In the 1990s, when community policing was the overriding philosophy of policing in the United States, the use of police paramilitary units continued to rise, causing some observers to argue that the police were becoming militarized, as evidenced by SWAT units and joint task forces.

- In the aftermath of 9/11, the United States became focused on homeland security, and the police followed in kind by preparing for future attacks through the use of the National Incident Management System and the Incident Command System. They also worked toward preventing future terrorist attacks through counterterrorism programs, intelligence-led policing, and the use of fusion centers.

Critical Thinking Questions

1. List the differences between police strategies, operations, and tactics and how they are also related.

2. For several decades the police held many assumptions that certain approaches to policing worked, namely, random patrols, rapid response, and criminal investigation technology. Discuss what research revealed and how that affected policing.

3. The broken windows theory is considered one of the most important crime theories in modern times. Detail the theory and, assuming the theory is sound, describe the role police have in regard to crime and disorder.

4. It is said that, to understand community policing, you must understand its many dimensions and how it has developed over time. What are the four dimensions and three generations of community policing?

5. What is problem-oriented policing, and what application does the SARA model have in regard to this police strategy?

6. There are numerous targeted policing programs, and each is slightly different from the others. What common focal points are found in all of these targeted methods?

7. CompStat is said to have been highly successful when used by the New York City Police Department, but it was not initially developed as a police strategy. Why was it developed, and what relationship does it have to other police strategies?

8. What is meant by the militarization of the police?

9. Since 9/11, many observers have argued that the United States has left the community policing era and entered an era of homeland security. How has 9/11 changed American policing, and what role do the police play in homeland security?

Key Terms

aggressive patrols (223)

blue wall of silence (216)

calls-for-service (212)

community policing (215)

CompStat (230)

counterterrorism (234)

Crime Prevention
Through Environmental
Design (227)

crime-specific
policing (226)

differential police
response (213)

directed patrols (223)

displacement effect (223)

evidence-based
policing (229)

four dimensions
of community
policing (217)

fusion centers (235)

hot spots policing (226)

intelligence-led
policing (235)

officer-initiated
contacts (212)

Omnibus Crime Control
and Safe Streets
Act of 1968 (207)

Operation Ceasefire (226)

police crackdowns (224)

police paramilitary
units (233)

police strategies (206)

predictive
policing (230)

preventive
patrol (212)

problem-oriented
policing (220)

pulling-levers
policing (229)

SARA model (221)

saturation
patrol (224)

special response
teams (232)

Special Weapons
and Tactics
(SWAT) (232)

split patrols (213)

stop and frisk (225)

tactical patrol (226)

targeted
policing (223)

team policing (223)

three generations (216)

zero-tolerance
policing (224)

$SAGE edgeselect™

edge.sagepub.com/payne

Sharpen your skills with SAGE edge select!

With carefully crafted tools and resources to encourage review, practice, and critical thinking, SAGE edge select gives you the edge needed to master course content. Take full advantage of open-access key term flashcards, practice quizzes, and video content. Diagnostic pre-tests, a personalized study plan, and post-tests are available with an access code.

8

ISSUES IN POLICING

© alessandro0770/Veer

ON AUGUST 9, 2014, OFFICER DARREN WILSON was patrolling the streets of Ferguson, Missouri, when he stopped a group of young people walking in the road and asked them to walk on the sidewalk. During the routine stop, an altercation between Wilson and one of the youth, Michael Brown, ensued. Witnesses' descriptions of the incident differed. Some witnesses reported a scene in which Brown raised his hands in the air and the officer unloaded his weapon into the body of unarmed Black man. The officer reported a different scene, one that characterized Brown as an aggressive assailant who had physically threatened the officer. Soon after, protesters organized and rioted in response to what they perceived to be police brutality. A grand jury reviewed evidence and listened to testimony for 25 days over a three-month period. The grand jury decided not to bring criminal charges against Officer Wilson. Again, protestors organized, but this time their anger increased. Police cars and buildings were set afire; stores were looted; and traffic was stopped as protestors blocked main roads in Ferguson.

Protests occurred in other major cities as well. Not everyone might agree with the grand jury's recommendation, but the Michael Brown case is symbolic of the strain that exists between police and members of the minority community. In Ferguson, for example, police-community relations were most certainly tenuous. From a law enforcement perspective, the police are charged with enforcing laws, and, while putting their own lives in danger, there are times when the police must use deadly force in an effort to promote community safety. Many police critics, however, question whether minorities are targeted disproportionately in use-of-force cases. This is a debate that will continue.

The Ferguson shooting highlights the many issues involved in policing in a democracy. The police face many external and internal issues in performing their jobs. This chapter focuses on the issues facing police today and how our society balances police power with citizens' rights.

LEARNING OBJECTIVES

After reading this chapter, students will be able to:

8.1 Explain how political, legislative, economic, social, and technological factors influence policing

8.2 Identify the source of the police subculture

8.3 Explain variables that impact police discretion

8.4 Identify types of police stress

8.5 Compare and contrast four types of police misconduct

ADMISSIBLE or INADMISSIBLE Evidence

Read the statements that follow. If the statement is true, circle *admissible*. If the statement is false, circle *inadmissible*. Answers can be found on page 518.

1. **Admissible Inadmissible** Federalism is the constitutional relationship between the 50 state governments and the national (federal) government located in Washington, D.C.

2. **Admissible Inadmissible** When police officers make an arrest, they are not legally authorized to search a person until they have secured a search warrant from a judge or magistrate.

3. **Admissible Inadmissible** According to the U.S. Supreme Court landmark case of *Miranda v. Arizona* (1966), as soon as police arrest an individual, they must notify the individual of his or her Miranda rights.

4. **Admissible Inadmissible** Evidence suggests that there is no difference between male and female police officers in the performance of their duties.

5. **Admissible Inadmissible** The use-of-force continuum states that police officers may use only the same amount of force that a suspect uses against them.

(Continued)

(Continued)

6. **Admissible   Inadmissible**   Posttraumatic stress disorder is a strong emotional reaction to one particular incident that can cause numerous emotional problems.

7. **Admissible   Inadmissible**   *Noble-cause corruption* refers to police misconduct committed by police officers who operate under the notion that the (good) end justifies the means.

8. **Admissible   Inadmissible**   Citizen review boards come into existence whenever a police department does not have an internal affairs unit.

➡ External Issues

External issues, which can also be called pressures or influences on the police, come from outside the police organization and profession (see Figure 8.1). These issues come in many different forms but can best be categorized using the acronym *PEST* (political, economic, social, and technological).[1] Political issues include government influences over the police, such as laws and court decisions that tell the police what they can and cannot do, as well as public opinion and media perspectives of the police. Economic issues include the influences that money can have on the police, whether through budget increases or, more likely, budget cuts, as well as grant-funding opportunities. Social influences include our changing American culture and how it prompts the police to change how they carry out their mission, or how changes in culture may change the police mission itself. Finally, technology, which is a neutral entity, but can be used for good or bad by different parties, raises issues often centered on freedom versus security. These four external influences over the police can be seen as good or bad or, perhaps more accurately, as presenting opportunities or threats to the police.[2] They have also created new job opportunities in the policing field (see the "Help Wanted" box in this chapter).

CAREER VIDEO
Community Relations Specialist

HELP WANTED: FORENSIC AUDITOR

DUTIES:

- Participates in and in some cases leads work involving the research, analysis, and/or evaluation of information to assist Office of Inspector General (OIG) auditors and investigators with conducting investigations, audits, evaluations, and other reviews.

- Uses sophisticated software tools to perform analysis of government databases and open source information, in support of the OIG's mission to enhance economy, efficiency, and effectiveness as well as to search for anomalies, questionable connections, trends, and patterns that may be indicative of fraud, waste, or abuse in the board of governors of the Federal Reserve System or Consumer Financial Protection Bureau programs and activities, to include delegated functions.

- The information collected and reports generated may be used to prosecute cases, pursue civil or administrative judgments, or assist with identifying or developing audit findings.

REQUIREMENTS: Bachelor's degree; effective skills in research, analysis, and oral and written communication

ANNUAL SALARY: $76,100–$139,300

Adapted from USAJOBS.gov. Retrieved from https://www.usajobs.gov/GetJob/ViewDetails/379257500

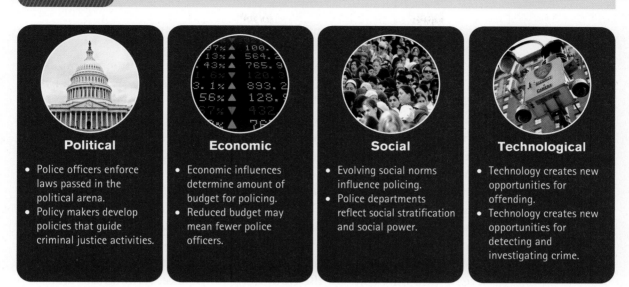

FIGURE 8.1   External Influences on Policing

Political
- Police officers enforce laws passed in the political arena.
- Policy makers develop policies that guide criminal justice activities.

Economic
- Economic influences determine amount of budget for policing.
- Reduced budget may mean fewer police officers.

Social
- Evolving social norms influence policing.
- Police departments reflect social stratification and social power.

Technological
- Technology creates new opportunities for offending.
- Technology creates new opportunities for detecting and investigating crime.

© iStockphoto.com/manley099; © iStockphoto.com/adrian825; © iStockphoto.com/MaestroBooks; © iStockphoto.com/Michael Krinke

Political Influences

In the majority of U.S. cities, the police chief is appointed by the mayor and city council and serves at their will and pleasure. This means that a police chief can be removed from office for political reasons, not just for performance issues. In counties across the United States, most sheriffs are elected, so they are very familiar with how politics influences their jobs and the entire sheriff's office. These politicians also determine the budgets for the police departments; they pass regulations to which the police must adhere; and they pass local city ordinances that the police must enforce. They can also influence the police department by advocating for the enforcement or nonenforcement of some law or the adoption or discontinuance of a particular police policy or strategy.

Legislative Laws

Cities and counties must follow state and federal law, but they often find that these laws do not cover all of their local concerns and therefore they must pass local laws known as *local ordinances*. Because the police department will be responsible for the enforcement of many of these local ordinances, passage of these new laws has an impact on the police department. For example, many cities have a problem with the homeless and aggressive panhandling. Numerous cities have passed local ordinances to make this type of activity illegal. For instance, in Atlanta, Georgia, the city council passed a ban on panhandling in the tourist area after dark or within 15 feet of an ATM, bus stop, or the like.[3] After the ordinance went into effect, the police were ordered to enforce the law. Two days later, the Atlanta Police Department announced that it would round up all of the homeless after dark and place them in a shelter. The local law quickly became divisive; many observers saw this as harassment on the part of the police and a

VIDEO
Police and Sit-Lie Ordinance

violation of people's civil rights, whereas others saw it as justified because it enhanced the safety and security of the tourist areas in Atlanta. Either way, the city council's passage of the local ordinance and the expectation that the police department would enforce it, created a difficult situation for the police.

Although the police typically work for the local municipal or county government, they are also required to enforce *state law* and abide by any state law that oversees police (peace) officers. The first part of this is easy to understand, for whenever a crime is committed in a city or county, it is state law that the police are enforcing. Homicides, rapes, robberies, and burglaries are all based on state statutes, and it is under these codes that the police are authorized to make arrests. State legislatures also have the authority to pass laws that oversee the police and instruct them on what they can and cannot do. Every state has a department or commission that oversees police training and certification. The state legislature has the power to mandate the number of hours required for police officer certification, how many hours of training are needed for recertification every year, who may conduct the training, and the like. In addition, state law may dictate how the police perform their jobs, such as in the Commonwealth of Virginia, where state law mandates that police officers, when operating emergency vehicles responding to an emergency, must run both lights *and* sirens.

The police may find that they must adhere to *federal law* as well. In many cases, federal laws mandate such things as hiring practices and employment procedures. For instance, the Civil Rights Act of 1964, under Title VII, provides the legal basis for fair employment in the United States and it applies to every police department in the country. It makes it unlawful for a police department to discriminate against any individual with respect to employment because of sex, age, color, national origin, or religion. This law was passed to stop discrimination against minorities and women in employment, including police employment, and every police department and sheriff's office in the United States must be in compliance with this federal law. Another example of how a federal law may become binding on local law enforcement is the Brady Handgun Violence Prevention Act's background check requirement for new gun purchases. When the act first became federal law, the only entity that existed to perform so many background checks was local law enforcement. After the bill passed, local police departments were overburdened with having to conduct background checks without any additional resources provided by Congress to carry out the mandated law.

In other cases, federal laws may create problems for the police in performing some function, or state and federal law may come into conflict. The United States operates under the system of **federalism**, which refers to the division of power among federal and state governments. Sometimes federal and state laws conflict. For instance, even after Colorado and Washington legalized the sale of marijuana, federal law still stated that marijuana was illegal. Another recent issue related to federalism is the national debate over the enforcement of federal immigration laws. In some jurisdictions, local

federalism: The issues of shared powers between the national and state governments and how, oversight of these powers is determined.

police and sheriffs are being asked to take on a larger role by checking the immigrant status of those they come in contact with and turning over any illegal immigrants to federal law enforcement. This requirement is being challenged in the courts because immigration law is argued to fall under the purview of the federal government, not state and local agencies.[4] Yet Congress has been unable to pass any immigration reform legislation, so local governments have to deal with this issue. Many of these governments have decided that since immigration law is federal law, the local police have no jurisdiction; therefore, they are prohibited from enforcing these laws.

The fact that the United States Constitution specifies that the federal government is responsible for immigration, and by extension its enforcement, has made it difficult for local officials to respond to immigration.

Wikimedia Commons

Judicial Decisions

The legislative branch of the government may make the law, but the judicial branch serves as a check on the legislature's actions by ensuring that laws passed are constitutional. The U.S. Supreme Court serves as a check on the U.S. Congress, and the state supreme courts serve as checks on state legislatures. These supreme courts also have the power, through their decisions, to determine whether or not police behavior is constitutional. The U.S. Supreme Court's decisions have had the broadest impact on police policies and procedures; when the Supreme Court decides a case, it affects every police department in the United States at the federal, state, and local levels. Therefore, it is important to understand how the U.S. Supreme Court influences what the police can and cannot do.

The Supreme Court typically finds itself hearing cases on appeal that deal with alleged violations of rights provided by the U.S. Constitution. These rights are found in the first 10 amendments to the Constitution, also known as the Bill of Rights. These rights were incorporated into the U.S. Constitution as a means of providing citizens with certain protections against government intrusion into their lives, and the most likely entity to intrude is the police. Although many of these amendments can have some bearing on policing, some are more likely than others to involve police officers. For instance, many cases center on the police violating a person's First Amendment right to freedom of speech or to peaceable assembly. Yet the majority of cases that involve the police pertain to the Fourth Amendment (the right of the people against unreasonable searches and seizures), and some cases center on protections found in the Fifth and Sixth Amendments, mostly the right against self-incrimination (Fifth) and the right to legal counsel (Sixth). Let's start with the amendment that has the most bearing on what the police do: the Fourth Amendment.

The Fourth Amendment

The Fourth Amendment provides for the "right of the people to be secure in their persons, houses, papers, and effects, against unreasonable searches and seizures." We, as Americans, have an implied right to privacy against

In most cases, police officers must have a search warrant in order to search our homes. If they don't have a warrant, defense attorneys may try to have the evidence excluded at trial.

© AP Photo/Mary Murphy, Pool

the government conducting unreasonable searches and taking either us or our stuff away. Typically we think of the police as the most likely government agent that will conduct a search or seizure, but the Fourth Amendment applies to any government agent or government action against the people. What is not protected against is another citizen's trying to conduct a search or take our property. For that we have civil law.

The Fourth Amendment says that, for the police to conduct a search, they must have **probable cause**, which is presented before a judge or magistrate, in order to secure an arrest warrant or a search warrant. *Probable cause* has been defined by the U.S. Supreme Court as more than just a hunch or suspicion. It is said to exist when "the fact and circumstance within [the officer's] knowledge and of which they [have] reasonably trustworthy information [are] sufficient to warrant a prudent man in believing that the [suspect] had committed or was committing an offense."[5] In other words, to obtain an arrest warrant, the police must have some kind of factual information that leads them to believe that a person has committed a crime, or that a person is hiding contraband (something illegal). If the police have probable cause, then, and only then, can they search us, take our property, and/or take us to jail.

Warrantless Searches

Although the concept behind the Fourth Amendment sounds good, in reality it is often hard to carry out. The complexity arises because it is not always convenient or practical for a police officer to secure an arrest warrant before making an arrest. Therefore, the U.S. Supreme Court, over time, has issued rulings that have allowed for searches and seizures to be conducted without warrants. This does not mean that the standard of probable cause is lessened. Officers still need probable cause. And, in most cases, officers will still secure the arrest warrant or search warrant from a judge or magistrate. There are, however, *exceptions* to the Fourth Amendment that allow the police to conduct searches and seize people or property without a warrant. These exceptions consist of consent searches, searches incident to arrest, plain-view searches, automobile searches, and searches dealing with exigent circumstances (see Figure 8.2).[6]

The first exception to the warrant requirement is for **consent searches**. In these cases, police officers are allowed to conduct a search without a warrant because the individual waived his or her Fourth Amendment rights. Essentially, the police may ask an individual if they may search the person's house or car. If the person refuses, he or she has retained his or her Fourth Amendment rights. Someone who allows the police to conduct the search has given consent, effectively waiving his or her Fourth Amendment rights. Two major requirements go along with consent searches. The first is that the consent cannot be "the result of duress or

probable cause: The evidence that a reasonable person would believe to indicate criminal behavior.

consent searches: Legal searches conducted without a warrant, when an individual has waived his or her Fourth Amendment rights.

coercion, express or implied."[7] The police cannot surround a person's car with six other officers and their patrol cars with guns drawn and ask for consent to search the car. That would constitute *duress*. *Coercion* is more subtle and might involve holding on to someone's driver's license and registration and asking if they can search the person's car. The person does not feel free to go and might believe he or she was coerced into consenting to the search; hence, the person would not be giving true consent. The second requirement is that, once a person gives consent, that person has the ability to restore his or her Fourth Amendment rights. For example, if someone consents to have a police officer search his or her car, and after searching the interior of the car, the officer wants to search the trunk, the person has the right to say, "No, I no longer consent to the search." In addition, the restoration of one's Fourth Amendment rights does not provide an officer with probable cause to believe the person is hiding something in the trunk.

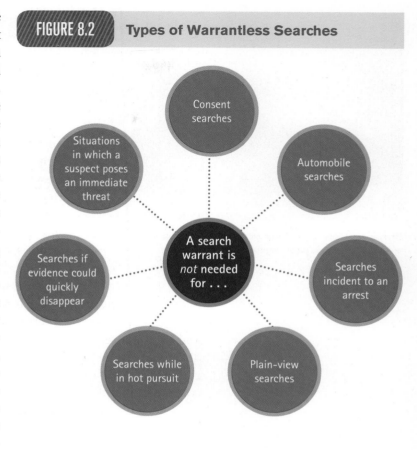

FIGURE 8.2 **Types of Warrantless Searches**

A search warrant is *not* needed for . . .

- Consent searches
- Automobile searches
- Searches incident to an arrest
- Plain-view searches
- Searches while in hot pursuit
- Searches if evidence could quickly disappear
- Situations in which a suspect poses an immediate threat

The next exception relates to **searches incident to arrest**. If a police officer arrives at a call and finds someone has committed a crime, say burglarizing a home or robbing a bank, the officer is allowed to make the arrest without a search warrant and conduct a search incident to arrest. These events must, however, occur in the proper order: probable cause, arrest, and *then* search incident to arrest. This warrantless search is limited in scope, and, according to the U.S. Supreme Court, is permitted only "to remove any weapon that the person might seek to use in order to resist arrest or effect his escape" and "to seize any evidence on the arrestee's person in order to prevent its concealment or destruction."[8] As with consent searches, two major requirements accompany searches incident to arrest. The first is that the search must be contemporaneous to the arrest. In other words, it must occur at the time of the arrest. The other major requirement relates to the extent of the search. The Court ruled that "a warrantless search 'incident to a lawful arrest' may generally extend to the area that is considered to be in the 'possession' or under the 'control' of the person arrested."[9] Whatever is within reach of the person at the time of the arrest, often called

searches incident to arrest: Legal searches conducted without a warrant, after police officers have placed a person under arrest.

Police officers do not need a search warrant in order to conduct a search that is incident to th arrest.

© LUCY NICHOLSON/Reuters/Corbis

Here, a Secret Service officer searches a vehicle after it managed to get past one of the road blocks protecting the White House campus.

© BRENDAN SMIALOWSKI /Getty Images

the arm-span rule, is allowed to be searched without a warrant. In other words, if the police arrest a suspect in the garage, they can search most of the garage, but not the rest of the house. To do that, the police would need a search warrant.

Another exception to the warrant requirement is known as **plain-view searches**. The police are authorized to conduct a search when an illegal item (contraband) is seen by the police officer in plain view. As with the two preceding warrantless exceptions, there are two requirements involved for the plain-view search to be legal. First, the police officer has to have the legal right to be wherever the contraband is located. If the officer is on public property, then it is legal, but if he or she is on private property and has no right to be there, then it would not be allowed. Second, the item has to be truly in plain sight and visible. If the officer has to move something to see it, then it is not truly in plain view, and the seizure of the item would not be in keeping with the plain-view doctrine.[10] If the police officer sees something in plain view and that officer has the legal right to be there, then no warrant is required to seize the contraband in plain view.

The fourth warrantless search authorized by court decisions is the *automobile search*. Due to the rather mobile nature of a car, it is unrealistic for a police officer to tell the driver to "wait there" while going to secure a search warrant for the vehicle. This case actually came up during Prohibition, when cars were being used to run alcohol (contraband) from illegal stills into the cities. The Supreme Court in the case of *Carroll v. U.S.* (1925) stated that the warrantless search was authorized because the evidence could have been destroyed or simply driven away. This became known as the *Carroll doctrine*. The Court, however, was very explicit in that probable cause must still be present before the search can be conducted, and it had to be a vehicle that was truly mobile and easily moved (a car on blocks or an immobile mobile home does not qualify!). Numerous other cases have helped to clarify many of the nuances of an automobile search, such as how far the search is allowed, or the reasonableness standard. For instance, you are not allowed to search for stolen tires in the glove compartment.

The final exception involves **searches based on exigent circumstances**. Exigent circumstances are those situations that are typically emergencies or very unusual incidents. Typically three categories of circumstances are recognized: hot pursuit, escape and/or presenting a danger to others, and evanescent evidence. In the case of *hot pursuit*, numerous factors must be in place for the warrantless search to be justified: The police must be legally justified in pursuing the suspect in the first place; a serious offense must have just occurred (no hot pursuit for someone who tore up a parking ticket!); the pursuit must truly be hot and immediately after the crime occurred; and the scope of the search is greatly limited to the suspect and where any weapon or contraband may be found (where the suspect may have tried to get rid of it during the pursuit). The second category of exigent circumstances, related to *escape and/or presenting a danger to others,* refers to situations when taking the time to secure the warrant would present a clear and present danger to the community if the police officers did not act immediately. The final exigent circumstance is known as *evanescent* (something that quickly fades or disappears) *evidence.* In this case, a warrantless search is authorized because the evidence could be destroyed easily and quickly (for example, flushing drugs down a toilet). The idea behind these exigent circumstances is that the police, acting on probable cause but under extreme circumstances, must have the authority to conduct the warrantless search.

Police officers must be well trained in order to determine whether they can search for evidence without a warrant. Circumstances are not always entirely clear, and decisions must be made rather quickly. The "Ethical Decision Making" box in this chapter provides a scenario for your review.

The police will often conduct another type of search called an **administrative search**, or an *inventory search*, but these are not searches in the sense of the Fourth Amendment. Rather, they are administrative in nature and done as part of routine police duties. For instance, if a police officer arrests a driver for driving while intoxicated (DWI) and there were no passengers in the car, the officer must have the car towed. Because items in the car need to be accounted for, the officer is required by departmental policy to conduct an inventory of the vehicle's contents. This is not a search for contraband but simply a search for accountability purposes. If, however, the officer comes across contraband, he or she, having the legal right to have found it, may use it as evidence for purposes of probable cause and then secure a search warrant to search the rest of the vehicle for similar contraband.

All five of these warrantless searches, as well as the actual search warrant obtained from a judge or magistrate, are based on probable cause, circumstances under which the police have some evidence that a crime has been committed and contraband is located someplace. Often, however,

administrative search: Searches conducted without a warrant for inventory purposes, when police take property, into their possession for legal purposes.

ETHICAL DECISION MAKING

WHAT IS A "REASONABLE" SEARCH?

Chandra Katz is a criminal justice student taking online courses while working as a police officer at the local university. Officer Katz is patrolling the streets adjacent to the residence halls when she sees someone climbing into one of the windows. Katz wants to make sure that the individual is not a burglar. She knocks on the apartment door and no one answers. She turns the knob and learns the door is unlocked. She opens the door and walks in. A group of students (not criminal justice majors, we hope) is sitting in the living room smoking marijuana.

YOU DECIDE

1. Can Katz search the apartment? Why or why not?

2. Should Katz arrest the students? Explain.

3. Would it matter if the students were older, or if they lived in Colorado? Explain.

Police officers must read the Miranda warnings to suspects prior to questioning them about their involvement in a crime.

Wikimedia Commons

when the police begin conducting an investigation, they do not have facts or evidence but only a suspicion or hunch. A suspicion or hunch is often based on an officer's past experience, but it still does not amount to probable cause The police in these circumstances are said to have a **reasonable suspicion**. In the event that an officer has a reasonable suspicion that someone has committed or is about to commit a crime, he or she has the ability to conduct a *stop and frisk* (see Chapter 7).

Fifth and Sixth Amendment Rights

The cases described in this chapter so far have related to constitutional challenges to the Fourth Amendment, but many Supreme Court cases have dealt with the Fifth and Sixth Amendments, especially when it comes to confessions and interrogations. The key aspect of the Fifth Amendment is that no person "shall be compelled in any criminal case to be a witness against himself, nor be deprived of life, liberty, or property without due process of law." In this regard, people cannot be forced into confession and they have the right not to say anything to the police, for if they say something, they may be acting as a witness against themselves. In addition, a person accused of a crime has a right to due process, which means he or she is afforded certain protections. These protections show up in the Sixth Amendment, which allows persons accused of a crime "to be informed of the nature and cause of the accusation." In other words, they have to be told why they were arrested, and they also have the right to "assistance of counsel for his defence [*sic*]." If you have ever watched a police drama on television, you can see where this is going. Most of this concept is encapsulated in the famous Miranda warning (see Figure 8.3).

reasonable suspicion:
The legal standard of proof by which a reasonable person would suspect that someone might be engaged in criminal behavior; leads to an investigative detention.

FIGURE 8.3   Miranda Warning

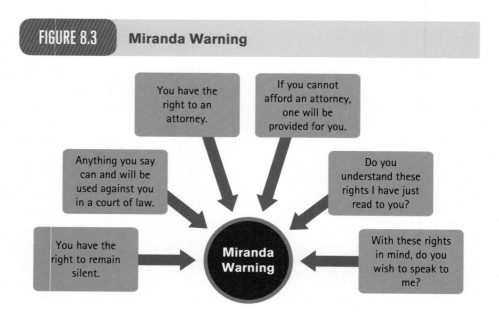

- You have the right to an attorney.
- If you cannot afford an attorney, one will be provided for you.
- Anything you say can and will be used against you in a court of law.
- Do you understand these rights I have just read to you?
- You have the right to remain silent.
- With these rights in mind, do you wish to speak to me?

Miranda Warning

The Miranda warning is derived from the U.S. Supreme Court case of *Miranda v. Arizona* (1966). In this case, Ernesto Miranda was arrested for the kidnapping and rape of a girl. Brought into the station by the police, he was questioned for two hours and, after confessing, signed a statement to that effect. He was, however, never told that he had the right to remain silent under the Fifth Amendment or the right to counsel under the Sixth Amendment. Miranda was convicted and sentenced to 20 to 30 years in prison, but his lawyers appealed his case. The Arizona Supreme Court upheld his conviction. It was then appealed to the U.S. Supreme Court. In the landmark case, the Supreme Court overturned Miranda's conviction. The Court stated that Miranda's rights under the Fifth and Sixth Amendments had been violated and therefore his confession could not be used in a court of law.

Miranda addressed two key factors about police procedures. First, the Miranda warning and the rights encapsulated within it do not become necessary until a person is taken into custody. What constitutes custody can be a bit murky, but essentially it means when a person has been arrested. For instance, the police may have a suspicion that someone committed a crime but no evidence. They then conduct what is known as a *Terry stop*, a temporary detention that allows the police to conduct a pat-down for public safety and to identify an individual. They ask the suspect questions. At this point, the person is not in custody of the police, but then again, he or she is not free to go. Perhaps the suspect then says something that gives the officer probable cause to make the arrest, which the officer does by placing handcuffs on the suspect and telling the individual he or she is under arrest. At this point, for purposes of Miranda, the suspect is in custody and, before questioning, the individual must be read the Miranda warning. This raises the second major factor in the *Miranda* decision: What constitutes interrogation? If the officer asks the suspect his or her name and address, without reading the Miranda warning, would that be a violation? The answer is no. Administrative questions are different from the interrogation of a suspect for a crime. The Miranda warning must be read only when questions pertain to the individual's involvement in the crime.

The Supreme Court's decisions, based on the protections found especially in the Fourth, Fifth, and Sixth Amendments to the Constitution, not only ensure the protection of civil liberties but also help to define police policies and procedures. For example, Supreme Court decisions have influenced when the police can and cannot search, whether they are allowed to enter private property when in hot pursuit of a suspect, and what they must say to crime suspects before interrogating them (that is, the Miranda warning). The government at all three levels (federal, state, and local) and in all three branches (legislative, executive, and judicial) has a profound influence over the police, but several other entities also exert political influence over the police.

The Miranda warnings are named after Ernest Miranda, whose conviction was overturned after the Supreme Court ruled that the failure to tell Miranda about his right to remain silent violated Miranda's rights.

© AP Photo, File

FEATURE VIDEO
Witness to Innocence Introductions

Economic Influences

Police departments often face economic influences on a daily basis. They can accomplish a lot and can carry out much of the political desires of politicians, the media, and the public if they have the money and resources to do so. However, these days, more and more police departments are expected to "do more with less." In times of austerity, police departments face tough choices about how to provide policing services with diminishing resources.

There have been some common trends in terms of how police departments are responding to these issues. The first set of approaches tend to be the extreme but include various means of reorganizing the police departments themselves, essentially consolidating them. To avoid duplication of management, the various agencies may consolidate under one management organization, public safety, which then oversees police, fire, and emergency medical technicians (ambulances).[11] Another form of police consolidation involves the merger of two or more organizations into one. Finally, police departments are sometimes dissolved, which means that either the local sheriff's office or the state police pick up responsibility for providing police services. A less extreme method for dealing with economic austerity falls into the category of sharing services and resources. Examples include shared SWAT teams and training facilities and the contracting of existing police for services in areas that can't support their own departments.

Two other means for dealing with austerity measures involve either reorganizing internally or seeking external funds. In the case of reorganizing internally, police departments may convert positions that were staffed by police officers to civilian positions, which are usually less expensive because the pay, benefits, and costs associated with outfitting a civilian are less than for a police officer. This is known as **civilianization**. Another means of reorganizing internally is to develop various positions, whether by sworn officers or civilians, into multitasking positions. For instance, detectives assigned to investigating gangs and organized crime may also be assigned to homeland security units because of their skill set.

Finally, the seeking of **external funds**, such as grants and budgetary supplements, has become more popular over the past 20 years. Both the states and the federal government have tried to influence American policing through various grant-funding projects. The federal government in the mid-1990s provided hiring grants for those departments willing to move toward community policing, whereas more recently the Department of Homeland Security has offered grants to police departments wanting to become better prepared to respond to terrorist attacks or natural disasters. Police departments may also seek funding from other sources, such as agencies that fund research. They can obtain budgetary resources to implement a program or technology in exchange for allowing researchers to evaluate its success. In other cases, they may simply lobby the local or state government to provide more funds in order to advance similar projects.

Grant funding has raised some questions about the funds that police departments receive and the programs they implement. Some observers think that this is all about what the latest need is in policing. Prior to 2001, there was little concern for police engaging in a war on terror, but

VIDEO
Robert Bates Speaks

civilianization: The practice of transferring job duties of police officers to nonsworn, civilian personnel.

external funds: Grants and budgetary supplements police departments seek from external sources.

that changed after 9/11. Now police need funding to prevent, prepare for, and recover from terrorist attacks. This is known as *contingency theory*.[12] Others think that whenever the federal government or various research organizations create grant-funding opportunities, police departments chase after these dollars whether or not they really want to implement the subject of the grant. This is known as resource dependency theory.[13] Both of these theories are simply different perspectives that try to explain police behavior, but they create an interesting debate: Are the police responding to a need, or are they chasing money?

Social Influences

Policing has witnessed numerous social changes throughout its history. These changes have helped to shape modern police work. Social changes related to women, race, juveniles, and societal norms are particularly relevant to policing.

Women and Policing

As women have gained equal rights to men, we have seen women in policing change with the societal changes. In the mid- to late 1880s, society was very male oriented, and as a reflection, policing was a male-oriented profession. At the turn of the century, society became more open to the contributions of women, but working women were limited to the "helping" professions: teaching, nursing, or caring for the young and the old.[14] Police departments began to reflect this change by hiring "police matrons," who were limited to dealing with female prisoners, youth, and the elderly.[15] Especially after the civil rights and women's movements of the 1950s to the 1970s, women gained more balanced rights. Once again, policing reflected this change in society, by law, accepting women as full-fledged police officers in 1972. The fear, of course, was that women could not perform effectively as police officers, yet study after study has put that concern to rest.

AUTHOR VIDEO
Women and Race

In the end, although women often carry out their duties differently than male officers, there is no difference between men and women in job performance.[16]

In the United States today, just under 12% (or 1 in 8) of police officers are women (see Figure 8.4). Larger cities tend to hire more female police officers and more females as civilian workers. This trend has remained stable over time despite efforts to increase the proportion of female police officers.

There is no difference between the way female and male police officers perform their duties.

© Hill Street Studios/Blend Images/Corbis

Race and Policing

In regard to race, the story is similar. In the mid- to late 1800s, a few police departments employed minorities to

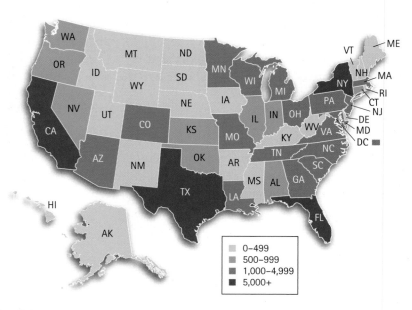

Number of Female Law Enforcement Officers, by State, 2013

Bureau of Justice Statistics

police their own communities, but once Jim Crow laws took effect (see Chapter 6), it was rare to see a police department hire anyone of color.[17] In those rare instances, the officer was typically still assigned to a neighborhood of his own race. It was almost unheard of for a police chief to hire a Black officer and assign him to work a mostly White neighborhood. Jim Crow laws began to fall in the 1950s and 1960s, and after passage of civil rights laws, minorities were hired and given the same assignments as White police officers. Just as with women police officers, there were concerns about the performance of minority police officers, but the research continually finds little difference. In fact, one argument in the 1970s was that if police departments hired Black officers, they would be more lenient on Black suspects. This turns out *not* to be the case. In fact, if anything, they tend to be a bit more severe when arresting black suspects.[18]

Approximately 25% (or 1 in 4) of the police officers in the United States are racial or ethnic minorities. The majority tend to be Black/African American (11.9%) and Hispanic/Latino (10.3%). Although the numbers remain relatively low, police departments across the country have been actively recruiting minority police officers since the mid- to late 1990s.

Juveniles and Policing

Social changes have also shaped how the police respond to cases involving juveniles. Prior to the early 1900s, juvenile suspects were handled much the same way as adult suspects. With the creation of the juvenile court system and reformers advocating for more lenient handling of juveniles, this changed in this early 1900s. A major shift in the 1960s, recognizing the existence of child abuse as a social phenomenon, broadened the jurisdiction of the police over juveniles. Today, police work with juveniles in at least three different situations: (a) when juveniles are suspects, (b) when juveniles are in need of protection from their parents, and (c) when providing community service activities.

Many researchers have examined how police respond to juvenile offenders. It is perhaps not surprising that the juvenile's demeanor is one of the strongest predictors of whether officers will take juveniles into custody. It makes sense. If juvenile suspects are rude to officers, they are more likely to be arrested. Police officers have different options when working with juvenile suspects than they might have with adult suspects. For example, an officer could choose to notify the suspect's parents and drop the case upon notification. Imagine if the police tried this option with a 25-year-old offender! Also, juveniles have slightly different rights than adult offenders. As an illustration, before beginning to question a juvenile who has been taken into custody, police are expected to make a good faith effort to locate and notify the juvenile's parents or guardians.

Police officers will also work with juveniles who need protection from their parents or guardians. In these cases, police officers will work closely with child protective services workers to ensure that children are removed from their homes as safely as possible. Three barriers sometimes arise in these cases. First, police officers and social workers have different orientations, and these differences can make it harder to work together. Second, police officers are adequately prepared (and trained) to work with offenders, but they receive much less training on working with victims. Third, the police can be viewed negatively by juveniles out of fear.

Police officers also work with juveniles in various community service activities. In some cases, police officers will visit local schools to give crime prevention talks. In other situations, juveniles might visit the police department or join a youth police academy. These efforts are intended to promote prosocial norms and improve the way that police are viewed by young people.

Societal Norms and Policing

Shifts in societal norms regarding topics as disparate as tattoos, gay marriage, and marijuana legalization have had an impact on policing. For example, 20 or 30 years ago, the only people who had tattoos were ex-convicts, sailors, and members of biker gangs. Today, tattoos are as ubiquitous as cell phones. Thirty years ago, police could use tattoos as *heuristic devices*, or judgmental shortcuts, to determine that the person they were dealing with, if he or she had a tattoo, might be dangerous. That no longer applies, as so many people have them. The police have to learn to be more discerning about types of tattoos, to determine whether they represent someone's fancy or markings for gang membership.

As American society becomes more accepting of homosexuality and gay marriage, police departments and police officers have been affected by these changes. Among the issues that departments need to address are the provision of same-sex partner benefits and gender-identity discrimination in the workplace.[19]

Police officers must be able to differentiate between gang tattoos and "normal" tatoos. One of these photos is a gang tattoo and the other is not.

Wikimedia Commons

Finally, consider again the legalization of marijuana in several states. This change can have an impact on police departments regarding how they enforce the laws. In this case, smoking marijuana may be legal, but what about driving under the influence of marijuana?[20] As with alcohol, how does one know when someone is too impaired to drive? Another related consideration is in the hiring of police officers. If departmental policy prevents the hiring of someone who has engaged in recreational marijuana use, yet marijuana is now a legal substance in that state, can the police department still bar a user from employment with the agency?[21] All of these social influences, and many others, will have a profound impact on the police.

Technological Influences

The final external influence on the police is technology. Remember that technology is a neutral creation, something created in someone's mind to do something and then made a reality through engineering, design, and trial and error. It is neither good nor bad. How people use that technology is what may translate into something used for good or something used for evil. That places technology into two primary categories, that which is used by the police and that which is used by criminals.

Policing's adaptation of technology to criminal investigation has a long history.[22] In the late 1800s, police departments used street-corner callboxes to relay information to officers in the field. August Vollmer adopted technologies such as bicycle and motor vehicle patrols, early computers, and the hard sciences by way of the first crime lab for criminal investigations, in both the Berkeley and Los Angeles Police Departments. Vollmer was also instrumental in the adoption of the polygraph (lie detector) and two-way radios, and he mentored his police officers in the development of these new technologies. Over time, patrol vehicles have adapted to onboard computers, dashboard cameras, and GPS tracking systems, all of which have been designed to enhance policing. More recent technologies, such as iPads, drones, and gunshot detection systems, have all been fielded to police officers. Each time a new technology is fielded to the police, it

AUTHOR VIDEO
Media's Influence on Policing

changes and influences how police work is conducted.[23] Some careers in law enforcement, for example, were developed specifically in response to technological advancements.

Criminals, however, also adapt to new technology. Identity theft, fake websites to steal credit card information, and ATM reader devices installed at real ATMs are adaptations of technology for criminal purposes. In turn, the police have had to adapt to the technology in order to investigate these types of criminal violations. For example, the police have had to learn how to use social media, since many pedophiles now use this technology to find new victims.

As discussed in the preceding section, broader societal shifts have influenced the way that police officers operate. This is also the case with technology. Social media didn't exist a few short years ago, yet this technology has redefined what was historically known as the "smoking gun." Facebook posts, tweets, and Instagram photos sometimes provide police the evidence they need to charge suspects with crimes. See the "Criminal Justice and the Media" box in this chapter for an example.

A possible third category of policing-related technology use involves the potential for the police to abuse technology for personal reasons or gains. Such abuse could include using databases to find information on people not related to the performance of their duties, employing street-corner cameras to invade people's privacy, or using stun guns as a mechanism for police brutality. In other cases, there is the threat that police departments may use the technology

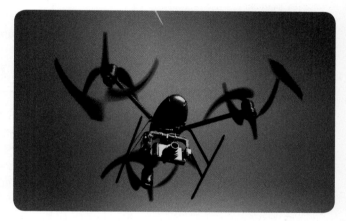

Some law enforcement agencies have used drones to search for criminal evidence from the sky.

© Staff/Reuters/Corbis

CRIMINAL JUSTICE and the **MEDIA:**
INSTAGRAM POST LEADS TO FELONY CHARGES

One 19-year-old man learned the hard way that the police actually search Instagram accounts. He had been under observation by the police for a few offenses when officers decided to look at his social media postings. On Instagram, officers found a photo of the man holding two guns. Using the photo as probable cause, the officers subsequently searched the offender's home and found enough evidence to file 142 charges against the man, who reportedly led a burglary ring. As another indication of the power of social media, the sheriff's office announced the execution of the search warrant on its Facebook page. In all, 32 viewers "liked" the page announcing this case.

Instagram led to an arrest for this suspect after police used the photo to support a search warrant. The search resulted in evidence implicating the offender in a burglary ring.

Instagram account of Depree Johnson, duce22ceritfied

http://www.nydailynews.com/news/crime/man-instagram-leads-142-felony-charges-article-1.1547932#VZCI5ElqHymCQ0fC.97

available to them to conduct investigations, but that, by employing the technology, they may violate Americans' civil rights. Recent controversies include the police's use of technology to look at cell phone usage and to track people's movements without obtaining a search warrant and the use of drones to look for criminal activity on the ground.[24] These technological advancements carry with them the possibility that our civil rights will be violated, especially our protections against unreasonable searches and seizures, as found in the Fourth Amendment.

BEYOND A REASONABLE DOUBT 8.1

Which of the following PEST categories is the proper one for criminal laws that the police enforce?

(a) Political, (b) Economic, (c) Social, (d) Technology

The answer can be found on page 521.

➡ Internal Issues

The police also face a number of internal issues or pressures. First, there is a pervasive *police subculture* that—again, though not inherently good or evil—can prove to be both beneficial and harmful to society. Second, *patrol-related issues*, or life-on-the-street factors, have a profound impact on the police. Finally, there are *police officer issues*, or personal issues such as dealing with high levels of stress; facing threats, injuries, and death on a routine basis; and simply trying to always do the right thing, day-in and day-out (see Figure 8.5). Given that these internal issues can be seen as both opportunities and threats, they generally reflect a combination of the strengths and weaknesses of the police officer, the organization, and the profession.[25]

Police Subculture

The police certainly have a subculture, but it is an elusive thing to understand. It is not as well defined as the rules and regulations the police must follow, since the subculture consists more of unwritten rules. Nor are police officers required to follow these unwritten rules; they just do. Think about how you walk down the hallway to your class. You walk on the right-hand side of the hall. There is no law that says you have to walk on the right-hand side, but it is a shared custom that most of us follow because it creates a sense of order in the hallway. Or, if there is an elevator in your building, what do you do when you get on it? You turn around and face the doors, then look at the floor, the ceiling, the number panel, or your cell phone. This is a shared norm. No one looks at the other people on the elevator or, worse, stands facing the back of the elevator (try that some time and see how fast people exit the elevator).

When a group of people have the same customs, norms, and values, what is known as a *culture* is present (if you have taken a sociology class, this should sound familiar). A *subculture* is a group of people who live within the larger culture, and although they share the same values, norms,

VIDEO
Death in
St. Augustine

and customs as the greater culture, they also have their own unique ways of doing things. They have their own customs, values, and norms. Think about police officers. Wherever you go, aren't they roughly the same? How can that be when so many towns, cities, counties, and states have their own police forces? It is because all police officers, all over the United States, have shared experiences that help to create the **police subculture**. There are certain things about being a police officer that every police officer has in common, regardless of the agency for which he or she works. The major things they share are the dangers of working the street, control of territory, the use of force, and solidarity.[26] (See Figure 8.6.)

One of the most common traits that all police officers share is the dangers they face on the job.[27] Nearly every police officer starts off his or her policing career on patrol, and regardless of the size of the town or city in which he or she serves, that officer faces the *potential* for danger because he or she wears the uniform. Police officers know that at any moment, they may receive a call-for-service that could instantly place their lives in danger, whether it is an armed suspect, a high-speed pursuit, or the unpredictability of a domestic

FIGURE 8.5   **Internal Factors Influencing Police Work**

police subculture: The values and traditions that are particular to police officers.

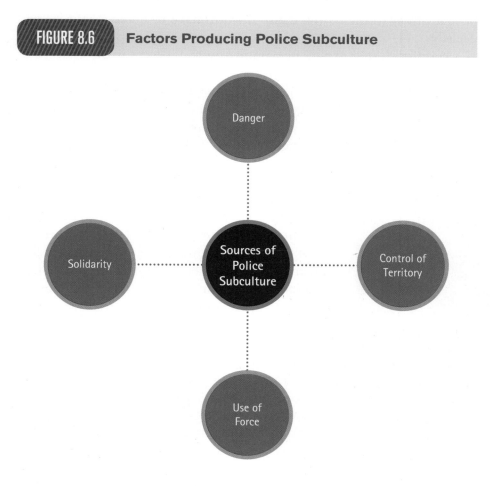

FIGURE 8.6   **Factors Producing Police Subculture**

dispute. Policing can be a hazardous job, which is an experience all police officers have in common. Note here that we said *"potential* for danger," not necessarily danger itself. Policing is a dangerous profession, but police officers do not face serious dangers every shift, every week, or even every month. Some experience more danger than others, such as those in large urban environments over those in rural counties. So police officers do not necessarily share the same *level* of real danger, but they all share the *potential* for danger.

An element of the shared sense of danger is the unpredictability of calls-for-service.[28] Officers often go through long periods of total boredom, and then something happens and they find they themselves in a police pursuit, a fight, or some other terror-inducing situation. This adds to the high level of potential danger because one minute the officer is reading a newspaper or talking with a citizen, and the next instant he or she is in the fight of his or her life. There is no time to prepare for the encounter, which adds to the dangerousness of the situation. In fact, what pushes this to the extreme is the fact that police are sometimes called upon to make split-second decisions, knowing full well that their decision will be criticized and talked about for weeks, months, or potentially years to come.[29] Knowing that these things happen, but not knowing *when* they will happen, contributes to all police officers' developing a strong suspicion of the people they encounter on the street, always wondering if the next person they encounter is going to be the one that is unpredictable, pose a threat to them, and cause them to have to make a split-second decision.

Another shared experience among police officers is the concept of control of territory.[30] Police officers on patrol typically work a beat, a geographically defined area they are responsible for controlling. Multiple concepts are wrapped up together in this concept. The first is **territorial control**, or as one author calls it "dominion," which is the exercise of command and control over their territory, or their beat. Control, then, is another element in that the police work to control crime and criminals in their beats and to maintain a sense of order, typically called **order maintenance**. All of this leads back to the police using their authority to keep people in line. Although most people stay within the law of their own accord, police must use coercion to keep the more law-breaking-minded individuals from actually breaking the law. When coercion no longer works, the police must then resort to arrest. All police officers, regardless of where they work, all understand the sense of territorial control and coercion, and they all use it to maintain order.

Another trait all police officers have in common is their authorization by the state to use force when necessary. No other government agency is authorized to use force against citizens, not even the U.S. military. The mere fact that police officers are authorized

territorial control: The exercise of command and control over a territory or beat by police officers.

order maintenance: The maintenance of territorial control over a specific area or beat by police officers.

Police agencies are the only government agencies authorized by the state to use force.

© Jewel Samad/AFP/Getty Images

the **use of force** gives them something in common, but the reality is that, while working the street, they often will have to use force. This is an experience they all share. Force can involve using a commanding voice; laying hands on someone; carrying out unarmed self-defense; using the baton, tear gas, pepper spray, or Taser; and, in extreme cases, using a firearm, namely, the use of deadly force. Not all police officers find themselves in **deadly force** encounters, but at some point in their careers they will assert force over suspects who do not comply with their authority or resist arrest.

Another common experience that all police officers share is the concept of solidarity.[31] Although solidarity is not unique to the police (that is, many other professionals, such as firefighters, military soldiers, and emergency room nurses, share this trait), it is especially dominant in the police subculture. Solidarity is the simple reality that police officers stick together; they watch each other's backs; they typically feel comfortable talking only to one another; and they do not turn on their fellow officers. This last point is often known as the blue wall of silence, in that police officers are reluctant to "rat out," or tell on another officer. There is a moral reason for this, as well as a practical one. Police officers have to trust one another, and if an officer loses that trust, he or she may lose the support of fellow officers. If that happens, at the very least it can make the work environment uncomfortable; at the extreme, it can be life threatening, especially if officers are unwilling to back up an officer who violated the blue wall of silence. All of this centers on trust in that officers must trust each other, but they also develop a distrust of everyone else, creating an "us-versus-them" mentality. In addition, to maintain the blue wall, there is the implied realization that police officers must maintain a sense of secrecy among them. The phrase "thin blue line" has been used to describe this police officer solidarity (see Figure 8.7). This phrase has been used to refer to the danger officers face, their efforts to separate good people from bad people, and the practice of using a blue ribbon to commemorate police officers killed in the line of duty.

Patrol-Related Issues

The police subculture is often the result of the encounters police face in performing their duties. Whether it is criminal activity or traffic enforcement, police officers spend much of their time working patrol and dealing with people. These interactions with citizens create many of the patrol-related issues that officers will face on the job. This is because no two police encounters, whether making criminal arrests or giving tickets, will ever be the same. There are laws the police can enforce that are uniform, and there are policies and procedures to guide them, but when people are involved, there can be no automated response. This is why the police must be able to exercise discretion in the performance of their duties. **Discretion** refers to the flexibility the police

VIDEO
Grateful for Force

use of force: The authority for police to use force when necessary.

deadly force: The authority for police to use force that can cause death when their lives or the lives of other citizens are placed in immediate jeopardy.

discretion: A police officer's ability to decide whether to apply the law or not.

FIGURE 8.7   **The Thin Blue Line: Police Solidarity**

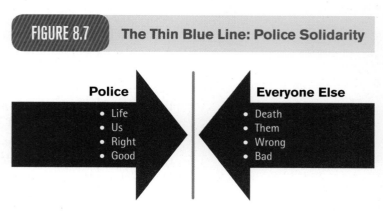

Police
- Life
- Us
- Right
- Good

Everyone Else
- Death
- Them
- Wrong
- Bad

have in making decisions. In addition to the external influences we discussed earlier (for example, the law, public opinion, social norms), many other factors will affect police officers' discretion when they perform their duties on the street. Scholars have generally placed these factors into four categories: organizational, neighborhood, situational, and individual.[32]

Organizational variables are the conditions set by the police department that can influence an officer's decision making, such as the bureaucratic nature of the agency, the shifts worked (that is, fixed or rotating), and the area (beat or sector) in which the officer is assigned. These factors can influence an officer's decision making in the way the factors come together. Think of an officer on the midnight shift, assigned to the outskirts of town, in a warehouse district where no one lives or works at night. The assignment can leave the officer feeling isolated and bored. Now think of that officer being assigned to the evening shift, after having just rotated off of midnights, in the most crime-ridden area in the city, on a foot patrol, without a partner. Exhausted from working midnights, now the officer must be extra vigilant when working a potentially dangerous assignment. Each of these organizational factors, all out of the officer's hands, will have an influence on his or her discretion and decision making.

Neighborhood variables include location, as in the preceding scenario. For example, one neighborhood was an isolated, low-crime area; the other was a highly populated, high-crime area. Other neighborhood variables found to influence officers to make more arrests, use force, and engage in more encounters are more racially diverse neighborhoods, more economically depressed neighborhoods, and the level of crime and deviance known in the neighborhood. Perhaps counterintuitively, the police are more likely to use their discretion not to arrest in high-crime areas and to choose to arrest in low-crime areas. Think in terms of a neighborhood that often has rapes, robberies, and homicides; catching a juvenile with a marijuana joint is not going to be considered serious. By contrast, think of a very safe neighborhood that rarely has any crime at all; that marijuana joint just became a very serious crime there.[33]

Situational variables include the suspect, the victim, and witnesses.[34] First, there is a difference in outcomes depending on whether the police are summoned to a call or they initiated the encounter themselves. In the former case, the police often focus on the suspect and the victim, whereas in the latter case, they tend to focus on their own perspective and the suspect. Police are more likely to make an arrest when they initiate the call. Other variables include the demeanor and attitude of the suspect and the victim. A hostile suspect is more likely to be arrested. If the victim is upset and hostile toward the suspect, the suspect is more likely to be arrested. To some degree, police feed off of witnesses as well. Their demeanor may influence the officer to arrest or not arrest. In addition, the relationship between the suspect and the victim will also play a role. Other factors include, age, sex, and race. Suspects who are young, male, and Black tend to be more likely to be arrested, whereas older, White females are least likely to be arrested. Research on the issue of race is highly mixed. Much of the research shows that Blacks are more likely to be arrested, but the findings have varied.

Some researchers have argued the issue is not race, but rather that black youth are more likely to be hostile toward the police. Others have said the situation is primarily the result of race, hence, the term *racial profiling*. Additional situational variables that lead to arrest are the seriousness of the offense (the more serious the crime, the more likely an arrest); the suspect's mental state (the more mentally unstable, the less likely police will arrest or the more likely they will do a mental commitment); and the presence of others (the more people watching, the more the police feel they must make an arrest).

Individual variables refers to the characteristics of the police officer.[35] The officer's age, race, education, and experience level will influence police officer discretion and decision making. Younger officers are more likely than older officers to initiate police-citizen contacts and to make arrests. Along with age typically go experience and education, both of which have similar findings to the outcomes for age. When it comes to race, the research is mixed, but much of it has found that White officers are more likely to make arrests overall (of anyone), whereas Black officers are more likely to treat Black suspects more severely. Some research suggests that when the likelihood of arrest is broken down by race, there is a greater chance overall that the police officer will make an arrest when he or she is of the same race as the suspect. It should be noted that sex was left off the list of individual variables, not because it has not been studied, but because the majority of the studies have found no discernible difference between male and female officers when it comes to arrest. The "Criminal Justice and College Students" box provides an exercise to help explain those factors that influence decision making.

Police Officer Issues

In addition to patrol-related issues, police officers themselves face a number of issues. The first, the inherent dangers within policing itself, has already been discussed to some degree. Police officers are authorized to use force and are typically taught the **use-of-force continuum** (see Figure 8.8).

> **use-of-force continuum:** The concept that, as force escalates, officers are authorized to use force that is just above the level of force being used against them.

CRIMINAL JUSTICE and **COLLEGE STUDENTS**

DECISIONS, DECISIONS, DECISIONS . . .

Although we typically use the term *discretion* to refer to decisions made by criminal justice officials, in reality we all have and use discretion in making our own decisions. Just as certain factors influence decisions made by police officers, certain factors influence our own decisions as well. As an example, make a list of the ways in which organizational, neighborhood, situational, and individual factors influenced your decision to pick your major. Then meet with a small group of your classmates and discuss with one another how various factors shaped your decision making. Also, consider how police officer discretion is different from "college student" discretion.

FIGURE 8.8   **Use-of-Force Continuum**

Lethal

Harmful

Threshold

Tactical

Professional

Officer Assessment

Assaultive (Serious Bodily Harm/Death)

Assaultive (Bodily Harm)

Resistant (Active)

Resistant (Passive)

Compliant

Subject Action

Risk Perception Categories

Officer Selection

Deadly Force

Defensive Tactics

Compliance Techniques

Contact Controls

Cooperative Controls

Officer Assessment

National Institute of Justice

This continuum reflects an understanding of the escalation of force that is authorized, typically moving from verbal commands to placing hands on a suspect to unarmed self-defense to use of baton, pepper spray, tear gas, or Taser, and finally the use of a firearm. Police are typically taught that they may use one level of force above the suspect's, so that if the suspect strikes an officer with his or her fist, the officer may use the baton. In addition, police officers are taught that they do not necessarily have to go through each step. For example, if the suspect has a knife, deadly force would be authorized. At the highest level, a police officer is authorized to use deadly force when the officer faces a situation in which his or her life or the life of a citizen is in danger. Although many people believe that the police in the United States often use deadly force, it appears to be employed only rarely.[36]

The other side of the equation—the number of people who assault, injure, and kill police officers—is perhaps more prevalent. In the 10-year period 2003–2013, the number of police officers assaulted averaged 57,892 per year, with 15,483 being injured in these assaults. Suspects use guns, knives, automobiles, and the like in these assaults. Sadly, on average, 154 police officers lose their lives each year in the line of duty. The reality, however, is that not all police officers lose their lives in deadly force encounters. Many die from such things as accidental falls, heart attacks, and automobile accidents.

One can only imagine the stress that all of this can cause police officers.[37] Researchers have typically categorized police stressors into four groups: internal stress, organizational stress, operational stress, and external stress. Although police officers would not use these labels to refer to the types of stress they confront, the labels provide a framework for understanding the sources of stress. **Internal stress** refers to officers' own personal stress, including the difficulties of making ends meet at home, family relations, fears of inadequacy, feelings of isolation, and the like. **Organizational stress** comes from the police department itself and can include difficulties with management and the problems inherent within a bureaucracy. **Operational stress** (sometimes called occupational stress) comes from specific job assignments, shift work, and dealing with criminals on the street. **External stress** is caused by those things outside of law enforcement, such as negative press coverage, negative public opinion, and laws or policies that police officers perceive will make their jobs more difficult.

The problem with all of this stress is that there are consequences. Stress is cumulative; it builds over time. Eventually, people have difficulties dealing with high levels of stress, and either they begin having personal difficulties because of it or they resort to other methods for dealing with the stress. Studies on police stress have shown that stress in officers can lead to marital and family problems, higher rates of divorce, consumption of alcohol and drugs, and, in extreme cases, suicide. Although a lot of the stress that officers face is cumulative, some of it can come from one tragic incident, such as arriving at the scene of a child fatality or a mass murder such as a school shooting. That one incident can be too much for one person to handle, and it can create a condition known as **posttraumatic stress disorder (PTSD)**. PTSD is a strong emotional reaction to one particular incident that can cause numerous emotional problems (anxiety, guilt, anger), which can turn into physical ailments (headaches, loss of sleep, ulcers).

Like anyone who suffers from stress (and that is all of us), police officers must learn to deal with the added stresses of the job. We already know that a careful diet, exercise, rest, meditation, counseling, and church attendance can decrease stress levels, if people avail themselves of these efforts. In addition, because police officers often talk only to other police officers, many police departments provide mandatory **critical-incident stress debriefing** sessions after a major incident; during these sessions, police officers who have been trained in counseling methods talk to the police officers who were involved in the incident.[38]

Although the topics discussed here are serious and policing can be rather tragic, what often gets lost is the fact that police officers who stay in policing are generally satisfied with their careers. If not, most would not stay. In fact, although many people are weeded out of policing in the academy and field training officer programs, many leave policing after discovering either other interests or that policing is not for them. Those who stay often do so because they enjoy the job, and although many do suffer burnout, most retire with no regrets for having served a career in law enforcement.[39]

internal stress: Factors that cause stress in police officers that lie inside their immediate control.

organizational stress: The stress caused by the organization, that is, the police department, for which an individual works.

operational stress: The stress associated with performing one's regular job duties.

external stress: Factors that cause stress in police officers that lie outside of their control.

posttraumatic stress disorder (PTSD): The psychological and physical distress caused by witnessing or experiencing a major catastrophic event.

critical-incident stress debriefing: A system by which trained police officers conduct debriefings of officers involved in major incidents.

TABLE 8.1	Confidence in Institutions

I am going to read you a list of institutions in American society. Please tell me how much confidence you, yourself, have in each one—a great deal, quite a lot, some, or very little?

June 7-10, 2012

	GREAT DEAL %	QUITE A LOT %	SOME %	VERY LITTLE %	NONE %	NO OPINION %	GREAT DEAL & QUITE A LOT %
The Military	43	32	18	5	1	1	75
Small Business	30	33	29	6	-	-	63
The Police	26	30	28	15	1	-	56
Church/Organized Religion	25	19	29	22	4	1	44
The Medical System	20	21	34	23	3	-	41
U.S. Supreme Court	15	22	38	20	2	3	37
The President	17	20	27	32	4	1	37
Public Schools	11	18	40	28	2	1	29
Newspapers	10	15	41	29	3	2	25
Banks	9	12	42	33	2	1	21
Television News	11	10	39	34	4	1	21
Organized Labor	11	10	37	34	4	4	21
Big Business	9	12	40	34	4	2	21
HMOs	8	11	44	29	3	6	19
U.S. Congress	6	7	34	47	5	1	13

Gallup Poll. (2013). Confidence in Institutions

VIDEO
Law and Disorder

police misconduct: Police behavior that is in violation of departmental policies and procedures, is a misuse of power and authority, or is a violation of the law.

Police Misconduct and Accountability

Although incidents of **police misconduct** are the exception and not the rule, each time they occur, they diminish policing as a whole.[40] Many people argue that police misconduct is typically committed by immoral individuals, but when one of those individuals commits misconduct, it makes all police officers look bad. This is known as the *rotten apple theory* because, as they saying goes, "one rotten apple spoils the barrel." Other people theorize that when police misconduct occurs, it is because the police organization allows it to happen, consciously or unconsciously, and since it goes through the entire department or various units, it is systemic. Hence, the alternative to the rotten apple theory is the *systemic theory* of police misconduct.

The majority of police misconduct is believed to involve primarily greed or violence.[41] In this case, police officers become greedy and simply want to commit misconduct to make money, or they are brutal and violent and cannot control themselves. Another type of misconduct has been called **noble-cause corruption**. This involves police officers becoming obsessed with righting wrongs when the criminal justice system fails, so that they take it upon themselves to mete out punishment. They do not seek financial gain, nor is violence their sole purpose. They simply want to get criminals off the street to protect society. Looking at types of police misconduct, most researchers tend to categorize them into four different groups: abuse of authority, police corruption, occupational deviance, and police crime.

Abuse of authority occurs when officers exceed their authority. For instance, we have already discussed that police officers are authorized to use force. When police officers attempt to arrest a suspect, the suspect may resist arrest, and the police may have to use force to make the arrest. If an officer has a suspect fighting him or her, and the officer strikes the person in the thigh with the baton, this would be proper use of force. If the person was lying down on the ground with his or her arms spread out as told to do, and the officer strikes the suspect one more time, this would be an example of *excessive use of force*, which means more force was used than was necessary to make an arrest. However, if a suspect made not-threatening gestures and simply called the officer names, and the officer struck the suspect with the baton, this would be an example of a *total abuse of authority*, for officers are taught not to respond to name-calling.

Police corruption involves police officers receiving some type of material reward, such as goods, services, or cash, illegally or in violation of police policies. This can be something as simple as the taking of a gratuity, such as a free cup of coffee from a service station, if it is a violation of police policies to do so. It can also include such actions as making a drug bust and turning in the drugs but not the cash obtained during the seizure, or it could involve looking away while others commit these types of crimes.

Occupational deviance includes using one's position as a police officer for personal gain, for example, fixing a friend's ticket or using one's access to criminal and driving databases to gain information on a particular person for oneself or a friend. Another form of occupational deviance might involve clocking in for court duty and then going to the gym to work out.

The final category of police misconduct involves police officers committing crimes themselves, otherwise known as *police crimes*. The activity could have the air of being related to the job, such as kicking in someone's door and searching the house without a search warrant, or trading sexual favors for not arresting a prostitute. Or it could simply involve an officer committing a theft while on duty, such as

noble-cause corruption: Police misconduct committed in order to ensure justice is served on a criminal.

occupational deviance: Improper or illegal conduct carried out while performing one's job.

The movie *Training Day* depicted an assortment of police behaviors that would, by any measure, be defined as misconduct.

WARNER BROS. PICTURES / Album/Newscom

visiting a jewelry store and taking a watch while no one is looking, since no one would suspect a police officer of committing a crime.

Police departments in the United States use a number of means to try to prevent and control corruption. For example, they offer police ethics training in the academy and additional education through in-service training. In addition, many police academies and police departments not only present the **police code of ethics** to their officers, but many have officers sign a pledge that they will live up to the code. Police departments almost universally have a departmental manual that details their policies and procedures, and these will include what is and what is not acceptable behavior for police officers (for example, a gratuities policy will tell them what they are allowed to accept: nothing, only free cups of coffee, etc.). Moreover, traditional field supervision can keep police officers from stepping out of line and engaging in any type of misconduct.

There are, however, times when more formal mechanisms must be employed to oversee police behavior. When police misconduct is alleged, the police department's **internal affairs** unit will typically investigate the case. The members of internal affairs come from the ranks, often with investigative skills, and they report directly to the police chief so as to avoid any possible conflict of interest. Although the investigators being police officers could be a conflict of interest, these officers have a duty to investigate the case regardless of what the outcome might be, and they must report their findings to the police chief, who then must answer to the city manager, mayor, and/or city council.

Citizen review boards are another mechanism put in place by many jurisdictions because of concerns about the police investigating their own.[42] These boards are groups of citizens representing various interests in the community who either review the investigations and their conduct or, rarely, conduct their own investigations.

Although citizen review can go a long way in alleviating fears of police misconduct in the internal affairs process, citizen reviews present new problems that must be dealt with. They are often expensive and duplicative, and when a disagreement exists, it can create a politically difficult situation that will diminish either the role of the police chief or the role of the citizen review board. Citizen review boards tend to be well received by citizens, but they are not received well by police officers, which creates antagonism between the police and the public they serve.

police code of ethics: The code by which many police officers are asked to live, upholding good values with strong ethics.

internal affairs: An administrative office within the police department that is charged with investigating allegations of police misconduct.

citizen review boards: Official government boards, consisting of citizens outside of the police department, that conduct investigations, oversee police investigations, or serve as appellate bodies to outcomes of police misconduct allegations.

BEYOND A REASONABLE DOUBT 8.2

Which of the following terms is most closely associated with the idea that police officers have wide latitude in their decision-making process?

(a) Use-of-force continuum, (b) Police culture, (c) Police discretion, (d) Police misconduct

The answer can be found on page 521.

Just the Facts: Chapter Summary

- Police are influenced by four major categories of external issues that can be summarized with the acronym *PEST*, which refers to political, economic, social, and technological factors.

- Laws that the police enforce are local ordinances, state law, and federal law.

- Federalism involves the national and state governments sharing power, but conflicts may arise when the different governments have competing laws.

- Judicial decisions, based on rights found in the Bill of Rights, often create case law that defines police behavior.

- The Fourth Amendment protects people against unreasonable searches and seizures and requires officers to have probable cause to obtain a warrant in order to search or arrest.

- The Supreme Court has allowed exceptions to the warrant requirement, including consent searches, searches incident to arrest, plain-view searches, automobile searches, and searches dealing with exigent circumstances.

- The exigent circumstances for a warrantless search and seizure include hot pursuit, escape and/or presenting a danger to others, and evanescent evidence.

- Police officers have the right to conduct a temporary detention, a stop and frisk, if they have reasonable suspicion to believe a crime has occurred, is occurring, or is about to occur.

- The Fifth Amendment protects people's rights to due process and against self-incrimination, and the case of *Miranda v. Arizona* (1966) created the famous Miranda warning.

- Economic influences on the police have led to the consolidation of agencies, often by way of public safety consolidation, police consolidation, or simply the dissolution of an agency.

- Other methods agencies have used to save money are sharing services (resources), contracting services, civilianization, and multitasking officers.

- Seeking external funds and lobbying are other common strategies.

- Contingency theory argues that police seek new resources because of need; by contrast, resource dependency theory argues that police chase money because it is available.

- Social influences on the police include society's changing views of women, minorities, juveniles, and societal norms.

- Technology is used by criminals in the commission of crimes and by police to investigate crimes.

- Internal issues the police face include the police subculture, patrol-related issues, and police officer issues.

- The police subculture is a subset of the larger American culture, with its own unique norms, values, and beliefs. The key elements that shape these norms are the dangers of working the street, control of territory, the use of force, and police solidarity.

- Patrol-related issues include police use of discretion and their decision making, which is based on four sets of variables: organizational, neighborhood, situational, and individual.

- Police officer issues include use of force, deadly force, and stress.

- Police stress is derived from internal stress, organizational stress, operational stress, and external stress, with extreme cases resulting in posttraumatic stress disorder.

- Police misconduct can be either individual (rotten apple theory) or throughout the agency (systemic theory); it is often motivated by greed and violence but may also be a way to deal with criminals when the system does not, known as noble-cause corruption.

- Types of police misconduct can be categorized as abuse of authority, police corruption, occupational deviance, and police crimes.

- The various methods for controlling police misconduct include training, police codes of ethics, internal affairs, and citizen review boards.

Critical Thinking Questions

1. What does the following quotation mean: "Democracy is always hard on the police"?

2. Which factors (political, economic, social, technological) do you think influence police work the most? Explain.

PART III

THE COURTS

©istockphoto.com/david franklin

COURTS

CHARGES FILED ⟶ Prosecutor rejects case

INITIAL APPEARANCE ⟶ Charges Dismissed

Preliminary Hearing

Grand Jury

Charges Dismissed

BAIL/DETENTION HEARING

- Conditional Release
- Preventative Detention
- Released on Recognizance
- Pretrial Release Officer
- Third-Party Custody
- Property Bond
- Bail Bond

ARRAIGNMENT ⟶ Charges Dismissed

Diversion Program

Successful

Unsuccessful

Appeal

Pleads Not Guilty

Pleads Guilty

PLEA BARGAIN

SENTENCING

- Deter?
- Punish?
- Rehabilitate?

TRIAL

Jury Selection

Victim/ Witness Impact Statement

Convicted

Acquitted

9

AN INTRODUCTION TO THE COURTS

HISTORY, STRUCTURE, AND ACTORS

© alessandro0770/Veer

IN SEPTEMBER 2014, THE WEBSITE TMZ.COM posted a video of football star Ray Rice knocking out his then-fiancée in the elevator of a Las Vegas hotel. Rice had already been suspended from two games as a result of the incident, which occurred the prior spring. Initially charged with aggravated assault, Rice was permitted by the court to enter a pretrial intervention program that would eventually allow him to avoid a conviction. After the video surfaced, many observers questioned how the case avoided prosecution. The decision not to prosecute the case was the result of negotiations between prosecutors and defense attorneys, and these negotiations were overseen by a judge.

To shed some light on how the court process results in decisions such as this one, in this chapter we address the court system: its history, structure, and actors.

LEARNING OBJECTIVES

After reading this chapter, students will be able to:

9.1 Describe the history of the courts

9.2 Identify the different types of courts and the types of cases they hear

9.3 Distinguish among federal, state, and local courts

9.4 Outline the process by which the Supreme Court hears a case

9.5 Describe how lower courts are arranged and their relationships

9.6 Explain the many actors in a courtroom, called the courtroom workgroup, and how they interact with each other

9.7 Explain the influences of technology on increased efficiencies in court processes

➡ History of the Courts

The U.S. judiciary system was established in **Article III of the U.S. Constitution**. In that document, one supreme court was created, but no lower federal courts were established. Instead, Congress was given the power to create other federal courts as needed (in Article III, Section 1). Because Article III did not provide much detail about the structure and function of the new judicial branch, the first Congress passed the **Judiciary Act of 1789** to define a federal court structure.

ADMISSIBLE or INADMISSIBLE Evidence

Read the statements that follow. If the statement is true, circle *admissible.* If the statement is false, circle *inadmissible.* Answers can be found on page 518.

1. **Admissible   Inadmissible**   The U.S. Supreme Court has only appellate jurisdiction to hear cases that are appealed to it from lower courts.

2. **Admissible   Inadmissible**   The U.S. Supreme Court must hear every case that is appealed to it.

3. **Admissible   Inadmissible**   The United States has a dual court system, meaning that there are state courts and federal courts that hear different types of cases.

4. **Admissible   Inadmissible**   To maintain consistency, every state court is the same in terms of structure and personnel.

5. **Admissible   Inadmissible**   A drug court is an example of a trial court of limited jurisdiction.

6. **Admissible   Inadmissible**   The courtroom workgroup includes employees who work in the courts and who work together to ensure an efficient flow of cases.

7. **Admissible   Inadmissible**   Many states and the federal courts are using more advanced technology in the courtroom as a way to improve filings and access to relevant documents.

8. **Admissible   Inadmissible**   Recent federal laws have mandated that states allow felons to serve on a jury.

The court process unfolds within the confines of a courtroom.

© Tribune Content Agency LLC/Alamy

John Marshall created the power of judicial review.

© CORBIS

Article III of the U.S. Constitution: The section of the Constitution that defines the judicial branch of government, or the court system.

Judiciary Act of 1789: The law that set forth the United States' federal court structure and defined the jurisdiction and role of the federal courts.

The act set up a system that was led by one Supreme Court composed of a chief justice and five associate justices. There would be three circuit courts, each of which would be presided over by three judges: two supreme court justices and one district judge. Thirteen district courts were also defined in the act. One district judge would preside over these courts. These courts would be placed in each of the 11 states that had ratified the Constitution by then, with separate tribunals created for Maine and Kentucky, which at the time were part of Massachusetts and Virginia, respectively.

Note that the number of justices serving on the Supreme Court was determined by Congress, not the Constitution. Although it began with only six justices, the number has been fixed at nine since 1869.

The Judiciary Act also defined more clearly the jurisdiction and the role of the federal courts. Section 2 of Article III defined the authority of the federal courts, giving the Supreme Court jurisdiction over cases involving particular parties or subjects. The Judiciary Act gave the Supreme Court original jurisdiction in some cases and appellate jurisdiction in others. According to the Judiciary Act, the circuit courts would act as lower appellate bodies. Finally, the district courts were to serve as trial courts for the federal system; they would hear cases involving petty federal crimes and admiralty issues, forfeitures, and penalties as well as minor U.S. civil cases.

The role of the Supreme Court was defined even further in the case of *Marbury v. Madison*. The chief justice at the time, John Marshall, was forced to review the Judiciary Act in light of the U.S. Constitution. He determined that Section 13 of the act, which the case hinged upon, was unconstitutional. In doing so, he also more clearly defined the judicial branch's role in reviewing acts of Congress to determine if federal laws are in violation of the Constitution. Marshall, in essence, defined the Court's power of *judicial review*, which means the Supreme Courts acts as a check on the other branches of government.

BEYOND A REASONABLE DOUBT 9.1

Which of the following established and defined the U.S. judiciary system?

(a) The Judiciary Act of 1789, (b) The U.S. Constitution, (c) State constitutions, (d) Both a and b, (e) None of the above

The answer can be found on page 521.

➡ Types of Courts

Today's courts are established in one of two ways. Those established through a constitution are called *constitutional courts*, whereas those established through a legislative process are considered to be *legislative courts*. Although these courts are created in different ways, their functions are primarily equal.

There are other ways to distinguish among courts. Courts differ as to their *jurisdictions*, or their authority to hear a case. In other words, different types of cases will be heard in different types of courts. A court of general jurisdiction will have jurisdiction over general cases, which encompasses a variety of offenses. By contrast, a court of limited, or specific, jurisdiction will hear only a specific type of case. For example, a juvenile court will hear only cases in which the defendants are within a specific age range. Another example is a drug court, which hears cases revolving around violations of drug laws.

Another concept that determines where a case is heard is **venue**. This refers to the geographic area where the trial occurs. Most trials take place within the geographic boundaries in which an alleged offense occurred. If an offense occurred in Pennsylvania, but the offender has traveled to Ohio, the offender will be returned to Pennsylvania for the trial proceedings. Occasionally, a case will be moved from the place where the offense occurred. If, for example, a case received a great amount of publicity prior to the trial, the proceedings may be held in another location to ensure a more fair process. This is referred to as a *change of venue*. This will happen only if a defendant can show that he or she cannot obtain a fair trial in the geographic jurisdiction of the offense. In this case, a petition must be filed with the court to ask for a change of venue to a neutral jurisdiction and the judge must agree to move the trial.

Another distinction can be made between courts of original jurisdiction and courts of appellate jurisdiction. Courts with **original jurisdiction** are those that hear the case initially or for the first time. Courts with **appellate jurisdiction** are those that hear appeals of rulings by courts with original jurisdiction. These courts do not hear cases first. They only review cases that were originally decided by a lower court.

Finally, a distinction is made between federal courts and state courts. Cases involving defendants charged with violating federal law, such as treason or counterfeiting money, will be heard in a federal court. A state court will hear cases related to violations of state offenses, such as murder or car theft. The two-court system is called a **dual court system** (see Figure 9.1).

VIDEO
Judge Denies
Change of Venue

venue: The place where a case is heard, typically the court located in the same geographic area in which the criminal behavior occurred.

original jurisdiction: Courts that hear cases initially or for the first time.

appellate jurisdiction: Courts responsible for hearing cases that have already been heard in a lower court but are being appealed for a legal reason.

dual court system: The simultaneous existence of two court systems, federal and state.

— BEYOND A REASONABLE DOUBT 9.2 —

A court's venue describes _____.

(a) the type of case and geographic area of the trial, (b) the expertise of the judge, (c) the type of jury that will be seated in the case, (d) how many jurors will be on the jury, (e) none of the above

The answer can be found on page 521.

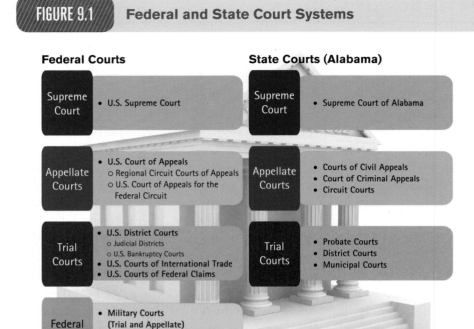

FIGURE 9.1   **Federal and State Court Systems**

© iStockphoto.com/alexsl

U.S. Supreme Court: The highest court in the United States; it is largely an appellate court but also has original jurisdiction in some cases.

Article III of the Constitution defines the federal courts.

© iStockphoto/alptraum

➡ Federal Courts

The federal court system is defined in Article III of the U.S. Constitution: "The judicial power of the United States, shall be vested in one supreme Court, and in such inferior Courts as the Congress may from time to time ordain and establish." Today, the federal court system comprises a Supreme Court, appeals courts, and district courts. The federal courts hear cases involving violations of acts of Congress (federal law). They hear both criminal and civil cases in which federal law was violated, such as cases involving kidnapping, smuggling, or drug trafficking. If there is a conflict between two states or between parties from different states, the case will be heard in a federal court.

U.S. Supreme Court

The **U.S. Supreme Court** is the highest court in the nation. It is largely an appellate court, as it hears mostly cases on appeal from lower courts. However, it also has the jurisdiction to hear some cases first, giving it original jurisdiction as well. As the highest appellate tribunal in the country, it is the ultimate decision maker in interpreting the Constitution, acts of legislative bodies, and treaties. It is the only federal court established by constitutional mandate rather than federal legislation. The Supreme Court is composed of the chief justice and a number of associate justices who are chosen, or fixed, by Congress. Today that number stands at nine.

The Supreme Court has original jurisdiction in cases that involve treaties made by the federal government, controversies in which the U.S. government is a party, and disputes between two states. The Court also has original jurisdiction with discretionary cases, which means that the Court may accept a case even though it is not required to do so. Examples include cases brought by a state against another state (for example, over a boundary), disputes between a state and a foreign government, cases involving a foreign government, or cases involving a foreign diplomat or ambassador.

The Supreme Court is probably known more for its appellate jurisdiction, which is how most cases reach the Court. Cases heard on appeal typically involve a losing party (either defense or plaintiff) who believes a substantial mistake was made in the original, lower court's ruling. Some cases are appealed if they raise a significant legal question, such as whether the evidence should not have been presented in court because it was gathered illegally. In either case, the Supreme Court is asked to review the case and make a ruling. Appellate cases typically come from a U.S. court of appeals or a state supreme court. The Supreme Court will review the facts of a case and determine if it contains an important legal question. If so, the Court will agree to hear the case. The "Criminal Justice and the Media" box in this chapter demonstrates how this process unfolds.

The U.S. Supreme Court is the highest court in the land.
Wikimedia Commons

The Supreme Court justices can choose which cases they will consider, depending on the legal significance of the case. There are, however, some appellate cases the Court must review. For example, the Court must review cases in which a lower federal court declares an act of Congress (a piece of legislation) to be unconstitutional, and the federal government is a party. Similarly, the Court must hear cases involving state laws ruled unconstitutional by the U.S. court of appeals. Finally, if a state's highest court holds a federal law to be invalid or unconstitutional, the Supreme Court must hear the case.

In certain situations, a lower appellate court may file a **writ of certification**. Through this process, the lower court justices request that the Supreme Court justices respond to a question about a federal law or clarify an issue with the federal law. The justices review the request and can either accept the question certified to them, or they can dismiss it. The writ of certification is not used frequently by the lower courts.

writ of certification: A legal document in which the Supreme Court justices are asked to respond to a question about a federal law or to clarify an issue with the federal law.

CRIMINAL JUSTICE and the **MEDIA:**

SISTER WIVES LAWSUIT

Kody Brown and his four wives lived in Salt Lake City, Utah, where they practiced polygamy as part of their church, the Apostolic United Brethren. They were forced to leave Utah and move to Nevada because they feared being criminally prosecuted for their polygamist lifestyle. They became known openly as a polygamist family after appearing on a television show called *Sister Wives* on the TLC Network. The family filed a federal lawsuit in July 2011, suing the state of Utah and the county where they lived in an effort to overturn the state's bigamy law, claiming the law was unconstitutional. In Utah, bigamy is a third-degree felony punishable by up to five years in prison. It is reported that tens of thousands of Mormon fundamentalists practice polygamy in Utah. Although Utah officials claimed they would not prosecute polygamists if they were not committing other crimes, Brown and his family chose to file the case nonetheless.

The Browns' attorney argued that under previous U.S. Supreme Court rulings, private relationships between consenting adults are protected by the U.S. Constitution. He based this argument on a decision from the Supreme Court in which a sodomy law in Texas was struck down. The Browns sought to persuade a federal judge to overturn Utah's bigamy law as being unconstitutional. This meant that Utah officials had to prove that polygamy was harmful and therefore should be banned.

In December 2013, a county attorney in Utah announced that his office would not seek to prosecute the Brown family for being polygamists. He explained that the office would no longer attempt to prosecute families who chose this lifestyle unless there was evidence of other crimes, or if a party in the marriage was under the age of 18. At the same time, U.S. District Judge Clark Waddoups ruled that the provision in Utah that forbids cohabitation with another person was unconstitutional because it was a violation of the First Amendment to the U.S. Constitution. While it remains illegal to marry more than one person, it is no longer illegal to cohabitate in what appears to be a marital relationship.

Procedure

If an appellant seeks to have his or her case reviewed by the Supreme Court, the process begins with the appellant filing a legal petition with the Court that describes the facts of the case and the events surrounding it (see Figure 9.2). Upon receipt, the petition is reviewed by the Court clerk. The clerk ensures that the appeal was filed properly and that technical or procedural rules were followed. The rules are sometimes quite precise—even outlining the specific size of paper to be used as well as the font type that needs to be used. Appellants who cannot afford to meet the standards can be granted exceptions. These appeals are called ***in forma pauperis*** briefs.

If an appeal meets the technical standards, it is given a **docket number**, which is simply an identification number that allows individuals to easily track the appeal through the process. Copies of each case are provided to the justices. The justices' clerks begin the work of summarizing the documents for their respective justices. Because there may be thousands of documents to read, most of the clerks work together to read the appeals and summarize each case in a memo. When the memos are completed, the justices may ask their own clerks for their ideas about the cases. The justices then rely on the memos, the clerks' opinions, and other information as they decide whether a case should be granted a full hearing by the Court.

in forma pauperis: The waiving of costs associated with a criminal defense, for appellants who cannot afford to pay.

docket number: The identification number assigned to a case.

FIGURE 9.2   How a Case Gets to the Supreme Court

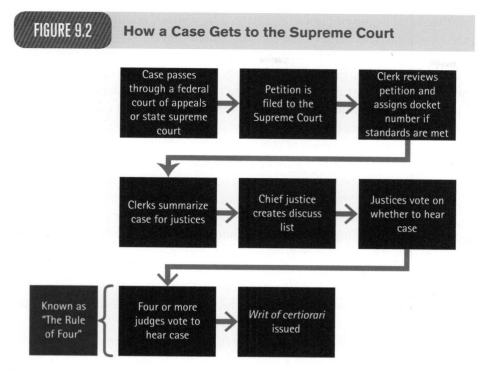

The chief justice plays a special role in this process. He creates a "discuss list," or a list of cases he feels are significant and deserve to be heard. Other justices may add cases to the list but are not permitted to remove any. If a case is not on placed on the list, it is denied a hearing. This means the decision of the lower court is final.

At this point, the justices meet privately to discuss the cases before them and choose the cases they will hear. If four of the nine justices vote to accept a case for review, the case moves forward. This is called the **Rule of Four**: Four justices must agree that there is a significant legal question underlying the case (see Figure 9.2). If this happens, the Court issues a *writ of certiorari* (which means "to be informed"). This is a demand that the lower courts involved provide transcripts of the proceedings from their courts to the Supreme Court for review. Most cases heard by the Court arrive through this process. If the justices do not grant *certiorari*, it means that the decision of the lower court stands.

If the Court grants *certiorari*, the attorneys on both sides in the case will present written and oral arguments in defense of their positions. The appellant (who is asking for a review of the lower court ruling) must provide the requested written documentation within 45 days after certiorari is granted. The respondent (who is supporting the lower court's ruling) has 35 days in which to respond to the appellant's brief. The guidelines for the written documents are very specific. There must be 40 copies of the briefs, which cannot exceed 15,000 words. They must include, among other things, a description of the issue under review and a list of the parties involved in the suit. Written briefs can also be submitted by interested parties or organizations. Called **amicus curiae briefs** (or "friends of the court" briefs), these provide the justices with another point of view, or

Rule of Four: The rule stipulating that four of the nine Supreme Court justices must agree to hear a case in order for it to move forward.

***amicus curiae* briefs:** Also known as "friends of the court" briefs, are submitted by interested parties to the U.S. Supreme Court to provide the justices with other perspectives or legal arguments about the case at hand.

another legal argument about the case. The written documents are examined by the justices prior to the oral argument phase.

Attorneys for each side then appear in front of the Court to present their oral arguments. They typically have only about 30 minutes each to provide the justices with their arguments. During that time, the justices can interrupt the attorneys to ask questions or clarify facts. Because it is not a trial, there is no jury, nor are witnesses called.

After the attorneys present their arguments, the justices meet to discuss the case and vote on it in a process called the "conference." Their discussions and deliberations are private, with no taping system, stenographers, or video cameras. It is thought that this is necessary because the justices are to make their decisions based only on the law—not on public opinion. Unlike the president and Congress, justices should not be concerned about what the public wants. They do not depend on the public to remain in their positions. It is also important to maintain a high level of secrecy about the decision, because the outcome may have important political or social ramifications.

After discussing and deliberating the case, the justices vote on the outcome of the case. When the justices come to a decision, their judgment is made public in a written opinion. One justice is assigned to write the Court's decision. If the chief justice sides with the majority, he will select one associate justice to write the opinion for the case. Occasionally, the chief justice will write the decision. On those occasions when the chief justice sides with the minority, then the most senior member of the Court who voted with the majority will assign the task. The opinion is a description of the Court's legal reasoning for its conclusion. The opinion also describes the rules of law that were applied and how they were applied to the case and their final resolution. It can often take months for the decision to be made public. After a draft is written, it will be circulated amongst the other justices for comments. It may be changed or edited to satisfy other justices.

If the decision of the Court is not unanimous (not all of the justices agree with the final outcome), then the written opinion is called a **majority opinion**, which is the opinion of the majority of the justices. Some justices may agree with the final decision but not the legal reasoning for that choice. In that case, a justice can opt to write a *concurring opinion*, which is a decision that comes to the same conclusion as the majority decision but may have a different logic or something to add to the argument. Other justices may disagree with the majority decision entirely. In that case, they can opt to write a *dissenting opinion*. This is an opinion that differs from the majority. Neither the concurring nor the dissenting opinion has an impact on the final decision of the case, but they may show alternative legal reasoning to that presented in the majority opinion. Another type of opinion is the ***per curiam* opinion**, which is a brief, unsigned opinion indicating that the Court agrees with part of a lower court ruling but disagrees with other parts. These are most often used if the Court agrees to hear a case but does not choose to give it a full hearing.

In the decision, the justices can affirm the decision of the lower court, reverse it, or remand it. If the court chooses to affirm the lower court decision, it means that they agree that the lower court decision was correct (that the correct decision was made and/or rules followed), and the

majority opinion: A decision by an appellate court that describes the finding of the majority of the justices.

***per curiam* opinion:** A legal opinion from an appellate court that is a brief, unsigned document in which the court agrees with part of a lower court ruling but disagrees with other parts.

case is finalized. If the Court decides to reverse a lower court decision, the conviction is overturned and the case is returned (or remanded) to the lower court. For example, it could decide that a procedure was not followed correctly, and the case must be retried in the lower court, this time with the correct procedure. Sometimes, such serious errors are made in the original trial that the lower court's decision is completely overturned. In other cases, the Supreme Court may reverse the lower court decision only "in part." If the court reverses "in part," it means that the case is sent back to the court of original jurisdiction (the lower court) and retried only with the particular modifications required.

Once the written opinions of the justices are completed, the Court then publicly announces its decision from the bench. The Office of the Clerk of the Court makes the report public and places it online. The official record of the Court's decision is called the *United States Reports*. Table 9.1 outlines some recent Supreme Court decisions.

TABLE 9.1   **Recent Decisions of the U.S. Supreme Court**

CASE	TOPIC	DESCRIPTION
District of Columbia v. Heller (2011)	Second Amendment gun rights	Dick Heller was a licensed special police officer for the District of Columbia. For his job, Heller carried a gun in federal office buildings but was not allowed to have one in his home. The U.S. Supreme Court held in a 5–4 decision that the Second Amendment to the U.S. Constitution protects an individual's right to possess a firearm for traditionally lawful purposes, such as self-defense within the home and within federal enclaves. It was the first Supreme Court case in U.S. history to decide whether the Second Amendment protects an individual's right to keep and bear arms for self-defense.
Trevino v. Thaler (2013)	Effective counsel	Carlos Trevino was convicted of capital murder in Texas state court and sentenced to death after the jury found insufficient mitigating circumstances to warrant a life sentence. Neither new counsel appointed for his direct appeal nor new counsel appointed for state collateral review raised the claim that Trevino's trial counsel provided ineffective assistance during the penalty phase by failing to adequately investigate and present mitigating circumstances. The U.S. Supreme Court held that death row inmates in Texas can raise claims of ineffectiveness of counsel for the first time in federal court if they did not have a meaningful chance to raise the claims in state appeals.
Dan's City Used Cars, Inc. v. Pelkey (2013)	Federal Aviation Administration Authorization Act	Robert Pelkey's car was towed from his apartment complex for failure to move it during a snowstorm. At the time, Mr. Pelkey was quite ill and eventually was sent to the hospital to have his left foot amputated. When he returned home and was made aware that his car was towed, Pelkey sued for violations of the Consumer Protection Act, a statute concerning liens, and a negligence claim based on the common law duty of a bailee. The trial court granted summary judgment in favor of Dan's, holding that the Federal Aviation Administration Authorization Act of 1994 (the Act) preempted Pelkey's claims. The U.S. Supreme Court held that the Federal Aviation Administration Act of 1994 does not preempt the state law because the claims are not "related to" the transportation of property. That phrase limits the scope of the preemption solely to transportation, rather than the disposal of property that occurs after the transportation, with which Pelkey's claim was concerned.
Thomas More Law Center v. Barack H. Obama, President of the United States	Affordable Health Care Act	In 2010, Congress enacted the Patient Protection and Affordable Care Act in order to increase the number of Americans covered by health insurance and decrease the cost of health care. One key provision is the individual mandate, which requires most Americans to maintain minimum essential health insurance coverage. For individuals who are not exempt, and who do not receive health insurance through an employer or government program, the means of satisfying the requirement is to purchase insurance from a private company. The case was heard by the Sixth Circuit Court of Appeals. The panel of three judges ruled that the individual mandate was a "Constitutional exercise" of the power of the federal government. This decision marked the first appellate court ruling on the Affordable Care Act.

Excerpted from each Court decision.

When the Court makes a ruling in a case, the new rule, policy, or procedure becomes a precedent that must be followed by all lower courts. The Supreme Court is a court of last resort, meaning that there is no way to appeal a Supreme Court decision.

Current Court

Today, there are eight associate justices and one chief justice serving on the Supreme Court. The current chief justice is John Roberts. With Roberts at

TABLE 9.2	Today's Supreme Court	
JUSTICE	**VIEWS**	**QUOTE FROM A JUDICIAL DECISION**
John Roberts 	Conservative	When police mistakes leading to an unlawful search are the result of isolated negligence attenuated from the search, rather than systemic error or reckless disregard of constitutional requirements, the exclusionary rule does not apply. *Herring v. United States* (07-513)
Samuel Alito	Conservative	It is one thing for the criminal "to go free because the constable has blundered" . . . (Cardozo, J.). It is quite another to set the criminal free because the constable has scrupulously adhered to governing law. Excluding evidence in such cases deters no police misconduct and imposes substantial social costs. We therefore hold that when the police conduct a search in objectively reasonable reliance on binding appellate precedent, the exclusionary rule does not apply. *Davis v. United States* (09-11328)
Stephen Breyer	Liberal	Our examination of history and purpose thus reveals nothing special enough about the job or about its organizational structure that would warrant providing these private prison guards with a governmental immunity. The job is one that private industry might, or might not, perform; and which history shows private firms did sometimes perform without relevant immunities. The organizational structure is one subject to the ordinary competitive pressures that normally help private firms adjust their behavior in response to the incentives that tort suits provide—pressures not necessarily present in government departments. *Richardson v. McKnight* (96-318)
Ruth Bader Ginsburg 	Liberal	Skilling failed to establish that a presumption of prejudice arose or that actual bias infected the jury that tried him. Jurors, the trial court correctly comprehended, need not enter the box with empty heads in order to determine the facts impartially. *Skilling v. United States* (08-1394)

JUSTICE	VIEWS	QUOTE FROM A JUDICIAL DECISION
Elena Kagan 	Liberal	These statements suggest that the court may have calculated the length of Tapia's sentence to ensure that she receive certain rehabilitative services. And that a sentencing court may not do. As we have held, a court may not impose or lengthen a prison sentence to enable an offender to complete a treatment program or otherwise to promote rehabilitation. *Tapia v. United States* (10-5400)
Anthony Kennedy 	Swing	Campbell, who is white, filed a timely pretrial motion to quash the indictment on the grounds the grand jury was constituted in violation of his equal protection and due process rights under the Fourteenth Amendment and in violation of the Sixth Amendment's fair-cross-section requirement. Campbell alleged a longstanding practice of racial discrimination in the selection of grand jury forepersons in the Parish. His sole piece of evidence is that, between January 1976 and August 1993, no black person served as a grand jury foreperson in the Parish, even though more than 20 percent of the registered voters were black persons. . . . We find Campbell, like any other white defendant, has standing to raise an equal protection challenge to discrimination against black persons in the selection of his grand jury. *Campbell v. Louisiana* (96-1584)
Antonin Scalia 	Conservative	Where, as here, a defendant who is convicted of murder and sentenced to life imprisonment succeeds in having the conviction set aside on appeal, jeopardy has not terminated, so that a life sentence imposed in connection with the initial conviction raises no double-jeopardy bar to a death sentence on retrial. *Sattazahn v. Pennsylvania* (01-7574)
Sonia Sotomayor 	Liberal	This case presents the question whether the age of a child subjected to police questioning is relevant to the custody analysis of *Miranda v. Arizona* . . . (1966). It is beyond dispute that children will often feel bound to submit to police questioning when an adult in the same circumstances would feel free to leave. Seeing no reason for police officers or courts to blind themselves to that commonsense reality, we hold that a child's age properly informs the *Miranda* custody analysis. *J. D. B. v. North Carolina* (09-11121)
Clarence Thomas 	Conservative	Although a search or seizure of a dwelling might be constitutionally defective if police officers enter without prior announcement, law enforcement interests may also establish the reasonableness of an unannounced entry. *Wilson v. Arkansas* (94-5707)

VIDEO
Supreme Court
Landmark Rulings

the helm, the court has a conservative majority. Four of the justices (Alito, Thomas, Scalia, and Roberts) are conservative. Four (Sotomayor, Breyer, Kagan, and Ginsburg) tend to hold liberal to moderate views on issues. One justice (Kennedy) is a conservative but sometimes votes with the liberal justices. He is considered to be a "swing vote" in controversial cases. His ideological alignment may change depending on the case and the issues involved.

Each of the justices on the Supreme Court was appointed by the president of the United States and then approved by the members of the Senate in a very political process. When a vacancy occurs on the Court, the president will nominate a replacement who will decide future cases with the same political ideology as himself. That means that conservative presidents will, more than likely, nominate conservative justices and liberal presidents will, more than likely, nominate liberal justices to the bench. The process becomes more complicated, however, when the nominee faces Senate approval. If the president's political party does not have a majority in the Senate, then the president will have to choose a nominee who is more centrist in his or her decisions or ideology.

Of course, a nominee's qualifications for office are essential. In 2005, when Justice Sandra Day O'Connor resigned from the Court, President George W. Bush had to nominate a replacement. He first chose Harriet Miers, who had been his personal lawyer when he was governor of Texas. She was also deputy chief of staff and legal counsel to the president while he was in the White House. But she did not have a strong record of written briefs, which was a concern to members of the Senate. They were unsure as to how she would vote. It took only 23 days for her to withdraw her name from consideration.

As a replacement, President Bush nominated Samuel Alito, a former law clerk for Justice Antonin Scalia. His written briefs demonstrated clearly that he supported a conservative political ideology. The Senate at the time had a majority of Republican members, and they backed the nomination, whereas the Democratic members did not. Alito was eventually confirmed in a 58–42 vote in the Senate.

Members of the Senate not only look at a nominee's party ideology and qualifications, but they are also influenced by different interest groups who seek to influence who is placed on the Court. For instance, members of the legal community get involved in the nomination process. The American Bar Association rates nominees and lobbies Congress in an attempt to support or weaken congressional support for a nominee. Law professors and other well-respected lawyers also evaluate nominees and make those appraisals public. Other interest groups make their feelings known. Labor groups and civil rights groups (such as the ACLU) are often engaged in the process. The reason for this involvement is simple: If they can influence the membership of the Court, it may have an impact on future Court decisions regarding issues of concern to the group's membership.

Although justices must base their decisions on the laws and the U.S. Constitution, they interpret those documents differently depending on their ideologies. For example, liberal justices tend to emphasize due process rights more than conservative justices, who tend to focus more on strict punishment. Liberal justices tend to support an active government role in controlling business and economic activity as well as social matters. They tend to give more support to human rights, matters of privacy, and freedoms of religion, speech, and press. Conservative justices have a strong belief in following precedents and a narrow view when interpreting the Constitution. They believe in limited government involvement whereby government activity should be restricted to functions that support and protect citizens' liberty.

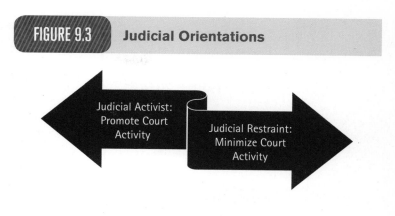

FIGURE 9.3   **Judicial Orientations**

Judicial Activist: Promote Court Activity

Judicial Restraint: Minimize Court Activity

The justices also differ regarding how they think a justice should make a decision (see Figure 9.3). Some justices follow the policy of *judicial restraint*, which is the idea that the justices should be less active in reviewing cases from the legislatures and Congress. Under this premise, the Court should not become involved in the roles of the other branches unless absolutely necessary. When in doubt, the actions taken by elected officials should take precedent. Courts should impose remedies that are tailored narrowly to correct specific legal wrongs. This perspective holds that precedents should be followed as a way to keep jurists from impulsive decision making.

Others justices follow the policy of *judicial activism*, according to which judges are more active in reviewing policies that come to them. An activist judge believes the proper role of the Court is to uphold independent positions in deciding cases, to review the actions of the other branches of government vigorously, to be willing to strike down policies that are unconstitutional, and to impose remedies for legal wrongs when necessary. Under this premise, the Court should make changes in public policy and use its power to declare acts of Congress invalid, when necessary.

Lower Federal Courts

In addition to the U.S. Supreme Court, other federal courts exist to help process defendants accused of criminal acts. The U.S. Constitution, in Article III, Section 1, declares that the judicial power of the United States shall be invested in one Supreme Court and in "such inferior Courts as the Congress may from time to time ordain and establish." Based on that, the Congress has created many lower federal courts over time.

U.S. Courts of Appeal

The **U.S. courts of appeals** are also called intermediate appellate courts or circuit courts of appeals. These courts were originally created in the Judiciary Act of 1789 as three circuit courts but were redesigned by Congress in 1891. They are the courts of last resort for most appeals in the federal court system since most cases either are not appealed to the Supreme Court or are not granted *certiorari* by the Supreme Court.

U.S courts of appeals: Also called intermediate appellate courts, or U.S. circuit courts of appeals, these are the courts of last resort for most appeals in the federal court system; they review cases appealed to them from the federal courts within a given district.

FIGURE 9.4   U.S. Courts of Appeals Caseload: Appeals Filed, Terminated, and Pending During June 2013–June 2014

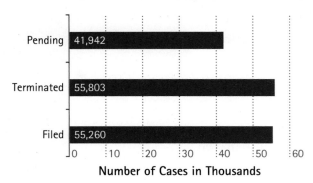

United States Courts

The court of appeals within a given district reviews cases appealed to it from the federal trial (district) courts. The courts of appeals were intended to reduce the number of appeals from the district courts that had to be heard by the Supreme Court. Thus, the courts of appeals have the power, or jurisdiction, to review the decisions of the district courts. They also review orders of federal administrative bodies such as the Food and Drug Administration (FDA), the National Labor Relations Board (NLRB), or the Securities and Exchange Commission (SEC). The caseload of the courts of appeals is shown in Figure 9.4.

Today, there are 13 courts of appeals, each presided over by a court of appeals judge. The United States is divided into 13 regions, or circuits, each of which has a court of appeals associated with it (see Figure 9.5). Each circuit is identified by a number. Eleven of the circuits include three or more states. One circuit encompasses the District of Columbia, and one (the U.S. Court of Appeals for the Federal Circuit) hears cases from the federal government, so it is a jurisdictional rather than a geographic circuit. The circuit courts are generally found in larger metropolitan areas, and appellants must travel to that location to have their cases heard. Each circuit has at least six permanent judges available to hear cases on a rotating basis. Typically, panels of three judges hear cases, but in some important cases, all of the judges may participate. When this happens, the case is said to be heard *en banc*.

FIGURE 9.5   Map of Federal Circuit Courts

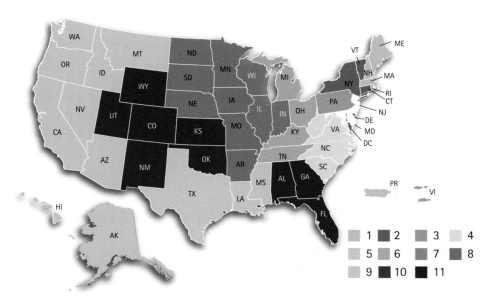

Federal Bar Association

The U.S. courts of appeals have appellate jurisdiction and can review records and documents related only to decisions made in the lower federal district courts (not state courts). A litigant in a lower federal case who believes that the decision of the lower court was incorrect may appeal his or her case to the court of appeals in the circuit in which the federal district court is located. The courts of appeals do not retry cases or make decisions concerning the guilt or innocence of those charged with crimes. They do not determine issues of fact that might or might not support conviction or dismissal. Instead, these courts only analyze judicial decisions (both statutory and constitutional) and consider constitutional issues surrounding the cases to determine if the decisions of the trial court were legally correct.

If the justices determine that no errors of law were made at the district court level, then the court upholds (or affirms) the decision of the lower court. If the court of appeals finds an error, it returns the case to the trial court. The trial court can either retry the case or dismiss it.

U.S. Court of Appeals for the Federal Circuit

The **U.S. Court of Appeals for the Federal Circuit** (or the thirteenth circuit court) was established by the Federal Courts Improvement Act of 1982. This court hears many types of cases. It has national jurisdiction, meaning that it hears cases from all across the United States. It also hears appeals from the district courts in patent cases, contract cases, and other civil actions in which the United States is a defendant. Moreover, this court also hears appeals stemming from the U.S. Court of International Trade, the U.S. Court of Federal Claims, and the U.S. Court of Veterans Appeals. The justices on the court are responsible for reviewing administrative rulings of different agencies, such as the U.S. Patent and Trademark Office, the U.S. International Trade Commission, the secretary of commerce, and the U.S. Merit Systems Protection Board.

The U.S. Court of Appeals for the Federal Circuit is based in Washington, D.C., but may occasionally hear cases where any court of appeals usually sits. The court consists of 12 circuit judges who sit in panels of three or more on each case. In special situations, the justices may also sit *en banc* (with all of the justices present).

U.S. District Courts

U.S. district courts were created by the Judiciary Act of 1789. These courts are the general trial courts for the federal system, and they are the courts of original jurisdiction for federal cases. This means that a defendant charged with a federal offense would have his or her case heard in district court first, marking the entry point for the federal court system. The district courts are courts of general jurisdiction, which means they hear both civil and criminal cases. District courts may also serve as appellate courts for cases tried before a U.S. magistrate. They also have appellate functions in dealing with certain writs of habeas corpus (formal requests for a judge to review an offender's sentence). Although decisions made by district court judges can be appealed to appellate courts, most cases never move beyond these courts.

U.S. Court of Appeals for the Federal Circuit: Also referred to as the thirteenth circuit court, this body hears cases from all across the nation related to patent cases, contract cases, and other civil actions in which the United States is a defendant, as well as appeals.

U.S. district courts: General trial courts, and the courts of original jurisdiction, for the federal system.

Defendants in district court cases may have been charged with violating federal law. Criminal offenses would include counterfeiting, assassination or attempted assassination of the president or another top government official, international drug trafficking, or interstate kidnapping or human trafficking. The plaintiff in these cases is the United States, and evidence against the defendant is presented by a U.S. attorney. District court trials include examining witnesses and documents to determine the facts of a case. A jury may be present, unless a defendant chooses to have a bench trial, in which case the facts are decided by the presiding judge.

Civil cases heard in U.S. district courts are limited to lawsuits in which the damages are valued at $10,000 or more in which a federal question is raised, lawsuits involving citizens of two or more states, or lawsuits in which a citizen of one state sues another state. Civil cases heard by district courts also include questions involving citizenship rights or rights of alien immigrants, lawsuits between citizens who reside in different states, lawsuits in which one state is suing another state or a citizen who lives in another state, or lawsuits involving the federal government.

There are 94 district courts spread across the United States. There is at least one district court in each state, with some of the larger states (like New York and California) having more. The number of federal district judges ranges from 2 to 28, depending on the caseload. Only one judge is usually required to hear and decide a case in a district court, but in some cases three judges may be seated. These courts handle thousands of cases each year. Figure 9.6 shows the caseloads for the U.S. district courts.

Federal Magistrates

Federal magistrates, formerly called United States commissioners, were created in the Federal Magistrates Act of 1968. They have jurisdiction over minor federal misdemeanor offenses, but they also issue arrest warrants or search warrants to federal law enforcement officers (such as FBI and DEA agents), conduct preliminary hearings, and set bail for defendants being released until trial. The jurisdiction of magistrates was expanded in 1976, when they were given the authority to review civil rights and habeas corpus petitions and make recommendations to district court judges.

There are currently 452 federal magistrates. Federal magistrates are lawyers who are appointed by district court judges for eight-year terms. There are also part-time magistrates who serve four-year terms.

Other Federal Courts

Other federal courts have jurisdiction over special areas. For example, the U.S. Court of Federal Claims hears cases in which the U.S. government has been sued for damages. The U.S. Court of International Trade handles cases involving appeals of U.S. Customs and Border Protection rulings, and the U.S. Court of Appeals for the Armed Forces hears appeals of military courts-martial. There is also a U.S. Tax Court, which ensures that citizens pay their taxes and determines liabilities for outstanding taxes.

federal magistrates: Officials who have the authority to hear cases that involve minor federal misdemeanor offenses as well as to issue arrest or search warrants to federal law enforcement officers, conduct preliminary hearings, and set bail for defendants.

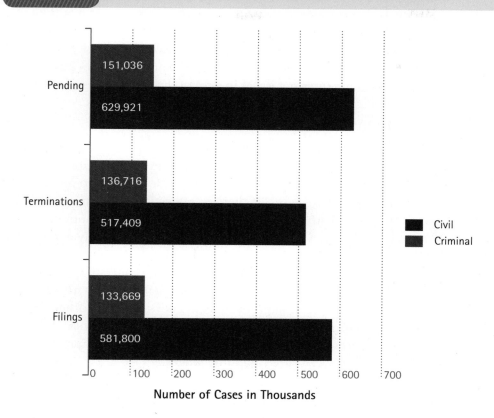

FIGURE 9.6 U.S. District Courts: Cases, June 2013–June 2014

Number of Cases in Thousands

United States Courts

➡ State Courts

Under the U.S. Constitution, each state has the right to create its own criminal justice (and judicial) systems. As a result, there is some variation in the court systems from state to state. The systems differ in the number of courts, the names of the courts, and the jurisdiction of those courts. Each state has its own unique court structure, but for the most part they parallel the federal court structure. Most states created a three-tiered system that includes courts of limited jurisdiction, courts of general jurisdiction, and appellate courts. But states refer to these courts differently. For example, the major trial courts in California are called superior courts, but in Texas they are referred to as district courts.

State trial courts hear cases in which a defendant has violated a state law (as opposed to a federal law). These include offenses such as murder (not including murder of a president, top government official, or candidate for office), rape, car theft, and underage drinking. Since most criminal offenses tend to be state offenses, the state courts must handle the majority of criminal offenders. In fact, 80% to 90% of criminal cases are handled in state courts. State appellate courts interpret issues in light of their own state constitutions.

State Supreme Courts

State supreme courts (sometimes called state judicial court or supreme court of appeals) are usually the court of last resort in the state. They hear cases on appeal from lower state courts to provide answers to questions of legal significance in state cases. If there is a question concerning the interpretation of a state statute or state constitution, the state supreme court will make a ruling. Typically, few state cases are successfully appealed to the U.S. Supreme Court, so state supreme court decisions are typically final. Like the U.S. Supreme Court, state supreme courts have discretion over the cases they hear. In some states, death penalty cases are automatically reviewed by the state supreme court. They may have other powers, such as issuing judicial assignments, confirming the nomination of judges, and reviewing cases of alleged judicial misconduct. State supreme courts are composed of between three and nine judges.

Lower State Appellate Courts (Intermediate Appellate Courts)

States also have established lower state appellate courts, which are most often called **intermediate appellate courts** but also called courts of appeals. They are typically organized regionally but sometimes across several counties. These courts are used by many states as a way to reduce the caseloads of the state supreme court. They review the decisions from lower court proceedings and decisions using trial records, appellate briefs submitted by each side, and arguments made by legal counsel. Thus, defendants may appeal if they believe the procedures used in the original case violated their constitutional rights, or if an error was committed in the original case. In some states, these courts are limited by law to hearing cases arising from specific lower courts or cases involving less than a specified dollar value. The judges in these courts usually sit on panels of three to nine.

state supreme courts: Usually the court of last resort in the state; hears cases on appeal from lower state courts.

intermediate appellate courts (state): Also called courts of appeals, these courts review decisions from lower court proceedings if a party to the original case believes that either the procedures followed during the trial stage or the decision rendered by the lower court was unconstitutional.

State supreme courts are the highest courts in each state.

Trial Courts

Trial Courts of General Jurisdiction

Trial courts of general jurisdiction, which are also called major trial courts or felony courts in some states, preside over criminal cases and serious civil cases. In Pennsylvania and Ohio, they are called the court of common pleas. They usually have exclusive jurisdiction over more serious felony offenses. In these courts, trials generally last a few days, or even weeks or months. A judge presides over the hearing, with the prosecution and the defense taking adversarial roles. Trial courts of general jurisdiction are considered to be courts of record because

Trials are well-orchestrated procedures in what are known as trial courts.

© REUTERS/Jahi Chikwendiu/POOL

trial transcripts are maintained to record all proceedings. These are the entry points to the court structure in the state systems.

Trial Courts of Limited Jurisdiction

The *trial courts of limited jurisdiction*, also called municipal, county, misdemeanor, or justice courts, are usually courts of limited jurisdiction. They hear cases of very specific origin, yet they hear the majority of cases that go to court. They include special courts such as juvenile courts, domestic violence courts, family courts, and probate courts (handling divorce, estate, and custody issues). These courts usually hear cases regarding infractions or minor misdemeanor offenses, such as shoplifting, traffic violations, or violations of municipal ordinances. They sometimes also hear preliminary proceedings of more serious felony cases (for example, probable cause hearings to determine whether a trial should be held).

Defendants in lower courts have the same rights as those in major trial courts, even though proceedings may be less formal. However, there is often more of an emphasis on disposing of cases quickly by relying on routines. This is called "assembly line justice." Defendants in these courts can enter a plea and agree to pay a fine for their offenses in a matter of minutes with little attention. Since these courts are not courts of record, there is no transcript or recording of events. The punishment involved in these cases is usually small. Most involve a fine of $1,000 or less and possible incarceration of 12 months or less in the local jail.

In most states, lower court judges are elected by voters through a campaign process. In other states, the judges are appointed by the governor and then confirmed by a judicial appointment committee made up of representatives from the state legislature and/or the judiciary. The appointed judge must then be confirmed by voters in the next general election.

JOURNAL
Focus on the Family

---

trial courts of general jurisdiction (state): State courts that have jurisdiction over general cases.

Magistrate Courts

Magistrates are members of the bar who oversee police courts, traffic courts, and/or municipal courts. They are usually limited to hearing specific types of cases and can, in some states, issue warrants and conduct bail hearings. Cases heard in magistrate courts can be appealed to the court of general jurisdiction or major trial court.

BEYOND A REASONABLE DOUBT 9.4

Which of the following are types of state courts?

(a) Supreme courts, (b) Lower appellate courts, (c) Trial courts, (d) Only b and c, (e) All of the above

---

The answer can be found on page 521.

➡ Actors: Courtroom Workgroup

Many people play crucial roles within the court to ensure that the judicial process is carried out in a timely yet fair and just manner. Courtroom personnel are called the **courtroom workgroup**. Although each member of the courtroom workgroup has a distinct role and responsibility, they share the same values and goals and often cooperate with one another to reach that goal: the efficient disposition of cases through the court. The courtroom workgroup includes professional members, such as the judge, prosecutors, defense attorneys, and other personnel who regularly work in a courtroom and have specific tasks in the process, as well as nonprofessional members, such as jurors, witnesses, victims, and the media. For example, defense counsel present evidence to show the defendant is innocent, whereas prosecutors present evidence to show the defendant is guilty. At the same time, the members of the courtroom workgroup also develop crucial relationships based on their roles that help to process cases. They frequently interact informally with one another about cases, which keeps the flow of cases moving and increases cooperation among the members of the group.

Professional Members

Judges

The role of the judge is to ensure that justice is served fairly throughout the trial process. To do this, the judge presides over the courtroom proceedings during hearings to guarantee the laws are followed and the conduct of the courtroom actors is appropriate. Theoretically, the judge is the most powerful figure in the courtroom. The judge is certainly the most visible actor in the judicial system.

Trial judges and appellate judges have different roles in the courtroom (see Figure 9.7). Trial judges serve as neutral arbiters to determine the guilt or innocence of a defendant charged with violating the law. To this extent, they must supervise the jury selection process, rule on motions, interpret and decide questions of law (questions about evidence), instruct (or "charge") the

JOURNAL
Courtroom Workgroups and Sentencing

AUTHOR VIDEO
Courtroom Workgroup, Misconceptions

courtroom workgroup: The collection of court personnel, who each have their own distinct roles but also work together to ensure that cases run smoothly through the system.

jury, sentence those offenders found guilty of their crimes, ensure that a defendant's guilty plea is voluntary, and preside over the plea-bargaining process (in which the defendant pleads guilty in return for reduced charges or punishment; see Chapters 10 and 11). If a jury trial is waived, the judge may decide matters of fact after a hearing. In addition to these responsibilities, the judge also has administrative roles. These include supervising support staff, preparing the budget, and managing cases. Judges play a prominent role in seeing that justice is served. Their rulings and sentencing decisions influence the actions of other courtroom actors, including defense attorneys, prosecutors, probation officers, and court clerks.

Among other things, judges preside over activities occurring in the courts.

© REUTERS/Robert E. Klein/Pool

Appellate judges have very different responsibilities and duties, compared with trial judges. Appellate judges must review the acts of lower courts to determine if there is a basis for an appeal. They review the trial records, trial brief, notice of appeal, and other matters submitted with the appeal to determine if the appeal was properly presented and the appropriate issues are properly brought before the court. They also preside over oral arguments and are involved in negotiating a decision among the justices considering the appeal. Finally, they must write an opinion that explains the logic and reasons for the decision.

As mentioned earlier, magistrate judges on the federal level were created by the Federal Magistrates Act of 1968 to replace U.S. commissioners. In 1990, the title of U.S. magistrate judge was coined in the Judicial Improvements Act. Magistrate judges are appointed by the judges of the district court and serve for eight-year terms, but they can be removed for "good cause" if needed. The exact duties of the magistrate judges are defined by the judge in the district court. In general, these judges can conduct all proceedings in a jury or nonjury civil matter, enter a judgment in the case, and/or conduct a trial of someone accused of a misdemeanor offense.

The qualifications to serve as a judge vary from state to state and court to court. Most states require that judges have law degrees and are licensed to practice law in their jurisdictions. They also require that a judge be a resident of the state in which he or she is employed, be a member of the state bar association, and be at least 25 years old but no more than 70 years old.

FIGURE 9.7 Trial Judges Versus Appellate Judges

Trial Judges	Appellate Judges
• Supervise jury selection • Rule on motions • Decide legal issues • Instruct jury • Oversee guilty pleas • Sentence guilty offenders • Perform administrative functions	• Review acts of lower courts • Decide if defendant was treated fairly • Review appeal notices • Review trial • Preside over oral arguments • Write judicial opinions

Courtrooms are designed in a way to separate those involved in court hearings: the judge, prosecutor, defense, jury members, and members of the public.

Wikimedia Commons

Law Clerks

Many judges in both state and federal courts hire **law clerks** to assist in various duties in the court, such as researching cases, reviewing documents, summarizing cases, preparing cases, and writing documents. The exact duties depend on the individual judge and type of court. In some cases, law clerks have a lot of contact with attorneys and witnesses or other courtroom workgroup members.

Prosecutors

The prosecution in the courtroom has the responsibility of enforcing the law by filing criminal charges against someone accused of a crime and then presenting the state's case against that defendant.

Prosecutors exist at the federal, state, and local levels. At the federal level, they are called U.S. attorneys and are responsible for prosecuting federal offenses in the federal court system. After being appointed by the president and then confirmed by the Senate, they are assigned to a U.S. district court. They are involved in all aspects of the trial process: investigations, arrests, initial appearances, grand juries, preliminary hearings, information and indictments, arraignments, pretrial motions, trials, sentencing, appeals, parole and probation decisions, and parole revocation hearings.

At the state level, the prosecutor may be referred to as a district attorney, state's attorney, county attorney, or prosecuting attorney. Whatever the title, this is the person (or group of people) to whom the police present their case about an alleged offender. Once the prosecutor receives this evidence, he or she will review it and decide what charges, if any, to file against the defendant. Because of this power, the prosecutor has a great deal of discretion, or the ability to choose the appropriate course of action. The prosecutor is the only actor with the authority to refer criminal charges against a defendant. A case does not begin until the prosecutor files the charges with the court.

Once the charges are filed, the prosecutor has a central part in the trial process. Prior to the trial, the prosecutor will take part in bail negotiations that help to determine whether a defendant will remain in custody until trial or will be released. Moreover, the prosecutor will help to collect evidence by interviewing witnesses and others involved in the case. They take part in pretrial hearings and motion procedures and are part of the plea-bargaining negotiations.

During the trial, the prosecutor presents evidence and witnesses to prove the defendant's guilt. Prosecutors seek a conviction for those accused of criminal offenses. They sometimes must work with police to subpoena

law clerks: Court employees who keep cases progressing smoothly by completing tasks such as researching cases, reviewing documents, summarizing cases, preparing cases, or writing documents.

prosecutor: A primary actor in the courtroom who is responsible for filing criminal charges and then presenting the state's case against that defendant to a judge and/or jury in the hopes of proving the defendant's guilt.

witnesses to ensure they appear. If a defendant is found guilty, the prosecutor recommends a sentence to the judge. If a case is appealed, the prosecutor will defend the case to the appellate court. If a defendant on probation is found to have violated terms of that probation, the prosecutor is responsible for presenting that evidence to the judge and possibly recommending the revocation of parole.

In most states today, the prosecution does not have the resources to convict every defendant who is charged with a criminal offense. This means they must choose to prosecute only those serious cases where there is enough solid evidence to secure a conviction. It also means that they have a great deal of choice, or discretion, to decide to pursue a case. Prosecutors often drop charges against a defendant if the evidence against the defendant is inadequate, or even weak. They may also choose not to proceed with a case because of a lack of probable cause, or even for political reasons (for example, if the defendant is a well-known community or business leader), or because the prosecutor's caseload includes more serious cases.

Prosecutors and the Police The prosecutor must develop positive working relationships with law enforcement, especially because prosecutors rely on the police to provide both the suspects and the evidence necessary to convict offenders. In return, police rely on prosecutors to get offenders off the streets. Thus, most prosecutors and police have to develop positive working relationships, given that they depend on each other to reach their goals. The prosecutor can give the police many perks: legal advice; limited unnecessary court appearances; information on the disposition of the case; preparatory information for pretrial appearances; and training for both new and experienced police in securing warrants, interrogating suspects, and conducting lineups.

Prosecutors and Other Courtroom Actors Prosecutors must also develop positive working relationships with many other courtroom actors. For example, although a case can still be prosecuted if the victim does not press charges, prosecutors rely on statements and evidence from victims and witnesses to aid in the prosecution of offenders. (See the "Help Wanted" box in this chapter.)

Another key courtroom actor with whom the prosecutor must work is the judge. This relationship is critical for many reasons. First, if the judge and the prosecutor have a positive working relationship, the judge may be more inclined to make rulings in the prosecutor's favor. Second, the prosecutor and the judge must work together in the plea-bargaining process. The judge may be more willing to accept plea bargains from a prosecutor with whom he or she has a positive working relationship. The prosecution and defense must also work together in the plea-bargaining process, so they also must form a working relationship. Finally, the prosecutor must work with the media, especially if the prosecutor is an elected official. The media can scrutinize the behavior of prosecutors and make that information public, either to the detriment or to the advantage of the prosecutor. For example, if a prosecutor campaigned on a "law and order" platform, the media will

HELP WANTED: PROSECUTOR

DUTIES:

- Analyzes new cases received from the U.S. Attorneys' Offices and Department components charging a crime punishable by death. Section attorneys advise the attorney general's capital case review committee in its factual and legal evaluation of cases submitted to the department for review regarding whether the death penalty should be sought in each capital-eligible case.

- Litigates all phases of federal capital cases, including pretrial litigation; provides guidance in selecting death-qualified juries; and helps construct penalty-phase evidentiary presentations. Section attorneys act as co-counsel in federal capital trials, assisting with the preparation of capital-eligible cases for department review, providing guidance on death-penalty–related aspects of the pretrial and trial process.

- Provides training on the department's capital case litigation. Section attorneys provide legal, procedural, and policy guidance to U.S. Attorneys'

Offices and Department components handling capital investigations and prosecutions.

- In collaboration with U.S. Attorneys' Offices, section attorneys advise in the preparation of legal memoranda, such as proposed legislation, amendments, regulations, testimony, briefing materials, public statements, and correspondence on capital punishment issues.

- Collects and maintains trial and appellate materials related to federal capital prosecutions. Section attorneys partner with U.S. Attorneys' Offices in the development and management of current information and materials, which acts as a resource center for capital prosecutors.

- Assists in the development of department policies and procedures related to federal capital prosecutions.

REQUIREMENTS: J.D. degree

ANNUAL SALARY: $124,995–$157,100

Adapted from USAJOBS.gov. Retrieved from https://www.usajobs.gov/GetJob/ViewDetails/380741100

CAREER VIDEO
Legal Assistant

defense attorney: An attorney who represents a person accused of a crime; he or she attempts to obtain an acquittal throughout all stages of the adjudication process.

watch for the prosecution to sentence more defendants more harshly. Or if a prosecutor, during a campaign, made a promise to get tough on drunk drivers, the media may keep an eye open for that. The media may apply pressure to prosecute certain cases that may generate publicity and public reaction even if the case is not as strong as typically desired for prosecution.

Defense Attorneys

Under the Sixth Amendment to the U.S. Constitution, every person accused of a crime has the right to adequate legal counsel. The defense counsel is an attorney and an officer of the court but also a representative of the defendant. The defense is the legal counterpart to the prosecuting attorney. The goal of the defense is to secure an acquittal for the defendant. The **defense attorney** must ensure that a client is properly represented at all stages of the criminal justice system (starting with arrest then to the initial appearance, preliminary hearing, arraignment, pretrial, trial, sentencing, and appeal). The defense also must see that the client's rights are not violated, and that the case is presented in the most favorable light possible, within legal boundaries. The defense must ensure that the prosecution proves its case in court or has substantial evidence of guilt before a defendant pleads guilty or is convicted and sentenced. Even if the accused admits his or her guilt to the defense attorney, the defense has the right to force the government to prove the accused's guilt beyond a reasonable doubt. The defense is required to use any legal method to prevent the accused's conviction or, in the case of conviction, to obtain the lightest sentence possible for the accused. However, the defense cannot present false evidence, allow perjury to be committed, or break the law in defending the accused.

Defense attorneys face many ethical decisions each day as they carry out their roles in the justice system (see the "Ethical Decision Making" box in this chapter).

It is the defense attorney's responsibility to represent the defendant's interests during the criminal justice process. Defense attorneys do not have to prove innocence, but they are obligated not to lie to the court. For example, if the defense attorney knows that the defendant committed the crime that he or she is on trial for, the defense attorney cannot allow the defendant to take the stand and state that he or she did not commit the crime.

Many times, the defense attorney is a private attorney who has been hired by the defendant for representation in court. However, even defendants who are indigent do not go without representation. The U.S. Constitution guarantees that if a defendant cannot afford an attorney, the state must provide one. States and the federal government use several different methods to provide the required legal counsel to indigent defendants: public defenders, assigned counsel, and contract counsel.

Public Defenders **Public defenders** are used by 30 states and the federal government. A public defender is an attorney who is employed by the state or federal government to serve as legal counsel for poor defendants. Sometimes a state has a statewide public defender's office headed by a chief public defender who oversees the office. In the majority of states,

> **public defender:** An attorney who provides legal representation for defendants who cannot afford private legal counsel.

ETHICAL DECISION MAKING

DEFENSE DILEMMA

Jill Jacobs is a self-employed defense attorney who recently completed law school. In an effort to make ends meet, she has offered her services to virtually anyone who contacts her.

One day, a gang member named "Hoolio" asks Jacobs to represent him on a burglary charge. After discussing rates, Hoolio tells Jacobs that he will not be able to pay her with money but that he can give her a 70-inch smart TV.

Later, Jacobs is reading Hoolio's arrest report when one item jumps out at her: Hoolio was accused of stealing a 70-inch smart TV.

YOU DECIDE

1. How should Jacobs proceed? Explain.
2. Does a career as a defense attorney interest you? Why or why not?

It is the bailiff's responsbility to maintain order in the court.

© ZUMA Press, Inc / Alamy

the public defender's office is organized on the county level of government, and each office is autonomous.

In most states, public defender's offices have extremely high caseloads, so they are unable to spend much time on each case. As a result, they are sometimes criticized for being not as legally qualified as they should be. They sometimes have a poor image among clients for being young and inexperienced and for not putting much preparation time into their cases prior to trial. However, public defenders are trained and competent attorneys who often have many years of experience. They often have also developed working relationships with the prosecution and judges that will help a defendant obtain the best possible outcome.

Assigned Counsel **Assigned counsel** refers to private attorneys assigned by the court to represent defendants in need of legal counsel. In about half the counties in the United States, all attorneys practicing in the local court are placed on a list, which the judge then uses to select an attorney for a defendant. Attorneys are usually reimbursed from the state for their representation. This system is often used in rural areas that do not have a high enough caseload to support a public defender's system.

Contract System The **contract system** of providing public counsel is a relatively new method. It is the sole method for providing public counsel in six states but is used by other states as a supplement to their public defender systems. In this case, a government office (either a county or a township, for example) will invite private law firms to submit proposals regarding the costs for establishing a public defender system. The government then selects the firm with the lowest bid for providing that service. Some firms agree to provide legal representation for a set number of cases for a determined fee. The chosen law firm is responsible for providing indigent defendants with representation in court.

Bailiff

The **bailiff** is also called the "court office." Bailiffs are usually armed law enforcement officers who keep order in the courtroom, announce the judge's entry into the courtroom, call witnesses, prevent the escape of the accused, and take charge of the jury when it is not in the courtroom. For example, the bailiff will supervise the jury when it is sequestered and guarantee that no outside influences are brought near the jury. They sometimes act as "gofers" for the judge and jury. In a federal courtroom, the bailiff is a deputy U.S. marshal.

assigned counsel: Court-assigned private attorneys who represent indigent defendants.

contract system: A method of providing counsel to indigent defendants whereby private law firms prepare an estimated cost for providing legal counsel, and the firm with the lowest bid to represent these offenders is awarded the responsibility.

bailiff: A courtroom employee, typically an armed law enforcement officer, who maintains order in the courtroom and ensures that the defendant is not able to escape or harm others.

Stenographer

It is the responsibility of the court **stenographer** (also known as court recorder or court reporter) to record all events that go on during the trial, including the testimony of witnesses, oral arguments, objections, rulings by the judge, the judge's instructions, and any verbal comments made during the court proceedings. The official trial record is often taken on a stenotype machine or audio recorder and may later be transcribed. This is essential if an appeal is made. In courts where there is no clerk, the court reporter lists all exhibits offered into evidence.

Court Clerks

The court clerk assists the judge by performing administrative duties. The clerk is responsible for docketing cases, collecting court fees, arranging a jury pool, issuing jury summonses and subpoenaing witnesses for both the prosecution and the defense, and maintaining court records of criminal cases, including all pleas and motions made before and after the trial. The clerk administers the oath to jurors and witnesses (swears them in), marks evidence as instructed by the judge, and keeps a log of what exhibits have been admitted. The clerk also maintains custody of the evidence admitted. The clerk is the official record keeper of the court and is responsible as custodian for all legal documents filed with the court.

Court Administrators

The report of the 1967 President's Commission on Law Enforcement and Administration of Justice found "a system that treats defendants who are charged with minor offenses with less dignity and consideration than it treats those who are charged with serious crimes." A few years later, the National Advisory Commission on Criminal Justice Standards and Goals recommended that all courts with five or more judges should create the position of trial court administrator to facilitate the smooth functioning of the courts.[1]

Administrators are trained personnel who assist judges in administrative and nonjudicial functions such as record keeping, scheduling of cases, case flow analysis, data gathering and analysis, personnel administration, research and planning, space utilization, facilities planning, and budget preparation and management. In some cases, the administrator is becoming increasingly involved with juror management to help reduce the time jurors waste waiting to be called or to deal with the excessive number of requests to be excluded from jury service. Overall, the administrator is essential for more effective and efficient court operation.

Nonprofessional Members

Jurors

The Sixth Amendment to the U.S. Constitution guarantees a defendant the right to an impartial jury made up of one's peers. A jury is composed of citizens with no personal knowledge of the dispute or any personal stake in

stenographer: A court employee who records all events that occur during a trial.

the outcome of the trial. The role of the jury is to decide the facts of a case based only on the evidence presented at the trial and to determine the guilt or innocence of the defendant. In some cases, juries recommend a sentence or penalty to be imposed. **Jurors** have enormous power in the courtroom and as players in the courtroom workgroup.

Because the jury is made up of community members, public sentiment may play a part in verdicts. If jurors feel a charge is too harsh, they may decide a defendant is not guilty. If they have the impression that the police officers in the community, as a whole, do not treat people fairly, they may find a defendant not guilty (or guilty of a lesser offense). If they have the impression that the prosecution is treating a particular group more harshly than others, they may find a defendant not guilty. In the end, the jury's perceptions of the defendant, the events, and the members of the courtroom workgroup all come together to influence its decision.

Not all members of a community can serve as jurors. There are certain qualifications for jury service. For instance, a person must be at least 18 years old to be called for jury duty, except in Mississippi and Missouri, where a person must be at least 21 years old. Some states have an upper age limit for jury duty, ranging from 65 to 75 years. Some states have no maximum age stipulation. In all states, jurors must be citizens of the United States, and in most states, jurors must be able to read, speak, and understand English.

Other factors may disqualify a juror from service. Those who have been convicted of a felony are disqualified in all states except Colorado, but many states have provisions for former felons to serve if they have been pardoned, if their civil rights have been restored, or after a certain period of time has passed since the offense. Many states have exempted those in particular careers from serving on a jury. Judicial officers (that is, judges and attorneys), elected officials, medical personnel, active-duty military personnel, clergy, and law enforcement officers are excluded in different states.

States use different methods to choose juries, but most have developed a master list that is used to draw jurors. These are based on driver's licenses records, tax rolls, voting lists, telephone directories, and other sources. Juries today are more representative of the community than they were in the past. The due process clause of the Fifth and Fourteenth Amendments prohibits juries that exclude members of the defendant's racial, gender, ethnic, or religious group. These groups, once excluded from juries, now play an important role in making sure the interests of all groups are represented.

> **jurors:** Citizens who, after hearing the evidence from both sides of a case, determine the guilt or innocence of a defendant and, in some cases, also recommend an appropriate sentence.

States use different strategies to select juries. Regardless of which strategy is used, the process can be quite time consuming.

Witnesses

Witnesses provide evidence about the facts of a case to the best of their knowledge. They can present evidence to support either the prosecution's case or the defense's. The attorney calling the witness to testify will interview the witness at length before the trial so that he or she is aware of the information the witness can provide. Thus, the relationship between the witnesses and the defense and prosecution is essential to the efficient functioning of the court.

Victims

Victims of criminal acts are key players in the courtroom workgroup. These individuals may be the person who was harmed as the result of a crime or the surviving friends and relatives of a victim (in the case of a death). The victims are essential to the trial process because they can provide needed evidence to prosecute an offender. Thus, they must have strong relationships with many other courtroom actors. Probably the most important relationship is with the prosecutor, who must develop a trusting relationship with the victim in order to have the evidence needed to bring charges against the defendant. If a victim does not trust the prosecutor, he or she may withhold evidence or not be forthcoming with information. Although the victim will not have any formal discussions with jurors in the courtroom, it is vital that the victim be portrayed as believable to the jury, especially if the victim takes the stand to tell his or her side of the story. The same holds true for a judge. The victim and the judge should have no contact during the trial process (whether or not the victim is called to testify), but the victim must be able to prove his or her story to the judge. Because the whole trial revolves around the victim's story and the evidence provided, the victim is a key player in the courtroom workgroup.

Media

The members of the media do not work in the courtroom, but they are sometimes considered to be part of the courtroom workgroup because they can influence what goes on before, during, or even after a trial. Before the trial, if the media coverage of the crime and/or defendants is too intense or biased, the judge may determine there is no way a defendant can get a fair trial in that court and order a change of venue. This means the case will be heard in a different location, with a different set of court personnel. During a trial or deliberations, jurors are asked to ignore media coverage of a case. Jurors who do not may be excused. After the trial, in the time between the verdict and sentencing, media coverage may influence the public's opinions of the events and the defendant, and thus the actions of the judge upon sentencing. Thus, because the media can influence the activities of the court to such a great extent, they are sometimes included as members of the courtroom workgroup.

Members of the media are in many ways a part of the courtroom workgroup.

flickr

VIDEO
Technology in the
Courtroom

➡ Technology

One way the courtroom workgroup is able to communicate more efficiently is with increased technology. In recent years, technology has become essential for online communication, research, and case management in many courts. State and federal courts are using technology both to improve access to documents and to streamline filings of documents. It is also used for word processing and tracking financial transactions such as fines. Improvements in technology allow for better communication of critical information between personnel within the court as well as between multiple other agencies that may be involved in cases. Court personnel use electronic means to carry out the necessary daily functions of the court and have come to rely on technology.

Traditionally, case documents were submitted on paper. Now courts are accepting electronic filings, or e-filing, of documents with digital signatures. These documents can be either e-filed or scanned into the system. The electronic version of that document is then accepted as the original. If properly used, e-filing can be a reliable and highly secure method to send and receive legal documents.

There are many advantages to e-filing of documents. With paper copies, only one person can view the document at a time. When documents are stored electronically, multiple users can view them from their personal workstations simultaneously. Those needing to see the documents can also access them much more quickly than they can when paper copies of the documents are stored. They are much more convenient, as there can be desktop access as opposed to waiting for file-room retrieval. Moreover, the information in the electronically stored documents can be found easier and more quickly because the data can be searched by different words and phrases.[2]

It is much easier to organize the electronic copies and maintain them over time. There is less chance that the electronic copies will be lost or damaged, compared with paper copies that can be damaged, misfiled, lost, or stolen. As a result, there will be more confidence that the court's files will be complete. Moreover, the electronic storage of documents is much more secure. There can be duplicate records, required password access, and heightened security over sealed records.[3]

CRIMINAL JUSTICE and **COLLEGE STUDENTS**

TECHNOLOGY AND THE COURTS

List three ways that technology has influenced a decision you made today. Did you happen to write the answers on a piece of paper, or did you use technology to record your answers? Next, review your list and identify how the technological influences on your life potentially influence the courts. Finally, consider two technological strategies that may be used to improve the courts. For example, could the courts e-mail jurors or witnesses instead of using postal mail? Explain how your own ideas about technology might advance court processes as well as the potential drawbacks. Discuss your ideas with a small group of classmates.

Another benefit to using technology is that it can be very cost effective. This is especially important in times when courts face severe budget cutbacks. The files are also easier to store. When documents are stored electronically, it takes far less space to store them. As courts see the number of filings continue to grow, they face the need for more storage space.[4]

Electronic filing of documents is more environmentally friendly, as much less paper is used. There can be built-in scheduling and updating of cases to ensure easier tracking of cases. Finally, there can be time savings with data entry.[5]

The courts are integral to the criminal justice system. Technological advancements have changed the way that the courts function, but there is certainly room for additional applications of technology to improve the operation of the courts. (See the "Criminal Justice and College Students" box in this chapter.)

AUTHOR VIDEO
Technology in the Courtroom

BEYOND A REASONABLE DOUBT 9.5

The courtroom workgroup includes _____.

(a) judges, (b) prosecutors, (c) media, (d) only a and b, (e) all of the above

The answer can be found on page 521.

Just the Facts: Chapter Summary

- The judiciary system is defined in Article III of the U.S. Constitution. It was further defined in the Judiciary Act of 1789, parts of which were declared to be unconstitutional by Chief Justice John Marshall.

- In *Marbury v. Madison*, the Court's power of judicial review was established.

- The United States is considered to have a dual court system, which means there are both federal and state courts.

- A court of general jurisdiction can hear a variety of general cases; a court of limited jurisdiction hears only a specific type of case.

- A court with original jurisdiction will hear that case first; a court of appellate jurisdiction hears only cases on appeal from lower courts.

- Federal courts hear violations of the federal code, whereas state courts hear cases concerning violations of state laws.

- The federal court system comprises a Supreme Court, appeals courts, and district courts.

- The U.S. Supreme Court is the highest court in the United States. It has both original and appellate jurisdiction.

- The Supreme Court decides what cases it will hear, and there is a specific procedure for making that choice.

- The courtroom workgroup is composed of actors who have distinct responsibilities yet have created informal working relationships that help the courts function efficiently. The workgroup includes judges, the prosecution, the defense, law clerks, jurors, the bailiff, the stenographer, court clerks, court administrators, witnesses, victims, and the media.

Critical Thinking Questions

1. Explain how Article III of the Constitution and the Judiciary Act of 1789 affected the creation of the courts.

2. How did *Marbury v. Madison* help to define the role of the courts?

3. What is a dual system of courts?

4. What is the difference between appellate and original jurisdiction?

5. What types of cases must be heard in the U.S. Supreme Court? Give examples of each.

6. What is the process for having a case heard in front of the Supreme Court?

7. What are the different types of state courts?

8. What are different types of methods for providing legal counsel to indigent offenders? Which one is best?

9. What is the courtroom workgroup, and who are the primary actors in it?

10. How can technology be used in the courtroom?

Key Terms

amicus curiae briefs (279)

appellate jurisdiction (275)

Article III of the U.S. Constitution (273)

assigned counsel (298)

bailiff (298)

contract system (298)

courtroom workgroup (292)

defense attorney (296)

docket number (278)

dual court system (275)

federal magistrates (288)

in forma pauperis (278)

intermediate appellate courts (state) (290)

Judiciary Act of 1789 (273)

jurors (300)

law clerks (294)

majority opinion (280)

original jurisdiction (275)

per curiam opinion (280)

prosecutor (294)

public defender (297)

Rule of Four (279)

state supreme courts (290)

stenographer (299)

trial courts of general jurisdiction (state) (291)

U.S. courts of appeals (285)

U.S. Court of Appeals for the Federal Circuit (287)

U.S. district courts (287)

U.S. Supreme Court (276)

venue (275)

writ of certification (277)

$SAGE edgeselect™

edge.sagepub.com/payne

Sharpen your skills with SAGE edge select!

With carefully crafted tools and resources to encourage review, practice, and critical thinking, SAGE edge select gives you the edge needed to master course content. Take full advantage of open-access key term flashcards, practice quizzes, and video content. Diagnostic pre-tests, a personalized study plan, and post-tests are available with an access code.

10

THE JUDICIAL PROCESS

© AP Photo/Red Huber, Pool

© alessandro0770/Veer

IN 2008, CASEY ANTHONY'S TWO-YEAR-OLD DAUGHTER, Caylee Anthony, was reported missing in Florida after the girl had been missing for many weeks. A few months later, even though there was no body, Casey was charged with first-degree murder. The little girl's body was found a few months later in nearby woods.

Casey was given a trial like any other defendant who had been accused of a crime. In that trial, the prosecution presented multiple pieces of evidence to demonstrate Casey's guilt. The defense refuted that evidence in its attempt to show that Casey was not guilty of the crime. The jury, which had been brought in from a neighboring county because of pretrial publicity, was composed of 12 seated jurors and 5 alternates (9 women and 8 men). After hearing the evidence, they found Casey to be not guilty of most of the crimes with which she had been charged. The judge sentenced Casey to a punishment relevant to the offenses of which she was found guilty.

LEARNING OBJECTIVES

After reading this chapter, students will be able to:

10.1 Describe the judicial process in the United States

10.2 Explain the pretrial process that occurs prior to the actual trial

10.3 Describe bail and different methods of granting bail

10.4 Outline the key stages in a trial

10.5 Explain how juries are chosen and the jury's role in a trial

10.6 Describe the factors considered in sentencing

10.7 Outline the purpose and process of appeals

10.8 Compare and contrast the process for juvenile courts and adult courts

10.9 Identify the rights of defendants throughout the judicial process

The Casey Anthony case clearly demonstrates the **judicial process** that exists in the United States. The *judicial process* entails the steps involved once someone has been accused of a crime, as the case travels through the court system, until he or she is found guilty or innocent. Certain rules determine what the judge, the prosecutor, the defense, and others can do. The judicial process is an adversarial one. The prosecutor, who advocates for the government (or the state), tries to prove a defendant's guilt, and the defense attorney, who advocates for the defendant, tries to prove the defendant's innocence. The goal of both sides is to convince the judge or jury that their perspective on the case is the correct one. The judge oversees the action in the courtroom and

ADMISSIBLE or INADMISSIBLE Evidence

Read the statements that follow. If the statement is true, circle *admissible*. If the statement is false, circle *inadmissible*. Answers can be found on page 518.

1. **Admissible   Inadmissible**   The police have a significant amount of discretion, or choice, when deciding to arrest an individual who breaks the law.

2. **Admissible   Inadmissible**   A prosecutor can take as long as he or she needs before having an initial appearance for a suspect.

3. **Admissible   Inadmissible**   A grand jury hears evidence in a courtroom and decides whether a person accused of a crime is guilty.

4. **Admissible   Inadmissible**   In a preliminary hearing, the prosecution must show that a crime was committed and that the accused committed the act.

5. **Admissible   Inadmissible**   Bail is a system that ensures the defendant will appear for his or her trial.

6. **Admissible   Inadmissible**   Most people agree that preventive detention is a good policy because it ensures the safety of the community.

7. **Admissible   Inadmissible**   For the most part, the plea-bargaining process does not include judges.

8. **Admissible   Inadmissible**   The prosecutor is responsible for "charging" the jury, or explaining the law as it applies to the case at hand.

The act of arrest is the first official stage of the justice process.

© ZUMA Press, Inc. / Alamy

judicial process: The progression of a case through the judicial system.

ensures that the defendant's due process rights are protected and that the prosecution and the defense follow all legal mandates. This system is depicted in Figure 10.1.

➡ Arrest/Booking

The judicial process begins with an arrest by a law enforcement officer of a person who allegedly has violated a local, state, or federal law. The police have a great amount of discretion as to whom they arrest. An arrest is the first formal point of contact between the state (the courts) and the accused. Upon being arrested, an alleged offender is booked into jail. During booking, the law enforcement agency records a description of the events that led to the arrest and possible charges against the suspect. The agency typically records the suspect's personal information (name, address, contact information) and physical description (age, weight, hair and eye color, tattoos). It may take a mug shot (photograph) and collect the suspect's fingerprints. Any personal property is taken from the suspect and stored until he or she is released. The suspect

FIGURE 10.1 Judicial Process Flowchart

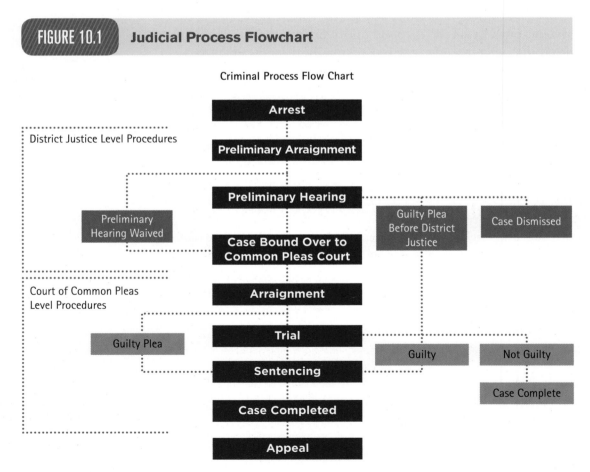

U.S. Department of Justice

BEYOND A REASONABLE DOUBT 10.1

Which of the following steps is involved in booking a suspect?

(a) Collecting the suspect's personal information, (b) Taking the suspect's mug shot, (c) Assigning an attorney to the suspect, (d) a and b, (e) All of the above

The answer can be found on page 521.

is asked about his or her medical background, and a brief mental evaluation may be performed. The suspect may have the opportunity to make a collect phone call, depending on the policy of the jail. An attorney may be assigned to a defendant at this stage.

➡ The Charging Decision

After a suspect is arrested and booked, the state's prosecutor (sometimes called the district attorney) must review the evidence gathered by law enforcement and decide if that person should be charged with a criminal offense and, if so, which offense (or offenses). The **charging** decision depends mainly on the seriousness of the crime as well as on the quality and quantity of the evidence against the suspect. The prosecutor may reject a case if the evidence is insufficient or of poor quality, if witnesses will not cooperate, or if the offense is minor (a misdemeanor). In this case, the charges against the suspect may be dropped and he or she can go free.

If the prosecutor decides to file charges, he or she must also decide at this time if the defendant is a candidate for pretrial release or for bail. The prosecutor will take many factors into consideration, such as the nature of the offense, the dangerousness of the defendant (his or her potential to commit further harm to people or property in the community), the defendant's risk of fleeing, and the defendant's family structure and ties to the community. If it is determined that a defendant is not a threat to the community, he or she may be released from the court's custody to await trial. If the prosecutor believes the defendant may be a threat, or if the offense was particularly dangerous, the defendant will remain in jail.

The choices made by the prosecutor at this stage of the judicial process are critical for the defendant. The prosecutor has significant discretion to influence the defendant's fate. By determining if charges will be brought, what charges will be applied, or if a defendant is held in jail or permitted to return home, the prosecutor may have an impact on whether the individual will have a criminal record and what punishments he or she may receive.

BEYOND A REASONABLE DOUBT 10.2

Who determines what charges will be filed against a suspect?

(a) The defense, (b) The police, (c) The prosecutor, (d) The judge, (e) The jury

The answer can be found on page 521.

VIDEO
Sticker and Chloroform

charging: The state's prosecutor (often the district attorney) decides what charges, if any, should be formally brought against the suspect.

➡ Pretrial

In the early stages of the judicial process, different labels are used to describe the individual who has been arrested. Essentially, he or she goes from being a citizen, to a suspect, to a defendant (see Figure 10.2). If a suspect is charged with a crime, or multiple crimes, he or she may face a criminal trial. However,

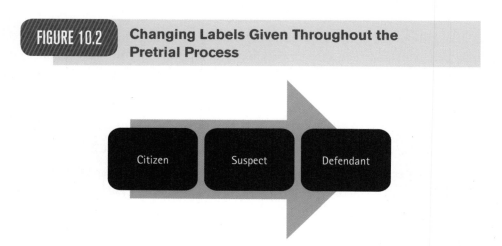

FIGURE 10.2 — **Changing Labels Given Throughout the Pretrial Process**

Citizen   Suspect   Defendant

many steps in the process occur before the actual trial as a way to ensure a defendant's rights are being preserved. This is known as the *pretrial process*.

Many actors are involved in the pretrial process (see Figure 10.3). The prosecutor, as the representative of the state, has the goal of proving a defendant guilty (or having the defendant plead guilty) within legal boundaries. It is much more efficient if a prosecutor can obtain a guilty plea during the pretrial process. The state will not have to pay to house the offender prior to trial, or for a trial itself. At the same time, the defense counsel is trying to obtain the defendant's release during the pretrial process by providing the best possible defense. If the prosecutor offers a "deal," the defense counsel must decide whether to recommend this plea negotiation to the defendant (see later discussion of plea bargaining). The judge is another primary actor in the pretrial process. The judge must oversee legal proceedings and ensure that any deals are made willingly and that they are legal and fair. The judge must ensure that a defendant is treated justly and fairly and that his or her due process rights are being preserved.

Initial Appearance

The initial appearance, or initial hearing, is usually held shortly after a defendant's arrest, and is often held in a lower court or even a magistrate's court. In this step of the judicial process, a judge formally informs the defendant of the charge(s) brought against him or her by the prosecutor. The court also informs the defendant of his or her constitutional rights, such as the right to remain silent and to have legal defense appointed to the case if he or she cannot afford to hire an attorney.

The law requires that a defendant must appear before a magistrate "without unnecessary delay" or "in a timely manner." But a question arises: What

FIGURE 10.3   Actors in the Pretrial Process

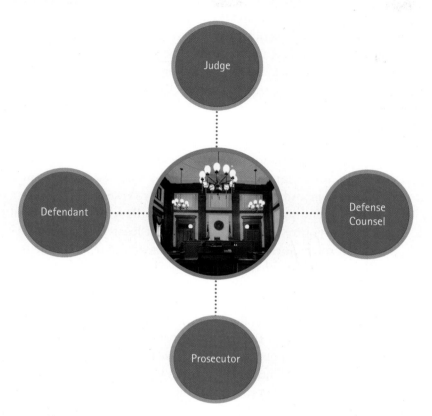

© iStockphoto.com/JPLDesigns

is meant by "a timely manner"? The U.S. Supreme Court attempted to answer this question in *McNabb v. United States* (1943). In this case the justices ruled that a confession is not admissible if it was obtained without a prompt appearance before a magistrate after an arrest was made. In other words, if an unreasonable delay occurs between an arrest and the initial court appearance, then a confession obtained during that delay would be inadmissible. Over time, 48 hours became the standard for the maximum delay between an arrest and a first appearance. The 48-hour rule was formalized in *County of Riverside (California) v. McLaughlin* (1991). In this case, the Supreme Court found that arraignments held within 48 hours of arrest, excluding weekends and holidays, satisfied the speedy trial standard. Moreover, delays may exceed the 48-hour rule and still be constitutional if the state can demonstrate that the delay was caused by an extraordinary circumstance or emergency.

Grand Jury

According to the Fifth Amendment to the U.S. Constitution, "No person shall be held to answer for a capital, or otherwise infamous crime, unless on a presentment or indictment of a Grand Jury." The **grand jury** is a system that helps to determine the appropriate charges that should be brought against an accused individual. A grand jury is a group of 16 to 23 (usually 19) people who hear the evidence and determine if that evidence is sufficient

grand jury: Citizens who hear evidence against a person accused of a crime and help to determine the appropriate charges that should be brought against that person.

for the state to hold an individual and bring charges against him or her. The primary purpose of the grand jury is to determine whether there is probable cause that a crime has been committed and the accused should be held for trial. It is a way to check the behavior of the prosecutor and ensure the state is not bringing charges for political or personal reasons against someone who is, in fact, innocent. It is a way to force the prosecutor to justify holding the defendant and depriving that individual of his or her freedom.

In the federal system, every person accused of a crime has the right to have his or her case heard in front of a grand jury. States vary in this regard. Some states use the grand jury system, but others do not. Some use a grand jury system for only certain types of cases, such as capital crimes. Pennsylvania does not allow for grand juries at all.

The members of a grand jury are typically selected at random from voter registration lists and other databases. They serve for anywhere from 1 to 18 months, depending on the state, and usually for several days of the week. Most states require a grand juror to be at least 18 years old, a U.S. citizen, a resident of the jurisdiction for at least one year, and able to read and write English.

The grand jury process is unlike a trial in many ways (see Figure 10.4). First, the grand jurors hear evidence only from the prosecutor, who tries to show that there is a strong probability that the defendant committed the crime. Second, in most cases, neither the defense attorney nor the defendant attends the hearing. Sometimes, the defense is not aware that a grand jury proceeding is taking place. Third, a defendant's guilt does not have to be proven beyond a reasonable doubt. It must be proven that there is a likelihood that the defendant committed the offense. Fourth, the prosecutor may rely on evidence that might be inadmissible in a trial, including hearsay. Fifth, in some states, the grand jury members can call and question their own witnesses.

If the majority of the grand jury members endorse or agree with the charges brought by the prosecutor, based on the evidence, then there is probable cause for the charges to be brought. The grand jury will present an *indictment*, or *true bill*, which is a formal, written accusation presented against a defendant. It alleges that the accused committed a specific offense and that a trial should be held to determine if there is enough evidence for conviction. If the members of the grand jury do not believe there is probable cause to believe the accused committed the alleged offenses, then the grand jury will fail to indict the defendant. This is called *no bill*. If this happens, a prosecutor has the option of presenting the case to another grand jury.

In recent years, some scholars have debated whether the grand jury process is fair to the defendant because he or she is given few due process rights.[1] It is easy for the prosecutor to persuade grand jury members of a defendant's guilt because he or she has can present such a wide array of evidence, some of which may not be admitted in trial. Additionally, the grand jury hears testimony secretly, without the accused or his or her attorney present. The defense does not have the opportunity to present evidence.

The American Bar Association has suggested some reforms of the grand jury system as a way to make it more efficient. Its recommendations call for allowing jurors to take notes during the trial, allowing jurors to

VIDEO
Grand Jury
Orientation

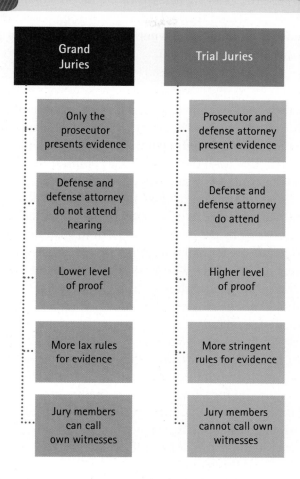

FIGURE 10.4 **How Grand Juries Differ From Trial Juries**

Grand Juries	Trial Juries
Only the prosecutor presents evidence	Prosecutor and defense attorney present evidence
Defense and defense attorney do not attend hearing	Defense and defense attorney do attend
Lower level of proof	Higher level of proof
More lax rules for evidence	More stringent rules for evidence
Jury members can call own witnesses	Jury members cannot call own witnesses

ask questions, using juries composed of 12 people, requiring unanimous decisions, and showing more concern for the privacy of jurors.[2]

Preliminary Hearing

Some states have abolished the grand jury system and instead use a **preliminary hearing** to determine if there is probable cause for the accused to be brought to trial. In this hearing, the state has to prove that a crime was committed and the accused committed that act. A judge presides to ensure the proceedings run smoothly. The prosecution presents its case and calls witnesses to show probable cause against the defendant, and then the defendant has the right to present evidence and cross-examine witnesses as a way to present favorable evidence.

After the evidence has been presented, the judge will determine whether there is probable cause for a trial. If he or she so determines, the prosecutor must file a *bill of information* with the court. This outlines the charges against the defendant. This also happens if the defense waives the hearing. The hearing is typically waived by the majority of defendants, so this step in the judicial process is simply skipped. This is helpful to the courts, because it is one less formal appearance that has to occur.

preliminary hearing: The stage in the criminal justice process (in some jurisdictions) when a judge determines whether probable cause exists to suggest that the suspect committed a crime in the judge's jurisdiction.

The preliminary hearing gives the judge an opportunity to review the methods by which the police gathered the evidence to ensure that it was done legally. It also enables the judge to review the prosecution's evidence against a defendant to determine whether there is sufficient evidence and probable cause has been established.

Bail

Bail is a monetary bond paid by the defendant after arrest as a way to obtain his or her release after arrest and before trial. If the defendant can post the bail amount set by the judge or the prosecutor, then he or she will be released from jail and can remain free until the trial. At that point, if the defendant fails to appear in court for trial, he or she may forfeit the money posted for bail. In general, bail acts as an insurance policy to guarantee the defendant will show up for trial. The bail amount can be set shortly after the defendant's arrest or at the preliminary hearing by the presiding judge or magistrate. All states and the federal government allow for bail, except in cases of serious or violent offenses.

Many states do not place a limit on the amount of bail a judge may set, but it is written in the Eighth Amendment of the U.S. Constitution that "excessive bail shall not be required." Although this clause does not grant the right to bail to all defendants, it nonetheless ensures that the bail amount is not to be excessive. But what is meant by "excessive"? The Supreme Court addressed this issue in *Stack v. Boyle* (1951), in which the justices decided that bail must be set at an amount no greater than that which would ensure the defendant will show up for future court proceedings. Although the justices did not establish exact amounts, they implied that each case, or each defendant, should be judged separately, taking into account the defendant's character, the evidence against him or her, the offense, and the defendant's ability to pay cash bail. In addition, bail cannot be used as punishment, nor may it be used to coerce or threaten a defendant. The average bail amount for those arrested for felonies in the state of California is represented in Figure 10.5.

Defendants who are unable to pay for their bail are placed in detention (usually a jail) until their trial date. In some cases, defendants must spend weeks or even months in a pretrial detention center where the conditions are sometimes very poor. They are unable to spend time with their families or friends, may risk losing their jobs and are therefore unable to support their families, and are unable to look for evidence for their cases. In addition, holding a defendant in jail for long periods results in serious financial burdens on local and state governments, and on taxpayers, to pay the cost of confinement. As a result, many pretrial release programs have been developed that allow more defendants to be released from jail and avoid pretrial detention.

It became clear that those defendants without spare cash were being discriminated against under the bail system. Defendants who had more resources were able to gain release under the bail system, whereas those without resources were detained, sometimes for long periods. Consequently, many states established nonmonetary options as a way for defendants to obtain pretrial release. One of those methods was a *pretrial release officer.* The pretrial release officer interviews defendants who have been arrested on criminal charges and obtains information about them, including the complaint made against them by the victim; the charges brought by the

JOURNAL
Price on Prisoner
Release

bail: A monetary bond that is paid by a defendant after an arrest as a way to obtain release before the trial.

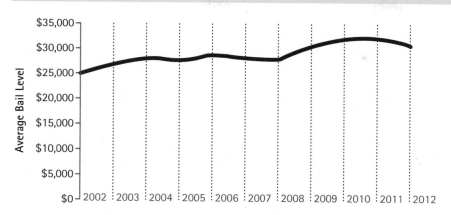

FIGURE 10.5   **Average Bail Amount for Felonies in California, 2002–2012**

Note: Author's calculations using annual bail schedules for Los Angeles, San Bernardino, Riverside, San Diego, Orange, Marin, Alameda, Solano, Tulare, San Mateo, San Luis Obispo, and Contra Costa counties.

Public Policy Institute of California

prosecutor; the report of the arresting officer; the suspect's prior record; and information from family members, employers, friends, probation or parole officers, or other agencies that might have had contact with the individual. They also seek information on the defendant's community ties, overall stability, risk of flight, and history of drug or alcohol abuse.

After gathering the information, the officer decides whether the defendant should be released prior to the trial. Release does not depend on the defendant's financial ability to pay bail. Under this system, all defendants, regardless of their income or wealth, may be released into the community. This helps defendants, but it is also cheaper for the community.

There are other alternatives for nonmonetary pretrial release. For example, under *third-party custody*, a criminal defendant is released to the custody of a third person who promises that the defendant will appear in court at the scheduled time. This type of pretrial release is most common with juvenile defendants who have been released to the custody of their parents or other guardians. Under *conditional release*, the judge releases the defendant with the stipulation that the defendant agrees to follow specified conditions. For example, a defendant must promise not to leave the area (for example, the county) or associate with particular people (convicted felons, gang members) and, in certain cases, must promise to attend a drug treatment program or maintain employment. If the defendant is found to be in violation of these conditions, he or she can be returned to custody.

With a *property bond*, a defendant substitutes other items of value in place of cash when posting bail. These items can include land, houses, automobiles, or stocks, as collateral. If the individual does not appear, the item becomes the property of the

Bail bonds agents provide bail to defendants in exchange for a fee.

Wikimedia Commons

police department. Another option for nonmonetary release involves unsecured bail or bond. In this situation, a defendant will pay no money to the court but is liable for the full amount of bail if he or she fails to appear. The different types of pretrial release and the frequency with which they are used are shown in Figure 10.6.

Congress first addressed the issue of fairness of bail through the Bail Reform Act of 1966. Members of Congress supported options for nonmonetary pretrial release for those arrested for criminal acts. They indicated that the courts should release defendants under the least restrictive conditions needed to ensure their return to court. In doing so, they indicated their support for releasing defendants simply on their promise that they would return to court when needed. This became known as *release on your own recognizance*, or ROR.

In 1984, Congress revisited the bail system and amended the 1966 law. The Bail Reform Act of 1984 required that the pretrial release decision also take into account the safety of the community. It also allowed judges to place dangerous federal defendants in pretrial detention without bail if they found that no conditions of release would ensure the defendant's appearance at trial. In other words, a judge could refuse bail if the accused was charged with a violent offense, had a serious criminal record, or was considered to be a danger to the community (likely to commit crimes while awaiting trial) or a flight risk (likely to leave the area). Another key feature of the act was its establishment of a no-bail presumption for certain types of cases. Under this stipulation, defendants accused of certain offenses would not be provided with the option of bail.

The U.S. Supreme Court reviewed the Bail Reform Act in *United States v. Salerno* (1987). The justices decided that Congress created the act as a way to prevent further danger or harm to the community and not as a way

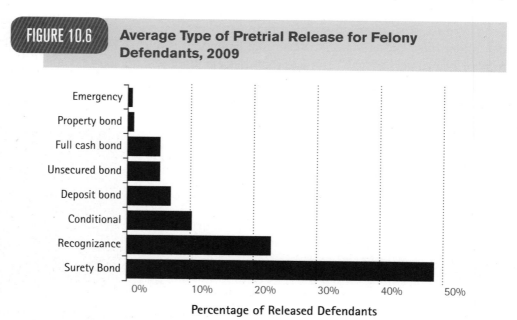

FIGURE 10.6   **Average Type of Pretrial Release for Felony Defendants, 2009**

Percentage of Released Defendants

Note: Data obtained from the 75 largest counties in the United States.

Bureau of Justice Statistics

to punish dangerous individuals. After this decision, many states passed laws similar to the Bail Reform Act. Now, in many states, a judge must determine the likelihood that an accused will be present for trial and consider the safety of the community when deciding whether or not to release a defendant from custody prior to trial. This is known as a *judicial release*.

Preventive Detention

If a defendant is charged with a serious violent crime, is believed to be a flight risk, or is considered to be dangerous to the community, he or she may be held in jail until trial. This is known as **preventive detention**. Preventive detention denies bail to certain defendants who are considered to be potentially dangerous.

The trend toward allowing some defendants to be held in preventive detention is often criticized because it is said to deprive defendants of their liberty even if they have not been proven guilty. Under preventive detention, a defendant who has not committed a crime could spend a year or more in jail. Nonetheless, the Supreme Court ruled in *Schall v. Martin* (1984) that preventive detention was constitutional. The justices decided that the pretrial detention of accused juvenile offenders did not violate their due process rights, even though one was held for 17 days, because probable cause had been established and showed that the juvenile committed the offense. Moreover, other procedural safeguards were provided during the juvenile's confinement. Thus, the justices decided in favor of preventive detention.

Arraignment

The next step in the judicial process is called arraignment. In this step, a defendant is brought before the judge to respond to the grand jury indictment or bill of information. The prosecutor reads the charges that have been brought against the defendant in open court. At the same time, the defendant is informed of his or her right to have an attorney appointed if he or she cannot afford one. This is the also the first stage of the trial process, and it occurs shortly after the indictment has been declared by the grand jury.

Once the charges are read, the defendant is asked to respond and make a plea (a defendant's response to a criminal charge). No matter how serious or minor the offense, all defendants must enter a plea. At the arraignment, a defendant has three plea options: guilty, not guilty, or nolo contendere (no contest).

A defendant who pleads guilty is admitting to all the facts alleged to have occurred, as well as their legal implications. By pleading guilty, the defendant is waiving several rights: the right to a trial by a judge or a jury, the right to remain silent, the right to confront the witnesses against him or her, and the right to require the prosecution to establish guilt beyond a reasonable doubt by admissible evidence. However,

> **preventive detention:** The act of holding a defendant prior to the trial if it is believed that he or she may be a flight risk or dangerous to the community.

At the arraginemnt, suspects are notified of their charges and asked to enter a plea.

© Pool/Getty Images

a trial judge is not required to accept a guilty plea. A judge can enter a plea of not guilty on behalf of the accused if he or she feels that the plea was not voluntary or that the defendant did not fully understand the implications of the plea. The judge may also believe that there is no factual basis for a guilty plea.

If a defendant pleads guilty and the judge accepts the plea, no trial date will be set. Instead, the judge will set a sentencing date. In most cases, a defendant must wait several weeks for the sentencing phase. In capital cases, the accused cannot enter a plea of guilty if the state is requesting the death penalty. See the "Criminal Justice and the Media" box in this chapter for an example of an unusual guilty plea.

If a defendant chooses to plead not guilty, that defendant is denying any guilt. The defendant then places the burden of proving guilt beyond a reasonable doubt on the prosecution. If a defendant pleads not guilty, the judge sets a date for trial.

The third type of plea is nolo contendere, or no contest. This is essentially a guilty plea, but the defendant is admitting criminal liability for purposes of this proceeding only. By entering a nolo plea, the accused waives the right to a trial just as if he or she had pled guilty. But this plea allows the defendant to avoid the implications of guilt in other proceedings, such as in civil court, where the accused may also be liable. This plea means that the accused did not formally admit to committing the act, which allows the defense to later claim that there was no guilty verdict. That being said, a

CRIMINAL JUSTICE and the MEDIA:
PLEADING GUILTY ON YOUTUBE

Matthew Cordle, 22, posted a three-and-a-half-minute video on YouTube in which he said, "I killed a man." When the video starts, the face of the confessor is blurred out of focus while he describes the events of the night of June 22, 2013. Cordle admits that he was out with a friend and drinking heavily. On the way home, he drove his Toyota Tundra the wrong way on a freeway and hit a Jeep. In the other car was a 61-year-old man, Vincent Canzani, who was declared dead at the scene. In the video, Cordle's face becomes clear as he continues to speak. Through the YouTube video, Cordle took responsibility for the events of that night. He told viewers, "Don't be like me." He claimed to have spoken to lawyers who told him to lie as a way to avoid punishment. But Cordle instead chose to produce the video and post it on a website called "because I said I would." He claimed that if he was charged with criminal offenses as a result of the video, he would plead guilty. County prosecutors reviewed the video and Cordle's confession and decided to present the evidence to the grand jury to determine if he should be indicted for aggravated vehicular homicide. They eventually charged Cordle with that crime, as well as for operating a vehicle while under the influence of alcohol. In the end, Cordle was sentenced to six months for driving under the influence of alcohol and six years for aggravated vehicular homicide. The sentencing judge also revoked Cordle's driving privileges for the rest of his life.

The goal of the video, according to Cordle, was to help others make better choices, and to convince them not to drink and drive.

Castillo, M. (2013). Drunken driving video confession: "I killed a man." Retrieved from http://www.cnn.com/2013/09/06/us/youtube-drunken-driving-confession/index.html

plea of "no contest" results in a conviction and the defendant can be given the same sentence that would have resulted from a guilty plea. This plea is available only in about half the states and in federal cases.

Pretrial Motions

Pretrial motions are requests, either oral or written (called petitions), that are made to a court seeking a finding, a decision, or an order. Motions can be made before trial, during trial, or even after trial. Types of motions include motions to dismiss, motions to suppress evidence, motions to reduce bail, and motions to discover what evidence the other side has. These motions can play a big role in the outcome of the case.

Plea Bargaining

Sometime before the trial occurs, the defense and the prosecution may enter into negotiations called **plea bargaining** (see Chapter 11). In a plea bargain, a defendant can give up the right to a trial in exchange for a reduction in the charges or sentence. In essence, some form of lenience is promised in exchange for a guilty plea. The prosecutor and the defense discuss terms under which the defendant will enter a plea of guilty. They can negotiate the sentence or the charges. In about 90% of cases, the prosecution and the defense are able to negotiate a plea. They are able to strike a bargain concerning the official charges to be brought and the nature of the sentence the state will recommend to the court.

There are four primary actors in the plea-bargaining process. The first actor is the prosecutor, who can have the most power in the process. Prosecutors have many options, including a reduction of the original charge; a dismissal of some charges; a recommendation of probation or another, more lenient, form of punishment; an agreement to make no recommendation as to sentence or not to oppose a defense plea of leniency; an agreement to dismiss charges against a codefendant; or the stipulation of a specific sentence, such as restitution or incarceration at a particular correctional institution. In short, the prosecutor determines the concessions to be offered in the plea bargain, if any.

Most prosecutors are more willing to negotiate a plea in a minor crime than in a more serious one. They are typically more interested in negotiating a plea when the state's case against the defendant is weak. This is because a plea bargain will guarantee a "conviction" for the prosecutor, who most likely is concerned with maintaining a high conviction rate.

The second actor is the defense counsel. The defense counsel is required to advise the defendant about the plea negotiations. The defense must be knowledgeable about the facts of the case and the evidence and be able to advise the defendant of the alternatives. The defense must ensure that the accused understands the plea-bargaining process, what it means to plead guilty, and the ramifications of doing so. The defense counsel must also keep the defendant informed of any developments and discussions with the prosecutor regarding plea bargaining.

The third actor in the plea-bargaining process is the defendant. A defendant will often agree to plea bargain because it can result in a reduced charge or a less severe punishment.

pretrial motions: Requests, either oral or written (called petitions), that are made to a court seeking a finding, a decision, or an order.

plea bargaining: A system in which the defendant gives up his or her right to a trial in exchange for a reduction in charges or the sentence imposed.

The fourth actor in the plea-bargaining process is the judge. Some judges are very involved in the process, whereas others stay more distant. Sometimes their involvement is limited by state law. Every state judge, however, has the duty to question the defendant at the end of the negotiations as a way to ensure that he or she was not coerced into pleading guilty by either the defense attorney or the prosecutor. Federal judges are prohibited from participating in plea negotiations, as outlined in the Federal Rules of Criminal Procedures.

In some states, the victim is allowed to participate as a fifth actor in the plea-bargaining process. The prosecution may pay close attention to what the victim requests in terms of the plea bargain. However, most state statutes do not require that the prosecutor defer to the victim's wishes, and there are no legal consequences if the victim's request is not given top priority. That means that the judge will uphold the victim's wishes in some cases, but in others it will not. Some observers have argued that a victim or the victim's family should have the authority to approve of any plea negotiation between the prosecutor and the defense attorney in criminal homicide cases, but others argue that the negotiation decision should remain with legally trained professionals.

BEYOND A REASONABLE DOUBT 10.3

What is the purpose of pretrial hearings and motions?

(a) So the attorneys can get to know the defendant's background, (b) To ensure a defendant's rights, (c) To allow the defense and the prosecution to build better cases, (d) To give the judge some information about the case, (e) To allow a jury to be chosen

---

The answer can be found on page 521.

➡ Trial

FEATURE VIDEO
The Trial Process

All defendants, regardless of their social standing, their economic status, or the nature of the alleged offense, have the right to a trial, as guaranteed under the U.S. Constitution. The premise in all trials is that the defendant is innocent until proven guilty by the state (the prosecutor). Even if a defendant did commit the crime, he or she is considered to be innocent under the law unless a prosecutor can prove the charges with enough evidence to convince a jury (or a judge) of a defendant's guilt "beyond a reasonable doubt."

The trial is an adversarial process whereby each party vies against the other. The prosecution tries to show the defendant's guilt; the defense tries to show the defendant's innocence; and both sides provide their evidence in front of a neutral judge and jury. With help, legal assistants ensure that the attorneys have the information they need in court (see the "Help Wanted" box in this chapter). Whereas the lawyers on both sides are active, the judge plays a more passive role. The judge oversees the trial process to ensure that a defendant's basic rights are protected. During the trial, power is held by attorneys, judges, and other actors in the system, such as the jury.

HELP WANTED: PARALEGAL SPECIALIST ASSISTANT

DUTIES:

- Review and organize complex factual material and other documentary data for investigations and trials.

- Perform legal research in a variety of areas, often involving complex legal issues and interpretation of statutes and rules.

- Provide advice on the most efficient method for preparing legal documents.

- Use tables and citation checking with efficiency.

- Prepare a variety of substantive legal documents to include extradition requests, grand jury and trial subpoenas, interrogatory requests, and documentation relevant to acquiring evidence or testimony.

- Develop and enter various case material into a computer database.

- Prepare charts, graphs, and tables to illustrate results.

- Prepare, develop, compile, or maintain jury instructions in preparing for trial.

- Prepare exhibits for trial, which typically include a wide range of visual materials.

- Provide litigation case management and organize cases for court presentation.

REQUIREMENTS: Associate degree or a certificate

ANNUAL SALARY: $57,982–$75,836

Adapted from USAJOBS.gov. Retrieved from https://www.usajobs.gov/GetJob/ViewDetails/363982300

Jury Selection

Before the trial begins, a jury must be selected. A jury is a group of citizens chosen to listen to the evidence presented by the prosecution and the defense and to determine the guilt or innocence of the offender. The process of **jury selection** is one of the most important steps in a criminal trial. The make-up of a jury can have a major impact on whether a defendant is found guilty (and then must face a prison term or some other punishment) or not guilty (in which case, he or she goes free). The study of juries and jury selection has become an essential component of our understanding of juries and their behavior.

The first step in selecting an impartial jury is to create a random list of names of people who are eligible to serve on a jury. This list of potential jurors is called the *jury panel*. It is imperative that the jury panel consist of a fair cross-section of the community and that all groups be represented. (See the "Ethical Decision Making" box in this chapter.)

Once a list of potential jurors is compiled, the court clerk or court administrator randomly chooses names of people who can serve on a jury. The court then uses the list to choose the final jury. The list must contain the names of many more people than are actually needed for the jury, given that many of the panel will not be chosen or will be unable to serve for various reasons.

The citizens on the panel are contacted and asked to arrive at the courthouse at a specific time and date. The group of people who come to serve as

AUTHOR VIDEO
Jury Selection Process

jury selection: The process by which an impartial jury is chosen to hear the evidence in a trial; includes the voir dire process, when potential jurors are questioned.

ETHICAL DECISION MAKING

THE CALL FOR JURY DUTY

Eddie Loft is preparing to celebrate his birthday with a well-earned vacation in the Pocono Mountains. After reviewing the nonrefundable plane reservations he made two days earlier, Eddie proceeds to open the day's mail. He is surprised to see something from the courthouse and opens that envelope first.

The sentence "You are being summoned for jury duty" is printed in bold letters across the top of the envelope. Reading the letter, Eddie quickly realizes that he is being summoned to serve at the same time that he had planned on vacationing.

After connecting the dates, Eddie remembers that he had asked to be excused from jury duty on two prior occasions. After the second excusal, he was told that a third one would be granted only for serious health reasons.

YOU DECIDE

1. If you were Eddie, would you try to get out of jury duty a third time? Why or why not?

2. Why do you think individuals avoid jury duty?

prospective jurors is called a *venire*. The attorneys involved in the case, both the defense and the prosecution, question the potential jurors in a process called *voir dire*. In some states, the attorneys must submit their questions to the judge, who then questions the jury members. In other jurisdictions, the attorneys question the prospective jurors themselves. In either situation, the potential jurors may be asked in open court about their background, family status, profession, or any other factor that the attorneys believe may predict their ability to serve, as well as how they may judge the defendant. The attorneys try to determine if a potential juror has a bias or prejudice toward the defendant, and they attempt eliminate all members who might have a reason not to render an impartial decision. When the questioning is done, the attorneys can then select jurors who they feel are acceptable.

Both the prosecution and the defense have challenges that allow them to select jurors that are likely to support their sides. There are two types of challenges. A *challenge for cause* is a request by either the prosecution or the defense to remove a potential juror from serving because of a concern about that person's ability to be fair and impartial or to follow the judge's instructions. This is intended to keep people who seem to have a conflict of interest or bias against the defendant off the jury. A challenge for cause must be ruled on by the judge, and if it is accepted, the potential juror is excused. There is no limit to the number of challenges for cause allowed, but the presiding judge must determine if the reasoning is valid.

The second type of challenge is a *peremptory challenge*. This is an objection to a prospective juror that may be exercised without any cause

The jury is charged with determining guilt or innocence.

© REUTERS/Jane Rosenberg

whatsoever. The attorneys are not required to provide a reason or an explanation for why they want a potential juror dismissed. One of the lawyers may simply not like a juror's answer, or may believe that a potential juror will be unfavorable to his or her side. Or the attorneys may have mapped out some sort of strategy and desire a specific type of juror. The number of peremptory challenges allowed for each side is limited by law. In most cases, the defense has more than the prosecution. In federal cases, each side is typically allowed between one and three challenges per jury, depending on the offense. In a death penalty case, up to 20 challenges are permitted.

Because they have little involvement in the political system, college students may assume that they are not potential jurors. Although rules for jury selection vary across the states, college student status does not prohibit one from serving on a jury.

Individual states can determine the number of people needed to make up a jury for a criminal trial. Traditionally, a jury is made up of 12 people, and most states today still use juries of 12 people with one or two alternates who can fill in for jurors who are forced to leave the trial process early due to illness, accident, or some other reason. There is no ruling by the Supreme Court that indicates that a jury must be made up of 12 people.

The Supreme Court has decided, however, that a six-person jury is fair and constitutional. In *Williams v. Florida* (1968), the justices declared that 12-person juries were the result of historical accident or tradition and that smaller, 6-person juries do not deprive a defendant of his or her constitutional right to a trial by jury. Therefore, the smaller jury is constitutionally permissible. After this ruling, some states chose to use 6 jurors instead of 12. Not only do these juries take less time to select, but they also save money.

Critics of the 6-person jury argue that the smaller juries will result in more convictions because it will be easier to convince 6 people, rather than 12, of a defendant's guilt. Critics also argue that if a jury is to be a microcosm of society and reflect the divergent values in our society, a smaller jury may not allow that. For instance, smaller juries may reduce the opportunity for minority group representation on the jury.

VIDEO
How Juries Are Fooled by Statistics

Opening Statements

The trial process begins with opening statements. The prosecution goes first. In the opening statement, the prosecution does not present evidence but rather simply informs the jury members about the general outline or objectives of the case. This helps jurors know what to expect and helps them understand the trial. The prosecution may talk about the evidence that it plans to introduce and what it seeks to prove from that evidence. When the prosecution is done, the defense can then choose to present an opening statement or it may wait until after the prosecution has presented all of its evidence. This allows the defense to hear the prosecution's case before beginning. If the defense chooses to make an opening statement, it will present a summary of the evidence it plans to present and how it will refute the state's (prosecutor's) case against the defendant.

Presentation of Evidence

After opening statements by both sides are completed, the prosecutor begins the trial and presents evidence against the defendant. The prosecution must prove the defendant's guilt "beyond a reasonable doubt." The prosecution may call witnesses to testify or present physical evidence to show the defendant's guilt. Evidence can be presented through testimony by eyewitnesses who have been "sworn in" and who have promised to describe what they know to the jury. Other witnesses may be those who have any knowledge of the case, including expert witnesses. Other evidence such as records, any property seized during arrest, photographs, reports, physical evidence (fingerprints, DNA, weapons, blood testing), and sworn statements or depositions may also be used as evidence.

After each witness is questioned by the prosecution, the defense can then cross-examine that witness. The defense's goal is to impeach, or discredit, the prosecution's witness. The defense will often try to make the witness confused or angry, and then provide conflicting testimony. When the defense has completed the cross-examination of the witness, the prosecutor may then conduct a *redirect examination* to clarify or correct any points that may have been muddied or still seem unclear. After all of the witnesses and other evidence has been presented, the prosecution rests its case.

The defense then has an opportunity to present its case. The defense can present contrary evidence that will rebut or cast doubt on the evidence presented by the prosecution, an alibi, or even some mitigating factors to explain the defendant's actions. The defense seeks to challenge the credibility or the legality of the state's case. Like the prosecution, the defense can also call witnesses or present evidence. The defense needs not to prove the defendant innocent of the charges but that the state did not prove the defendant's guilt beyond a reasonable doubt.

After the defense has presented its case, it then rests. The prosecution can then present rebuttal evidence, after which the defense may offer a *surrebuttal.*

JOURNAL
Justifying Proof Structure

Throughout the trial, the judge serves as a disinterested party and ensures that both sides are allowed to present their cases fully to the jury. He or she rules on motions by the prosecutor or the defense regarding evidence that is submitted or the kinds of questions that are asked. The judge does not present any evidence or take an active role in the trial. In some states, the judge is allowed to ask questions of witnesses and make comments to the jury about the credibility of the evidence.

Trials are structured to give both sides the opportunity to present their cases.

© AP Photo/Atlanta Journal-Constitution, Kent D. Johnson, Pool

Closing Arguments

After both sides have presented their evidence to the jury and rested their cases, they each have the opportunity to present closing arguments. This enables both sides to summarize their cases and emphasize to the jury the evidence in favor of their side. The prosecution gives its closing argument first, followed by the defense. The defense attorney will attempt to point out to the jury the weaknesses in the prosecution's case and assert that the prosecution has not proved beyond a reasonable doubt that the defendant committed the crime charged. Since the burden of proof is on the prosecution, the prosecutor then has a second opportunity to present its case and gets to make the final argument. The prosecutor usually reviews the evidence to the jury and attempts to convince the jury that the offense was proven beyond a reasonable doubt. No new evidence is admitted during closing arguments, and it is unethical for counsel to indicate a personal belief regarding whether or not the accused is guilty.

Jury Instructions

After closing arguments are finished, the case is "handed over" to the jury. Before that happens, a judge must provide instructions to the jury members. This is the step during which the judge explains the law to the jurors, which is critical since most are unfamiliar with the technicalities of the law. The process of **jury instructions** is also called *charging the jury*. In essence, the judge tells the jury about the specific elements of the offenses with which the defendant is charged or of any lesser offenses that may be relevant. For example, the judge might instruct a jury about the differences between first-degree and second-degree murder. The judge may also discuss the types of evidence that are necessary to prove each element of the offense or lesser offenses and procedural matters such as the voting process. The judge typically instructs the jurors about the burden of proof required to convict a defendant on criminal charges (that is, beyond a reasonable doubt) or even about any criminal defenses used in the trial (for example, insanity).

> **jury instructions:** When the presiding judge explains the law to the jurors and informs them about the specific elements of the offenses with which the defendant is charged or of any lesser offenses that may be relevant.

The instructions given by the judge can affect the outcome of the case. If the judge gives the jurors highly technical instructions that are confusing, they may be less likely to find a defendant guilty. The same can happen if the judge gives the jury a narrow description of an offense. The judicial instructions can often be confusing to the jury, especially in long or complicated cases. Verdicts can be appealed based on the instructions given to the jury, so the judge must take particular care at this stage of the process.

Attorneys on both sides are given an opportunity to submit written requests to the judge for particular instructions they want to be given. Usually the instructions cover the presumption of innocence and the burden of proof, evidentiary problems, a definition of the offense or offenses, and information about any of the defenses used in the trial. The judge may

During jury instruction, judges tell jurors the specific elements of a law that should be considered during deliberations.

© Tim Pannell/Corbis

summarize the evidence for the jury members, help them recall details, or try to reduce complicated evidence, but the judge may not give opinions on any issue of fact in the case or favor either side.

Jury Deliberations

The members of the jury then retire to the jury room to deliberate about the facts of the case and decide the verdict. **Jury deliberations** are done in private, with no outside observers or assistance. The jury members choose a fellow juror to serve as the *foreman*, or the leader of the group, to lead the debate. The jurors must apply the law to the facts as described in the judge's instructions.

During deliberations, jurors can ask to examine any items of evidence that were entered into the trial or even portions of the transcript for clarification. They can even ask the judge for additional instructions or clarification of legal questions if they are unclear as to the law in the case. But they cannot ask to recall a witness or for additional evidence.

After they discuss the evidence, jurors will each vote on the defendant's guilt. In most states, the vote must be unanimous to find a defendant guilty. If the vote is not unanimous, the jurors will continue to deliberate. If they do not reach a verdict by the end of the day, the judge will send them home with instructions not to discuss the case with anyone, read anything about the case in the newspaper, or watch television programming related to the case. If there has been a great deal of media attention or public interest in the case, the jurors are sequestered. This means that they will not have contact with anyone other than the other jurors and the bailiff. The jurors will spend the night in a hotel (at the state's expense) and are kept apart from family, friends, and the general public until they reach a verdict.

Once the jurors agree on a verdict, they (and the other participants in the trial) reenter the courtroom. The foreman will read the verdict to the court. The verdict will be either "guilty" or "not guilty." They may find the defendant guilty of some charges and not guilty of others. If the jury decides the defendant is not guilty, the judge releases the defendant and he or she goes free, unless other charges are pending.

If the jury finds the defendant guilty, it means that the jury members deem, beyond a reasonable doubt, that the defendant committed the offense charged. In that case, he or she will be returned to custody until a sentencing hearing is held. If a judge believes that the jury has not followed the court's instructions, he or she can refuse to accept the guilty verdict. If the judge accepts the verdict, however, the defense counsel can then file motions to set aside the verdict or to ask for a new trial. The defense may claim jury tampering or misconduct, or the availability of new evidence, among other things, as reasons why the defendant should be granted a second trial.

If jurors cannot reach a verdict, then it is called a *hung jury*. In this case, the jury is excused. The prosecutor must then decide whether to bring the defendant to trial again (retry the case) at a later date or dismiss the charges.

After the verdict is announced, either the defense or the prosecution may request to poll the jury. When this happens, the judge will ask each member of the jury if the verdict announced by the foreman was indeed his or her verdict. The purpose for polling the jury is to determine if any of the jury members were pressured by others on the jury.

jury deliberations: The stage in the trial process, after the attorneys present their closing arguments, when the members of the jury privately discuss the facts of the case to decide the verdict.

The answer can be found on page 521.

➡ Sentencing

If a defendant either pleaded guilty or was found guilty by a jury, the next step in the judicial process is **sentencing** by the judge or jury. This is the stage in which the punishment or penalty is formally imposed on the defendant.

The sentencing hearing is one of the most important steps in the judicial process. It is said that deciding on a sentence for a guilty offender is one of a judge's most difficult responsibilities. The judge seeks to impose a sentence that will punish, rehabilitate, incapacitate, and deter offenders, all at once. Sometimes multiple sanctions are imposed. In most states and in the federal system, the sentence is decided solely by the presiding judge. However, in some states, a defendant can choose to be sentenced by a jury.

Because the sentencing phase of the judicial process is so vital to the defendant, the Supreme Court has decided many cases regarding this phase. In *Mempa v. Rhay* (1967), the Court labeled the sentencing hearing as a "critical stage" of the justice system because the defendant is at risk of losing his or her rights and interests. Thus, the Court held that the offender had the right to be represented at sentencing.

Although the judge makes the final decision about the sentence, the prosecutor, the defense, and the probation department have the opportunity to make recommendations. The offender has the right to address the court prior to sentencing. The offender may ask for a lesser sentence or even a pardon. In some states, the victim or the victim's family may speak and give a *Victim Impact Statement* that describes the effect the crime has had on their lives. Each of these actors tries to influence the final sentence of the court.

Another influence on the court's sentencing decision is the **pre-sentence investigation** (PSI). The PSI is completed by a probation officer who interviews the offender's family, friends, and others to discover more about the offender's background (see Figure 10.7). The PSI provides the judge with detailed information on the offender, including family background (childhood and current family situation), employment history, and arrest record; reports describing the current offense (the official or police version, the offender's version, and sometimes the victim's version of the facts); any previous pre-sentence reports (if available); and psychiatric or psychological reports. In some states the PSI can include a sentencing recommendation from the reporting officer.

The judge has many options for sentencing an offender. These include fines, probation (or conditional liberty), confinement in jail or another correctional facility, community service, intermediate sanctions, diversion

JOURNAL
Probation Officers
Sentencing

sentencing: The stage of adjudication, after a defendant either pleaded guilty or was found guilty, whereby punishment is formally imposed.

pre-sentence investigation: Written by a probation officer, this document provides the judge with detailed information about the offender prior to the sentencing phase of a trial.

FIGURE 10.7   Pre-Sentence Investigation Report Process

Probation officer interviews multiple parties.

The officer provides the judge with detailed information about the offender's background

Judge uses the report to decide how to sentence the offender.

programs, or even death. The amount of discretion that judges have to impose sentences differs among states and depends on the kind of sentencing structure the state has imposed.

BEYOND A REASONABLE DOUBT 10.5

Why did the Supreme Court define the sentencing phase of the trial as a "critical stage"?

(a) Because many people are involved in the process, (b) Because the defendant is at risk of losing his or her freedom, (c) Because the Court has made many decisions about the sentencing phase, (d) Because most defendants are not sentenced fairly, (e) None of the above

---

The answer can be found on page 521.

➡ Appeals

appeal: The process by which a second court reviews the conviction or sentencing decision made by a lower court.

After a trial and sentencing have occurred, a defendant has the right to **appeal** his or her case or to ask another court to review the events surrounding the original case. In an appeal, the burden of proof changes from the prosecutor to the defense, which must demonstrate why a conviction should be overturned or a sentence reduced. It may be something as simple as an error, such as the lack of a speedy trial. Or it could relate to the admission of illegally gathered evidence. An appeal is reviewed by an appeals court, which can consider only procedural questions and questions of law—not any facts related to a defendant's guilt or innocence. Usually if there is a harmless error, a defendant is less likely to win his or her appeal. If the defendant pleaded guilty, most grounds on which a defendant could base an appeal are invalid.

An appeal is started by the losing side of a case, which becomes known as the *appellant*. The first official step of an appeal occurs when the appellant files a formal notice of appeal with the trial court that heard the original case. Typically, this is done within a month or two of the verdict. The court then sends a copy of the notice to the *appellee*, the side that won the case. The appellant is responsible for transmitting all of the records of the trial court, including a transcript of the trial, to the appeals court for review.

The appellant's lawyer must submit a legal brief describing the reasons for the appeal. The appellee then responds to the appellant's arguments and typically requests that the lower court decision be upheld. In some cases, the two sides make oral presentations of their opinions in the appellate court. After the presentation of the arguments from each side, the appeals court makes a determination on the case and issues a written opinion. Appellate courts have five options. They can:

- Affirm, or uphold, the lower (trial) court ruling
- Modify the lower court ruling (change a part of the ruling but not reverse it in total)
- Reverse the lower court ruling (set aside the verdict of the trial court, with no further court action necessary)
- Remand the case, or send it back to the lower court, without overturning the original ruling (if this happens, the appellate court will instruct the lower court to conduct a new trial)
- Reverse the lower court decision and remand the case (overturn the lower court ruling and require further action by the lower court, such as a new trial)

If the appellate court overturns the trial court decision, it does not mean that the defendant goes free. Most often, the case is remanded to the lower court. This means that the prosecutor must decide whether to try the case again. If the appellate court does not overturn the trial court decision, the defendant can request that the state supreme court (or a higher appellate court) review the case.

If an offender is sentenced to a term in custody, he or she can petition for a **writ of habeas corpus**. This is a judicial procedure in which an offender's sentence is reviewed to determine whether it is fair and whether the person is being held illegally. If a judge finds the person is being held improperly, the writ may be granted and the person released. A convicted offender may claim that his or her imprisonment is improper because one of his or her constitutional rights was violated during the investigation or

FEATURE VIDEO
Appeals Process

writ of habeas corpus: A judicial procedure in which an offender's sentence is reviewed to determine whether it is fair or whether the person is being held illegally.

trial stage. A writ of habeas corpus is not an appeal. It can be filed only by someone who is imprisoned, and it can address only constitutional issues rather than technical errors.

In recent years, a lot of attention has been given to the large number of prisoners' cases being filed and clogging the federal court system. In particular, the idea that there should be a shorter time between an offender's conviction and execution in death penalty cases became popular. Thus, in 1996, Congress passed the **Anti-Terrorism and Effective Death Penalty Act**, which placed a one-year time limit on any defendant filing a habeas corpus petition. It also placed increased restrictions on a federal court's ability to overturn a state court's criminal conviction. The statute was later tested and upheld by the Supreme Court.

BEYOND A REASONABLE DOUBT 10.6

What happens when an appeal is filed?

(a) The case is then heard by an appellate court, (b) The defense must prove why a decision should be overturned, (c) There may be a concern about either the decision or the sentence, (d) All of the above, (e) None of the above

---

The answer can be found on page 522.

▶ Juvenile Court Process

Juvenile offenders are treated differently from adults in the U.S. court system. The underlying premise for the juvenile court system is to treat the underlying causes of the juvenile's criminal behavior. This way, the juvenile will not commit more crimes and thus be deterred from becoming an adult repeat offender. In most states, a juvenile offender is one who is under the age of 18 when the offense is committed. When a juvenile is brought into the court by law enforcement, he or she is referred to the intake division, where officials review the facts of the case and the possible criminal charges against the juvenile. They will then, in consultation with probation officers, school officials, social service representatives, or other professionals, determine the most appropriate course of action. Most times, if it is reasonable, officials attempt to divert the offender from further contact with the criminal justice system. Thus, in many cases, officials may determine that the best option would be to settle the case informally. The juvenile may be returned to his or her home under the supervision of parents or guardians. If the charges are more serious, the juvenile may be detained. In this case, there must be a *detention hearing*.

The judicial process is also different for juveniles than for adults. Instead of an arraignment, a juvenile will have an **initial appearance**, or initial hearing. Here, the formal charges against the juvenile are presented. The juvenile is informed of his or her legal rights, such as having legal representation appointed. If necessary, conditions for bail may be discussed. Most of the time, this is the last stage of the court process for juveniles, as

Anti-Terrorism and Effective Death Penalty Act: Passed by Congress in 1996, this law set a one-year time limit on any defendant seeking to file a habeas corpus petition and placed restrictions on a federal court's ability to overturn a state court's criminal conviction.

initial appearance (juveniles): A legal proceeding in the juvenile justice system in which a young suspect is asked to appear to hear the formal charges against him or her and to be informed of his or her legal rights.

most admit to the facts and events surrounding the charges. Then the judge must decide on a punishment or treatment.

If a juvenile refutes or disagrees with the facts presented, there is an **adjudication** hearing. This stage is similar to a trial in the adult court, but there is no jury present to hear the evidence, only a judge, who listens to the evidence and makes a decision. The adjudication process was originally intended to be an informal, nonadversarial process. It was intended as an opportunity for the judge to be presented with not only the facts of the crime but also relevant information about the juvenile, including his or her educational status, family and social situation, or any other dynamics that would help the judge fully understand

The juvenile court was established on different principles from the criminal court.

© ZUMA Press, Inc / Alamy

the events and the child. In these hearings, juveniles were not necessarily provided the same rights as adults, since they were not considered to be "on trial." However, in recent years, this has changed. The adjudication process for juveniles is much more technical (and even adversarial) than in the past. Juveniles are now afforded many of the same procedural rights granted to adults.

After hearing the evidence in the adjudication process, the judge enters a judgment. This would be similar to a verdict in the adult court. If the crime is serious, and if there is evidence against the offender, he or she could be declared to be delinquent. Just like in an adult trial, the judge will then hand down a sentence. This is done in a *dispositional hearing* (like a sentencing hearing for adults). The judge has many options, such as placing the juvenile in a residential facility, referring him or her to an outside social agency (for treatment or counseling), or referring the offender to a term of community service. The judge has great leeway when making this decision.

In some cases, a juvenile may commit an extremely violent or serious offense. In this case, he or she may be sentenced to an adult court in a process referred to as a *bind over*. In the case, the juvenile is bound over to an adult court, where he or she will be put on trial and sentenced as an adult. For this to happen, there must be a **waiver**, as the juvenile judge waives his or her jurisdiction over the case.

BEYOND A REASONABLE DOUBT 10.7

What does it mean when a juvenile who has committed a serious offense is bound over?

(a) The juvenile will be sent immediately to an institution, (b) The juvenile will be bound in restrictive clothing and handcuffs when appearing in the courtroom, (c) The juvenile will go through the adult court system, (d) The juvenile will be placed with his or her parents, (e) The police will refer the juvenile to a community corrections facility

The answer can be found on page 522.

adjudication: A proceeding in the juvenile justice system that is similar to a trial in the adult system, but the evidence is presented to a judge rather than a jury.

waiver: The process by which a juvenile offender who commits an extremely violent or serious offense can be tried in an adult court if the juvenile judge waives his or her jurisdiction.

➡ Defendants' Rights

Throughout the entire trial process, all defendants are given certain rights, regardless of the charges against them. **Defendants' rights** are described in the U.S. Constitution and the Bill of Rights. It was important to the founding fathers that those people accused of wrongdoing have due process rights and receive a fair trial. The Fifth and Sixth Amendments, in particular, set out rights guaranteed to those people charged with a criminal offense. These amendments guarantee the defendant the right to counsel, the right to a public trial, the right to a speedy trial, the right to a trial by an impartial jury of his or her peers, the right to confront any prosecution witnesses, and the right against double jeopardy and self-incrimination. (See the "Criminal Justice and College Students" box in this chapter).

Right to Counsel

In the Sixth Amendment, defendants are guaranteed the right to counsel. The Supreme Court has made multiple decisions that ensure that a defendant has legal counsel in a state trial. For instance, in the case of *Powell v. Alabama* (1932), nine Black youths in Scottsboro, Alabama, were arrested and charged with raping two young White women. On the day their trial was to begin, their appointed attorney refused to represent them in court. The judge asked any attorney in the courtroom that day to serve as the defendants' legal counsel, but every one declined. By the time a willing attorney was found, the attorney was given no opportunity to review the facts of the case and only 30 minutes to meet with the defendants before the hearing began. In a very short time, the boys were tried, convicted, and then sentenced to the death penalty. Upon review, the Supreme Court concluded that the need to have a defense attorney is so vital to ensuring a fair trial that when the trial court failed to appoint adequate legal counsel, the defendants were denied due process of law.

Another case in which the Supreme Court expanded the right to counsel was *Gideon v. Wainwright* (1963), in which the justices decided that a person charged with a felony in a state court has the constitutional right to counsel (see the "Criminal Justice Pioneer" box in this chapter). Prior

---

AUTHOR VIDEO
Students and the Judicial Process

---

defendants' rights:
The rights guaranteed to defendants in a criminal case, as defined by the U.S. Constitution and the Supreme Court.

CRIMINAL JUSTICE
and **COLLEGE STUDENTS**

JUDICIAL PROCEEDINGS ON CAMPUS

Every college has a process for handling violations of the college's honor code or general rules for students. Use the Internet to locate information about your college's judicial proceedings. Review the process. How is this process similar to the criminal justice process? How is it different? In a similar way, how are the rights given to students similar to or different from those given to defendants in the criminal justice process? Share your answers with your classmates.

CLARENCE EARL GIDEON

CRIMINAL JUSTICE PIONEER

Clarence Earl Gideon was an unlikely hero. He was a man with an eighth-grade education who ran away from home when he was in middle school. He spent much of his early adult life as a drifter, spending time in and out of prisons for nonviolent crimes.

Gideon was charged with breaking and entering with the intent to commit a misdemeanor, which is a felony under Florida law. At trial, Gideon appeared in court without an attorney. In open court, he asked the judge to appoint counsel for him because he could not afford an attorney. The trial judge denied Gideon's request because Florida law only permitted appointment of counsel for poor defendants charged with capital offenses.

At trial, Gideon represented himself—he made an opening statement to the jury, cross-examined the prosecution's witnesses, presented witnesses in his own defense, declined to testify himself, and made arguments emphasizing his innocence. Despite his efforts, the jury found Gideon guilty and he was sentenced to five years imprisonment.

Gideon sought relief from his conviction by filing a petition for writ of habeas corpus in the Florida Supreme Court. In his petition, Gideon challenged his conviction and sentence on the ground that the trial judge's refusal to appoint counsel violated Gideon's constitutional rights. The Florida Supreme Court denied Gideon's petition.

Gideon next filed a handwritten petition in the Supreme Court of the United States. The Court agreed to hear the case to resolve the question of whether the right to counsel guaranteed under the Sixth Amendment of the Constitution applies to defendants in state court.

State Archives of Florida

Reprinted from United States Courts. (n.d.). Facts and case summary: Gideon v. Wainwright. Retrieved from http://www.uscourts.gov/educational-resources/get-involved/constitution-activities/sixth-amendment/right-counsel/facts-case-summary-gideon.aspx

to this case, some states did not provide legal counsel to indigent defendants in misdemeanor cases. The Supreme Court, however, concluded that the Sixth Amendment right to be represented by counsel when a person is being tried for a crime in a state court to be among the fundamental rights guaranteed by the Fourteenth Amendment. This includes the right of an indigent defendant to have counsel assigned by the court.

Another case that helped define defendants' right to counsel was *Argersinger v. Hamlin* (1972). In the *Argersinger* case, the Supreme Court held that no person can be imprisoned for any offense, misdemeanor or felony, without representation by counsel at trial. The Court decided that all defendants facing a possible jail sentence are entitled to be represented by legal counsel in their trials and that the state must provide a lawyer if the defendant wants one and cannot afford one.

Right to a Public Trial

Under the Sixth Amendment, the accused has the right to a public trial. This guarantee was made by the founding fathers so that legal proceedings would not be carried out in secret, since officials will be more forthright if the public can observe their actions. In addition, in an open trial, witnesses are less likely to lie, since their conduct is under public scrutiny.

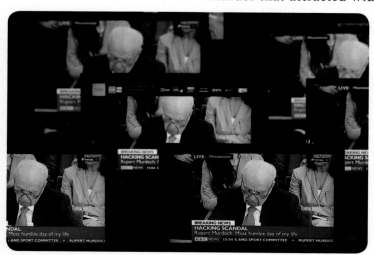

The right to a public trial has been debated for many years. When the public is invited into the courtroom, it can lead to hostility and anger. Witnesses may feel pressured to act in a certain way, jury bias may result, or other behavior may result that produces prejudice either for or against the defendant. The presence of media in the courtroom may disrupt court proceedings or alter the behavior of the judge, prosecutor, defendant, jury members, and others.

At the same time, the First Amendment to the U.S. Constitution guarantees a free press. The courts have been forced to find ways to balance the rights of the media to cover trials against the rights of the state and the accused to proceed through the trial in a fair, orderly, and efficient way.

A Supreme Court case that helped to define the media's role in criminal proceedings was *Estes v. Texas* (1965). Estes was under indictment in Texas for swindling. The case received massive pretrial publicity, even on the national level. Because of the publicity, the judge allowed for a change of venue. Estes filed a motion to prevent telecasting, radio broadcasting, and news photography. The judge allowed the hearing to be carried live on television and radio and with news photography. Furthermore, the jury received a lot of media attention during the two days of the pretrial hearing. Four of the jurors later selected at the trial had seen or heard all or part of the broadcasts. The cameramen in various parts of the courtroom caused considerable disruption with their equipment. Estes was convicted of the offense and sentenced.

Estes appealed the verdict to the U.S. Supreme Court, claiming harm because of pretrial publicity. After hearing the case, the justices reversed the conviction, saying that the bright lights, strands of television cable, and activities of the news groups at the preliminary hearing and, to a lesser degree, at the trial were excessive in relation to the public's interest in the news. Moreover, all of the media had prevented a thorough search for the truth and denied Estes a fair trial.

The Court continued to address the issue of media coverage of trials. In 1976, the Supreme Court reviewed a case concerning a multiple murder that attracted widespread coverage in the media. The trial judge ordered the media to refrain from publishing or broadcasting accounts of any confessions or admissions that were made by the accused to law enforcement officers or others. The press argued that the judge's order violated their constitutional guarantee of freedom of the press. In *Nebraska Press Association v. Stuart* (1976), the Court decided that trial court judges could not issue gag orders that prohibit the press from reporting about criminal cases, as long as the defendant's right to a fair trial and an impartial jury was provided. As a result, members of the press are allowed into most state courtrooms even today.

The Court further defined the role of the media in court proceedings in *Gannett Co. v. DePasquale* (1979). The Supreme Court found

Judicial proceedings often garner extensive media coverage, but some argue that this level of publicity affects the outcome of trials.

© DAVID MOIR/Reuters/Corbis

that denying the public access to a trial did not violate First, Sixth, or Fourteenth Amendment rights. In this case, defendants in a second-degree murder, robbery, and grand larceny case asked that the public and the press be excluded from a pretrial hearing on a motion to suppress an involuntary confession and some physical evidence. They argued that the adverse publicity would jeopardize their chance to receive a fair trial. The Supreme Court held that in cases in which the trial judge had adequately considered the balance of the right of the defendant to a fair trial against the right of the press and public to attend a suppression hearing, the order closing the hearing to the press and public was constitutional.

When the media cover criminal cases, it can lead to a greater understanding of the judicial process for citizens, although sometimes media coverage can be misleading. It also makes justice system officers accountable to the public. However, this right has to be weighed against a defendant's right to a fair trial.

Right to a Speedy Trial

According to the Sixth Amendment, all defendants in criminal prosecutions have the right to a speedy trial. This guarantees that a defendant's trial should not be unduly delayed and that a suspect should not be held in custody indefinitely. Once a person is accused of a crime, that person may lose his or her freedom if incarcerated while awaiting a trial. Further, when criminal charges are brought against an individual, it harms the person's reputation within his or her community. The guarantee to a speedy trial ensures that charges against the accused are decided promptly and brought to closure quickly.

Some evidence indicates that speedy trials can help to deter additional crime in the community. When there are long delays between arrest and trial, there may be more chance of a plea bargain, which may reduce the deterrent effect of punishments. Moreover, many criminals commit more crime when they are free on bail and in the community. Finally, the longer the time between the crime and the trial, the more difficult it is to secure a conviction.

Because the Sixth Amendment does not define what is meant by "speedy trial," Congress set standards in the **Speedy Trial Act of 1974**. As defined in this law, there should be no more than 30 days between arrest and indictment, no more than 10 days between indictment and arraignment, and no more than 60 days between arraignment and trial. In general, the Speedy Trial Act guarantees that a suspect in the federal judicial system will be brought to trial within 100 days. The law was amended in 1979 to encourage states to adopt similar timelines.

Until recently, the "speedy trial" clause in the Constitution applied only to cases in the federal system. The guarantee was made applicable to the states in the case of *Klopfer v. North Carolina* (1967). Professor Klopfer was a professor of zoology at Duke University who was indicted by a grand jury for criminal trespass after a sit-in demonstration at a segregated motel and restaurant. At his first trial, the jury could not agree on a verdict and the judge

Speedy Trial Act of 1974: A law passed by Congress that defines a "speedy trial" so that there should be no more than 30 days between arrest and indictment, no more than 10 days between indictment and arraignment, and no more than 60 days between arraignment and trial.

declared a mistrial. When a year went by with no additional movement by the prosecutor, Klopfer demanded that either a new trial be held or the charges against him be dismissed. At that point, the prosecutor requested that the judge place the case on the inactive trial docket. The judge granted the prosecutor's request and Klopfer appealed. The U.S. Supreme Court struck down the law that allowed a judge to place a case on the inactive docket, stating that the procedure clearly denied the defendant the right to a speedy trial, a fundamental right under the Sixth Amendment.

In another case, *Strunk v. United States* (1973), the Court again faced issues surrounding the definition of a speedy trial. In this case, Strunk was charged with the federal offense of transporting a stolen automobile from Wisconsin to Illinois. At his trial, Strunk did not call any witnesses or take the stand. He was found guilty and sentenced to prison. He filed a motion claiming that he had been denied his right to a speedy trial because there was a 10-month delay before his case was heard. The district court denied the motion. The Supreme Court declared that the charges should be dismissed because of the failure to provide a speedy trial.

The speedy trial concept was defined further by the Supreme Court in the case of *Doggett v. United States* (1992). In 1980, Doggett was indicted on federal drug charges but left the country before U.S. Drug Enforcement Administration (DEA) agents could arrest him. The DEA discovered later that Doggett was imprisoned in Panama, so they requested that he be brought back to the United States, but they never followed up on his status. DEA agents soon discovered that Doggett had left Panama for Colombia but made no additional attempts to find him. They were not aware that Doggett had reentered the United States in 1982 and married, earned a college degree, found employment, and was living a lawful life openly under his own name. The U.S. Marshals Service eventually located him in 1988, eight and a half years after his indictment. Doggett moved to dismiss the indictment on the grounds that the government's failure to prosecute him earlier violated his Sixth Amendment right to a speedy trial.

The Court found that a delay of eight and a half years between indictment and arrest is prejudicial to a defendant and therefore required that the charges be dismissed. They explained that an eight-year delay between indictment and trial could show denial of speedy trial even though there was no proof of actual prejudice. In cases with extraordinary delays, the Court wrote, the longer the delay, the less evidence of prejudice is needed.

The right to a speedy trial may be denied in today's courts because of the problem with court backlogs. So many cases are waiting to be heard in the courts that there is often a lengthy wait between arrest and trial. Among the many reasons for the problem are the large number of people now suing someone in civil court, the fact that civil lawsuits can be brought by anyone at any time for any reason, and even the expansion in border policing. Federal and state courts are buckling under the strain of the resulting caseloads. Among the many options created to help reduce

VIDEO
11 Years in Guantanamo

backlogs are mediation, dispute resolution, drug courts, diversion to a civil court, and pretrial diversion.

Right to a Jury Trial and an Impartial Jury

Under the Sixth Amendment, defendants have the right to a jury trial and an impartial jury. This means that the jurors at the trial must not be prejudiced in any way before the trial begins or during the trial process. Jurors cannot be friends or relatives of the victim, the defendant, or any courtroom personnel. They also cannot be biased against a particular religion or race.

Witnesses play a key role in the trial.

© AP Photo/Atlanta Journal-Constitution, Kent D. Johnson, Pool

Every state has created rules to make jury trials available to all defendants, regardless of their crimes. Some states allow for jury trials in all criminal cases except minor ones such as for petty theft or traffic offenses. In most states, defendants can opt between a jury trial or a bench trial. In *Duncan v. Louisiana* (1968), the Supreme Court ruled that the right to a jury trial extended to cases heard in state courts and federal courts, and that this right must be provided to all suspects who have been accused of a serious crime (a felony). In *Baldwin v. New York* (1970), the Court decided that if a suspect is facing a possible sentence of more than a short period (more than six months), the accused has a constitutional right to a jury trial, and one must be offered. When the sentence is shorter than six months, there is no right to a jury trial, though some states may still authorize them for these less serious cases.

Right to Confront Witnesses

The Sixth Amendment provides the accused with the right to be confronted with witnesses against him or her. The intent is to restrict the admissibility of hearsay evidence against a defendant. This requires that witnesses must testify in open court while facing the accused. It is more difficult to tell lies about people to their faces than behind their backs. The theory is that witnesses are less likely to lie or give false testimony if they must face the accused during testimony. Additionally, it provides the opportunity for the defense to cross-examine witnesses, determine their biases, and attempt to determine their validity.

The U.S. Supreme Court addressed this issue in *Coy v. Iowa* (1988). In this case, two young females were cross-examined behind a screen, with the defendant on the other side of the screen. This Supreme Court ruled that the screen blocked the sight of the witness and therefore violated the defendant's right to confront witnesses. The Court overturned the defendant's conviction, stating that the screen violated his Sixth Amendment right to confront witnesses face-to-face who were providing evidence against him. In making this decision, the Court also limited the protection available to child victims of sexual crimes at the trial stage. Two years later, in *Maryland v. Craig* (1990), the Supreme Court decided that child abuse victims could testify using closed-circuit television if a determination was made that face-to-face confrontation with the accused would traumatize the child.

Double Jeopardy

The Fifth Amendment says that a defendant cannot be put on trial twice for the same offense (**double jeopardy**). The Supreme Court has guaranteed that an accused will not face multiple prosecutions for the same offense or multiple punishments for the same crime. If a defendant was tried once for a crime, he or she cannot be charged with the same crime again. If a jury finds the accused not guilty, the prosecution cannot appeal to have the decision reversed. In short, there cannot be multiple trials for the same offense. However, a defendant can be the target of a civil suit after a criminal trial. A defendant can also be acquitted of violating a state criminal law and then be tried for violating federal law. Both trials can relate to the same act.

The Supreme Court decided what was meant by double jeopardy in *Bartkus v. Illinois* (1959). Bartkus was tried and acquitted in a federal district court for robbing a federally insured bank. On almost the same evidence, he was then tried and convicted in an Illinois state court for violation of a state robbery statute. The Supreme Court held that the cooperation of federal law enforcement officers and the Illinois officials did not violate the double jeopardy clause. Further, the state prosecution after a prior acquittal for a federal offense, on substantially the same evidence, did not violate the due process clause of the Fourteenth Amendment.

Pleading the Fifth

The Fifth Amendment states that no person "shall be compelled in any criminal case to be a witness against himself." This means that a defendant has the right not to testify at a trial if his or her testimony would reveal participation in illegal behavior. This right against self-incrimination is known as "pleading the fifth." It is well accepted that an individual's decision to plead the fifth cannot be used against him or her.

In concluding the discussion about judicial process, it is important to reiterate that the process is guided by legal precedents and constitutional protections. Table 10.1 summarizes the significant cases that have helped to characterize this process.

double jeopardy: According to the Fifth Amendment to the U.S. Constitution, a defendant cannot be put on trial twice for the same offense.

BEYOND A REASONABLE DOUBT 10.8

Where are defendants' rights in the courtroom, such as the right to counsel or the right to a speedy trial, described?

(a) The U.S. Constitution, (b) The Bill of Rights, (c) The Judiciary Act, (d) Both a and b, (e) All of the above

The answer can be found on page 522.

TABLE 10.1	Significant Court Cases Related to the Judicial Process
CASE	**FINDING**
Powell v. Alabama (1932)	Defendants have right to counsel in death penalty cases.
McNabb v. United States (1943)	If there is an unreasonable delay in the period between arrest and initial court appearance, then a confession obtained during that delay would be inadmissible.
Stack v. Boyle (1951)	Bail must be set at an amount no greater than would ensure that the defendant would show up for future court proceedings.
Gideon v. Wainwright (1963)	Those charged with a felony in a state court have the constitutional right to counsel.
Estes v. Texas (1965)	Court found that the media had prevented a thorough search for the truth and denied Estes a fair trial.
Klopfer v. North Carolina (1967)	Struck down law allowing judges to place cases on inactive dockets.
Mempa v. Rhay (1967)	Defendants have the right to be represented at sentencing.
Duncan v. Louisiana (1968)	Right to jury trial applies in state and federal court cases involving felonies.
Williams v. Florida (1968)	Juries do not have to include 12 jurors.
Baldwin v. New York (1970)	Defendant has right to jury trial if facing six or more months incarceration.
Argersinger v. Hamlin (1972)	No person can be imprisoned for any offense, misdemeanor or felony, without representation by counsel at trial.
Strunk v. United States (1973)	Delay of 10 months until trial violates right to speedy trial.
Nebraska Press Association v. Stuart (1976)	Judges could not issue gag orders that prohibit the press from reporting about a criminal case, as long as the defendant's right to a fair trial and an impartial jury was provided.
Gannett Co. v. DePasquale (1979)	Denying the public access to a trial did not violate First, Sixth, or Fourteenth Amendment rights.
United States v. Salerno (1987)	Bail Reform Act defined as a way to prevent further danger or harm to the community and not as a way to punish dangerous individuals.
Maryland v. Craig (1990)	Child abuse victims could testify using closed-circuit television if a determination was made that face-to-face confrontation with the accuser would traumatize the child.
County of Riverside v. McLaughlin (1991)	Arraignments that were held within 48 hours of arrest, excluding weekends and holidays, satisfied the Speedy Trial standard.
Doggett v. United States (1992)	Delay of eight and a half years between indictment and arrest is prejudicial.

Just the Facts: Chapter Summary

- An arrest is the first formal contact between the state and the accused. It is the only way defendants are brought into the court system.

- A prosecutor determines what charges to bring against a defendant based on the evidence collected by the police. The prosecutor also decides whether a defendant should be given the chance to make bail.

- In the initial appearance, the judge informs the defendant of the charges brought against him or her. This must happen in a "timely manner."

- A grand jury is a group of people who hear evidence against a defendant to determine if there is probable cause that a crime has been committed and the accused should be held for trial.

- In some states, a preliminary hearing is used to determine if there is evidence that a crime was committed and that the accused committed the crime; a judge presides over this type of hearing.

- Bail enables a defendant to be released in the period before a trial is held. If a defendant does not appear on the scheduled trial date, he or she can lose the bail money bond. Other options for pretrial release include conditional release, judicial release, or release on one's own recognizance.

- Preventive detention is a way to hold dangerous offenders in custody prior to trial.

- In the arraignment stage, a defendant is brought before a judge to respond to the charges brought against him or her. The defendant can plead guilty, not guilty, or nolo contendere (no contest).

- Pretrial motions are hearings that occur prior to the trial stage, such as a motion for discovery, a motion to change the venue of the case, or a motion for dismissal.

- In the plea-bargaining process, the defense and the prosecution negotiate for a reduced sentence in return for a guilty plea from the defendant.

- A trial is an adversarial process in which the prosecution and the defense vie against each other.

- A jury is a group of community members selected to determine the defendant's guilt or innocence.

- The prosecution must prove a defendant's guilty beyond a reasonable doubt in order to achieve a guilty verdict.

- A guilty verdict can be appealed if there is a procedural question or a question of law.

- An appellate court can affirm the lower court ruling, modify the lower court ruling, reverse the lower court ruling, remand the case to the lower court, or reverse the lower court decision and remand the case for further action.

- Every defendant has rights to counsel, to a public trial, to a speedy trial, to a jury trial (with an impartial jury), to confront witnesses, to avoid double jeopardy, and to avoid self-incrimination (by pleading the Fifth).

Critical Thinking Questions

1. What factors do prosecutors use when determining the charges to bring against a suspect? Is such discretion a positive thing? How much discretion should a prosecutor have in this regard?

2. What steps are involved in the pretrial process? Are these steps necessary for a fair trial?

3. Should states eliminate or revise the grand jury system? If so, how should this be done?

4. The bail process has been criticized for favoring wealthy offenders. What are some ways the bail system could be changed to address this criticism?

5. Should we allow people to be detained before trial (that is, before they are found guilty of their offenses)?

6. What is the purpose of plea bargaining? Is it a good or bad thing? Explain.

7. Explain the trial process. What roles do the prosecution, defense, judge, and jurors play in this process?

8. What is the purpose of closing arguments in a trial?

9. What is the appellate process for those who seek to have their trial outcomes reviewed by another court?

10. The rights of defendants have expanded in recent years. What are these rights, and why are they important?

Key Terms

adjudication (331)

Anti-Terrorism and
    Effective Death
    Penalty Act (330)

appeal (328)

bail (314)

charging (309)

defendants' rights (332)

double jeopardy (338)

grand jury (311)

initial appearance
    (juveniles) (330)

judicial process (308)

jury deliberations (326)

jury instructions (325)

jury selection (321)

plea bargaining (319)

preliminary hearing (313)

pre-sentence
    investigation (327)

pretrial motions (319)

preventive detention (317)

sentencing (327)

Speedy Trial Act of
    1974 (335)

waiver (331)

writ of habeas
    corpus (329)

$SAGE edgeselect™

edge.sagepub.com/payne

Sharpen your skills with SAGE edge select!

With carefully crafted tools and resources to encourage review, practice, and critical thinking, SAGE edge select gives you the edge needed to master course content. Take full advantage of open-access key term flashcards, practice quizzes, and video content. Diagnostic pre-tests, a personalized study plan, and post-tests are available with an access code.

(c) legal issues related to the courts, and (d) court innovations. Within each of these general areas, several specific issues arise as well. A full understanding of these issues is helpful in identifying the importance of the courts, court officials, and court processes in the broader criminal justice system.

► Issues Stemming From Overcrowding

A serious problem facing the U.S. criminal justice system is **court overcrowding**, in which an overwhelming number of unresolved cases are on the court's docket. In other words, the number of cases on the court's calendar exceeds the capacity of the court to hear them. When a court's caseload is so full that cases cannot be heard in a timely manner, a backlog of cases results. Of course, attorneys need a suitable period of time after a client's arrest in which to prepare adequately for trial, but sometimes that time period is too long. Some **court backlogs** contain thousands of cases, which can delay trials by three years or longer.

There are many adverse consequences for defendants when cases are not heard in a reasonable time (see Figure 11.1). Backlogs may deny defendants their constitutional rights to a speedy trial. They are unable to continue with their daily lives while they wait for their trial to take place. Some defendants may be held in jail or another holding facility until the trial, preventing them from maintaining a job or family relationships. Even defendants who are not being held before trial may need to return to court frequently for hearings or to meet with officials. Many defendants suffer economic hardships from a delayed trial because they cannot hold employment and are denied an income during this time.

court overcrowding: A situation in which there are too many cases for the courts to hear.

court backlogs: The sometimes-long delay between arrest and a trial for some defendants.

| FIGURE 11.1 | **Consequences of Court Overcrowding** |

Violates constitutional rights

Punishes individuals before incarceration

Accrues economic costs

Affects credibility of criminal justice system

© iStockphoto.com/Rich Legg

Long delays in the court process can negatively affect the credibility of the justice system. When cases are not heard quickly, confidence in the judicial system declines among the general public. It appears to outsiders that criminals are not being held accountable for their offenses. Crime victims are especially affected. Many feel mistreated and have the impression that justice is not being served.

Long delays between the time of the offense and the trial can also have an impact on the trial itself. As time goes on, witnesses move away or die, and evidence may disappear. In some cases, the lack of evidence allows guilty defendants to go free.

A great deal of waiting occurs in the courts.

© AP Photo/Akron Beacon Journal, Karen Schiely

Sources of Overcrowding

There are many reasons for court overcrowding (see Figure 11.2). One is the increased demands on the court for more preliminary hearings, trials, and sentencing hearings. There must be an adequate number of court personnel to manage the increased number of cases. Unfortunately, in many cases, the manpower and other court resources needed to process these new cases are lacking. Many jurisdictions report an insufficient number of judges to preside over cases. Others report a need for additional defense attorneys, because many more defendants cannot afford attorneys. Some jurisdictions report a lack of prosecutors to bring cases to trial. Most courts also lack the funding needed to hire more personnel. A similar problem is a lack of physical courtroom space, forcing a delay in trials and hearings. Without adequate personnel and courtroom space, trials cannot take place.

In some places, court backlogs result from delays stemming from the crime labs used to test evidence. The number of requests from law enforcement and court personnel for evidence to be analyzed is growing because of an increased reliance on forensic evidence to solve and prosecute crimes. Crime labs cannot keep up with the increased demand for evidence testing, yet trials cannot move forward without the results of the testing.

Solutions to Overcrowding

Long delays appear to have become an accepted part of the legal system. Most people expect that there will be some lag between the offense and the trial, and it has become part of the court culture. However, because long backlogs can have such damaging effects, many recommendations have been made to address the problem. One obvious solution is to hire more court personnel. If there

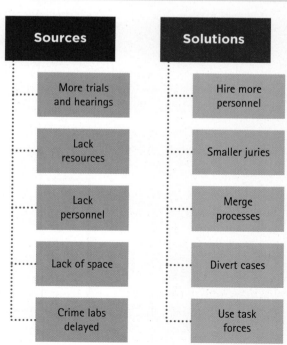

FIGURE 11.2 **Sources of Overcrowding and Solutions**

Sources	Solutions
More trials and hearings	Hire more personnel
Lack resources	Smaller juries
Lack personnel	Merge processes
Lack of space	Divert cases
Crime labs delayed	Use task forces

are more judges, prosecutors, defense attorneys, and even support personnel (clerks, bailiffs), cases could be processed through the system more quickly. Additional scientists and crime lab analysts should also be hired to speed up analysis of forensic material. However, the lack of funds available to courts may make these solutions prohibitive.

Some observers have argued that changes in the jury system would help. If a smaller jury was required, jury selection would not take so long. It has also been suggested that modifications be made in the method by which jurors are chosen. Limiting the pretrial questioning of prospective jurors by attorneys would also speed up the process.

Another suggestion is that preliminary hearings be merged with arraignments, or even eliminated. With fewer pretrial stages in the process, the trial would occur sooner after the alleged crime and the process would move more quickly.

Some states have chosen to move cases out of the courts and put them into mediation, leaving the courtrooms for serious criminal cases. In mediation, the parties involved attempt to work out their differences with a trained mediator instead of in a hearing in front of a judge. Mediation is often very successful in divorce or juvenile cases.

In some places, task forces made up of experienced attorneys have been developed to assist in districts where the courts are overloaded. These attorneys will help prosecutors or defense attorneys prepare for hearings (or even appear at hearings) for a short period of time as a way to help get some cases off the docket. In some jurisdictions, judges have stepped in temporarily to hear cases. For example, overcrowded courts in Brooklyn, New York, used state supreme court justices to hear bench trials as a way to reduce backlogs.[2] In other jurisdictions, volunteer lawyers have stepped up to assist defendants. This is sometimes called "pro bono" work, or volunteer hours.

Another suggestion to reduce court backlogs is to reduce the number of cases being heard in the courts. One way this can happen is by removing selected cases from the courts. Many states have created specialty courts, such as drug courts and mental health courts, that hear certain cases (see "Issues Related to Innovations in the Courts," later in this chapter). These courts help to streamline the process for those defendants whose cases are heard there, and they also free up time in the general or criminal courts.

BEYOND A REASONABLE DOUBT 11.1

Which of the following is a consequence of court overcrowding and backlogs?

(a) Denial of defendants' right to a speedy trial, (b) Defendants having difficulty continuing with their lives while they wait for trial, (c) Defendants having difficulty maintaining family ties if held in jail, (d) Defendants needing to return to court for multiple pretrial hearings, (e) All of the above

The answer can be found on page 522.

➡ Issues Related to Court Processes

Overcrowding is perhaps the most far-reaching issue affecting the courts. Related to the overcrowding problem are specific processes in the courts that affect case outcomes. Three aspects of court processing warrant discussion here: plea bargaining, sentencing models, and judicial appointment strategies.

Plea Bargaining

One solution to court overcrowding is plea bargaining, in which a defendant pleads guilty in return for reduced charges or punishment (see Chapter 10). Since there is not enough time, space, or personnel to hold a trial for every person who is arrested or charged with a crime, plea bargaining is a way to ensure that an offender will be punished without the process of a trial. With a plea bargain, the police and prosecution save time because there is no need to collect, organize, and present evidence to a jury. If an assistant prosecutor is used in the plea-bargaining process, it frees up time on the part of the lead prosecutor to focus on more serious cases.[3] The judge does not need to preside over a trial, and the defense does not need to organize and present a case on the offender's behalf. Since there is no need for a trial, the courtroom and its personnel are available for other cases. Figure 11.3 shows that in 2010, 89% of cases involved a plea bargain, as opposed to 2% of cases in which defendants were convicted through a trial process.

Although plea bargaining has become an accepted part of the criminal justice system, not everyone agrees with its use (see Figure 11.4). Debate continues over the extent to which plea bargaining should be used and the proper role it should play in criminal trials. Proponents of plea bargaining argue that

VIDEO
The Plea

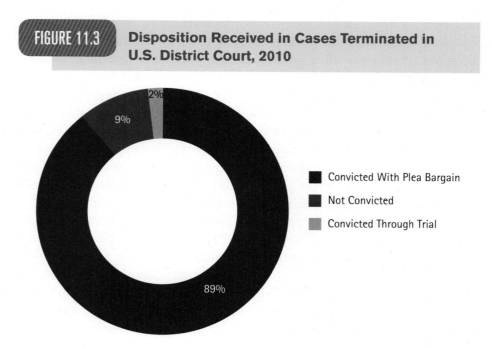

FIGURE 11.3 **Disposition Received in Cases Terminated in U.S. District Court, 2010**

- Convicted With Plea Bargain
- Not Convicted
- Convicted Through Trial

2%
9%
89%

Bureau of Justice Statistics

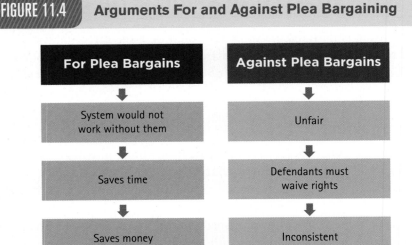

FIGURE 11.4   **Arguments For and Against Plea Bargaining**

For Plea Bargains	Against Plea Bargains
System would not work without them	Unfair
Saves time	Defendants must waive rights
Saves money	Inconsistent

it is an essential part of our judicial system to such an extent that it has even become functional for the court system. They argue that the criminal justice system could not possibly provide the number of trials needed if every criminal defendant were to demand one. If every person accused of a crime wanted a full trial, the court system would collapse. Proponents of plea bargaining also point out that the state actually benefits from plea bargaining. They point out that each guilty plea saves hundreds and sometimes thousands of dollars that would be spent on a trial. Plea bargains also save time for court personnel, police, and citizens who would be required to appear in court as witnesses and jurors. Plea bargaining also helps the state "win" weak cases.

There are also strong opponents of plea bargaining, some of whom go so far as to argue for the abolition of the practice. Some opponents argue that plea bargaining is not fair to society or to defendants. By pleading guilty, most defendants waive their rights not only to a jury trial but also to appeal questions of evidence admissibility. Some critics argue that plea bargaining is not fair to society because it allows guilty offenders to return to the community without sufficient punishment. Additionally, negotiated pleas may soften the potential deterrent effect of the law. The idea that justice is open to negotiation is repugnant to critics of plea bargaining. Moreover, the process lacks consistency. Criminal courts vary from one jurisdiction to the next in the frequency of plea bargaining; the role of the prosecutor, the defense, and the judge in the process; the time at which plea negotiations occur; and whether the bargaining focuses on the charge or the sentence.

The Supreme Court has made some key decisions concerning plea bargaining. In *Santobello v. New York* (1971), the Court mandated that the prosecution must follow through with its end of the plea bargain with a defendant when it comes to the sentence recommendation. In that case, the defendant, Santobello, agreed to withdraw his not-guilty plea to two felony counts after negotiating with a prosecutor. After the prosecutor agreed not to make a recommendation about a possible sentence, the defendant entered a guilty plea to a lesser, included offense. When it came time for the sentencing hearing, a different prosecutor pointed out the defendant's criminal record and recommended a maximum sentence to the judge, which was imposed. The defense counsel objected on the basis that the prosecution violated the plea agreement. Santobello tried at that point to withdraw his guilty plea, but the judge refused to allow that and sentenced him to the maximum term in prison, citing Santobello's prior criminal record as the reason for the extended prison term. Santobello appealed to the Supreme Court, asking for a clarification about the plea-bargaining process. The Court agreed to review the case and ruled that prosecutors must make their plea-bargained sentence recommendations known in court. However, the judge is not obligated to award the recommended sentence.

Part of the plea bargain process includes offenders being required to sign that they agree to the terms of the plea deal.

© JOHN KUNTZ/The Plain Dealer /Landov

The Supreme Court revisited the plea-bargaining process in *Brady v. United States* (1970). In that case, the Court upheld the defendant's right to counsel during the plea-bargaining process. Brady was charged with kidnapping and faced a penalty of death. Brady first entered a not-guilty plea but then waived a jury trial, which would have reduced the possibility of a death sentence if he were convicted. The judge did not want to try the case without a jury. Brady then changed his plea to guilty after the codefendant in the case confessed and agreed to testify against him. The judge accepted Brady's plea after ensuring that the plea was voluntary. Later, Brady claimed his not-guilty plea was *not* voluntary. In its decision, the Supreme Court stressed the need for defense counsel during the pleading process. The Court sought to prevent coercion in cases involving guilty pleas and altered the standards regarding voluntary statements.

There have been calls for reforming the plea-bargaining process so that defendants' due process rights and constitutional protections are not violated during the process. One suggestion has been that legislatures should reduce the maximum punishments allowed for offenses. This would limit the ability of prosecutors to adjust the charges. The prosecution would not be able to overcharge defendants and then use plea bargaining to reduce the punishment of almost all of the defendants who are charged with a crime. Another suggestion focuses on increasing the quality of public defenders to ensure that the quality of defense is higher and there is less reliance on plea bargaining. Many people support making the plea-bargaining process more transparent, with many of the negotiations conducted openly and in the presence of all participants. In this way, the defendant will not feel as if a deal is being made without his or her consent or knowledge.

In 1975, the state of Alaska eliminated plea bargaining. After the new law was in effect for five years, a study was conducted to determine what effect the law had on the system and the defendants.[4] The ban on plea bargaining increased the severity of sentences in minor cases that would have been dealt with informally before the ban, but it appeared to have no significant effect on the outcome of serious cases.

Sentencing Models

FEATURE VIDEO
Goal of Sentencing

The way in which judges sentence convicted offenders has been an issue of debate for many years. Television shows provide a glimpse into how judges sentence wrongdoers, but the depiction is often more for entertainment value (see the "Criminal Justice and the Media" box in this chapter). Some people believe that judges need to have wide discretion in the sentencing process so that they can tailor sentences to individual offenders. However, this practice led to abuse by some judges who sentenced offenders based on considerations other than the facts of the case. Reforms in sentencing policies have been geared toward decreasing the discretion of judges. Despite these reforms, inequities in sentencing remain. Sentencing options are described in the sections that follow (see Figure 11.5).

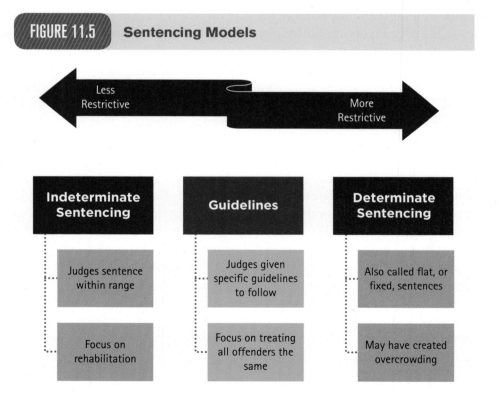

FIGURE 11.5   Sentencing Models

Less Restrictive ←→ More Restrictive

Indeterminate Sentencing	Guidelines	Determinate Sentencing
Judges sentence within range	Judges given specific guidelines to follow	Also called flat, or fixed, sentences
Focus on rehabilitation	Focus on treating all offenders the same	May have created overcrowding

CRIMINAL JUSTICE and the **MEDIA:**

JUDGES ON TELEVISION

The number of television shows featuring judges "in action" has grown substantially over the past two decades. One of the earliest court shows was *People's Court*. First airing in 1981, *People's Court* typically featured disputes between acquaintances, and Judge Joseph Wapner would hear arguments from both sides before making a decision, all within a 15-minute segment. In later episodes, Harvey Levin, who went on to found the website TMZ.com, provided legal insight and interviews from members of the public watching the case unfold.

The success of *People's Court* resulted in many similar shows and celebrity judges, including *Judge Wapner's Animal Court*, *Judge Hatchett*, *Divorce Court*, *Moral Court*, *Judge Joe Brown*, and *Judge Judy*, to name a few. *Judge Judy* has been highlighted as the "richest" celebrity judge, reportedly remaking nearly $50 million a year.

The behavior of these judges is not the same as what you would find in a criminal court. In fact, in many cases, if prosecutors, defense attorneys, defendants, or witnesses were treated in court the way these celebrity judges treat participants, accusations of misconduct would likely follow. Kimball (2005) uses the term *syndic-court judge* to describe these judges and explains, "Because the behavior of a syndic-court judge has Nielsen ratings as a standard, they are allowed to engage in acts that would generally not be appropriate

Judges in the criminal justice system rarely behave the way that judges behave on syndicated court television shows.

© DAMIAN DOVARGANES/AP/Corbis

in court. The more 'straight-talking' that a judge appears, which often means being as mean as possible to unlikable litigants, the better ratings he or she receives" (p. 150).

You are encouraged to watch an episode of a court show and then attend a criminal trial to watch a judge in action. Doing so will demonstrate how "syndic-court judges" have a knack for theater.

Kimball, P. Z. (2005). *Syndi-court justice: Judge Judy and exploitation of arbitration*. American Bar Association. Retrieved from http://www .americanbar.org/content/dam/aba/migrated/dispute/essay/syndicourtjustice .authcheckdam.pdf

Indeterminate Sentencing

In the 1970s, most states had an **indeterminate sentencing** system whereby a possible sentence for an offense was given as a range of time (minimum to maximum). The actual sentence depended on the seriousness of the crime. Under this system, a judge could impose a sentence that was not less than the established minimum and not more than the established maximum. For example, an offender would be sentenced to two to five years in prison after conviction of a crime. After serving a certain time in prison, the inmate would appear in front of a parole board or other authority, which would determine whether to grant the inmate's release. The offender's behavior while in prison would determine the exact release date. This system was based on the assumption that inmates should be held in prison until they are "cured" or "rehabilitated."

indeterminate sentencing: A system of sentencing that gives a range of time; the actual sentence depends on the seriousness of the crime.

Over time, problems developed with indeterminate sentences. There were abuses by the parole boards in determining release dates, and there was great disparity in the sentences offenders served for similar offenses. It soon became apparent that minorities, the poor, and other disadvantaged groups typically received harsher punishments for similar offenses. As a result, states began to use other methods to assist judges in sentencing offenders. One of those was sentencing guidelines.

Sentencing Guidelines

Under **sentencing guidelines**, judges are provided with specific sentences that must be imposed on offenders. These are based on the seriousness of the offense and characteristics of the offender (such as prior record). It was hoped that guidelines removed discretion from judges and the parole authority, making sentencing of offenders more fair and equal. That meant that offenders would be treated the same, regardless of their economic standing, race, or other characteristics.

Minnesota was the first state to create sentencing guidelines, and the federal government adopted them in November 1987. Since then, many states have opted to create guidelines. While individual state sentencing guidelines systems differ in their design and operation, most states have developed a grid to help judges determine the proper sentence. On these grids, one axis ranks the type of offense, while the other refers to the offender's criminal history. The intersection of these characteristics provides a judge with the sentence that should be imposed.

There are many different approaches to guidelines, but two primary forms of sentencing guidelines have developed: presumptive and voluntary. *Presumptive guidelines* establish appropriate sentences for certain crimes. It is understood that judges should impose the suggested sentences, and when they choose to "depart" from the guidelines, they must provide an explanation. These departures are then subject to appellate review. *Voluntary guidelines* are simply suggestions that the judge may accept if he or she wishes to do so.

It has been argued that, although guidelines succeed in limiting judges' discretion in the sentencing process, they have created punishments that are often too harsh. In those cases, judges are dissuaded from departing from the guidelines and using a lesser sentence. Instead, the discretion to alter a sentence to an individual offender is shifted from the judge to the prosecutor, who may choose to file particular criminal charges against an offender based on the possible punishment rather than the facts of the case. Furthermore, it is said that sentences imposed under guidelines are based on a defendant's prior record and behavior rather than the conviction charge in the case at hand.

sentencing guidelines: A theory of sentencing according to which judges are provided with specific sentences that must be imposed, based on the seriousness of the offense and characteristics of the offender.

At the sentencing hearing, defendants learn what sanctions they will receive.

Most research on sentencing guidelines seems to show that different methods have little or no effects on judicial sentencing patterns of offenders. At the same time, the guidelines were shown to reduce sentence disparities and to diminish gender and racial bias and discrimination in sentencing.

Determinate Sentencing

Determinate sentencing, often called "fixed" sentencing, has also become a popular method for sentencing offenders in recent years. In this type of sentencing scheme, a fixed, or definite, time for a sentence is imposed on a convicted offender. This means that both the offender and correctional personnel are aware of the exact length and nature of an offender's punishment. There are three types of determinate sentences: flat-time sentences, presumptive sentences, and mandatory sentences.

In *flat-time sentencing*, the judge has only a small amount of discretion in determining the length of an offender's sentence. There is no possibility for a judge to either reduce or increase an offender's sentence once an offender is incarcerated.

Presumptive sentencing allows a judge to impose a typical sentence for a crime but provides the judge the opportunity to vary the sentence to accommodate any aggravating or mitigating circumstances involved. In states that use these sentencing structures, the legislature "presumes" the sentence, and then any judge must explain why he or she does not impose the presumed term.

Mandatory sentencing provides the judge with a required term of incarceration for a certain crime. Offenders must be sentenced to a specified amount of prison time for an offense, with no option of probation, suspended sentence, or immediate parole eligibility. However, inmates often still get credit for good behavior while in prison under mandatory sentencing, which can reduce a mandatory sentence by up to one-third or more of the sentence imposed.

Another type of mandatory sentence is dictated by **three-strikes laws**, sometimes called habitual offender laws. These arrangements require that any offender convicted of a third felony must be sentenced to a lengthy term in prison. The crime does not have to be violent or dangerous. It must simply be categorized as a felony offense.

Generally, the public supports the idea of "three strikes." One national poll found that more than 8 out of 10 Americans supported life sentences for felons convicted three times.[5] That being said, these laws may not have the expected effect that politicians sought. Under three strikes, many more inmates are being sentenced to prison for long times. Some prisons are quickly becoming overcrowded. When this happens, officials must find ways to free up space. Because these felons cannot be released early (even though most are nonviolent drug offenders), prison administrators must release other violent offenders early. More information on three strikes is presented in Figure 11.6.

Truth in Sentencing

Offenders usually do not serve the entire sentence that is imposed by a judge after conviction. There is usually a discrepancy between the sentence imposed by the court and the time actually served by the offender. This is

> **JOURNAL**
> Indeterminate and Determinate Sentencing

determinate sentencing: Also called "fixed" sentencing, a method for sentencing convicted offenders in which a fixed, or definite, sentence is imposed.

three-strikes laws: Also called habitual offender laws, these laws require that any offender convicted of a third felony must be sentenced to a lengthy term in prison.

FIGURE 11.6   Arguments For and Against Three Strikes

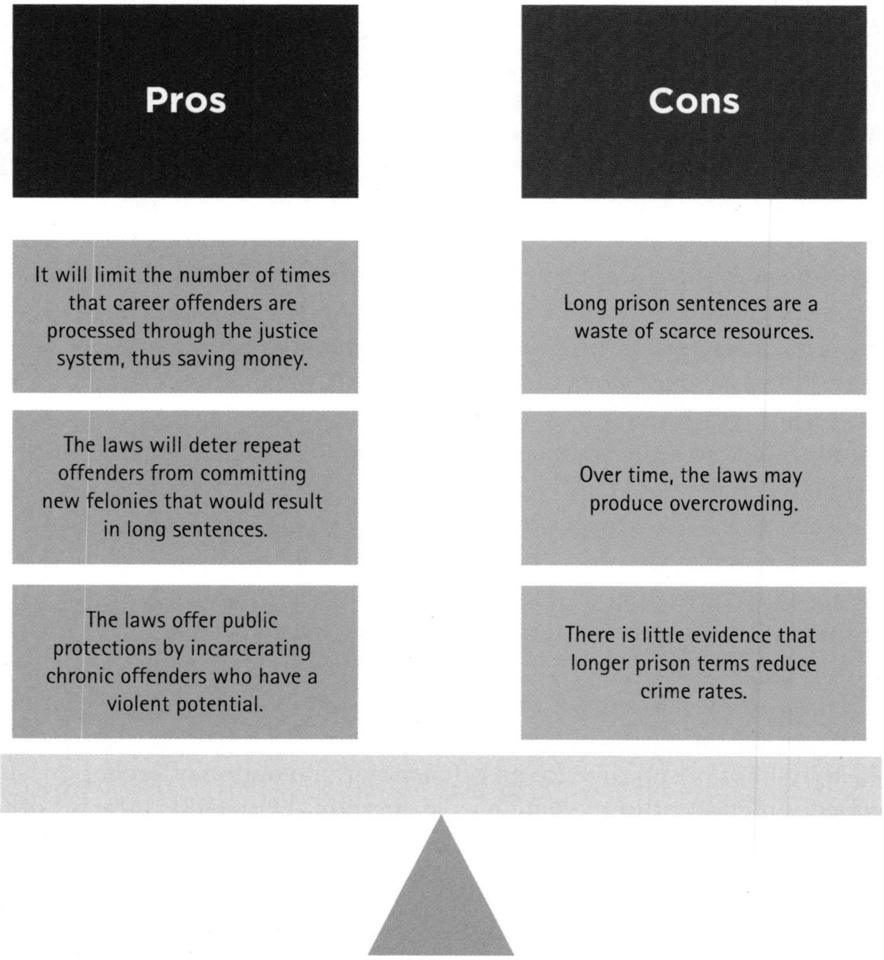

Pros	Cons
It will limit the number of times that career offenders are processed through the justice system, thus saving money.	Long prison sentences are a waste of scarce resources.
The laws will deter repeat offenders from committing new felonies that would result in long sentences.	Over time, the laws may produce overcrowding.
The laws offer public protections by incarcerating chronic offenders who have a violent potential.	There is little evidence that longer prison terms reduce crime rates.

because an offender may receive time off because of good behavior or have multiple sentences that run concurrently. As a result, it may appear that offenders are not being punished for their crimes as intended.

Because so many offenders were being released early, **truth-in-sentencing laws** were passed by many state legislatures. These laws require offenders to serve substantial portions of their sentences. The federal government supported this movement and, in 1984, passed the Comprehensive Crime Control Act, which practically eliminated good time credits for inmates. However, the longer sentences placed extra burdens on states, forcing them to house inmates for longer times in already overcrowded facilities. In 1994, Congress passed the Violent Crime Control and Law Enforcement Act, in which it authorized $4 billion in grant money to help states build additional state prisons and jails. Four years later, in 1998, Congress passed legislation that required states to develop truth-in-sentencing laws so that those convicted of violent offenses would serve at least 85% of their terms. They also provided money to states that already had truth-in-sentencing laws requiring offenders to serve a specific percentage of their sentences.

truth in sentencing: A sentencing system that forces offenders to serve the majority of the sentence imposed by a judge after conviction.

BEYOND A REASONABLE DOUBT 11.3

Which of the following sentencing models gives judges specific sentences that should be imposed on offenders based on the seriousness of the offense and the characteristics of the offender?

(a) Indeterminate sentencing, (b) Guidelines, (c) Determinate sentencing, (d) Mandatory sentences, (e) Truth in sentencing

---

The answer can be found on page 522.

Judicial Election Versus Appointment

There is great debate as to the best method for placing judges on the bench so that the most qualified person is serving in that position. Although it is imperative that judges have independence, there must also be accountability. Judicial independence allows a judge to make decisions objectively and free from political pressure, whereas judicial accountability makes judges responsible to the people. There are different ways to select judges: election (partisan and nonpartisan), merit selection, and appointment by an executive or legislature.

VIDEO
Sandra Day
O'Connor Speaks

Elections

Many states have chosen to elect their judges. Electing judges is a way in which the public, or the voters, can "choose" who will serve in those positions. This means that the people agree that the judge is competent and reflects the values of the people he or she is serving. If a judge makes decisions that seem logical to the public, he or she is usually reelected. If those decisions are illogical or wasteful, the judge can be voted out of office. This method for choosing judges allows for great judicial accountability because judges must be responsive to the needs of the public, or they can lose their judgeships by losing reelection.

partisan elections: Elections in which the candidate's political party affiliation is clearly identified.

nonpartisan elections: Elections in which the candidate's political party affiliation is not identified.

The judicial election process can be either partisan, in which case a candidate's political party is identified, or nonpartisan, in which case party affiliation is not identified. In **partisan elections**, members of political parties will nominate candidates for judicial office. The candidates then run campaigns with party identifications in the general election. After a term in office, the judges must seek reelection in a partisan reelection. Some states, particularly Pennsylvania and Illinois, hold retention elections for incumbent judges. In **nonpartisan elections**, no party affiliation is attached to the judicial candidates on the ballot. Typically, the top two candidates in a nonpartisan primary qualify for the general election.

Not long ago, judicial elections were relatively low-key and low-cost events. The campaigns focused on candidates' backgrounds,

Judicial campaigns are run essentially the same way as other political campaigns.

© Jill Ann Spaulding/Getty Images

qualifications to hold office (experience), and reputations for fairness. But this has changed. In recent years, judicial elections have become incredibly expensive, and the outcomes may be influenced by who spends the most money. Because candidates must campaign for support (and votes), they must raise money to pay for media coverage (television, radio, and print ads), mailers, and other tactics.

To pay for their campaigns, judicial candidates must rely on contributions from groups or individuals. This can include corporations, law firms, and other attorneys who may appear before them as litigants. Some people in the legal profession may make contributions to judicial candidates, hoping that they will receive favorable treatment from that judge at a later date. Interest groups may also contribute, with the same hope of support from a judge who is elected. Special interest groups may attempt to influence the outcome of a race by supplying a candidate with lots of money.

Groups contribute money to the campaigns of judicial candidates that they believe are sympathetic to their views, or they may try to defeat candidates whose views they oppose. In one 2000 election, Citizens for a Strong Ohio spent more than $4 million on television ads in an effort to oust Justice Alice Resnick. Trial attorneys and unions contributed large sums to the judge in an effort to keep her in office, and in the end Resnick remained in office.[6]

Until recently, judicial candidates could not discuss issues or cases before the court or even hypothetically in public. But that changed with the Supreme Court ruling in *Republican Party of Minnesota v. White* (2002). The justices decided that the Minnesota Supreme Court's canon of judicial conduct that prohibited judicial candidates from speaking about their views on legal or political issues violated the First Amendment's freedom of speech clause. In other words, the First Amendment protects the right of judicial candidates to discuss positions on issues. The decision loosened the standards on judicial campaign speech and opened the scope of acceptable judicial political activity.

Critics of judicial elections claim that voters do not have the information necessary to make a choice about the qualifications of the candidates. Most judicial campaigns tend to be low visibility, with minimal press coverage (when candidates were not allowed to discuss their views, there wasn't much for the press to cover). This means that voters typically have had little information about the candidates on which to base their choices. Some voters use party identification (if available), or maybe a family name, a newspaper endorsement, an American Bar Association rating, or incumbency as a way to make their decisions. Others simply refrain from voting for the judge at all.

Merit

Some states have opted to seat qualified judges based on a merit plan, also called the Missouri Plan. This plan was created in 1940 in Missouri as a way to remove politics from the judicial selection process, thus providing more judicial independence. **Merit selection** involves a combination of elections and appointments. When a judicial vacancy occurs, a nominating panel of attorneys (chosen by the state bar association), non-lawyers (chosen by the governor), and/or some judges provides the state's governor with a list of several candidates who are qualified to fill the position. The

---

AUTHOR VIDEO
Judges Elected v.
Judges Appointed

---

merit selection: Also called the Missouri plan, this is a method of seating judges whereby a nominating panel provides the state's governor with a list of candidates, and the governor then selects one of those candidates and appoints him or her to the position.

governor then selects one of those candidates and appoints him or her to the position. After that nominee serves as a judge for a short time, the new judge must run in a retention election. In that election, the judge does not face an opponent. Instead, he or she must run on his or her record. The question on the ballot is simply "Should X be retained in office?" The party affiliation does not appear on the ballot. Instead, the incumbent is assessed on his or her performance. If a judge has committed abuses or has voted in a way the public doesn't like, he or she may be voted out. However, voter turnout is typically low and incumbents generally win. Politics still plays a significant role in merit selection. There may be organized opposition from attorneys, members of the media, interest groups, or the general public.

Executive/Legislative Appointment

In some states and the federal government, judges are appointed by an executive (governor or president) and then confirmed by another body: the U.S. Senate (in the case of federal nominees) or the state senate or some other official entity. In some states (such as Virginia and South Carolina), the legislature appoints judges. In some states, appointed judges must then face election.

The **executive/legislative appointment** process for judges is a reaction to the problem of an uninformed electorate. Many voters are not aware of the court system and issues related to the courts, so knowledgeable groups such as bar associations may be more qualified to choose those judges. Trained individuals from the legal community such as law professors, current members of the bench, and citizen groups are able to advise legislators and executives as to the most qualified judges. Moreover, more and better-qualified lawyers would be willing to seek judicial positions if they did not have to go through the election process.

However, a great deal of politics is involved in the appointment process. Although executives base their nominations on a candidate's merit (strong legal credentials and unquestioned ethical behavior), they also tend to choose people who have been active in the political system and who support their political party. The policy preferences of the nominees are crucial. Appointments can also be used as rewards for party loyalty and friendship. Some observers argue that, in this system, judges who are dependent on the person who appoints them cannot be relied on to render fair and effective decisions.

BEYOND A REASONABLE DOUBT 11.4

What was the finding in the Supreme Court case *Republican Party of Minnesota v. White*?

(a) Judges should be appointed because it leads to a more diverse judiciary, (b) Judges should be elected because it leads to a more representative judiciary, (c) Justice White's party affiliation should not have been identified during the election, (d) The canon of judicial conduct in Minnesota violated a candidate's First Amendment rights, (e) States could decide how they wanted to seat justices

The answer can be found on page 522.

executive/legislative appointment: A method of seating judges in which the governor of a state appoints justices, who are then confirmed by another body, such as a legislature.

➡ Legal Issues Related to the Courts

Courts are not simply settings in which legal issues are resolved. In fact, within the court process a number of specific issues arise that have very real implications for our efforts to promote fairness and justice. Three legal issues that are especially relevant include the court as a law maker, misconduct in the courts, and strategies for defending criminal defendants.

Court as a Law Maker

A judge's loyalty to the person who appointed him or her, the judge's personal ideology, or other personal factors are not to supposed to be the basis for judicial decisions. When judges make their decisions, they are to make them based only on the law. The role of the appellate courts is to review the acts of the legislature to ensure they are fair and constitutional or to clarify points in a law. Some observers have pointed out that as the courts decide cases and make rulings that interpret the law, they are making new rules that must be followed, describing how things should be done from then on, or even establishing new standards. In doing so, they are effectively making new laws and policies.

In the past, the decisions handed down by the Supreme Court have affected how the courts, corrections, and law enforcement systems operate. These decisions sometimes have long-term impacts on the criminal justice system as well as on others not associated with the system. When judges make new policy, it is called *judge-made law*. Policy is made by both trial-level justices and appellate justices on the federal and state levels, as both are responsible for clarifying legislation and/or defining terms that may be unclear.

One example of judges' policy-making powers revolves around the procedures by which offenders are arrested. When the Supreme Court justices decided *Miranda v. Arizona*, they created new guidelines that law enforcement must follow when they arrest people. Since then, every person brought into the system through arrest must be provided their Miranda rights, as defined by the Supreme Court.

Another example of judge-made law concerns prison overcrowding. In 1980, the Supreme Court decided *Ruiz v. Estelle*, a case concerning conditions in the correctional facilities in Texas. The Supreme Court declared that seriously overcrowded prisons are cruel and unusual punishment, which violates the Eighth Amendment to the Constitution. Its decision in the case required the state to make numerous changes in its prison operations, including ending the use of "tenders" (trusted inmates) to carry out administrative tasks, increasing the number of corrections officers, retraining of veteran officers, revising the procedures for handling inmate grievances, changing the methods used to classify inmates, improving the health system, and providing a single cell for each inmate.

Over time, the Supreme Court has also made decisions on racial segregation, pornography, appropriate law enforcement activities, the rights of criminal defendants, specific punishment strategies, and procedures regarding capital punishment. It could be argued that the courts are the only body that can make policy in these areas because these are highly controversial topics. Since the courts are insulated from politics and cannot suffer repercussions resulting from their actions, they are able to step in and make policies without political backlash. In other words, they can make policy in areas where it is politically unfeasible for politicians to act. Legislators may have to concern themselves with the public's reaction to a particular decision and may be hesitant to show support for either side of a proposal. Federal appellate judges (like the Supreme Court) do not have this concern because they are appointed and do not need to worry about public opinion.

Critics of judge-made law contend that laws should be made only by elected officials. If a bad policy is made by an elected official, voters can hold the official accountable at election time. Since judges are not always elected, they are not held accountable in the same way.

BEYOND A REASONABLE DOUBT 11.5

Judge-made law refers to which of the following?

(a) Judges working with Congress to get bills passed, (b) The procedure by which judges are approved in the nominating process, (c) Judges making policy as part of their decisions, (d) None of the above

---

The answer can be found on page 522

Misconduct in the Judicial System

Many courts must deal with misconduct on the part of courtroom personnel. **Misconduct** is any behavior by an attorney or a judge that is in conflict with the established rules of professional conduct. Most often, misconduct revolves around the abuse of an individual's power. In some circumstances, the misconduct can be punishable by disciplinary measures, including disbarment (formally banned from practicing law). In other cases, misconduct might be defined as potentially unethical but not necessarily illegal (see the "Ethical Decision Making" box in this chapter).

The legal profession is "self-governing," or "self-regulated," meaning that attorneys' behavior is regulated by others attorneys in the field rather than an outside agency. The organization that defines appropriate and proper conduct for the legal profession is the American Bar Association (ABA). The standards are established by the ABA Standing Committee on Ethics and Professional Responsibility. According to the ABA's *Lawyers' Manual on Professional Conduct*:

> As members of the bar and officers of the court, lawyers are beneficiaries of the privilege of the practice of law and also are subject to higher duties and responsibilities than are non-lawyers. A lawyer's fiduciary duties arise from the lawyer's status as a member of the legal profession and are expressed, at least in part, by the applicable rules of professional conduct.

judicial misconduct: Any behavior by an attorney or a judge that is in conflict with the established rules of professional conduct.

ETHICAL DECISION MAKING

IS THIS MISCONDUCT?

Heather Grace is a young prosecutor with hopes of one day becoming a judge. One afternoon, her boss tells her that she is going to be the lead prosecutor on a case against Thomas Allen Leslie, a well-known businessman in the community who goes by the nickname TAL. The charges against TAL are fraud, bribery, and conspiracy.

Grace's boss comments, "I knew this fool when I was in college. He's been getting into things he shouldn't all along. It's about time we got this jerk."

Grace is curious about her boss's prior relationship with TAL. She asks, "How well did you know him when you were in college?"

Her boss responds, "We got to know each other real well. But then he stole my girlfriend and married her. I can't wait to see this idiot burn at the stake."

A bit of concern passes through Grace when she hears her boss say, "Keep me in the loop on everything about this case. We need to nail him. You do well on this one, and I will make sure that you are taken care of."

YOU DECIDE

1. Should Grace tell any of her coworkers about her boss's connection to TAL? Why or why not?

2. Would you treat this case any differently than you would treat other cases? Explain.

The American Bar Association has developed *Model Rules of Professional Conduct*, which serves as a model for state bar associations to formulate their own ethical guidelines. The rules of conduct have been adopted by state courts around the United States. Violations of the rules are monitored by disciplinary committees or state bar associations. Some states have established commissions to review the behavior of lawyers. Attorneys found to have violated the codes can be considered guilty of misconduct. They are then subject to some form of discipline, such as private reprimands, public censure, or suspension of the ability to practice law. If the offense is serious enough, the misbehaving attorney can be disbarred, or permanently denied the ability to practice law in that jurisdiction. The state supreme court is the final arbiter regarding professional conduct in most states. Complaints against attorneys are fairly common, but prosecutions are relatively rare. The media tend to depict many attorneys as unethical and unscrupulous. Such a portrait is inaccurate and misleading. The vast majority of judges, prosecutors, and defense attorneys are honest professionals. The few of them who break the occupational rules reflect poorly on the entire legal system.

Misconduct by Judges

Under Article III of the U.S. Constitution, judges on the federal and state level are appointed "during good behavior." This means they serve until they step down, retire, pass away, or are impeached for wrongdoing. Judges who are corrupt, unethical, or misbehaving can be removed from office through impeachment, recall elections, or resolutions of the legislature, depending on the state. If found guilty, judges can be barred temporarily or permanently from practice.

It is important for judges to be independent in order for them to fulfill their constitutional role of reviewing laws to determine if they are fair.[7] Judges should not make decisions based on outside factors such as public opinion, interest group involvement, or business interests. Judges must have the independence to make these decisions without being fearful of repercussions. This is provided through life tenure without salary diminution and protection against arbitrary removal from office. However, judicial behavior is checked by other branches.[8]

Misconduct by Prosecutors

Misbehavior by prosecutors can be just as serious as judicial misbehavior since prosecutors have the power to take away people's freedom. There are many ways in which prosecutors can misbehave. Prosecutors can bring more serious charges than the evidence warrants. They can also withhold important exculpatory evidence (favorable evidence) from the defense (called a Brady violation), lie in court, or make incriminating but improper or inadmissible remarks in front of juries (called the *harmless error* doctrine—when improper statements are made by prosecutors that do not render sentencing proceedings unfair).[9] Some prosecutors have tried to use inadmissible evidence in a trial, knowing that it was not permitted.[10] In other situations, unethical prosecutors have attempted to coax witnesses into giving false or misleading testimony.

Prosecutor misconduct can occur for many reasons. Prosecutors are typically under pressure to win cases. This is especially important for elected prosecutors, who must run on their records of being tough on criminals and skilled at putting criminals behind bars. The job of prosecutor is sometimes used as a stepping-stone to other jobs. Thus, the need to have an impressive winning record is essential for those who want to move up. Another explanation for misconduct is that prosecutors sometimes face great public pressure for a conviction, especially in more serious cases. Thus, they may be more likely to cut procedural corners and rely on belief in defendants' guilt to justify their misconduct.[11]

Misconduct can also be the result of incompetence or poor training. It could also be related to abuse of prosecutorial power and too much prosecutorial discretion, allowing for trumped-up criminal charges against defendants.

There are also inadequate penalties for misconduct. Like judges, prosecutors rely on themselves to police other prosecutors. Although it is possible for someone to file charges against a prosecutor, it rarely happens. And any charges would need to be brought by another prosecutor, and it seems unlikely that a prosecutor would pursue charges against a colleague. Those who misbehave are rarely, if ever, professionally disciplined. If the behavior is not serious, a prosecutor may be cautioned not to act the same way again. If the offense is serious, a prosecutor could be reported and his or her convictions overturned. Although overturning a conviction may ensure due process for a defendant, it does not punish the prosecutor responsible for the wrong.

Moreover, misbehaving prosecutors are not personally liable for their misconduct in the courtroom. The Supreme Court made this clear in *Imbler v. Pachtman* (1976). In this decision, the justices declared that prosecutors

JOURNAL
Misconduct in Prosecution

FEATURE VIDEO
Challenges with the Prosecutor

are immune from damages in a civil suit. This means that a prosecutor is protected from any civil liability that might arise from his or her misconduct related to a trial.

Misconduct by Defense Attorneys

Judges and prosecutors are not the only legal professionals who occasionally misbehave. Some defense attorneys also are guilty of misconduct. The ABA *Model Rules of Professional Conduct* includes guidelines regarding the attorney-client relationship. According to the ABA, a lawyer is professionally responsible for violations involving "violence, dishonesty, breach of trust, or interference with the administration of justice" (*Model Rules of Professional Conduct*, Rule 3). Thus, according to the rules set forth by the ABA, a defense attorney could be guilty of misconduct if she or he fails to provide competent representation to a client before, during, or after a trial; to act with diligence and promptness regarding a client's case; or to keep a client informed of legal proceedings. If a defense attorney charges too many fees or overbills a client, the attorney may be guilty of misconduct.

Another area of concern is sexual relations between defense attorneys and their clients. Although the ABA *Model Rules of Professional Conduct* does not address this issue directly, the ABA's Standing Committee on Ethics and Professional Responsibility did so in 1992. That year, it issued a formal opinion in which it made it clear that an attorney's sexual relationship with a client "may involve unfair exploitation of the lawyer's fiduciary position and presents a danger that the lawyer's ability to represent the client adequately may be impaired."[12] If a physical relationship between the defense attorney and a client exists, the "objective detachment" that is necessary for the defense to provide adequate legal representation no longer exists. In addition, the ABA made it clear that a physical relationship between a client and a defense attorney introduces a clear conflict of interest into a case, possibly compromising the attorney-client privilege. Any information exchanged between the client and an attorney that is not part of their legal relationship may not be protected under attorney-client privilege.

Defense attorneys can be guilty of misconduct if there is a conflict of interest and they do not step down from a case. This may happen if an attorney, for example, could negatively affect one client by representing another client. Further, attorneys cannot make deals for the acquisition of book, film, or media rights to clients' stories. Defense attorneys are also not permitted to represent clients if the opposition is a family member. They cannot misuse a client's money (misappropriation of client funds) by stealing from a client, mixing the attorney's money with that of the client, or controlling client funds without authorization. Other examples of misconduct by all types of attorneys include the following:

- Failing to keep client information confidential (attorney-client privilege)
- Committing a criminal act

- Bringing a frivolous, or unnecessary, lawsuit
- Making false statements to the court
- Providing false evidence before or during a hearing or trial
- Obstructing another party's access to evidence
- Bribing or intimidating a judge or juror
- Making statements outside of court that will influence a court proceeding or about a witness's credibility or character
- Advertising their services in a way that is false, deceptive, or misleading
- Failing to report the possible misconduct of other lawyers

Attorneys found guilty of misconduct can be censured or reprimanded by a judge. They can be disbarred if the offense is serious. One strategy used to try to limit misconduct is to hire ethical attorneys (see the "Help Wanted" box in this chapter).

CAREER VIDEO
Professor

HELP WANTED: U.S. TRIAL ATTORNEY

DUTIES:

- Analyzes new cases received from the U.S. Attorneys' Offices and Department components charging a crime punishable by death. Section attorneys advise the attorney general's capital case review committee in its factual and legal evaluation of cases submitted to the department for review regarding whether the death penalty should be sought in each capital-eligible case.

- Litigates all phases of federal capital cases, including pretrial litigation; provides guidance in selecting death-qualified juries; and helps construct penalty-phase evidentiary presentations. Section attorneys act as co-counsel in federal capital trials, assisting with the preparation of capital-eligible cases for department review, providing guidance on death-penalty-related aspects of the pretrial and trial process.

- Provides training on the department's capital case litigation. Section attorneys provide legal, procedural, and policy guidance to U.S. Attorneys'

Offices and Department components handling capital investigations and prosecutions.

- In collaboration with U.S. Attorneys' Offices, section attorneys advise in the preparation of legal memoranda, such as proposed legislation, amendments, regulations, testimony, briefing materials, public statements, and correspondence on capital punishment issues.

- Collects and maintains trial and appellate materials related to federal capital prosecutions. Section attorneys partner with U.S. Attorneys' Offices in the development and management of current information and materials, which acts as a resource center for capital prosecutors.

- Assists in the development of department policies and procedures related to federal capital prosecutions.

REQUIREMENTS: J.D. degree

ANNUAL SALARY: $124,995–$157,100

Adapted from USAJOBS.gov. Retrieved from https://www.usajobs.gov/GetJob/ViewDetails/362714000

BEYOND A REASONABLE DOUBT 11.6

Which of the following is an example of misconduct by attorneys?

(a) Bringing a frivolous lawsuit, (b) Making false statements in court, (c) Bribing a judge, (d) Providing false evidence, (e) All of the above

The answer can be found on page 522.

Defending Clients

Ethical attorneys are expected to represent their side (whether it is the prosecution or the defense) to the best of their ability. Criminal defense attorneys frequently receive a great deal of flak for representing suspected offenders. However, defendants have a constitutional right to such representation. Defense attorneys have an assortment of legal defenses they can use to represent their clients. These defenses center on the intent of the defendant. If the defendant did not have the intent to commit a crime, then he or she cannot be held responsible (and punished) for the criminal act (see Figure 11.7).

Entrapment

If the defense can show that the offender was induced to commit crime by law enforcement, the defense of *entrapment* may be used as an "excuse" or reason why the crime was committed. This means that a law enforcement officer created an opportunity for a crime where there otherwise would not have been one and that the offender was persuaded to commit the act by the police. However, it is legally permissible for law enforcement to provide opportunities for crime with undercover agents. The question for the jury becomes the police's role in the offense: Did the police go too far or make it too easy for the offender to commit an offense that he or she otherwise would not have committed?

self-defense: A legal defense, according to which a crime is committed in order to save oneself or someone nearby from death or great harm.

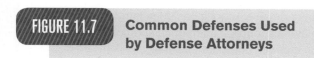

FIGURE 11.7 **Common Defenses Used by Defense Attorneys**

Entrapment

Insanity

Self-defense

Mistake of fact

Stand your ground

Duress

Castle doctrine

Necessity

© iStockphoto.com/OJO_Images

Self-Defense

Self-defense is probably the most well-known defense to a criminal act. One could argue that the criminal offense occurred in order to ensure the defendant's own safety in the face of certain injury or harm. Legally, the self-defense argument can be used only if the defendant had no "path of retreat" or alternative to the use of force. The defense must show that the offender believed that he or she was in immediate danger of being harmed by another person and had no other option but to use harm to protect himself or herself. Moreover, the extent of the injury must be reasonable with the degree of the perceived threat.

Stand Your Ground and the Castle Doctrine

Related to self-defense are the "stand your ground" and castle doctrine defenses. *Stand your ground laws* have been passed in many states. They allow people the right to use deadly force to defend themselves if they believe that it is necessary to prevent death or great bodily harm to themselves or to another person, or to prevent the commission of a felony, even outside of a person's home. Under the law, a person does not have to retreat or back away from a dangerous person or situation but can use violence (even deadly violence) to "stand their ground." A person who feels threatened can "meet force with force." Many such laws were passed after the terrorist attacks of September 11, 2001, when many people felt unsafe and had less confidence that the criminal justice system could protect citizens. There was also a general perception that the courts were more concerned with providing due process rights to offenders rather than rights to victims of crime. In some places, there was also a decrease in gun legislation, allowing for concealed-carry licenses or even open-carry laws.[13]

The Supreme Court has supported these laws. In *Beard v. United States* (1985), the Court ruled that a man involved in a murder did not provoke an assault and had reasonable grounds to believe (in good faith believed) that the attacker (deceased) intended to take his life or do him great bodily harm. The defendant was not obliged to retreat.

A similar defense passed in some states is the *castle doctrine*, sometimes called "line in the sand" or "no duty to retreat" laws. In these states, a person does not have a duty to retreat in situations in which his or her home is attacked. In other states, this also includes locations outside the home. Generally, a person has no duty to retreat from a place where a defender may legally be. These laws differ from state to state. In Ohio, "someone claiming self-defense must prove his or her case by a preponderance of evidence. Florida, by contrast, requires merely that the person establish reasonable doubt of guilt . . . the legal difference is significant."[14]

Critics argue that stand your ground laws reduce murder rates and violent crime,[15] whereas others say they increase homicide rates.[16] One study found that there was an increase in the number of injuries and homicides of White males and higher rates of visits to hospital emergency rooms and discharges for gun injuries in those states where these laws were enacted.[17] In Florida, after the law was passed, the rate of justifiable homicides in the state tripled, from an average of 13.2 per 100,000 people between 2001 and 2005 to an average of 42 per 100,000 between 2006 and 2012. At the same time, the state's violent crime rate decreased.[18]

Similarly, according to a report by the Mayors Against Illegal Guns coalition, in states where these laws were passed, claims that shootings were justified increased sharply and overall homicide rates rose. States with stand your ground laws have seen their justifiable homicide rates rise by an average of 53% in the five years following passage; in states without such laws, justifiable homicides fell by an average of 5%.[19]

Critics of these laws say that they make it difficult to prosecute someone who is charged with shooting another because of the claim of self-defense. In these cases, the shooter only needs to argue that he or she felt threatened. Critics also say these laws "open the door to random public violence and vigilantism disguised as quasi-legal action."[20] They also say that it "encourages

George Zimmerman shot Trayvon Martin, a 17-year-old unarmed African American, killing him. Zimmerman was a neighborhood watch volunteer who claimed that Martin physically attacked and restrained him. The Stand your Ground law in Florida reads, "A person who is not engaged in an unlawful activity and who is attacked in any other place where he or she has a right to be has no duty to retreat and has the right to stand his or her ground and meet force with force, including deadly force if he or she reasonably believes it is necessary to do so to prevent death or great bodily harm to himself or herself or another or to prevent the commission of a forcible felony."

© Handout/Getty Images

VIDEO
Oklahoma's Stand Your Ground

and justifies violent and fatal escalation of altercations instead of promoting peaceful resolution."[21] They point out, further, that someone can shoot innocent people who really aren't dangerous, such as children.

Although the National Rifle Association (NRA) supports these laws and says that people have a fundamental human right to defend themselves, the law enforcement community does not agree. They argue that these laws may encourage the use of deadly force by untrained people.[22]

Necessity

The **necessity** defense refers to an illegal act committed to prevent an even greater harm. This means that a person had to commit a crime in order to avoid another larger injury or hurt. For example, a police officer may be forced to shoot a student who is threatening others with a gun as a way to protect those others. In this case, a crime was committed to prevent a greater harm. Another example is if someone has to trespass on a person's property in order to give that person medical assistance. To use this defense, three elements need to be present. First, the defendant must show that he or she acted in a way to avoid a significant risk of harm to the victim or property. Second, the defendant must show that there was no lawful way that the harm could have been prevented. Third, the harm that was avoided was more than that caused by breaking the law.

Duress

The defense may try to show that its client committed a crime because he or she was under *duress*, or was coerced by another person to do so. It is illegal to use a threat or coercion to induce another to act (or to refrain from acting) in a manner he or she otherwise would not, especially if there is no way of escaping or avoiding the act. The defense must prove that there was a reasonable fear, and that the fear was of imminent serious bodily harm (or even death). An example would be making a person commit a theft by threatening to kill the person if he or she does not.

Mistake of Fact

A **mistake of fact** has to do with an offender truly not knowing a crucial fact. A common example is if an older male did not know a female's true age and had sexual relations with her. She may have told him, or even shown identification to verify, an age older than the truth. Another example is if a medicine is mislabeled and was given to a patient. In that case, it may be a mistake of fact and could be used as a legal defense.

In some cases, intoxication can be a defense. To use this defense, it must be demonstrated that the intoxication (either by drugs or alcohol) was not voluntary or self-induced. This could occur if someone was tricked into ingesting the substance. Generally, if a person is voluntarily intoxicated, or voluntarily ingests drugs, then he or she is responsible for his or her actions. Although voluntary intoxication may be used as a mitigating factor to reduce the seriousness of a charge, it is not an excuse for criminal behavior.

necessity: A criminal defense, according to which an illegal act is committed to prevent an even greater harm.

mistake of fact: A legal defense having to do with an offender's truly not knowing a crucial fact that results in criminal behavior.

Insanity

If a defendant was insane at the time of the crime, he or she was not able to form the intent, or the *mens rea*, necessary to be guilty of the crime. This means the offender did not know what he or she was doing or that what he or she was doing was wrong. The burden of proof is on the defendant to prove insanity, not on the prosecution to prove the defendant's sanity. States use different standards for proof of mental instability, and the standard changes as more is learned about the concept of being "insane."

Proving legal insanity is not easy to do in a courtroom. One method used to do so is the *McNaughten rule*. This standard was named after Daniel McNaughten, a woodworker from Glasgow, Scotland, who, in 1843, tried to assassinate Sir Robert Peel, the British prime minister. McNaughten missed Peel and instead killed Edward Drummond, Peel's secretary. During the trial, medical professionals testified that McNaughten did not know what he was doing when he shot Drummond. McNaughten was found not guilty by reason of insanity, the first person for whom this defense was used.

This case set the standard of proof for determining insanity in a courtroom. The focus is on the offender's ability to distinguish between right and wrong. If the offender is not able to know the difference, he or she is assumed to have a mental defect or disability. Eventually, the McNaughten rule became widely known as the "right-from-wrong" test.

Other states use a different standard to define insanity in offenders. Some states have chosen to use the *irresistible impulse standard*. Under this rule, if a defendant knew that what he or she was doing was wrong but could not help himself or herself, or if the defendant was unable to control his or her actions, then the defendant may be declared insane and may not be held accountable for the offense. This is currently the standard in 18 states.

A third standard for determining insanity in an offender is the *Durham rule*. The Durham rule was the result of *Durham v. United States* (1954). Monte Durham was a defendant who had a long record that included mental illness and criminal activity. At the age of 26, he and two of his friends broke into a home. He was later found guilty of the crime but appealed his conviction based on the idea that the criminal behavior was the product of his "mental disease or defect." The standard for insanity established in this case is that "a person is not criminally responsible for their behavior if their illegal actions were the result of some mental disease or defect." Therefore, based on the Durham rule, jurors must decide that the defendant's criminal behavior was the product of mental deficiencies or defect. The Durham rule is sometimes difficult to use because it does not define what a "mental disease or defect" really is.

A few states follow the *substantial capacity rule* for determining if an offender had a decreased mental capacity at the time a crime was committed. Because this standard is presented in the Model Penal Code of the American Law Institute, it is referred to as the MPC rule or the ALI rule. It simply states that insanity is the lack of a substantial capacity to control one's behavior. Thus, a defense attempting to prove insanity must show that a defendant lacked "the mental capacity needed to understand the wrongfulness of his act, or to conform his behavior to the requirements of the law." Generally speaking, the MPC rule combines the McNaughten rule with the irresistible impulse standard. This standard does not require that the defendant have total mental incompetence. The question becomes, what is meant by a "substantial mental capacity?"

In 1972, another standard for determining insanity resulted from the *United States v. Brawner* case. This criterion, called the *Brawner rule*, places responsibility for deciding insanity with the jury. In this case, the jury must decide if a defendant should be held responsible for a criminal act. However, most juries are given few guidelines on how to determine insanity. Since very few jurors have any experience with mental disease, it becomes very difficult for them to make this determination.

If it can be determined that a criminal defendant was unconscious at the time of the offense, he or she may be able to use that as a defense. For example, sleepwalking may result in unintentional offenses.

Some defendants are found guilty but mentally insane (GBMI). In these cases, an offender will be held responsible for the crime, but it is recognized that some mental illness played a role in the behavior. If a person is found to be GBMI through a court proceeding, a judge may impose any sentence allowable under the law for the crime. But the offender will also receive mandated psychiatric treatment as part of the criminal sentence. If the offender completes the treatment successfully, he or she will be placed in the general population in a correctional facility to serve the remaining portion of his or her sentence.

Temporary insanity is sometimes used as a criminal defense. In these cases, the offender must prove that he or she was insane for only a short time. But since the offender is no longer "insane," there is no need for psychiatric treatment and he or she does not receive any treatment.

In federal cases, standards were established in the Insanity Defense Reform Act of 1984 after the assassination attempt on President Reagan. The new law substantially revised the federal insanity defense. The law defined insanity as a condition in which the defendant was suffering under a "severe mental disease or defect" and, as a result, "was unable to appreciate the nature and quality or the wrongfulness of his acts." In the federal system, the burden of proof is on the defendant to demonstrate a mental disease or defect if this defense is to be used.

Other Defenses

In some cases, age or immaturity can be used as a criminal defense. Young children cannot form the intent to commit a crime. Most childhood experts believe that a child cannot reason logically until around the age of seven. Thus, if a young person commits a criminal offense, most states will not charge that person criminally. Under common law, a person between the ages of 7 and 14 is not criminally liable for his or her crimes. In some states, a 17-year-old will be treated as an adult, whereas in others the offender must be 16 or 18. Until a person reaches that age, he or she is considered a juvenile and the case will be heard in a juvenile court, unless the case is remanded to the adult court.

Over time, many other defenses have been attempted as a way to excuse criminal behavior. These include premenstrual syndrome (PMS), chemical imbalances, or even an excessive ingestion of sugar. The latter defense was attempted in 1978 by Dan White after he was accused of shooting San Francisco Mayor George Moscone and City Councilman Harvey Milk. It was quickly labeled the "Twinkie defense."

Dan White's "Twinkie defense" was protested for being a travesty against the ideals of justice.

© Susan Gilbert/San Francisco Chronicle/Corbis

Criminal justice officials use their professional judgment at each stage of the justice process to decide whether to define behaviors as crimes. In doing so, they follow legal definitions of crime, although social, political, and ethical factors might influence the decisions to label behaviors as criminal. In addition, broader societal changes will influence the viability of specific legal defenses.

BEYOND A REASONABLE DOUBT 11.7

Which of the following is an example of a criminal defense?

(a) Entrapment, (b) Duress, (c) Insanity, (d) Intoxication, (e) All of the above

---

The answer can be found on page 522.

➡ Issues Related to Innovations in the Courts

Societal changes have led to changes in the way certain types of offenders are processed through the courts. Some of the changes are the result of research and evidence that specific types of offenders might fare better if their cases were handled in settings responsive to their offenses. Consider the evolution of **specialty courts**, also called "problem-solving courts." The intent of these courts is to address the root causes of certain criminal behavior to reduce the probability of continued criminal behavior by the defendant. These courts emphasize one offense type or category of offender, such as juveniles, gun offenses, family courts, and drug courts (sometimes DWI courts). Specialty courts do not exist in every state. They vary as to their exact jurisdictions and how they are organized and operate.

In most specialty courts, the same judge, prosecutor, and defense team will be part of every case. This way, they will become experts in that specific area. They will become well versed in relevant ideas or concepts and will not have to spend extra time getting up to speed during a trial. They will also know if experts are reliable and should be believed. They may also be aware of the newest research findings. As a result, what might otherwise become a lengthy and complex trial may be much shorter. The verdicts reached by the courts may be more accurate, timely, and efficient.

AUTHOR VIDEO
Specialty Courts

specialty courts: Also called problem-solving or alternative courts, these courts attempt to reduce the probability of recidivism by diverting the defendant from trial and placing him or her in a treatment program.

Instead of the usual adversarial setting found in a courtroom, the specialty courts use a team approach to address the cause of the defendant's action. Usually this involves the judge, prosecutor, defense, a case manager, treatment providers, and the defendant (or guardian, if applicable). In most cases, the team will consult and devise a plan for the defendant to receive treatment in lieu of a term in jail. If the defendant completes the required treatment, the charges will be dropped or reduced. If the treatment is not fulfilled, the offender can be placed on trial for the original charges, or could be placed in custody.

Many supporters of specialty courts believe that they are an innovative way to handle offenders who committed a crime because of some problem or deficiency that, if treated or solved, will prevent that person from reoffending. Others disagree and argue that these courts are simply a way to "widen the net" of state control because police will cast a wider net and arrest more people in order to get them into treatment.

Juvenile Courts

Until the late 1800s, juvenile offenders were treated the same as adults in criminal courts. Upon arrest, juveniles were held alongside adult offenders in jails until trail. When that time came, young offenders were tried in the same courts as adult offenders, regardless of their offenses. Offenders who were very young, under the age of seven, were considered by the courts to lack both the mental capacity and the moral responsibility to be liable for their crimes. This was sometimes called the "infancy defense." Under it, offenders aged 7 to 14 could be criminally liable if the prosecutor could prove that the juvenile was mentally and morally mature. Any young offender who was over age 14 was generally thought to be accountable for any criminal acts.[23] If found guilty in a courtroom, these juveniles would then be sentenced to a term in an adult facility or even executed if the crime was grim.

However, in the late 1800s, a group of reformers sought to change the way the courts handled juvenile offenders. They believed that juveniles had different needs than adults and sought to make the court a place where young criminals could receive treatment or rehabilitation instead of punishment. This way, juveniles might be prevented from becoming adult criminals. One recommendation made by the reformers was to separate juvenile defendants from adults during the time before a trial and after sentencing so that they would not be "further criminalized" by their contact with grown, sometimes more dangerous (or more experienced) offenders. Another recommendation was to keep court records confidential as a way to minimize the stigma associated with being a juvenile offender. Finally, reformers also recommended removing juveniles from adult courts so that judges could give young offenders individual attention.

Officials in Cook County, Illinois, listened to the reformers and in 1899 established a separate court to

Juvenile suspects are processed through the courts in a way similar to how adult suspects are processed.

hear only cases involving young offenders. Called a "children's court," it had jurisdiction over young offenders (under the age of 16) who were charged with committing crimes. The court also heard cases in which the child was homeless, in need of public support, or neglected.[24] The underlying purpose of these courts was not to punish offenders in the same way that adults were punished but instead to rehabilitate them. Because the defendants were not "found guilty" and punished as in the adult court, officials did not see the need to protect the constitutional, due process rights of the juveniles.

This attitude changed in the 1960s. *Kent v. United States* (1966) was the first case to examine the extent to which juveniles should be granted rights in **juvenile court**. The defendant in this case, Morris A. Kent, Jr., was 14 when he was arrested in Washington, D.C., and charged with housebreaking, robbery, and rape. Because of his age, Kent was first referred to the juvenile court. However, because of the seriousness of his crime, the juvenile court waived its jurisdiction and sent Kent's case to the adult court. Even though Kent's legal counsel filed a motion for a hearing on the waiver to the adult court, the juvenile court chose not to have such a hearing. In the adult court, Kent was indicted, tried, and convicted on six counts of housebreaking and robbery. He was subsequently acquitted on two counts of rape by reason of insanity. Kent's conviction was appealed to the U.S. Supreme Court. In their decision, the justices asserted that the juvenile court must conduct a hearing before a juvenile is transferred to an adult criminal court for a trial.

Another landmark case to test the rights of juvenile defendants was *In re Gault* (1967) ("in the matter of Gault"). This case revolved around a 15-year-old juvenile from Arizona, Gerald Gault, who was charged by law enforcement with making an obscene phone call to a female neighbor. The "Criminal Justice Pioneer" box in this chapter provides an overview of the case. He was later convicted in court and given an indeterminate sentence for his crime, which meant that Gault could remain in prison until he turned 21. The case was appealed to the U.S. Supreme Court, which decided that juveniles are entitled to the following:

- Adequate notice of the precise nature of the charges brought against [them]

- Notice of the right to counsel and, if indigent, the right to have counsel appointed

- The right to confront and cross-examine witnesses

- The privilege against self-incrimination[25]

Over time, Supreme Court cases have defined the rights of juveniles in the courts. Some of these cases are outlined in Table 11.1.

Today's juvenile court is still focused on the belief that juvenile offenders should be treated differently from adult offenders. Most professionals believe that young people have not yet fully developed either physically and mentally, and some juveniles face serious environmental, social, and educational deficiencies that, if corrected, may prevent them from becoming adult offenders. Moreover, many experts believe that juveniles are easier

juvenile courts: Courts established in the late 1800s that treated young offenders differently from adults, focusing on treatment and rehabilitation as opposed to punishment.

TABLE 11.1   Supreme Court Cases and Juvenile Rights

COURT CASE	FINDING
In re Gault (1967)	Juveniles have the right to an attorney in juvenile proceedings. If a minor cannot afford an attorney, he or she has the right to be represented by a state-appointed attorney. A juvenile must be provided with notice of the delinquency charges he or she faces.
In re Winship (1970)	Juveniles must be proved guilty beyond a reasonable doubt.
McKeiver v. Pennsylvania (1971)	The right to a jury trial is not required by the U.S. Constitution in delinquency cases, although a state could provide a jury if it wished.
Breed v. Jones (1975); *Swisher v. Brady* (1978)	The Constitution's double jeopardy clause prevents a juvenile court from transferring a youth to a criminal court after previously finding him or her delinquent.
Fare v. Michael (1979)	A youth's Miranda rights regarding self-incrimination are not invoked by his or her request to see a probation officer during custodial interrogation by the police.
Schall v. Martin (1984)	A youth can be subjected to "preventive detention" while awaiting trial.

National Crime Justice Reference Service

to rehabilitate than adults. Thus, whereas the goal of adult courts tends to be punishment of those found guilty of crimes, juvenile courts focus more on the rehabilitation of young offenders.[26] They do this by uncovering the underlying cause of the criminal behavior and the most appropriate way to address it.

Teen Courts

Teen courts, sometimes referred to as youth courts, have become a popular method in some states to manage young, first-time offenders who have been charged with minor misdemeanor crimes such as theft, simple assault, or possession of alcohol. In these courts, young people are involved in determining the facts of the case and suggesting an appropriate punishment. Although there is an adult judge in the courtroom who oversees the proceedings, a youth judge presides. Other young people serve as attorneys, jurors, clerks, and other court personnel. The young people acting as attorneys present their cases to the youth judge and jury, who then must decide the appropriate punishment for the defendant. In some places, the teen court is set up so that there are no youth attorneys. In those places, the facts are presented to a jury composed of young people. In those situations, the youth jury asks questions of the defendant. Most of the time, the defendant must admit to the charges against him or her before the case will be heard in the teen court.

Most teen courts do not determine the guilt or innocence of a youth offender but rather simply determine a punishment. Because the offenses are minor, the punishments are typically community service, apology letters or essays, teen court jury duty, drug or alcohol classes, or monetary restitution to the victim. Community service and apology letters are the two most commonly awarded sanctions.[27] One might question whether similar courts could be developed for college students (see the "Criminal Justice and College Students" box in this chapter).

teen courts: Sometimes referred to as youth courts, these courts allow young people to determine the facts of a case and suggest an appropriate punishment while an adult judge in the courtroom oversees the proceedings.

GERALD GAULT

A READERS THEATER MONOLOGUE FROM THE UNITED STATES COURTS WEBSITE

Hey, I'm Jerry Gault. All the talk about phones these days is about texting while driving. Well, in my day the big thing was making crank calls on these old things. Reminds you of the old Alfred Hitchcock movies, doesn't it?

Well, if I had my own blog today, this is what I'd be writing about my case that went all the way to the Supreme Court. I'd call it: *My Fight for Your Rights*. Just a year after the Supreme Court decided in Mr. Gideon's case, I got in trouble with the law in a small town in Arizona.

It was the morning of June 8, 1964, and I was 15. What really happened depends on who you believe, but what I told the judge was that my buddy Ron Lewis was over at my parents' trailer house where I lived. I'm getting ready for work when I hear my man Ronnie in the next room talking on the phone. He's using some pretty raunchy language. So I walk over, take the phone off him, hang it up, and kick him out of the trailer.

The next thing I know the county sheriff shows up and hauls **me** off to jail. I'm already on probation, so this is not good. The cops don't tell me what's up. They don't give me my rights. Nothin'.

I hear later that a lady in the trailer park says she got a crank phone call. To tell you the truth, I wouldn't recognize her if she was standing in this courtroom today. The Constitution says you're supposed to be able to confront your accuser in court. Didn't happen in my case. She didn't show up at any of my hearings, even though my parents asked her to.

But anyways, when my parents get home from work that night, they freak out when they can't find me anywheres. They call my boss, my friends, and the hospital. Finally, they track me down at the county Children's Detention Home. But they aren't allowed to come get me.

The next morning, I land in court—no attorney, no parents, nothin'. Just me and Judge Robert McGhee.

When it comes to deciding what to do with me, the Judge says he'll "think about it" and they put me back in the slammer for a few **more** days. Then, out of the blue, they let me out. They don't tell me why and I'm not pushin' it.

That day my Mom gets a note from the superintendent of the juvenile detention home telling her that the Judge has set a hearing for that coming Monday to sentence me on my "delinquency." I'm thinkin': "What the heck . . . ." One day I'm on my way to work and the next thing I know they're talkin' reform school?!!" Judge McGhee says I'm a "delinquent child" and sends me to the State Industrial School. He's not letting me out until I turn **21!**

I was charged with making lewd phone calls. If an adult had been convicted of the same thing, he woulda got a maximum prison sentence of two months and a fine of $5 to $50. I got sent away for six years to what is, essentially, a prison for kids.

Looking back on it, the process was more obscene than the phone call:

1. I wasn't told the charges against me.
2. My parents were kept in the dark.
3. No rights, no attorney. Nothing like what they call due process—doing things the straight up way.

My parents ended up taking my case to the Arizona Supreme Court. But that Court decided that, because I was a juvenile, what the trial judge did was okay and they let it stand. So we took our case to the U.S. Supreme Court.

I finally got justice there. The Supreme Court ruled in my favor. They said the trial court did me wrong and that kids have rights, too. Justice Abe Fortas wrote the opinion. Remember, he was the attorney who won for Clarence Gideon. He wrote a great one-liner in the opinion for me. He said: "Under our Constitution, the condition of being a boy does not justify a Kangaroo court." The opinion was 8-to-one **in my favor**. Yeah!!!

Reprinted from UScourts.gov. Retrieved from http://www.uscourts.gov/educational-resources/get-involved/constitution-activities/sixth-amendment/right-counsel/re-enactment.aspx

CRIMINAL JUSTICE and **COLLEGE STUDENTS**

DESIGNING A COLLEGE STUDENT COURT

Imagine the dean of students at your college hired you to create a college student court similar to the specialty courts that have been created across the United States. Identify four types of misconduct by college students that you would have handled by the court. What penalties would you give to those found guilty of wrongdoing? Who would be involved in the court? How would your court be different from other specialty courts? Discuss your answers with three classmates.

VIDEO
Drug Courts

Drug Courts

In the mid-1980s, many state and local courts faced overcrowding problems largely as the result of drug-related cases. Research on drug offenders indicated that drug offenders, when released from prison, were likely to commit more crime and that longer prison terms did not help them break their addictions. However, it became clear that offenders who participated in treatment programs were likely to stop using drugs and avoid additional prison time once released from custody.

The first **drug court** opened in Miami, Florida, in 1989 as an experiment by the Dade County, Florida, Circuit Court. It was so successful that many other cities established similar courts (see Figure 11.8). Although the courts are all unique, they have many similarities. In most places, certain defendants can be referred to drug courts in lieu of traditional courts. They

FIGURE 11.8   **Drugs Courts in the United States, 2013**

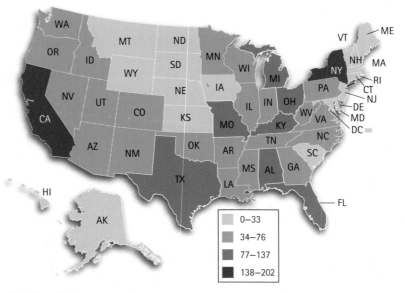

Legend:
- 0–33
- 34–76
- 77–137
- 138–202

National Crime Justice Reference Service

drug courts: Alternative courts for drug offenders that allow the offender to participate in treatment programs in lieu of a criminal conviction and sentencing.

are identified soon after arrest and placed in the program early in the judicial process. The offenders are usually nonviolent offenders whose crimes were, at least in part, the result of their drug addiction. They must agree to take part in the drug court option and abide by the rules set forth.

The drug court approach was supported by researchers for the National Association of Criminal Defense Lawyers who, in 2009, found that drug addiction should be treated as a medical or public health problem as opposed to a criminal matter. They suggested that the leniency offered to drug-addicted defendants by drug courts was preferable to the punishment in a traditional court, and more successful. The report included some recommendations, as listed below:

1. Defendants should not be required to plead guilty to receive placement in a drug treatment program. If they did this, they would give up their constitutional rights and protections. This is important because these defendants may end up in a trial proceeding if they do not complete the required elements of the drug program.

2. Admission criteria for participating in the drug court should be objective and fair, and not controlled by prosecutors.

3. Drug courts must incorporate strong ethical frameworks. Defense lawyers must not be required to surrender their obligation to defend their clients.[28]

In the drug court, the prosecution and defense operate in a nonadversarial way, meeting often as a team, as a way to help the offender. The offender may be required to participate in weekly (or even daily) counseling or therapy sessions, education programs, and frequent urinalysis or drug testing, vocational programs, or medical services. Throughout, the offender must appear before the drug court judge for status updates. After the participant finishes the initial therapy and is no longer using illicit drugs, he or she is typically expected to maintain certain conditions such as keeping a job, paying bills, and having a sponsor. In some programs, drug court participants may be expected to perform community service activities.

Research shows that drug courts are very successful in treating addiction and the resulting criminal behavior. The results of many studies indicate that most offenders in the drug court program will remain in their drug treatment programs and successfully break their drug addictions. Moreover, most offenders do not commit new crimes and do not return to prison. One study found that the proportion of offenders rearrested for felony offenses dropped from 40% before participating in the drug court program to only 12% after participation. In another location, the rearrest rate for felony offenses dropped from 50% to 35%. Another benefit of drug courts is that court backlogs have been reduced in counties that have initiated them. These counties have also experienced a cost savings because of the drug courts. On average, there was a public savings of $6,744 per offender.[29]

Mentally ill individuals are frequently arrested for behaviors that can be attributed to their mental illnesses. Many jurisdictions across the United States created mental health courts to improve the way that the justice system processes these cases.

REUTERS/Lucy Nicholson

Mental Health Courts

Mental health courts were another type of specialty court that appeared in the late 1990s as a way to reduce court backlogs as well as to help offenders suffering from mental illnesses. In large part they were a response to the large number of mentally ill individuals who were being held in jails and prisons where they did not receive any mental health treatment. These courts divert mentally ill offenders from the prison or jail and place them in some type of community treatment program in the hopes that they will receive assistance and thus be less likely to return to prison or jail.

These courts have become essential as the number of mentally ill offenders in the United States has increased dramatically in the past 25 years. Police sometimes take people with mental disorders to jail as a way to get them off the street and protect the community, a trend called the "criminalization of mental illness." Regrettably, most jails lack any kind of services for many of these people and even when services are available, they are typically minimal. Nor do jails refer these individuals to community treatment services when they leave the jail. Often, they return to the jail.

Mental health courts have a dedicated judge, prosecutor, and defense counsel who work in a nonadversarial team approach. Offenders who agree to have their cases diverted to the mental health court are required to participate in treatment, take any necessary medications, find employment, or fulfill other conditions as determined by the officials. Offenders are supervised through judicial hearings and also through direct supervision in the community to ensure they are complying with the rules. If needed, an offender's treatment plan can be altered. If the offender completes the treatment plan successfully, the initial charge(s) will be dropped or reduced.

Many research studies show that mental health courts are effective in reducing future criminal behavior by program participants. One study focused on the courts in Seattle, where offenders could "opt in" or "opt out" of the program. In the end, offenders who "opted-in" had fewer criminal bookings over an average nine-month period after entry into the court, compared to the "opt-outs."[30] Another study followed a random control group who participated in a mental health court in Santa Barbara, California. Here, offenders were randomly assigned for 18 months to either the mental health court with community treatment or a traditional criminal court with treatment as usual. After a period of one year, offenders assigned to the mental health court had fewer convictions for new offenses, compared with the control group.[31] Moore and Hiday found that participants in the mental health courts had a rearrest rate half that of similar defendants not in the program.[32]

mental health courts: Specialty courts that help those offenders suffering from mental illnesses and divert mentally ill offenders from the jail/prison and place them in treatment programs instead.

CORRECTIONS

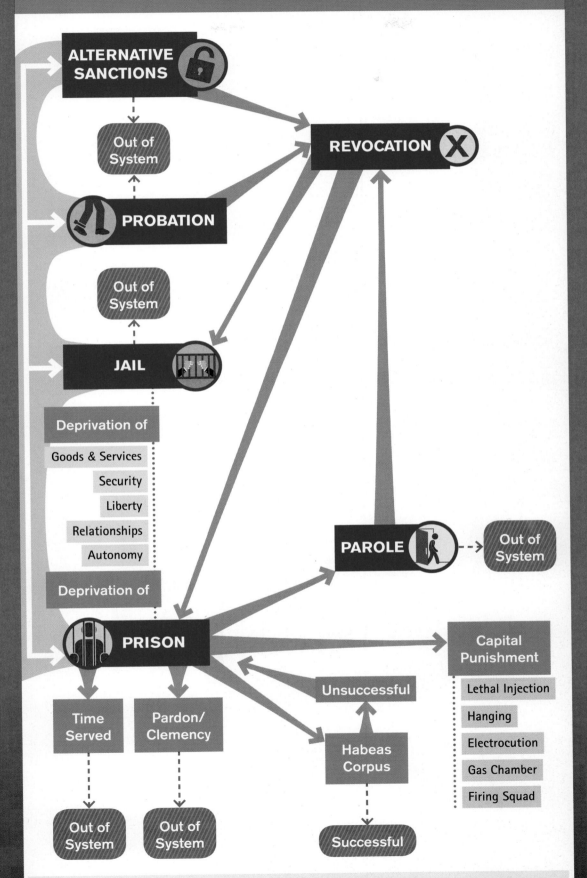

ALTERNATIVE SANCTIONS

Out of System

PROBATION

Out of System

JAIL

REVOCATION

Deprivation of

Goods & Services

Security

Liberty

Relationships

Autonomy

Deprivation of

PAROLE

Out of System

PRISON

Time Served

Pardon/ Clemency

Unsuccessful

Habeas Corpus

Capital Punishment

Lethal Injection

Hanging

Electrocution

Gas Chamber

Firing Squad

Out of System

Out of System

Successful

12

AN INTRODUCTION TO CORRECTIONS

HISTORY, STRUCTURE, AND ACTORS

© Jessica Miller

© alessandro0770/Veer

EASTERN STATE PENITENTIARY IS LOCATED in downtown Philadelphia, Pennsylvania. Opened in 1829, the prison appears on the outside to resemble a medieval fortress. Inside the imposing building, the prison operated on the concept that inmates should be isolated from other prisoners and guards. The inmates were not permitted to leave their cells or communicate in any way with each other. They were housed in private cells that each had an individual exercise area. Meals were provided through small holes in the cell door. When it was necessary for inmates to leave their cells, hoods were placed over their heads. They were provided a Bible to read and were allowed to perform menial work such as shoemaking or weaving in their own cells. It was thought that the inmates would reflect on their crimes and become penitent (thus, the name penitentiary).

Many tourists came to the prison to wonder at the grand architecture. Debate raged over the effectiveness of the institution's methods. Philosophers Alexis de Tocqueville and Gustave de Beaumont supported the philosophy of the prison, but the English author Charles Dickens did not. Over time, the practice of isolating the inmates began to crumble, and inmates slowly were permitted contact with others. By 1909, inmate baseball teams played each other for recreation.

Due to increasing costs of maintaining the institution, the prison was closed in 1971. The City of Philadelphia purchased the site and considered demolishing the buildings but abandoned those plans. The prison was opened to the public for tours beginning in 1994.

Today, tourists can visit the prison and see for themselves what it must have been like to be imprisoned there. Visitors are immediately struck by the massive stone wall that surrounds the buildings. Upon entering the prison, visitors notice the air is chilly and dank. The buildings are clearly showing their age. Paint is chipping off the walls and cell bars. Some cells have been painted and made to appear as they did in the 1800s. Most cells, however, remain untouched, covered with years of dirt. An occasional cell has the remnants of a sink and toilet used by the inmates housed there. As visitors walk through the unlit cellblocks, the tour guide tries to explain what it was like to be housed in the prison, isolated from any other human contact for months at a time. Some inmates went crazy because of the lack of human contact. It is not easy to comprehend what it must have been like to live in such a cold, dark place for many years.

LEARNING OBJECTIVES

After reading this chapter, students will be able to:

12.1 Compare and contrast the goals of punishment

12.2 Identify three historical eras leading to the current strategies for punishing offenders

12.3 Describe four types of prisons

12.4 Delineate the differences among federal, state, and local corrections

12.5 Compare and contrast juvenile facilities with adult institutions

12.6 Describe the role of wardens in prisons

12.7 Identify the behaviors of corrections officers

ADMISSIBLE or INADMISSIBLE Evidence

Read the statements that follow. If the statement is true, circle *admissible*. If the statement is false, circle *inadmissible*. Answers can be found on page 518.

1. **Admissible   Inadmissible**   *Restitution* refers to efforts to punish offenders as severely as necessary to stop future crime

2. **Admissible   Inadmissible**   Debtor's prisons were places where individuals who could not pay their debts were incarcerated at night; prisoners were expected to perform hard labor during the day to pay off their debts.

(Continued)

(Continued)

3. **Admissible   Inadmissible**   Beccaria argued that in order for people to live in relative peace, they must give up some of their liberties to the government so that criminal laws may be established and offenders may be punished.

4. **Admissible   Inadmissible**   The Western Penitentiary was built near Los Angeles and opened in 1976.

5. **Admissible   Inadmissible**   Three-strikes laws are a form of indeterminate sentencing.

6. **Admissible   Inadmissible**   Following military structures, the individual who runs a prison is known as a commander.

7. **Admissible   Inadmissible**   Jails typically hold offenders who have been convicted of low-level misdemeanors and sentenced to terms of under one year.

8. **Admissible   Inadmissible**   Under current laws in the United States, offenders can be banished to another country as part of their punishment.

The system of housing inmates found in the Eastern State Penitentiary was innovative for its time. Prisons have not always been a mainstay of corrections in the world, or in the United States. In fact, the philosophy of punishment has undergone numerous changes over time. Before the establishment of prisons, punishment in early America tended to be more brutal and quick, involving everything from corporal punishment to the death penalty. The first jails in the United States were used only as a means of pretrial detention. It was through the experience with these facilities that the idea of sentencing people to jails and prisons began to take hold and the penitentiary system began to rise. However, the system was fraught with problems, and calls for reform were made. These reforms attempted to fix some of the problems, but the United States eventually reverted to a punishment mode, and prisons reflected just that. Once again, in the 20th century, reforms were called for, but they too failed and crime continued to rise. The end of the 20th century saw another prison-building boom, and the United States criminal justice system once again focused on punishment. The practice of punishment in America is always in a state of flux, changing as society changes its views on what is appropriate and what is necessary.

Understanding the history of punishment in America also helps us understand how we got to where we are today. In assessing the state of what has been called the prison-industrial complex, we see that this did not just develop overnight but rather was created over approximately 200 years. We can also be sure that there will continue to be changes in the future, based on new reforms, which, like past reforms, will change the direction of corrections. Therefore, it is also important that we understand the modern state of corrections in the United States.

This chapter introduces students to the corrections subsystem of the criminal justice system. To provide a framework for understanding the corrections system, we focus first on the goals of punishment and the history of corrections. We then examine the way that corrections agencies are structured, both politically and geographically.

Goals of Punishment

The activities that take place within a corrections institution depend to a large extent on the goals the administrators (and, to some extent, political leaders) have for the facility, the inmates, and the criminal justice system overall. Many goals of the criminal justice system have been identified, none of which consistently stands out over another. Instead, the goals ebb and flow as they become more or less popular politically.

VIDEO
A Living Death

Retribution

One of the goals of the system is to punish offenders, which is sometimes called **retribution**. This is a way to discipline offenders by restricting their freedom and ability to make choices. It is based on the idea of "just deserts." Individuals should be held accountable for their actions, and therefore offenders should be punished in a way that is proportionate to their offenses. This means that the punishment an offender receives is the product of his or her offense. Under this premise, punishments should be the same for people who commit similar crimes.

Rehabilitation

The goal of **rehabilitation** is based on the idea that criminals commit crime because they are lacking something or are deficient in some way. It is necessary for prisoners to change or modify so that they do not commit more offenses. This means that prison programs must improve the skills, education, and/or self-confidence of inmates so that they do not commit more criminal acts once released. This can be attempted through vocational and education programs, counselors, and inmate services. A common mode of rehabilitation is drug and alcohol treatment programs for inmates with addiction problems. The goal of rehabilitation is linked to the medical model—that something is wrong or lacking in the offender and that programs can solve what is wrong, just as someone who is sick can receive treatment for an illness. Once inmates are treated, they can rejoin society and not commit another crime.

retribution: The correctional goal of punishing or disciplining criminal offenders by restricting their freedom and ability to make choices.

rehabilitation: The correctional goal of making a criminal into a productive citizen.

reintegration: The correctional goal of moving inmates from the prison environment and integrating them back into society so that they can become productive citizens.

Reintegration

The goal of **reintegration** means that inmates must understand that conforming is necessary to fit into society, so prison officials must work with offenders so that they can make the transition from prison life to life in the community. Prison administrators need to help inmates learn how to fit back into society so that they don't commit more crimes. To do this effectively, some prisons allow inmates to work outside the prison but return to the prison nights and

While prisons have changed over time, one aspect that has remained the same is their purpose: separate convicted offenders from the community.

© Reuters /Jason Redmond /Landov

weekends, and some offenders live in halfway houses that allow them to be half in prison yet half in society at the same time.

Incapacitation

Another goal of the criminal justice system (and punishment) is **incapacitation**, which involves keeping offenders from committing more crimes by putting them in prison or jail. An inmate can also be incapacitated through house arrest or electronic monitoring. The theory here is simple: Inmates can't commit more crimes while they are in prison or under a form of punishment. When a dangerous criminal is sentenced to spend time in a facility, his or her opportunity for committing more crime on the streets is eliminated.

Deterrence

The goal of deterrence is based on the idea that punishment exists to deter future crime. According to this perspective, it is important to know the appropriate punishment for offenses because a punishment that is too lenient or too harsh won't be an effective deterrent. This is based on the assumption that people are rational actors who weigh the costs and benefits of their actions. In doing so, they factor in the cost of committing a crime, and they should conclude that the cost outweighs any benefit they may obtain from the crime.

There are two types of deterrence. One is **specific deterrence**, whereby an individual offender is discouraged from committing a second crime because he or she was punished for the first offense. In other words, an offender does not reoffend because he or she has learned a lesson. This can be likened to a child who learns not to commit bad behavior because he or she was punished by a parent previously for misbehaving.

The second type of deterrence is **general deterrence**. In this case, a person does not commit a crime because he or she saw another person punished for doing so. The person learns by observation not to duplicate that same offense at the risk of being punished in the same way. When a person who committed a crime is punished severely, it makes an example of him or her, and those in the general public who may be considering committing the same crime will be dissuaded from doing so. This means that punishment is a signal to others.

Restitution

Restitution occurs when an inmate reimburses society for the harm done by the offense. An offender can pay back victims for any losses that occurred during the crime, or pay a fine, forfeit property, or perform community service. Sometimes this is called *restoration* or *community justice*. It is based on the idea that crime is a disruption of the community's peace, and the punishment aims to restore the community to its original state before the crime was committed.

AUTHOR VIDEO
The Goal of Punishment

incapacitation: The correctional goal of putting a person in jail or prison so that he or she is unable to commit further crime.

specific deterrence: The correctional goal of discouraging offenders from committing additional crimes because they were punished for the first offense.

general deterrence: The correctional goal of dissuading people from committing a crime because they have seen another person punished for doing so.

restitution: The correctional goal of having an inmate pay his or her victim for any losses that occurred during the crime, or to pay a fine, forfeit property, or perform community service as a way to reimburse the community.

——— BEYOND A REASONABLE DOUBT 12.1 ———

Which of the following goals of punishment refers to efforts to hold offenders accountable for their actions?

(a) Retribution, (b) Restitution, (c) General deterrence, (d) Specific deterrence, (e) None of the above

The answer can be found on page 522.

➡ History of Punishment

There are many ways to assess the history of punishment. Perhaps the simplest is to look at punishment prior to the time when prisons were used as punishment and the time after prisons had become commonly used forms of punishment. That division occurred at around 1826, when the first penitentiary was built in the United States. Another way to define different periods of punishment is to divide time by century. Prior to the 19th century, punishment typically ranged from fines, to corporal punishment, to banishment and execution; imprisonment was not an option. The 19th century saw the rise of the penitentiary system, to include the eventual problems of overcrowding and prisons serving as breeding grounds for criminality. In the 20th century, the focus was primarily on reforming the system.[1] The century-based approach gives a good general overview, but it misses some of the more subtle changes that have occurred over time. A more complete understanding of the history of punishment can be obtained by looking at the various eras of punishment (see Figure 12.1).[2]

JOURNAL
Reclaiming Crime Prevention

Punishment Before Prisons

Corrections throughout world history prior to the 17th and 18th centuries tended to focus on corporal punishment, banishment, and death.[3] Imprisonment in the "dungeons," a form of prison, was generally relegated to political prisoners, and the only jails that existed were **debtor's prisons**

debtor's prisons:
An early form of prison, for those who could not pay their debts.

FIGURE 12.1   Eras of Punishment

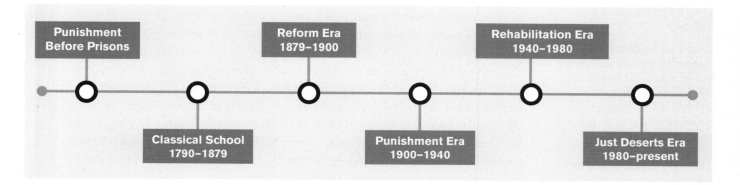

Punishment Before Prisons

Classical School 1790–1879

Reform Era 1879–1900

Punishment Era 1900–1940

Rehabilitation Era 1940–1980

Just Deserts Era 1980–present

The stocks (depicted above) and pillory were one of the early forms of colonial corporal punishment.

© Bettmann/Corbis

corporal punishment: A form of physical punishment intended to inflict pain as a means of retribution for an offense.

stocks and pillories: Punishment devices used before prisons; stocks sat low to the ground and locked a person's ankles in place, forcing the person to remain in an upright position, whereas pillories locked a person's neck and wrists into place, forcing the individual to remain standing.

or gaols (pronounced "jails"), where individuals who could not pay their debts were incarcerated at night and performed hard labor during the day to pay off their debts. In England, the need for cheap labor to perform often strenuous and hazardous tasks grew in the 16th and 17th centuries; thus, imprisonment at the oars of ships or in the mines became a common means of punishment.[4] Eventually oar-driven ships were replaced by wind- and steam-driven ships, and many of the older ships became prison hulks sitting in dock along the Thames River.[5] Abandoned mines also became penitentiaries for criminals during this time. In addition to the use of old ships and mines as prisons during these two centuries, England also employed the death penalty, corporal punishment, and eventually the transportation of criminals to the colonies as the most common means of dealing with the crime problem.

The system of corrections in the British colonies in America was supposed to be a direct application of the system of punishment used in England. However, punishment quickly became dependent on each colony's adaptation of the English code of law.[6] Most punishment for petty crimes consisted of forms of **corporal punishment**. Typical types of punishment consisted of whipping, branding, and confinement to either the pillory or the stocks.[7] The sentences were carried out in public view—often in a carnival atmosphere. The purpose was twofold: to punish the offender and to deter others. These types of punishment were only for persons committing minor offenses.[8] However, "neither in theory nor in practice was colonial law very bloodthirsty," and sentences were often commuted or punishment was minimized.[9]

The use of the whipping post was quite common throughout the colonies, but it was especially prevalent in the Delaware colony.[10] In one particular county, Sussex, the whipping post was painted red and called "Red Hannah." An example of its use was against Agnieta Hendriks, who was given 27 lashes on April 3, 1769, for the crime of giving birth to three "bastard" children. She proved unrepentant for her ways and was convicted in November 1780 for having another child out of wedlock. She was then given the punishment of 37 lashes and a five-year banishment from the community.

Although the whipping post was found throughout many of the colonies, it was the **stocks and pillories** that were perhaps the most common means of corporal punishment. The stocks were wooden boards with two holes through which to put the prisoner's feet, whereas the pillory forced the prisoner to stand with his or her head and arm through holes in wooden boards (most people mix up the terms). Any number of crimes ended in confinement in the village square in one or the other for hours, days, or, on some occasions, weeks. These were often painful forms of punishment and humiliating in that everyone in the village would see the individual on display and could taunt, jeer, or throw spoiled vegetables at the prisoner.

A common punishment throughout the colonies at the time was the branding of an adulterer with the letter "A" on the forehead. Other letters were also used, to identify various transgressions.[11] A thief would often be branded with a "T" and a drunkard with the letter "D." In the East Jersey Codes of 1668 and 1675, it was mandated that a letter "T" be branded on the hand for someone sentenced for burglary, that an "R" be branded on the forehead if the person was convicted for a second offense, and, of course, that the scarlet letter "A" be used for adultery.[12]

Other forms of punishment found in the early colonial period included the "ducking stool," whereby an individual would be tied to a chair and immersed under water, or "carting," whereby an individual was tied to the back of a wagon and dragged through the streets.[13] Another means of punishment was the "dame's bridle" or the "gossip's helm," typically used to punish people (mostly women) for such crimes as gossiping, scolding, or witchcraft. The bridle was a metal frame that went around the head with a metal spike that entered the mouth over the tongue. If the person spoke, the spike would spear the tongue and cause pain. In addition, iron masks or iron collars were used on an individual while he or she was chained to a wall. In some cases, the punishment was **banishment** from the community, which in most instances meant a sentence of death, because of the environment and distance from other villages. Another possible sentence was death itself.[14]

For more serious crimes, generally defined as an offender's being unable to pay his or her debts, the individual would be sentenced to debtor's prison. In fact, there were so many debtors during the colonial era that "one historian has estimated that the Americans owed English merchants almost 6 million pounds on the eve of the revolution."[15] If the criminals were not punished through corporal methods or with debtor's prison, they would mostly likely be hung for their crimes. Property crimes such as counterfeiting and larceny, as well rape, robbery, and murder, would often result in death by hanging.

AUTHOR VIDEO
History of Punishment

BEYOND A REASONABLE DOUBT 12.2

The _____ forced the prisoner to stand with his or her head and arms through holes in wooden slats.

(a) Stocks, (b) Pillory, (c) Post, (d) Time out stand, (e) None of the above

The answer can be found on page 522.

Classical School Era (1790–1879)

The Enlightenment of the late 18th century led the way for a reexamination of the factors related to crime and punishment. A little known Italian by the name of Cesare Beccaria published a book in 1764 titled *Dei Delitti E Delle Pene (On Crimes and Punishments)*, which generated dialogue for reforming the penitentiary system.[16] Previously, religion was the only lens through which people understood crime and punishment. Beccaria presented a system, which came to be known as the Classical School (see Chapter 5), based on the concept of a *contractual society*. According to Beccaria's system, for people to live in relative peace, they must give up some of their liberties to the government so that criminal laws may be established and offenders may

banishment: The act of forcing a member of a community to leave and never return as a means of punishment for some offense.

be punished. These laws must come from the legislature. The role of the judge in a criminal case is simply to mete out justice. The guiding principles for a justice system should be the presumption of innocence and the protection of the rights of all parties involved. In terms of punishments, then, Beccaria wrote that they should be based on retribution for the harm done to the individual, proportionate to the seriousness of the crime, and prompt and certain. Ultimately, Beccaria believed that the purpose of criminal law was to prevent crimes, rather than to punish them.

Once America became independent from England, corporal punishment practices were abandoned and the death penalty was minimized. However, this left the need for an alternative. In 1786, the Pennsylvania legislature took the first step by authorizing funds to build a prison that allowed "the courts to inflict solitary confinement in a cell during day and night, upon those guilty of capital crimes."[17] As a result, the Walnut Street Jail became the first jail in the United States that used confinement as a punishment rather than as a means of pretrial detention. In 1790, the Pennsylvania legislature changed the Walnut Street Jail from a county jail to a state penitentiary, complicating the management of the prison. Difficulties arose in keeping prisoners isolated, sharing costs between the state and local governments, and, of course, handling overcrowding.[18]

The Walnut Street Jail became the model jail in America. Alcohol was banned from the jail, women and debtors were separated into their own building, children were separated from adults, meals were improved, and an infirmary was opened. Inmates were put to work, rather than sitting around idle; those who were apprentices on the outside were encouraged to continue their trades; and in 1798 a prison school was established. In addition, the head jailor was placed on salary, thus eliminating the old system of the jailor collecting "fees" from the inmates. Moreover, a **classification system** was created in 1797, which determined the danger each inmate posed to other inmates and society and thus separated them based on these categories. Finally, a board of inspectors was established to inspect the prisons. As a result, the Walnut Street Jail improved dramatically from its previous poor conditions.

Like all prisons, however, the Walnut Street Jail fell victim to a number of problems. In 1797, several inmates protested their conditions by setting fire to the building that housed the prison industry programs. As a result, the inmates remained idle for a number of years, thus contributing to more violent encounters among them. In addition, the popularity of sentencing offenders to the Walnut Street Jail increased, and the jail became grossly overcrowded.[19] This created difficulties in keeping the offenders separated by age, and

This photo, from 1907, shows two offenders in a pillory and one tied to a whipping post.

© George Grantham Bain Collection

GOAL, in Walnut Street PHILADELPHIA.

Walnut Street Jail was the first jail in the United States to use confinement as a punishment rather than as a form of pretrial detention.

© William Birch and Son

gender, and seriousness of crime. It also became difficult to keep the jail clean and orderly. In fact, the debtor's quarters had become so overcrowded and filthy that the board of inspectors made repeated requests for the city magistrates to stop sending vagrants to the Walnut Street Jail because they could not be adequately fed, clothed, or housed. By the turn of the century, the Walnut Street Jail was on a downward spiral that continued with each successive year. In 1820, a riot by over 200 inmates inside the jail forced armed citizens to climb over the walls and surround the offenders; ultimately, the state militia had to quell the riot.

Western Penitentiary housed inmates in solitary confinement.

WordPress

At the turn of the century, the Pennsylvania Prison Society realized that the Walnut Street Jail was overcrowded. In 1803, it made a plea to the Pennsylvania legislature to construct a new facility to accommodate the increasing number of inmates. The society argued that when the jail had been built, it was not designed to conform to either the concepts of **solitary confinement** or for prison industry and that a new prison could be built with these ideas in mind. The legislature later authorized the appropriations to build two new penitentiaries. In 1817, it appropriated $60,000 to build a penitentiary in western Pennsylvania, and in 1821, it appropriated $100,000 to build a penitentiary in eastern Pennsylvania. Although the money to build the Western Penitentiary was allocated in 1817 and the funds to build the Eastern Penitentiary were allocated in 1821, the two penitentiaries did not open until 1826 and 1829, respectively.

According to Gustave de Beaumont and Alexis de Tocqueville, writing in 1833,

> The principles to be followed in the construction of these two establishments were, however, not entirely the same as those on which the Walnut Street prison had been erected. In the latter, classification formed the predominant system, to which solitary confinement was secondary. In the new prisons the classifications were abandoned, and a solitary cell was to be prepared for each convict. The criminal was not to leave his cell day and night, and all labor was denied to him in his solitude. Thus absolute solitary confinement, which in Walnut Street was but accidental, was now to become the foundation of the system adopted for Pittsburgh (the Western Penitentiary) and Cherry-Hill (the Eastern Penitentiary).[20]

The penitentiary system in the United States had become the standard practice. The Western Penitentiary was built near Pittsburgh and opened in 1826. It was intended to house inmates from the western portion of the state. The prison emphasized solitary confinement and consisted of 190 individual cells that were very small and dark. Later, a debate within the legislature ensued, and it was decided that the prisoners would be required to perform hard labor. The only problem was that by the time the legislature

classification system: The method by which prisons separate offenders, especially based on categories of sex, crime type, and dangerousness.

solitary confinement: A type of incarceration in which a prisoner is sentenced to his or her own cell so as to have no other contact with the other inmates and only limited contact with corrections officers.

Like Western Penitentiary, Eastern Peniteniary housed inmates in solitary confinement.

Adam Jones

made its decision, the prison already had been built. It was not designed for inmates to perform labor in their cells and, as a result, inmates had to be brought together during the day to perform their labor. Not being satisfied with this setting, the legislature appropriated additional funds to build new cells that would allow for inmates to labor in solitary confinement. These larger cells were built, but the prison organization had already become accustomed to bringing the inmates together to labor, so prison officials never fully instituted the new system.

The Eastern Penitentiary, which opened in 1829, was built in a cherry orchard, so it has often been referred to as the "Cherry Hill Penitentiary."[21] As a result of the prison's Philadelphia location, the Pennsylvania legislature appointed several members of the Philadelphia Prison Society to oversee its construction by placing them on the board of commissioners. This allowed for the construction of the prison to conform to the ideas of the reformers from the very beginning and not to repeat the "mistakes" of the Western Penitentiary. For example, the Eastern Penitentiary was constructed so that the cells were large enough for the inmates to labor in solitary confinement. A typical inmate would be brought into the prison and placed in a cell in solitary confinement with no rations available to him. After a few days or weeks of this lifestyle, if the inmate had not requested work, prison officials would ask if he wanted work. Almost invariably inmates would request work, and then they were taught the trade they would practice in their cells. The inmates remained in solitary confinement and had no contact with other inmates, but they were allowed to have visitors on occasion.

The Eastern Penitentiary quickly fell victim to the problems found in the Walnut Street Jail. Even so, it was becoming renowned for its ability to "control prisoners and its humanity." The system used in the Eastern Penitentiary became widely known as the **Pennsylvania system**, as it was fast becoming contrasted to the **New York system** in the late 1820s and early 1830s.[22] New York, facing similar problems to Pennsylvania, had opened a prison in Auburn. The Auburn prison was built very much on the same philosophy as the Pennsylvania prisons: Keep offenders separated, have them adhere to strict silence, and generally keep them isolated under all conditions. The difference, however, was in how the prison industry worked. Whereas the Pennsylvania system kept inmates isolated in their cells during the day, the New York system allowed the prisoners to come together, under strict silence, and labor alongside one another. However, it was the inward difference that perhaps mattered most. The Pennsylvania system was built with the Quaker religion in mind. A part of this religion was the belief that people could change, that they could be reformed and therefore become productive citizens. The New York system, by contrast, was not constructed with any specific religious principles in mind, and those running the prison were less inclined to believe anyone could be reformed. As a result, the Pennsylvania

Pennsylvania system: The prison system in which inmates were kept in solitary confinement, even during hard labor.

New York system: The system of penitentiaries which confined inmates to their cells at night, but brought them together to work communally during the day.

system was aimed at reform, while the New York system was largely about punishment. The Pennsylvania system became known for its separate labor system, and the New York system became known for its silent system.

A number of other penitentiaries were built and opened during this time. Maryland and Massachusetts opened theirs in 1829, and Tennessee and Vermont followed in 1831.[23] The next year, Georgia and New Hampshire opened their penitentiaries, and "between 1834 and 1837 Louisiana and Missouri built penitentiaries, as did Ohio and New Jersey."[24] Going into the early 1840s, Mississippi, Alabama, Michigan, Indiana, and Illinois opened theirs. As soon as the penitentiaries opened, however, they began to face problems of overcrowding and discipline issues and often resorted to corporal punishment to deal with the problems of discipline. The prison system of the Classical School Era was badly in need of reform.

Reform Era (1879–1900)

Some reform-minded individuals were aware of the growing problem with America's penitentiary system.[25] Enoch Cobb Wines, a former college president and minister who was appointed secretary of the New York Prison Association in 1862, and Theodore Dwight, a member of the New York elite and first president of the Columbia School of Law, were among the first to point out the need for sweeping reforms. They visited 15 penitentiaries, 16 reform schools, and numerous jails throughout the northern United States and into Canada and conducted a survey of 45 prison wardens.

Auburn Prison followed the same practice of isolating inmates from one another. But unlike the prisons in Pennsylvania, inmates spent the days in hard labor working with one another.

© Photo Archives online by Eastern Kentucky University

Wines and Dwight found the penitentiary system in the United States to be very poor. They commended several institutions for their prison systems, such as the Massachusetts penitentiary system, and the individual work of people such as Zebulon R. Brockway at the Detroit House of Corrections. Overwhelmingly, though, they found the prisons to be poorly run and poorly maintained.

In 1867, other like-minded reformers began discussing how they could advance their ideas for penitentiary reform. Wines organized the National Congress on Penitentiary and Reformatory Discipline, which met in Cincinnati, Ohio, in 1870. Rutherford B. Hayes, the governor of Ohio and future U.S. president, was the meeting's official chairman. Delegates from 24 states, totaling 237 participants and consisting of wardens, judges, and prison reform advocates, attended. The only three states that did not send delegates were North Carolina, South Carolina, and Tennessee.

The congress issued a declaration of principles, which consisted of 37 tenets of penal reform and became the cornerstone of the prison reform movement. It also drafted a charter to establish the National Prison Association, which was incorporated in New York in 1871, with Wines as its first secretary. To give the association some credibility and visibility, the association's organizers asked Hayes to serve as its leader.

Created in 1876, the Elmira reformatory was known for its emphasis on reform rather than punishment.

© Douglas Grundy/Three Lions/Getty Images

The most notable reform that came out of the National Prison Association's calls for improvement was the opening of the Elmira Adult Reformatory in New York. The governor of New York had read and supported Wines and Dwight's *Report on the Prisons and Reformatories of the United States and Canada* and asked the New York legislature to appropriate funds for the building of a new reformatory. The legislature approved the appropriations, and as the Elmira reformatory went into the building phase, it was able to incorporate a number of the recommendations from the National Congress on Penitentiary and Reformatory Discipline's declaration of principles. The intent of the Elmira reformatory was to incorporate the indeterminate sentence, whereby judges based sentencing decisions on individual circumstances an industrial education process and a form of postrelease supervision to assist inmates in transferring from the reformatory back to the community. The person chosen to lead the Elmira reformatory was an individual who had been at the forefront of the call for reforms, Zebulon R. Brockway.

Brockway's 1876–1900 tenure as the superintendent of the Elmira reformatory marked a new beginning in the prison reform movement. Brockway was instrumental in putting into place a three-stage system for prisoners. The incoming prisoner would be interviewed in order to determine two things: the reason for his past crimes and deviance and the education level and work to which he was best suited. In the second stage, the prisoner would exist in a very regimented system that focused on his academic and industrial education. This regimen would occur six days a week; on Sunday the prisoners would attend church, which was mandatory, and rest. In the third stage, the prisoner would be required to secure a job in the community before he was able to be paroled. Once released and under parole, the individual would be required to follow specific rules and would be supervised. Any violations of the parole would result in the individual's returning to the Elmira reformatory.

Brockway used a simple **mark system** to classify prisoners. The prisoners would begin in the middle or "second" grade, and then their behavior would determine their movement either up to first grade or down to third grade. Third-grade prisoners were treated with little respect and strong discipline. They wore red uniforms, were moved about in lockstep, and had almost no privileges. Second-grade prisoners had a limited number of privileges, wore typical prisoner garb, and had access to some of the prison's offerings. First-grade prisoners had the most privileges: They received better food, could send and receive mail daily, and had the rights of extended hours at bedtime and in the library. Once in the first grade, if a prisoner continued exhibiting good behavior and earned enough credits, then after six months the individual could go before the parole board. If the individual was approved for parole and could find a position in the community, he

mark system: A simple classification system that gave prisoners rewards (marks) for good behavior, which were associated with more freedoms in prison.

would move into the third stage of the Elmira reformatory's system. This system of rewards and punishments and the movement toward reform through various stages became known as the *Elmira system*, and Brockway ultimately received credit for the implementation and advancement of the indeterminate sentence under this system. Although this system marked the beginning of the *reformatory movement*, it was not until the last quarter of the 19th century that it began to spread rapidly as the preferred method of penology.

As a result of these and other innovations, the Elmira reformatory was regarded as the most advanced prison in the world, and visitors came from all over to observe and study the reformatory's practices.[26] Elmira's success resulted in the construction of other reformatories across the country, including those in Michigan (1877), Colorado (1890), and Wisconsin (1899). All of this led to Brockway's election as the president of the National Prison Association in 1897 and his recognition as the premier prison innovator of the late 19th century, whose influence lasted well into the 20th century.

The Elmira reformatory, despite its many innovations, reforms, and successes under Brockway, also faced many of the same problems that have plagued all prisons at one time or another: overcrowding, understaffing, and abuse.[27] In 1893, the New York State Board of Charities investigated complaints of abuse by former inmates of the Elmira reformatory. The specific charges were directed not only against the staff of the reformatory but also at Brockway himself. He admitted the charges of beatings and solitary confinement, but he maintained that they caused no permanent harm and, therefore, did not rise to the level of brutality. The New York State Board of Charities issued its report in 1894 and alleged that brutality did exist within the reformatory, in part due to Brockway's management style. This set off political protest and caused the governor of New York to appoint a committee to investigate the allegations.

The committee issued its report, stating that the allegations were unfounded. Controversy continued to surround the Elmira reformatory. In 1899, these continued allegations forced then-governor Theodore Roosevelt to appoint three new managers for the Elmira reformatory, whom he charged to investigate the complaints. These managers issued their report in early 1900, and their findings were similar to those of the New York State Board of Charities. In the end, several of Brockway's staff were fired, new reforms were recommended, and eventually, in July 1900, Brockway resigned.

Punishment Era (1900–1940)

Corrections, at the beginning of the 20th century, witnessed a continued growth in the building of new reformatories, although prison populations across the country remained stable.[28] This allowed for more people to be sentenced to prison, and with more inmates came more prison laborers who could be leased out to farmers and industries to work, while the prisons kept their wages. As a result, the focus remained on punishing offenders and not rehabilitating or treating them.

There were some attempts at reform during this period, such as the use of the *good-time laws*. Early in the 20th century, the movement was

While prison chain gangs still are used for certain types of manual labor, they are much less common today than they were in the past.

toward a parole system. Previously, certain inmates had earned early release through good behavior, but now all prisoners would reach a particular point in their prison sentences when they would be eligible for parole. The individual's penitentiary history would then be reviewed to determine whether the prisoner would be released early. Upon release, the individual on parole would usually become the responsibility of a local county or city probation office. Two of the earliest release systems were in California in 1909 and Wisconsin in 1913, when prisoners convicted of misdemeanors could be released from prison early on a sort of parole, by performing prison labor to complete the last one-fourth of their sentences.

In the South, the **convict leasing system** was on the decline in the last decade of the 19th century.[29] But a number of states delayed abolishing the practice. On one hand, the system paid for itself quite well and was both politically and economically beneficial to the government and prison, as well as to the business hiring the convict labor. On the other hand, the abusive conditions under which convicts worked and lived, coupled with the fact that obtaining labor from those imprisoned necessitated taking away a potential job from someone who was not, created a deplorable system. As more and more prison reform associations began to appear at the state level in such states as Georgia, Tennessee, and Virginia, the negatives of convict leasing were clearly starting to outweigh the benefits. The call for the abolition of the program grew, and more and more states abolished the practice. The question for wardens, however, was what to do with the inmates now that they were no longer being leased.

Initially, the answer was to return to the older practice of local farming by having the prisoners grow the food that would feed them, thus cutting costs in running and maintaining the prison. This would quickly grow into larger farms whereby the produce could be sold on the market and at a profit, allegedly to be used for running the prison. As a result, the new prison industry of southern **prison plantations** was born. Prisoners became agricultural workers, growing fruits and vegetables, as well as cotton.

In addition to the southern prison plantations, another movement from the convict leasing program was to "lease" the prisoners for state projects. A key allegation that triggered calls for reform consisted of abolishing this relationship with private business. This resulted in the birth of the *state-use system*, whereby prison labor was acceptable if it was being used for the construction of public projects. Clearly the biggest project for prison labor at the beginning of the 20th century was the construction of new roads. Prisoners were chained together and worked during the day, clearing land and constructing roads. Thus was born the *chain gang*. By the end of the Progressive Era, prisons from 20 states were using chain gangs of prisoners to build roads.[30]

Corrections during this era also began to witness more changes in terms of prison construction and reforms, only to be hit hard by the Great Depression. A spurt of prison construction came about in

convict leasing system: A system whereby penitentiaries, for a small fee, leased out prisoners to labor in factories and fields.

prison plantations: Prisons that had inmates farm the surrounding lands to provide food for the prisoners; excess food was sold to run the prison.

the 1920s and continued into the 1930s, creating large prisons often referred to as the "big house." These huge new prisons were being built in Jackson, Michigan; San Quentin, California; Stateville, Illinois; as well as in other towns across the country. These prisons, which could hold thousands of inmates, were built with industrial labor in mind, and assembly lines were constructed for inmate labor. However, as a result of the Great Depression, prison industry ground to a halt.

As the United States entered the Great Depression of the 1930s, Congress passed the Hawes-Cooper Act, which "divested prison products of their interstate character on arrival at destination, thus making them subject to state law."[31] This legislation allowed states to regulate the prison industry, and, as the country sank further into the Depression, the nation became far more hostile to prison labor, especially when there were similar jobs in the private sector. In 1935, with support from President Franklin D. Roosevelt's administration, Congress passed the **Ashurst-Sumners Act**, which prohibited any transportation company from transporting goods made in prison industries, effectively eliminating prison labor. After 1935, prisons returned to the old ways of simply warehousing prisoners, most of whom became idle.

Although the Depression curtailed prison industries, it did nothing to curtail the prison-building movement. One example of this movement can be found in Virginia's state penitentiary. Although opened in 1800, the prison had not been changed throughout the 19th century. In 1902, the inmates were authorized to build a new cellblock, which opened in 1905, but this was the limit of any reform until the 1960s. In 1925, plans were drawn up to change the structure of the Virginia penitentiary, and in 1928, the original building was demolished. The prisoners were moved to the cellblock that had opened in 1905, and new cellblocks were built, along with a women's cellblock and a new shop where inmates labored during the day.[32] Despite the Depression, and largely because of the rise in crime during the 1920s and 1930s, prison building and expansion were common during this era.

The federal government became heavily involved in prison construction in the late 1920s when it began building a women's penitentiary in Lewisburg, West Virginia, which opened in the early 1930s. The federal government also began building the famous Alcatraz prison in 1934. Located in the San Francisco Bay on an island made of rock, Alcatraz became known derisively as "the rock." It was built as a maximum-security prison to house inmates who either were at a high risk of escape or had attempted a previous

> **Ashurst-Sumners Act:** A Depression-era act (1935) that prohibited any transportation company from transporting goods made in prison industries, in order to eliminate prison labor.

Located in San Francisco Bay, Alcatraz Prison was created in 1934 to house maximum security inmates and inmates who tried to escape from other prisons. It closed in 1963 because it was too expensive to operate.

© Cameron Davidson/Corbis

escape. The average sentence on Alcatraz was only five years, and despite persistent rumors, there were neither torture chambers in the prison nor "man-eating" sharks in the waters surrounding it. Alcatraz was difficult to escape from because of its location so far from land and the frigid temperatures of the bay, which typically caused hypothermia before the escapee even made it halfway across. The two most famous prisoners of Alcatraz were Al Capone and Robert Stroud (the "Birdman of Alcatraz," who kept no birds on the rock). Although hailed as the most secure of prisons, Alcatraz was eventually shut down in 1963 because of its high operating expenses.

The federal government created the Bureau of Prisons in 1930, which had its operational control under the U.S. Department of Justice. Sanford Bates, a well-known advocate for advancing the field of corrections, was originally hired in 1926 to serve as the superintendent of federal prisons. When the Bureau of Prisons was created, President Herbert Hoover appointed Bates as its first director. At first, because the Bureau of Prisons was so far behind in running and maintaining facilities, it borrowed operational practices from state penitentiaries and applied them to its federal penitentiaries. Eventually, Bates was able to advance the federal prisons through such measures as the diagnosis and classification of offenders and the use of psychologists to determine both the capabilities of inmates and their needs for treatment and rehabilitation (see the "Criminal Justice Pioneer" box in this chapter).

BEYOND A REASONABLE DOUBT 12.3

The _____ Act prohibited any transportation company from transporting goods made in prison industries, effectively eliminating prison labor.

(a) Hawes-Cooper, (b) Ashurst-Sumners, (c) Antitrust, (d) Great Depression, (e) All of the above

---

The answer can be found on page 522.

Rehabilitation Era (1940–1980)

The post–World War II era witnessed renewed reforms. The postwar reforms, which were largely the result of "a combination of forces— including a growing willingness on the part of the state to commit fiscal resources, the rising importance of humanitarian rhetoric and human-rights language following the Holocaust, a relatively low crime rate during the 1950s, and the prestige of the social sciences—led to expanded efforts to achieve rehabilitation within prisons."[33] Prisoners began to receive some therapeutic treatment, were given access to libraries, and were able to enroll in education programs. In addition, several of the new prisons being built, like Soledad Prison in California, began to look less like penitentiaries and more like modern high schools. Finally, many prisoners began to assert their individual rights, and the prisoners' rights movement was beginning to form during the 1950s and would come to fruition in the 1960s.

SANFORD BATES

Sanford Bates was born July 17, 1884, in Boston, Massachusetts. After being recognized as a capable administrator, Bates was appointed the first commissioner of the Massachusetts Department of Correction by Governor Calvin Coolidge in 1919. After almost 10 years as commissioner, Bates helped establish two new juvenile delinquent institutions and sponsored progressive legislation. He also was influential in the establishment of the largest Massachusetts prison colony at Norfolk.

In 1929, Bates accepted a job in Washington, D.C., as superintendent of federal prisons. With the establishment of the federal Bureau of Prisons in 1930, Bates's title was changed to director. As director of the Bureau of Prisons, Bates supported prisoner rehabilitation and penal reform. Fifteen new federal prison institutions became part of the bureau under Bates, and he worked to establish social work facilities and prison libraries.

In 1936, Bates wrote *Prisons and Beyond*, which was a detailed framework on prison reform and administrative technique. By 1940, he had become the head of the New York state parole system, and then in 1945 he became commissioner of institutions and agencies for New Jersey. While in New Jersey, he oversaw construction of a state mental hospital and a nursery for special needs children, and he introduced plans for a new 1,200-bed penitentiary.

Significantly, Bates was involved with international corrections and was a liaison on behalf of the United States at several foreign conferences. He was appointed as delegate to the International Prison Congress in 1925 and represented the United States on the International Prison Commission in 1932. From 1946 to 1951, Bates served as president of the International Penal and Penitentiary Congress, and in 1951, he was a member of the UN Commission on Crime Prevention. He was appointed official delegate to the UN Conference on Crime held in London in 1960.

Sanford Bates was the first director of the U.S. Bureau of Prisons.

© Repository: Library of Congress Prints and Photographs Division

Bates retired in 1954 but continued working as a corrections consultant for many state and federal correctional agencies. He worked as special consultant to the War Department, the American Bar Association, and the American Law Institute. Bates became special assistant to the President's Commission on Crime and Law Enforcement in 1966.

With his extensive knowledge and experience in criminal justice, Bates became known as the "Dean of American Corrections." From prisoner rehabilitation to progressive juvenile delinquent treatment, Sanford Bates helped frame the modern correctional field.

Adapted from Shotwell, T. (2013). Sanford Bates collection, 1906–1972, Thomason Special Collection & Sam Houston State University Archives. Retrieved from https://archon.shsu.edu/?p=collections/findingaid&id=2&q=

The American correctional system passed from one corrections philosophy to another during the 1960s. This was due largely to the many social changes occurring at that time.[34] As the United States entered the nationalization era, the correctional philosophy was still one of rehabilitation, as it had been for most of the 20th century. However, the new philosophy that began to take hold in the early 1960s argued that correctional agencies entered "an era of reintegration," in which the philosophy was to move prisoners back into society through various programs. The focus of this movement was for corrections to "be advocates for offenders."[35] Although rehabilitation programs were still being advocated during the 1960s, a number of reforms marked the reintegration movement.

Just Deserts Era (1980–Present)

As the United States had to deal with an increase in crime in the 1960s and 1970s, presidents and governors, beginning in the early 1970s, saw the building of more prisons as the answer to the growing crime problem. During the 1970s, funds were allocated, plans were made, and prisons began to be built. This trend continued unchecked throughout the 1980s and 1990s, as more and more money was allocated at the federal, state, and local levels for building more prisons and jails. Because of the continued increase in crime, prisons were overcrowded. Although this situation might have been alleviated somewhat in the early 1980s, the advent of the "war on drugs" meant that prisons began to fill with those convicted of everything from bringing drugs into the country, to dealing drugs in the cities, to simply being drug users. Convictions increased, and prison populations exploded. The building of prisons could not keep up. Prisons in states such as California and New York were operating at nearly double their capacity, and only a few states, such as Utah and North Dakota, were operating at even slightly less than capacity.

In the United States, approximately 700,000 individuals were serving time in prisons and jails at the federal, state, and local levels by the mid-1980s. Today, more than 2.2 million individuals serve time in prisons and jails. Despite the significant drop in crime beginning in the early 1990s, prisons continued to be built and inmate populations continued to rise. The most ignored fact of this rise is that, although most Americans believed that hardened criminals were the ones being sent to prison, most of the additional offenders were imprisoned for misdemeanors and a large portion of those were for minor drug offenses. Also, although most Americans thought that the new prisons would keep offenders locked up for longer periods of time, such as 20 years or more, most offenders served, on average, 5–7 years.

A confluence of factors contributed to the rise in inmate populations at a time when crime rates were declining. As a result of the perception that rehabilitation programs of the 1960s and 1970s had grossly failed, the public and politicians began to favor increased use of incarceration. In addition, career criminals, or *repeat offenders*, were targeted in the 1980s, and their sentences were longer than what many would have received if not for tougher standards on repeat offenses. These changes contributed to the passage of *three-strikes laws*, which are really a form

Rehabilitation programs exist in prisons across the United States, but the emphasis on rehabilitation today is much less than it was in the 1960s.

of determinate sentencing (see Chapter 11). In terms of sentencing, many states and the federal government reformulated their sentencing guidelines, restricting judges to formulas for meting out punishment, which tended to result in longer sentences than most judges would have prescribed on their own. Moreover, attempts at curtailing the use of plea bargaining contributed to more cases proceeding to trial and ultimately to more defendants being sentenced to prison. Mandatory sentencing for drug violations also contributed heavily to the increase in inmate populations in the United States.

Modern efforts to punish offenders very much reflect prevailing societal trends and innovations. The just deserts ideology supports punishment on the grounds that punishment is deserved. At the same time, technological innovations have altered the way that sanctions are administered, both in prisons and jails and outside in the community. The use of webcams to allow inmates to communicate with the outside world is an example of one such innovation (see the "Criminal Justice and the Media" box in this chapter).

➡ Structure of Corrections

Today's correctional facilities can be classified according to the security level of the institution (minimum, medium, maximum, and super-maximum, or supermax) or the level of government that runs the facility (federal, state, and

CRIMINAL JUSTICE and the **MEDIA:**
WEBCAMS AND PRISON VISITATION

Reflecting broader technological trends, some prisons are now allowing inmates to have "web visits" with family members, friends, and others. These visits are highly regulated and aim to strengthen ties between inmates and the community. Prisons vary in how they design the web visits. The Pinal County Sheriff's Office uses the following webcam procedures:

In an effort to encourage inmates/detainees to maintain contact and communication with their families and friends, regular visitation privileges are afforded to the PCSO and DHS/ICE populations. The Pinal County Sheriff's Office has recently launched a state-of-the-art web video visitation system known as iWebVisit.com.

Visitors are now able to conduct remote video visitation from your home, office or remote location over the Internet. You now can conduct an Internet Video Visit with inmates currently housed at the Pinal County Sheriff's Office by using a computer equipped with high-speed Internet and a webcam. This new technology "Remote Video Visitation" will offer increased remote visiting hours and visiting frequency with the convenience of seven-day availability.

The Pinal County Sheriff's Office is proud to offer this service and is dedicated to helping connect loved ones from around the world to those entrusted in our custody.

Services may be interrupted or suspended due to operational issues at the direction of the Sheriff or Chief Deputy of the Adult Detention Center (ADC). Discrimination on the basis of a disability or other protected classes is strictly prohibited. Onsite visitors shall check in upon entry and may be subject to search and/or canine barrier screening. All visits must be scheduled 24 hours in advance. You can schedule in person at the facility or online at iWebVisit.com.

Reprinted from Pinal County Sheriff's Office. (2014). Retrieved from http://www.pinalcountyaz.gov/sheriff/ad/pages/visitation.aspx.

local). In addition, the juvenile corrections system operates independently of the adult system.

Prison Types, by Security Level

Minimum-security prisons typically house low-risk, nonviolent, first-time offenders (such as white-collar criminals) who have been sentenced to shorter stays in the institution. These facilities also house inmates who have already served some time in a higher-security institution but are close to their release dates. Minimum-security prisons often have dormitory-style housing with fewer rules to govern inmate behavior. This gives the inmates more freedom of movement within the facility. Because these inmates are less "hardcore" (less likely to be career criminals), it is thought that they are more likely to be rehabilitated. Thus, many institutions provide treatment programs, educational options, and even jobs for the inmates. Visitors are a common sight at these buildings. These inmates are usually trusted by the guards and administration and are not seen as escape threats. Thus, many minimum-security facilities do not have armed guards or high walls with electric fences. The inmates are summoned to events and meals by bells.

Medium-security prisons hold both violent and nonviolent offenders at the same time. The institutions usually have high walls but few, if any, guard towers. Although most medium-security institutions have a common living area where the inmates can congregate or watch television, they have more rules that regulate inmate behavior. Medium-security facilities offer inmates fewer privileges, less freedom of movement, and fewer rehabilitative programs, compared with minimum-security institutions. Inmates also have fewer visitor privileges and less personal contact with those from the outside.

Maximum-security prisons are considered to have some of the most dangerous, high-risk, violent offenders, sometimes with a record of prior escape attempts. Thus, the buildings are constructed to discourage escape attempts. Their facilities often look like fortresses, with high walls, guard towers, and electric fencing or barbed wire. Most facilities are on a permanent state of lockdown whereby prisoners can leave their cells only if accompanied by a corrections officer or other prison employee. Video cameras throughout the institution monitor inmates' actions at all times. There are many rules to synchronize inmate behavior. Offenders have only minimal visitation privileges with few or no options for rehabilitative programs. Usually the inmates spend a great deal of time alone in their cells, each of which will have a built-in bed and desk with a metal sink and toilet. Examples of this kind of prison include Sing Sing and Attica in New York, Joliet and Stateville in Illinois, and Folsom and Alcatraz in California.

Supermax prisons provide a relatively new level of security for the worst prisoners. These inmates are violent and disruptive and are considered to be a danger to the facility staff and other inmates. Thus, they are allowed little human contact. They are housed in their cells for the majority of the day. If they must leave their cells, they are shackled and accompanied by a corrections officer. These inmates are considered to be beyond

---

minimum-security prisons: Correctional facilities that hold low-risk, nonviolent, first-time offenders; they provide dormitory-style housing and few rules to govern inmate behavior.

medium-security prisons: Correctional facilities with high walls but few, if any, guard towers and in which inmates are permitted to congregate, watch television, and take part in rehabilitative programs.

maximum-security prisons: High-security correctional facilities that hold some of the most dangerous, high-risk, violent offenders, some of whom have a record of prior escape attempts.

supermax prisons: Correctional facilities in which offenders, typically guilty of violent crimes, are confined in their cells for 23 hours each day and are not able to associate with other inmates.

the scope of rehabilitation, so these programs are typically nonexistent or limited in supermax prisons.

An example of a supermax prison is Pelican Bay, located on the California coast near the Oregon border. Opened in 1989, the prison has as its mission to hold California's "most serious criminal offenders in a secure, safe, and disciplined institutional setting."[36] The designed capacity of the institution is 2,280, yet it currently holds 2,700 potentially violent criminals. To manage the prison, the institution employees 1,054 custody staff and almost 500 support staff. Its annual budget is over $190 million.

Pelican Bay holds some inmates in a general population setting, but it also holds inmates in the Security Housing Unit (SHU), which is designed for inmates for whom there are serious management concerns, such as gang members and violent inmates. An electric fence surrounds the entire perimeter of this section of the prison. The cells of the SHU are approximately 8 feet × 10 feet. The walls are made of concrete and have no windows. Inmates are housed in their cells for at least 22 hours a day. Three meals a day are delivered to the inmates through a slot in the cell door. The "Help Wanted" box in this chapter lists the duties of one type of employee working in Pelican Bay.

All doors in the prison are electronically controlled by an armed corrections officer who sits in a central control booth. The officer allows one prisoner at a time to the shower area or to a court-mandated five hours of outdoor exercise each week in an area referred to as the "dog run."

There are some unique programs found within the prison. One is the Psychiatric Services Unit (PSU), designed to treat inmates who have mental disorders. Another is a minimum security support facility where nonviolent offenders are held outside of the tight security of the main prison. The prison also has a firehouse in which inmates serve as firefighters.

In addition to these programs, one prison industry is available for inmates at Pelican Bay. The California Prison Industry Authority oversees the laundry operation in the prison and employs approximately 18 inmates. This operation performs laundry services for the prison as well as for the Del Norte School District. The prison also operates a literacy program for inmates seeking a high school diploma or college-level courses through distance learning with local colleges. For those seeking career training, the prison has a Career Technical Education program that focuses on training inmates in computer literacy. Inmates who qualify have the option to work in the kitchen, as a groundskeeper, in the maintenance group, as clerks, or in other duties. Inmates with addiction problems can participate in support groups such as Alcoholics Anonymous and Narcotics Anonymous. Inmates who may be close to being released from prison are provided additional assistance through the Family Reunification Liaison, who helps inmates prepare for release into the community.

Some experts have criticized Pelican Bay as being cruel and unusual punishment for the harsh conditions and long periods of isolation and lack of contact with others. They report that these inmates are more likely to suffer from depression, anger, and suicide.[37]

HELP WANTED: PELICAN BAY COUNSELOR POSITION

DUTIES:

- Processes inmate marriage requests and correspondence course requests.
- Processes CDCR Form 1074, Request for Correspondence Approval.
- Documents inmate infractions on disciplinary reports.
- Processes inmate certified mail requests.
- Completes special projects as directed by the CCII.
- Interviews inmates and evaluates their adjustment and progress.
- Counsels inmates on personal, institutional, and family issues.
- Processes CDCR Form 193, Trust Withdrawal Orders.
- Makes a cell-by-cell caseload contact a minimum of two (2) times per month.
- Attends Annual Peace Officer Training (40 hours) and On the Job Training Module (12 hours).

- Attends mandatory training for Peace Officers and Correctional Counselors for new policy/procedures and/or revised policy/procedures, as they occur.
- Accesses DECS to determine whether the inmate has a disability and what, if any, accommodation is required.
- Ensures reasonable accommodations are afforded to inmates with disabilities (e.g., vision, speech, hearing impaired, non-English speaking, and learning disabled).
- Ensures equally effective communication during inmate general contacts and due process events.
- Provides direct and meaningful classification of inmates.

REQUIREMENTS: Bachelor's degree

ANNUAL SALARY: $5,033–$7,734

Adapted from USAJOBS.gov. Retrieved from http://jobs.spb.ca.gov/wvpos/more_info.cfm?recno=590777

CAREER VIDEO
Corrections Sargent

Prison Types, by Government Level

All levels of government (federal, state, and local) have some type of corrections systems, usually as part of the executive branch of the government. Federal facilities are responsible for holding people convicted of federal offenses such as major drug trafficking, bank robbery, or counterfeiting currency. State correctional facilities oversee offenders who committed state-level offenses such as car theft, assault, or murder. Local correctional institutions secure offenders who committed minor offenses or are awaiting trial.

Federal Prison System

The federal prison system is operated by the Bureau of Prisons, which is found within the U.S. Department of Justice. The bureau oversees all federal offenders who have been sentenced to a stay in a federal correctional facility. Inmates on probation or parole are overseen by the Administrative Office of the U.S. Courts.

The Bureau of Prisons was established on May 14, 1930. The first director, Sanford Bates, was appointed by President Herbert Hoover and was given the task of reorganizing the prison system that then existed, which comprised only 11 institutions. Those institutions housed some of the worst criminals in the nation and were severely overcrowded. Bates made the federal system much less corrupt and established standards for the institutions that would later be used by states as well.

Today, the Bureau of Prisons is responsible for operating 119 prisons across the country that house approximately 219,000 inmates. The Bureau of Prisons has eight divisions that assist in overseeing program areas and operations, including the National Institute of Corrections (see Figure 12.2). The bureau is located in Washington, D.C.

A breakdown of federal inmates shows that the majority of inmates (59.5%) are White, with an average age of 39 years. The majority (74.1%) are U.S. citizens. Most inmates are sentenced to serve between 5 and 10 years (see Figure 12.3), and most (46.8%) are there after being sentenced for drug offenses (see Figure 12.4).

Federal prisons are categorized into one of five security levels: ADMAX through minimum security, as described in the preceding section. The **ADMAX prison** is the supermax-style prison for the federal government. The federal government's only ADMAX prison, in Florence, Colorado, opened in 1995. This ultra-maximum-security prison is sometimes referred to as "the Alcatraz of the Rockies." It is designed to hold 575 inmates. The inmates in the facility are generally violent offenders

ADMAX prison: The super-maximum-security prison for the federal government.

FIGURE 12.2   Bureau of Prisons Organizational Chart

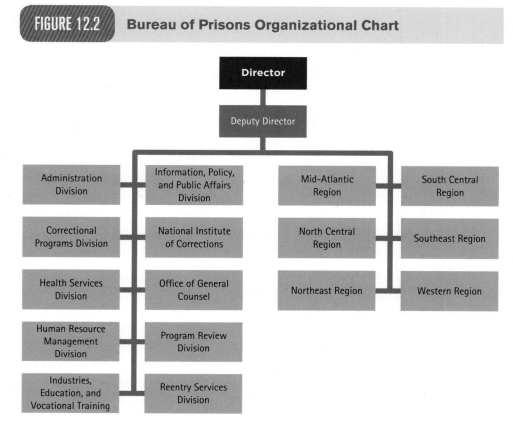

Federal Bureau of Prisons

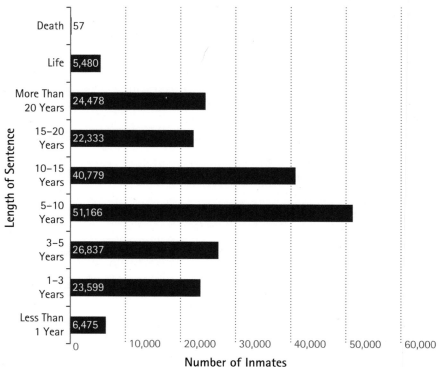

Federal Bureau of Prisons

(sometimes high-profile offenders) who have been convicted of federal offenses such as organized crime or terrorism. The inmates are confined in their cells for 23 hours per day and are not able to associate with other inmates in the facility. After a period of time, it is hoped that the inmates can be moved to a section of the prison that has less security. Corrections officers there use electronic controls to operate the heavy steel doors found in the prison. The doors can be sectioned off in the event of a riot or other emergency. Closed-circuit television provides inmates with exercise classes, educational classes, or religious services broadcast into their cells. Some famous inmates housed in Florence include Theodore Kaczynski (the "Unabomber"), Robert Hanssen (an FBI agent who spied for the Soviets), Terry Nichols (who took part in the Oklahoma City bombing), and Richard Reid (the "shoe bomber").

High-security (maximum-security) federal prisons are referred to as *U.S. penitentiaries*. Their main goal is security. Thus, there are secured perimeters and few rehabilitation programs for the inmates, who are in secure environments with little freedom of movement. Medium-security federal prisons are called *federal correctional institutions*. They have electronic fences but a lower ratio of guards to inmates. The third tier of federal prisons are the federal **prison camps** (sometimes called "Club Fed"), which hold nonviolent offenders who are not considered to be prone to escape. These inmates have more freedom of movement and live

prison camps: Minimum- and low-security federal correctional facilities that have few guards with limited fences; they hold nonviolent offenders who are not considered to be escape threats.

FIGURE 12.4 **Federal Inmates by Offense Type, 2014**

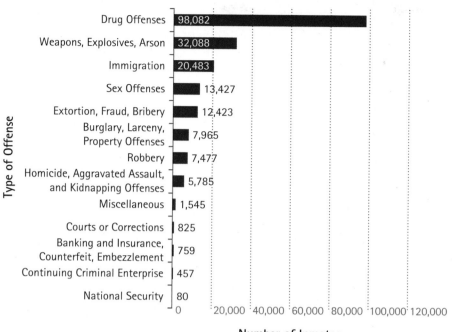

Federal Bureau of Prisons

in dormitory-style housing (see the "Criminal Justice and College Students" box in this chapter).

Another type of federal prison is called an *administrative facility*. These facilities have special missions and are designed to house inmates from all security categories. Usually these institutions serve as jails for the federal system and are usually found in large cities near the courthouse. Some facilities hold inmates who are awaiting a federal trial, whereas others serve as medical centers for prisoners who need serious medical attention.

CRIMINAL JUSTICE and **COLLEGE STUDENTS**

CLUB FED OR CLUB DREAD?

It is commonly suggested that some prisons are "too lenient" on offenders or "too nice" for prisons. One prison in South Dakota, the Mike Durfee State Prison, was a former college campus that was converted to a state prison. The prison maintained the college's open environment, but make no mistake about it, the prison was truly a prison and not a college campus after the transition.

Think of a college campus that you are familiar with. Could that campus be converted into a prison? List three aspects of the campus that would make it similar to a prison. Next, consider whether you would want to be confined to that campus for a year or more, with limited contact with the outside world. Would you feel as if you were spending time in a country club or a prison? Explain. Share your answers with a small group of classmates.

In addition to the traditional prison settings, the Bureau of Prisons oversees inmates sentenced to community corrections facilities. In some cases, the federal government contracts with residential reentry centers (or *halfway houses*) to house inmates who are close to their release dates. This enables offenders to reintegrate into society slowly. In the halfway house, staff will help inmates find employment, offer them financial advice, and provide other services that will help offenders establish contacts within the community. It is hoped that offenders will be able to transition into the community more easily and be less likely to commit more crime.

Thousands of federal inmates are housed in these different levels of institutions. The number of federal inmates has grown each year over the past 10 years, to a current level of just under 200,000 inmates (see Figure 12.5).

BEYOND A REASONABLE DOUBT 12.4

The federal prison system is operated by the _____.

(a) Federal Bureau of Investigation, (b) Bureau of Justice Assistance, (c) Department of Federal Punishment, (d) Federal Bureau of Prisons, (e) All of the above

---

The answer can be found on page 522.

State Corrections

Each state has developed its own system for holding convicted offenders, so the organization and operation of the facilities varies from state to state. There is also variation in the security types, the sizes of the institutions (and the populations), money allocated, and the services provided to inmates. However, the administration of the prisons in each state is part of the state's executive branch. Moreover, most states have an agency or bureaucracy that

VIDEO
Prison State

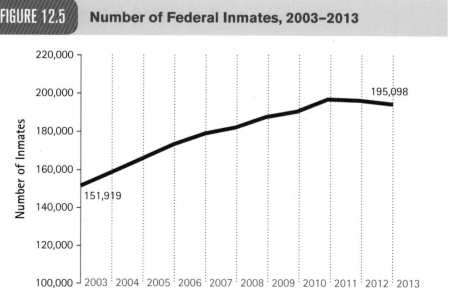

FIGURE 12.5   **Number of Federal Inmates, 2003–2013**

The U.S. Department of Justice, Office of Justice Programs, Bureau of Justice Statistics

is devoted to overseeing the state institutions and the treatment of inmates within those institutions. For example, in Arkansas, there is a Department of Correction, which consists of five divisions, including the Administrative Services Division, Construction and Maintenance Division, Health and Correctional Programs Division, Institutions Division, and Operations Division. State-level institutions hold inmates convicted of state-level offenses such as murder, assault, car theft, domestic violence, or sex offenses.

The number of inmates held in state prisons is presented in Figure 12.6. The state inmate population continued to grow until 2009, after which the number of inmates started to decline. Louisiana has far more inmates per 100,000 residents than any other state (see Figure 12.7). The states with the next highest incarceration rates are Oklahoma, followed by Mississippi and Alabama. The states with the lowest incarceration rates are Minnesota and Maine.

As a way to save money, some states have contracted with private corporations to house their prisoners. Sometimes, these private corporations will finance and build a facility and then contract with the state's correctional authorities to provide services. The private companies claim that they are able to build and run their prison facilities as effectively and humanely as the state but at a lower cost to taxpayers. Some can even run the prisons at a profit. The two companies most likely to run these prisons are the Corrections Corporation of America (CCA) and the GEO Group (formerly Wackenhut Corrections Corporation).

Some observers express fears that companies that run correctional facilities for profit will cut corners and in the end provide poor services to inmates or even inadequate security. It is thought that the companies will accept more inmates than they should, provide fewer services, and even have fewer guards. Nonetheless, the number of private facilities (both confinement facilities and community-based facilities) has increased in recent years. See the "Ethical Decision Making" box in this chapter for an illustration of the issues that might arise for private prisons.

FIGURE 12.6 **Number of State Inmates, 2003–2013**

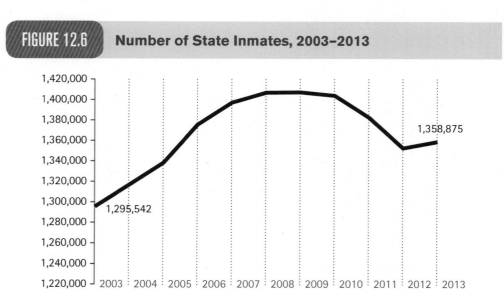

The U.S. Department of Justice, Office of Justice Programs, Bureau of Justice Statistics

FIGURE 12.7 Incarceration Rate by State

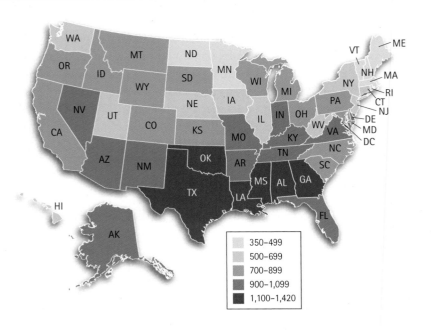

350–499
500–699
700–899
900–1,099
1,100–1,420

Local Corrections

In addition to federal and state corrections, there are also local-level correctional facilities. Most of the county-level corrections systems are

ETHICAL DECISION MAKING

PRIVATE PRISONS

Roberto Damien was appointed judge after a successful career as a prosecutor. After a few months on the bench, he went fishing with Bill Jameson, a former college roommate. Jameson is the CEO of a private prison company that houses prisoners for the state.

"How is business?" Damien asks Jameson.

"Why don't you tell me?" Jameson quips back.

"Well it seems to me like we are sending fewer people to prison," Damien remarks. "I don't know if demographic changes have made this happen, or if evidence-based practices are paying off, but I have seen a difference."

Hinting that he wants the judge to sentence more offenders to prison, Jameson responds, "When you needed campaign money for your prosecutor elections, you remember that I was your biggest contributor, right?"

"What are you getting at?" asks Damien.

YOU DECIDE

1. Should the judge continue in this conversation? Why or why not?

2. What factors influence judges' sentencing decisions?

jails that operate under the authority of cities, counties, or towns, but they can also be administered by law enforcement agencies such as the county sheriff. Most often, jails hold offenders who have been convicted of low-level misdemeanors and sentenced to terms of under one year. They also hold pretrial detainees who cannot post bail, those already found guilty in a trial but awaiting the sentencing phase, and probationers and parolees who have broken the terms of their release. In some places, jails hold juveniles who are pending a transfer to a juvenile facility, or state offenders if the prisons are overcrowded. Usually the inmate turnover in these facilities is high since so many of them are being held temporarily or for such short periods. The typical activities of jail personnel are depicted in many television shows, such as *Jail* and *Lockup*.

Juvenile Corrections Facilities

Juveniles who have been found guilty of criminal offenses will be punished in a way that is commensurate with their offenses. Typically, first-time offenders or those who commit status offenses will be placed on probation or diverted to a placement outside of the criminal justice system. In this case, juveniles will remain in the home (sometimes under electronic monitoring) but be required to meet specific conditions such as attending school or counseling sessions. They may be required to fulfill community service hours as part of their punishment.

Young people who commit more severe crimes may be placed in residential programs run by probation departments or social service agencies, such as group homes. Here, juveniles must meet certain conditions similar to those required of juveniles placed on probation. However, they have more freedom to be in the community.

Another option for juvenile corrections pertains to those who are repeat offenders or who commit serious offenses. These facilities, called training schools, are more like adult facilities. Juveniles in these settings have limited freedom and are required to participate in programs designed to treat or rehabilitate them. Moreover, these juveniles often are required to participate in aftercare programs to help them readjust to the community.

VIDEO
Kid in Jail

➡ Actors in Corrections

Although many actors are pivotal to the successful operations of prisons, wardens and corrections officers are especially important.

Wardens

In general, prison **wardens** oversee the operations of the prison facility and ensure that the policies established by the legislatures are carried out. The job of warden entails many duties. One is to keep the prison safe for

wardens: Correctional administrators who oversee the operations of a prison facility and ensure that the inmates are safe and treated fairly while keeping the facility escape proof to protect the community.

JOURNAL
Prison Warden Job
Stress

the inmates, while keeping it escape proof to protect the community. This part of the job is more difficult as the number of "difficult-to-manage" inmates continues to rise. Wardens must also supervise treatment programs since they are expected to rehabilitate inmates to ensure that prisoners are less likely to reoffend. Additionally, wardens must manage hundreds of employees throughout the facility, including guards, administrative staff, and other workers, while also managing multimillion-dollar budgets.[38]

Prison wardens are required to make policy decisions that can influence the structure, culture, and activities of the prison institution and its inmates. Although some decisions are influenced by laws, wardens have a great deal of discretion to make policies as they see fit. A warden must understand the prison culture (the institution's history, staff, inmates, community) when making these critical decisions.[39]

The job of a prison warden is becoming more difficult as they must now cooperate with many more outsiders than ever before. They must learn to operate in highly political environments.[40] They must work with state legislatures, executives, and bureaucrats to avoid losing state allocations. They must also work with these groups to ensure that laws that affect prisons are useful and effective.

They must also develop positive relationships with the media, which act as a "watchdog" over the prison operations and the warden alike. Wardens must be ready for increased inmate litigation, and they must work well with unions for corrections officers and other personnel. It is important for wardens to be aware of the public's concerns about potential risks to the community.

Wardens must now be concerned with the spread of sexually-transmitted infections, including HIV, within prisons.[41] They must also develop emergency plans and even conduct realistic training scenarios to deal with the threat of terrorism. They must also manage the gang-related violence that is responsible for most of the crime that occurs in prison, as well as smuggled drugs and contraband, assaults on both inmates and staff, corruption of staff, and rule violations—all serious management problems.[42]

Corrections Officers

Corrections officers have the task of supervising inmates in jails and prisons. They are responsible for maintaining order within the correctional facilities on a daily basis. They must also protect the inmates from harm during their stays. Corrections officers have a lot of influence on the daily events within a prison because they have daily contact with inmates.

In most prisons, there is a constant threat of inmate violence against other inmates or the corrections officers. It is imperative that corrections officers keep order to reduce the chance of violence erupting. One way they do that is through a threat of punishment—they can punish offenders who do not follow the rules. Officers can also deny recreation privileges (for example, television) or place prisoners in administrative segregation cells.

JOURNAL
Correctional Officer
Use of Force

corrections officers:
Employees in correctional facilities who maintain order within the facility.

If necessary, corrections officers can use force against an inmate to gain compliance. Corrections officers are trained to use offensive or defensive physical contact against inmates. In some cases, corrections officers can apply restraints to a misbehaving inmate as a way to either preserve or restore order. In some prisons, corrections officers can use chemical agents such as pepper spray against misbehaving offenders. Some officers carry weapons that can be used during disturbances, but others do not because the weapons can be used against them.

The qualifications needed to be a corrections officer differ by state. Most states require that a potential officer have at least a high school diploma, be at least 18 or 21 years old, and have no felony convictions. Some states require a written and/or oral interview or exam. Some require a medical exam or physical fitness assessment and/or a personality assessment to determine the candidate's emotional status, to identify any biases he or she might have, and to see how the candidate might react to stressful situations.

BEYOND A REASONABLE DOUBT 12.5

_____ are responsible for maintaining order within correctional facilities on a daily basis.

(a) Corrections officers, (b) Security officers, (c) Inmate staff, (d) Governors, (e) All of the above

---

The answer can be found on page 522.

Just the Facts: Chapter Summary

- The criminal justice system has many goals, including retribution, rehabilitation, reintegration, incapacitation, deterrence (specific and general), and restitution.

- The five main eras of punishment are the Classical School Era (1790–1879), the Reform Era (1879–1900), the Punishment Era (1900–1940), the Rehabilitation Era (1940–1980), and the Just Deserts Era (1980–present).

- Prior to the building of prisons and incarceration, punishment consisted of fines, corporal punishment, banishment, or death.

- Gaols were typically used as debtor's prisons or were for pretrial detention.

- Common forms of corporal punishments included whipping posts, stocks and pillories, branding, iron masks, and the ducking stool.

- Cesare Beccaria changed the world's thinking about crime and punishment.

- The Walnut Street Jail was the first jail in America that began to use its facility as a means of punishment.

- Early prisons attempted to control prisoners through silence and solitary confinement, although some attempted to bring inmates together to work. The former became known as the Pennsylvania system, whereas the latter was the New York system.

- The South took a different approach from the North, by using convicts for labor and leasing them to plantations and farms.

- The 1950s and 1960s were marked by many prison reforms aimed at rehabilitation and reintegration of prisoners.

- Prisons can be categorized by their security level: minimum-security, medium-security, maximum-security, and supermax prisons.

- Federal prisons are operated by the Bureau of Prisons, found within the U.S. Department of Justice.

- Every state has developed its own system for corrections, but each typically has a system with minimum-, medium-, and maximum-security prisons.

- Local-level corrections are typically jails that hold offenders who are sentenced to less than one year or who are awaiting trial.

Critical Thinking Questions

1. Describe what punishment was like before the building of prisons.

2. Who was Cesare Beccaria, and what impact did he have on our thinking about crime and punishment?

3. Compare and contrast the Pennsylvania system with the New York system.

4. What prison reforms happened in the United States in the late 1800s? Were they successful?

5. How did the treatment of prisoners change in the 1960s?

6. Why did the United States return to a punishment orientation in the late 20th century (the Just Deserts Era)?

7. What types of rehabilitation/treatment services should be provided at correctional facilities?

8. Compare and contrast private prisons and public prisons, with an aim toward identifying which strategy is most effective.

9. What should be the primary goal of the criminal justice system? Should the focus of the prisons be on rehabilitation, punishment, or something in between?

Key Terms

ADMAX prison (405)
Ashurst-Sumners
    Act (397)
banishment (389)
classification
    system (390)
convict leasing
    system (396)
corporal punishment (388)

corrections officers (412)
debtor's prisons (387)
general deterrence (386)
incapacitation (386)
mark system (394)
maximum-security
    prisons (402)
medium-security
    prisons (402)

minimum-security
    prisons (402)
New York system (392)
Pennsylvania
    system (392)
prison camps (406)
prison plantations (396)
rehabilitation (385)
reintegration (385)

restitution (386)
retribution (385)
solitary confinement (391)
specific deterrence (386)
stocks and pillories (388)
supermax prisons (402)
wardens (411)

$SAGE edgeselect™

edge.sagepub.com/payne

Sharpen your skills with SAGE edge select!

With carefully crafted tools and resources to encourage review, practice, and critical thinking, SAGE edge select gives you the edge needed to master course content. Take full advantage of open-access key term flashcards, practice quizzes, and video content. Diagnostic pre-tests, a personalized study plan, and post-tests are available with an access code.

PUNISHING OFFENDERS IN PRISONS, JAILS, AND THE COMMUNITY

© alessandro0770/Veer

FORMER NEW YORK CITY POLICE COMMISSIONER BERNARD KERIK was sentenced to four years in prison in February 2010 after being convicted of tax fraud. Two years into his prison sentence, he told a reporter, "Going to prison is like dying with your eyes open . . . . You watch your world pass before your very eyes, and no matter how good, bad, tragic or horrific . . . all you can do is watch from afar."[1] It is important to recognize that his punishment is his separation from society. To be sure, being separated from society, regardless of the location of the prison, is a punitive experience. Inmates cannot leave when they want, eat what they want, or take showers when they want. Every aspect of their existence is controlled or restricted. Other inmates report experiences similar to Kerik's, whether they are incarcerated in minimum-, medium-, or maximum-security prisons. Kerik, like most other inmates, was eventually released into the community to serve part of his sanction under community supervision.

LEARNING OUTCOMES

After reading this chapter, students will be able to:

13.1 Distinguish jails from prisons

13.2 Describe how inmates experience incarceration

13.3 Explain how inmates are released from prison

13.4 Identify how probation and parole are structured in the United States

13.5 Describe five challenges that probation and parole officers confront on their jobs

13.6 Explain the various roles of juvenile probation officers

13.7 Evaluate the usefulness of various types of sanctions

To help readers to fully understand how we punish offenders, in this chapter we focus on the incarceration experience, the process by which inmates are released back into the community, the structure of probation and parole, and types of alternative sanctions.

➡ The Incarceration Experience

Incarceration refers to the act of holding someone in a setting for the purposes of detention or incarceration. In the criminal justice

---

ADMISSIBLE or INADMISSIBLE Evidence

Read the statements that follow. If the statement is true, circle *admissible*. If the statement is false, circle *inadmissible*. Answers can be found on page 519.

1. **Admissible Inadmissible** Before being released from prison, inmates undergo a classification process to make sure they are ready to return to the community.

2. **Admissible Inadmissible** The term *prisonization* describes the way that inmates experience the prison's socialization process.

3. **Admissible Inadmissible** The main difference between jails and prisons is that jails have a stronger focus on rehabilitation.

4. **Admissible Inadmissible** Administrative probation refers to situations in which juveniles are sentenced to probation in their schools.

5. **Admissible Inadmissible** House arrest has been found to be a punitive experience.

6. **Admissible Inadmissible** Shock incarceration refers to sentencing strategies that impose a quick stint of incarceration to be followed by release into the community.

7. **Admissible Inadmissible** Day reporting centers are locations where inmates must go during the day to show corrections officers that they are staying out of trouble.

8. **Admissible Inadmissible** One of the criticisms of alternative sanctions is that the sanctions widen the net of criminal justice control.

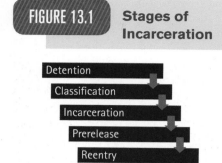

FIGURE 13.1   Stages of Incarceration

Detention

Classification

Incarceration

Prerelease

Reentry

incarceration: The act of holding someone in a setting for the purposes of detention or incarceration.

detention: The process by which offenders are held before determinations of guilt are made.

classification: The process by which a determination is made about where offenders will be incarcerated and the types of programs that will be made available to them.

reentry: The process during which an offender becomes reintegrated into the community at large.

prison: An institution that houses offenders who have been convicted of felonies.

Jails are often designed much differently than prisons.

© Darren Banks/Splash News/Newscom

system, five stages of incarceration exist: detention, classification, incarceration, prerelease, and reentry (see Figure 13.1). **Detention** refers to the process by which offenders are held before determinations of guilt are made. Detention typically occurs in a jail or detention facility (for juveniles). Those being detained are called detainees, rather than prisoners, to describe their status.

After offenders are convicted and sentenced to prison, they will go through the **classification** process. Classification varies across jurisdictions, but it generally entails determining the needs of offenders, identifying their security level, and determining where they will be incarcerated and the types of programs that will be made available to them. In some states, all convicted offenders may be sent to a specific location where classification occurs. In other states, classification may be done in part of a particular institution. Classification also serves to orient inmates to the incarceration experience. Recall your own orientation to college. You were taught what to expect from the college experience, regardless of whether you were enrolled in an online college or were attending a residential college.

In this context, the incarceration experience refers to the time that offenders spend in jail or prison after their sentence has begun. The nature of the incarceration experience will be discussed in more detail later in this chapter.

Prerelease refers to the process by which offenders are prepared for reentering society. This, too, could be done in different ways depending on the jurisdiction's laws and policies. In some states, offenders may go through programs or services within the prison where they served their sentences. In other places, offenders may be sent to a different facility that is designed as a stepping-stone between the prison and the community. In those settings, offenders may be allowed to work but are still supervised by corrections staff. As an illustration, many criminal justice students do internships in the last semester of their coursework to prepare them for their careers. Still students, interns are basically "living in two worlds." In a similar way, offenders in prerelease settings are "living in two worlds."

Reentry refers to the process by which an offender reenters society. It includes the offender's release from jail or prison as well as the length of time the offender spends becoming reintegrated into the community. These topics are also addressed further later in this chapter.

Our discussion of the incarceration experience addresses the following themes: (a) the difference between jail and prison, (b) the prison subculture, (c) the pains of imprisonment, and (d) prison and jail architecture.

Distinguishing Jail From Prison

To the layperson, there may be very little difference between jails and prisons. After all, both are institutions where offenders are incarcerated. In reality, a number of differences exist between the types of institutions. Whereas **prisons** house inmates who have been convicted of committing felonies, at the most basic level, **jails** hold (a) pretrial offenders awaiting trial who were not granted bail or pretrial release and (b) offenders who have been convicted of misdemeanors and sentenced to jail for less than 12 months as part of their punishment. Because of the shorter sentences, jail populations turn over more quickly, which has implications for management of the offender population. In addition, offenders in jails experience "less isolation from the outside community."[2] In particular, offenders awaiting trial and those sentenced for misdemeanors are housed in jails that are typically not far away from the offender's home (assuming the offender committed the crime in the same jurisdiction where he or she lives). When sentenced to prison, offenders eventually may be housed hours away from their families, homes, and communities.

Inmates in prisons are often much more restricted than inmates in jails.

REUTERS/Lucy Nicholson

According to the Bureau of Justice Statistics, besides detaining offenders and housing misdemeanants, jails also are used to perform the following functions:

- Remit probation, parole, and bail-bond violators and absconders

- Temporarily detain juveniles pending transfer to juvenile authorities

- Hold mentally ill persons pending transfer to appropriate mental health facilities

- Hold individuals for the military, for protective custody, for contempt, and for the courts as witnesses

- Release inmates to the community upon completion of sentence

- Transfer inmates to federal, state, or other authorities

- House inmates for federal, state, or other authorities because of crowding of their facilities

- Sometimes operate community-based programs as alternatives to incarceration[3]

One of the criticisms of jails is that they are unable to provide effective treatment to offenders. There are several reasons why jails are not conducive for rehabilitation.[4] First, for detainees who have not been convicted, questions arise regarding the legality of forcing or mandating treatment for people who are assumed innocent until proven guilty. Second, offenders are typically not in jail long enough for certain types of treatment to be effective. In addition, the physical design of detention facilities is such that they are not built with treatment needs in mind.

It is common to hear claims that treatment is not provided because policy makers are not supportive of treatment initiatives in jails. Such a claim

VIDEO
Jail v. Prison

jail: Institutions that hold pretrial offenders awaiting trial who were not granted bail or pretrial release and offenders who have been convicted of misdemeanors and sentenced to jail for less than 12 months.

CRIMINAL JUSTICE and **COLLEGE STUDENTS**

MEASURING THE INMATE CODE

Criminologists James Garofalo and Richard Clark developed an inmate subculture scale that measured the adherence of jail inmates to the inmate subculture. The scale includes five scenarios and asks inmates about their reactions to the scenarios. Read the scenarios below and determine how you, in your role as a college student, might respond to the scenario. Next, determine how you think incarcerated offenders might be expected to respond. What are the similarities and differences between how you might respond and how offenders might respond?

Item 1: Two inmates are planning an escape. They threaten a third inmate, Jones, with a beating unless he steals a wire cutter for them from the place he is assigned to work. Jones thinks they mean business. He gets the wire cutter, but is caught trying to smuggle it into his cell. If he doesn't describe the whole situation, he will probably be charged with an escape attempt. He can avoid this by blaming the other two inmates. What should Jones do?

    A. Clear himself by telling about the escape plans of the other two inmates

    B. Keep quiet and face the consequences

    C. Don't know/No opinion

Item 2: Smith and Long are friends in the same jail. Smith has some cash that was smuggled into the jail by a visitor. Smith tells Long that he thinks the guards are suspicious of him, and he asks Long to hide the cash for a few days. How do you personally feel about Long's hiding the money?

    A. Strongly approve

    B. Approve

    C. Disapprove

    D. Strongly disapprove

    E. Don't know/No opinion

Item 3: Johnson knows that two guys are threatening to beat up another guy, Martin, because Martin won't help them cover up their gambling operation in the jail. Martin is afraid to tell anyone. Johnson has an opportunity to pass this information on to a guard without anyone else finding out. What should Johnson do?

    A. Tell the guard about Martin's problem

    B. Mind his own business and keep quiet

    C. Don't know/No opinion

Item 4: Hill is awaiting trial on a burglary charge. Another guy in the jail tells Hill that he knows a lawyer who can almost certainly get him off without a prison sentence. In return for putting Hill in contact with this lawyer, the other guy wants Hill to help him smuggle some pills into the jail. Hill believes that, without this lawyer, he will probably get a prison sentence on the burglary charge. What should Hill do?

    A. Accept the other guy's bargain

    B. Reject the offer so he can avoid the risk of being caught smuggling pills

    C. Don't know/No opinion

*Item 5: If you were being hassled by some other guy being held here, how would you handle it?

    A. Retreat/avoid

    B. Tell guard

    C. Talk it out

    D. Fight

    E. Handle by self

    F. Depends on situation

    G. Other

    H. Don't know/No opinion

*Item 5 eliminated from final subcultural scale.

Source: Reprinted from Garofalo, J., & Clark, R. D. (1985). The inmate subculture in jails. *Criminal Justice and Behavior, 12*(4), 415–434, p. 417.

some inmates may reflect attitudes consistent with a prison culture, not all inmates necessarily do. In effect, inmates may hold varying beliefs and values, just as members of the outside community do.

The Pains of Imprisonment

In his classic book, *The Society of Captives*, Gresham Sykes offered this rather obvious conclusion: "Imprisonment . . . is painful."[12] While seemingly an obvious statement, to fully show how imprisonment is painful, Sykes described five **pains of imprisonment** that arise during the incarceration experience (see Figure 13.3):

FEATURE VIDEO
Pains of Imprisonment

- **Deprivation of autonomy.** Inmates give up complete control over their lives and are "subject to a vast body of rules and commands that are designed to control."[13]

- **Deprivation of goods and services.** Inmates lose access to goods and services accessible in the world at large. In Sykes's words, "The average inmate finds himself in a harshly Spartan environment which he defines as painfully depriving."[14]

- **Deprivation of liberty.** Inmates lose certain civil rights, such as the right to vote in some states.

- **Deprivation of heterosexual relationships.** Inmates lose physical and psychological relationships with their significant others.

pains of imprisonment: The five deprivations that offenders experience during incarceration are: autonomy, goods and services, liberty, heterosexual relationships, and security.

deprivation of autonomy: The pain of imprisonment that involves inmates giving up complete control over their lives.

deprivation of goods and services: The pain of imprisonment that involves inmates losing access to goods and services accessible in the world at large.

deprivation of liberty: The pain of imprisonment that involves inmates losing certain civil rights, such as the right to vote in some states.

deprivation of heterosexual relationships: The pain of imprisonment that involves inmates losing physical and psychological relationships with their significant others.

FIGURE 13.3   Pains of Imprisonment

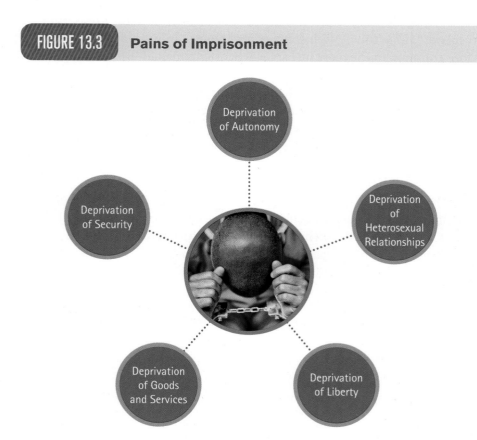

© iStockphoto.com/SeanShot

- **Deprivation of security.** Inmates live in a seemingly unsafe environment. One inmate quoted by Sykes said, "The worst thing about prison is you have to live with other prisoners."[15]

The degree to which inmates experience these "pains" varies across offenders and institutions. Responses to the pains include a heightened suicide risk, problems sleeping, anxiety, depression, and violence.[16] Simply being around individuals who are feeling the pains can exacerbate the consequences experienced by inmates. Shelley Listwan and her coauthors wrote, "Inmates do not have to be personally victimized for prisons to have criminogenic effect."[17] Moreover, a study by the same researchers of 1,613 offenders who recently were released from prison found that experiencing certain types of strain in prison increased the likelihood of reoffending. In particular, having negative relationships and perceiving the prison environment as severe increased the likelihood of reoffending.

Efforts to mitigate these pains are used to reduce the likelihood that inmates are harmed or act out aggressively as a way to cope with the pains. Visitation policies, for example, can reduce the pains of incarceration. Prison visitation serves many different purposes.[18] First, the visits allow inmates to maintain contact with their family members, which is believed to benefit offenders and families. Also, the visits are believed to reduce the stress of prison life. In addition, the visits provide inmates an external form of social support. As well, maintaining contact with family members during incarceration will potentially help offenders better adjust to life outside prison when they are released. In turn, these positive consequences should lower inmates' risk of reoffending.

Conjugal visits refer to visits during which inmates are permitted to spend "alone time" with spouses and engage in intimate relationships. More common in the past, just six states offer conjugal visits.[19] Proponents of such visits argue that beyond the positive contributions of visitations noted earlier, conjugal visits are an effective tool to promote prosocial behavior by inmates. In particular, it is believed that by promising inmates conjugal visits if they behave, the inmates will be more prone to abide by prison rules. Opponents see conjugal visits as rewarding inmates for wrongdoing. At times, conjugal visits have become a political issue in those states that still have them.

Criminal justice professor Jeanne Stinchcomb used a rather novel class assignment to teach her students about the pains of imprisonment. In particular, she essentially turned her students into prisoners for 48 hours, asking them to confine themselves to their homes as if they were inmates themselves. Stinchcomb asked students to follow certain rules during this period, including the following:[20]

1. No watching television or using a computer, CD player, or stereo. (Handheld devices were not yet created or they would have been banned as well!)

2. No use of any weightlifting or exercise equipment, or recreational games.

3. Only three 20-minute trips to the kitchen/refrigerator per day.

deprivation of security: The pain of imprisonment that involves inmates living in a seemingly unsafe environment.

conjugal visits: Visits during which inmates are permitted to spend "alone time" with spouses and engage in intimate relationships.

4. No use of anything from the medicine cabinet (e.g., aspirin) without prior approval.

5. Except for one 5-minute phone call per day, no verbal or physical contact with anyone from outside who does not live in the facility.

After completing their confinements, students told Stinchcomb about their experiences with boredom, anxiety, silence, claustrophobia, fatigue, and hunger. Here is a sampling of the comments students made to the professor after confining themselves for 48 hours:

- I wasn't prepared for the boredom that set in.

- I just wanted to jump out of my skin.

- A deafening silence is ringing in my ears.

- I had a feeling of suffocation.

- [I decided] to end my misery and go to sleep.

- Dinner—I thought it would never come.[21]

Students learned firsthand that being separated from society is punitive, regardless of the prison environment or prison design.

Prison and Jail Architecture

At the most basic level, prisons are designed to house offenders in a way that will keep them from trying to escape. Robert Morris and John Worrall cite three common architectural designs of prisons: telephone pole design, campus facility design, and mixed design.[22] The **telephone pole design** typically has one or two long corridors with parallel rows of shorter corridors ("poles") that intersect through the longer corridors. These are typically multistory structures, and the first prison of this type in the United States was built in 1914. The corridors are very long, but the "poles" in theory "increased security and restricted movement of inmates outside of the corridors."[23]

The **campus facility design**, by contrast, includes several separate buildings constructed inside a large area. Students attending a residential university might imagine how their own campuses could be similar to these types of prisons. Versions of these institutions began to appear in the United States in 1980. Morris and Worrall point out that "such prisons typically consist of several small housing and operations buildings that allow for the direct supervision of inmates."[24] These facilities are cheaper to build, with no high walls or towers.

The mixed design prison has a combination of features found in the telephone pole design and the campus facility designs. The facilities are located in areas of the prison that are most conducive to effective administration of institutional activities. Again, think of a residential college campus. Typically, the classroom buildings, dormitories, student center, and other buildings are situated in a way that most effectively promotes the collegiate experience. Just as the design of college communities might

telephone pole design: Type of architectural design of prisons that typically has one or two long corridors with parallel rows of shorter corridors ("poles") that intersect through the longer corridors.

campus facility design: A common architectural design for prisons; includes several separate buildings constructed inside a large area.

Telephone Pole Design, exterior and cells:

Image property of the California Department of Corrections and Rehabilitation; © Image Source/Corbis

Mixed Design, exterior and cells:

Image property of the California Department of Corrections and Rehabilitation; Hicks, Robert A., creator. This image or media file contains material based on a work of a National Park Service employee, created as part of that person's official duties.

Campus Design, exterior and cells:

Pole designs, mixed designs, and campus designs are the most common designs used for prisons.

Image property of the California Department of Corrections and Rehabilitation; author: Bob Jagendorf.

affect student learning, the design of prisons affects the inmate social culture.[25] Also, design type may influence the types of nonviolent misconduct inmates engage in while incarcerated.[26]

The type of design will be determined in part by the types of offenders housed in the institution. For low-level offenders who pose little threat of escape, prisons might be more open. For more dangerous offenders, prisons are typically designed with the utmost concern given to the need to keep offenders incarcerated.

Describing the importance of prison design, one architect wrote,

> Prison design is so extremely backward that history and precedent are of no positive use to the socially minded designer. . . . The architect, when basing his design on precedent, has taken the cell block within the cell house as the model for the maximum security prison. Were the modern architect to approach the problem without any encumbering knowledge of historical methods, he might decide that one of the surest and least expensive ways of preventing escape would be to house this class of offenders in the upper stories of a tall building.[27]

Consider that the architect wrote these comments more than 80 years ago. They are relevant today, however, because they demonstrate that prisons are designed based on the architectural skills and construction abilities of a particular time period. One would expect that technological advancements have shifted the design of jails and prisons. Goldberg and Weber use the phrase "intelligent jail" to refer to the way that intelligence and technology should be used to build modern jails that are safe, cost effective, and efficient.[28] The intelligent jail has qualities distinct from many past jails. These include

- Floor plans that reflect the community's overall criminal justice philosophy, with safety emphasized the most.

- Control posts that are strategically located to allow staff to carry out tasks efficiently.

- Housing pods that are designed differently based on types of offenders (e.g., sex offenders and inmates convicted of driving under the influence would need different types of housing).

- Technology used to improve safety and reduce workload (e.g., voice-activated locks, touchscreen computers, closed caption television).

- Video visitation programs used to allow offenders to communicate with the outside world, without allowing physical contact.

Building new jails or prisons in these ways may cost more, but the higher costs are upfront costs rather than administrative costs. It is believed that, in the long run, intelligent jails are cheaper to administer and consequently more cost effective. As one author notes, "We need to develop environments that aid rather than hinder coping."[29] Although this author was referring to coping of inmates, the environment should also be such that employees are able to do their jobs in the safest way possible. Balancing the needs of corrections staff and inmates in building prisons ensures that institutions fulfill the purpose of housing offenders. The environment should not be the punishment; after all, it is the time away that is supposed to be punitive. The "Help Wanted" box in this chapter lists the duties of corrections officers in one recent job advertisement. Note that none of the duties requires that corrections officers punish offenders.

HELP WANTED: CORRECTIONS OFFICER

DUTIES:

- Provides supervision, care, and correctional treatment of inmates. Incumbent is concerned with maintenance of institution security contributing to the health and welfare of the inmates and the promotion of good public relations.

- Enforces rules and regulations governing facility security, inmate accountability and inmate conduct to ensure judicial sanctions are carried out and inmates remain in custody. From time to time, may be authorized to carry firearms and to use physical force, including deadly force, to maintain control of inmates.

- During institution emergencies or other periods of heavy workload or limited staff, may be required to work long and irregular hours, unusual shifts, Sundays, holidays, and unexpected overtime. Information as to operations and procedures is provided by post orders, Bureau of Prisons program statements, local supplements, custodial manual, internal correspondence, and staff meetings. Incumbent must be flexible and have a broad knowledge base to use own initiative in the resolution of problem situations.

REQUIREMENTS: Bachelor's degree

ANNUAL SALARY: $39,012–$51,702

Adapted from USAJOBS.gov. Retrieved from https://www.usajobs .gov/GetJob/ViewDetails/362628200

BEYOND A REASONABLE DOUBT 13.1

The _____ argues that values are developed because of things that are missing in the prison environment and as a result of the oppressive environment found in prisons.

(a) importation model, (b) subcultural theory, (c) deprivation model, (d) pains of imprisonment theory, (e) none of the above

The answer can be found on page 522.

➤ Releasing Inmates Back Into the Community

FEATURE VIDEO
Reentry Challenges

Inmates leave jail or prison in one of several different ways: (a) They complete the maximum sentence they were expected to serve, (b) they complete the minimum sentence they were expected to serve and abided by jail or prison rules, (c) they are paroled by a parole board, (d) their sentences are overturned on appeal, (e) they are pardoned by the governor or president, (f) their sentences are commuted by the president or governor, or (g) they die in jail or prison (see Figure 13.4). In reality, few inmates serve the full sentence they are given. Most often they serve the minimum expected sentence, are released because of good-time credits, or are paroled.

The amount of time offenders actually serve varies across jurisdictions. States with mandatory minimum policies stipulate that convicted offenders must serve a certain amount of time before release decisions can be made. Some states award good-time credits, which essentially mean "time off for

FIGURE 13.4   How Inmates Leave Prison

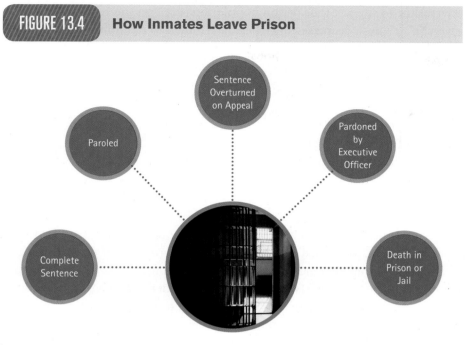

© istockphoto.comfhogue

good behavior." The advantage of good-time credits is that they potentially make it easier to supervise offenders who are, in theory, more likely to behave if they believe they will get out early. The disadvantage is that the credits may not be applied equally and may be misused.

Figure 13.5 shows the admissions, releases, and prison populations between 1992 and 2013. Between 2009 and 2013, more inmates were released each year than were admitted to state prisons. Consequently, prison populations dropped over that timeframe; however, the decreases were minimal. Still, these decreases are unprecedented in modern times, prompting

FIGURE 13.5   Number of State and Federal Inmates Admitted and Released, 1978–2012

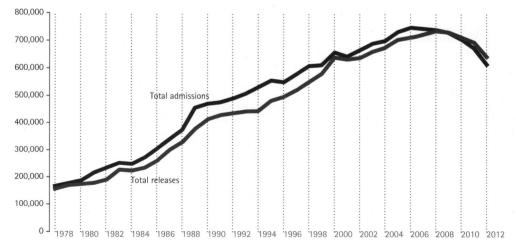

The U.S. Department of Justice, Office of Justice Programs, Bureau of Justice Statistics

one author to suggest that prison populations are "on the verge of a historic reversal."[30] These decreases have been attributed to the following factors:[31]

- Concerns about state budgets
- Shifts in political thinking
- Increased support for alternative sanctions
- Enhanced community supervision practices
- Changes to sentencing guidelines

These decreases were met with a slight increase (0.3%) in prison populations between 2012 and 2013 (see Figure 13.6).

As noted earlier, some inmates might have their sentences commuted or they may be pardoned. Having a sentence *commuted* means that the offender's original sentence is shortened. It does not mean that the system believes that the offender is innocent. The offender may have to serve some time incarcerated, but he or she will not need to serve the entire sentence. A *pardon*, by contrast, means that the sentence is forgiven and the offender is released from custody as soon as the pardon is issued.

FIGURE 13.6 Sentenced Prisoners State Versus Federal Inmates, 2003–2013

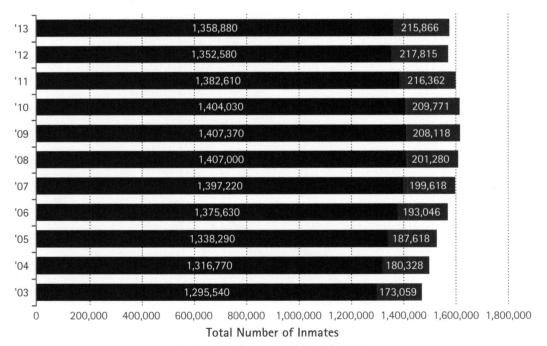

National Prisoner Statistics Program

Inmates are released either conditionally or without conditions. Conditionally released inmates are placed on parole or another version of community supervision and expected to abide by a host of rules designed to promote prosocial lifestyles. The difficult nature of the reentry process frequently results in many offenders returning to prison. These dynamics have been labeled "the revolving door" of prisons in reference to the way that some offenders leave prison only to return a short time later.

VIDEO
The Released

—BEYOND A REASONABLE DOUBT 13.2—

Which of the following explains why prison populations decreased in recent years?

(a) Concerns about state budgets, (b) Shifts in political thinking, (c) Increased support for alternative sanctions, (d) All of the above, (e) None of the above

---

The answer can be found on page 522.

➡ The Structure of Probation and Parole

Thus far, this chapter has focused on incarceration as a method for punishing offenders; however, far more individuals are punished through other methods. *Community-based sanctions* describes a range of punishments administered to offenders while they remain in the community. The vast majority of these sanctions fall under the categories of probation and parole. Although probation and parole are discussed in conjunction with each other, they are two different types of sanctions. **Probation** refers to a sanction imposed by the judge that provides for community supervision without any form of incarceration. John Augustus is recognized as the father of probation (see the "Criminal Justice Pioneer" box in this chapter). **Parole**, where it exists, involves a period of community supervision that is imposed after individuals have served a stint of incarceration. In some localities, probation offices are tied to the courts and parole departments are situated within the corrections department. In other localities, particularly rural areas, the same individuals responsible for supervising probationers may also be responsible for supervising parolees. Although different challenges may arise for probationers and parolees, the topics of probation and parole are discussed together as form of community-based corrections to provide a general overview of the two topics.

Figures 13.7 and 13.8 illustrate trends in community-based supervision since 2000. Table 13.1 shows probation and parole rates over the same timeframes. The number of offenders supervised in the community increased through 2007 but has been decreasing some since then. However, the number of individuals on some form of community sanction is still

probation: A sentence whereby an offender is free in the community but remains under the supervision of the court and must abide by certain requirements or risk being sent to prison.

parole: Community supervision imposed after individuals have served a stint of incarceration.

JOHN AUGUSTUS

John Augustus, the "Father of Probation," is recognized as the first true probation officer. Augustus was born in Woburn, Massachusetts, in 1785. In 1841, Augustus attended police court to bail out a "common drunkard," the first probationer. The offender was ordered to appear in court three weeks later for sentencing. He returned to court a sober man, accompanied by Augustus. To the astonishment of all in attendance, his appearance and demeanor had dramatically changed.

Augustus thus began an 18-year career as a volunteer probation officer. Not all of the offenders helped by Augustus were alcohol abusers, nor were all prospective probationers taken under his wing. Close attention was paid to evaluating whether or not a candidate would likely prove to be a successful subject for probation. The offender's character, age, and the people, places, and things apt to influence him or her were all considered.

Augustus was subsequently credited with founding the investigations process, one of three main concepts of modern probation, the other two being intake and supervision. Augustus, who kept detailed notes on his activities, was also the first to apply the term "probation" to his method of treating offenders.

By 1858, Augustus had provided bail for 1,946 men and women. Reportedly, only 10 of this number forfeited their bond, a remarkable accomplishment when measured against any standard. His reformer's zeal and dogged persistence won him the opposition of certain segments of Boston society as well as the devotion and aid of many Boston philanthropists and organizations. The first probation statute, enacted in Massachusetts shortly after his death in 1859, was widely attributed to his efforts.

Reprinted from New York Department of Probation. (n.d.). History of probation. Retrieved from http://www.nyc.gov/html/prob/html/about/history.shtml

FIGURE 13.7   **Number of Adults Under Community Supervision at Year End, 2000–2013**

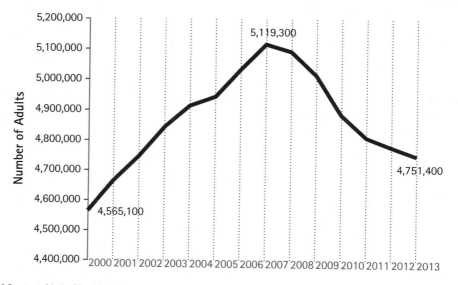

The U.S. Department of Justice, Office of Justice Programs, Bureau of Justice Statistics

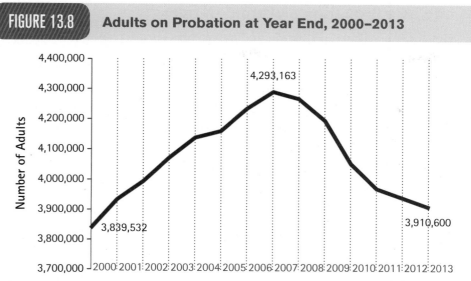

FIGURE 13.8   **Adults on Probation at Year End, 2000–2013**

The U.S. Department of Justice, Office of Justice Programs, Bureau of Justice Statistics

TABLE 13.1   **U.S. Adult Residents on Community Supervision, Probation, and Parole, 2000, 2005–2013**

YEAR	SUPERVISION	PROBATION	PAROLE
2000	1 in 46	1 in 55	1 in 291
2005	1 in 45	1 in 54	1 in 285
2006	1 in 45	1 in 53	1 in 283
2007	1 in 45	1 in 53	1 in 277
2008	1 in 45	1 in 54	1 in 279
2009	1 in 47	1 in 56	1 in 284
2010	1 in 48	1 in 58	1 in 281
2011	1 in 50	1 in 60	1 in 280
2012	1 in 50	1 in 61	1 in 284
2013	1 in 51	1 in 62	1 in 286

The U.S. Department of Justice, Office of Justice Programs, Bureau of Justice Statistics

high. More than 4.7 million individuals in the United States were on probation or parole in 2012. This equates to 1 in 50 residents. This means that someone in one of your classes likely is, or has been, under some form of community supervision.

To provide a general introduction to probation and parole, we examine the following topics: (a) life as a probation or parole officer, (b) probation and parole caseloads, (c) daily challenges facing probation and parole officers, (d) juvenile probation, and (e) pros and cons of probation and parole.

Life as a Probation or Parole Officer

Generally speaking, probation and parole officers are responsible for supervising offenders and ensuring that they abide by their conditions of probation or parole. According to one study, supervision, surveillance, and investigation were the types of tasks that probation and parole officers were most frequently required to perform.[32] The American Probation and Parole Association has classified probation activities into the following categories:[33]

- Assessment and case planning
- Conducting home visits
- Conducting workplace visits
- Communicating with treatment providers and collateral contacts
- Reporting to court as needed
- Holding offenders accountable through strict monitoring of conditions
- Enforcing conditions through arrest and formal sanctioning

A significant amount of probation and parole officers' time is spent in assessment and case-planning activities. The pre-sentence report is one area where probation officers conduct assessment activities. This report is essentially a biography about a specific offender (based on interviews with the offender, family members, collateral contacts, and others) that concludes with a sentencing recommendation to the judge. It is estimated that, on average, each pre-sentence report takes six to seven hours to complete. The pre-sentence report is designed to fulfill the following functions:[34]

- Assist the judge in sentencing
- Help probation officers with supervision and treatment strategies
- Assist in determining how offenders are classified and treated in prisons
- Provide the parole board with information
- Serve as a source of data for researchers

Researchers have probably not taken advantage of these reports as much as they could. One ethnographic study found that material included in the reports is presented or structured in a way that legitimates the officer's initial perceptions of the offender.[35] In other words, it is believed that some officers might use the reports to present a picture of offenders that they believe will be consistent with the sentencing recommendations they expect to recommend. Said one probation officer:

> Bottom line, it's the sentencing recommendation that's important. That's what the judge and everybody wants to see. I start thinking about the recommendations as soon as I pick up the court referral. Why wait? The basic facts aren't going to change.[36]

Assessment and case planning is an ongoing process for probation and parole officers. They will continue to assess offenders under their supervision and revise offender plans accordingly. Some probation officers turn to social media in their assessment and case-planning efforts (see the "Criminal Justice and the Media" box in this chapter).

Conducting **home visits** is another part of probation and parole officers' routine. Depending on the level of probation (discussed below), officers will make unannounced home visits to check in on family members and their loved ones. Theoretically, these visits are designed to ensure that offenders are abiding by their conditions of probation or parole. Occasionally, even with these visits, offenders may be engaging in criminal acts that go unnoticed during home visits.

The case of Jaycee Dugard is illustrative. Dugard was kidnapped by Philip Garrido and sexually assaulted over a period of 18 years. Garrido was a registered sex offender, which would have required periodic visits from probation officers. However, the officers never noticed any evidence of Garrido's ongoing offenses. Dugard was locked in a shed in the backyard, along with two children she had after Garrido got her pregnant on two separate occasions.

The Garrido case is not typical, but it highlights the need to use multiple strategies to supervise offenders. Home visits alone—whether frequent or infrequent—are not enough to supervise offenders. Indeed, officers will also spend a significant amount of their time visiting offenders at their places of work to ensure that offenders remain gainfully employed.

In addition to case planning, home visits, and workplace visits, probation and parole officers spend a great deal of their time communicating with treatment providers and collateral contacts. These collateral contacts might include family members, neighbors, friends, or others who have

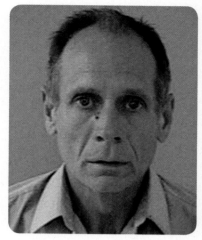

Philip Garrido's probation did not deter him from committing additional sex crimes.
El Dorado Sheriff's Office

VIDEO
System Failure in Jaycee Dugard

home visits: Visits made by community corrections officers to ensure that offenders are abiding by the conditions of their probation or parole.

CRIMINAL JUSTICE and the MEDIA:
PROBATION OFFICERS AND SOCIAL MEDIA

For most of us, reading Facebook, checking Instagram, or reading tweets while at work goes against our workplace rules. For probation officers, however, social media has become a powerful tool that officers can use to keep an eye on their probationers. In the words of one officer, "I can gauge what's going on in their lives. I see people partying or using drugs and alcohol. . . . If people are told not to search the Internet or use electronic devices, they have to be compliant with that order" (WCVB.com, 2013). Think about the types of pictures people post in social media. These posts provide an insight into our daily lives and allow probation

officers to make a "home visit" without even leaving the office. In one case, a probationer was so brazen to taunt his officer after absconding. He posted the following on his Facebook page: "Fresh out of another state. Catch me if you can" (Bernstein, 2012). It did not take the officer long to track down this offender. The judge sent the Facebook poster to prison for 2.5 years.

WCVB.com. (2013). Probation officers keep tabs on offenders through social media. Retrieved from http://www.wcvb.com/news/local/boston-south/Probation-officers-keep-tabs-on-offenders-through-social-media/18003106#ixzz3C7Yqyt2B; and Bernstein, M. (2012). Probation officer answers Facebook taunt. Retrieved from http://www.oregonlive.com/portland/index.ssf/2012/06/probation_officer_answers_face.html

information about the probationer or parolee. One of the criticisms leveled against the probation agency in Garrido's case was that officers "never talked with neighbors and local law enforcement."[37]

Officers also spend a portion of their time reporting to court. These court visits could be for one of three reasons: (a) The visit could be a routine visit scheduled ahead of time, (b) the visit could be for a hearing to decide if the offender violated probation or parole, or (c) the visit could be held to decide whether to end the offender's supervision.

Officers also spend part of the time holding offenders accountable, monitoring their behavior, and deciding whether to cite them for violations. Probation and parole officers are not able to revoke an offender's probation or parole; this is a decision made by the judge. Still, an officer can recommend revocation, and a judge is likely to follow that recommendation. Research shows that officers will selectively decide which violations to refer to court. Selective enforcement, in this context, fulfills five functions:[38]

- Gives officers even more power and control over offenders because it shows that officers have the ability to decide if offenders should go to court

- Promotes behavioral change in offenders

- Allows officers to decide how to allocate their time and resources

- Allows officers to assess risk

- Promotes public safety

Probation and Parole Caseloads

When characterizing probation and parole by **caseload**, four different levels of probation or parole are typically identified: intensive supervision, traditional supervision, low supervision, and administrative supervision. **Intensive supervision** refers to situations in which officers supervise a small number of offenders who are deemed to be at a high risk for reoffending. These offenders are believed to be particularly dangerous to the community. It is believed by some that "small caseloads and close supervision would prompt needed change in the offender, protect the community, and assist offenders in successfully completing supervision."[39] An intensive supervision caseload might be around 20 offenders, whereas caseloads for other levels of probation are much higher. With the smaller caseloads, officers will be able to spend more time on specific supervisory tasks. A smaller caseload does not make it easier for officers; rather, they will need to focus even more closely on each offender's activities. In a similar way, the smaller caseload is experienced differently by the offenders. Consider your own class sizes in your college courses. Your experiences in smaller classes are likely much different from your experiences in larger classes.

Traditional supervision caseloads refer to situations in which officers supervise roughly 50 offenders at any given time. What this means is that

caseload: A model of probation and parole characterized by different levels, focusing on the number of offenders, rather than on the amount of work.

intensive supervision: The level of probation or parole at which caseloads include a small number of offenders who are deemed to be at a high risk for reoffending.

officers will, in theory, devote roughly 2.4 hours each month to each case in their caseloads.[40] This does not mean that they spend that amount of time with each offender, given that much of their time is spent planning and doing administrative activities. *Low supervision* caseloads entail situations in which officers supervise roughly 100 offenders. With these caseloads, officers are able to devote roughly 36 minutes per month to each offender. Again, this does not refer to time spent meeting with offenders. Clearly, these caseloads would include offenders who are not deemed to be serious threats to the community. Still, these large caseloads make it next to impossible for community corrections officers to engage in meaningful interactions with offenders.

Administrative supervision caseloads are even larger and may run up to 1,000 offenders in some places. It would be impossible for officers to truly supervise these offenders. Technology is frequently used to support these caseloads. For example, some jurisdictions use kiosks (similar to ATMs) and require offenders to check in at the kiosk at various times. Offenders assigned to these caseloads are judged to have no risk at all for reoffending. The main purpose of the sanction appears to be punishment and control, rather than treatment or supervision.[41]

Although it is common practice to assign offenders to specific probation or parole officers, not everyone favors this "caseload model" approach. Criminologist Todd Clear asserts that caseload models have the following consequences for probation and parole:[42]

- Caseloads promote individualism inasmuch as they force individual officers to work with individual offenders. In doing so, this inhibits the possibility of promoting a sense of community with offenders.

- Caseloads promote more paperwork to force officers to "cover your ass."

- Caseloads discourage officers from thinking innovatively.

- Caseloads promote "trail 'em and nail 'em philosophies."

Others have criticized caseload models for being bureaucratic in nature[43] and based on assumptions rather than research.[44]

A distinction can be made between caseload and workload models in probation and parole (see Table 13.2). Whereas a caseload approach focuses on the number of offenders, a **workload** model considers the amount of work completed by officers. Caseload and workload models also vary in the following ways:[45]

- In caseload models, cases are assigned based on offender characteristics. In workload models, cases are assigned based on the type of work.

- In caseload models, resources are assigned based on the number of offenders. In workload models, cases are assigned based on the amount of work that needs to be completed.

administrative supervision: The level of probation or parole at which caseloads may run up to 1,000 offenders in some places.

workload: A model of probation and parole that considers the amount of work completed by officers, rather than the number of offenders.

TABLE 13.2	Caseload Versus Workload Models	
	CASELOAD	**WORKLOAD**
Focus	Number of offenders to officers	Amount of effort for different tasks
Cases Assigned	Based on offender characteristics	Based on expertise of officer
Resources Assigned	Based on number of offenders	Based on types of tasks and amount of effort
Workload Distribution	Based on assumption that all offenders receive same effort	Recognizes need to distribute tasks based on offender's needs
Goals	Supervision/discourage rehabilitation	Supervision and rehabilitation in efficient manner
Innovative Thinking	Discouraged	Promoted
Accountability	For supervising offenders: blame assigned to offender	For completing tasks efficiently: intrinsic rewards assigned to officer
Evidence-Based Study	Focuses on the officer	Focuses on the strategies (or the case)

Department of Justice, Bureau of Justice Assistance

- Caseload models assume that offenders require the same amount of effort, whereas workload models recognize that different types of offenders require different amounts of effort.

- Workload models recognize that offenders require different types of services.

The two models are also based on different goals. Whereas the workload model promotes rehabilitation and supervision as a goal, caseload models promote supervision but discourage rehabilitation.[46] In addition, officers are accountable for completing different types of tasks in the two models. Officers working in a department following a caseload model are accountable for the behavior of specific offenders. In a workload model, officers are accountable for completing specific activities.[47] Finally, researchers would use different types of techniques to study the two models.

Daily Challenges Facing Community Corrections Officers

Probation and parole officers confront many different challenges in the daily course of their occupational routines. These barriers include[48]

- Traveling

- Home visit barriers

- Waiting

- Collaboration

- Cultural influences

- Rural barriers

- Low salaries

In terms of traveling, probation and parole officers spend a considerable amount of time driving. Whether to meet offenders, go to court, attend training, or another activity, many community corrections officers likely spend as much time out of the office as they do in the office. Traffic can be a problem in urban areas, and distance can be problematic in rural areas.

Once they arrive at offenders' homes, a new set of potential barriers arise for community corrections officers. Family members or offenders might have dogs, it might be hard to find somewhere to park, or the offender might not be home. The end result is that a long and routine trip may prove to be a waste of the officer's time.

Anecdotally, it is safe to suggest that community corrections officers will spend a great deal of their time waiting. If they want to meet with the offender's treatment provider in person, the officer will spend time in the treatment provider's office. Trips to the offender's worksite or relatives' homes may lead to similar "waiting" times. Perhaps most of the officer's "waiting" time will be time spent waiting for court hearings. No studies have determined how much time community corrections officers spend waiting in court, but a study of social workers (a similar occupation) found that social workers spend roughly 1.8% of their time waiting in court.[49] What this suggests is that out of every 50 working days, an entire day may be spent waiting. Excluding two weeks of vacation per year (for the new officer), this would further mean that five days a year may be spent waiting in court!

Collaboration issues are also confronted by community corrections officers. More so than in the past, community corrections officers are being asked, if not required, to form partnerships and work with officials from other agencies. Although working together can improve the ability of the justice system to supervise and treat offenders, for probation officers, collaborations can be quite time consuming and problematic. Mission distortion (when individuals exaggerate the mission of their agencies) and mission creep (when the missions of agencies "creep" into other agencies) are particularly problematic. Some observers might expect community corrections officers to focus exclusively on treating offenders, for example, when their primary responsibility is to supervise the offenders.

Cultural barriers may also make the job of community corrections officers more difficult. Consider situations in which officers need to communicate with offenders who do not speak their language. One expert writes:

> A probation officer conducting an interview in the same language as the defendant is able to understand the nuances of a conversation and can rely on his/her intuition to probe with follow-up questions. When working through an interpreter, nuances can be missed and intuition based on language lost.[50]

Another barrier that officers face has to do with the communities where they work and live. In particular, "rural barriers" refers to the fact that rural community corrections officers will confront different challenges than officers working in other communities. Challenges that rural officers confront include physical distance, isolation, lack of resources, and unique cultural and social dynamics.[51]

A final barrier that probation and parole officers confront has to do with their salaries. Probation and parole officers' salaries are not competitive, which may make it difficult to recruit or retain new officers. This has a direct bearing on supervision in that probationers may have problems developing relationships with their officers if there is turnover in the probation office.[52]

Juvenile Probation

When juveniles are sanctioned in the community, a probation or parole officer will be assigned to their cases. Juvenile probation and parole officers typically use different strategies to supervise juvenile offenders than those used by probation and parole officers who supervise adult offenders. The underlying philosophy of the juvenile court is *parens patriae*, which suggests that the state should take over as the parent in cases where parents have been unable to raise their children as law-abiding citizens. Consequently, the behavior of those in juvenile corrections mirrors this philosophy. Consider the duties of juvenile probation and parole officers illustrated in Table 13.3. Note the following differences between juvenile and adult probation officers:

- Juvenile officers "assist youth" whereas adult officers "supervise felons."

- Juvenile officers "help youth adhere to conditions" whereas adult officers "enforce conditions."

- Juvenile officers focus on the "youth's individual needs" whereas adult officers perform more administrative functions.

Not surprisingly, because of these differences, the caseloads for juvenile officers tend to be much smaller. After all, it is easier to serve as a parent for a few children than it is to be a parent in a really large family!

TABLE 13.3	Duties of Probation and Parole Officers in Louisiana
TYPE OF PROBATION OFFICER	**DUTIES**
Juvenile	Assists youth and families in navigating the juvenile justice system
	Supervises, advocates, refers, and coordinates services for youth and their families, to assist them in becoming productive citizens
	Helps youth adhere to the conditions set forth by the court and holds youth accountable for their actions
	Provides consistent management of services based on youth's individual needs
Adult	Supervises felons and misdemeanants through counseling
	Enforces conditions of supervision
	Conducts criminal justice social background investigations of offenders
	Conducts arrests
	Transports violators
	Prepares reports for courts and parole board
	Administers drug tests and evaluates results

State of Louisiana, Office of Juvenile Justice; Louisiana Department of Public Safety and Corrections

Pros and Cons of Probation and Parole

Probation and parole are justified on multiple grounds, including cost, treatment, punitiveness, and public safety. In terms of cost, it is much cheaper to supervise offenders in the community than it is to incarcerate them in jail or prison. By some estimates, it costs $28,948 a year to incarcerate offenders and $3,347 a year to supervise them in the community.[53] The higher costs are attributed to workload, health care, "room and board" costs, and supervision costs.

It is also believed that, compared with incarceration, probation and parole sanctions are more conducive to treatment strategies. While incarcerated, inmates may have little exposure to treatment programs. In contrast, offenders on probation and parole may have many different options for treatment.

With regard to punitiveness, a number of research studies have demonstrated that probation and parole are experienced as punitive sanctions. Although offenders are able to be free in the community, various restrictions make the sanction punitive. In fact, some types of offenders reportedly prefer incarceration over certain types of probation and parole.

Another advantage is that various types of probation and parole are able to provide public safety. When applied effectively, the level of control that officers have over probationers and parolees is such that the offenders are unlikely to reoffend. Of course, some offenders violate their probation or parole conditions, but officers more often than not are able to detect those violations and respond accordingly. Of course, probation and parole sanctions have been criticized. The most common criticisms relate to net widening, public safety concerns, truth-in-sentencing issues, and perceptions of lenience. *Net widening* refers to the belief that probation and parole sanctions may widen the net of criminal justice control. In particular, some critics believe that individuals may be placed on probation and parole when they should be given less serious sanctions.

Public safety concerns also surface with probation and parole sanctions. Although the sanctions exert a great deal of control over offenders, occasionally parolees or probationers commit additional violent offenses while under community supervision. Violent offending by probationers and parolees receives a great deal of media coverage when it occurs. This coverage, then, leads members of the public to question the effectiveness of probation and parole.

Truth-in-sentencing issues arise when offenders are released early from prison. Some people believe that offenders should serve every day of their sentences. When offenders leave prison early, those holding more punitive beliefs are likely to suggest that the sentencing ideals were not met.

In a related vein, although research shows that probation and parole sanctions are experienced as punitive, members of the public tend to view the sanctions as lenient. By itself, a lenient sanction is not problematic. However, when the sanctions are given to offenders who members of the public believe should be incarcerated, probation and parole are viewed in a less favorable light.

> **BEYOND A REASONABLE DOUBT 13.3**
>
> _____ involves a period of community supervision that is imposed after individuals have served a stint of incarceration.
>
> (a) Corrections, (b) Community corrections, (c) Probation, (d) Parole, (e) None of the above

The answer can be found on page 522.

➡ Types of Alternative Sanctions

The phrase *alternative sanctions* refers to a range of punishments that are believed to be less punitive than incarceration but more punitive than traditional probation or parole. These sanctions are sometimes referred to as community-based sanctions. Common alternative sanctions include the following:

- Home confinement
- House arrest with electronic monitoring
- Day reporting centers
- Boot camps
- Community service
- Work release

Home Confinement

Home confinement, also known as house arrest, refers to sanctions that require offenders to be at home either for portions of their sanctions or for their entire sanctions. As an alternative sanction, home confinement has been used for centuries in different countries. Some jurisdictions have levels of home confinement distinguished by the amount of time that offenders spend at home. The federal courts, for example, follow three restriction levels: curfew, home detention, and home incarceration. The curfew level requires offenders to be at home at specified times. The home detention level requires offenders to be at home all of the time "except for preapproved and scheduled absences, such as for work, school, treatment, church, attorney appointments, court appearances, and other court-ordered obligations."[54] The home incarceration level requires offenders to be on "lockdown"; they are permitted to leave only for court hearings and medical visits.

Home confinement can be used either as a pretrial detention strategy or as a sanction. When used as a pretrial detention strategy, offenders may be required to post bail to ensure that they will appear in court for trial. Some critics believe that, when used as a sanction, home confinement is not punitive. However, recall Stinchcomb's study. Her students were essentially on home confinement and still experienced the process as punitive.[55]

home confinement: Also known as house arrest; an alternative sanction that requires offenders to be at home either for portions of their sanctions or for their entire sanctions.

House Arrest With Electronic Monitoring

AUTHOR VIDEO
Pains of Electronic Monitoring

House arrest with electronic monitoring is a variation of the home confinement sanction. The distinction is that in house arrest with electronic monitoring sanctions, technology is used to monitor the offenders' whereabouts. This sanction is frequently referred to as "electronic monitoring" in reference to the fact that technology is being used to supervise offenders. The use of electronic monitoring in the United States began in Florida in 1984, when a local jurisdiction used electronic monitoring technology as part of the house arrest sanctions for low-risk offenders in that jurisdiction. The technology at the time was quite archaic in comparison with today's technology. In early versions of electronic monitoring, community corrections officers would call the home to ensure that offenders were at home when they were supposed to be. A device connected to the phone and an anklet worn by offenders would be used to determine if offenders were at home.

As technology changed, so too did the types of electronic monitoring tools available. Both passive and active monitoring technologies are used. Passive technologies require some action on the part of the offender or officer to identify the offender's whereabouts. Active technologies are able to monitor offenders' whereabouts at any given time. GPS technology is now frequently used to monitor offenders serving on electronic monitoring.

The use of electronic monitoring has spread over the past two decades. It is used at different phases of the justice process (as a pretrial tool and as a sanction after conviction), for offenders of different ages (juveniles and adults alike), and for different types of offenders. When electronic monitoring first surfaced as a tool, it was used primarily for low-risk offenders. In the past 10 years or so, electronic monitoring has been used more frequently as a tool to supervise more violent offenders, including sex offenders, gang members, and domestic violence offenders. For sex offenders, exclusion zones are sometimes developed with the technology, and probation or parole officers are notified by the technology if offenders enter those zones (including day cares, schools, and the like). For domestic violence offenders, electronic monitoring technologies have been used in ways that alert the authorities if offenders who are supposed to stay away from victims go near them.

It is not entirely clear how many offenders are electronically monitored each year. It is estimated that roughly 200,000 electronic monitoring units were in use in 2009.[56] By some estimates, one-fifth of all community-based supervision involves some form of electronic monitoring.[57]

Many criticisms have been leveled against electronic monitoring. Some critics have argued that the tool provides for net widening, suggesting that alternative sanctions simply increase the number of offenders under the control of the criminal justice system. Concerns about privacy and turning the home into a prison have also surfaced. With the use of more recent technologies, some critics have raised legal and ethical questions. Are officers legally liable if offenders commit serious offenses while they are being supervised? Can GPS tracking be used to identify a monitored suspect's presence at a particular crime scene? Does pretrial monitoring constitute cruel and unusual punishment? Although some people question whether

house arrest with electronic monitoring: An alternative sanction similar to home confinement; technology is used to monitor offenders' whereabouts.

the sanction is cruel and unusual punishment, others have suggested that the sanction is too lenient.

Supporters of house arrest with electronic monitoring cite several advantages associated with the sanction. First, offenders are able to live at home while serving their sanctions. Staying at home allows them to maintain their employment and build family relationships. Second, the sanction provides offenders much-needed structure that they otherwise would not receive. In addition, for less serious offenders, the sanction allows them to avoid the criminogenic environment of jails and prisons. In doing so, the possibility of receiving effective treatment increases. Finally, the sanction is viewed as a cost-effective alternative to incarceration. It is cheaper than jail and prison for many reasons, including the fact that offenders typically have to pay for the monitoring equipment and technology.

Some observers have questioned whether house arrest with electronic monitoring is punitive. Although the public may view the sanction as lenient, offenders who experience the sanction find it to be punitive. Research shows that electronically monitored offenders experienced pains of imprisonment similar to those experienced in prison.[58] In addition, the same study found that offenders experienced pains unique to the electronic monitoring sanction. These included monetary costs, family effects, "watching others" effects, and bracelet effects. Monetary costs refers to the "pain" that offenders experience having to pay in order to be punished. Family effects refers to the negative effects that family members experience when offenders are sentenced to house arrest with electronic monitoring. Watching others effects refer to the pain that offenders feel when they see others are able to do things that they are not able to do. Bracelet effects refer to the embarrassment or other types of discomfort that offenders feel when wearing the device. Offenders describe their experiences with electronic monitoring in ways that suggest they experienced deprivations similar to incarcerated offenders (see Table 13.4).

Although offenders experience the sanction as punitive, few offenders in these past studies said they would rather be in jail or prison. Offenders recognize that the sanction is less punitive than prison. However, they do experience deprivations on the electronic monitoring sanction.

Day Reporting Centers

Day reporting centers are locations where offenders are required to report on a daily basis as part of their sanctions. Also known as day treatment centers, day incarceration centers, and community resource centers and designed differently across jurisdictions, offenders might spend a small part of the day at the center, or they might be expected to spend several hours at the center each day participating in treatment.[59] The centers were initially created in Great Britain in the 1960s and eventually expanded to the United States.[60]

The centers were created to reduce jail populations and provide access to treatment and have been used as pretrial strategies as well as for probation and parole conditions.[61] Violent offenders would rarely be sentenced to day reporting centers as part of an initial sentence, though some might be expected

day reporting centers:
Locations where offenders are required to report on a daily basis as part of their sanctions.

TABLE 13.4	Pains of House Arrest With Electronic Monitoring	
PAIN	**WHAT IT MEANS**	**QUOTES FROM OFFENDERS**
Deprivation of Autonomy	Electronically monitored offenders lose their freedom and have very little control over decisions about movement.	"The only thing this lacks is bars on windows." "It has taught me a valuable lesson of what it is like to have my freedom taken away from you [*sic*]. Also, [I learned] not to take for granted as so many of us do. You don't realize what you've got until it's gone." "I feel like a dog on a leash."
Deprivation of Goods and Services	Electronically monitored offenders are not permitted to do activities outside of the home that others take for granted.	"At times it can be a hassle. . . . I lose a lot of money having to be back here on time. Used to be, I could stay [at work] until 11. It's an inconvenience". "I can't go shopping." "I do not like electronic monitoring because it is summertime and I can't enjoy it. It is like being at the beach and not being able to touch the sand, water, or look at the pretty girls."
Deprivation of Liberty	Electronically monitored offenders lose many of their rights, with some losing their right to vote.	"We lose our voting rights forever. But we're still taxed. Yet the constitution says there shall be no taxation without representation. Could you explain that one to me?" "Voting is a subject I don't discuss." "Can't vote"/"Don't vote"
Deprivation of Heterosexual Relationships	Electronically monitored offenders do not lose their ability to have relationships with others, but these relationships are certainly influenced by the sanction.	"My wife goes out more, leaves me alone more often, and is more friendly with men. She responds to me hatefully." "They get a free ride. I have to pay the phone and electric bill. If I don't, I'm back in jail and they know that."
Monetary Costs	Electronically monitored offenders usually have to pay to be on the sanction.	"My lawyer didn't explain to me how much the program costs. If it weren't for my mother, I would never be able to support myself and I would be forced to go back to jail. I can completely understand how someone who has no real job skills, no other financial support and a felony on their record would have a hard time making ends meet, and pay for the program, even if they can find a job. So, I am not making excuses, but I can see how people may feel trapped and forced to find illegal means to support themselves." "Jail costs the public a lot. Electronic monitoring costs the offender a lot."
Family Effects	The family members of electronically monitored offenders must change their actions when someone in their home is monitored.	"My fiancé is just as much on house arrest as I am." "Electronic monitoring has shifted a great deal of responsibilities outside the home onto my wife." "I live with my parents and the phone calls wake them up in the middle of the night or early in the mornings."
Watching Other Effects	Electronically monitored offenders see others engaging in activities that they would like to be doing.	"It is difficult due to the fact that you are tempted to leave the house because all of the direct temptations you encounter." "It's torture doing it. . . . You have to watch others get ready for the Garth Brooks concert and then they are going out the door and I have to say, 'Have a good time, I'll stay home tonight and baby-sit.'"
Bracelet Effects	Electronically monitored offenders often complain about having to wear the bracelet.	"I need bigger socks to cover it when I am at work." "I have to wear pants all the time." "I work in boots and it's uncomfortable." "I have a foreign object attached to my leg."

Payne, B. K. (2012). *White-collar crime: The essentials*. Thousand Oaks, CA: Sage Publication.

Payne, B. K. & Gainey, R. R. (1998). A qualitative assessment of the pains experienced by electronic monitoring. *International Journal of Offender Therapy, 42*(2), 149–163.

Boot camps in the justice system are administered much the same way that military boot camps are administered.

© Bettmann/CORBIS

to report to the centers as part of their parole or release conditions. Offenders reporting to the centers are expected to abide by various rules or conditions, which might include the following:[62]

- Approval of daily itineraries
- Adherence to curfews
- Submission to random drug tests
- Attendance of school or work
- Participation in treatment services

The centers have been hailed for filling "a gap between the security of imprisonment and the relative lack of supervision offered to offenders" in the community.[63] Some research shows that they potentially have a stronger deterrent effect than other forms of alternative sanctions and they are seen as cost-effective.[64] However, researchers have noted that the cost-effectiveness varies across program types[65] and offender types.[66]

Boot Camps

Boot camps are a form of *shock incarceration*, which refers to sentencing strategies that impose a quick stint of incarceration to be followed by release into the community. The idea is that "shocking" offenders will keep them from reoffending after they are released. Consider a situation when someone touches an electrical outlet and is shocked. That person won't touch that outlet again.

As a form of shock incarceration, boot camps are structured very much like military boot camps. Daily routines include a "demanding regimen of strict discipline, physical training, drills, inspections, and discipline."[67] Figure 13.9 illustrates the daily routine that juveniles follow in one such program. Advocates believe that boot camps promote positive change in offenders. The following positive qualities of boot camps have been cited:[68]

- Boot camps should reduce the number of prison beds.
- In theory, they should teach discipline and reduce impulsivity.
- By returning offenders to the community more quickly, these efforts should promote stronger attachments to the community.
- The programs may promote more prosocial attitudes on the part of offenders.

Various criticisms of boot camps have been leveled. Some critics have noted that military boot camps are designed to prepare soldiers for war and that a similar model may not be appropriate for offenders.[69] Others have called into question potential net-widening effects of the sanction. Perhaps the most

VIDEO
Boot Camp for Troubled Teens

boot camps: A form of shock incarceration; structured much like a military boot camp.

FIGURE 13.9   A Day in the Life of Boot Camp Participants

MINNESOTA CORRECTIONAL FACILITY–WILLOW RIVER/MOOSE LAKE WILLOW RIVER CHALLENGE INCARCERATION PROGRAM DAILY SCHEDULE

TIME	EVENT
5:30 am	Wake Up/Roll Call
5:35–5:45	Physical Training Preparation
5:45–6:35	Physical Training
6:35–7:00	Personal Cleanup
7:00–7:30	Breakfast Meal
7:30–7:45	Morning Flag Ritual
7:45–8:25	Barracks Maintenance/Offender Inspection
8:25–8:30	Program Readiness Preparation
8:30–9:55	Cognitive Skills Training/Barracks Inspection
10:00–11:55	Education Programming or Work Assignment
11:55–12:00	Roll Call
12:00–12:30	Lunch Meal
12:35–3:15	Work Assignment
3:15–3:30	Physical Training Preparation
3:30–4:30	Physical Training
4:30–4:55	Personal Cleanup
4:55–5:00	Roll Call
5:00–5:30	Evening Meal
5:30–6:00/6:15	Evening Flag Ritual/KP/Administration Building Cleanup/Program Readiness Preparation
6:00–7:00	Lecture or Acupuncture Treatment
7:00–8:00	Chemical Dependency Programming
8:00–9:00	Squad Meeting
9:00–9:25	Individual Offender Programming and Journal/Correspondence and Study Time
9:25–9:30	Personal Cleanup
9:30	Roll Call
9:35	Lights Out

National Institute of Justice

common criticism surrounding boot camps is whether they actually deter future criminal behavior. Doris McKenzie, perhaps the leading boot camp researcher, has concluded that boot camps are ineffective in reducing offending, "at least in the absence of therapeutic elements and aftercare components."[70]

Despite evidence suggesting that boot camps are ineffective, they remain a popular option. Their popularity led one author to suggest, "Now it is up to policy makers to admit that boot camps will never live up to their intended promise because of inherent flaws in its model. Clinging to false hope will only harm those that the juvenile justice system strives to protect."[71]

Community Service

Community service sanctions require offenders to perform some sort of work-related activity for a community agency. Typically, offenders receiving this sentence are sentenced to perform a specified number of hours working on community service. In some jurisdictions, community service is believed to be among the most common type of sanction used. The goals of community service include the following:[72]

- Hold offenders accountable for the harm they have caused to the community

- Provide communities with human resources that can improve the quality of life in public environments, business, and even individual residences

- Help offenders develop new skills through supervised work activities

- Allow victims a voice and occasionally some direct benefit by recommending the type of community service performed

Community service tends to receive a great deal of press attention when celebrities receive the sanction.

Some observers have noted that community service sanctions may be especially useful for white-collar offenders who have job skills that can be of benefit to the community. Sentencing convicted health care providers to work at a community health clinic, for example, would be beneficial to the community. Two general rules guide the assignment of community service locations. First, violent offenders should not be assigned to work in areas that are related to their crimes. For instance, a person convicted of abusing an older person should not be assigned to work in a nursing home. Second, the community service activities should be of value to the community. Offenders would not be assigned to work for a private business simply to improve the company's profits.

Offenders do not get "overtime" when assigned to community service. They are expected to work the number of hours indicated in their sentences. There is no "time and a half" for working weekends!

community service: An alternative sanction that requires offenders to perform some sort of work-related activity for a community agency.

work release: An alternative sanction that allows offenders to maintain jobs while they are incarcerated.

Work release programs allow inmates to work in the community during the day.

© Diez, Cherie/ZUMA Press/Corbis

Work Release

Work release programs allow offenders to maintain jobs while they are incarcerated. Technically speaking, work release programs are not alternatives to incarceration, but they are a form of community-based sanction because they permit incarcerated offenders to spend time in the community (at their jobs) while they are serving their incarceration. Vermont created the first work release program in 1906.[73] Today, work release programs are used across many different jurisdictions in the United States.

A few different varieties of work release programs exist. First, some offenders might be sentenced to work release immediately as part of their sanctions. In these situations, offenders are permitted to keep the jobs they had when they were convicted but are required to be incarcerated for a stated length of time. Second, some offenders might be assigned to work release after they have served a specified amount of time in jail or prison. In these situations, offenders typically would need to find jobs that they did not have prior to their incarceration. Third, in terms of locations, work release offenders might be incarcerated in jails or prisons, or they might be housed in work release centers, which are sometimes called *restitution centers* in reference to the way that income made by the inmates can be given back to the victims or the government.[74]

Work release is hailed as an appropriate community-based sanction for many different reasons. For example,

- In some jurisdictions offenders have to pay rent to live in the work release centers. Rather than having the government pay the entire incarceration cost, inmates pay some of the costs.

- Employment is potentially a protective factor against future crime.[75]

- While working, inmates are doing something productive rather than being unproductive. This also makes it easier to supervise offenders who are not on work release because corrections officers have fewer inmates to supervise during the day.

- Working while incarcerated will help inmates develop or hone their work-related skills.

- Having a job when released from jail or prison will assist with reentry.

- Leaving jail or prison to go to work each day would help to deal with the boredom associated with confinement.

- Working while incarcerated should build appreciation for work. As students, if you were on an educational release, one would expect that you would rather be in class than in prison during your release times. Hence, you would appreciate your courses even more than you do now!

- Typically, offenders have to save some of the money they make and send some back to their families. This means that offenders have money saved up when they are released from incarceration.

- Work release programs produce tax revenue for the state. Between 1995 and 2012, offenders on work release in New York paid $42.6 million in taxes.[76]

As is the case with other types of community-based sanctions, some observers criticize work release as being too lenient, even though offenders spend roughly two-thirds of their time incarcerated. The "Ethical Decision Making" box in this chapter shows how some of the issues that arise in jails may arise in work release centers.

ETHICAL DECISION MAKING

INTERACTING WITH INMATES IN A FAIR MANNER

Mary Beth Moore, a student taking an online Introduction to Corrections course, works as a cook in the local work release center as a way to make ends meet. She got the job after her uncle, a local car salesman, sold the sheriff a new automobile.

Moore is apprehensive about working in the jail, but the inmates and coworkers quickly put her at ease. She is the youngest worker in the kitchen, though she is the only one seeking a college degree.

Moore and her coworkers have a very clear job: prepare the food, distribute the meals, collect the food, and count the forks when they are returned to make sure that they get them all back. The inmates working in the kitchen clean up after each meal. It is Moore's job to make sure that the inmates complete their tasks.

One day Moore is talking to Nancy Walker, a likeable middle-aged drug addict who has been in and out of prison a dozen times. Walker is affectionately called "Bob" because she "bobbed" in and out of prison so regularly. Walker asks Moore about her college experience: "How many classes are you taking?"

Moore responds, "I have three this semester. I am taking them online so I can keep working and pay for my classes."

"What is your favorite class?" Walker asks.

"I really like my corrections class because it helps me understand my job," Moore responds.

"Do you keep your books or sell them back to the library?" Walker asks.

"Well, the library doesn't buy books, that would be the online bookstore," Moore responds. "Anyway, I never sell my books back because I want to keep them."

Walker then gets to the point, "My daughter is a criminal justice major and trying to raise her daughter who has epilepsy. The money she spends on her books could be used to buy her daughter the medicine she needs. Can my daughter borrow your books? I promise that she will give them back."

Moore is caught off guard. She has been trained not to befriend inmates or do them favors. "Let me think about it," she says just to end the conversation.

Nancy follows up with, "Think about it. Your generosity will make you have a safer work environment."

YOU DECIDE

1. Under what conditions, if any, should Moore lend the books to Walker's daughter?

2. If the books were e-books that required passwords, how might this make a difference in your response?

In addition to concerns about leniency, the occasional inmate escape from work release weakens the image that members of the public have regarding the programs. Also, some critics have argued that the politicization of work release programs may result in "work release participants, especially those with high-paying jobs, . . . vulnerable to the political processes."[77] The basis of this claim is that offenders might end up paying more if the fees charged are based on a percentage of the offender's salary. Essentially, the fees are similar to a tax. Despite these criticisms, work release remains a popular community-based sanction.

BEYOND A REASONABLE DOUBT 13.4

Which of the following is a form of shock incarceration?

(a) House arrest with electronic monitoring, (b) Day reporting centers, (c) Community service, (d) Work release, (e) Boot camps

The answer can be found on page 522.

Just the Facts: Chapter Summary

- Incarceration refers to the act of holding someone in a setting for the purposes of detention or incarceration. In the criminal justice system, five stages of incarceration exist: detention, classification, incarceration, prerelease, and reentry.

- Prisons house inmates who have been convicted of committing felonies; jails hold pretrial offenders awaiting trial who were not granted bail or pretrial release and offenders who have been convicted of misdemeanors and sentenced to jail for less than 12 months as part of their punishment.

- One of the criticisms of jails is that they are unable to provide effective treatment to offenders.

- Both prisons and jails house offenders, employ corrections staff, can be defined as total institutions, are designed securely, and are reliant on government funding.

- The prison subculture is characterized by "the adherence of inmates to a set of norms that reflect opposition to institutional rules and staff."

- Prisonization refers to the way that inmates experience the prison's socialization process.

- Five pains of imprisonment can arise during the incarceration experience: deprivation of autonomy, deprivation of goods and services, deprivation of liberty, deprivation of heterosexual relationships, and deprivation of security.

- Three common architectural designs for prisons are telephone pole design, campus facility design, and mixed design.

- Inmates leave jail or prison in one of several different ways: (a) They complete the maximum sentence they were expected to serve; (b) they complete the minimum sentence they were expected to serve and abided by jail or prison rules; (c) they are paroled by a parole board; (d) their sentences are overturned on appeal; (e) they are pardoned by the governor or president; (f) their sentences are commuted by the president or governor; or (g) they die in jail or prison.

- *Community-based sanctions* refers to a range of punishments administered to offenders while they remain in the community.

- Probation is a sanction imposed by the judge that provides for community supervision without any form of incarceration.

- Parole, where it exists, involves a period of community supervision that is imposed after individuals have served a stint of incarceration.

- Generally speaking, probation and parole officers are responsible for supervising offenders and ensuring that offenders abide by their conditions of probation or parole.

- The American Probation and Parole Association has classified probation activities into the following categories: assessment and case planning, conducting home visits, conducting workplace visits, communicating with treatment providers and collateral contacts, reporting to court as needed, holding offenders accountable through strict monitoring of conditions, and enforcing conditions through arrest and formal sanctioning.

- Four different levels of probation or parole are typically identified: intensive supervision, traditional supervision, low supervision, and administrative supervision.

- Probation and parole officers confront many different challenges in their occupational routines, including traveling, home visit barriers, waiting, collaboration, cultural influences, technological barriers, rural barriers, stress, and low salaries.

- The phrase *alternative sanctions* refers to a range of punishments that are believed to be less punitive than incarceration but more punitive than traditional probation or parole.

- In home confinement, also known as house arrest, offenders are expected to be at home either for portions of their sanctions or for their entire sanctions.

- House arrest with electronic monitoring is a variation of the home confinement sanction, in which technology is used to monitor offenders' whereabouts.

- Day reporting centers are locations where offenders are required to report on a daily basis as part of their sanctions.

- As a form of shock incarceration, boot camps are structured very much like military boot camps.

- Community service sanctions require offenders to perform some sort of work-related activity for a community agency.

- Technically speaking, work release programs are not alternatives to incarceration, but they are a form of community-based sanction because they permit incarcerated offenders to spend time in the community (at their jobs) while they are serving their incarcerations.

Prison yards provide opportunities for interaction between inmates. They also provide a potential setting for violent interactions between inmates.

© Reuters/Lucy Nicholson

FIGURE 14.1 **Patterns Surrounding Inmates' Rights**

- Change over time
- Inmates' Rights . . .
- Determined through constitutional interpretations
- Limited

➡ General Issues for Prisoners

Observers occasionally suggest that prison and jail sanctions are lenient and easy, but in reality, incarceration experiences result in many difficulties for inmates. In considering the issues particularly relevant to inmates, we focus on inmates' rights, danger in prison, sexual assaults in prison, and health care and incarceration.

Inmates' Rights

Some people wrongly assume that inmates lose all of their rights when they are incarcerated. This is far from the truth, but the assumption is somewhat understandable given the way that inmates' rights have evolved over time. Three fundamental aspects of inmates' rights are that they change over time; they are limited; and they are determined through court interpretations of the U.S. Constitution (see Figure 14.1).

Simply put, inmates are treated differently today than they were in the past, and these differences in treatment stem from interpretations about their rights. Definitions of **cruel and unusual punishment**, crucial to a protection offered through the Eighth Amendment, for example, have changed over time. According to the Supreme Court, cruel and unusual punishments are those that are "incompatible with the evolving standards of decency that mark the progress of a maturing society . . . or which involve the unnecessary infliction of pain."[2] Among the penalties used in the past are branding, whipping, cutting off individuals' ears, or tying offenders to a wooden horse in the middle of the town.[3] Evolving standards of decency have told us that these punishments are now cruel and unusual.

Although some people believe that inmates have no rights, others assume that inmates have the same rights as everyone else, that prison is "easy," and that inmates are just sitting around watching television in their cells. This is not the case. When sentenced to prison or jail, offenders forfeit certain rights, or their rights and privileges are restricted. Consider the following examples:[4]

- ➡ Inmates have a right to a certain amount of privacy, but not complete privacy.

- ➡ Inmates have a right to have visitors, but these rights are restricted as visitation is a privilege.

cruel and unusual punishment: Punishments that are "incompatible with the evolving standards of decency that mark the progress of a maturing society . . . or which involve the unnecessary infliction of pain."

- Inmates have a right to medical care, but the care only needs to be reasonable.

- Inmates have a right to be protected against cruel and unusual punishment, but they do not have a right to be protected against punishment (and if they are injured during security measures, the infliction of injury is not cruel and unusual if the security measures were in good faith).

- Inmates have a right to participate in media interviews, but these interviews can be restricted.

Specific punishments are determined by the courts, while the sanctions are imposed in the correctional setting.

© AP Photo/Atlanta Journal-Constitution/John Spink

- Inmates have a right to practice religion, but the religious practices can be limited if it is believed that they make it too difficult to secure the prison environment (for example, using sacrificial knives is prohibited, and practicing martial arts may be limited).

- Inmates have a right to receive and send mail, but this mail can be, and will be, opened and read by prison staff for security purposes unless it is privileged materials from their attorneys.

- Inmates have a right to file complaints to the courts.

- Inmates have a right to "reasonable" dietary needs related to religious beliefs.

In some institutions, inmates might have access to the Internet, but the access is limited and the websites they visit are closely monitored.

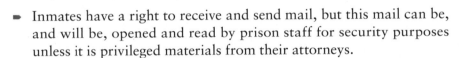

CRIMINAL JUSTICE and the **MEDIA:**
INMATE "PENPAL" WEBSITES

In a rather innovative archival study using websites, criminal justice scholar Richard Tewksbury read the personal advertisements of 1,051 prisoners posted on three websites (writeaprisoner.com, inmate-connection.com, and inmate.com) and compared the information that inmates posted about themselves with official information provided on state websites. He found that approximately one-third of the inmate ads included "at least one inaccurate reporting of the three pieces of basic personal information (age, release date, conviction offense)." Just two of the inmates lied about all three pieces of information. Tewksbury stressed that two-thirds of the inmates were, in fact, honest about the information they provided.

Would you consider being a penal with an inmate? What do you think some of the pros and cons would be?

Tewksbury, R. (2005). Personal ads from prisoners: Do inmates tell the truth about themselves? *Federal Probation, 69*(2), 32–34.

Some inmates might even find "penpals" through these websites (see the "Criminal Justice and the Media" box in this chapter).

Historically the courts avoided getting involved in inmate complaints. Referred to as the *hands-off doctrine*, the courts allowed corrections institutions and states to oversee their own practices. Traced to the 1871 Supreme Court decision of *Ruffin v. Commonwealth*, inmates were viewed as "slaves of the state" who had virtually no rights. In 1964, the Court's decision in *Cooper v. Pate* interpreted the Civil Rights Act of 1871 as suggesting that imprisonment should not result in the loss of constitutional rights as described under the Fourteenth Amendment and the "equal protection under the law" clause.[5] The resulting effect of the *Cooper* decision gave prisoners the right to challenge prison rules, policies, and procedures and opened up a number of court cases that argued for expanded rights for prisoners in many different areas. The decision paved the way for prisoners to file petitions, or formal complaints, that challenge some aspect of their incarceration.

After the *Cooper* decision, courts across the United States began to take a closer look at prison life. According to one author:

> They were shocked by what they saw. Courts declared some prisons to be "unfit for human habitation," "a dark and evil world completely alien to the free world," and "so inhumane and degrading as to amount to cruel and unusual punishment." . . . In 1974, the Court announced: "[t]here is no iron curtain drawn between the Constitution and the prisons of this country."[6]

What followed was a series of court decisions that expanded inmates' rights in the areas of health care, court access, and cruel and unusual punishment. Table 14.1 provides an overview of some of those decisions.

Generally speaking, types of petitions filed by inmates include civil rights petitions, habeas corpus petitions, motions to vacate sentences, and mandamus petitions. A *civil rights petition* (also known as a Section 1983 petition) alleges that corrections practices are violating the inmate's rights. A *habeas corpus petition* alleges that the inmate's incarceration is unlawful. A *motion to vacate sentence* alleges that the sentence is in violation of legal standards. A *mandamus petition* requests that the court order a specific action to be performed by a public entity on behalf on the inmate.[7]

Although the number of prison petitions filed in U.S. district courts increased after *Cooper*, they soared in the mid-1990s, peaking at more than 63,000 petitions filed alleging abuses of rights. Figure 14.2 shows the number of petitions filed over time.

Four factors contributed to this increase in the use of courts to resolve complaints by prisoners. First, the willingness of the courts to hear the cases in the first place created a foundation from which this increase could occur. Second, more attorneys began practicing law in this timeframe. Third, the number of inmates increased over this same period of time, suggesting that the rate of inmate complaints per total number of inmates did not increase to the same degree as the number of complaints. Finally, across the United States, a general culture supporting the use of civil courts to

TABLE 14.1 Significant Prisoner Rights Cases

CASE	ISSUE	DESCRIPTION	WHAT THE COURT SAID
Estelle v. Gamble (1974)	Medical care	Gamble was injured on his prison job and received substandard responses from the prison over the injury and in some cases was not permitted to see the doctor.	"We therefore conclude that deliberate indifference to serious medical needs of prisoners constitutes the 'unnecessary and wanton infliction of pain', *Gregg v. Georgia, supra*, at 173 (joint opinion), proscribed by the Eighth Amendment. This is true whether the indifference is manifested by prison doctors in their response to the prisoner's needs . . . or by prison guards in intentionally denying or delaying access to medical . . . care . . . or intentionally interfering with the treatment once prescribed." *Estelle v. Gamble* (75–929)
Pell v. Procunier (1974)	Freedom of speech	Four inmates and three journalists were denied face-to-face interviews and filed suit.	"A prison inmate retains those First Amendment rights that are not inconsistent with his status as prisoner or with the legitimate penological objectives of the corrections system, and here the restrictions on inmates' free speech rights must be balanced against the State's legitimate interest in confining prisoners . . . to deter crime, to protect society by quarantining criminal offenders for a period during which rehabilitative procedures can be applied, and to maintain the internal security of penal institutions. . . . Alternative means of communication remain open to the inmates; they can correspond by mail with persons (including media representatives), *Procunier v. Martinez*, 416 U.S. 396; they have rights of visitation with family, clergy, attorneys, and friends of prior acquaintance; and they have unrestricted opportunity to communicate with the press or public through their prison visitors." *Pell v. Procunier* (73–918)
Rhodes v. Chapman (1981)	Double celling inmates	Inmates alleged that housing two inmates in a 63-square-foot space was cruel and unusual.	"To the extent such conditions are restrictive and even harsh, they are part of the penalty that criminals pay for their offenses against society. . . . [T]he Constitution does not mandate comfortable prisons, and prisons of SOCF's type, which house persons convicted of serious crimes, cannot be free of discomfort. Thus, these considerations properly are weighed by the legislature and prison administration rather than a court." *Rhodes v. Chapman* (80–332)
Hudson v. McMillian (1992)	Excessive force	Hudson was beaten up by a correctional officer. The lower court said the injuries were not that serious and, as a result, that Hudson's rights were not violated.	"In the excessive force context, society's expectations are different. When prison officials maliciously and sadistically use force to cause harm, contemporary standards of decency always are violated. . . . This is true whether or not significant injury is evident. Otherwise, the Eighth Amendment would permit any physical punishment, no matter how diabolic or inhuman, inflicting less than some arbitrary quantity of injury. . . . That is not to say that every malevolent touch by a prison guard gives rise to a federal cause of action." *Hudson v. McMillian* (90–6531)
Farmer v. Brennan (1994)	Legal duty to protect inmates	Farmer, a transsexual, was housed with a traditional population and raped.	"The question under the Eighth Amendment is whether prison officials, acting with deliberate indifference, exposed a prisoner to a sufficiently substantial 'risk of serious damage to his future health'. . . . Being violently assaulted in prison is simply 'not part of the penalty that criminal offenders pay for their offenses against society.'" *Farmer v. Brennan* (92–7047)

(Continued)

TABLE 14.1 Significant Prisoner Rights Cases (Continued)

CASE	ISSUE	DESCRIPTION	WHAT THE COURT SAID
Pennsylvania Department of Corrections v. Yeskey (1998)	Disabilities	Yeskey was denied admission to a boot camp because of hypertension. Do the protections in Title II of the Americans With Disabilities Act extend to inmates?	"Assuming, without deciding, that the plain-statement rule does govern application of the ADA to the administration of state prisons, we think the requirement of the rule is amply met: the statute's language unmistakably includes State prisons and prisoners within its coverage . . . the plain text of Title II of the ADA unambiguously extends to state prison inmates" *Pennsylvania Department of Corrections v. Yeskey* (97-634)
Overton v. Bazzetta et al. (2003)	Visitation rights	Michigan passed a law prohibiting children from visiting unless the inmate had parental rights and restricting other types of visitors. A group of inmates filed suit.	"The fact that the regulations bear a rational relation to legitimate penological interests suffices to sustain them regardless of whether respondents have a constitutional right of association that has survived incarceration. This Court accords substantial deference to the professional judgment of prison administrators, who bear a significant responsibility for defining a corrections system's legitimate goals and determining the most appropriate means to accomplish them." *Overton v. Bazzetta* (02-94)
Cutter v. Wilkinson (2005)	Religion	Inmates argued that their non-mainstream religions were not accommodated as specified in the Religious Land Use and Institutionalized Persons Act of 2000.	"RLUIPA thus protects institutionalized persons who are unable freely to attend to their religious needs and are therefore dependent on the government's permission and accommodation for exercise of their religion. But the Act does not elevate accommodation of religious observances over an institution's need to maintain order and safety. An accommodation must be measured so that it does not override other significant interests." *Cutter v. Wilkinson* (03-9877)
Brown v. Plata (2011)	Prison population limits	A lower court ordered that the California state prison system reduce prison populations because of its inability to meet physical and health needs of inmates.	"The medical and mental health care provided by California's prisons falls below the standard of decency that inheres in the Eighth Amendment. This extensive and ongoing constitutional violation requires a remedy, and a remedy will not be achieved without a reduction in overcrowding. . . . The State shall implement the order without further delay." *Brown v. Plata* (09-1233)
Swarthout v. Cooke (2011)	Inmates' rights to parole	A federal court overturned the governor's decision to deny an inmate parole. The state appealed on the grounds that the federal court did not have legal standing.	"Whatever liberty interest exists is, of course, a state interest created by California law. There is no right under the Federal Constitution to be conditionally released before the expiration of a valid sentence, and the States are under no duty to offer parole to their prisoners." *Swarthout v. Cooke* (10-333)

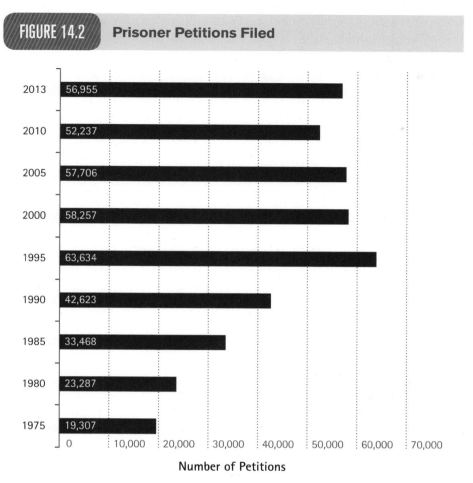

FIGURE 14.2   **Prisoner Petitions Filed**

Year	Number of Petitions
2013	56,955
2010	52,237
2005	57,706
2000	58,257
1995	63,634
1990	42,623
1985	33,468
1980	23,287
1975	19,307

Number of Petitions

U.S. Census Bureau, Statistical Abstract of the U.S.

resolve disputes was manifested during this time. Indeed, 117,320 lawsuits were filed in U.S. district courts in 1975. By 1985, 273,670 lawsuits were filed in U.S. district courts.[8] In other words, it was not just inmates who were using the courts to resolve civil matters!

In an effort to curb the number of lawsuits filed by inmates, Congress passed the **Prison Litigation Reform Act** (PLRA) in 1996. Among other things, this act required inmates to exhaust all administrative remedies and to pay a filing fee before filing suit. In addition, the law stipulated that higher fees would be paid by inmates who had a history (that is, three strikes) of filing frivolous lawsuits. As well, the PLRA restricted the amount of fees that attorneys could charge in these cases. The act seemed to have mixed success. Although filings decreased somewhat, as one researcher found, the law "seems to be making even constitutionally meritorious cases harder both to bring and win."[9]

Danger in Prison

In 1972, inmates at Attica prison in New York state rioted over poor prison conditions and took over part of the prison. Holding 42 corrections officers and staff hostage for four days, the inmates had many demands,

Prison Litigation Reform Act: A law requiring inmates to exhaust all administrative remedies and pay a filing fee before filing suit claiming that their rights have been abused.

some of which the government agreed to. However, the government was not willing to promise they would not hold the offenders accountable for taking the hostages nor would they remove the prison superintendent. The takeover became especially violent when authorities intervened and Governor Nelson Rockefeller sent state police into the prison. After the exchange of fire ended, 43 individuals were killed, including 33 prisoners and 10 corrections staff.

Less than a decade a later, violence erupted at the Penitentiary of New Mexico in Santa Fe. This riot was described by one reporter as "an inmate rebellion without a plan, without leadership, and without goals."[10] By the time the National Guard entered the prison, 33 inmates had already been brutally murdered. Several of the inmates were "snitches" who had been housed in a segregation unit. According to one reporter, "One was hung from the upper tier of the cellblock, another decapitated."[11] Though no guards were killed, they were beaten and tortured, and some were raped.[12]

More recently, inmates rioted for 11 hours in the California Institution for Men, injuring more than 250 inmates, 55 of whom required hospitalization. Inmates' gangs, divided between Black gang members and Latino gang members, fought one another for the duration of the riot.[13] Table 14.2 provides details surrounding other prison riots that have occurred across the United States.

Some prisons are notorious for the amount of violence that is reported to occur within them. Inmates at the Idaho State Correctional Center labeled the prison "Gladiator School" in reference to the seemingly high level of violence at the prison. A group of inmates sued the Corrections Corporation of America (CCA), which runs the prison, alleging that the "CCA had ceded control to prison gangs so that they could understaff the prison and save money on employee wages."[14]

Factors contributing to prison violence include violent histories, diet, structural factors, and situational factors. With regard to the first factor, consider that incarcerated offenders tend to have violent histories, both as victims and as offenders. In many ways, violence is a way of life for these offenders. These violent histories are related to the importation model discussed in Chapter 13.

Meager meals have also be linked to prison violence. A study of diet found that providing inmates with daily vitamin, mineral, and essential fatty acid supplements reduced violent incidents by inmates by 37%.[15] Nutritional experts have suggested various changes in diet to reduce the risk of violence related to food. Besides the addition of vitamin supplements, straightforward and less costly suggestions have included serving dinner slightly later so that offenders don't eat fatty snacks at night and minimizing the amount of time between dinner preparation and consumption so that the food does not lose its nutritional value.[16]

Structural factors related to the prison may also foster violence. Overcrowding, an abundance of free time, the experience of various deprivations, and prison culture are a few of the factors that may lead to violence. With regard to overcrowding, prison riots are often attributed to a high inmate-to-staff ratio. In terms of free time, the more time that

TABLE 14.2	Description of Prison Riots
LOCATION	**DESCRIPTION OF EVENTS**
Kirkland Correctional Institution (Kirkland, South Carolina)	The Kirkland facility was generally well managed at the time of the disturbance of April 1, 1986, and so was the riot's resolution. The riot began in a housing unit holding the prison's most violent and disruptive inmates. Inmates seized control of this unit, scaled the fence around it, and then used construction tools left on the grounds to release 700 general-population inmates. The riot command post functioned smoothly, resolving the disturbance in six hours.
U.S. Penitentiary (Atlanta, Georgia)	On November 10, 1987, the U.S. State Department announced that Cuba had agreed to reinstate a 1984 accord that would permit the repatriation of up to 2,500 Cuban nationals. Included would be Cubans who had fled in the 1980 Mariel boatlift but who, once released on "immigration parole," had been convicted of a crime and were now detained in one of two federal prisons. Three days after the announcement, the detainees seized control of the U.S. Penitentiary in Atlanta (part of the Bureau of Prisons, U.S. Department of Justice). Their principal demand was that they not be repatriated to Cuba. The uprising lasted 11 days, involved more than 100 hostages, and required protracted negotiations to resolve.
Mack Alford Correctional Center (Mack Alford, Oklahoma)	The riot that occurred at this medium-security institution between May 13 and 15, 1988, was preceded by a six-hour period during which Black and White inmates milled about in crowds, expressing antagonism toward each other and toward authorities. Despite attempts to defuse the situation, a corrections official was taken hostage late in the evening, marking the start of the riot. Over a two-hour period, inmates seized seven more hostages and took over two-thirds of the prison. No substantive issues were raised during the three-day disturbance, which was eventually resolved through a combination of negotiation, exhaustion on the part of the inmates, and defection by inmates who no longer wanted to participate.
Arizona State Prison Complex—Cimarron Unit (Tucson)	This one-hour disturbance by inmates at the Cimarron Unit of the Arizona State Prison Complex at Tucson [on June 21, 1990] initially pitted inmates against inmates. It began as a fight over a cigarette lighter and escalated into a large, racially divided brawl. When prison administrators intervened, inmates turned on them, and force had to be used to end the disturbance.
Idaho State Correctional Institution (Boise)	The Idaho State Correctional Institution (ISCI) houses medium-custody inmates as well as close-custody inmates (those who are dangerous and difficult to manage), inmates in administrative segregation and detention, and those awaiting execution. On September 28, 1988, inmates in a close-custody housing unit refused to return to their cells after having been observed drinking a homemade alcoholic beverage. They then used an unsecured table to break into the unit's control center. The riot was eventually brought under control by an ultimatum and riot squad deployment.
Pennsylvania State Correctional Institution (Camp Hill)	Since 1975 Camp Hill had been an adult correctional facility, housing minimum- and medium-security inmates. On October 25, 1989, inmates returning from an exercise yard in the late afternoon overwhelmed correctional staff and seized eight hostages. The riot ended through negotiations, and inmates were confined to cells. The next day the superintendent met with the inmates to discuss their grievances. In a development unknown to him, many of the cells to which the inmates had been confined were not secure, permitting the start of a second riot later that same day. Five more hostages were taken. Negotiations were again attempted, but the riot finally ended when state police forcibly entered the compound.

Resolution of Prison Riots : Strategies and Policies by Useem, Camp, and Camp (1995) Tab. "Description of Prison Riots." By permission of Oxford University Press, USA.

offenders have on their hands, the more time they have to engage in inappropriate activities. Deprivations may lead to violence inasmuch as the deprivations lead to frustrations among inmates, who use violence as a strategy to cope. As well, prison culture (and prison management styles) "can also play a role in prison violence."[17]

Situational factors also contribute to prison violence. The nature of interactions between individuals, some of whom are already disposed to violence, may lead to violence. For example, it has been suggested that inmate-on-inmate violence occurs because of the values that inmates bring into prisons, whereas inmate-on-staff violence is the result of deprivations in prison.[18] In addition, inmates may find themselves in situations where they deem violence to be the appropriate response. A study by Stephen Light found that violence toward prison staff is tied to perceptions of being treated unfairly or inconsistently.[19] According to Light, "Conduct by an officer that is defined as inconsistent with

Correctional officers spend a significant portion of their time searching for contraband.

flickr/Jim Tourtellotte

accepted practices or as arbitrary, capricious, spiteful, unnecessary, or petty may be viewed as an occasion for resistance."[20]

Related to situational factors, some observers have argued that contraband (that is, goods that inmates are not supposed to have in prison but that are trafficked into the institution) provides an opportunity for violence. Similar to the way that the presence of illegal drugs in neighborhoods is tied to violence, contraband (and efforts to sneak it in and sell it) may create situations in which violence is used.

Prisons and jails are dangerous locations. They house individuals with violent histories, offer little programming, provide meager meals, and possess structural features that promote gang involvement. Given that reality, five factors explain why there is not even *more* violence in prisons and jails:[21]

- ➡ Professionalization of prison staff better prepares the staff to deal with inmate violence.

- ➡ Prison classification strategies that use valid risk assessment tools to predict violence can be useful in deciding which programs inmates should be offered.

- ➡ Modern technology is used to monitor inmates more closely.

- ➡ Evidence-based policies are used to support programming initiatives.

- ➡ Separating offenders who are prone to violence (for example, gang members) reduces violence.

Prisons have become much safer than in the past. In 1980, 54 out of 100,000 inmates were victims of homicide, compared with roughly 5 out of 100,000 inmates currently.

Sexual Assaults in Prison

Sexual assault in prison has been described as "one of America's older, darkest, and yet most open, secrets."[22] Increased concern about sexual violence in prisons surfaced after the Supreme Court ruled in *Farmer v. Brennan* that the prison was responsible for the rape of a transsexual inmate who was housed in the general prison population.

About a decade after the *Farmer* case, Congress passed the Prison Rape Elimination Act of 2003 in an effort to curb sexual violence prisons. The major provisions of the act include the following:[23]

- ➡ Adherence to a zero-tolerance standard for the incidence of inmate sexual assault and rape

- ➡ Development of standards for detection, prevention, reduction, and punishment of prison rape

- Collection and dissemination of information on the incidence of prison rape
- Award of grant funds to help state and local governments implement the purposes of the Act

The Bureau of Justice Statistics (BJS) was charged with collecting data on the extent of sexual violence in prisons through random samples of offenders. The results from a recent effort by the BJS show that inmate-on-inmate sexual assaults are the most common allegations, and across all varieties, the allegations are infrequently substantiated. This does not mean that the acts did not occur; it simply means the allegations could not be substantiated.

Similar to sexual assaults outside of prison, those occurring in prison frequently are conducted out of a desire for power and control rather than because of sexual desires. The varieties of sexual assault have been classified according to offender-victim relationships (staff-on-inmate sexual assaults, inmate-on-inmate sexual assaults) and type of behavior performed (for example, anal rape, oral rape). Table 14.3 provides definitions

TABLE 14.3   Sexual Assault Definitions

SEXUAL ASSAULT TYPE	BUREAU OF JUSTICE STATISTICS DEFINITION
Inmate-on-Inmate Sexual Victimization	Involves sexual contact with a victim without his or her consent or with a victim who cannot consent or refuse
Nonconsensual Sexual Acts	The most serious victimizations, including
	Contact between the penis and the vagina or the penis and the anus, including penetration, however slight
	Contact between the mouth and the penis, vagina, or anus
	Penetration of the anal or genital opening of another person by a hand, finger, or other object
Abusive Sexual Contacts	Less serious victimizations, including
	Intentional touching, either directly or through clothing, of the genitalia, anus, groin, breast, inner thigh, or buttocks of any person
	Incidents in which the intent was to sexually exploit (rather than to harm or debilitate)
Staff-on-Inmate Sexual Victimization	Includes both consensual and nonconsensual acts perpetrated on an inmate by staff.
	Staff includes employees, volunteers, contractors, official visitors, or other agency representatives. Family, friends, and other visitors are excluded.
Staff Sexual Misconduct	Includes any act or behavior of a sexual nature directed toward an inmate by staff, including romantic relationships. Such acts include
	Intentional touching of the genitalia, anus, groin, breast, inner thigh, or buttocks with the intent to abuse, arouse, or gratify sexual desire
	Completed, attempted, threatened, or requested sexual acts
	Occurrences of indecent exposure, invasion of privacy
	Staff voyeurism for sexual gratification
Staff Sexual Harassment	Includes repeated verbal statements or comments of a sexual nature to an inmate by staff. Such statements include
	Demeaning references to an inmate's sex or derogatory comments about his or her body or clothing
	Repeated profane or obscene language or gestures

The U.S. Department of Justice, Office of Justice Programs, Bureau of Justice Statistics

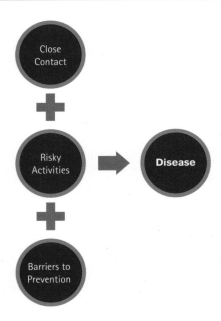

FIGURE 14.3   Sources Leading to Disease in Correctional Institutions

Close Contact

+

Risky Activities

+

Barriers to Prevention

→ Disease

used by the BJS. Prison rapes are similar to other sexual assaults in that the offender and the victim tend to know each other. They are different from the vast majority of other sexual assaults (with the exception of marital rape) in that the victim lives with the offender. This dynamic places victims at continued risk for victimization.

Health Care and Corrections Institutions

Prisons and jails are hotbeds for disease and illness. Compared with community settings, those in institutional settings have higher rates of illnesses such as HIV/AIDS and tuberculosis. Three factors make inmates in prison and jail environments particularly susceptible to disease (see Figure 14.3). First, inmates are in close contact with one another for extended periods of time. Think of a time when you were on an airplane and the person next to you sneezed. You could get off that plane and away from the "sneezer" in a relatively short period of time. In prison, there is no escaping these illnesses.

Second, inmates frequently engage in risky activities (like unprotected sexual activities) that may increase their likelihood of experiencing various illnesses. Some groups of inmates may bring diseases into the jail environment, whereas others may contract diseases while they are incarcerated. In either case, engaging in certain risky activities increases the risk of disease.

Third, until recently, efforts to prevent disease in institutional communities lagged behind efforts in community-based settings. Efforts to prevent disease in prisons and jails have been expanding over time, but in general, a greater emphasis is typically placed on protecting the community from disease rather than protecting inmates from disease.

Some individuals ask why we should be so concerned with inmates' health. Society needs to pay attention to inmates' health for several reasons. First, providing health care to those in need is simply the right thing to do. Of course, some observers might contend that inmates have committed a crime and access to health care should be forfeited. A quotation attributed to Sanford Bates, the first director of the Federal Bureau of Prisons, is worth sharing in response to this contention: "Individuals are sent to prison as punishment, not for punishment."[24] Deprivation of health care would fall into the "for punishment" category.

Second, in terms of disease prevention, remember that most inmates will eventually leave prison. When they do, any diseases they contracted while in prison have the potential to become public health problems in the community.

Inmates have a right to medical care while incarcerated.

© Reuters/Robert Galbraith

Third, with regard to reintegration efforts, attention should be given to the ties between good health and the ability to engage in prosocial behavior. Those who leave prisons and jails with illnesses may have problems getting or keeping jobs. Or problems paying for medication or accessing health care on the outside may provide a motive for subsequent offending. When inmates leave institutions in good health, these problems are minimized.

Fourth, legal factors also drive the need to provide health care to inmates. In reality, legal factors are probably the set of factors that drive most corrections officials' decisions to provide health care. The Supreme Court scrutinized health care delivery in prisons in the past and, in 1972, even declared one state's entire system of prison medical facilities to be in violation of the Eighth Amendment protections against cruel and unusual punishment (*Newman v. Alabama*).[25] Four years later, the Court ruled that providing inadequate health care resulted in "unnecessary and wanton infliction of pain" for inmates (*Estelle v. Gamble*).[26] As a result, prisons are now expected to provide at least reasonable health care to inmates.

Finally, providing health care to inmates also makes economic sense. In short, it is cheaper to treat minor illnesses and diseases, or to prevent them in the first place, than it is to provide care for full-blown illnesses. A great portion of prison and jail budgets is spent on providing health care to inmates. Prison doctors, nurses, aides, and other health care workers are on the payrolls of all prisons and jails.

Evidence indicates that health care officials have done a good job reducing and controlling the spread of illness in prisons and jails. Figure 14.4a shows the declines in HIV/AIDS cases among federal and state prison inmates and the rate of AIDS-related deaths among this population. Figure 14.4b shows the rate of AIDS-related deaths (for 15–55 year olds) in state prisons in comparison to national rates in the community. In 2009, for the first time ever, the rate of prison deaths from AIDS-related illnesses was actually lower than the rate found in the national population.

JOURNAL
Project START

FIGURE 14.4a Rate of HIV/AIDS Cases and AIDS-Related Deaths Among State and Federal Prison Inmates, 2001–2010

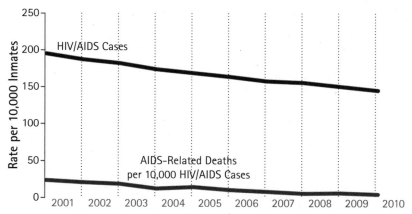

The U.S. Department of Justice, Office of Justice Programs, Bureau of Justice Statistics

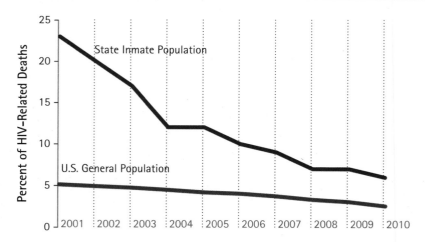

FIGURE 14.4b   Rate of HIV/AIDS cases and AIDS-related Deaths Among State Prison Inmates Ages 15-54, 2001–2010

The U.S. Department of Justice, Office of Justice Programs, Bureau of Justice Statistics

---

BEYOND A REASONABLE DOUBT 14.1

Which Supreme Court case gave prisoners the right to challenge prison rules, policies, and procedures?

(a) *Cooper v. Pate*, (b) *Miranda v. Arizona*, (c) *Gideon v. Wainwright*, (d) *Escobedo v. Illinois*, (e) None of the above

The answer can be found on page 522.

➡ General Issues for Corrections Employees

Like other criminal justice employees, those who work in corrections may find their careers difficult but rewarding. Among the key issues facing corrections employees are correctional misconduct and stress experienced by corrections employees.

Correctional Misconduct

Similar to other professions, the field of corrections is not immune from misconduct by its employees. However, much less research has focused on **correctional misconduct** in comparison to other forms of workplace offending. Bernard McCarthy conducted one of the first studies on correctional misconduct.[27] The varieties of misconduct he examined included stealing from the institution, drug smuggling, and transporting contraband into the prison.

Physical abuse is another type of correctional misconduct. The level of authority that officers have over inmates creates a dynamic in which some

VIDEO
Stanford Prison Experiment

correctional misconduct:
Illegal acts committed by corrections professionals.

officers may use unnecessary power to control the offenders. Zimbardo's Stanford Prison Experiment, discussed in Chapter 2, illustrates this point (recall that the experiment was canceled because students acting as guards in the experiment exerted too much power and control over the students acting as inmates). Consider also abuses occurring in military prisons. The torture occurring at Abu Ghraib made international headlines when photos surfaced showing military officials sexually degrading prisoners. The level of authority created a foundation from which these abuses occurred.

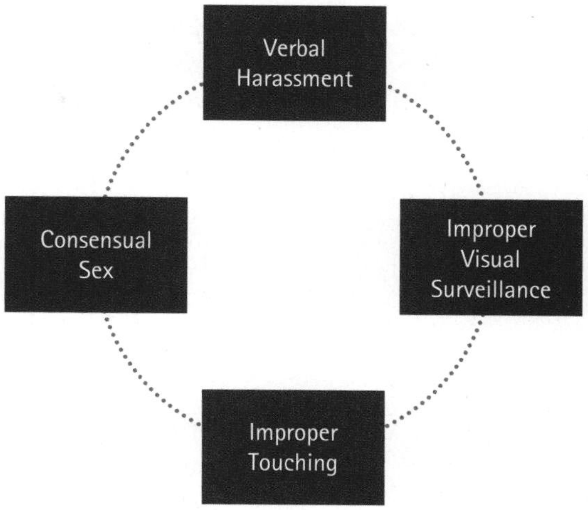

Sexual misconduct by corrections officials includes verbal harassment, improper visual surveillance, improper touching, and consensual sex[28] (see Figure 14.5). So-called *consensual relations* are the most common incidents of sexual misconduct between corrections officers and inmates.[29] Bear in mind, however, that the word *consensual* is misleading in the context of sexual misconduct by corrections officers. The corrections employee has a great deal of power over inmates or probationers, and many states have laws stipulating that sexual relations between officers and offenders are prohibited. These laws exist, in part, because it is recognized that offenders are unable to truly consent in such relationships.[30]

In some cases, the inmate, probationer, or parolee may be the one initiating the relationship. The term **turner** is used to describe "inmates who befriended employees and used that friendship to ultimately coerce employees into rule infractions."[31] Robert Worley and his coauthors identified three types of turners. *Heart-breakers* engage corrections officials in relationships in order to develop long-term relationships with them; *exploiters* engage in the relationship in order to gain access to goods and services or privileges they otherwise would not be able to access; and *hell-raisers* "cause trouble and create hell for the prison system" just for the fun of it.[32] When the relationships are discovered, the most common result is the firing of the employee; criminal prosecutions are relatively infrequent.[33]

A variety of explanations have been offered for correctional misconduct. For example, corrections officers have a great deal of authority and work alone for much of their time. As well, the demand for contraband in prisons provides an incentive for corrupt officers to engage in misconduct. In addition, low morale among corrections staff, many of whom work in stressful environments, may result in misconduct.[34] Strategies suggested to prevent sexual misconduct by corrections officers, and all forms of correctional misconduct, include developing clear policies that are enforced as needed, improving the quality of workers, enhancing supervisory practices, implementing various social control mechanisms, and providing ethics training to officers and staff.[35]

As with other types of misconduct, we do not know how often correctional misconduct occurs. Inappropriate relationships appear to be the most

FIGURE 14.5 Types of Sexual Misconduct by Corrections Officials

turner: A term used to describe an inmate who befriends corrections employees in order to manipulate them into breaking the rules.

frequent type of correctional misconduct. A study of 501 corrections employees in Texas found that "when asked to respond to the item 'some employees have inappropriate relationships with inmates' the mean score was 4.49 on a scale ranging from 1 to 5, with five meaning 'strongly agree.'"[36] Despite this high level of agreement, it seems safe to suggest that the vast majority of corrections professionals are honest and hard-working employees. The few who are dishonest leave unwarranted marks on the entire profession.

Stress

Working in corrections can be a stressful job. Factors that produce stress for those working in prisons and jails include environmental factors, situational factors, biological factors, and work/home factors. *Environmental factors* refers to the condition of the prison or jail and ways that the condition itself may lead to stress for corrections officers. Officials will be inside, with little exposure to sunlight, and greatly restricted in their own abilities to move around (see Figure 14.6). Remember that corrections officers are working in a place designed to keep its inhabitants isolated from society, and while they are working there, they too are isolated and may experience "pains" similar to those that are experienced by inmates.

Situational factors refers to various parts of the corrections officers' daily routines that may contribute to stress. For example, officers face constant threats of violence and danger. They are expected to perform long hours for a relatively low salary. In addition, because they are working out of the public eye, community support is minimal. Boredom is also a frequent part of the corrections officer's routine (just as boredom is part of the inmate's daily routine). The lack of mental activities that challenge officers to use their skills can produce stress.

Biological factors refers to the physical and biological demands placed on corrections officers that can make the job stressful. For example, shift work can produce stress. Also, whereas workers in many other occupations can stop working and eat when they are hungry, corrections officers' work hours are much more regimented. In addition, the sedentary work style of some officers can result in stress.

Work/home factors refers to conflicts that corrections officers can experience between their work roles and their roles as husbands, wives, fathers, mothers, sons, daughters, or other family roles. When at work, officers must be in control and exert authority. Turning off their "corrections officer" behaviors may be difficult when they get home. Also, a lack of family support for corrections officers can be problematic in the workplace and the home. For instance, work/home conflict has been found to reduce job satisfaction for corrections officers.[37] This, in turn, could produce stress.

FIGURE 14.6   **Factors Producing Stress in the Corrections Profession**

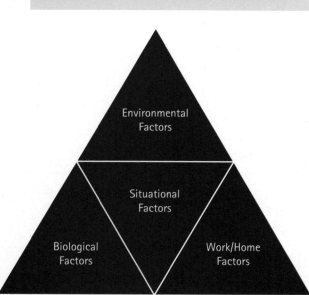

Probation and parole officers also have stressful jobs. After all, any wrongdoing by the offender could be blamed on the officer's failure to supervise the offender. Sources of stress include high caseloads, working with potentially dangerous offenders, paperwork demands, lack of recognition, lack of input into decision making, unrealistic expectations of supervisors, and lack of preparation.[38] Research shows that better prepared probation and parole officers experience lower levels of stress,[39] and the ability to participate in workplace decision making also reduces stress.[40]

BEYOND A REASONABLE DOUBT 14.2

Which of the following would be an example of sexual misconduct by corrections officers?

(a) Verbal harassment, (b) Improper visual surveillance, (c) Improper touching, (d) Consensual sex, (e) All of the above

---

The answer can be found on page 522.

➡ Issues Related to Working With Different Types of Offenders

Corrections employees work with many different types of offenders. Each type of offender may present different issues for corrections workers as well as for the offenders themselves. The populations that warrant consideration in this context are juveniles, women, sex offenders, and mentally ill offenders.

Juvenile Corrections

Juvenile corrections refers to the practices used to punish, detain, and house juveniles who have been charged with an offense, adjudicated as a delinquent, or convicted of a crime if their case was waived to adult court. Strategies used to punish juveniles vary across jurisdictions and communities.

Juvenile offenders are incarcerated in juvenile group homes, in juvenile detention centers, in juvenile institutions, or in juvenile wings of adult prisons or jails. Group homes tend to be managed much like a regular home, and they house fewer children. Sometimes, juveniles in group homes have been abandoned by their parents or are status offenders such as runaways or truants. Juvenile detention centers, also known as juvie, are facilities that house juveniles who are awaiting disposition of their cases. Juvenile institutions are facilities that house juveniles for longer periods of time, with some juveniles sentenced to these facilities until they are 21 years old. When housed in adult prisons or jails, juveniles are separated from adult inmates in order to protect them.

Juvenile detention facilities serve many of the same purposes as adult facilities.
© AP Photo/David Goldman

A number of issues arise when considering the institutionalization of juvenile offenders. Juveniles frequently have histories of abuse and neglect that, if untreated in institutions, may lead to more problems. Also, when juveniles are housed in prisons or jails, even when separated from adults, the stigma may do them more harm than good. One author team identified the following "dangers of detention" for juveniles:[41]

- Detention can increase recidivism.

- Congregating delinquent youth together negatively affects their behavior and increases their chance of reoffending.

- Detention pulls youth deeper into the juvenile and criminal justice system.

- Detention can slow or interrupt the natural process of "aging out of delinquency."

- Detention makes mentally ill youth worse.

- Detention puts youth at greater risk of self-harm.

- Formerly detained youth have reduced success in the labor market.

- Detention is expensive—more expensive than alternatives to detention.

As in adult prisons, violence is a very real problem in juvenile institutions. Some observers have argued that the behavior of corrections staff in juvenile institutions could lead to violence. Using force, ignoring violence, and inducing violence are ways that staff have been implicated in violent incidents. One survey of 100 offenders found that one-third of the juveniles "had directly experienced or witnessed guards offering an incentive to a juvenile offender to intimidate or assault another inmate."[42]

Women and Corrections

In considering women and the corrections experience, attention can be given to women as corrections employees, women as inmates, and women as offenders on community-based sanctions.

Female Corrections Officers

For the most part, the corrections field has been a male-dominated profession. This trend has changed in recent years, with more women entering the field. In 1984, one-fifth of corrections employees were women; by 2005, roughly one-third of corrections employees in state and federal corrections institutions were women.[43]

Researchers have examined differences in the ways that female and male corrections staff function. Generally, research shows that, compared with male corrections officers, female officers are better able to diffuse violent situations,[44] are more likely to experience work/home conflict,[45] and demonstrate more concern about victimization by inmates.[46] Although more women have entered the corrections workforce, experts suggest that female corrections officers "continue to encounter issues of tokenism, sex role stereotyping, paternalistic behavior, exclusion from informal social networks, and both verbal and sexual harassment."[47]

Female Inmates

Gender differences are also seen in the experiences of inmates. Imogene Moyer was one of the first criminologists to study female inmates. After interviewing offenders and staff for a few months, she lived in a female prison for three months in order to gain direct insight about the experiences of female inmates. Her research illuminated the experiences of female offenders while they are incarcerated. One of her observations was that, although the prison looked similar to a college campus, the regimentation and rules enforced on the inmates made it clear that punishment and control were central to the institution's mission.[48]

Female corectional institutions may be designed differently than institutions for male inmates, but their purpose is the same: regimentation and control.

© Jim Lo Scalzo/Epa/Newscom

She also found that the prison tended to promote sex role stereotypes and provided programming in line with gender roles. Such programming, she implied, would result in inmates having job skills that would place them in a disadvantaged position upon their release. For example, inmates were prepared for service occupations such as beauticians, cooks, and housekeepers. Elsewhere, Moyer concluded that changes in the female prison structure over time had "reinforced traditional sex-role stereotypes of women as dependent children."[49] Moyer and others believe that prison programs frequently focus on teaching female offenders how to fulfill stereotypical, and sometimes degrading, gender roles that place them in subservient positions to males.

Whereas male prisons are characterized as having prison gangs, researchers have described how female inmates develop relationships similar to those found in families. Referred to as "**pseudo family groups**,"[50] these relationships develop in part as coping mechanisms for female inmates. Although some of these relationships may be sexual in nature, the majority are more familial in nature than they are intimate.[51]

One issue that some female inmates face involves their roles as mothers (for those inmates who have children). An inmate who enters prison pregnant will give up custody of her child when the child is born, whereas those who already have children give up custody upon admission. In many of these cases, the mother may have already been the sole provider for the child. Prison programming efforts have been developed to help incarcerated mothers maintain contact with their children. These initiatives have several benefits, including the following:[52]

- ➡ Help family bonds
- ➡ Help inmates cope with the pains of imprisonment
- ➡ Potentially protect inmates against the negative qualities of the prison environment
- ➡ Improve the likelihood of successful reentry

JOURNAL
Feelings of Safety

pseudo family groups:
The relationships that female inmates develop with each other; the majority are more family type in nature than they are intimate.

Female Probationers and Parolees

With regard to females on community-based sanctions, as with the incarceration experience, females tend to experience certain types of sanctions differently than males do. Because female probationers and parolees have different needs than male probationers and parolees, some agencies have developed specific female probation units. The vast majority of females on probation have histories of abuse, often at the hands of their former spouses or parents. Consequently, probation services may target strategies to address the consequences of victimization.

For mothers who are on probation, many may be in need of parenting services in order to help protect their children from the types of abuses that led to the mother's own offending.[53] In addition, many of these women are single parents and in need of parenting programs that promote healthy relationships with their children.

Specific types of alternative sanctions are also experienced differently by female offenders. For example, females on electronic monitoring may experience more shame from the electronic monitoring bracelet.[54] As well, work release programs for single mothers become problematic when the mothers have to find child care, and fines for those living on single incomes are difficult to pay. In addition, for those women leaving prison, it has been found that reentry initiatives rarely focus on child care services, health care, counseling, housing needs, or substance abuse services.[55]

One of the reasons that female offenders experience probation differently than males likely has to do with the types of offenses females commit. In general, females tend to commit less serious offenses than males. With different criminal backgrounds and conviction offenses, females may be assigned different types of supervision conditions than males. As a result, these conditions of probation and parole would require different investigatory and supervisory strategies by probation and parole officers.[56]

Feminist criminologists have noted that criminal justice is dominated by male-oriented research studies and theories. Several problems arise from this narrow focus on male offenders. First, it cannot be assumed that the theories that explain male behavior can be used to explain female behavior. Second, the types of responses and treatment strategies used for male offenders may not be appropriate or useful for female offenders. Third, the consequences of male and female offending may vary based on offender type, but these consequences cannot be understood if researchers fail to study female offending. Finally, ignoring female offending limits our understanding about crime and criminal justice in general. More specifically, just as medical doctors study rare diseases to better understand all types of disease, we can better understand all types of crime by studying crimes perpetrated by females as well as males.

Sex Offenders and Corrections

Sex offenders are among the most vilified offender group. In prisons, jails, and community-based corrections, sex offenders, as a group, present different types of issues for corrections employees than do other types of offenders. In prisons, four qualities of sex offenders result in the need to supervise these offenders differently than other offenders: (a) Sex offenders are stigmatized, (b) sex offenders tend to have histories of being victimized, (c) sex offenders tend to receive long prison sentences, and (d) sex offenders face a number of restrictive policies upon their release from incarceration (if they are released).

In terms of the stigma that sex offenders face, across the board, law-abiding citizens and offenders alike seem to view sex offenders as especially evil. No other offender group is viewed with the same level of hatred. For prison and jail officials, the task at hand is to create environments that protect sex offenders from victimization at the hands of fellow inmates. Some observers may wonder about the need to protect offenders; however, both moral and legal reasons warrant such protection. Recall that when offenders are sent to prison, the punishment is the time away from society, rather than the prison experience itself. Legally, prison and jail officials can be sued if inmates are victimized and it can be shown that staff could have prevented the victimization.

The histories of victimization among sex offenders are relevant for corrections staff when considering strategies to treat and rehabilitate sex offenders. It is well accepted in the research literature that many sex offenders were once victims themselves. Recognizing that this relationship exists does not condone sex offending; however, identifying this relationship provides a foundation for more appropriate treatment.

In addition, sex offenders tend to receive particularly long prison sentences. The length of their sentences means that officials will need to supervise (and protect) these offenders in different ways than would be the case for other offenders. Many sex offenders will grow old in prison, which presents a whole different set of issues (discussed in Chapter 15).

Finally, sex offenders, if and when their prison sentences end, face a number of restrictive policies that have implications for their supervision in the community. These policies are strikingly more restrictive than the types of policies used for other offenders. Consider the restrictiveness of the following sex offender policies:

- **Civil commitment laws** are used to commit sex offenders in institutions after their incarceration dates. Mechanisms used to commit mentally ill offenders are used to commit sex offenders for indeterminate periods of time as long as this confinement includes a treatment component.

- *GPS monitoring laws* allow for the use of electronic monitoring for certain types of sex offenders. Using GPS technology, officers can monitor sex offenders' locations.

- **Exclusion zone policies** stipulate places sex offenders cannot go, such as playgrounds, day cares, libraries, or school zones.

- **Registry laws** require sex offenders to register with the state police, and information about registered sex offenders is typically available online.

civil commitment laws: Laws used to commit sex offenders in institutions after their incarceration dates.

exclusion zone policies: Policies that stipulate places sex offenders cannot go.

registry laws: Laws that require sex offenders to register with the state police; information about registered sex offenders is typically available online.

- *Chemical castration laws* allow officials to use drugs to control sex offenders' impulses.

- *Polygraph policies* allow probation and parole officers to force sex offenders to take polygraphs so that officers can determine whether they are being honest about efforts to avoid offending.

Some states have also developed policies calling for mandatory probation sentences to be awarded either in addition to prison sentences or instead of prison sentences. In some states, lifetime probation sanctions are given to sex offenders. The result of these laws is that probation and parole officers are now working with sex offenders more so today than ever before. To address the increase in the number of sex offenders on probation and parole, some agencies have developed specific sex offender probation units. In smaller localities, sex offenders on probation are supervised by general probation officers.

It can be particularly challenging for community corrections officers to supervise sex offenders. Liability concerns for officers surface if sex offenders commit new crimes while on community supervision. In addition, whereas community corrections officers may be able to relate to, identify with, or even understand certain types of offenders, this is not the case with sex offenders.[57] As well, officers will need to work with officials from other systems in supervising sex offenders. Based on these considerations, issues that arise in working with sex offenders include the following:

- Interagency conflict
- Lack of understanding about the mental health system
- Lack of understanding about sex offender treatment
- Lack of understanding about "clinical criteria predicting recidivism"[58]

Mentally Ill Offenders

In 1963, President John F. Kennedy signed into law the **Community Mental Health Act**, which aimed at deinstitutionalizing mentally ill individuals and treating the majority of them in the community rather than in state hospitals. On the surface, such a move likely sounds compassionate and empathetic. Because available community services were insufficient, however, the result of this widespread deinstitutionalization movement has been a dramatic increase in the number of mentally ill individuals sent to jails and prisons and placed on community-based sanctions. As one sheriff told a reporter, "Society was horrified to warehouse people in state hospitals, but we have no problem with warehousing them in jails and prisons."[59]

Indeed, estimates suggest that more than half of all incarcerated inmates suffer from some form of mental illness.[60] Four issues are prevalent among this group of offenders. First, the vast majority of them do not receive the treatment they need while incarcerated. Second, for some offenders, having a mental illness while incarcerated may elevate their risk of victimization. Third, some observers may question whether incarcerating mentally ill

chemical castration laws: Laws that allow officials to use drugs to control sex offenders' impulses.

Community Mental Health Act: An act, that aimed at deinstitutionalizing mentally ill individuals and treating the majority of them in the community rather than in state hospitals.

individuals is equivalent to criminalizing a health problem. Fourth, most of those who are mentally ill while incarcerated will be released back into the community, and they have a high risk of returning to prison or jail.

To improve community supervision of offenders with mental health issues, some agencies have developed mental health units in order to centralize the supervision and treatment of this group of offenders. Some jurisdictions develop these units in conjunction with mental health courts, while others develop them as separate units. Typically, mental health probation units will provide officers with smaller caseloads composed solely of individuals with mental health problems.[61] Certainly, offenders with mental health issues will have much different needs than other offenders. Some of them may have more than one mental health problem; many will have multiple treatment needs; and many have housing needs.[62] In addition, the supervision strategy is typically less punitive, requiring more meetings between officers and offenders, more supervision, and more conditions placed on them.[63]

Because mentally ill offenders are watched more closely than other offenders while they are on probation and parole, they are more likely be caught violating their conditions of release.[64] Drawing attention to this dilemma, one author team writes:

> When they are behaving no worse than offenders without mental illness, it seems inappropriate to use incarceration to achieve social control over offenders with mental illness, regardless of whether this is motivated by fear or paternalism. It is important to remain mindful of our tendency to more closely watch offenders with mental illness and to more forcefully respond to their behavior. Even if evidence-based strategies in mental health and corrections are ideally matched to subgroups of offenders with mental illness, these individuals will continue to "fail" as long as we maintain an unusually high threshold for their success.[65]

BEYOND A REASONABLE DOUBT 14.3

_____ laws are used to commit sex offenders in institutions after their incarceration dates.

(a) Civil commitment, (b) Registry, (c) Exclusionary, (d) Inclusionary, (e) None of the above

---

The answer can be found on page 522.

➡ Issues Related to Punishment Strategies

A number of issues related to specific punishment strategies and policies continue to be the subject of significant debate among policy makers and criminal justice scholars. These issues include the death penalty, recidivism, criminogenic sanctions, support for treatment, and restorative justice.

Death Penalty

Every now and then you may see a Western television show or movie depicting the "bad guy" being sentenced to death. The offender has a noose placed around his neck while standing on a platform in the center of town; the executioner has the floor moved out from beneath the offender's feet, and the offender falls toward the ground but does not fully reach the ground. The rope breaks the offender's neck and the offender dies hanging from the noose. This depiction is probably not far off base.

The **death penalty** (also known as capital punishment) has been used throughout time. Our modern laws governing the death penalty can be traced to *Furman v. Georgia*, a Supreme Court case that outlawed the death penalty on grounds that the penalty was arbitrary and capricious. The Court ruled this way because it believed that allowing juries to decide both guilt and the death penalty at the same time constituted cruel and unusual punishment in violation of the Eighth and Fourteenth Amendments. Justice Potter Stewart wrote in his concurring opinion that "these death sentences are cruel and unusual in the same way that being struck by lightning is cruel and unusual."[66]

As a result of the *Furman* decision, state laws governing the death penalty were voided in 40 states. The state of Georgia changed its state law to provide for a two-stage decision process in death penalty cases (a stage in which guilt is determined and a stage in which the sanction is decided). This new law was upheld by the Supreme Court in *Gregg v. Georgia*.[67]

Some individuals oppose the death penalty because they believe the sanction is a cruel and unusual punishment. For some individuals, definitions of cruel and unusual are tied to the method of death. The most common method is lethal injection, which is generally regarded as the most humane method. Other methods include the electric chair (authorized in eight states), the gas chamber (authorized in three states), hanging (authorized in three states), and firing squad (authorized in two states).[68] Figure 14.7 shows the number of executions across the United States, and Figure 14.8 shows the number of individuals sentenced to death by each method in the United States since 1976.

Related to the "unusual" part of "cruel and unusual," some people oppose the death penalty because they believe that the application of the death penalty is discriminatory. Available evidence suggests that this belief may have some merit. Studies have found that Blacks are more likely than Whites to receive the death penalty. Supporters of the death penalty typically counter this finding by suggesting that when other variables are factored in (such as seriousness of the offense, criminal histories, and so on), the significance of race is minimized. Others have found, however, that even when including these other variables, the death penalty is differentially applied when considering victims' race. A study of 352 death penalty cases in North Carolina, for example, found that "the odds of a death sentence for those suspected of killing Whites are approximately three times higher than the odds of a death sentence for those suspected of killing Blacks."[69] Other researchers have found that "the race of the defendant and victim are both pivotal," at least in some jurisdictions.[70]

death penalty: A sanction that calls for the end of the offender's life.

FIGURE 14.7   Number of Executions by State, 2015

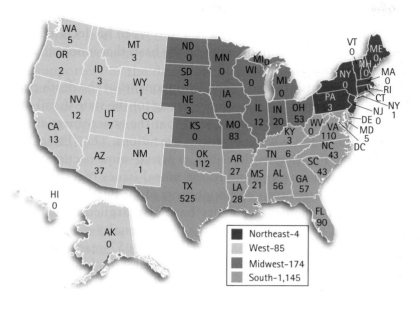

Northeast-4
West-85
Midwest-174
South-1,145

FIGURE 14.8   Execution Methods in Death Penalty Cases, 1973–2014

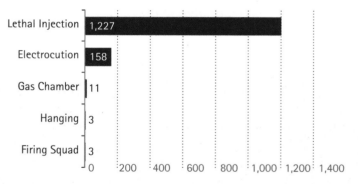

Lethal Injection 1,227
Electrocution 158
Gas Chamber 11
Hanging 3
Firing Squad 3

Death Penalty Information Center

Another criticism of the death penalty is that innocent individuals have been sentenced to death. It has been reported that, since 1973, 140 individuals who had been sentenced to death were exonerated and freed from death row.[71] Supporters of the death penalty point out that the fact that these offenders were exonerated reflects the belief that the system worked. Opponents counter that some innocent individuals have been executed. Supporters of the death penalty suggest that more innocent individuals are protected by sentencing murderers to death than are wrongfully executed, and they add that those rare wrongful executions are unfortunate consequences of our justice process. In the words of one author team that supports the death penalty, "If the poor fellow had a fair trial and was

With regard to demographic factors, research has found that males[78] and those who are married[79] are more likely to support the death penalty. By contrast, racial minorities are more likely to oppose the death penalty.[80] According to one author team, "The gap between Blacks and Whites with regard to capital punishment is enduring."[81]

In terms of education, the **Marshall hypothesis**, traced to Supreme Court Justice Thurgood Marshall, suggests that the more informed individuals are about the death penalty, the less likely they will be to support it. The results of this research are mixed. Perhaps the most conclusive evidence suggests that education about the death penalty may shift attitudes in the short term, but long-term effects do not appear to exist.[82] In simple terms, you may decide today (because of exposure to a criminal justice class) that you do not support the death penalty, but 10 years from now, the impact of education on your attitudes will dissipate.

Geographical factors also influence support for the death penalty. On one level, research shows that areas with high rates of violence tend to be areas that demonstrate more support for the death penalty.[83] Laws supporting the death penalty and decisions to apply the death penalty appear to be shaped, at least in part, by geography. All told, the death penalty is illegal in 17 states and the District of Columbia, and 19 states rarely use the death penalty, even though they have laws that would allow for its use. Fourteen states, most of them in the South, apply death penalty statutes more frequently (see Figure 14.7).[84]

Recidivism

The Bureau of Justice Statistics created a Prisoner Recidivism Analysis Tool that allows users to examine recidivism rates for a sample of offenders from 15 states released from prison in 1994. The tool is available to the public online.[85] A simple search of all of the offenders found that two-thirds of them were arrested again within three years and 39.2% were reincarcerated. The BJS tool should be updated with more current recidivism data in the near future. By all indications, the recidivism rate for offenders is still high, though it may not be as high as it was in the past.

In 2012, nearly 500,000 offenders were on parole. Of those inmates, 58% completed their parole successfully and one-fourth were sentenced back to prison either for a new offense or for violating their parole. This may seem like a high number of offenders returning to prison, but the percentage of parolees returning to prison has actually decreased since 2008, when a third of parolees returned to prison.

Reentering society is not an easy process for offenders. Certain factors have been found to improve the likelihood of successful reentry. For example, a strong family network has been found to reduce the likelihood of returning to prison.[86] It is not simply being married or being a parent that reduces the likelihood of reoffending. Instead, the strength of family relationships is important. Consequently, some experts have suggested that reentry efforts should focus on the entire family and not just the offender.[87] In addition, other factors such as employment and participation in evidence-based treatment programs also ease the reentry experience.

Marshall hypothesis: The idea that the more informed individuals are about the death penalty, the less likely they will be to support it.

In some places, when offenders leave prison they are given reentry guides to assist in their return to society. A review of 13 such guides found that they fall short in their efforts to help.[88] Six of the guides were difficult or very difficult to read. Also, the guides have been criticized for being outdated, void of research, and too general.

Some authors have examined reentry as if it were a separate part of the justice process. Others have argued that in order to understand reentry, one must examine the entire criminal justice process. Criminologist Michael Hallett wrote:

> While prisoner reentry programs emerged only as it became painfully obvious that recidivism was increasing and not decreasing, the real lesson is that "getting tough" on offenders did just that—made it harder, not easier for criminals to return to a normal life . . . the horrendous policies of the past three decades made it tougher for former prisoners to construct anything approximating a normal life.[89]

Many observers would argue that a high recidivism rate is an indication that the criminal justice system has failed. An alternative perspective suggests that it is shortsighted to assume that a long history of experiences by offenders can be offset by one corrections experience. One question that arises is whether offenders are any different at all after incarceration. As one author team wrote, "Corrections administrators and practitioners need to reexamine the commonly held assumption that any intervention is better than no intervention at all."[90]

Criminogenic Sanctions

Criminogenic sanctions refers to the possibility that, rather than deterring crime, certain sanctions might actually *cause* crimes. This is especially a concern in prisons. Although, as one author team noted, "there is general consensus that imprisonment should not be damaging [and] prisons should not change individuals for the worse,"[91] the possibility exists for some offenders and some sanctions. Six dimensions have the potential to produce criminogenic sanctions: (a) the prison environment, (b) learning from other offenders, (c) perceptions of fairness, (d) community consequences of incarceration, (d) lack of treatment, and (e) release strategies.

In terms of the environment, the harsh conditions found in prisons have been cited as a source of future crime. In this sense, rather than preventing crime, these conditions may actually breed crime. Indeed, Beccaria, in writing about deterring crime more than 250 years ago, advised against sanctions that are too severe. Instead, he noted that the sanction should be slightly more severe than the pleasure offenders get from committing the crime. For many offenders, the prison environment appears to violate Beccaria's recommendation.

With regard to learning, being around other types of offenders for long periods of time (and in a spartan environment) produces the opportunity for convicted offenders to learn about crime. Traced to learning theory, the idea is that offenders might learn about strategies for new crimes, reasons

JOURNAL
High Cost of Ignoring Science

to commit new crimes, and opportunities for new crimes. This dynamic is not limited to prisons. It has been reported that batterer treatment programs, when not managed correctly, might result in batterers learning from one another about strategies to control and abuse their partners without getting caught.

Perceptions of fairness have also been tied to criminogenic sanctions. Tom Tyler has written extensively about procedural justice and the importance of fairness and legitimacy in the application of the law.[92] From this perspective, if inmates perceive their sanctions to be unfair, they may be at a higher risk of reoffending. Sanctions that are experienced as too severe, then, run the risk of producing crime rather than deterring it.

Prison sanctions can also be criminogenic when considering the impact that sanctions have on urban communities. Recall from Chapter 5 that incarcerating high numbers of minorities from urban neighborhoods weakens the social capital found in those neighborhoods. With more single-parent homes and fewer fathers available to help raise children, the potential for crime increases. Michelle Alexander likened this mass incarceration to former policies that formally segregated minorities and suppressed them in many different ways. In particular, in *The New Jim Crow,* Alexander skillfully and masterfully asserted that mass incarceration, in effect, has the same consequences that Jim Crow laws had on minority populations in years past.[93] Perhaps one day we will look back on our current incarceration policies and hold them in the same level of contempt that we now hold Jim Crow laws.

Release strategies and reentry processes (or rather, the lack of reentry efforts) also may contribute to crime. When these processes are weak, offenders are essentially going from a harsh environment full of regimentation and control to an environment where their needs are not met and there is nothing stopping them from reoffending. With this sort of a framework, it might be more appropriate to ask, Why don't even more offenders commit new crimes? Consider how difficult it is for felons to access federal

FEATURE VIDEO
Education in Prison

CRIMINAL JUSTICE and **COLLEGE STUDENTS**

INCARCERATION AND FINANCIAL AID

Federal regulations prohibit incarcerated individuals from consolidating their federal student loans while they are incarcerated. Inmates can, however, apply for loan deferments, allowing them to defer payment of loans they took out prior to their incarceration. Once released, individuals may be eligible for new federal student loans, though convictions for certain drug offenses and some types of sex offenses may result in limited access to student loans. With this information as a backdrop, list three reasons why financial aid should be tied to conviction and incarceration as well as three reasons why it shouldn't. Should inmates be able to take college courses while incarcerated? Would it make a difference if the course was offered online? Discuss your answers with your classmates.

aid for college. The "Criminal Justice and College Students" box in this chapter considers how financial aid rules are related to college students and incarceration.

Returning Home: Understanding the Challenge of Prisoner Reentry was an Urban Institute Study focusing on prisoner reentry in Maryland, Illinois, Ohio, and Texas. The researchers examined how reentry was experienced by offenders, their families, and communities. The results, based on a study of 1,450 incarcerated offenders and 2,600 interviews following release, led the researchers to make the following recommendations:[94]

AUTHOR VIDEO
Education in Prison

- Develop individualized case management approaches for offenders

- Deliver intensive services immediately upon release

- Broaden the focus to include family and community contexts

- Reinvent postrelease supervision

- Implement comprehensive reentry strategies, not programs

These recommendations have direct ties to our society's punishment goals.

Treating Offenders

Rehabilitation was, for the most part, an accepted philosophy of punishment for the better part of the 20th century. This changed in the 1960s and 1970s, when a law-and-order philosophy promoted more punitive responses to criminal behavior. Then, in 1974, a well-known report, known as **Martinson's report**, evaluated various treatment efforts and offered this rather straightforward conclusion: Nothing works. Martinson wrote, "The rehabilitative efforts that have been repeated so far have had no appreciable effect on recidivism."[95] The report provided fodder for conservatives to call for stricter responses to criminal behavior and was a serious blow to rehabilitative efforts. In considering why "nothing works," four possible explanations surface: unrealistic expectations, implementation issues, problems measuring success, and lack of evidence-based treatment strategies.

Unrealistic expectations potentially explain why "nothing works" in terms of rehabilitation. In particular, when evaluating treatment strategies, it may be expected that all individuals receiving the treatment become law-abiding citizens. This is an extraordinarily high bar. After all, when offenders are sent to prison, and then continue offending after their release, it is rare that individuals blame the prison experience for failing. So, on the one hand, treatment strategies are defined as failures because offenders reoffend, but when former inmates reoffend, the vast majority of the public does not view prison as failing. Indeed, the response is to say that the offender should have received "more prison." Few individuals have said (out loud anyway) that when treatment fails, offenders should have simply received "more treatment."

Implementation issues also help to explain why some treatment programs do not work. In particular, programs may be designed in ways that are destined for failure. For example, when drug treatment occurs in prisons,

Martinson's report: A report that found, essentially, that efforts to rehabilitate offenders had no significant effect on recidivism rates.

a number of issues arise for inmates. One author team has identified the following issues:[96]

- Some inmates may feign abuse problems in order to participate in treatment programs.

- Treatment is often tacked on at the end of a prison sentence, whereas it should be given earlier.

- Treatment is separated from community services, whereas the treatment should be integrated with the community.

- The admission criteria for treatment programs are too restrictive.

For these programs to work, they must be implemented in a way that is responsive to available evidence.

Many treatment programs may be viewed as failures because of difficulties measuring success. Community-based sanctions, for example, are designed to do more than simply prevent crime. From this perspective, a more appropriate way to measure success might be to focus on whether offenders were able to pay their rent and find employment.[97] Describing this orientation, criminologists Susan Turner and Joan Petersilia wrote:

> Adopting more realistic outcome measures may make it more possible to bridge the gap between public expectations for the justice system and what most practitioners recognize as the system's actual capacity to control crime. By documenting what corrections programs can accomplish, we can move towards integrating [community-based sanctions] into a more balanced corrections strategy.[98]

In other words, by setting more realistic measures of success, treatment programs can be implemented more effectively, and more fairly.

A lack of evidence-based treatment strategies is also problematic in developing and implementing treatment programs. Frequently, treatment strategies that work for one group of offenders are replicated for other groups of offenders, with little thought given to offenders' needs, risks, and responsiveness to treatment. The task at hand is for practitioners to balance offenders' needs with available resources and treatment strategies in a way that responds to the actual causes of the offending. This is certainly a difficult task, but one worth devoting our efforts toward. Indeed, in some careers, this is precisely what workers try to do (see the "Help Wanted" box in this chapter).

Restorative Justice

restorative justice: A philosophy of crime prevention that focuses on restoring the victim and the offender in a way that best serves the greater community the victim.

Restorative justice is a relatively new philosophy of crime prevention that focuses on restoring the victim and offender in a way that best serves the greater community. This orientation was formalized in the 1970s by writers such as John Braithwaite, Mark Umbreit, Howard Zehr, and Gordon Bazemore, who were critical of the punitive nature of the criminal justice system. From a restorative justice orientation, punishing the offender takes a back seat to making the victim whole, shaming the offender, and then

HELP WANTED: DRUG ABUSE TREATMENT SPECIALIST

DUTIES:

- The incumbent provides individual and group counseling/therapy to inmates with drug abuse problems within the Bureau of Prison's treatment framework. He or she is also responsible for the education of prison staff about drug abuse, drug abuse treatment, and the local prison program.

- The incumbent administers eligibility and psychosocial assessments as the basis for individual treatment planning. The incumbent is responsible for providing residential and/ or nonresidential treatment to offenders who volunteer for treatment and are diagnosed with a drug use disorder.

- Along with all other correctional institution employees, the incumbent is charged with responsibility for maintaining security of the institution. The staff's correctional responsibilities precede all others required by this position and are performed on a regular and recurring basis.

REQUIREMENTS: Bachelor's degree

ANNUAL SALARY: $52,830–$80,414

Adapted from USAJOBS.gov. Retrieved from https://www.usajobs.gov/GetJob/ViewDetails/367347200

reintegrating the offender into the community. The foundational principles of restorative justice practices include the following:[99]

JOURNAL
Restorative Justice Projects

- The victim and offender communicate through an open dialogue.

- The dialogue includes discussion about the harm from the act.

- The dialogue also focuses on why the offender committed the act.

- At some point, the offender should offer an unsolicited apology and accept fault for the act.

- As a result of the dialogue, the victim will have a better understanding about why the crime occurred.

- Restitution and reparations are facilitated by those with skills in these areas.

- The offender is separated from the action.

- The focus is on the future and rebuilding the community, not on punishing the offender.

Although some people are very supportive of restorative justice strategies, disagreement exists about the types of offenses that could be addressed through this framework. For instance, it may be much easier to make reparations for property offenses than for violent offenses. Should the victim and the offender be expected to engage in a dialogue in sexual assault cases or domestic violence cases? Do some victims gain satisfaction out of knowing that offenders are punished? Are victims more vulnerable when they engage in dialogues with offenders? These are just a few questions that arise with restorative justice strategies. Still, restorative justice efforts remain a popular alternative for addressing victimization and offending.

Just the Facts: Chapter Summary

- Three fundamental aspects of inmates' rights are that they change over time, they are limited, and they are determined through court interpretations of the U.S. Constitution.

- Definitions of cruel and unusual punishment, crucial to protection offered through the Eighth Amendment, have changed over time.

- In 1964, the Supreme Court's decision in *Cooper v. Pate* interpreted the Civil Rights Act of 1871 as suggesting that imprisonment should not result in the loss of constitutional rights as described under the Fourteenth Amendment and the "equal protection under the law" clause.

- Factors contributing to prison violence include violent histories, diet, structural factors, and situational factors.

- Five factors explain why there is not even more violence in prisons and jails: professionalization of prison staff, prison classification strategies, modern technology, evidence-based strategies, and separating potentially violent offenders.

- Society needs to pay attention to inmates' health for moral reasons; to prevent disease, in anticipation of reintegration efforts; for legal reasons; and for economic reasons.

- Similar to other professions, the field of corrections is not immune to misconduct by its employees.

- Misconduct by corrections staff includes stealing from the institution, drug smuggling, transporting contraband into the prison, physical abuse, and sexual misconduct.

- Factors that produce stress for those working in prison include environmental factors, situational factors, biological factors, and work/home factors.

- For probation and parole officers, sources of stress include high caseloads, working with potentially dangerous offenders, paperwork demands, lack of recognition, lack of input into decision making, unrealistic expectations of supervisors, and lack of preparation.

- Juvenile probation and parole officers typically use different strategies to supervise juvenile offenders than are used by probation and parole officers who supervise adult offenders.

- Juvenile offenders are incarcerated in juvenile group homes, in juvenile detention centers, in juvenile institutions, or in the wings of adult prisons or jails.

- In 1984, one-fifth of corrections employees were women; by 2005, roughly one-third of corrections employees in state and federal corrections institutions were women.

- Whereas male prisons are characterized as having prison gangs, researchers have described how female inmates develop relationships similar to those found in families.

- In prisons, four qualities of sex offenders result in the need to handle sex offenders differently than other offenders: (a) sex offenders are stigmatized, (b) sex offenders tend to have histories of being victimized, (c) sex offenders tend to receive long prison sentences, and (d) sex offenders face a number of restrictive policies upon their release from incarceration (if they are released).

- Estimates suggest that more than half of all incarcerated inmates suffer from some form of mental illness.

- Modern laws governing the death penalty can be traced to *Furman v. Georgia*, a Supreme Court case that outlawed the death penalty on grounds that the penalty was arbitrary and capricious.

- *Criminogenic sanctions* refers to the possibility that, rather than deter crime, certain sanctions might actually cause crimes.

- Six dimensions have the potential to produce criminogenic sanctions: (a) the prison environment, (b) learning from other offenders, (c) perceptions of fairness, (d) community consequences of incarceration, (e) lack of treatment, and (f) release strategies.

- Rehabilitation was, for the most part, an accepted philosophy of punishment for the better part of the 20th century.

Critical Thinking Questions

1. Describe the types of rights that inmates have and why these rights are important.

2. What factors make prisons and jails violent?

3. Describe the types of sexual violence occurring in prisons and jails.

4. How do prison health care decisions impact the community?

5. Why are corrections jobs stressful?

6. What are some arguments for and against the death penalty?

7. Does prison cause crime? Explain.

8. Does rehabilitation "work"? Explain.

Key Terms

chemical castration
  laws (476)

civil commitment
  laws (475)

Community
  Mental Health
  Act (476)

cruel and unusual
  punishment (456)

correctional
  misconduct (468)

death penalty (478)

exclusion zone
  policies (475)

Marshall
  hypothesis (482)

Martinson's
  report (485)

Prison Litigation
  Reform Act (461)

pseudo family
  groups (473)

registry laws (475)

restorative justice (496)

turner (469)

$SAGE edgeselect™

edge.sagepub.com/payne

Sharpen your skills with SAGE edge select!

With carefully crafted tools and resources to encourage review, practice, and critical thinking, SAGE edge select gives you the edge needed to master course content. Take full advantage of open-access key term flashcards, practice quizzes, and video content. Diagnostic pre-tests, a personalized study plan, and post-tests are available with an access code.

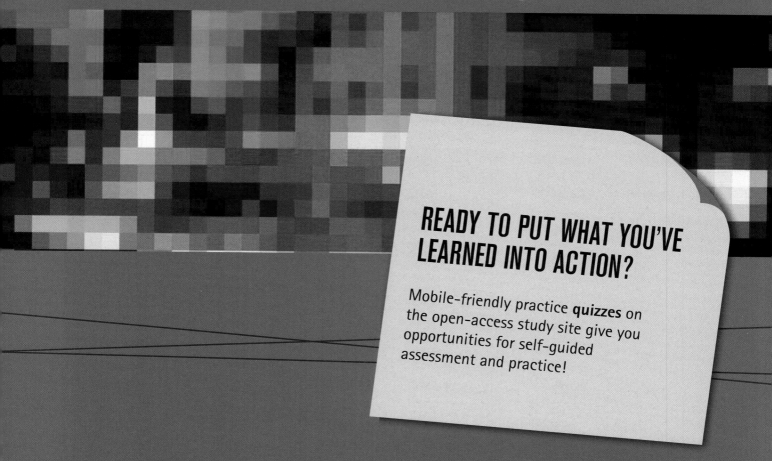

PART V

CONTEMPORARY CHALLENGES

Chapter 15 • Current and Future Criminal Justice Issues

15

CURRENT AND FUTURE CRIMINAL JUSTICE ISSUES

© alessandro0770/Veer

"I'M NOT REMOTELY INTERESTED in presiding over a $180 million ego bath that we both know will be the career-defining debacle for both of us. I'm not destroying my career over a minimally talented spoiled brat who thought nothing of shoving this off her plate for 18 months so she could go direct a movie." The "spoiled brat" referred to the writer's views about actress Angelina Jolie. The comment was shared in a private e-mail one Hollywood producer wrote to another producer. The word *private* might be misleading given that the e-mail was made public after a group calling itself the Guardians of Peace hacked into the Sony Pictures e-mail system. That e-mail, along with many others, was shared by national news outlets including CNN, Fox News, and NBC News.

Although the e-mails provided entertainment fodder for many, in reality the group had committed very serious crimes. The hackers attributed their displeasure with Sony Pictures to the movie company's decision to film and release a movie about a bungled attempt to assassinate North Korea's president, Kim Jong-un. It was not immediately clear whether the hackers came from outside the United States, but two weeks before the Christmas Day release of the movie, the hackers threatened terrorist acts if the film was released. Movies have been the subject of protests in the past, but this took protesting to a new level.

LEARNING OBJECTIVES

After reading this chapter, students will be able to:

15.1 Discuss how crime varies across countries

15.2 Distinguish between domestic and international terrorism

15.3 Identify how technology has influenced criminal justice and crime

15.4 Discuss how demographic changes will influence criminal justice in the future

15.5 Identify successful and unsuccessful gun violence reduction policies

15.6 Discuss three reasons drugs should be legalized and three reasons they should not be

15.7 Assess whether criminal justice policies are evidence-based policies

The criminal justice system of today is much different from the criminal justice system of years past. As well, because history teaches us valuable lessons, it seems safe to suggest that the criminal justice system of the future will be much different from our modern justice system. In this chapter, we address

ADMISSIBLE or INADMISSIBLE Evidence

Read the statements that follow. If the statement is true, circle *admissible*. If the statement is false, circle *inadmissible*. Answers can be found on page 519.

1. **Admissible   Inadmissible**   International research shows that the vast majority of countries have nearly identical victimization rates.

2. **Admissible   Inadmissible**   The U.S. Patriot Act permitted indefinite detention of terrorism suspects, unprecedented access to financial records of individuals or businesses suspected of terrorism, and the use of wiretaps without court orders in these cases.

3. **Admissible   Inadmissible**   Although official statistics portray a low victimization rate for older persons, self-report surveys and data from adult protective services officials reflect a much higher rate.

4. **Admissible   Inadmissible**   *Computer crime* and *cybercrime* refer to the same behaviors.

5. **Admissible   Inadmissible**   With regard to gun crimes, pulling-levers policies are targeted efforts by law enforcement and prosecutors to identify and send a message to specific individuals and groups at risk of gun violence so that they know these offenses will not be tolerated.

6. **Admissible   Inadmissible**   Research fails to show a link between type of drug offender and type of crime.

7. **Admissible   Inadmissible**   *Right- and left-wing extremism terrorism* refers to situations in which terrorists are motivated by mental health problems.

8. **Admissible   Inadmissible**   Evidence-based policies are those that are supported by empirical research.

493

various trends in criminal justice with an aim toward understanding what the future holds for the criminal justice system. For those of you thinking about working in the criminal justice system, this chapter will shed some light on what is in store for you in the years ahead. For others, as citizens, a general understanding about these issues will help you to understand them when you encounter them in the future. The topics addressed in this chapter include international issues, terrorism, technology and criminal justice, aging and the criminal justice system, and the evolution of criminal justice policies.

▶ International Issues

Not so many decades ago, when your parents were born perhaps, we lived in a world where it was difficult for individuals to communicate with those from other countries, and it was equally difficult for individuals to travel to those other countries. With technological changes, the size of our world has, in a way, shrunk. More so than ever in our history, the events occurring in one country have very real implications for what occurs in our country and in every other country, for that matter. We now live in a global world that encourages us to look beyond our borders to understand human behavior.

Crime occurs in every country in the world, but this does not mean that crime is the same everywhere. Definitions of crime, responses to crime, and potential risk factors for crime vary across countries. With regard to *definitions of crime*, different countries have different definitions of law violations. Criminal justice students from the United States participating in study abroad programs are often surprised to see the variation in laws between their home country and their host countries. Those visiting Amsterdam, in the Netherlands, for instance, will find that prostitution is legal and marijuana use, at least until recently, was tolerated. Those visiting other countries, such as Saudi Arabia, Pakistan, and Iran, will find that alcohol consumption is illegal.

Different countries also have different *responses to crime*. As is discussed later in this chapter, the United States has the highest incarceration rate in the world. As one commentator noted, "The United States has less than 5 percent of the world's population. But it has almost a quarter of the world's prisoners."[1] In the United States, 751 out of every 100,000 individuals are in prison. By comparison, in Japan, 63 out of 100,000 individuals are incarcerated. The factors that have led to our high prison population will be addressed in more detail later, as well. For now, it can simply be suggested that different countries choose to respond to crime in different ways. To be sure, although we have a high incarceration rate, some other countries have sanctions that would, by U.S. standards, be considered arbaric. Consider the well-publicized 1994 case of Michael Fay, who at 19 years old was convicted of vandalism in Singapore and given "caning" as a punishment.

The prostitution laws of Amsterdam demonstrate the way that definitions of crime vary across countries.

© Atlantide Phototravel/Corbis

The caning involved four strikes with a rattan cane against Fay's backside. Fay later won the dubious notoriety of being "the only minimum-wage worker on *People* magazine's '25 Most Intriguing People' list."[2] Incidentally, Fay later developed an addiction to butane, which he described as a strategy he used to cope with the long-term stress he experienced from the caning.

The *risk factors for crime* may vary across countries as well. For instance, research comparing homicide and suicide rates in the United States and Japan found that the impact of female labor force participation and unemployment on violence varied between the two countries, leading the authors to conclude that "different theories may be necessary to account for the variation in rates of personal violence in different societies."[3] Put simply, the reasons that individuals commit crime in one country might be different from the reasons that individuals commit crime in another country.

Victimization rates also vary across countries. As one author team writes, "Countries such as Colombia and Sierra Leone can have above 50 homicides per 100,000 people per year, while other countries, such as Austria and Iceland, can have less than 1."[4] To improve cross-national comparisons, Jan Van Dijk and his colleagues developed the **International Crime Victimization Survey** (ICVS) in 1989 to assess victimization rates in different parts of the world. Since the survey was created, it has been conducted six times. The results show differences in victimization rates for each victimization type across all countries, suggesting that the presence of specific factors in each country influences victimization risk. Figure 15.1 shows the assault and threat victimization rates for respondents from 10 countries included in the most recent ICVS. Northern Ireland had the highest rate and Japan had the lowest rate. Approximately 1 in 200 respondents from Japan reported experiencing an assault or threat, compared with 1 in 15 respondents from Northern Ireland. Low victimization rates are found for other offenses in Japan as well.[5]

Globalization also has made it easier for individuals to travel from country to country. At the same time, it has become easier for offenders to transport victims across borders and countries. **Human trafficking** refers to offenses in which individuals are relocated without their consent. Human trafficking victims are most frequently forced into different forms of labor. The U.S. Trafficking Victims Protection Act of 2000 has identified the following types of "severe" human trafficking:

- Sex trafficking in which a commercial sex act is induced by force, fraud, or coercion, or in which the person induced to perform such act has not attained 18 years of age

- The recruitment, harboring, transportation, provision, or obtaining of a person for labor or services, through the use of force, fraud, or coercion for the purpose of subjection to involuntary servitude, peonage, debt bondage, or slavery[6]

International Crime Victimization Survey: A survey created in 1989 to assess victimization rates in different parts of the world.

human trafficking: Offenses in which individuals are relocated without their consent.

Japan typically has among the lowest victimization rates across the world.
©iStockphoto/vichie81

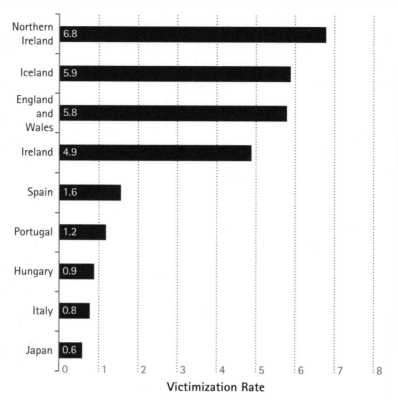

FIGURE 15.1   **Assault and Threat Victimization Rates for Respondents From 10 Countries (top five rates and lowest five rates), 2004–2005**

UNICRI, UNODC

To date, little research has been conducted on human trafficking. The existing research typically links human trafficking to other organized crimes including drug trafficking, money laundering, and gambling. In some cases, human trafficking victims are forced into prostitution rings that are advertised on the Internet.

Recognizing the similarities and differences between crimes and criminal justice responses across the globe helps us to better understand our own crime problem and how and why our criminal justice system operates as it does. The "Criminal Justice and College Students" box in this chapter encourages you to think even more about cross-cultural variations related to crime and criminal justice.

BEYOND A REASONABLE DOUBT 15.1

Which of the following countries has the lowest victimization rate?

(a) China, (b) Japan, (c) Canada, (d) United States, (e) Australia

---

The answer can be found on page 522.

CRIMINAL JUSTICE and **COLLEGE STUDENTS**

IT'S A SMALL WORLD, BUT I WOULDN'T WANT TO HAVE TO PAINT IT

One of comedian Steven Wright's famous one-liners goes like this: "It's a small world, but I wouldn't want to have to paint it." The first part of the quotation reminds us how connected we all are, while the second part points to the vastness of our world. Using this as a framework, write down three ways that you think crime is similar across countries. Next, write down three ways that crime varies across cultures. Share your answers with a group of your classmates. Are there similarities and differences between what you and your fellow students wrote down?

➡ Terrorism

Generally speaking, **terrorism** refers to activities that individuals engage in to create terror and panic in specific groups of individuals. Although victims of terrorism may experience direct physical harm, the goal of terrorists is to create emotional terror in a broader group of individuals. The U.S. government defines terrorism as "premeditated, politically motivated violence perpetrated against noncombatant targets by subnational groups or clandestine agents."[7] Experts typically classify terrorism into categories of **domestic terrorism** and **international terrorism**. Here is how the FBI defines these two types of terrorism:

- ➡ Domestic terrorism is the unlawful use, or threatened use, of force or violence by a group or individual based and operating entirely within the United States or Puerto Rico without foreign direction committed against persons or property to intimidate or coerce a government, the civilian population, or any segment thereof in furtherance of political or social objectives.

- ➡ International terrorism involves violent acts or acts dangerous to human life that are a violation of the criminal laws of the United States or any state, or that would be a criminal violation if committed within the jurisdiction of the United States or any state. These acts appear to be intended to intimidate or coerce a civilian population, influence the policy of a government by intimidation or coercion, or affect the conduct of a government by assassination or kidnapping. International terrorist acts occur outside the United States or transcend national boundaries in terms of the means by which they are accomplished, the persons they appear intended to coerce or intimidate, or the locale in which their perpetrators operate or seek asylum.[8]

Terrorism has always been a concern, at least on some level, but in the aftermath of September 11, 2001—when terrorists overtook four airplanes

terrorism: Activities that individuals engage in to create terror and panic in specific groups of individuals.

domestic terrorism: Terrorists acts occurring in the United States with no connections to foreign entities.

international terrorism: Terrorist acts committed with a specific connection to foreign entities.

and crashed them into the World Trade Center, the Pentagon, and a field in Pennsylvania—public concern and the government's interest in suppressing and controlling terrorism heightened dramatically. With the passage of the U.S. Patriot Act, government officials were given additional tools to respond to terrorism, some say at the expense of individual rights. In particular, the act allows the government more leeway in gathering evidence in investigations targeting terrorist activities. For example, the act permitted indefinite detention of terrorism suspects, unprecedented access to financial records of individuals or businesses suspected of terrorism, and the use of wiretaps without court orders in these cases.

VIDEO
TEVUS Database

The National Consortium for the Study of Terrorism and Responses to Terrorism (START), at the University of Maryland, created the Global Terrorism Database to track terrorism incidents across the world and over time. The database includes information on more than 125,000 terrorist incidents occurring since 1970. In 2013, 11,952 terrorism incidents occurred across the world. In the United States, 15 terrorism incidents occurred and eight individuals were killed in these incidents.

With regard to terrorist incidents occurring on U.S. soil, the vast majority are committed by domestic terrorists. In fact, between 2002 and 2005, of the 24 recorded incidents in the United States, all but one was initiated by a domestic terrorist.[9] Of the 23 incidents on U.S. soil, all but one "were committed by special interest extremists active in the animal rights and environmental movements."[10] Of course, not all domestic terrorist incidents focus on these issues. The Boston Marathon bombing in March 2013 by brothers Dzhokhar and Tamerlan Tsarnaev were traced to the brothers' radical Islamic beliefs. The terrorists set off two bombs near the finish line of the marathon, killing three people and injuring more than 260 individuals. The police chase leading to the capture of the brothers unfolded on national television.

Two explosions went off near the finish line of the 117th Boston Marathon on April 15, 2013. In 2015, Dzhokhar Tsarnaev was sentenced to the death penalty for his involvement.

© David L. Ryan/The Boston Globe/Getty Images

In addition to classifying terrorism as domestic versus international terrorism, experts have further classified terrorism into the following categories: religious terrorism, single-issue terrorism, right- and left-wing extremism, and cyberterrorism.[11] *Religious terrorism* includes actions tied to or based on religious beliefs or religious opposition. The recent actions by ISIS can be viewed as a form of religious terrorism. Also known as the Islamic State of Iraq and Syria, ISIS carried out multiple acts of terrorism in an effort to develop an Islamic government in parts of Iraq and Syria. In addition to public executions, extortion, and crucifixions, the group received widespread attention in the United States after releasing videos of hostages being beheaded.

Single-issue terrorism includes actions intended to draw attention to a specific issue the terrorists support or oppose. Consider cases in which offenders target violence against abortion providers. The terrorists in these incidents are focused solely on their opposition to abortion. In the words of one offender serving prison time: "Abortionists are killed because they are serial murderers of innocent children who must be stopped, and they will continue to be stopped."[12]

Right- and left-wing extremism terrorism refers to actions motivated by terrorists' extreme political beliefs. Timothy McVeigh and Terry Nichols's bombing of the Oklahoma City Federal Building on April 19, 1995, is an example of this

The destruction caused by Timothy McVeigh in Oklahoma City is an example of domestic terrorism.

© BOB DAEMMRICH/AFP/Getty Images

type of terrorism. The incident killed 168 individuals and injured another 642. McVeigh, who received a Bronze Star for his military service in the Gulf War, authorized a biography titled *American Terrorist*. Providing 75 hours of interviews to journalists Lou Michel and Dan Herbeck, McVeigh attributed the bombing to his discontent with the standoffs the federal government had with White supremacist Randy Weaver in Ruby Ridge, Idaho, in 1992 and the Branch Davidian cult in Waco, Texas, in 1993.[13] The Ruby Ridge standoff lasted 10 days and resulted in the shooting of Weaver's wife and 14-year-old son by law enforcement officers and the death of a federal marshal; the Waco standoff lasted 51 days and resulted in the deaths of 76 members of the cult, including 20 children, and 4 law enforcement officers.[14]

Cyberterrorism is discussed in more detail in the next section. This newer form of terrorism uses computer networks and computer software to perpetrate the terror.

Types of acts used in terrorist incidents include bioterrorism, physical violence, bombings, hostage taking, and psychological threats. *Bioterrorism* involves the use of biochemical weapons such as anthrax or other harmful chemicals. *Physical violence* includes beheadings, torture, and other harmful behaviors. *Bombings* involve the detonation of various types of bombs, many of which are crudely made. *Hostage taking* refers to situations in which terrorists kidnap victims and hold them in an effort to gain some advantage or benefit from the broader group. *Psychological terrorism* occurs when terrorists simply threaten harm in an effort to create terror.

Concerns about terrorism have reshaped criminal justice practices since 9/11. New policies, revised practices, and new laws have changed how the United States responds to concerns about terrorism. The Department of Homeland Security was created in 2002 through an integration of 22 different federal agencies. The "Help Wanted" box in this chapter shows an example of the types of jobs available in this area.

CAREER VIDEO
Director of IT and Electronic Security

HELP WANTED: CUSTOMS AND BORDER PROTECTION OFFICER

DUTIES:

- Enforcing customs, immigration, and agriculture laws and regulations

- Detecting and preventing terrorists and weapons of mass destruction from entering the United States

- Facilitating the flow of legitimate trade and travel

- Conducting inspections of individuals and conveyances

- Determining the admissibility of individuals for entry into the United States

- Preventing the illegal entry of individuals and prohibited goods and smuggling of illegal drugs and other contraband

REQUIREMENTS: Bachelor's degree or equivalent experience

ANNUAL SALARY: $31,628–$39,179

Adapted from USAJOBS.gov. Retrieved from https://www.usajobs.gov/GetJob/ViewDetails/372309100

CAREER VIDEO
Jail Administrator

BEYOND A REASONABLE DOUBT 15.2

_____ terrorism refers to actions motivated by terrorists' extreme political beliefs.

(a) Right- and left-wing extremism, (b) Single issue, (c) Domestic, (d) Cyber, (e) None of the above

The answer can be found on page 522.

AUTHOR VIDEO
Future of Criminal Justice and Technology

➡ Technology and Criminal Justice

Technology has had, and will continue to have, a dramatic impact on criminal justice. Among other things, technology has changed the way criminal justice officials gather and secure evidence, how criminal justice data are stored, how trials are conducted, how offenders are punished, and how crimes are committed. This last area, in particular, has been of great interest to criminal justice officials.

The phrase **cybercrime** refers to a wide range of computer-related behaviors that are criminally illegal. A computer can be the target of an offense (as it is in cases of sabotage), a tool used in the commission of a crime (as in piracy or cyber-fraud), or incidental to an offense.[15] Florida and Arizona were the first states to create laws covering computer crime, in 1978. Florida's Computer Crime Act "defined all unauthorized access as a third degree felony regardless of the specific purpose."[16] By the end of the 1980s, most states and the federal government had passed computer crime laws.

All evidence suggests that cybercrime is rampant. The 2008 Computer Crime and Security Survey found that computer crimes on average cost half a million dollars per incident and that many of the offenses are perpetrated

cybercrime: Criminally illegal computer-related behaviors.

by someone working in the company that is victimized.[17] More recently, the 2012 Internet Crime Complaint Center annual report, published by the Federal Bureau of Investigation (FBI), received more than 289,000 complaints and estimated that computer crimes reported to the complaint center cost more than $525 million that year. The "Criminal Justice and the Media" box in this chapter describes a computer crime that increased during this time.

Generally speaking, there are five types of computer offenses (see Figure 15.2). **Cyber theft** includes incidents in which the offender uses a computer to steal something from an individual, the government, or a business. Items stolen include funds, information, and intellectual property.[18] **Unauthorized access** occurs when offenders gain access illegally to computer databases to which they do not have legitimate access (*hackers* do this for fun, whereas *crackers* do it to sabotage). Virus introduction is a variety of computer crime in which offenders pass viruses on to others, and these are generally done for recreational reasons, pride, or profit.[19] **Software crimes** include instances when the computer software is a primary part of the offense. Four overlapping types of software crimes exist: theft of software, counterfeiting software, copyright violations of computer software, and piracy.[20] **Internet crimes** refers to a range of offenses in which the offender uses the Internet to perpetrate his or her

cyber theft: A type of computer crime in which the offender uses a computer to steal something from an individual, the government, or a business.

unauthorized access: Computer crime in which offenders gain access illegally to computer databases to which they do not have legitimate access.

software crimes: Crimes in which computer software is a primary part of the offense.

Internet crime: A range of offenses in which the Internet is used to perpetrate offenses.

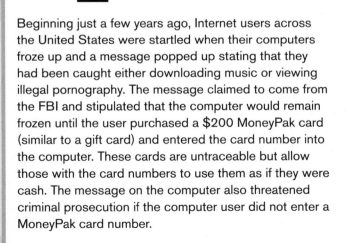

CRIMINAL JUSTICE and the MEDIA:
FBI'S RANSOMWARE VIRUS

Beginning just a few years ago, Internet users across the United States were startled when their computers froze up and a message popped up stating that they had been caught either downloading music or viewing illegal pornography. The message claimed to come from the FBI and stipulated that the computer would remain frozen until the user purchased a $200 MoneyPak card (similar to a gift card) and entered the card number into the computer. These cards are untraceable but allow those with the card numbers to use them as if they were cash. The message on the computer also threatened criminal prosecution if the computer user did not enter a MoneyPak card number.

What was actually happening was that the computer had become infected with a type of *ransomware*. In some cases, the virus even turned on the computer's webcam and showed a video of the user on the screen. This really made it seem as if the computer user was being watched by someone.

Criminal justice officials offer the following advice to guard against ransomware:

- **Backup, backup, backup.** Regularly backup your files and keep these backups in an offline location that is not connected to the Internet.

- **Be careful what you click.** Be careful about e-mail attachments that you open and the links you click. As a rule, you should never open an unsolicited e-mail from a source you do not recognize.

- **Use anti-virus software.** Install anti-virus software and keep it up to date.

- **Stay on top of software updates.** Keep your operating system and other software up to date with the newest patches.

Adapted from Schuette, B. (n.d.). Consumer alert: Computer ransomware. Retrieved from http://www.michigan.gov/ag/0,4534,7-164-17337_20942-324685–,00.html

offenses (e.g., consumer fraud, fake e-mails, ransomware, extortion). Figure 15.3 illustrates patterns surrounding Internet crime complaints received by the FBI in 2012.

FIGURE 15.2   Types of Cybercrimes

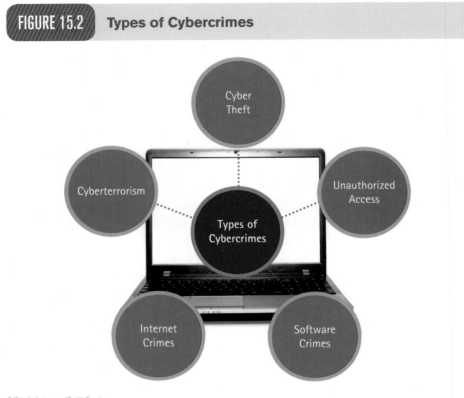

© iStockphoto.com/GetUpStudio

FIGURE 15.3   Patterns Surrounding Internet Crime Complaints Received by the FBI in 2013

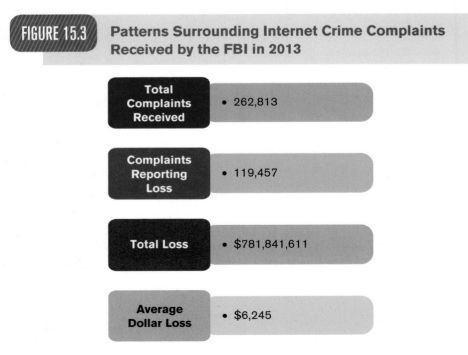

Federal Bureau of Investigation

Cyberterrorism is perhaps the most serious form of computer crime. This includes instances when offenders use computers to commit terrorist acts. Illustrating the potential for harm from these offenses, consider the following two examples described by Barry C. Collin, of the Institute for Security and Intelligence, who coined the phrase *cyberterrorism*:

VIDEO
Cyber Warfare

- A CyberTerrorist will remotely access the processing control systems of a cereal manufacturer, change the levels of iron supplement, and sicken and kill the children of a nation enjoying their food. That CyberTerrorist will then perform similar remote alterations at a processor of infant formula. The key: the CyberTerrorist does not have to be at the factory to execute these acts.

- A CyberTerrorist will attack the next generation of air traffic control systems, and collide two large civilian aircraft. This is a realistic scenario, since the CyberTerrorist will also crack the aircraft's in-cockpit sensors. Much of the same can be done to the rail lines.[21]

Although the preceding two examples were hypothetical, there have been numerous cases in which computers have been used to commit acts of terrorism. Consider the examples cited in this blog posting:

Last year, cyber terrorists used a deadly virus to attack the information network of Aramco, the Saudi oil company, and annihilated all of the data on 35,000 desktop computers. The screens of the infected computers were left with the vision of a burning American flag. A group called the Cutting Sword of Justice claimed credit for the attack. Two months ago, computer hackers hacked the Twitter account of The Associated Press and sent a tweet stating that there had been two explosions at the White House and that President Barack Obama was injured. Within two minutes, the stock market dropped by 143 points. The Syrian Electronic Army later claimed credit for the attack.[22]

Perhaps not surprisingly, "the threat posed by terrorists, nation-states, and criminal groups conducting computer network operations against the United States" is viewed as a "top national security threat" by the FBI.[23] The enormous threats that cyberterrorists pose have led to the development of cyberterrorism law enforcement units.

Several dynamics surrounding computer crimes make them difficult for law enforcement agencies to address. Because computer crimes happen so quickly, they have been called "hit and run" offenses.[24] Also, they are often international in scope, creating jurisdictional issues. In addition, with the constant changes in types of computer crimes, it is difficult for officials to identify warning signs. As well, victims of computer crimes may not realize that they have been victimized until a long time after the crime occurred.[25] Computer offenders are able to use their technical knowledge to hide their offenses. In fact, it has been suggested that computer criminals' "technical knowledge is the equivalent of the stereotypical ski mask that conventional

cyberterrorism: The most serious form of computer crime; includes instances when offenders use computers to commit terrorist acts.

offenders wear in old cops-and-robbers movies."[26] Computer criminals don't hold guns to commit their crimes; they hold tablets, laptops, and other electronic devices to carry out their trade.

BEYOND A REASONABLE DOUBT 15.3

Which of the following is a type of cybercrime?

(a) Theft, (b) Unauthorized access, (c) Virus introduction, (d) Internet crimes, (e) All of the above

---

The answer can be found on page 522.

➡ The Aging of the Criminal Justice System

VIDEO
America's Incarcerated

In 1900, three million Americans were over the age of 65. By 2008, 39 million Americans were in this age category.[27] It is a simple fact: Individuals are living longer today than they were in years past. This means three things for the criminal justice system: There will be more older persons *working* in the criminal justice system; there will be more older *offenders* in the criminal justice system; and there will be more older *crime victims*.

A higher number of older offenders presents issues for law enforcement, the courts, and corrections. For corrections, in particular, the higher number of older incarcerated offenders leads to issues regarding the management of older offenders, many of whom have health problems or are in danger of being victimized in prison. Older offenders are commonly protected in prison by segregating them in older offender units. In terms of health issues, these can be especially expensive to address. Older inmates are sometimes placed on house arrest with electronic monitoring under the premise that they are better off in the community. In these cases, the older offenders need to pay for their own health care. In some situations, it has been reported that older sex offenders have been released from prison only to be placed in nursing homes, where other nursing home residents might be at risk.

Older crime victims present a number of challenges in criminal justice. One general problem that older crime victims face is that many people are unfamiliar with elder abuse. Experts have described several varieties of elder abuse. *Elder physical abuse* refers to behaviors such as hitting, slapping, kicking, withholding medication from an older person, and overmedicating elderly persons. *Elder neglect* refers to situations in which individuals who have a legal duty to provide care to an elderly person fail to do so, with *active neglect* referring to intentional neglect and *passive neglect* characterizing unintentional neglect. *Elder sexual*

Older inmates have many different needs than younger inmates do. These differences may present challenges to prison and jail administrators.

© Andrew Burton/Staff/Getty Images

abuse refers to situations in which individuals perform illegal and inappropriate sexual activities against older persons, including engaging in sexual relations, voyeurism, and inappropriate touching. *Elder financial abuse*, or financial exploitation, refers to instances in which offenders steal from older persons. *Elder emotional abuse* includes instances in which offenders engage in psychologically or verbally abusive acts targeted at an older person. In one case, for example, a nursing home employee repeatedly tormented a nursing home resident by telling the resident that the employee was going to have sex with the resident's granddaughter. Patronizing speech, such as calling older persons "pretty," "young," "beautiful," or other words that the speaker does not mean, has been cited as an example of verbal abuse. As an analogy, if someone called one of the authors "skinny," he would be offended.

Official statistics show that older persons have the lowest victimization rate of any age group. As a result, criminologists have tended to ignore elder abuse in their research. Political issues, methodological issues (a sample is hard to find), and conceptual issues (the problem is vaguely defined) are additional reasons why elder abuse has been ignored by criminologists. Recognizing that the study of elder abuse requires an interdisciplinary effort, the term *gero-criminology* reflects the empirical response to elder abuse that brings together various researchers and practitioners to better understand the problem.[28]

Although official statistics portray a low victimization rate for older persons, self-report surveys and data from adult protective services officials reflect a much higher victimization rate. In addition, because of physical frailties and the inability to accumulate wealth, it has been suggested that the consequences of certain types of elder abuse are much more serious than the consequences of forms of victimization experienced in other life stages. Research shows that the consequences of neglect can be far more serious than the consequences of physical abuse and that cases of financial abuse have been increasing in recent years. Perpetrators in these offenses include adult offspring, grandchildren, other relatives, professionals hired to provide care to older persons, and those who seek out older persons to victimize. Historically, abuse cases have been attributed primarily to caregiver strain, though in recent years it has been recognized that certain types of elder abuse are likely caused by specific factors. For example, although caregiver strain might cause a person to hit someone, it should not cause someone to steal from an older person. It is believed that people who have Alzheimer's disease or related forms of dementia are more likely to experience physical aggression at the hands of caregivers.[29]

BEYOND A REASONABLE DOUBT 15.4

Instances in which offenders intentionally fail to provide care to older persons are known as _____.

(a) exploitation, (b) emotional neglect, (c) passive neglect, (d) active neglect, (e) none of the above

The answer can be found on page 522.

FEATURE VIDEO
Spreading Awareness

➡ The Evolution of Criminal Justice Policies

Criminal justice policies have evolved over time and will continue to evolve. In many ways, these policies shift as political values and belief systems change over time. Policies are also shaped by changes in understanding about different types of crime. By focusing on two current controversial policies (gun control policies and drug law policies), this section provides a backdrop for considering how evidence-based criminal justice policies will become more common in the future.

Gun Control Policies

Most individuals, Republican and Democrat alike, seem to agree that gun violence is a serious problem in the United States. Between 1993 and 2011, gun violence was attributed to nearly 70% of all homicides. Of those homicides, 70% to 80% were committed with handguns, and handguns were used in 90% of all nonfatal firearm offenses.[30] A review of gun violence data from the same time period highlighted the following patterns:

- ➡ Firearm-related homicides declined 39%, from 18,253 in 1993 to 11,101 in 2011.

- ➡ Nonfatal firearm crimes declined 69%, from 1.5 million victimizations in 1993 to 467,300 victimizations in 2011.

- ➡ For both fatal and nonfatal firearm victimizations, the majority of the decline occurred during the 10-year period from 1993 to 2002.[31]

This decline in gun violence is likely of little comfort to the families and friends of the more than 11,000 individuals killed by firearms each year. Although most people agree that gun violence is a serious problem, great disagreement centers on how to respond to it. Some people argue that citizens should be able to carry weapons to protect themselves from gun violence; others argue that gun possession should be restricted in an effort to reduce gun violence.

Policies used to control gun violence include background check policies, possession policies, pulling-levers policies, and enhanced penalties for offenses involving firearms. **Background check policies** require gun distributors to conduct background checks on gun purchasers before finalizing sales. These laws prohibit people with felony convictions for different types of offenses from owning guns. Critics of the policies argue that offenders who use guns in crimes frequently buy their weapons on the black market rather than from legal distributors. Supporters of the policies point out that, in the absence of such policies, guns would be even more readily available to potential offenders.

Somewhat related, **possession policies** generally regulate the possession of weapons. Certain types of firearms are illegal in virtually all states, firearms cannot be carried in certain places such as schools or universities

background check policies: Policies that require gun distributors to conduct background checks on gun purchasers before finalizing the sale.

possession policies: Policies that generally regulate the possession of weapons.

in many states, and certain kinds of individuals cannot legally carry handguns. For instance, in Virginia, people who have certain types of criminal histories, have been civilly committed, have been dishonorably discharged from the military, or have a protective order against them are prohibited from either purchasing or carrying firearms. Other restrictions found in different states focus on limiting access of young people to guns. For instance, in Virginia, guns must be locked up in the presence of children, juveniles must have parental permission to possess handguns, and handguns cannot be sold to those under age 18.[32]

Critics dismiss these policies on the grounds that only law-abiding citizens follow the laws in the first place and that offenders will carry guns regardless of these restrictions. Still, the policies send a message about the tolerance of guns.

Pulling-levers policies are used by law enforcement and prosecutors to identify and send a message to specific individuals and groups at risk of gun violence so that they know these offenses will not be tolerated. Part of sending the message may involve carrying out the threat against a high-profile offender to show potential offenders in the community that criminal justice officials mean business. In these situations, law enforcement and prosecutors work closely with community partners to ensure that those most at risk of future offending "get the message." Figure 15.4 shows a poster that was used as part of one city's pulling-levers efforts. The posters were hung in locations that potential gun offenders were believed to frequent. Other cities have even placed such notices on their public transportation buses.

Confiscated guns, such as those shown here, are eventually melted into scrap metal.

© Ralf-Finn Hestoft/Corbis

FIGURE 15.4   **Sample Text From a Pulling-Levers Poster**

Problem

VIOLENT GANG MEMBER

Solution

ARMED CAREER CRIMINAL CONVICTION

Future Address

FEDERAL CORRECTIONAL INSTITUTE,
MAXIMUM SECURITY FACILITY

If you have a criminal record and are arrested with a gun or even a single bullet, you could face a mandatory minimum sentence of 15 years to life with no parole.

Center for Problem-Oriented Policing; ©iStockphoto.com/jeff giniewicz

pulling-levers policies: With regard to gun crimes, targeted efforts by law enforcement and prosecutors to identify and send a message to specific individuals and groups at risk of gun violence so that they know these offenses will not be tolerated.

Pulling levers practices often involve implementation of **penalty enhancement policies**. These policies stipulate that offenders who use a gun in their offenses can receiver longer and stiffer jail and prison sentences because they used a gun. If someone robs me with a spatula pointed at my back, this would elicit one type of sanction. If another offender robs me with a gun, this could elicit a stiffer penalty in many states and at the federal level.

Several years ago, a handful of cities across the United States implemented programs based partly on pulling-levers and penalty enhancement ideals. Among these programs were Project Exile (Richmond, Virginia), Project Ceasefire (Kansas City, Missouri), and Operation Ceasefire (Boston, Massachusetts). These programs called for specific law enforcement and prosecutorial strategies to reduce gun violence in each city. The common features of the programs were that they allowed for increased efficiency in prosecuting offenses involving guns, called for stiffer penalties for drug offenders who used weapons in their offenses, and promoted interagency collaboration between the various systems involved in responding to violent crimes.[33]

Boston's Operation Ceasefire was hailed as a model gun violence intervention program (see Chapter 7). According to Braga, youth violence decreased two-thirds in Boston after the project was implemented.[34] Richmond's Project Exile also received widespread acclaim. The program specified that gun cases that in the past were prosecuted locally could be prosecuted in federal court. The use of federal courts allowed for quicker case processing, longer penalties, and prison sentences in isolated federal penitentiaries. The media were used to help get the message to offenders that the gun offenses would be punished more severely.[35] Ultimately, the aim of Project Exile was "to get guns out of the hands of those who are carrying them illegally, felons who are most likely to use weapons in the commission of a crime."[36] With the media attention, and because the program targeted criminals who used guns, it received widespread public support.[37]

Project Exile was touted a success immediately after its implementation when homicide rates fell dramatically in Richmond. Within one year, the number of gun-involved robberies was down one-third and the number of offenders who were carrying guns when they were arrested was cut in half.[38] The apparent success of Project Exile and the other gun-reducing programs led to federal funding being made available so that other cities could develop similar programs.

Critics have cited some drawbacks with the policies based on penalty enhancement. The increased sentences are seen by some critics as a tool to control minorities and, based on this, the system is seen as a tool for racial discrimination. Others have suggested that the policies are not as successful as they appear to be and that decreases in homicide rates were more a function of demographics than of anything else. Despite these criticisms, because the policies focus on criminals who use guns, rather than on the "average" gun owner, the policies have received widespread public support.

One firearms policy by itself cannot be expected to be a panacea, but the combination of firearms policies is a better indicator of the ability of the policies to prevent violence. A recent study considering the restrictiveness of state firearms policies found a direct relationship between restrictiveness and

VIDEO
Operation Ceasefire

penalty enhancement policies: Policies stipulating that offenders who use a gun in committing an offense can receive longer and stiffer jail and prison sentences because they used a gun.

suicide rates—leading the researchers to suggest that more restrictive states "have the potential to reduce the suicide rate."[39] In a similar fashion, another study found that the more available guns are in a state, the higher the likelihood of unintentional deaths by firearms.[40] Policies controlling the availability of guns, then, should reduce the likelihood of injuries from firearms.

After reviewing dozens of studies on gun and violence policies, Sherman concluded that just two strategies have conclusively demonstrated "what works": gun crime hot spots law enforcement and background checks.[41] Other researchers examining state background checks have also demonstrated the success of the policies. One study found that "states with less stringent background checks on firearms purchases were significantly associated with firearms homicides."[42]

The War on Drugs and Drug Legalization

Drug laws govern the possession, use, sales, and trafficking of drugs. In the United States, most of the major drugs (heroin, cocaine, and marijuana) that are now illegal were legal through the early 1900s. Between the early 1900s and 1970s, a number of state laws were passed that criminalized different drugs in varying ways. In 1970, the **Comprehensive Drug Abuse and Control Act** created the most comprehensive federal legislation governing drug laws. By the 1980s, the federal government officially declared its "war on drugs" with a series of laws that greatly stiffened the penalties for various drug offenses. First Lady Nancy Reagan even appeared on the popular television show *Diff'rent Strokes* to help educate young people about the travails of drugs. Apparently the teen actors on the series did not get the message as two of them eventually faced drug problems later in their own lives.

As shown in Figure 15.5, the number of drug arrests increased dramatically between 1980 and 2012. More than three times as many offenders were arrested for drug offenses in 2007, compared with 1980. Many

> **Comprehensive Drug Abuse and Control Act:** Comprehensive federal legislation governing drug laws.

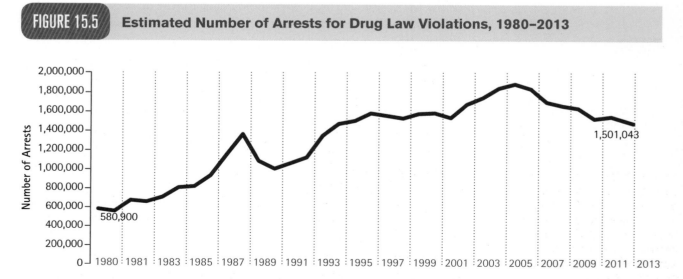

FIGURE 15.5   **Estimated Number of Arrests for Drug Law Violations, 1980–2013**

The U.S. Department of Justice, Office of Justice Programs, Bureau of Justice Statistics

After marijuana was legalized in Washington, entrepreneurs opened marijuana shops to meet the demand for legal marijuana.

© Gilles Mingasson/Getty Images

criminologists point to the war on drugs as the source of our country's imprisonment boom. Essentially, nearly a million more individuals were brought into the criminal justice system for drug offenses in 2012 than in 1980.

Most criminal justice scholars agree that drugs and crime are related, but they may disagree on the reasons for the link. One author team has cited the following possible relationships between drugs and crime: Drugs cause crime; crime causes drugs; the relationship is a coincidence; or the same factors that cause drugs also cause crime.[43]

Research shows a link between type of drug offender and type of crime.[44] In particular, heavier drug users are more likely than nonusers to be involved in property offenses, and drug traffickers are more likely to be involved in crimes against persons. Research also shows that, with the introduction of crack cocaine in the late 1980s, types of urban offenders shifted, with robberies increasing and burglaries and home break-ins decreasing.[45] In addition, some observers have pointed out that "open air drug dealing" (which refers to drug dealing that occurs in open areas rather than behind closed doors) leads to the following problems: traffic congestion, too much noise, higher rates of disorderly conduct, begging, loitering, vandalism, littering, and public drug use.[46]

The illicit drug business has been compared to legitimate businesses. One similarity is that just as legitimate businesses may employ numerous employees in order to function, drug dealers often rely on fellow "employees" in their trade: *Lookouts* watch for law enforcement and alert drug dealers when the police are nearby, *holders* hold drugs for the dealers, *steerers* make referrals to dealers in exchange for cash, *touts* find customers for dealers, and *middlemen* move the drugs and money between respective parties.[47]

It is common in the United States to debate the legalization of drugs (see Table 15.1). This debate remains a popular issue, particularly for drugs such as marijuana. Indeed, in 2014, Colorado and Washington legalized the recreational use of marijuana, and other states are likely to make similar decisions in the near future. One entrepreneur viewed the decision to legalize marijuana from a businesslike perspective:

> Making a business illegal doesn't get rid of the efforts of entrepreneurs to pursue it. Everyone knows that entrepreneurs are selling marijuana for recreational use in all 48 states where it is illegal. Making a business legal makes it easier for policy makers to tap entrepreneurial efforts to benefit society. Colorado and Washington are using taxes and regulation to channel pot entrepreneurship more productively than other states, where policy makers are wasting resources trying to stop it, and, consequently, driving it underground.[48]

JOURNAL
Legalize It?

TABLE 15.1	Arguments for and Against Drug Legalization
FOR LEGALIZATION	**AGAINST LEGALIZATION**
• Drug use is a right. • Drug laws are biased. • The war on drugs costs too much. • Government can tax drugs. • The war on drugs creates crime. • Legalization would make drugs safer.	• Drug use is wrong and immoral. • Drug use is harmful to users. • Drug use harms the social fabric. • Drug use would increase among juveniles. • Drug use is tied to crime.

Payne, B. K., & Gainey, R. R. (2005). Drugs and policing: A scientific perspective. Springfield, IL: Thomas.

By all accounts, this perspective holds some weight. Colorado received $2 million from taxes placed on recreational marijuana use, and it was estimated that the state would recoup more than $40 million from recreational and medicinal sales in new tax revenue in the first year of the new law.[49] Somewhere out there, one expects that a criminal justice graduate student is preparing a thesis or dissertation searching for evidence regarding the success of this new effort. After all, success should not be measured in dollars alone. See the "Ethical Decision Making" box in this chapter for a scenario assessing your own beliefs about whether a criminal justice student should smoke marijuana.

Criminal Justice and Evidence-Based Policy

Increased recognition of the importance of evidence-based practices has improved the criminal justice system and will continue to do so. Over the past decade or two, criminal justice researchers and criminologists have

ETHICAL DECISION MAKING

STUDY ABROAD AND MARIJUANA

Criminal justice major John Johnson is excited to be on a study abroad trip to Amsterdam. It is his first time out of the country. After arriving, he is quickly introduced to the many parts of the city that differ from what he experienced growing up in the United States. One evening during his free time, he ventures into a cannabis club to see what the club looks like on the inside.

After entering the club, he is amazed at how relaxed the environment seems. He remembers very clearly that his parents and his professor told him he should not smoke marijuana on his trip, even though it is legal to do so in Amsterdam. The fact that he has been told not to smoke marijuana makes him want to smoke it even more.

YOU DECIDE

1. Would it be wrong if Johnson smokes marijuana in the club? Why or why not?

2. How might his decision to smoke marijuana impact his future career choices in the United States?

become more instrumental in determining the efficacy of criminal justice policies. **Evidence-based policies** refers to policies supported by empirical research. Criminologist Robert Bohm argued in his 1993 presidential address to the Academy of Criminal Justice Sciences that the discipline has "done a poor job of educating" about issues related to criminal justice.[50] He cited several policies (e.g., the death penalty, the war on drugs, and prison construction) that are based on myths to which policy makers adhere in their efforts to develop and implement crime control policies. Bohm challenged scholars to focus more on what they can do to influence policy. In his own address to the same academy, Gennaro Vito said, "Our purpose is to provide information that can serve as a basis for policy—policy that is effective, policy that produces a just result. We are not merely technocrats. Our aim is to help people live safely in society."[51]

In the 2000s, greater attention was given to the need for evidence in developing criminal justice policies. In another presidential address to the Academy of Criminal Justice Sciences, Todd Clear made an impassioned plea for using criminal justice research to influence policy: "No legislature dealing with the field of medicine would ever pass any legislation without consulting the American Medical Association. Yet criminal justice legislation is routinely enacted without any word from those who study the process and effects of criminal justice action. This must change."[52] About a decade later, it seemed that the discipline was, in fact, taking a stronger role in testing, developing, implementing, and revising criminal justice policies and practices.

Clear later became the president of the American Society of Criminology. In his address to that organization, he highlighted several changes in the discipline that demonstrated a commitment to evidence-based criminal justice:

- ➡ The journal *Criminology and Public Policy* was created in the early 2000s by the American Society of Criminology. It quickly became one of the top journals in the field.

- ➡ The *Journal of Experimental Criminology* was created and has published numerous criminal justice experiments testing programs and topics directly related to criminal justice policy.

- ➡ The Campbell Crime and Justice Collaboration Group was created in 2000. This group has overseen more than two dozen systematic reviews of criminal justice topics by focusing on past criminal justice studies that adhered to strict rules of the scientific method.

- ➡ Criminal justice scholars have increasingly published meta-analyses, which are similar to the systematic reviews conducted by the Campbell Collaboration. These meta-analyses were done in an effort to identify "the impact of various interventions or outcomes."[53]

Clear summarized the focus on evidence-based policy by stating, "It suddenly seems that everyone in the policy-making world, from professional associations to the White House, has accepted the importance of the evidence-based paradigm."[54]

VIDEO
Todd Clear

evidence-based policies:
Policies supported by empirical research.

Research by itself will not, however, necessarily influence or change criminal justice policies. Joan Petersilia pointed out that "empirical results must be weighed against political and economic constraints."[55] In terms of political constraints, certain types of criminal justice or crime policies likely will not change even in the face of great evidence demonstrating that the policy is a failure, and many effective programs may never be implemented on a widespread basis. In terms of economic costs, some programs or strategies that would reduce crime are simply too costly to implement. The political and economic constraints are often joined together as factors that restrain policy making. Treatment programs for sex offenders are illustrative. Some treatment programs relying on individual therapy have been deemed to be effective for sex offenders.[56] These programs are expensive, however, and legislators are viewed as being "for sex offenders" when they support anything other than punitive approaches to dealing with this group of offenders. Certainly, legislators weigh a range of factors when considering new laws and policies. Evidence is just one factor, albeit an important one.

BEYOND A REASONABLE DOUBT 15.5

The _____ created the most comprehensive federal legislation governing drug laws.

(a) War on Drugs Act, (b) Comprehensive Drug Abuse and Control Act, (c) U.S. Patriot Act, (d) Pulling Levers Act, (e) Homeland Security Act

---

The answer can be found on page 522.

➡ Concluding Remarks

AUTHOR VIDEO
Futures in Criminal Justice

Criminal justice seniors and graduate students are frequently asked on their final or comprehensive examinations to describe what the criminal justice system will be like three or four decades from now. The authors took their own examinations roughly two decades ago. Even at that time, had we predicted what the criminal justice system would "look like" in 2014, we never would have predicted certain features of our governmental efforts to control behavior. Among other things, we never would have predicted that

- A Department of Homeland Security would be created to focus on various crimes, including terrorism.

- Traveling through airports would require a wide range of intrusive searches to protect everyone on airplanes.

- New technologies would allow criminal justice officials to track offenders in real time.

- New technologies would make it incredibly easy for offenders to victimize others across the world.

- A federal law would be passed allowing individuals' rights to be circumvented in the name of terrorism investigations.

The list could go on and on. It is impossible to predict with great accuracy what is in store for the criminal justice system. Indeed, the system is incredibly flexible, adapting to changes in other systems in a way that helps to move our society forward. This unpredictability and flexibility makes criminal justice careers especially exciting.

At the risk of oversimplifying the future of criminal justice, there are a few things we can predict:

- Terrorism will continue to be a matter of concern for criminal justice officials.

- The global nature of our lives will lead to even more issues related to transnational crime and criminal justice.

- Gun violence will continue to be a national issue, though the trend related to the decreasing number of gun crimes is expected to continue.

- The number of older offenders, criminal justice professionals, and crime victims will increase.

- Other states will begin to legalize marijuana, though it is not expected that other types of drugs will be legalized any time soon.

- The discipline of criminal justice will have a stronger role in helping to formulate, implement, and evaluate evidence-based policies.

- Some of you will become criminal justice professionals and leaders in the field of criminal justice.

This last point is especially exhilarating for us. With the appropriate education, which you are now receiving, and the skills you will develop, you can play a central role in promoting public safety. In making the world safer for others, you will join a select group of professionals, and we will all look up to you. It is our hope that the information contained in this book will help those of you on a path to a criminal justice career as well as those of you who will be involved only tangentially with the criminal justice system. Whichever path you choose, we wish you the best!

Just the Facts: Chapter Summary

- The federal government defines terrorism as "premeditated, politically motivated violence perpetrated against noncombatant targets by subnational groups or clandestine agents."

- Experts typically classify terrorism as domestic terrorism or international terrorism.

- Definitions of crime, responses to crime, and potential risk factors for crime vary across countries.

- *Human trafficking* refers to offenses in which individuals are relocated without their consent.

- A computer can be the target of an offense, a tool used in the commission of a crime, or incidental to an offense.

- Between 1993 and 2011, gun violence was attributed to nearly 70% of all homicides. Of those homicides, 70% to 80% were committed with handguns, and handguns were used in 90% of all nonfatal firearm offenses.

- Policies used to control gun violence include background check policies, possession policies, pulling-levers policies, and enhanced penalties for offenses involving firearms.

- As the population ages, there will be more older persons working in the criminal justice system, more older offenders in the criminal justice system, and more older crime victims.

- Drug laws govern the possession, use, sales, and trafficking of drugs.

- In 2014, Colorado and Washington legalized the recreational use of marijuana, and other states will likely make similar decisions in the near future.

- Criminal justice researchers and criminologists have become more instrumental in helping to determine the efficacy of criminal justice policies.

Critical Thinking Questions

1. Describe how crime is an international issue. How have societal changes shaped the international nature of crime?

2. Select three countries that you would like to visit. Rank those countries from the most safe to least safe. What factors influence your ranking?

3. How does terrorism impact the lives of college students?

4. How are computers related to crime?

5. Describe how crime and victimization are different for older and younger persons.

6. How can gun control policies influence gun violence?

7. Should marijuana be legal? Explain.

8. What does the phrase "evidence-based policy" mean?

Key Terms

background check policies (506)
Comprehensive Drug Abuse and Control Act (509)
cybercrime (500)
cyberterrorism (503)
cyber theft (501)

domestic terrorism (497)
evidence-based policies (512)
human trafficking (495)
International Crime Victimization Survey (495)

international terrorism (497)
Internet crime (501)
penalty enhancement policies (508)
possession policies (506)

pulling-levers policies (507)
software crimes (501)
terrorism (497)
unauthorized access (501)

$SAGE edgeselect™

edge.sagepub.com/payne

Sharpen your skills with SAGE edge select!

With carefully crafted tools and resources to encourage review, practice, and critical thinking, SAGE edge select gives you the edge needed to master course content. Take full advantage of open-access key term flashcards, practice quizzes, and video content. Diagnostic pre-tests, a personalized study plan, and post-tests are available with an access code.

Chapter 1

1. Inadmissible (False)
2. Inadmissible (False)
3. Inadmissible (False)
4. Admissible (True)
5. Admissible (True)
6. Admissible (True)
7. Admissible (True)
8. Inadmissible (False)

Chapter 2

1. Inadmissible (False)
2. Inadmissible (False)
3. Admissible (True)
4. Admissible (True)
5. Admissible (True)
6. Inadmissible (False)
7. Inadmissible (False)
8. Admissible (True)

Chapter 3

1. Inadmissible (False)
2. Admissible (True)
3. Inadmissible (False)
4. Inadmissible (False)
5. Admissible (True)
6. Admissible (True)
7. Inadmissible (False)
8. Admissible (True)

Chapter 4

1. Inadmissible (False)
2. Admissible (True)
3. Inadmissible (False)
4. Inadmissible (False)
5. Admissible (True)
6. Admissible (True)
7. Inadmissible (False)
8. Admissible (True)

Chapter 5

1. Inadmissible (False)
2. Admissible (True)
3. Admissible (True)
4. Inadmissible (False)
5. Admissible (True)
6. Inadmissible (False)
7. Admissible (True)
8. Admissible (True)

Chapter 6

1. Inadmissible (False)
2. Inadmissible (False)
3. Admissible (True)
4. Inadmissible (False)
5. Admissible (True)
6. Inadmissible (False)
7. Inadmissible (False)
8. Admissible (True)

Chapter 7

1. Inadmissible (False)
2. Inadmissible (False)
3. Inadmissible (False)
4. Admissible (True)
5. Admissible (True)
6. Inadmissible (False)
7. Admissible (True)
8. Admissible (True)

Chapter 8

1. Admissible (True)
2. Inadmissible (False)
3. Inadmissible (False)
4. Admissible (True)
5. Inadmissible (False)
6. Admissible (True)
7. Admissible (True)
8. Inadmissible (False)

Chapter 9

1. Inadmissible (False)
2. Inadmissible (False)
3. Admissible (True)
4. Inadmissible (False)
5. Admissible (True)
6. Admissible (True)
7. Admissible (True)
8. Inadmissible (False)

Chapter 10

1. Admissible (True)
2. Inadmissible (False)
3. Inadmissible (False)
4. Admissible (True)
5. Admissible (True)
6. Inadmissible (False)
7. Inadmissible (False)
8. Admissible (True)

Chapter 11

1. Inadmissible (False)
2. Admissible (True)
3. Inadmissible (False)
4. Admissible (True)
5. Admissible (True)
6. Admissible (True)
7. Inadmissible (False)
8. Inadmissible (False)

Chapter 12

1. Inadmissible (False)
2. Admissible (True)
3. Admissible (True)
4. Inadmissible (False)
5. Inadmissible (False)
6. Inadmissible (False)
7. Admissible (True)
8. Inadmissible (False)

Chapter 13

1. Inadmissible (False)
2. Admissible (True)
3. Inadmissible (False)
4. Inadmissible (False)
5. Admissible (True)
6. Admissible (True)
7. Inadmissible (False)
8. Admissible (True)

Chapter 14

1. Inadmissible (False)
2. Admissible (True)
3. Admissible (True)
4. Inadmissible (False)

5. Admissible (True)
6. Inadmissible (False)
7. Inadmissible (False)
8. Inadmissible (False)

Chapter 15

1. Inadmissible (False)
2. Admissible (True)
3. Admissible (True)
4. Admissible (True)
5. Admissible (True)
6. Inadmissible (False)
7. Inadmissible (False)
8. Admissible (True)

Chapter 1

1.1 (d) legislature

1.2 (a) juvenile police officers

1.3 (a) crime control

1.4 (d) August Vollmer

Chapter 2

2.1 (d) deviance

2.2 (d) surveys

2.3 (d) on-site administration

2.4 (a) Quasi-experiment

Chapter 3

3.1 (c) to determine where hospitals should be placed

3.2 (a) the Federal Bureau of Investigation

3.3 (b) July

Chapter 4

4.1 (d) crime typology

4.2 (a) Carnal knowledge

4.3 (b) burglary

4.4 (d) status offenses

4.5 (a) Organized crime

Chapter 5

5.1 (e) routine activities theory

5.2 (a) Conflict

5.3 (c) social control theory

5.4 (e) all of the above

Chapter 6

6.1 (d) states

6.2 (a) Political Era

6.3 (c) 18,000

Chapter 7

7.1 (a) Kansas City Preventive Patrol Experiment

7.2 (c) targeted policing

7.3 (a) Crime Prevention Through Environmental Design

7.4 (d) Compstat

Chapter 8

8.1 (a) political

8.2 (c) police discretion

Chapter 9

9.1 (d) both a and b

9.2 (a) the type of case and geographical area of the trial

9.3 (e) all of the above

9.4 (d) all of the above

9.5 (e) all of the above

Chapter 10

10.1 (e) all of the above

10.2 (c) the prosecutor

10.3 (b) to ensure a defendant's rights

10.4 (b) voir dire

10.5 (b) the defendant is at risk of losing his or her freedom

10.6 (d) all of the above

10.7 (c) the juvenile will go through the adult court

10.8 (d) both a and b

Chapter 11

11.1 (e) all of the above

11.2 (a) a defendant had a right to counsel during plea bargaining

11.3 (b) guidelines

11.4 (d) that the canon of judicial conduct in Minnesota violated a candidate's First Amendment rights

11.5 (c) when judges make policy as part of their decisions

11.6 (e) all of the above

11.7 (e) all of the above

Chapter 12

12.1 (a) retribution

12.2 (b) pillory

12.3 (b) Ashurst-Sumners

12.4 (d) Federal Bureau of Prisons

12.5 (a) corrections officers

Chapter 13

13.1 (c) deprivation model

13.2 (d) all of the above

13.3 (d) parole

13.4 (e) boot camps

Chapter 14

14.1 (a) *Cooper v. Pate*

14.2 (e) all of the above

14.3 (a) Civil commitment

Chapter 15

15.1 (b) Japan

15.2 (a) Right- and left-wing extremism

15.3 (e) all of the above

15.4 (d) active neglect

15.5 (b) Comprehensive Drug Abuse and Control Act

accomplice hypothesis: A hypothesis explaining gender differences in crime, according to which, female involvement in crime is often in the role of an accomplice.

adjudication: A proceeding in the juvenile justice system that is similar to a trial in the adult system, but the evidence is presented to a judge rather than a jury.

ADMAX prison: The super-maximum-security prison for the federal government.

administrative searches: Searches conducted without a warrant for inventory purposes, when police take property, such as an automobile, into their possession for legal purposes.

administrative supervision: The level of probation or parole at which caseloads may run up to 1,000 offenders in some places.

adolescence-limited offenders: Offenders whose antisocial behavior is temporary and does not extend beyond adolescence.

age-crime curve: A line graph that illustrates the percentage of crimes committed by members of different age groups; crime is most prevalent from ages 18 to 24.

aggressive patrols: The use of the law to investigate potential crimes by way of officers' presence, through heavy enforcement of the law, and stop and frisks.

amicus curiae briefs: Also known as "friends of the court" briefs, these are submitted by interested parties to the U.S. Supreme Court to provide the justices with other perspectives or legal arguments about the case at hand.

anomie theory: A theory that suggests that crime is produced by normlessness or confusion.

Anti-Terrorism and Effective Death Penalty Act: Passed by Congress in 1996, this law set a one-year time limit on any defendant seeking to file a habeas corpus petition and placed restrictions on a federal court's ability to overturn a state court's criminal conviction.

appeal: The process by which a second court reviews the conviction or sentencing decision made by a lower court.

appellate jurisdiction: Courts responsible for hearing cases that have already been heard in a lower court but are being appealed for a legal reason.

archival research: The use of archives to conduct scientific endeavors.

arraignment: The first stage of the trial process, in which a defendant appears before the judge to respond to charges against him or her by pleading guilty, not guilty, or nolo contendere (no contest).

arrest: The first formal point of contact between the courts and the accused; when a suspect is taken into custody by law enforcement officers under suspicion that he or she violated a local, state, or federal law.

arson: A crime in which an individual intentionally sets a structure on fire; common law defines it as a crime only if the structure was someone else's dwelling place, whereas state laws treat arson as an intentional burning of any structure or property, including the offender's own property and nonresidential structures.

Article III of the U.S. Constitution: The section of the Constitution that defines the judicial branch of government, or the court system, and reads, "The judicial power of the United States, shall be vested in one supreme Court, and in such inferior Courts as the Congress may from time to time ordain and establish."

Ashurst-Sumners Act: A Depression-era act (1935) that prohibited any transportation company from transporting goods made in prison industries, in order to eliminate prison labor.

assault: The attempt or threat to inflict harm on another person.

assigned counsel: Court-assigned private attorneys who represent indigent defendants.

background check policies: Policies that require gun distributors to conduct background checks on gun purchasers before finalizing the sale.

bail: A monetary bond that is paid by a defendant after an arrest as a way to obtain release before the trial.

bailiff: A courtroom employee, typically an armed law enforcement officer, who maintains order by tasks such as announcing the judge's entry into the courtroom, calling witnesses, assisting the jury when not in the courtroom, and ensuring that the defendant is not able to escape or harm others.

banishment: The act of forcing a member of a community to leave and never return as a means of punishment for some offense.

battery: An actual completed assault; in many states, "assault and battery" has been merged into the offense of "assault."

blue wall of silence: The concept that police officers protect their own and will not divulge any wrongdoing on the part of another officer.

booking: A formal description of the events and possible charges against the suspect are recorded; fingerprints and a mug shot are taken; and other information, such as the suspect's personal information and physical description, is recorded.

boot camps: A form of shock incarceration; structured much like a military boot camp.

bounding: The process of asking about victimization within a specific amount of time in order to reduce the likelihood of double-counting of a specific instance of victimization.

Bow Street Runners: The Bow Street magistrates' office developed by Henry Fielding in 1749 that served as an early police force, patrolling the Bow Street District and investigating crimes.

broken windows theory: The theory that minor crimes and disorder send a signal to people that a community does not care, thus inviting an unwanted element that engages in more serious crime.

burglary: A crime defined in common law as "the breaking and entering the house of another in the night-time, with intent to commit a felony therein, whether the felony be actually committed or not"; in state law, it is defined as breaking and entering during the daytime and into places other than a house.

calls-for-service: The phone calls placed to the police for which a police officer is dispatched.

campus facility design: A common architectural design for prisons; includes several separate buildings constructed inside a large area.

career criminal: A member of the small group of offenders who appear to commit the vast majority of offenses.

caseload: A model of probation and parole characterized by different levels, focusing on the number of offenders, rather than on the amount of work.

charging: The state's prosecutor (often the district attorney) decides what charges, if any, should be formally brought against the suspect, based on the evidence gathered by law enforcement.

chemical castration laws: Laws that allow officials to use drugs to control sex offenders' impulses.

child abuse: Also known as child maltreatment; crimes of violence perpetrated against a child by someone who has power over the child.

child sexual abuse: Sexual abuse committed against a child.

chivalry hypothesis: A hypothesis explaining gender differences in crime, according to which, females and males may be treated differently by criminal justice officials and this differential treatment may, in fact, insulate females from future offending.

citizen review boards: Official government boards, consisting of citizens, outside of the police department, that conduct investigations, oversee police investigations, or serve as appellate bodies to outcomes of police misconduct allegations.

civil commitment laws: Laws used to commit sex offenders in institutions after their incarceration dates.

civilianization: The practice of transferring job duties of police officers to nonsworn, civilian personnel.

Classical School: Adherents of the theory that crime is the result of free choice on the part of the individuals.

classification: The process by which a determination is made about where offenders will be incarcerated and the types of programs that will be made available to them.

classification system: The method by which prisons separate offenders, especially based on categories of sex, crime type, and dangerousness.

clearance rate: The percentage of crimes that were "solved," either by arrest or exceptional means.

common couple violence: Occasional "outbursts" of violence that either males or females may perpetrate against their spouses.

Community Mental Health Act: An act, signed by president John F. Kennedy in 1963, that aimed at deinstitutionalizing mentally ill individuals and treating the majority of them in the community rather than in state hospitals.

community policing: A philosophy and strategy of policing aimed at bringing the police and community together in partnerships to address the problems specific to their neighborhoods.

community service: An alternative sanction that requires offenders to perform some sort of work-related activity for a community agency.

complete observer: A role for researchers in which they do not participate with the research subjects; they only observe.

complete participant: A role for researchers in which they participate in activities with the research subjects but do not identify themselves as researchers.

Comprehensive Drug Abuse and Control Act: Comprehensive federal legislation governing drug laws.

CompStat: A managerial method for holding police managers accountable for the crimes and disorder that occur in their jurisdictions.

concentric zone theory: A theory developed by Park and Burgess that divided the city into a series of concentric zones with the assumption that crime is more likely to occur in the zones with more disorder.

conflict theory: The theory that crime is caused or influenced by the actions and decisions of those with power.

conjugal visits: Visits during which inmates are permitted to spend "alone time" with spouses and engage in intimate relationships.

consent searches: Legal searches conducted without a warrant, when an individual has waived his or her Fourth Amendment rights.

constable: In the early English system of policing, the individual selected to oversee the watch and ward; today, the type of law enforcement officers who work for the courts and may have arrest powers.

contract system: A method of providing counsel to indigent defendants whereby private law firms prepare an estimated cost for providing legal counsel, and the firm with the lowest bid to represent these offenders is awarded the responsibility.

convict leasing system: A system whereby penitentiaries, for a small fee, leased out prisoners to labor in factories and fields.

corporal punishment: A form of physical punishment intended to inflict pain as a means of retribution for an offense.

corporate crime: Instances when employees break rules in order to benefit the corporation; distinguished from occupational crime, which is done by the worker for his or her own benefit.

correctional misconduct: Illegal acts committed by corrections professionals.

corrections officers: Employees in correctional facilities who maintain order within the facility.

counterterrorism: The strategy, tactics, and techniques used by police departments (and others) to stop terrorist threats and acts.

court backlogs: The sometimes-long delay between arrest and a trial for some defendants, sometimes due to overcrowding or delays from the crime labs used to test evidence.

court overcrowding: A situation in which there are too many cases for the courts to hear; caused by increased demands on the court for more legal proceedings, an inadequate number of court personnel, a lack of courtroom space, and an increased number of cases.

courtroom workgroup: The collection of court personnel, such as the judge, bailiff, defense, and prosecution, as well as jurors, the victim, witnesses, and the media, who each have their own distinct roles but also work together to ensure that cases run smoothly through the system.

crime clock: Data reported in *Crime in the United States*, providing a general breakdown of how frequently crime occurs, assuming that crime occurs at the same frequency every day of the year, at each time of day.

crime control model: A model characterizing the criminal justice system, according to which cases are processed with a primary focus given to the need to protect the public.

Crime Prevention Through Environmental Design: The reshaping of the environment to control the problems of crime and disorder.

crime-specific policing: A police strategy for targeting specific offenses committed by particular offenders at specific places and times.

criminal justice system: A phrase used to describe the three main components of criminal justice: the police, the courts, and corrections.

criminal law: The branch of law that prescribes formal punishment for the violation of society's rules, or offenses against the state, in contrast to civil law, which proscribes punishment for violations against the individual.

criminal negligence: A type of intent in which individuals fail to act in a reasonable way, and this failure to act can be connected to harmful results.

criminology: The academic study of crimes and the circumstances surround them.

critical-incident stress debriefing: A system by which trained police officers conduct debriefings of officers involved in major incidents.

cruel and unusual punishment: Punishments that are "incompatible with the evolving standards of decency that mark the progress of a maturing society . . . or which involve the unnecessary infliction of pain."

cyber theft: A type of computer crime in which the offender uses a computer to steal something from an individual, the government, or a business.

cybercrime: Criminally illegal computer-related behaviors.

cyberterrorism: The most serious form of computer crime; includes instances when offenders use computers to commit terrorist acts.

dark figure of crime: A phrase used to describe the amount of crime that is not reported to police.

date rape: Synonymous with acquaintance rape, in which victims and offenders know one another, are not married, and are not related; perhaps a misnomer in that it seems to suggest that the rape occurs as part of a date.

day reporting centers: Locations where offenders are required to report on a daily basis as part of their sanctions.

deadly force: The authority for police to use force that can cause death when their lives or the lives of other citizens are placed in immediate jeopardy.

death penalty: A sanction that calls for the end of the offender's life.

debtor's prisons: An early form of prison, for those who could not pay their debts.

defendants' rights: The rights guaranteed to defendants in a criminal case, as defined by the U.S. Constitution and the Supreme Court.

defense: A legal strategy that defendants use to establish that they should not be found guilty of a specific crime.

defense attorney: An attorney who represents a person accused of a crime in the courtroom; he or she attempts to obtain an acquittal for that defendant throughout all stages of the adjudication process.

deprivation of autonomy: The pain of imprisonment that involves inmates giving up complete control over their lives.

deprivation of goods and services: The pain of imprisonment that involves inmates losing access to goods and services accessible in the world at large.

deprivation of heterosexual relationships: The pain of imprisonment that involves inmates losing physical and psychological relationships with their significant others.

deprivation of liberty: The pain of imprisonment that involves inmates losing certain civil rights, such as the right to vote in some states.

deprivation of security: The pain of imprisonment that involves inmates living in a seemingly unsafe environment.

detention: The process by which offenders are held before determinations of guilt are made; typically occurs in a jail or detention facility (for juveniles).

determinate sentencing: Also called "fixed" sentencing, this is a method for sentencing convicted offenders in which a fixed, or definite, sentence is imposed.

determinism: A principle of science, according to which behavior is caused or influenced by preceding events.

deterrence theory: Based on the classical school, the theory that offenders choose to commit crime as a result of their free will.

differential police response: The use of different types of responses for different types of calls in order to deal with a high call volume versus low number of police resources.

directed patrols: A police strategy in which police officers select a specific problem area for crime and/or disorder and spend shift downtime in that location.

discretion: A police officer's ability to decide whether to apply the law or not, for example, to stop a citizen, to issue a warning, to issue a ticket, or to make an arrest.

displacement effect: The movement of the criminal element out of one area and into another when police conduct aggressive policing or crackdowns.

docket number: The identification number assigned to a case, so that interested persons can easily track the case through adjudication.

domestic terrorism: Terrorists acts occurring in the United States with no connections to foreign entities.

domestic violence courts: Specialty courts that hear cases involving violence between individuals who are involved in an intimate relationship and who physically, emotionally, sexually or verbally abuse their partners.

double jeopardy: According to the Fifth Amendment to the U.S. Constitution, a defendant cannot be put on trial twice for the same offense.

driving while Black: The belief that Black drivers are more likely than White drivers to be stopped by police.

drug courts: Alternative courts for offenders addicted to drugs that allow the offender to participate in treatment programs in lieu of a criminal conviction and sentencing.

dual court system: The simultaneous existence of two court systems, federal and state.

due process model: A model characterizing the criminal justice system that emphasizes the protection of defendants' rights and is driven by respect for the "formal structure of the law."

elder abuse: Violence targeted at an elderly person; it can include emotional abuse, financial abuse, neglect, physical abuse, or sexual abuse.

elder sexual abuse: Situations in which individuals perform illegal and inappropriate sexual activities targeted against older persons included engaging in sexual relations, voyeurism, and inappropriate touching.

ethical neutrality: A principle of science, according to which criminal justice researchers should not allow their own ethical beliefs (or ideas about right and wrong) to guide their research efforts.

evidence-based policing: The use of data and facts (that is, the evidence) to guide the deployment of police in order to resolve crime and disorder in a community.

evidence-based policies: Policies supported by empirical research.

exclusion zone policies: Policies that stipulate places sex offenders cannot go, such as playgrounds, day cares, libraries, or school zones.

executive/legislative appointment: A method of seating judges in which the governor of a state appoints justices, who are then confirmed by another body, such as a legislature.

external funds: Grants and budgetary supplements police departments seek from external sources.

external stress: Factors that cause stress in police officers that lie outside of their control.

federal magistrates: Officials who have the authority to hear cases that involve minor federal misdemeanor offenses as well as to issue arrest warrants or search warrants to federal law enforcement officers, conduct preliminary hearings, and set bail for defendants being released until trial.

federalism: The issues of shared powers between the national and state governments and how, through intergovernmental relations, oversight of these powers is determined.

four dimensions of community policing: An interpretation of community policing that includes a philosophy of policing, a strategy for policing, a method of tactical deployment, and a means by which to best organize a department.

frankpledge system: The early English system for kin policing that organized 10 families into tithings and 10 tithings into hundreds in order to police their own.

fusion centers: Federally funded and locally staffed shared centers that collect data and share it in real time with the intent of assisting in police investigations.

gender role hypothesis: A hypothesis that explains gender differences in crime, according to which, different norms for the behavior of boys and girls may lead to differences in criminal behavior.

general deterrence: The correctional goal of dissuading people from committing a crime because they have seen another person punished for doing so.

general intent: A type of intent in which the suspect intended to commit the crime but may not have intended the specific consequences.

general strain theory: The theory that crime is caused by the way individuals respond to frustrations they encounter.

grand jury: Citizens who hear evidence against a person accused of a crime and help to determine the appropriate charges that should be brought against that person.

GLOSSARY

GLOSSARY

hate crimes: Situations in which one is targeted for victimization because of demographic characteristics (including gender, race, and the like), religion, health status, or sexuality; hating people is not illegal, but victimizing people because of that hatred is illegal.

home confinement: Also known as house arrest; an alternative sanction that requires offenders to be at home either for portions of their sanctions or for their entire sanctions.

home visits: Visits made by community corrections officers to ensure that offenders are abiding by the conditions of their probation or parole.

homeland security: The mechanisms put into place after the terrorist attacks of 9/11 in order to better respond not only to terrorist attacks but also to natural disasters.

homicide: The killing of one human being by another; may be criminal or justifiable.

hot spots policing: The concentration of police forces on a specific geographic location known to have a high incidence of crime and disorder.

house arrest with electronic monitoring: An alternative sanction similar to home confinement; technology is used to monitor offenders' whereabouts.

hue and cry: The requirement for good people to shout and come to the aid of people in distress from a crime.

human trafficking: Offenses in which individuals are relocated without their consent.

identity theft: Stealing someone else's background; can be perpetrated through other crimes such as forgery, credit card fraud, and the like.

in forma pauperis: The waiving of costs associated with a criminal defense, such as legal counsel or filing fees, for appellants who cannot afford to pay.

incapacitation: The correctional goal of putting a person in jail or prison so that he or she is unable to commit further crime.

incarceration: The act of holding someone in a setting for the purposes of detention or incarceration; includes five stages: detention, classification, incarceration, prerelease, and reentry.

indeterminate sentencing: A system of sentencing that gives a range of time (minimum to maximum); the actual sentence depends on the seriousness of the crime.

initial appearance: The stage in the criminal justice process when the suspect appears before a magistrate or similar official to be formally notified of the charges, advised of his or her rights, and notified of bail decisions (in some jurisdictions); in minor cases, summary trials may be held before the judge at this point, with the judge determining guilt or innocence and sentencing cases in which guilt is determined.

initial appearance (juveniles): A legal proceeding in the juvenile justice system in which a young suspect is asked to appear to hear the formal charges against him or her and to be informed of his or her legal rights.

institutional anomie theory: The theory that structural factors related to strain or anomie contribute to overall crime rates in a society.

intelligence-led policing: A policing model based on assessment and management of risk by collecting data and converting it into actionable intelligence for the police.

intensive supervision: The level of probation or parole at which caseloads include a small number of offenders who are deemed to be at a high risk for reoffending.

intermediate appellate courts (state): Also called courts of appeals, these courts review decisions from lower court proceedings if a party to the original case believes that either the procedures followed during the trial stage or the decision rendered by the lower court was unconstitutional.

internal affairs: An administrative office within the police department that typically reports directly to the police chief and is charged with investigating allegations of police misconduct.

internal stress: Factors that cause stress in police officers that lie inside their immediate control.

International Crime Victimization Survey: A survey created in 1989 to assess victimization rates in different parts of the world.

international terrorism: Terrorist acts committed with a specific connection to foreign entities.

Internet crime: A range of offenses in which the Internet is used to perpetrate offenses (e.g., consumer fraud, fake e-mails, ransomware, extortion).

involuntary manslaughter: Situations in which reckless acts lead to unintentional killings.

jail: Institutions that hold pretrial offenders awaiting trial who were not granted bail or pretrial release and offenders who have been convicted of misdemeanors and sentenced to jail for less than 12 months as part of their punishment.

Judiciary Act of 1789: The law that set forth the United States' federal court structure and defined the jurisdiction and role of the federal courts.

judicial misconduct: Any behavior by an attorney or a judge that is in conflict with the established rules of professional conduct, often revolving around the abuse of an individual's power.

judicial process: The progression of a case through the judicial system.

jurisdiction: The geographic area and boundaries where police have the authority of office to enforce the law.

jurors: Citizens who, after hearing the evidence from both sides of a case, determine the guilt or innocence of a defendant and, in some cases, also recommend an appropriate sentence to be imposed on the defendant.

jury deliberations: The stage in the trial process, after the attorneys present their closing arguments, when the members of the jury privately discuss the facts of the case to decide the verdict.

jury instructions: The stage in the trial process when the presiding judge explains the law to the jurors and informs them about the specific elements of the offenses with which the defendant is charged or of any lesser offenses that may be relevant.

jury selection: The process by which an impartial jury is chosen to hear the evidence in a trial; includes the voir dire process, when potential jurors are questioned.

justifiable homicide: Homicides in which the killing is justified in the eyes of the law; includes cases in which a police officer or a citizen kills another person who is in the process of committing a felony.

juvenile courts: Courts established in the late 1800s that treated young offenders differently from adults, focusing on treatment and rehabilitation as opposed to punishment.

juvenile delinquency: Illegal behaviors committed by individuals under age 18.

juvenile justice system: The system through which cases involving juvenile offenders are processed.

kin policing: An early form of policing that relied on family and clans to be responsible for the behaviors of their people.

labeling theory: The theory that labeling individuals contributes to future offending and that expectations of individuals, whether positive or negative, may lead individuals to meet those expectations.

larceny: A crime defined by legal scholars as the taking of someone's else's property with intent to keep the property.

law clerks: Court employees who keep cases progressing smoothly by completing tasks such as researching cases, reviewing documents, summarizing cases, preparing cases, or writing documents.

learning theory: A theory that suggests that criminal behavior is learned just as other behavior is learned.

life-course-persistent offenders: Offenders who continue to engage in crime throughout life.

life course theory: An interdisciplinary developmental theory that explains human behavior by examining how past events put individuals on certain trajectories for future behaviors.

majority opinion: A decision by an appellate court that describes the finding of the majority of the justices.

mala in se offenses: Crimes considered to be inherently evil (for example, murder, rape, incest).

mala prohibita offenses: Crimes that are illegal simply because a particular government chooses to make the behaviors illegal.

manslaughter: Killings that are intentional but in response to some form of provocation, or perceived provocation, though words alone are not enough; typically classified as voluntary or involuntary manslaughter.

marital rape: Instances in which spouses (typically husbands) sexually assault their wives; some state laws require the use of force in order for the act to be classified as rape, in which case threat of force is not be enough.

mark system: A simple classification system that gave prisoners rewards (marks) for good behavior, which were associated with more freedoms in prison.

Marshall hypothesis: The idea that the more informed individuals are about the death penalty, the less likely they will be to support it.

Martinson's report: A report that found, essentially, that efforts to rehabilitate offenders had no significant effect on recidivism rates.

mass murders: Crimes committed by individuals who kill a large number of victims all at once.

maximum-security prisons: High-security correctional facilities that hold some of the most dangerous, high-risk, violent offenders, some of whom have a record of prior escape attempts.

medium-security prisons: Correctional facilities with high walls but few, if any, guard towers in which inmates are permitted to congregate, watch television, and take part in rehabilitative programs.

mental health courts: Alternative or specialty courts that developed to help those offenders suffering from mental illnesses and that divert mentally ill offenders from the jail/prison and place them in treatment programs instead.

merit selection: Also called the Missouri plan, this is a method of seating judges whereby a nominating panel provides the state's governor with a list of candidates, and the governor then selects one of those candidates and appoints him or her to the position; new judges must run on their records in a retention election after a few years.

Metropolitan Police Act of 1829: The act that created the first formally recognized police department in the world in London, England.

middle-class measuring rod: The types of values that school children are expected to demonstrate and adhere to in their scholastic endeavors.

minimum-security prisons: Correctional facilities that hold low-risk, nonviolent, first-time offenders; they provide dormitory-style housing and few rules to govern inmate behavior.

mistake of fact: A legal defense having to do with an offender's truly not knowing a crucial fact that results in criminal behavior, such as a mislabeled medicine that is given to a patient.

motor vehicle theft: Instances in which individuals steal automobiles (as opposed to thieves stealing items *from* automobiles).

municipal police: The predominant type of law enforcement agency in the United States, representing a municipal government such as a town or city.

murder: Certain classifications of homicide; *first-degree murder* typically describes premeditated and deliberate homicides and *second-degree murder* typically describes unplanned but intentional homicides.

National Crime Victimization Survey: A survey that collects information directly from residents of the United States to assess their victimization experiences.

National Incident-Based Reporting System: A national crime reporting system developed in the late 1980s in an effort to provide more detail about crime incidents.

necessity: A criminal defense, according to which an illegal act is committed to prevent an even greater harm.

negligent homicide: Accidental (or unintentional) killings in which the offender should have reasonably known that his or her behavior could lead to someone's death.

neutralization theory: The theory that juveniles tend to know right from wrong, but they engage in delinquent acts after rationalizing (or neutralizing) their behavior as appropriate in specific situations.

New York system: The system of penitentiaries based on the Auburn prison in New York state, which confined inmates to their cells at night, but brought them together to work communally during the day.

night watch: In the early English system of policing, a semiformal guard for nighttime.

noble-cause corruption: Police misconduct committed in order to ensure justice is served on a criminal.

nonpartisan elections: Elections in which the candidate's political party affiliation is not identified.

objectivity: A principle of science, according to which scholars must not let their values drive their research endeavors.

occupational deviance: Improper or illegal conduct carried out while performing one's job.

officer-initiated contacts: The police function by which police officers initiate investigations rather than wait for calls-for-service.

Omnibus Crime Control and Safe Streets Act of 1968: A federal law that provided funding for state and local police.

Operation Ceasefire: A program in Boston that was aimed specifically at reducing youth gun violence by targeting the few offenders who caused most of the problems.

operational stress: The stress associated with performing one's regular job duties.

order maintenance: The maintenance of territorial control over a specific area or beat by police officers.

organizational stress: The stress caused by the organization, that is, the police department, for which an individual works.

organized crime: Offenses committed by networks or organizations formed for the sole purpose of engaging in illegal practices.

original jurisdiction: Courts that hear cases initially or for the first time.

pains of imprisonment : According to Sykes, the five deprivations that offenders experience during incarceration: autonomy, goods and services, liberty, heterosexual relationships, and security.

parenting hypothesis: A hypothesis explaining gender differences in crime, according to which, differences in males and females result from different ways that boys and girls are treated by their parents.

parole: Community supervision imposed after individuals have served a stint of incarceration.

parsimony: A principle of science, according to which scientists must create the simplest explanation possible in examining the topics under study.

Part I offenses: Criminal homicide, forcible rape, robbery, aggravated assault, burglary, larceny–theft, motor vehicle theft, and arson.

Part II offenses: Offense that are technically less serious than Part I offenses, though most criminologists agree that such a statement is misleading given the breadth of offenses.

participant as observer: A role for researchers in which they participate in the activities, but the research subjects know that they are being observed.

partisan elections: Elections in which the candidate's political party affiliation is clearly identified.

patriarchal terrorism: A type of violence that happens in families; refers to "systematic male violence" over time.

patronage system: A politically corrupt system in the 19th century, by which government positions (including as police officers) were handed out for political gain; see also *spoils system*.

penalty enhancement policies: Policies stipulating that offenders who use a gun in committing an offense can receive longer and stiffer jail and prison sentences because they used a gun.

Pennsylvania system: The prison system in which inmates were kept in solitary confinement, even during hard labor.

per curiam opinion: A legal opinion from an appellate court that is a brief, unsigned document in which the court agrees with part of a lower court ruling but disagrees with other parts.

plagiarism: Stealing the intellectual property of another.

plain-view searches: Legal searches conducted without a warrant, when contraband is in plain view of the police.

plea bargaining: A system in which the defendant gives up his or her right to a trial in exchange for a reduction in charges or the sentence imposed.

police code of ethics: The code by which many police officers are asked to live, upholding good values with strong ethics.

police-community relations: Developed in 1955 and implemented throughout the 1960s, the program that educated police officers on the varying needs of the populations they serve.

police crackdowns: Shows of force by the police to concentrate on specific crime problems, locations, or persons.

police misconduct: A general term used to describe police behavior that is in violation of departmental policies and procedures, is a misuse of power and authority, or is a violation of the law.

police paramilitary units: Specially trained and outfitted police units for use in high–risk situations; commonly called SWAT (Special Weapon and Tactics) teams.

police strategies: Broad concepts for how best to deploy the police in order to effectively reduce crime and disorder.

police subculture: The values and traditions that are particular to police officers.

Positivist School: Adherents of the theory that crime is caused by factors beyond choice.

possession policies: Policies that generally regulate the possession of weapons.

posttraumatic stress disorder (PTSD): The psychological and physical distress caused by witnessing or experiencing a major catastrophic event.

GLOSSARY

predictive policing: A police strategy that uses empirical data and attempts to make predictions about what crimes are likely to occur, where, and when.

preliminary hearing: The stage in the criminal justice process (in some jurisdictions) when a judge determines whether probable cause exists to suggest that the suspect committed a crime in the judge's jurisdiction.

pre-sentence investigation: A report written by a probation officer, this document provides the judge with detailed information about the offender prior to the sentencing phase of a trial.

pretrial detention: Holding an inmate in prison prior to a trial if he or she is deemed to be a flight risk or to have the potential to commit additional crimes.

pretrial motions: Requests, either oral or written (called petitions), that are made to a court seeking a finding, a decision, or an order.

preventive detention: The act of holding a defendant prior to the trial if it is believed that he or she may be a flight risk or considered to be dangerous to the community.

preventive patrol: The police strategy by which police officers patrol their beats with the intention that their presence would deter crime.

prison: An institution that houses offenders who have been convicted of committing felonies.

prison camps: Minimum- and low-security federal correctional facilities that have few guards with limited fences; they hold nonviolent offenders who are not considered to be escape threats.

Prison Litigation Reform Act: A law requiring inmates to exhaust all administrative remedies and pay a filing fee before filing suit claiming that their rights have been abused.

prison plantations: Prisons that had inmates farm the surrounding lands to provide food for the prisoners; excess food was sold to run the prison.

prison subculture: A set of values and norms found in prisons and jails.

prisonization: The phrase used to characterize the way that inmates experience the prison's socialization process.

probable cause: The evidence that a reasonable person would believe to indicate criminal behavior.

probation: A sentence whereby an offender is free in the community but remains under the supervision of the court and must abide by certain requirements or risk being sent to prison.

problem-oriented policing: A concept for police response developed by Herman Goldstein and widely implemented using the SARA model; it applied problem-solving methods to police work.

prosecutor: A primary actor in the courtroom who is responsible for filing criminal charges against a person accused of criminal behavior, based on the evidence presented by the police, and then presenting the state's case against that defendant to a judge and/or jury in the hopes of proving the defendant's guilt.

prostitution: Situations in which individuals provide sexual behaviors in exchange for money; illegal in all states except for Nevada.

pseudo family groups: The relationships that female inmates develop with each other; the majority are more family type in nature than they are intimate.

public defender: An attorney who provides legal representation for defendants who cannot afford to retain their own private legal counsel.

public order crime: A class of crimes that appear to be victimless but are classified as crimes because of the belief that they harm the public order in some way.

pulling-levers policies: With regard to gun crimes, targeted efforts by law enforcement and prosecutors to identify and send a message to specific individuals and groups at risk of gun violence so that they know these offenses will not be tolerated.

pulling-levers policing: A strategy for the implementation of multiple programs at the same time or in succession in order to address a specific problem of crime or disorder.

rape: By common law, when a man had carnal knowledge (e:g:, sexual contact) through force with a woman to whom he was not married.

rational choice theory: The theory that offenders decide to commit crimes for specific purposes.

reasonable suspicion: The legal standard of proof by which a reasonable person would suspect that someone might be engaged in criminal behavior; leads to an investigative detention.

reentry: The process during which an offender becomes reintegrated into the community at large.

registry laws: Laws that require sex offenders to register with the state police; information about registered sex offenders is typically available online.

rehabilitation: The correctional goal of making a criminal into a productive citizen.

reintegration: The correctional goal of moving inmates from the prison environment and integrating them back into society so that they can become productive citizens.

restitution: The correctional goal of having an inmate pay his or her victim for any losses that occurred during the crime, or to pay a fine, forfeit property, or perform community service as a way to reimburse the community.

restorative justice: A philosophy of crime prevention that focuses on restoring the victim and the offender in a way that best serves the greater community; punishing the offender takes a back seat to making the victim whole, shaming the offender, and reintegrating the offender into the community.

retribution: The correctional goal of punishing or disciplining criminal offenders by restricting their freedom and ability to make choices.

revolving door: A phrase that refers to the recidivism rate for offenders.

robbery: The taking of another person's property by force or threat of force; typically defined as a violent crime.

routine activities theory: The theory that crime occurs when three things occur at the same time and in the same location: a motivated offender is present, capable guardians are absent, and vulnerable targets are present.

Rule of Four: The rule stipulating that four of the nine Supreme Court justices must agree to hear a case based on a significant legal question in order for it to move forward.

SARA model: The four-step model created to instruct police officers on problem-oriented policing; the four steps are scanning, analysis, response, and assessment.

saturation patrol: The use of a high number of officers as a show of force to deal with crime at a specific location, at a specific time, and involving specific people.

searches based on exigent circumstances: Legal searches conducted without a warrant, typically when evidence may be destroyed or a person faces imminent danger.

searches incident to arrest: Legal searches conducted without a warrant, after police officers have placed a person under arrest.

self-control theory: The theory that a lack of self-control is the main factor behind deviant behavior.

self-defense: A legal defense, according to which a crime is committed in order to save oneself or someone nearby from death or great harm.

sentencing: The stage of adjudication, after a defendant either pleaded guilty or was found guilty, whereby punishment is formally imposed.

sentencing guidelines: A theory of sentencing according to which judges are provided with specific sentences that must be imposed, based on the seriousness of the offense and characteristics of the offender (such as prior record).

serial killings: Crimes committed by individuals who kill several victims over a period of time.

sheriff: In the early English system of policing, the king's representative of law and order; this role was later adopted in the United States, developing into the county sheriff.

Sheriff's Department/Office: The highest law enforcement position in a county, providing police services to county residents.

skepticism: A principle of science, according to which scientists must question and re-question everything.

social control theory: A theory that asserts that individuals commit crime because of weak bonds to societal institutions.

social disorganization theory: The theory that a community's or neighborhood's level of disorganization contributes to the crime rate in that community or neighborhood.

software crimes: Crimes in which computer software is a primary part of the offense (e.g., theft, counterfeiting, copyright violations, and piracy).

solitary confinement: A type of incarceration in which a prisoner is sentenced to his or her own cell so as to have no other contact with the other inmates and only limited contact with corrections officers.

southern subculture of violence: A phrase used to characterize the higher crime rate in the South, suggesting that Southerners are socialized to accept, and use, violence in certain situations.

special jurisdiction police: Police agencies that do not represent a city, county, or state, but rather have a unique jurisdiction or law enforcement responsibility.

special response teams: A variety of special units designed to respond to high-risk situations needing special skills, weapons, and tactics.

Special Weapons and Tactics (SWAT): The original name for police paramilitary units, created by the Los Angeles Police Department.

specialty courts: Also called problem-solving courts or alternative courts, these courts attempt to reduce the probability of continued criminal behavior by diverting the defendant from trial and placing him or her instead in a treatment program.

specific deterrence: The correctional goal of discouraging offenders from committing additional crimes because they were punished for the first offense and have learned their lesson.

specific intent: A type of intent in which a suspect intended to commit an act, and specific consequences can be associated with that act.

Speedy Trial Act of 1974: A law passed by Congress that defines a "speedy trial" so that there should be no more than 30 days between arrest and indictment, no more than 10 days between indictment and arraignment, and no more than 60 days between arraignment and trial.

split patrols: The policing strategy that involves splitting the police patrol into two groups; one is responsible for calls-for-service, and the other conducts police patrols and investigations.

spoils system: A politically corrupt system in the 19th century, by which those in political power shared in extortion and bribery money; see also *patronage system.*

state crime : crime occurring in a government organization.

state police: A law enforcement agency that represents the state government, often through state-level criminal investigations and the highway patrol.

state supreme courts: Usually the court of last resort in the state; hears cases on appeal from lower state courts to provide answers to questions of legal significance in state cases.

status offenses: A class of offenses that are illegal for juveniles but not adults.

stenographer: A court employee who records all events that occur during a trial, including the testimony of witnesses, oral arguments, objections, rulings by the judge, the judge's instructions, and any verbal comments made during the proceedings.

stocks and pillories: Punishment devices used before prisons; stocks sat low to the ground and locked a person's ankles in place, forcing the person to remain in an upright position, whereas pillories locked a person's neck and wrists into place, forcing the individual to remain standing.

stop and frisk: Based on the Supreme Court case of *Terry v. Ohio* (1968), which allows officers, based on a reasonable suspicion, to stop and detain a person for purposes of a field investigation.

subcultural theory: The theory that subcultural factors contribute to criminal and delinquent behavior.

summary offenses: Minor offenses that the justice system is able to handle fairly quickly (for example, disorderly conduct, public drunkenness, many traffic offenses).

supermax prisons: Correctional facilities in which offenders, typically guilty of violent crimes, are confined in their cells for 23 hours each day and are not able to associate with other inmates.

tactical patrol: The use of patrol officers, often in plainclothes, to respond to potential threats of crime and disorder.

team policing: An early 1970s program that assigned officers permanently to neighborhoods to work with citizens; a forerunner to community policing.

teen courts: Sometimes referred to as youth courts, these courts allow young people to determine the facts of a case and suggest an appropriate punishment while an adult judge in the courtroom oversees the proceedings.

telephone pole design: Type of architectural design of prisons that typically has one or two long corridors with parallel rows of shorter corridors ("poles") that intersect through the longer corridors.

telescoping: Situations in which respondents "indirectly identify the timing of past events."

terrorism: Activities that individuals engage in to create terror and panic in specific groups of individuals.

thief-taker system: In the early English system of policing, the government's practice of paying criminals to turn in other criminals; known more formally as the parliamentary reward system.

third degree: A 19th-century police practice that involved using force to keep people in line and beating confessions out of people.

three generations: The breakdown of the era of community policing into three generations of development, consisting of innovation, diffusion, and institutionalization.

three-strikes laws: Also called habitual offender laws, these laws require that any offender convicted of a third felony must be sentenced to a lengthy term in prison.

transferred intent: A type of intent in which an individual may be held liable for the behavior of others on the assumption that the individual's behavior contributed to the crime.

trial: A legal proceeding in which evidence is presented to a jury or a judge to prove that a defendant committed a crime, alongside evidence that he or she did not, with the underlying premise that the defendant is innocent until proven guilty beyond a reasonable doubt by the state.

trial courts of general jurisdiction (state): State courts that have jurisdiction over general cases.

tribal police: Police agencies that oversee law enforcement on Native American reservations.

truth in sentencing: A sentencing system that forces offenders to serve the majority of the sentence imposed by a judge after conviction.

turner: A term used to describe an inmate who befriends corrections employees in order to manipulate them into breaking the rules.

unauthorized access: Computer crime in which offenders gain access illegally to computer databases to which they do not have legitimate access.

Uniform Crime Reports: A program administered by the FBI as a strategy to collect data about crimes that are reported to the police.

U.S. Court of Appeals for the Federal Circuit: Also referred to as the thirteenth circuit court, this body hears cases from all across the nation related to patent cases, contract cases, and other civil actions in which the United States is a defendant, as well as appeals from the U.S. Court of International Trade, the U.S. Court of Federal Claims, and the U.S. Court of Veterans Appeals, among others.

U:S courts of appeals: Also called intermediate appellate courts, or U.S. circuit courts of appeals, these are the courts of last resort for most appeals in the federal court system; they review cases appealed to them from the federal courts within a given district.

U.S. district courts: General trial courts, and the courts of original jurisdiction, for the federal system.

U.S. Supreme Court: The highest court in the United States; it is largely an appellate court but also has original jurisdiction in some cases.

use of force: The authority for police to use force when necessary:.

use-of-force continuum: The concept that, as force escalates, officers are authorized to use force that is just above the level of force being used against them, typically ranging from presence to the use of deadly force.

venue: The place where a case is heard, typically the court located in the same geographic area in which the criminal behavior occurred.

voluntary manslaughter: Killings that are intentional but in response to some form of provocation, or perceived provocation.

waiver: The process by which a juvenile offender who commits an extremely violent or serious offense can be tried in an adult court if the juvenile judge waives his or her jurisdiction.

ward: In the early English system of policing, a semiformal guard for daytime.

wardens: Correctional administrators who oversee the operations of a prison facility and ensure that the inmates are safe and treated fairly while keeping the facility escape proof to protect the community.

wedding cake model: An analogy used to describe the flow of cases through the criminal justice system.

white-collar crime: A crime committed by individuals as a part of their legitimate occupation.

work release: An alternative sanction that allows offenders to maintain jobs while they are incarcerated.

workload: A model of probation and parole that considers the amount of work completed by officers, rather than the number of offenders.

writ of certification: A legal document in which the Supreme Court justices are asked to respond to a question about a federal law, or to clarify an issue with the federal law.

writ of habeas corpus: A judicial procedure in which an offender's sentence is reviewed to determine whether it is fair or whether the person is being held illegally.

zero-tolerance policing: Based on the broken windows theory that small matters of crime and disorder left unchecked send a signal to the criminal element that the community does not care; instead, this strategy enforces the law on petty crimes and disorder through a no-tolerance policy.

Chapter 1

1. Duke, A. (2012). Lindsay Lohan enters probation "homestretch." *CNN.* Retrieved from http://articles.cnn.com/2012-02-22/entertainment/showbiz_lindsay-lohan-probation_1_court-judge-stephanie-sautner-steve-honig-lohan-lawyer-shawn-holley?_s=PM:SHOWBIZ

2. Boydell, C. L., & Connidis, I. A. (1982). Social system's approach to criminal justice: An overview. In C. L. Boydell & I. A. Connidis (Eds.), *The Canadian criminal justice system.* Toronto, Canada: Holt, Rinehart and Winston of Canada, pp. 3–27.

3. U.S. Bureau of Justice Statistics. (2012). *The justice system.* Retrieved from http://bjs.ojp.usdoj.gov/content/justsys.cfm/

4. Packer, H. L. (1968). *The limits of the criminal sanction.* Stanford, CA: Stanford University Press.

5. Ibid., p. 5.

6. Ibid., p. 6.

7. Ibid., p. 7.

8. Cloud, J. (2011). How the Casey Anthony murder case became the social-media trial of the century. *Time U.S.* Retrieved from http://www.time.com/time/nation/article/0,8599,2077969,00.html

9. Walker, S. (2006). *Sense and nonsense about crime and drugs: A policy guide.* Belmont, CA: Wadsworth, p. 38.

10. Ibid.

11. Ibid., p. 43.

12. Ibid., p. 44.

13. Petersilia, J. (1991). Policy relevance and the future of criminology. The American Society of Criminology, 1990 presidential address. *Criminology, 29*(1), 1–15.

14. Foster, J. P., Magers, J. S., & Mullikin, J. (2007). Observations and reflections on the evolution of crime-related higher education. *Journal of Criminal Justice Education, 18*(1), 123–136.

15. Wellford, C. (1997). *The challenge of crime in a free society: Looking back, looking forward.* Symposium of the 30th anniversary of the President's Commission on Law Enforcement. Washington, DC: U.S. Government Printing Office, p. 1.

16. President's Commission on Law Enforcement and the Administration of Justice. (1967). *The challenge of crime in a free society.* Washington, DC: U.S. Government Printing Office.

17. Ibid., p. 291.

18. U.S. Department of Justice. (1996). *LEAA/OJP: 30 years of federal support to state and local criminal justice.* Washington, DC: U.S. Government Printing Office, p. 3.

19. Durham, A. M., III. (1992). Observations on the future of criminal justice education: Legitimizing the discipline and serving the general university population. *Journal of Criminal Justice Education, 3*(1), 35–52.

20. Castellano, T. C., & Schafer, J. A. (2005). Continuity and discontinuity in competing models of criminal justice education: Evidence from Illinois. *Journal of Criminal Justice Education, 16*(1), 60–78.

21. U.S. Department of Justice. (1996). *LEAA/OJP: 30 years of federal support to state and local criminal justice.* Washington, DC: U.S. Government Printing Office.

22. Foster, J. P., Magers, J. S., & Mullikin, J. (2007). Observations and reflections on the evolution of crime-related higher education. *Journal of Criminal Justice Education, 18*(1), 123–136, p. 134.

23. Ibid.

24. Finckenhauer, J. O. (2005). The quest for quality in criminal justice education. *Justice Quarterly, 22*(4), 413–426.

25. Ibid., p. 419.

26. Hale, D. C. (1998). Delivered at the 34th annual meeting of the Academy of Criminal Justice Sciences, Louisville, Kentucky, March, 1997. Criminal justice education: Traditions in transition. *Justice Quarterly, 15*(3), 385–394.

27. Castellano, T. C., & Schafer, J. A. (2005). Continuity and discontinuity in competing models of criminal justice education: Evidence from Illinois. *Journal of Criminal Justice Education, 16*(1), 60–78.

28. Southerland, M. D., Merla, A. V., Robinson, L., Benekos, J., & Albanese, J. S. (2007). Ensuring quality in criminal justice education: Academic standards and the reemergence of accreditation. *Journal of Criminal Justice Education, 18*(1), 87–105.

29. Bierstedt, R. (1970). *The social order.* New York: McGraw-Hill.

30. U.S. Department of Health and Human Services. (2000). *OPRR guidance on research involving prisoners.* Retrieved from http://www.hhs.gov/ohrp/archive/humansubjects/guidance/prison.htm

31. Clark, R. (2014, April 30). Remembering Stephanie Neiman. Retrieved from http://www.news9.com/story/25392928/remembering-stephanie-neiman-oklahoma-murder-victims-tragic-story

32. Cruise, G. (2014, June 19). Alleged sexual assault victim disapproves of university's response. WHSV.com. Retrieved from http://www.whsv.com/news/headlines/Alleged-Sexual-Assault-Victim-Disproves-of-Universitys-Response-263722991.html

33. Payne, B. K. (2012). *White-collar crime: The essentials.* Thousand Oaks, CA: Sage.

34. Baum, K., & Klaus, P. (2005). *Bureau of Justice Statistics special report on the violent victimization*

NOTES

of college students, 1995–2002. Washington, DC: U.S. Department of Justice.

35. Fisher, B. S., Daigle, L. E., & Cullen, F. T. (2010). *Unsafe in the ivory tower: The sexual victimization of college women.* Thousand Oaks, CA: Sage.

36. Mustaine, E. E., & Tewksbury, R. (2000). Comparing lifestyles of victims, offenders and victim-offenders: A routine activity theory assessment of similarities and differences for criminal incident participants. *Sociological Focus, 33*(3), 339–362.

37. Zane State College Criminal Justice Program. (n.d.). General information: Prospective criminal justice students. Retrieved from http://www.zanestate.edu/files/Prospective_CriminalJustice_Student_Packet.pdf

38. Payne, B. K., Blackwell, B. S., & Collins, S. C. (2011). Exploring the ties between career satisfaction and education: Trait versus situational approaches. *Journal of Criminal Justice Education, 21*(1), 77–92.

39. Payne, B. K., & Chappell, A. (2008). Using student samples in criminological research. *Journal of Criminal Justice Education, 19*(2), 175–192, p. 183.

Chapter 2

1. Sanchez-Jankowski, M. (1991). *Islands in the street: Gangs and American urban society.* Berkeley and Los Angeles: University of California Press, p. 9.

2. Ibid., p. 12.

3. Ibid., p. 13.

4. Tayman, J. (1991). Prof n the hood. *People, 36*(12). Retrieved from http://www.people.com/people/archive/article/0,,20110951,00.html

5. Tappan, P. (1960). *Crime, justice and correction.* New York: McGraw-Hill, p. 10.

6. Nemeth, C. P. (2012). *Criminal law* (2nd ed.). Boca Raton, FL: Taylor & Francis Group, p. 52.

7. Hemmens, C., Brody, D., & Spohn, C. (2009). *Criminal courts.* Newbury Park, CA: Sage, p. 60.

8. Ortmeier, P. J. (1999). *Public safety and security administration.* Boston, MA: Butterworth-Heinemann.

9. Sumner, W. G. (1906). *Folkways: A study of the sociological importance of usages, manners, customs, mores and morals.* Boston, MA: Athenaeum.

10. Kemp, R. S., & Kemp, C. H. (1978). *The developing child.* Cambridge, MA: Harvard University Press, p. 4.

11. American Medical Association. (n.d.). *Opinion 1.02. The relation of law and ethics.* Retrieved http://www.ama-assn.org/ama/pub/physician-resources/medical-ethics/code-medical-ethics/opinion102.page

12. Becker, H. S. (1963). *Outsiders: Studies in the sociology of deviance.* New York: The Free Press, p. 9.

13. Goode, E. (2014). *Drugs in American society.* New York: McGraw-Hill.

14. Merriman, S. A. (2007). *Religion and the law in America: An encyclopedia of personal belief and public policy.* Santa Barbara, CA: ABC-CLIO.

15. Quinney, R. (1974). *Critique of legal order: Crime control in capitalist society.* Boston, MA: Little, Brown.

16. Zajda, J., Majhanovich, S., & Rust, V. (2006). Education and social justice: Issues of liberty and equality in the global culture. *Humanities, Social Sciences and Law, 10,* 1–12, p. 5.

17. Center for Economic and Social Justice. (n.d). Defining economic justice and social justice. Retrieved from http://www.cesj.org/learn/definitions/defining-economic-justice-and-social-justice/

18. Barlow, M. H. (2013). Sustainable justice: 2012 presidential address to the Academy of Criminal Justice Sciences. *Justice Quarterly, 30*(1), 1–17.

19. Rothe, D. L. (2011). Complementary and alternative domestic responses to state crime. In D. L. Rothe & C. W. Mullins (Eds.), *State crime, current perspectives* (pp. 198–218). New Brunswick, NJ: Rutgers University Press.

20. Payne, B. K. (2012). *White-collar crime: The essentials.* Thousand Oaks, CA: Sage.

21. Jacobs, B. A., & Wright, R. (1999). Stick-up, street culture, and offender motivation. *Criminology, 37*(1), 149–174.

22. Taylor, S. S. (2009). How street gangs recruit and socialize members. *Journal of Gang Research, 17,* 1–27.

23. Jacques, S. (2010). The necessary conditions for retaliation: Toward a theory of non-violent and violent forms of drug markets. *Justice Quarterly, 27*(2), 186–205.

24. Gill, M., Bilby, C., & Turbin, V. (1999). Retail security: Understanding what deters shoplifters. *Journal of Security Administration, 22*(1), 29–40.

25. Copes, H., & Vieraitis, L. M. (2012). *Identity thieves: Motives and methods.* Boston, MA: Northeastern University Press.

26. May, D. C., & Wood, P. B. (2010). *Ranking correctional punishments: Views from offenders, practitioners, and the public.* Durham, NC: Carolina Academic Press.

27. Copes, H., & Vieraitis, L. M. (2012). *Identity thieves: Motives and methods.* Boston, MA: Northeastern University Press.

28. Fox, K. A., & Lane, J. (2010). Perceptions of gangs among prosecutors in an emerging gang city. *Journal of Criminal Justice, 36*(4), 595–603.

29. Ibid.

30. Ibid., p. 597.

NOTES

31. Thornberry, T. P., & Krohn, M. D. (2000). The self-report method for measuring delinquency and crime. *Measurement and Analysis in Criminal Justice, 4,* 33–83.

32. Tjaden, P., & Thomas, N. (1998*). Stalking in America: Findings from the National Violence Against Women Survey.* Washington, DC: U.S. Government Printing Office.

33. Pizzaro, J. M., Zgoba, K. M., & Jennings, W. G. (2011). Assessing the interaction between offender and victim lifestyle & homicide type. *Journal of Criminal Justice, 39*(5), 367–377.

34. Ibid., p. 374.

35. Spears, J. W., & Spohn, C. C. (1996). The genuine victim and prosecutors' charging decisions in sexual assault cases. *American Journal of Criminal Justice, 20*(2), 185–205.

36. Baker, S. M., Vaughn, M. S., & Topalli, V. (2008). A review of the powers of bail bond agents and bounty hunters: Exploring legalities and illegalities of quasi-criminal justice officials. *Aggression and Violent Behavior, 13*(2), 124–130.

37. Hartley, C. C. (2001). "He said, she said": The defense attack of credibility in domestic violence felony trials. *Violence Against Women, 7*(5), 510–544.

38. Barak, G. (2001). Newsmaking criminology: Reflections on the media. In J. Muncie & E. McLaughlin (Eds.), *The Sage dictionary of criminology.* London: Sage, p. 190.

39. Stinson, P. M. (2009). *Police crime: A newsmaking criminology study of sworn law enforcement officers arrested,* 2005–2007. Retrieved https://dspace.iup.edu/handle/2069/207

40. Britto, S., & Dabney, D. A. (2010). "Fair and balanced?" Justice issues on political talk shows. *American Journal of Criminal Justice, 35*(4), 198–218.

41. Ibid., p. 211.

42. Payne, B. K. (2012). You're so vain you probably think this keynote is about you: Expanding art and music in criminal justice. *American Journal of Criminal Justice, 37,* 291–305, p. 297.

43. Heckert, D. M. (1997). Lethal violence: A comparative analysis of the natural accoutrements of culture. *Justice Professional, 10*(2), 161–181.

44. Hemmens, C. (1999). Three's a darkness on the edge of town: Merton's five modes of adaptation in the lyrics of Bruce Springsteen. *International Journal of Comparative and Applied Criminal Justice, 23*(1), 127–137.

45. Martin, F., & Lee, A. (2011). *Being left out? The coverage of Latinos in criminal justice and criminology textbooks.* Presented at the Southern Criminal Justice Association, September 22, Nashville, TN.

46. Del Carmen, A., & Bing, R. L. (2000). Academic productivity of African Americans in criminology and criminal justice. *Journal of Criminal Justice Education, 11*(2), 237–249.

47. Ibid., p. 248.

48. Payne, B. K. (2011). *White-collar crime: A text reader.* Thousand Oaks, CA: Sage.

49. Sherman, L. W., & Berk, R. A. (1984). The specific deterrent effects of arrest for domestic assault. *American Sociological Review, 49*(2), 261–272.

50. Ibid., p. 270.

51. Sherman, L. W. (1992). The influence of criminology on criminal law: Evaluating arrests for misdemeanor domestic violence. *Journal of Criminal Law and Criminology, 83*(1), 1–45.

52. Clear, T. R. (2010). Policy and evidence: The challenge to the American Society of Criminology: 2009 Presidential address to the American Society of Criminology. *Criminology, 48*(1), 1–25.

53. Berg, B. L. (2009). *Qualitative research methods for the social sciences* (7th ed.). Boston, MA: Pearson.

54. Rosenhan, D. L. (1973). On being sane in insane places. *Science, 19*(179), 250–258.

55. Rossman, G. B., & Rallis, S. F. (2011). *Learning in the field: An introduction to qualitative research.* Thousand Oaks, CA: Sage, p. 103.

56. Cullen, F., Maakestad, W., & Cavender, G. (1987). *Corporate crime under attack: The Ford Pinto case and beyond.* Cincinnati, OH: Anderson Publishing.

57. Sutherland, E. H. (1937). *The professional thief.* Chicago, IL: Chicago University Press.

58. Ibid., p. 1.

59. Ridley, H. S. (1979). The professional burglar: A case study. *Criminal Justice Review, 4*(1), 85–94.

60. Klockars, C. B. (1974). *The professional fence.* New York: The Free Press; Steffensmeir, D. (1986). *The fence: In the shadow of two worlds.* Totowa, NJ: Rowman and Littlefield.

61. Vaughn, D., & Carlo, G. (1975). The appliance repairman: A study of victim responsiveness and fraud. *Journal of Research in Crime and Delinquency, 12,* 153–161.

62. Travis, L. W., III. (1983). The case study in criminal justice research: Applications to policy analysis. *Criminal Justice Review, 8*(2), 46–51, p. 49.

63. DeLisi, M. (2002). The Columbine High School massacre and criminal justice system response: An exploratory case study. *Social Science Journal, 39*(1), 19–29.

64. Ibid., p. 26.

NOTES

65. Calavita, K., Pontell, H., & Tillmann, R. (1997). The savings and loan debacle, financial crime, and the state. *Annual Review of Sociology, 23*(1), 19–38.

66. Oleson, J. C. (2004). Sipping coffee with a serial killer: On conducting life history interviews with a criminal genius. *Qualitative Report, 9*(2), 192–215.

67. Travis, L. W., III. (1983). The case study in criminal justice research: Applications to policy analysis. *Criminal Justice Review, 8*(2), 46–51.

Chapter 3

1. Blumstein, A., Cohen, J., & Rosenfeld, R. (1991). Trends and deviation in crime rates: A comparison of UCR and NCS data for burglary and robbery. *Criminology, 29*(2), 237–263, p. 238.

2. Chappell, A. T., Monk-Turner, E., & Payne, B. K. (2011). Broken windows or window breakers: The influence of physical and social disorder on quality of life. *Justice Quarterly, 28*(3), 522–540.

3. Blumstein, A., Cohen, J., & Rosenfeld, R. (1991). Trends and deviation in crime rates: A comparison of UCR and NCS data for burglary and robbery. *Criminology, 29*(2), 237–263, p. 238.

4. Rosen, L. (1995). The creation of the uniform crime reports: The role of social science. *Social Science History, 19*(2), 215–238, p. 215.

5. Ibid.

6. Ibid.

7. Federal Bureau of Investigation. (n.d.). *Crime in the United States, 2012.* Retrieved from http://www.fbi.gov/about-us/cjis/ucr/crime-in-the-u.s/2012/crime-in-the-u.s.-2012

8. Ibid.

9. Ibid.

10. Payne, B. K. (2012). *White-collar crime: The essentials.* Thousand Oaks, CA: Sage.

11. Gove, W., Hughes, M., & Geerken, M. (1985). Are uniform crime reports valid indicators of index crimes? An affirmative answer with minor qualifications. *Criminology, 23*, 451–501.

12. Ibid., p. 451.

13. Poston, B. (2012). Crimes underreported to the police include robbery and rape. *Journal Sentinel.* Retrieved from http://www.jsonline.com/watchdog/watchdogreports/crimes-underreported-by-police-include-robbery-rape-e567cu0-167448105.html

14. Ibid.

15. Rosenfeld, R. (2007). Transfer the uniform crime reporting program from the FBI to the Bureau of Justice Statistics. *Criminology & Public Policy, 6*(4), 825–833.

16. Ibid., p. 831.

17. Rand, M. (2006). The National Crime Victimization Survey: 34 years of measuring crime in the United States. *Statistical Journal of the United Nations, 23*, 289–301.

18. Ibid.

19. Ibid.

20. Ibid.

21. Ibid., p. 294.

22. Lee, L., & Carr, J. (2009). Evaluation of a 12-month reference period in the National Crime Victimization Survey (NCVS). Presented at the Federal Committee on Statistical Methodology Conference, Washington, DC.

23. NORC. (2009). Methodological research to support the redesign of the national crime victimization survey. Retrieved from http://www.norc.org/Research/Projects/Pages/methodological-research-to-support-the-redesign-of-the-national-crime-victimization-survey.aspx

24. Blumstein, A., Cohen, J., & Rosenfeld, R. (1991). Trends and deviation in crime rates: A comparison of UCR and NCS data for burglary and robbery. *Criminology, 29*(2), 237–263, p. 238.

25. Baumer, E. P., & Lauritsen, J. L. (2010). Long-term trends in the National Crime Survey (NCS) and National Crime Victimization Survey (NCVS). *Criminology, 48*(1), 131–185.

26. Ibid.

27. Ibid., p. 132.

28. Federal Bureau of Investigation. (n.d.). *Crime in the United States, 2012.* Retrieved April 21, 2014, from http://www.fbi.gov/about-us/cjis/ucr/crime-in-the-u.s/2012/crime-in-the-u.s.-2012

29. Maxfield, M. G. (1999). The National Incident-Based Reporting System: Research and policy applications. *Journal of Qualitative Criminology, 15*(2), 119–149.

30. Ibid.

31. Chilton, R., & Jarvis, J. (1999). Victims and offenders in two crime statistics programs: A comparison of the National Incident-Based Reporting System (NIBRS) and the National Crime Victimization Survey (NCVS). *Criminology, 15*(2), 193–205; Maxfield, M. G. (1999). The National Incident-Based Reporting System: Research and policy applications. *Journal of Qualitative Criminology, 15*(2), 119–149.

32. Maxfield, M. G. (1999). The National Incident-Based Reporting System: Research and policy applications. *Journal of Qualitative Criminology, 15*(2), 119–149, p. 120.

33. Moffit, T. E. (1993). Adolescence-limited and life-course persistent antisocial behavior:

A developmental taxonomy. *Psychological Review,* *100*(4), 674–701.

34. Wolfgang, M. E., Figlio, R. M., & Sellin, T. (1972). *Delinquency in a birth cohort.* Chicago: University of Chicago Press.

35. Glueck, S., & Glueck, E. (1930). *500 criminal careers.* New York: Knopf; Glueck, S., & Glueck, E. (1950). *Unraveling juvenile delinquency.* New York: Commonwealth Fund; Glueck, S., & Glueck, E. (1968). *Delinquents and nondelinquents in perspective.* Cambridge, MA: Harvard University Press.

36. Laub, J. H., & Sampson, R. J. (2003). *Shared beginnings, divergent lives: Delinquent boys to age 70.* Boston, MA: Harvard University Press.

37. Ibid., p. 569.

38. Donohue, J. J., III, & Levitt, S. D. (2001). The impact of legalized abortion on crime. The *Quarterly Economics Journal, 116*(2), 379–420.

39. Chamlin, M. B., Myer, A. J., Sanders, B. A., & Cochran, J. K. (2008). Abortion as crime control: A cautionary tale. *Criminal Justice Policy Review, 19*(2), 135–152; Lott, J. R., & Whitley, J. (2001). Abortion and crime: Unwanted children and out-of-wedlock births. *Economic Inquiry, 45*(2), 304–324.

40. Federal Bureau of Investigation. (n.d.). *Crime in the United States, 2013.* Retrieved from http://www.fbi .gov/about-us/cjis/ucr/crime-in-the-u.s/2013/crime-in-the-u.s.-2013/tables/3tabledatadecoverviewpdf/table_3_crime_in_the_united_states_offense_and_population_distribution_by_region_2013.xls

41. Cohen, D., Nibett, R. E., Bowdle, B. F., & Schwartz, N. (1996). Insult, aggression, and the southern culture of honor: An "experimental" ethnography. *Journal of Personality and Social Psychology, 70*(5), 945–960.

42. Ibid., p. 955.

43. Nisbett, R. E., & Cohen, D. (1996). *Culture of honor: The psychology of violence in the south.* Boulder, CO: Westview.

44. Barber, N. (2009). Is southern violence due to a culture of honor? *Psychology Today,* April 2. Retrieved from https://www.psychologytoday.com/blog/the-human-beast/200904/is-southern-violence-due-culture-honor

45. Miller, J. M. (2011). SCJA presidential address: Southern culture & crime: Considering a theoretical research program for the 21st century. *American Journal of Criminal Justice, 36*(4), 281–292.

46. Buchanan, P. J. (2007). The crime of color. Retrieved from http://buchanan.org/blog/pjb-the-color-of-crime-826

47. Gabbidon, S. L., & Greene, H. T. (2012). *Race and crime* (3rd ed.). Thousand Oaks, CA: Sage, p. 46.

48. Sampson, R. J., & Wilson, W. J. (1995). Towards a theory of race, crime, and urban inequity. In J. Hagen & R. D. Peterson (Eds.), *Crime and inequity.* Palo Alto, CA: Stanford University Press.

49. Ibid., p. 53.

50. Ibid., p. 51.

51. Gottfredson, M. R., & Hirschi, T. (1990). *A general theory of crime.* Palo Alto, CA: Sage.

52. Rose, D. R., & Clear, T. R. (1998). Incarceration, social capital, and crime: Implications for social disorganization theory. *Criminology, 36*(3), 441–480.

53. Miller, K. (2009). Race, driving, and police organization: Modeling moving and nonmoving traffic stops with citizen self-reports on driving practices. *Journal of Criminal Justice, 37*(6), 564–575.

54. Tillyer, R., & Hartley, R. D. (2010). Driving racial profiling research forward: Learning lessons from sentencing research. *Journal of Criminal Justice, 38*(4), 657–665.

55. Moon, B., & Corley, C. J. (2007). Driving across campus: Assessing the impact of drivers' race and gender on police traffic enforcement actions. *Journal of Criminal Justice, 35*(1), 29–37.

56. Ibid., p. 35.

57. Chappell, A. T., & Maggard, S. R. (2007). Applying Black's theory of law to crack and cocaine sentencing. *International Journal of Offender Therapy and Comparative Criminology, 51*(3), 264–278, p. 276.

58. Payne, B. K., & Gainey, R. R. (2009). *Family violence & criminal justice: A life-course approach* (3rd ed.). New Providence, NJ: Matthew Bender.

59. Wright, J. P., Tibbetts, S. G., & Daigle, L. E. (2008). *Criminals in the making: Criminality across the life course.* Thousand Oaks, CA: Sage.

60. Ibid., p. 170.

61. Mollenkott, V. R. (2007). *Omnigender: A trans-religious approach.* Cleveland, OH: Pilgrim Press, p. 22.

62. Dietz, T. L. (1998). An examination of violence and gender role portrayals in video games: Implications for gender socialization and aggressive behavior. *Sex Roles, 28*(5/6), 425–442.

63. Ibid., p. 438.

64. Schwartz, J., & Steffensmeier, D. (2007). The nature of female offending: Patterns and explanations. In R. Zaplin (Ed.), *Female offenders: Critical perspective and effective interventions.* Boston, MA: Jones & Bartlett.

65. Ibid., p. 58.

66. Scott, M. S. (2006). *Problem-oriented guides for police: Drunk driving.* Washington, DC: U.S. Department of Justice.

67. Payne, B. K., Berg, B. L., & Sun, I. Y. (2005). Policing in small town America: Dogs, drunks, disorder, and dysfunction. *Journal of Criminal Justice, 33*(1), 31–41.

68. Ibid.

69. Payne, B. K., & Thompson, A. R. (2008). Sexual assault crisis workers' perceptions of law enforcement. *International Journal of Police Science, 10*, 23–35.

70. Felson, M., & Poulsen, E. (2003). Simple indicators of crime by time of day. *International Journal of Forecasting, 19*(4), 595–601, p. 595.

71. Federal Bureau of Investigation. (n.d.). *Crime in the United States, 2012.* Retrieved from http://www.fbi.gov/about-us/cjis/ucr/crime-in-the-u.s/2012/crime-in-the-u.s.-2012

72. Office of Juvenile Justice and Delinquency Prevention. (2008). Juveniles as offenders: Time of day. Statistical briefing book. Retrieved from http://ojjdp.gov/ojstatbb/offenders/qa03301.asp?qaDate=2008

73. Barak, G. (2003). *Violence and nonviolence: Pathways to understanding.* Thousand Oaks, CA: Sage.

74. Schafer, J. A., Varano, S. P., Jarcis, J. P., & Cancino, J. M. (2010). Bad moon on the rise? Lunar cycles and incidents of crime. *Journal of Criminal Justice, 38*(4), 359–367.

75. Sorg, E. T., & Taylor, R B. (2011). Community-level impacts of temperature on urban street robbery. *Journal of Criminal Justice, 39*(6), 463–470, p. 463.

76. Harris, D. K., & Benson, M. L. (2000). Theft in nursing homes: An overlooked form of elder abuse. *Journal of Alder Abuse & Neglect, 11*(3), 73–90.

77. Cohn, E. G., & Rotton, J. (2003). Even criminals take a holiday: Instrumental and expressive crimes on major and minor holidays. *Journal of Criminal Justice, 31*(4), 351–360, p. 358.

78. Schafer, J. A., Varano, S. P., Jarcis, J. P., & Cancino, J. M. (2010). Bad moon on the rise? Lunar cycles and incidents of crime. *Journal of Criminal Justice, 38*(4), 359–367.

79. Payne, B. K., & Gainey, R. R. (2009). *Family violence & criminal justice: A life-course approach* (3rd ed.). New Providence, NJ: Matthew Bender.

80. Martin, R., Mutchick, R., & Austin, W. (2008). *Criminological thought: Pioneers past and present.* New York: Prentice-Hall.

81. American Psychological Association. (n.d.). Violence & socioeconomic status. Retrieved from http://www.apa.org/pi/ses/resources/publications/factsheet-violence.pdf

82. Ibid.

83. Quinney, R. (1970). *The social reality of crime.* Boston, MA: Little, Brown.

84. Tittle, C. R., Vilemez, W. J., & Smith, D. A. (1978). The myth of social class and crime. *American Sociological Review, 43*(5), 643–656.

85. Sampson, R. J., & Wilson, W. J. (1995). Towards a theory of race, crime, and urban inequity. In J. Hagen & R. D. Peterson (Eds.), *Crime and inequity.* Palo Alto, CA: Stanford University Press, p. 38.

Chapter 4

1. Interlandi, J. (2006). An unwelcome discovery. *New York Times.* Retrieved from http://www.nytimes.com/2006/10/22/magazine/22sciencefraud.html?pagewanted=all&_r=0

2. Dabney, D. (2004). *Crime types: A text reader.* Belmont, CA: Wadsworth.

3. Roberts, A. R., Zgoba, K., & Shahidulluah, S. M. (2007). Recidivism among four types of homicide offenders: An exploratory analysis of 226 homicide offenders in New Jersey. *Aggression and Violent Behavior, 12*(5), 493–507.

4. Federal Bureau of Investigation. (2005). *Serial murder: Multi-disciplinary perspectives for investigators.* Washington, DC: U.S. Department of Justice. Retrieved from http://www.fbi.gov/stats-services/publications/serial-murder

5. Alvarex, A. (1992). Trends and patterns of justifiable homicide: A comparative analysis. *Violence and Victims, 7*(4), 347–356.

6. Blumstein, A., & Rosenfeld, R. (1998). Explaining recent trends in US homicide rates. *Journal of Criminal Law and Criminology, 88*(1), 1175–1124.

7. Ousey, G. C., & Lee, M. R. (2007). Homicide trends and illicit drug markets: Exploring differences across time. *Justice Quarterly, 24*(1), 48–79.

8. Ibid.

9. Blumstein, A., & Rosenfeld, R. (1998). Explaining recent trends in US homicide rates. *Journal of Criminal Law and Criminology, 88*(1), 1175–1124.

10. Ibid., p. 1177.

11. Eng, J. (2012). Jobless rate up, but crime down: What gives? *U.S. News and World Report.* Retrieved from http://usnews.nbcnews.com/_news/2012/01/03/9925171-jobless-rate-up-but-crime-down-what-gives?lite

12. Braga, A. (2002). *Problem oriented policing and crime prevention.* Monsey, NY: Criminal Justice Press.

13. Ibid., p. 5.

14. U.S. Department of Health and Human Services. (2013). *Child maltreatment 2013.* Retrieved from http://www.acf.hhs.gov/sites/default/files/cb/cm2012.pdf#page=16

15. Payne, B. K., & Gainey, R. R. (2009). *Family violence and criminal justice: A life course approach* (3rd ed.). Cincinnati, OH: Anderson.

16. Straus, M. A., & Gelles, R. J. (1986). Societal change and change in family violence from 1975 to 1985 as revealed by two national surveys. *Journal of Marriage and the Family, 48,* 465–479.

17. Johnson, M. P. (1995). Patriarchal terrorism and common couple violence: Two forms of violence against women. *Journal of Marriage and the Family, 57*(2), 283–294.

18. Ibid., p. 283.

19. Walker, L. (1979). *The battered woman.* New York: Harper & Row.

20. Muller, R. (2013, June 22). Revealing the five types of stalkers. *Psychology Today.* Retrieved from http://www.psychologytoday.com/blog/talking-about-trauma/201306/in-the-mind-stalker

21. Mullen, P. E., Pathe, M., Purcell, R., & Stuart, G. W. (1999). Study of stalkers. *American Journal of Psychiatry, 156,* 1244–1249.

22. Payne, B. K., Berg, B. L., & Byars, K. (1999). A qualitative analysis of the similarities and differences of elder abuse definitions among four groups: Nursing home directors, nursing home employees, police chiefs and students. *Journal of Elder Abuse and Neglect, 19*(3/4), 63–85.

23. National Center for Education Statistics. (n.d.). *Indicators of school crime and safety: 2012.* Retrieved from http://nces.ed.gov/pubs2013/2013036.pdf

24. Segal, K., Couweia, J., & Brumfeld, B. (2013, October 21). Mother of girl accused of bullying Florida teen arrested on unrelated charges. *CNN.* http://www.cnn.com/2013/10/17/justice/rebecca-sedwick-bullying-death/

25. Unever, J. D., & Cornell, D. G. (2003). The culture of bullying in middle school. *Journal of School Violence, 29*(2), 5–27.

26. Weiler, R. M., Dorman, S. M., & Pealer, L. N. (1999). The Florida School Violence Policies and Programs Study. *Journal of School Health, 69*(7), 273–279.

27. Langton, L., & Planty, M. (2011). *Hate crime, 2003–2009.* Washington, DC: U.S. Department of Justice. Retrieved from http://www.bjs.gov/content/pub/pdf/hc0309.pdf

28. Thrasher, F. (1927). *The gang.* Chicago, IL: University of Chicago Press.

29. Federal Bureau of Investigation. (2011). *Latest gang threat assessment.* Retrieved from http://www.fbi.gov/news/stories/2011/october/gangs_102011

30. Amato, J. M., & Cornell, D. G. (2003). How do youth claiming gang membership differ from youth who claim membership in another group, such as a crew, clique, posse, or mob? *Journal of Gang Research, 10*(4), 13–23.

31. Federal Bureau of Investigation. (n.d.). *Crime in the United States, 2012.* Washington, DC: U.S. Department of Justice. Retrieved from http://www.fbi.gov/about-us/cjis/ucr/crime-in-the-u.s/2010/crime-in-the-u.s.-2010

32. Greenfield, L. A. (1997). *Sex offenses and offenders: An analysis of data on rape and sexual assault.* Washington, DC: U.S. Department of Justice. Retrieved from http://www.mincava.umn.edu/documents/sexoff/sexoff.html

33. Groth, A. N. (1979). *Men who rape.* New York: Plenum.

34. Payne, B. K., & Gainey, R. R. (2009). *Family violence and criminal justice: A life course approach* (3rd ed.). Cincinnati, OH: Anderson.

35. United States Conference of Catholic Bishops. (2004). *The nature and scope of sexual abuse of minors by Catholic priests and deacons in the United States 1950–2002,* p. 4. Retrieved from http://www.usccb.org/issues-and-action/child-and-youth-protection/upload/The-Nature-and-Scope-of-Sexual-Abuse-of-Minors-by-Catholic-Priests-and-Deacons-in-the-United-States-1950-2002.pdf

36. Rosetti, S. J. (1995). The impact of child abuse on attitudes toward God and the Catholic Church. *Child Abuse and Neglect, 19*(12), 1469–1481.

37. ElSohly, M. A., & Salamone, S. J. (1999). Prevalence of drugs used in cases of alleged sexual assault. *Journal of Analytical Toxicology, 23*(3), 141–146.

38. Fisher, B. S., Cullen, F. T., & Turner, M. G. (2000). *The sexual victimization of college women.* Washington, DC: U.S. Department of Justice. Retrieved from https://www.ncjrs.gov/pdffiles1/nij/182369.pdf

39. Payne, B. K., Ekhomu, J., & Carmody, D. (2009). Structural barriers to preventing and responding to sexual assaults. *Crime Prevention and Community Safety, 11,* 243–257.

40. Payne, B. K., & Gainey, R. R. (2009). *Family violence and criminal justice: A life course approach* (3rd ed.). Cincinnati, OH: Anderson.

41. Payne, B. K. (2011). *Crime & elder abuse: An integrated perspective.* Springfield, IL: Thomas.

42. Federal Bureau of Investigation. (n.d.). *Crime in the United States, 2013.* Washington, DC: U.S. Department of Justice.

43. Luckenbill, D. F. (1980). Patterns of force in robbery. *Deviant Behavior, 1*(3-4), 361–378.

44. Monk, K., Heinonen, J. A., & Eck, J. E. (2010). The problem of street robbery. *Center for Problem-Oriented Policing, 59.*

45. Ibid.

46. Ibid.

47. Wright, R. T., & Decker, S. H. (1997). *Armed robbers in action: Stickups and street culture.* Lebanon, NH: Northeastern University Press.

48. Ibid., p. 72.

49. Willis, K. (2006). Armed robbery: Who commits it and why? *Trends and Issues in Criminal Justice, 328*, p. 4.

50. Ibid.

51. Jacobs, B. A., & Wright, R. (2008). Moralistic street robbery. *Crime & Delinquency, 54*(4), 511–531.

52. Ibid., p. 511.

53. Federal Bureau of Investigation. (n.d.). *Crime in the United States, 2013.* Retrieved from http://www.fbi .gov/about-us/cjis/ucr/crime-in-the-u.s/2013/crime-in-the-u.s.-2013/property-crime/larceny-theft-topic-page

54. Mustaine, E. E., & Tewksbury, R. (1998). Predicting risks of larceny theft victimization: A routine activities approach. *Criminology, 36*(4), 829–857, p. 829.

55. Hollinger, R. (2014). *2012 NRSS executive summary.* Retrieved from http://lpportal.com/academic-viewpoint/item/2966-2012-nrss-executive-summary .html

56. Kansas Bureau of Investigation. (n.d.). *Types of shoplifters.* Retrieved from http://www.accesskansas .org/kbi/info/docs/pdf/Shoplifting.pdf

57. Newman, G. R. (2004). Identity theft. *Center for Problem Oriented Policing.* Retrieved from http:// www.popcenter.org/problems/identity_theft/

58. Ibid.

59. Federal Trade Commission. (2014). *FTC announces top national consumer complaints for 2013.* Retrieved from http://www.ftc.gov/news-events/ press-releases/2014/02/ftc-announces-top-national-consumer-complaints-2013

60. Newman, G. R. (2004). Identity theft. *Center for Problem Oriented Policing.* Retrieved from http://www .popcenter.org/problems/identity_theft/

61. Federal Bureau of Investigation. (n.d.). *Crime in the United States, 2013.* Washington, DC: U.S. Department of Justice.

62. Weisel, D. L. (1999). *Burglary of single-family homes.* Washington, DC: U.S. Department of Justice. Retrieved from http://www.cops.usdoj.gov/pdf/ e07021611.pdf

63. Ibid.

64. Cromwell, P., Olson, J. N., & Avary, D. (2002). Decision strategies of residential burglars. In P. Cromwell (Ed.), *In their own words: Criminals on crime* (3rd. ed.). Los Angeles, CA: Roxbury.

65. Robinson, M. (1998). The time period of heightened risk for repeat burglary victimization. *British Journal of Criminology, 38*(1), 76–85.

66. Poliv, N., Looman, T., Humphries, C., & Pease, K. (1991). The time course of repeat burglary victimization. *British Journal of Criminal Justice, 31*(4), 411–414, p. 411.

67. Harlow, C. W. (1988). *Motor vehicle theft* (Bureau of Justice Statistics special report). Washington, DC: U.S. Department of Justice.

68. Walsh, J. A., & Taylor, R. B. (2007). Predicting decade-long changes in community motor vehicle rates: Impacts of structure and surround. *Journal of Research in Crime and Delinquency, 44*(1), 64–90, p. 64.

69. Ibid., p. 80.

70. Lockwood, B. (2012). The presence and nature of a near-repeat pattern of motor vehicle theft. *Security Journal, 25*(1), 38–56.

71. Ibid.

72. Ibid., p. 38.

73. Klaus, P. (2004). *Carjacking, 1993–2002.* Washington, DC: U.S. Department of Justice.

74. Federal Bureau of Investigation. (n.d.). *Crime in the United States, 2013.* Washington, DC: U.S. Department of Justice.

75. Campbell, R. (2014). *Intentional fires.* Boston, MA: National Fire Protection Association. Retrieved from http://www.nfpa.org/~/media/Files/Research/ NFPA%20reports/Major%20Causes/osin tentional.pdf

76. Stambaugh, H., & Styson, H. (2003). *Special report: Firefighter arson.* Washington, DC: Department of Homeland Security, U.S. Fire Administration.

77. Hall, J. R., Jr. (2007). *Intentional fires and arson.* Boston, MA: National Fire Protection Association.

78. Ibid.

79. Johnson, K. D. (2004). *Underage drinking: Problem oriented guides for police.* Washington, DC: U.S. Department of Justice.

80. U.S. Department of Transportation. (2013). Traffic safety facts. Retrieved from http://www.nrd.nhtsa .dot.gov/Pubs/811870.pdf

81. Flowers, R. B. (1998). *The prostitution of women and girls.* Jefferson, NC: McFarland & Company.

82. Moye, D. (2012). Catarina Migliorini, woman auctioning her virginity, at odds with organizer over charity claims. *Huffington Post.* Retrieved from http://www.huffingtonpost.com/2012/10/05/ catarina-migliorini-virgin-auction_n_1936095 .html

NOTES

83. Fagen, C. (2009). Deflower deal guy pulls out. *New York Post*. Retrieved from http://nypost.com/2009/05/31/deflower-deal-guy-pulls-out-2/

84. Morris, N., & Hawkins, G. J. (1972). *The honest politician's guide to crime control*. Chicago, IL: University of Chicago Press.

85. Ibid., p. 3.

86. Kelling, G. L., & Wilson, J. Q. (1982). Broken windows: The police and neighborhood safety. *The Atlantic, 249*(3), 29–38.

87. Morris, N., & Hawkins, G. J. (1972). *The honest politician's guide to crime control*. Chicago, IL: University of Chicago Press.

88. Dabney, D. (2004). *Crime types: A text reader*. Belmont, CA: Wadsworth.

89. Sutherland, E. (1949). *White-collar crime*. New York: Holt, Rinehart, & Winston.

90. Clinard, M., & Quinney, R. (1973). *Criminal behavior systems: A typology*. New York: Holt, Reinhart, & Winston, p. 164.

91. Payne, B. K. (2012). *White-collar crime: The essentials*. Thousand Oaks, CA: Sage.

92. Ibid.

93. Payne, B. K. (2003). *Incarcerating white-collar offenders*. Springfield, IL: Thomas.

94. Gerber, J. (1994). "Club fed" in Japan? Incarceration experiences of Japanese embezzlers. *International Journal of Offender Therapy and Comparative Criminology, 7*(2), 163–174, p. 164.

95. Payne, B. K. (2012). *White-collar crime: The essentials*. Thousand Oaks, CA: Sage, p. 370.

96. Ibid.

97. Mullins, C. W., & Rothe, D. L. (2008). *Blood, power, and bedlam: Violations in international and criminal law in post-colonial Africa*. New York: Lang, p. 137.

98. Rothe, D. (2009). *State criminality: The crime of all crimes (issues in crime and justice)*. Lanham, MD: Lexington, p. xvii.

99. Rothe, D., & Friedrichs, D. (2006). The state of the criminology of crimes by the state. *Social Justice, 33*, 147–161.

100. Federal Bureau of Investigation. (n.d.). *Organized crime: Glossary of terms*. Washington, DC: U.S. Department of Justice. Retrieved from http://www.fbi.gov/about-us/investigate/organizedcrime/glossary

101. Federal Bureau of Investigation. (n.d.). *Organized crime: Overview*. Washington, DC: U.S. Department of Justice. Retrieved from http://www.fbi.gov/about-us/investigate/organizedcrime/overview

102. Ibid.

103. IMDb. (n.d.). Top 250. Retrieved from http://www.imdb.com/chart/top?ref_=nv_ch_250_4

Chapter 5

1. White, G. F. (1990). Neighborhood permeability and burglary rates. *Justice Quarterly, 7*(1), 57–67.

2. Higgins, G. E., Fell, B. D., & Wilson, A. L. (2007). Low self-control and social learning in understanding stdents' intentions to pirate movies in the United States. *Social Science Computer Review, 25*(3), 339–357.

3. Mustaine, E. E., & Tewksbury, R. (1998). Predicting risks of larceny theft victimization: A routine activities approach. *Criminology, 36*(4), 829–857.

4. Phillips, J. (2010). "Theories are like toothbrushes. . . ." American Counseling Association. Retrieved from http://my.counseling.org/2010/03/04/theories-are-like-toothbrushes/

5. Nagin, D. S., & Pogarsky, G. (2001). Integrating celerity, impulsivity, and extralegal sanction threats into a model of general deterrence: Theory and evidence. *Criminology, 39*, 404–430.

6. Paternoster, R. (2010). How much do we really know about criminal deterrence. *Journal of Law & Criminology, 100*(3), 765–824, p. 781.

7. Clark, R. V., & Cornish, D. B. (1985). Modeling offenders' decision making: A framework for research and policy. In M. Tonry & N. Morris (Eds.), *Crime and justice: An annual review of research* (Vol. 6). Chicago: University of Chicago Press.

8. Guerette, R. T., Stenius, V. M., & McGloin, J. M. (2005). Understanding offense specialization and versatility: A reapplication of the rational choice perspective. *Journal of Criminal Justice, 33*(1), 77–78, p. 79.

9. Bouden, R. (1998). Limitations of rational choice theory. *American Journal of Sociology, 104*(3), 817–828.

10. Guerette, R. T., Stenius, V. M., & McGloin, J. M. (2005). Understanding offense specialization and versatility: A reapplication of the rational choice perspective. *Journal of Criminal Justice, 33*(1), 77–87, p. 79.

11. Cohen, L. E., & Felson, M. (1979). Social change and crime rate trends: A routine activity approach. *American Sociological Review, 44*(4), 588–608.

12. Payne, B. K. (2012). *White-collar crime: The essentials*. Thousand Oaks, CA: Sage.

13. Ibid.

14. Casten, J. A., & Payne, B. K. (2008). The influence of social disorder and victimization on business owners'

decisions to use guardianship. *Journal of Criminal Justice, 36*(5), 396–402.

15. Coren, S., & Hodgson, S. (2011). *Understanding your dog for dummies.* Hoboken, NJ: Wiley.

16. Payne, B. K. (2012). You're so vain you probably think this keynote is about you: Explaining art and music in criminal justice. *American Journal of Criminal Justice, 37*(3), 291–305.

17. Holzman, H. R., Hyatt, R. A., & Dempster, J. M. (2001). Patterns of aggravated assault in public housing: Mapping the nexus of offense, place, gender, and race. *Violence Against Women, 7*(6), 662–685.

18. Kane, R. J. (2006). On the limits of social control: Structural deterrence and the policing of 'suppressible' crimes. *Justice Quarterly, 23*(2), 186–213.

19. Daigle, L. E. (2012). *Victimology: The essentials.* Thousand Oaks, CA: Sage.

20. Payne, B. K. (2011). *White-collar crime: A text reader.* Thousand Oaks, CA: Sage.

21. Parks, K. A., & Fals-Stewart, W. (2004). The temporal relationship between college women's alcohol consumption and victimization experiences. *Alcoholism: Clinical & Experimental Research, 28*(4), 625–629.

22. Ellis, L. (2005). A theory explaining biological correlates of criminality. *European Journal of Criminal Justice, 2*(3), 287–315.

23. Madden, S., Walker, J. T., & Miller, J. M. (2009). The BMI as a somatotopic measure of physique: A rejoinder to Jeremy E. C. Genovese. *Social Science Journal, 46,* 394–401, p. 395.

24. Ibid., p. 395.

25. Wright, R., & Miller, J. (1998). Taboo until today. *Journal of Criminal Justice, 26,* 1–19.

26. Rafter, N. (2004). Earnest A. Hooten and the biological tradition in American criminology. *Criminology, 42*(3), 735–772, p. 736.

27. Fishbein, D. H. (1992). The psychobiology of female aggression. *Criminal Justice and Behavior, 19*(2), 99–126.

28. Raine, A. (2002). The role of prefrontal deficits, low automatic arousal, and early health factors in the development of antisocial and aggressive behaviors in children. *Journal of Child Psychology and Psychiatry, 43*(4), 417–434.

29. Brennan, P. A., & Raine, A. (1997). Biosocial bases of antisocial behavior: Psychophysiological, neurological, and cognitive factors. *Clinical Psychology Review, 17*(6), 589–604, p. 591.

30. Raine, A. (2002). Biosocial studies of antisocial and violent behavior in children and adults: A review. *Journal of Abnormal Child Psychology, 30*(4), 311–326, p. 311.

31. Brennan, P. A., Mednick, S. A., & Volavka, J. (1995). *Biomedical factors in crime.* Washington, DC: CQ Press.

32. Raine, A. (2002). Biosocial studies of antisocial and violent behavior in children and adults: A review. *Journal of Abnormal Child Psychology, 30*(4), 311–326, p. 320.

33. Ellis, L. (2005). A theory explaining biological correlates of criminality. *European Journal of Criminal Justice, 2*(3), 287–315.

34. Dabbs, J. M., Carr, T. S., Frady, R. L., & Raid, J. K. (1995). Testosterone, crime and misbehavior among 692 male prison inmates. *Personality and Individual Differences, 18,* 627–633.

35. Wright, J. P., Beaver, K. M., DeLisi, M., Vaughn, M. G., Boisvert, D., & Vaske, J. (2008). Lombroso's legacy: The miseducation of criminologists. *Journal of Criminal Justice Education, 19*(3), 325–338.

36. Ibid., p. 326.

37. Brennan, P. A., Mednick, S. A., & Volavka, J. (1995). Biomedical factors in crime. In J. Q. Wilson & J. Petersilia (Eds.), *Crime* (pp. 65–90). San Francisco: ICS Press.

38. Wright, J. P., Beaver, K. M., DeLisi, M., Vaughn, M. G., Boisvert, D., & Vaske, J. (2008). Lombroso's legacy: The miseducation of criminologists. *Journal of Criminal Justice Education, 19*(3), 325–338.

39. Wright, J. P., Tibbetts, S. G., & Daigle, L. E. (2008). *Criminals in the making: Criminality across the life course.* Thousand Oaks, CA: Sage.

40. Park, R. E., & Burgess, E. (Eds.). (1925). *The city.* Chicago: University of Chicago Press.

41. Shaw, C., & McKay, H. (1942). *Juvenile delinquency and urban areas.* Chicago: University of Chicago Press.

42. Sampson, R., & Groves, W. B. (1989). Community structure and crime: Testing social disorganization theory. *American Journal of Sociology, 94,* 774–802.

43. Silver, E., & Miller, L. (2004). Sources of informal social contract in Chicago neighborhoods. *Criminology, 42,* 551–583.

44. Wilson, J., & Kelling, G. L. (1982). Broken windows. *Atlantic Monthly,* March 29, 38.

45. Ibid.

46. Cohen, A. K. (1955). *Delinquent boys: The culture of the gang.* New York: Free Press.

47. Miller, W. B. (1958). Lower class culture as a generating milieu of gang delinquency. *Journal of Social Issues, 14*(3), 5–19.

NOTES

48. Cloward, R., & Ohlin, L. (1961). *Delinquency and opportunity: A theory of delinquent gangs.* New York: Free Press.

49. Murphy, D. S., & Robinson, M. B. (2008). The maximizer: Clarifying Merton's theories of anomie and strain. *Theoretical Criminology, 12*(4), 501–521, p. 509.

50. Wolfgang, M. E., & Ferracuti, F. (1967). *The subculture of violence: Towards an integrated theory in criminology.* Thousand Oaks, CA: Sage.

51. Payne, B. K., & Gainey, R. R. (2005). *Family violence & criminal justice: A life-course approach* (2nd ed.). New Providence, NJ: Matthew Bender, p. 48.

52. Anderson, E. (1999). *Code of the streets: Decency, violence, and the moral life of the inner city.* New York: Norton.

53. Ibid., p. 34.

54. Ibid., p. 33.

55. Ibid., p. 34.

56. Jacques, S., & Wright, R. (2012). The code of the suburb & drug dealing. In F. Cullen & P. Wilcox (Eds.), *Oxford handbook of criminological theory.* New York: Oxford University Press.

57. Quinney, R. (1970). *The social reality of crime.* Boston, MA: Little, Brown, as cited in Martin, R., Mutchnick, R., & Austin, W. T. (1990). *Criminological thought.* New York: Macmillan.

58. Jacobs, D. (1979). Inequality and police strength: Conflict theory and coercive control in metropolitan areas. *American Sociological Review, 44*, 913–925, p. 922.

59. Rose, D., & Clear, T. (1998). Incarceration, social capital, and crime: Implications for social disorganization theory. *Criminology, 36*(3), 441–479.

60. Sampson, R. J., & Wilson, W. J. (1995). Toward a theory of race, crime, and urban inequality. In S. Gabbison & H. T. Greene (Eds.), *Race, crime and justice: A reader.* New York: Routledge.

61. Merton, R. K. (1938). Social structure and anomie. *American Sociological Review, 3*(5), 672–682.

62. Murphy, D. S., & Robinson, M. B. (2008). The maximizer: Clarifying Merton's theories of anomie and strain. *Theoretical Criminology, 12*(4), 501–521, p. 502.

63. Messner, S. F., & Rosenfeld, R. (1994) *Crime and the American Dream.* New York: Wadsworth.

64. Messner, S. F., & Rosenfeld, R. (1997). Political restraint of the market and levels of criminal homicide: A cross-national application of institutional-anomie theory. *Social Forces, 75*(4), 1393–1416.

65. Trahan, A., Marquart, J. W., & Mullings, J. (2005). Fraud and the American dream: Toward an understanding of fraud victimization. *Deviant Behavior, 26*(6), 601–620.

66. Schoeffer, A., & Picquero, N. L. (2006). Exploring white-collar crime and the American dream: A partial test of institutional anomie theory. *Journal of Criminal Justice, 34*, 227–235.

67. Laub, J. H., Sampson, R. J., & Sweeten, G. A. (2008). Assessing Sampson and Laub's life-course theory of crime. *Advances in Criminological Theory, 15*, 313–333, p. 314.

68. Ibid.

69. Payne, B. K., & Gainey, R. R. (2009*). Family violence and criminal justice: A life-course approach* (3rd ed.). Providence, NJ: Matthew Bender.

70. Laub, J. H., Sampson, R. J., & Sweeten, G. A. (2008). Assessing Sampson and Laub's life-course theory of crime. *Advances in Criminological Theory, 15*, 313–333.

71. Ibid., p. 323.

72. Ibid., p. 322.

73. Agnew, R. (1992). Foundation for a general strain theory of crime and delinquency. *Criminology, 30*(1), 47–88.

74. Agnew, R. (2001). Building on the foundation of general strain theory: Specifying the types of strain most likely to lead to crime and delinquency. *Journal of Research in Crime and Delinquency, 38*(4), 319–361, p. 321.

75. Agnew, R., Brezina, T., Wright, J. P., & Cullen, F. T. (2002). Strain, personality traits, and delinquency: Extending the general strain theory. *Criminology, 40*(1), 43–71.

76. Ibid.

77. Broidy, L., & Agnew, R. (1997). Gender and crime: A general strain theory perspective. *Journal of Research in Crime and Delinquency, 34*(3), 275–306.

78. Ibid., p. 287.

79. Hirschi, T. (1969). *Causes of delinquency.* Berkeley: University of California Press.

80. Gottfredson, M. R., & Hirschi, T. (1990). *A general theory of crime.* Stanford, CA: Stanford University Press.

81. Ibid., p. 5.

82. Ibid., p. 88.

83. Ibid., p. 90.

84. Gottfredson, M. R., & Hirschi, T. (1993). Commentary: Testing the general theory of crime. *Journal of Research in Crime and Delinquency, 30*(1), 47–54, p. 53.

85. Evans, T. D., Cullen, F. T., Burton, V. S., Head, J. R., Dunway, G., & Benson, M. L. (1997). The social

NOTES

consequences of self-control: Testing the general theory of crime. *Criminology, 35*(3), 475–504.

86. Lagrange, T. C., & Silverman, R. A. (1999). Low self-control and opportunity: Testing the general theory of crime as an explanation for gender differences in delinquency. *Criminology, 37*(1), 41–72.

87. Gottfredson, M. R., & Hirschi, T. (1993). Commentary: Testing the general theory of crime. *Journal of Research in Crime and Delinquency, 30*(1), 47–54.

88. Lagrange, T. C., & Silverman, R. A. (1999). Low self-control and opportunity: Testing the general theory of crime as an explanation for gender differences in delinquency. *Criminology, 37*(1), 41–72.

89. Grasmick, H. G., Tittle, C. R., Bursik, R. J., & Arneklev, B. J. (1993). Testing the core empirical implications of Gottfredson and Hirschi's general theory of crime. *Journal of Research in Crime and Delinquency, 30,* 5–29.

90. Gottfredson, M. R., & Hirschi, T. (1993). Commentary: Testing the general theory of crime. *Journal of Research in Crime and Delinquency, 30*(1), 47–54, p. 48.

91. Sykes, G., & Matza, D. (1957). Techniques of neutralization: A theory of delinquency. *American Sociological Review, 22*(6), 664–670.

92. Coleman, J. W. (1994). *The criminal elite: The sociology of white collar crime.* New York: St. Martin's Press.

93. Minor, W. W. (1981). Techniques of neutralization: A reconceptualization and empirical examination. *Journal of Research in Crime and Delinquency, 18*(2), 295–318.

94. Coleman, J. W. (1994). *The criminal elite: The sociology of white collar crime.* New York: St. Martin's Press.

95. Minor, W. W. (1981). Techniques of neutralization: A reconceptualization and empirical examination. *Journal of Research in Crime and Delinquency, 18*(2), 295–318.

96. Evans, R. D., & Porche, D. A. (2002). The nature and frequency of Medicare/Medicaid fraud and neutralization techniques among speech, occupational, and physical therapists. *Deviant Behavior, 26*(3), 253–270.

97. Gauthier, D. K. (2001). Professional lapses: Occupational deviance and neutralization in veterinary medical practice. *Deviant Behavior, 22*(6), 467–490.

98. Morris, R. G., & Higgins, G. E. (2008). Neutralizing potential and self-reported digital piracy: A multitheoretical exploration among college undergraduates. *Criminal Justice Review, 34*(2), 173–195.

99. Sutherland, E. H. (1939*). Principles of criminology* (3rd ed.). Philadelphia, PA: Lippincott.

100. Akers, R. L. (1973). *Deviant behavior: A social learning approach.* Belmont, CA: Wadsworth.

101. Martin, R., Mutchnick, R., & Austin, W. T. *Criminological thought: Pioneers past and present.* New York: Macmillan.

102. Winfree, L. T., & Bernat, F. P. (1998). Social learning, self-control, and substance abuse by eighth grade students: A tale of two cities. *Journal of Drug Issues, 27*(2), 539–558.

103. Lemert, E. (1951). *Social pathology.* New York: McGraw-Hill.

104. Triplett, R. (1993). The conflict perspective, symbolic interactionism, and the status characteristics hypothesis. *Justice Quarterly, 10*(4), 541–558.

105. Ibid., p. 553.

106. Bernburg, J. G., Krohn, M. D., & Rivera, C. J. (2006). Official labeling, criminal embeddedness, and subsequent delinquency. *Journal of Research in Crime and Delinquency, 43*(1), 67–88, p. 82.

107. Brennan, P. A., & Raine, A. (1997). Biosocial bases of antisocial behavior: Psychophysiological, neurological, and cognitive factors. *Clinical Psychology Review, 17*(6), 589–604, p. 589.

108. Herrnstein, R. (1995). Crimineogenic traits. In J. Q. Wilson & J. Petersilia (Eds.), *Crime.* San Francisco: Institute for Contemporary Studies Press, p. 62.

Chapter 6

1. Haberfeld, M. R., & Cerrah, I. (2010). *Comparative policing: The struggle for democratization.* Thousand Oaks, CA: Sage.

2. Archbold, C. A. (2013). *Policing: A text/reader.* Thousand Oaks, CA: Sage.

3. Diamond, J. (1997). *Guns, germs, and steel: The fates of human societies.* New York: Norton.

4. Ibid., p. 271.

5. Ibid.

6. Reith, C. (1952). *The blind eye of history.* London, England: Faber, p. 20; see also Reith, C. (1938). *The police idea.* Oxford, England: Oxford University Press; Reith, C. (1940). *Police principles and the problem of war.* Oxford, England: Oxford University Press; Reith, C. (1943). *British police and the democratic ideal.* Oxford, England: Oxford University Press; and Reith, C. (1948). *A short history of police.* Oxford, England: Oxford University Press.

7. Diamond, J. (1997). *Guns, germs, and steel: The fates of human societies.* New York: Norton, p. 272.

8. Ibid., p. 278.

NOTES

9. Morris, W. A. (1910). *The frankpledge system.* New York: Longmans, Green.

10. Oliver, W. M., & Hilgenberg, J. F. (2010). *A history of crime and criminal justice in America* (2nd ed.). Durham, NC: Carolina Academic Press.

11. Ibid.

12. Ibid.

13. Beattie, J. M. (2012). *The first English detective: The Bow Street Runners and the policing of London, 1750–1840.* New York: Oxford University Press.

14. Colquhoun, P. (1800). *A treatise on the police of the metropolis.* Retrieved from http://www.gutenberg.org/files/35650/35650-h/35650-h.htm

15. Emsley, C. (2009). *The great British bobby: A history of British policing from the 18th century to the present.* London, England: Quercus; Miller, W. R. (1999). *Cops and bobbies: Police authority in New York and London, 1830-1870* (2nd ed.). Columbus: Ohio State University Press.

16. Russell, F. (1975). *A city in terror: Calvin Coolidge and the 1919 Boston police strike.* Boston, MA: Beacon.

17. Oliver, W. M., & Hilgenberg, J. F. (2010). *A history of crime and criminal justice in America* (2nd ed.). Durham, NC: Carolina Academic Press.

18. Kelling, G. L., & Moore, M. H. (1988). The evolving strategy of policing. *Perspectives on Policing, No. 4.* Washington, DC: National Institute of Justice.

19. Oliver, W. M. (2007). *Homeland security for policing.* Upper Saddle River, NJ: Prentice Hall.

20. Kelling, G. L., & Moore, M. H. (1988). The evolving strategy of policing. *Perspectives on Policing, No. 4.* Washington, DC: National Institute of Justice.

21. Abbott, K. (2007). *Sin in the second city: Madams, ministers, playboys and the battle for America's soul.* New York: Random House.

22. Dash, M. (2007). *Satan's circus: Murder, vice, police corruption, and New York's trial of the century.* New York: Three Rivers Press, p. 50.

23. Skolnick, J. H., & Fyfe, J. J. (1993). *Above the law: Police and the excessive use of force.* New York: Free Press.

24. Kelling, G. L., & Moore, M. H. (1988). The evolving strategy of policing. *Perspectives on Policing, No. 4.* Washington, DC: National Institute of Justice.

25. National Commission on Law Observance and Enforcement. (1931). *Report on the enforcement of the Prohibition laws of the United States.* Washington, DC: U.S. Government Printing Office.

26. Carte, G. E., & Carte, E. H. (1975). *Police reform in the United States: The era of August Vollmer, 1905-1932.* Berkeley: University of California Press.

27. Ibid.

28. Gentry, C. (2001). *J. Edgar Hoover: The man and the secrets.* New York: Norton.

29. Hoover, L. T. (2014). *Police crime control strategies.* Clifton Park, NY: Delmar Cengage.

30. Kelling, G. L., & Moore, M. H. (1988). The evolving strategy of policing. *Perspectives on Policing, No. 4.* Washington, DC: National Institute of Justice.

31. Myer, R. W. (2013). Police-community relations. In K. J. Peak (Ed.), *Encyclopedia of community policing and problem solving* (pp. 284–288). Thousand Oaks, CA: Sage.

32. Oliver, W. M., Marion, N. E., & Hill, J. B. (2014). *Introduction to homeland security: Policy, organization, and administration.* Boston, MA: Jones & Bartlett Learning.

33. Ibid.

34. Ibid.; Oliver, W. M. (2007). *Homeland security for policing.* Upper Saddle River, NJ: Prentice Hall.

35. U.S. Senate. (2012). *Federal support for an involvement in state and local fusion centers.* Washington, DC: Author. Retrieved from http://www.hsgac.senate.gov/subcommittees/investigations/media/investigative-report-criticizes-counterterrorism-reporting-waste-at-state-and-local-intelligence-fusion-centers

36. Ibid.

37. Oliver, W. M. (2007). *Homeland security for policing.* Upper Saddle River, NJ: Prentice Hall; Oliver, W. M., Marion, N. E., & Hill, J. B. (2014). *Introduction to homeland security: Policy, organization, and administration.* Boston, MA: Jones & Bartlett Learning.

38. Oliver, W. M., Marion, N. E., & Hill, J. B. (2014). *Introduction to homeland security: Policy, organization, and administration.* Boston, MA: Jones & Bartlett Learning.

39. Struckhoff, D., & Scott, R. (2004). *The American sheriff.* Washington, DC: Justice Research Institute.

40. Bechtel, H. K. (1995). *State police in the United States: A socio-historical analysis.* Westport, CT: Praeger.

41. Rubenser, L., & Priddy, G. (2011). *Constables, marshals, and more: Forgotten offices in Texas law enforcement.* Denton: University of North Texas Press.

42. Luna-Firebaugh, E. (2007). *Tribal policing: Assessing sovereignty, seeking justice.* Tucson: University of Arizona Press.

43. Bumgarner, J. B. (2006). *Federal agents: The growth of federal law enforcement in America.* Westport, CT: Praeger; Bumgarner, J., Crawford, C., & Burns, R. (2013). *Federal law enforcement: A primer.* Durham, NC: Carolina Academic Press; Marion, N. E., & Oliver, W. M. (2015). *Federal law enforcement agencies in America.* Boston, MA: Jones & Bartlett.

NOTES

44. Bayley, D. H. (2006). *Changing the guard: Developing democratic police abroad.* New York: Oxford University Press.

45. Bureau of Justice Statistics. (n.d.). Local police. Retrieved from http://www.bjs.gov/index.cfm?ty=tp&tid=71

Chapter 7

1. Hoover, L. T. (2014). *Police crime control strategies.* Clifton Park, NY: Delmar Cengage.

2. President's Crime Commission on Law Enforcement and Administration of Justice. (1967). *The challenge of crime in a free society.* Washington, D.C.: U.S. Government Printing Office.

3. Kelling, G. L., Pate, T., Dieckman, D., & Brown, C. E. (1974). *The Kansas City Preventive Patrol Experiment: A summary report.* Washington, D.C.: Police Foundation.

4. Pate, T., Ferrara, A., Bowers, R., & Lorence, J. (1976). *Police response time.* Washington DC: Police Foundation.

5. Greenwood, P. W., Chaiken, J., & Petersilia, J. (1977). *The criminal investigation process.* Lexington, MA: Heath; National Institute of Law Enforcement and Criminal Justice. (1977). *The criminal investigation process: A dialogue on research findings.* Washington, D.C.: U.S. Government Printing Office.

6. Wilson, O. W., & McLaren, R. C. (1977). *Police administration* (4th ed.). New York: McGraw Hill.

7. Cordner, G. W. (1989). The police on patrol. In D. J. Kenney (Ed.), *Police and policing: Contemporary issues.* Westport, CT: Praeger; Gay, W. G., Schell, T. H., & Schack, S. (1977). *Routine patrol: Improving patrol productivity.* Washington, D.C.: National Institute of Justice.

8. Sparrow, M., Moore, M. H., & Kennedy, D. M. (1992). *Beyond 911: A new era for policing.* New York: Basic Books.

9. McEwen, T., Connors, E. F., & Cohen, M. I. (1986). *Evaluation of the Differential Police Response Field Test.* Washington, D.C.: U.S. Government Printing Office; Worden, R. E. (1993). Toward equity and efficiency in law enforcement: Differential police response. *American Journal of Police, 12,* 1–32.

10. Tien, J. M., Simon, J. W., & Larson, R. C. (1977). *An evaluation report of an alternative approach to police patrol: The Wilmington Split Force Experiment.* Cambridge, MA: Public Systems Evaluation.

11. Ibid.

12. *Law Enforcement News.* (1991). Faced with a crime wave, Houston cops "wave back": Intensive patrols hit the streets, but union blasts directive not to field calls for service. *Law Enforcement News,* December 15, p. 3.

13. Kelling, G. L., & Wilson, J. Q. (1982). Broken windows: The police and neighborhood safety. *Atlantic Monthly,* March 1. Retrieved from http://www.theatlantic.com/magazine/archive/1982/03/broken-windows/304465/

14. Kennedy, D. M. (2011). *Don't shoot: One man, a street fellowship, and the end of violence in inner-city America.* New York: Bloomsbury.

15. Kelling, G. L., & Wilson, J. Q. (1982). Broken windows: The police and neighborhood safety. *Atlantic Monthly,* March 1. Retrieved from http://www.theatlantic.com/magazine/archive/1982/03/broken-windows/304465/

16. Oliver, W. M. (2007). *Community-oriented policing: A systemic approach to policing.* Upper Saddle River, NJ: Prentice Hall.

17. Oliver, W. M. (2000). The third generation of community policing: Moving through innovation, diffusion, and institutionalization. *Police Quarterly, 3,* 367–388.

18. Cordner, G. W. (1995). Community policing: Elements and effects. *Police Forum, 5,* 1–8.

19. Roth, J. A., et al. (2000). *National evaluation of the COPS program—Title I of the 1994 crime act.* Washington, D.C.: U.S. Department of Justice.

20. Roh, S., & Oliver, W. M. (2005). Effects of community policing upon fear of crime: Understanding the causal linkage. *Policing: An International Journal of Police Strategies & Management, 28,* 670–683; Zhao, J. S., Scheider, M., & Thurman, Q. C. (2002). The effect of police presence on public fear reduction and satisfaction: A review of the literature. *Justice Professional, 15,* 273–299.

21. Goldstein, H. (1977). *Policing a free society.* New York: HarperCollins.

22. Goldstein, H. (1979). Improving policing: A problem-oriented approach. *Crime & Delinquency, 25,* 236–258.

23. Cordner, G., & Biebel, E. P. (2005). Problem-oriented policing in practice. *Criminology & Public Policy, 4,* 155–180; Weisburd, D., Telep, C. W., Hinkle, J. C., & Eck, J. E. (2010). Is problem-oriented policing effective in reducing crime and disorder? Findings from a Campbell systematic review. *Criminology & Public Policy, 9,* 139–172.

24. See, for instance, McGarrell, E. F., Chermak, S., & Weiss, A. (2002). *Reducing firearms violence through directed police patrol: Final report on the evaluation of the Indianapolis Police Department's Directed Patrol Project.* Washington, D.C.: U.S. Department of Justice; Sherman, L. W., et al. (1998). *Preventing crime: What*

works, what doesn't, what's promising. Washington, D.C.: National Institute of Justice.

25. Hoover, L. T. (2014). *Police crime control strategies.* Clifton Park, NY: Delmar Cengage.

26. Ibid.; McArdle, A., & Erzen, T. (2001). *Zero tolerance: Quality of life and the new police brutality in New York City.* New York: New York University Press.

27. Zimring, F. E. (2012). *The city that became safe: New York's lessons for urban crime and its control.* New York: Oxford University Press.

28. Worden, R. E., & McLean, S. J. (2008). *Tactical patrols: A synopsis.* Albany, NY: John F. Finn Institute for Public Safety.

29. Braga, A. A., & Weisburd, D. L. (2010). *Policing problems places: Crime hot spots and effective prevention.* New York: Oxford University Press.

30. Hoover, L. T. (2014). *Police crime control strategies.* Clifton Park, NY: Delmar Cengage.

31. Kennedy, D. M. (2011). *Don't shoot: One man, a street fellowship, and the end of violence in inner-city America.* New York: Bloomsbury.

32. Jeffery, C. R. (1977). *Crime prevention through environmental design.* Thousand Oaks, CA: Sage.

33. Peak, K. (2013). *Encyclopedia of community policing and problem solving.* Thousand Oaks, CA: Sage.

34. Braga, A. A., Kennedy, D. M., Waring, E. J., & Piehl, A. M. (2001). Problem-oriented policing, deterrence and youth violence: An evaluation of Boston's Operation Ceasefire. *Journal of Research in Crime and Delinquency, 38,* 195–226; Kennedy, D. M. (1998). Pulling levers: Getting deterrence right. *National Institute of Justice Journal, 7,* 2–8.

35. Sherman, L. (1998). Evidence-based policing. *Ideas in American Policing.* Retrieved from http://www .policefoundation.org/content/evidence-based-policing

36. Perry, W. L., et al. (2013). *Predictive policing: The role of crime forecasting in law enforcement operations.* Santa Monica, CA: Rand Corporation.

37. Pearsell, B. (2010). Predictive policing: The future of law enforcement? *NIJ Journal, 266.* Retrieved from http://www.nij.gov/journals/266/Pages/predictive.aspx

38. Bratton, W., & Knobles, P. (1998). *The turnaround: How America's top cop reversed the crime epidemic.* New York: Random House; Henry, V. E. (2002). *The CompStat paradigm: Management accountability in policing, business, and the public sector.* Flushing, NY: Looseleaf Law Publications; Maple, J., & Mitchell, C. (1999). *The crime fighter.* New York: Doubleday.

39. Jang, H. S., Hoover, L. T., & Joo, H. J. (2010). An evaluation of CompStat's effect upon crime: The Fort Worth experience. *Police Quarterly, 13,* 387–412.

40. Kraska, P. B. (2001). *Militarizing the American criminal justice system: The changing roles of the armed forces and the police.* Boston, MA: Northeastern; Kraska, P. B., & Cubellis, L. J. (1997). Militarizing Mayberry and beyond: Making sense of American paramilitary policing. *Justice Quarterly, 14,* 607–629.

41. U.S. Department of Homeland Security. (2008). *National Incident Management System.* Washington, D.C.: Author.

42. Oliver, W. M. (2007). *Homeland security for policing.* Upper Saddle River, NJ: Prentice Hall.

43. U.S. Senate. (2012). *Federal support for and involvement in state and local fusion centers.* Washington, D.C.: Author. Retrieved from http://www .hsgac.senate.gov/subcommittees/investigations/ media/investigative-report-criticizes- counterterrorism-reporting-waste-at-state-and-local- intelligence-fusion-centers

Chapter 8

1. PEST is sometimes associated with PEST analysis in the business world. For more information, see http://www .businessballs.com/pestanalysisfreetemplate.htm

2. The concept of opportunities and threats are often associated with SWOT (strengths, weaknesses, opportunities, and threats) analysis in the business world. For more information, see: http://www .businessballs.com/swotanalysisfreetemplate.htm

3. National Coalition for the Homeless. (2013). A dream denied: The criminalization of homelessness in U.S. cities. Retrieved from http://www.nationalhomeless .org/publications/crimreport/meanestcities.html

4. Hoffmaster, D. A., Murphy, G., McFadden, S., & Griswold, M. (2010). *Police and immigration: How chiefs are leading their communities through the challenges.* Washington, DC: Police Executive Research Forum.

5. *Beck v. Ohio,* 379 U.S. 89 (1964), p. 91.

6. Del Carmen, R., & Walker, J. T. (2011). *Briefs of leading cases in law enforcement* (8th ed.). Cincinnati, OH: Anderson Publishing.

7. *Schneckloth v. Bustamonte,* 412 U.S. 218 (1973).

8. *Chimel v. California,* 395 U.S. 752 (1969).

9. Ibid.

10. The original *Coolidge* case added a third requirement, the discovery of the contraband had to be in advertent, but this requirement was struck down in a later ruling, *Horton v. California* (1990).

11. Michigan State University. (2013). *Program on police consolidation and shared services.* Retrieved from http:// policeconsolidation.msu.edu/

12. Maguire, E. R. (2003). *Organizational structure in American police agencies: Context, complexity, and control.* Albany: State University of New York Press.

13. Ibid.

14. Duffin, A. T. (2010). *History in blue: 160 years of women police, sheriffs, detectives, and state troopers.* New York: Kaplan Publishing.

15. Ibid.

16. Morash, M., & Greene, J. R. (1986). Evaluating women on patrol: A critique of contemporary wisdom. *Evaluation Review, 10,* 231–255; Parsons, D., & Jesilow, P. (2001). *In the same voice: Women and men in law enforcement.* Santa Ana, CA: Seven Locks Press.

17. Barlow, D. E., & Barlow, M. H. (2000). *Police in a multicultural society: An American story.* Long Grove, IL: Waveland.

18. Brown, R. A., & Frank, J. (2006). Race and officer decision making: Examining difference in arrest outcomes between black and white officers. *Justice Quarterly, 23,* 96–126.

19. Barlow, D. E., & Barlow, M. H. (2000). *Police in a multicultural society: An American story.* Long Grove, IL: Waveland.

20. Barron, J. (2013). Colorado marijuana laws worries Cheyenne police chief. Retrieved from http://trib.com/news/local/crime-and-courts/colorado-marijuana-law-worries-cheyenne-police-chief/article_d11ed5c2-0535-5a46-9f1e-b150de8c8f75.html

21. City of Colorado Springs. (2013). Marijuana use policy: Recreational and medical marijuana. Retrieved from http://www.springsgov.com/Page.aspx?NavID=4887

22. Oliver, W. M., & Hilgenberg, J. F., Jr. (2010). *A history of crime and criminal justice in America* (2nd ed.). Durham, NC: Carolina Academic Press.

23. Schultz, P. D. (2013). The future is here: Technology in police departments. *Police Chief.* Retrieved from http://www.policechiefmagazine.org/magazine/index.cfm?article_id=1527&fuseaction=display&issue_id=62008

24. Fenton, J. (2014). Police, privacy advocates clash over cellphone tracking. *Baltimore Sun,* November 22. Retrieved from http://www.baltimoresun.com/news/maryland/baltimore-city/bs-md-ci-stingray-police-tactic-20141122-story.html#page=1; Dvorak, K. (2012). Homeland Security increasingly loaning drones to local police. *Washington Times,* December 10. Retrieved from http://www.washingtontimes.com/news/2012/dec/10/homeland-security-increasingly-loaning-drones-to-l/

25. For more on SWOT Analysis, see: http://www.businessballs.com/swotanalysisfreetemplate.htm

26. Crank, J. P. (1998). *Understanding police culture.* Cincinnati, OH: Anderson Publishing.

27. Ibid.

28. Ibid.; Manning, P. K. (1977). *Police work: The social organization of policing.* Cambridge, MA: MIT Press.

29. Crank, J. P. (1998). *Understanding police culture.* Cincinnati, OH: Anderson Publishing; Fyfe, J. J. (2001). The split-second syndrome and other determinants of police violence. In R. G. Dunham and G. P. Albert (Eds.), *Critical issues in policing* (4th ed., pp. 583–598). Prospect Heights, IL: Waveland.

30. Bittner, E. (1970). *The functions of police in modern society.* Washington, DC: National Institute of Mental Health; Crank, J. P. (1998). *Understanding police culture.* Cincinnati, OH: Anderson Publishing.

31. Bouza, A. (1990). *The police mystique: An insider's look at cops, crime, and the criminal justice system.* New York: Plenum; Crank, J. P. (1998). *Understanding police culture.* Cincinnati, OH: Anderson Publishing.

32. Riksheim, E. C., & Chermak, S. M. (1993). Causes of police behavior revisited. *Journal of Criminal Justice, 21,* 353–382.

33. Klinger, D. (1997). Negotiating order in patrol work: An ecological theory of police response to deviance. *Criminology, 35,* 277–306.

34. Roberg, R., Novak, K., Cordner, G., & Smith, B. (2012). *Police & society* (5th ed.). New York: Oxford University Press.

35. Ibid.

36. Klinger, D. (2004). *Into the kill zone: A cop's eye view of deadly force.* San Francisco, CA: Jossey-Bass.

37. Stevens, D. J. (2008). *Police officer stress: Sources and solutions.* Upper Saddle River, NJ: Prentice Hall.

38. Ibid.

39. Ibid.

40. Kappeler, V. E., Sluder, R. D., & Alpert, G. P. (1998). *Forces of deviance: Understanding the dark side of policing* (2nd ed.). Longrove, IL: Waveland.

41. Champion, D. J. (2001). *Police misconduct in America.* Santa Barbara, CA: ABC-CLIO.

42. Finn, P. (2001). *Citizen review of police: Approaches and implementation.* Washington, DC: National Institute of Justice.

Chapter 9

1. National Advisory Commission on Criminal Justice Standards and Goals. (1973). Records of the Law Enforcement Assistance Administration. Retrieved from http://www.archives.gov/research/guide-fed-records/groups/423.html

NOTES

2. McMillan, J. E. (2010). Electronic documents: Benefits and potential pitfalls. *Future Trends in State Courts 2010.* National Center for State Courts. Retrieved from http://www.ncsc.org; Carson, A. (2004). *Electronic filing and service: An evolution of practice.* Denver, CO: Justice Management Institute.
3. Ibid.
4. Ibid.
5. Ibid.

Chapter 10

1. Dillard, W. T., Johnson, S. R., & Lynch, T. (2003). *A grand façade: How the grand jury was captured by government* (Policy Analysis Paper No. 476). Washington, DC: Cato Institute; Alexander, R. P., & Portman, S. (1974). Grand jury indictment versus prosecution by information—An equal protection-due process issue. *Hastings Law Journal, 25*(4), 997–1016.
2. Carter, T. (2005). The verdict on juries. *ABA Journal,* April 28. Retrieved from http://www.abajournal.com/magazine/article/the_verdict_on_juries/print/

Chapter 11

1. Associated Press. (2011). Pennsylvania judge gets 28 years in "kids for cash" case. NBC News. Retrieved from http://www.nbcnews.com/id/44105072/ns/us_news-crime_and_courts/t/pennsylvania-judge-gets-years-kids-cash-case/#.VBXWOn7D9jo
2. Legal Aid Society. (2010). Criminal court backlogs hurt defendants, warns criminal defense chief Seymour James. Retrieved from http://www.legal-aid.org/en/mediaandpublicinformation/inthenews.
3. Ibid.
4. Clarke, S. H. (1997). *Alaska plea bargaining study, 1974–1976.* ICPSR07714-v2. Ann Arbor, MI: Inter-university Consortium for Political and Social Research [distributor], 1997. http://doi.org/10.3886/ICPSR07714.v2
5. Applegate, B. K., Cullen, F. T., Turner, M. G., & Sundt, J. L. (1996). Assessing public support for three-strikes-and-you're-out laws: Global versus specific attitudes. *Crime and Delinquency, 42.*
6. Marion, N., Farmer, R., & Moore, T. (2005). Financing Ohio supreme court elections 1992–2002: Campaign finance and judicial selection. *Akron Law Review, 38*(3), 567–623.
7. Edwards, H. T. (1989). Judicial misconduct and divining "good behavior" for federal judges. *Michigan Law Review, 87*(1), 765–796.

8. Ibid.
9. Balko, R. (2010). Misbehaving federal prosecutors. Retrieved from http://reason.com/archives/2010/09/27/misbehaving-federal-prosecutor
10. Gershman, B. L. (1986). *Why prosecutors misbehave.* Pace Law Faculty Publications, No. 540. Retrieved from http://digitalcommons.pace.edu/lawfaculty/540
11. Lucas, J. W., Graif, C., & Lovaglia, M. J. (2006). Misconduct in the prosecution of severe crimes: Theory and experimental test. *Social Psychology Quarterly, 69*(1), 97–107.
12. American Bar Association. (2014). *Model rules of professional conduct.* Washington, DC: Author.
13. Cohen, T. (2013, July 22). "Stand your ground" laws up to states, not Obama or Congress. CNNPolitics. Retrieved from http://www.cnn.com/2013/07/22/politics/stand-your-ground/index/html
14. Sullivan, S. (2013, July 15). Everything you need to know about "stand your ground" laws. *Washington Post.* Retrieved from http://www.washingtonpost.com/blogs/the-fix/wp/2013/07/15
15. Lott, J. R., Jr. (2010). *More guns, less crime: Understanding crime and gun control laws* (3rd ed.). Chicago: University of Chicago Press.
16. Cheng, C., & Hoekstra, M. (n.d.). Does strengthening self-defense law deter crime or escalate violence? Evidence from castle doctrine. Retrieved from http://econweb.tamu.edu/mhoekstra/castle_doctrine.pdf
17. McClellan, C., & Tekin, E. (2012). Stand your ground laws, homicides, and injuries. *Bulletin on Aging and Health.* NBER Working Paper No. 18187. Retrieved from http://www.nber.org/papers/w18187
18. Sullivan, S. (2013, July 15). Everything you need to know about "stand your ground" laws. *Washington Post.* Retrieved from http://www.washingtonpost.com/blogs/the-fix/wp/2013/07/15
19. Rousseau, M. (2013, September 16). Report: States with stand your ground laws have increased homicides, complicated prosecutions. Retrieved from http://www.metro.us/boston/news/2013/09/16/report-states-with-stand-your-ground-laws-have-increased-homicides-complicated-prosecutions/
20. Smith, S. (2013, July 15). "No: It would be one more reason to pull the trigger." In Sullivan, S. (2013, July 15). Everything you need to know about "stand your ground" laws. *Washington Post.* Retrieved from http://www.washingtonpost.com/blogs/the-fix/wp/2013/07/15
21. Ibid.
22. McVeigh, K. (2014, March 27). Critics say Georgia stand-your-ground gun law "recipe for unnecessary

killing." *The Guardian*. Retrieved from http://www
.theguardian.com/world/2014/mar/27/georgia-gun-
law-stand-your-ground; Gregg, J. P. (2012, March
28). Some police call N.H. "stand your ground" law a
bad idea. Retrieved from http://www.lawofficer.com/
article/news/some-police-call-nh-stand-your

23. Shepherd., R. (1999). The juvenile court at 100 years.
Juvenile Justice Journal. Retrieved from https://www
.ncjrs.gov/html/ojjdp/jjjournal1299/2.html

24. Ibid.

25. Ibid.

26. Ibid.

27. Vose, B., & Vannan, K. (2013). A jury of your peers.
Journal of Juvenile Justice, 3(1). Retrieved from http://
www.journalofjuvjustice.org/JOJJ0301/article07.htm

28. National Association of Criminal Defense Lawyers.
(2009). *America's problem solving courts*. Washington,
DC: Author, pp. 11–13.

29. National Institute of Justice, Office of Justice
Programs. (2008, May 12). Do drug courts work?
Findings from drug courts research. Retrieved from
http://www.nij.gov/topics/courts/drug-courts/pages/
work.aspx.

30. Trupin, E., & Richards, H. (2003). Seattle's mental
health courts: Early indicators of effectiveness.
International Journal of Law and Psychiatry, 26, 33–53.

31. Cosden, M., Ellens, J., Schnell, J., Yamini-Diouf, Y.,
& Wolfe, M. (2003). Evaluation of a mental health
court with assertive community treatment. *Behavioral
Sciences and the Law, 21*, 415–427; Cosden, M.,
Ellens, J., Schnell, J., & Yamini-Diouf, Y. (2005).
Efficacy of a mental health treatment court with
assertive community treatment. *Behavioral Sciences
and the Law, 23*, 199–214.

32. Moore, M. E., & Hiday, V. A. (2006). Mental health
court outcomes: A comparison of re-arrest severity
between mental health court and traditional court
participants. *Law and Human Behavior, 30*(6), 659–674.

Chapter 12

1. Alschuler, A. W. (2003). The changing purposes of
criminal punishment: A retrospective on the past
century and some thoughts about the next. *University
of Chicago Law Review, 70*, 1–22.

2. See, for instance, Morris, N., & Rothman, D. J. (1995).
*The Oxford history of the prison: The practice of
punishment in Western society*. New York: Oxford
University Press.

3. Foucault, M. (1977). *Discipline & punishment:
The birth of the prison*. New York: Vantage Books;

4. Morris, N., & Rothman, D. J. (1995). *The Oxford
history of the prison: The practice of punishment in
Western society*. New York: Oxford University Press.

4. Schwartz, M. D., & Travis, L. F., III. (1997). *Corrections:
An issues approach* (4th ed.). Cincinnati, OH: Anderson.

5. Ibid.

6. Hirsch, A. J. (1992). *The rise of the penitentiary:
Prisons and punishment in early America*. New Haven,
CT: Yale University Press.

7. Friedman, L. M. (1985). *A history of American law*
(2nd ed.). New York: Touchstone Books; Morris, N.,
& Rothman, D. J. (1995). *The Oxford history of the
prison: The practice of punishment in Western society*.
New York: Oxford University Press.

8. Foote, J. (1976). *Two hundred years of American
criminal justice*. Washington, DC: U.S. Government
Printing Office.

9. Friedman, L. M. (1985). *A history of American law* (2nd
ed.). New York: Touchstone Books, p. 70.

10. Caldwell, R. (1947). *Red Hannah: Delaware's whipping
post*. Philadelphia: University of Pennsylvania Press.

11. Walker, S. (1998). *Popular justice: A history of
American criminal justice* (2nd ed.). New York: Oxford
University Press.

12. Cole, S. A. (2001). *Suspect identities: A history of
fingerprinting and criminal identification*. Cambridge,
MA: Harvard University Press; Friedman, L. M. (1985).
A history of American law (2nd ed.). New York:
Touchstone Books.

13. Lewis, O. F. (1967). *The development of American
prisons and prison customs, 1776–1845*. Montclair, NJ:
Patterson Smith.

14. Haas, K. C. (1999). *Violence in America* (Vol. 1).
New York: Scribner's; Walker, S. (1998). *Popular
justice: A history of American criminal justice*
(2nd ed.). New York: Oxford University Press.

15. Fleming, T. (1997). *Liberty: The American Revolution*.
New York: Viking Press, p. 23.

16. Beccaria, C. (1767/1963). *On crimes and punishments*.
Henry Paolucci (trans.). Indianapolis: Bobbs-Merrill
Educational; retrieved from http://www.constitution
.org/cb/crim_pun.htm and http://www.la.utexas.edu/
research/poltheory/ beccaria/delitti/index.html

17. De Beaumont, G., & de Toqueville, A. (1833). *On the
penitentiary system in the United States and its
application in France*. New York: Augustus M. Kelley
(reprinted, 1970), p. 1.

18. Friedman, L. M. (1985). *A history of American law*
(2nd ed.). New York: Touchstone Books; Teeters, N. K.,
& Shearer, J. D. (1957). *The prison at Philadelphia—
Cherry Hill: The separate system of penal discipline*,

1829–1913. New York: Columbia University Press; Walker, S. (1998). *Popular justice: A history of American criminal justice* (2nd ed.). New York: Oxford University Press.

19. Barnes, H. E. (1968). *The evolution of penology in Pennsylvania: A study in American social history*. Montclair, NJ: Patterson Smith; Teeters, N. K. (1955). *The cradle of the penitentiary: The Walnut Street Jail at Philadelphia, 1773–1835*. Philadelphia: Temple University Press.

20. De Beaumont, G., & de Toqueville, A. (1833). *On the penitentiary system in the United States and its application in France*. New York: Augustus M. Kelley (reprinted, 1970), p. 5.

21. Walker, S. (1998). *Popular justice: A history of American criminal justice* (2nd ed.). New York: Oxford University Press.

22. Ibid.

23. Morris, N., & Rothman, D. J. (1995). *The Oxford history of the prison: The practice of punishment in Western society*. New York: Oxford University Press.

24. Ayers, E. L. (1984). *Vengeance and justice: Crime and punishment in the 19th-century American South*. New York: Oxford University Press, pp. 34–35.

25. Oliver, W. M., & Hilgenberg, J. F., Jr. (2010). *A history of crime and criminal justice in America* (2nd ed.). Durham, NC: Carolina Academic Press.

26. Ibid.

27. Walker, S. (1998). *Popular justice: A history of American criminal justice* (2nd ed.). New York: Oxford University Press.

28. Jenkins, P. (1986). A progressive 'revolution'? Penal reform in Pennsylvania, 1900–1950. In L. A. Knafla (Ed.), *Criminal justice history: An international annual*. (pp. 177–199). Westport, CT: Meckler.

29. Oliver, W. M., & Hilgenberg, J. F., Jr. (2010). *A history of crime and criminal justice in America* (2nd ed.). Durham, NC: Carolina Academic Press.

30. Walker, S. (1998). *Popular justice: A history of American criminal justice* (2nd ed.). New York: Oxford University Press; Zimmerman, J. (1951). The penal reform movement in the South during the Progressive Era, 1890–1917. *Journal of Southern History, 17*(4), 462–492.

31. Killinger, G. G., Wood, J. M., & Cromwell, P. (1979). *Penology: The evolution of corrections in America*. St. Paul, MN: West Publishing, p. 53.

32. Keve, P. W. (1986). *The history of corrections in Virginia*. Charlottesville: University Press of Virginia.

33. Meranze, M. (1999). *Violence in America* (Vol. 2). New York: Scribner's, p. 599.

34. Schwartz, M. D., and Travis, L. F., III (1997). *Corrections: An issues approach* (4th ed.). Cincinnati, OH: Anderson.

35. Ibid.

36. California Department of Corrections and Rehabilitation. Retrieved from http://www.cdcr.ca.gov/Facilities_Locator/PBSP.html

37. Haney, C. (2003). Mental health issues in long-term solitary and supermax confinement. *Crime and Delinquency, 49*, 124–156.

38. Ruddell, R., & Norris, T. (2008). The changing role of wardens: A focus on safety and security. *Corrections Today* (October), 36–39.

39. McCampbell, S. (2002). Making successful new wardens. *Corrections Today* (October), 130–133.

40. Ruddell, R., & Norris, T. (2008). The changing role of wardens: A focus on safety and security. *Corrections Today* (October), 36–39.

41. Hensley, C., & Tewksbury, R. (2005). Wardens' perceptions of prison sex. *Prison Journal, 85*(2), 186–197.

42. Marchese, J. J. (2009). Managing gangs in a correctional facility: What wardens and superintendents need to know. *Corrections Today* (February), 44–47.

Chapter 13

1. Richardson, C. (2012). Former NYPD commissioner Bernard Kerik says "prison is like dying with your eyes open." Retrieved from http://www.nydailynews.com/new-york/nypd-commissioner-bernard-kerik-prison-dying-eyes-open-article-1.1094542

2. Garofalo, J., & Clark, R. D. (1987). The inmate subculture in jails. *Criminal Justice and Behavior, 12*(4), 415–434, p. 417.

3. Bureau of Justice Statistics. (2014). *Local jail inmates and jail facilities*. Retrieved from http://www.bjs.gov/index.cfm?ty=tp&tid=12

4. Austin, J. (1999). As cited in Applegate, B. K., Davis, R. K., Otto, C. W., Surette, R., & McCarthy, B. J. (2003). The multifunction jail: Policymakers' views on the goals of local incarceration. *Criminal Justice Policy Review, 14*, 155–170.

5. Applegate, B. K., Davis, R. K., Otto, C. W., Surette, R., & McCarthy, B. J. (2003). The multifunction jail: Policymakers' views on the goals of local incarceration. *Criminal Justice Policy Review, 14*, 155–170, p. 161.

6. Irwin, J. (1985). *Jails: Managing the underclass in American society*. Berkeley and Los Angeles: University of California Press, p. xi.

NOTES

7. Gibbs, J. (1982). As cited in Klofas, J. M. (1990). The jail and the community. *Justice Quarterly, 7*(1), 69–102.

8. Garofalo, J., & Clark, R. D. (1985). The inmate subculture in jails. *Criminal Justice and Behavior, 12*(4), 415–434, p. 417.

9. RDAP Law Consultants. (n.d.). *The "never" rules of prison.* Retrieved from http://www.rdaplawconsultants.com/prison-life/the-never-rules/

10. Garofalo, J., & Clark, R. D. (1985). The inmate subculture in jails. *Criminal Justice and Behavior, 12*(4), 415–434, p. 416.

11. Proporino, F. J., & Zamble, E. (1984). Coping with imprisonment. *Canadian Journal of Criminology, 26,* 403–422.

12. Sykes, G. M. (2007). *The society of captives: A study of a maximum security prison.* Princeton, NJ: Princeton University Press, p. 78.

13. Ibid., p. 73.

14. Ibid., p. 68.

15. Ibid., p. 77.

16. Proporino, F. J., & Zamble, E. (1984). Coping with imprisonment. *Canadian Journal of Criminology, 26,* 403–422.

17. Listwan, S. J., Sullivan, C. J., Agnew, R., Cullen, F. T., & Colvin, M. (2013). The pains of imprisonment revisited: The impact of strain on inmate recidivism. *Justice Quarterly, 30*(1), 144–168, p. 162.

18. Tewksbury, R., & Connor, D. P. (2012). Inmates who receive visits in prison: Exploring factors that predict. *Federal Probation, 76*(3), 119–123.

19. Kenyon, J. (2013). Senator Nozzolio proposes bill to end conjugal visits in state prisons, put tax dollars to use elsewhere. Retrieved from http://www.cnycentral.com/news/story.aspx?id=956678#.U0MYI1Eb6_w

20. Stinchcomb, J. B. (2002). Prisons of the mind: Lessons learned from home confinement. *Journal of Criminal Justice Educations, 13*(2), 463–479, p. 470.

21. Ibid.

22. Morris, R. G., & Worrall, J. L. (2010). Prison architecture and inmate misconduct: A multilevel assessment. *Crime & Delinquency, 20*(10), 1–27.

23. Ibid., p. 3.

24. Ibid., p. 5.

25. Feld, B. (1981). A comparative analysis of organizational structure and inmate subcultures in institutions for juvenile offenders. *Crime and Delinquency, 27,* 336–363.

26. Morris, R. G., & Worrall, J. L. (2010). Prison architecture and inmate misconduct: A multilevel assessment. *Crime & Delinquency, 20*(10), 1–27.

27. Davidson, R. L. (1931). Prison architecture. *Annals of the American Academy of Political and Social Science, 157,* 33–39, pp. 33, 35.

28. Goldberg, L. T., & Weber, J. M. (2010). The two sides of an intelligent jail. *American Jails, 24*(4), 13–19.

29. Proporino, F. J., & Zamble, E. (1984). Coping with imprisonment. *Canadian Journal of Criminology, 26,* 403–422, p. 416.

30. Phelps, M. S. (2013). The paradox of probation: Community supervision in the age of mass incarcerations. *Law & Policy, 35*(1/2), 51–80.

31. Ibid.

32. Purkiss, M., Kifer, M., Hemmens, C., & Burson, V. S. (2003). Probation officer functions: A statutory analysis. *Federal Probation, 67*(1), 12–23.

33. DeMichele, M., Payne, B. K., & Matz, A. K. (2011). *Community supervision workload considerations for public safety.* Washington, DC: U.S. Department of Justice.

34. Administrative Office of the U.S. Courts. (1976). *The selective presentence investigation report.* Washington, DC: Author.

35. Rosencrance, J. (1988). Maintaining the myth of individualized justice: Probation presentence reports. *Justice Quarterly, 5,* 235–256.

36. Ibid., p. 242.

37. CNN Wire Staff. (2011). Federal report blasts probation officers' handling of Garrido case. Retrieved from http://www.cnn.com/2011/CRIME/07/09/california.garrido.probation/

38. Krebs, J. J., Jones, M., & Jolley, J. M. (2009). Discretionary decision making by probation and parole officers the role of extralegal variables as predictors of responses to technical violations. *Journal of Contemporary Criminal Justice, 25*(4), 424–441.

39. Clark-Miller, J., & Stevens, K. D. (2011). Effective supervision strategies: Do frequent changes of supervision officers affect probationer outcomes? *Federal Probation, 73*(3), 11–18.

40. DeMichele, M., Payne, B. K., & Matz, A. K. (2011). *Community supervision workload considerations for public safety.* Washington, DC: U.S. Department of Justice.

41. Ibid.

42. Clear, T. R. (1985). Managerial issues in community corrections. In Travis, L. (Ed.), *Probation, parole and community corrections.* Prospect Heights, IL: Waveland Press.

43. O'Neil, K. M. (2003). Organizational chance, politics, and the official statistics of punishment. *Sociological Forum, 18*(2), 245–267.

NOTES

44. DeMichele, M., Payne, B. K., & Matz, A. K. (2011). *Community supervision workload considerations for public safety.* Washington, DC: U.S. Department of Justice.

45. Ibid.

46. Clear, T. R. (1985). Managerial issues in community corrections. In Travis, L. (Ed.), *Probation, parole and community corrections.* Prospect Heights, IL: Waveland Press.

47. DeMichele, M., Payne, B. K., & Matz, A. K. (2011). *Community supervision workload considerations for public safety.* Washington, DC: U.S. Department of Justice.

48. Ibid.

49. Tooman, G., & Fluke, J. (2002). Beyond caseload: What workload studies can tell us about enduring issues in the workplace. *Protecting Children, 17*(3), 1–8.

50. Jensen, M. (2002). Reflections of a Southwest border probation chief. *Federal Sentencing Reporter, 14*(5), 225–259, p. 257.

51. McGrath, S. A. (2008). Making "what works" work for rural districts. *Federal Probation, 72*(2).

52. Clark-Miller, J., & Stevens, K. D. (2011). Effective supervision strategies: Do frequent changes of supervision officers affect probationer outcomes? *Federal Probation, 73*(3), 11–18.

53. U.S. Courts. (2013). Supervision costs significantly less than incarceration in the federal system. Retrieved from http://news.uscourts.gov/supervision-costs-significantly-less-incarceration-federal-system

54. U.S. Probation and Pretrial Services. (n.d.). Home confinement. *Courts & Community.* Retrieved from http://www.nhp.uscourts.gov/pdf/cchome.pdf

55. Stinchcomb, J. B. (2002). Prisons of the mind: Lessons learned from home confinement. *Journal of Criminal Justice Educations, 13*(2), 463–479.

56. DeMichele, M., & Payne, B. K. (2010). Electronic supervision and the importance of evidence based practices. *Federal Probation, 74*(2).

57. Martin, J. S., Hanrahan, K., & Bowers, J. H. (2009). Offenders' perceptions of house arrest and electronic monitoring. *Journal of Offender Rehabilitations, 48*(6), 547–570.

58. Payne, B. K., & Gainey, R. R. (1998). A qualitative assessment of the pains experienced by electronic monitoring. *International Journal of Offender Therapy, 42*(2), 149–163; Martin, J. S., Hanrahan, K., & Bowers, J. H. (2009). Offenders' perceptions of house arrest and electronic monitoring. *Journal of Offender Rehabilitations, 48*(6), 547–570.

59. Boyle, D. J., Ragusa, L., Lanterman, J., & Marcus, A. (2011). *Outcomes of a randomized trial of intensive community corrections program-day reporting centers-for parolees.* Washington, DC: National Institute of Justice.

60. Craddock, A. (2004). Estimating criminal justice system costs and cost-saving benefits of day reporting centers, *Journal of Offender Rehabilitation, 39,* 69–98.

61. Roy, S. (2004). Factors related to success and recidivism in a day reporting center. *Criminal Justice Studies, 1,* 3–17.

62. Roy, S. (2004). Factors related to success and recidivism in a day reporting center. *Criminal Justice Studies, 1,* 3–17, p. 4.

63. Champion, D. R., Harvey, P. J., & Schanz, Y. Y. (2011). Day reporting center and recidivism: Comparing offender groups in a western Pennsylvania county study. *Journal of Offender Rehabilitation, 50*(7), 433–446, p. 434.

64. Ibid.

65. Craddock, A. (2004). Estimating criminal justice system costs and cost-saving benefits of day reporting centers, *Journal of Offender Rehabilitation, 39,* 69–98.

66. Boyle, D. J., Ragusa, L., Lanterman, J., & Marcus, A. (2011). *Outcomes of a randomized trial of intensive community corrections program-day reporting centers-for parolees.* Washington, DC: National Institute of Justice.

67. Gowdy, V. B. (1996). Historical perspective. In MacKenzie, D. L., & Hebert, E. E. (Eds.), *Correctional boot camps: A tough intermediate sanction.* Washington, DC: National Institute of Justice, p. 2.

68. Wilson, D. B., MacKenzie, D. L., & Mitchell, F. N. (2008). *Effects of corrections boot camps on offending.* Oslo, Norway: The Campbell Collaboration.

69. Ibid.

70. Ibid., p. 20.

71. Muscar, J. E. (2008). Advocating the end of juvenile boot camps: Why the military model does not belong in the juvenile justice system. *U.C. Davis Journal of Juvenile Law & Policy Review, 12*(1), 1–50, p. 50.

72. National Institute of Justice. (2007). Community service. Retrieved from http://nij.gov/topics/courts/restorative-justice/promising-practices/Pages/community-service.aspx

73. Williams, V. L. (1996). *Dictionary of American penology.* Westport, CT: Greenwood Press.

74. Ibid.

75. Tripodi, S. J., Kim, J. S., & Bender, K. (2010). Is employment associated with reduced recidivism? The complex relationship between employment and

crime. *International Journal of Offender Therapy and Comparative Criminology, 54,* 706–720.

76. New York Department of Corrections and Community Supervision. (2013). *Temporary release program 2012 annual report.* Retrieved from http://www.doccs.ny.gov/Research/Reports/2013/TempReleaseProgram2012.pdf

77. Feldschreiber, S. (2003). Free at last? Work release participation fees and the takings clause. *Fordham Law Review, 72*(1), 207–250, p. 250.

Chapter 14

1. Oberg, T. (2014, September 30). FBI investigating case of inmate left in cell for weeks. Abc13.com. Retrieved from http://abc13.com/news/fbi-investigating-case-of-inmate-left-in-cell-for-weeks-/331720/

2. *Estelle v. Gamble,* U.S. 75-929 (1976).

3. Loomis, D., & Calhoun, G. (1895). *The judicial and civil history of Connecticut.* Boston: Boston History Co.

4. Nevada Department of Corrections. (n.d.). Constitutional rights of inmates. Retrieved from http://www.doc.nv.gov/sites/doc/files/training/south/2013_academy/week_1/inmate_constitutional_rights/Constitutional_Rights_of_Inmates.pdf

5. Oliver, W. M., & Hilgenberg, J. F., Jr. (2010). *A history of crime and criminal justice in America* (2nd ed.). Durham, NC: Carolina Academic Press.

6. Borchardt, D. (2012). The iron curtain redrawn between prisoners and the Constitution. *Columbia Human Rights Law Review, 43*(3), 469–529, pp. 469–470.

7. Neubauer, D. W., & Fradella, H. F. (2013). *America's courts and the criminal justice system.* Belmont, CA: Wadsworth.

8. U.S. Department of Commerce. (1975). *Statistical abstract of the United States, 1975.* Washington, DC: U.S. Government Printing Office; U.S. Department of Commerce. (1985). *Statistical abstract of the United States, 1985.* Washington, DC: U.S. Government Printing Office.

9. Schlanger, M. (2003). Inmate litigation. *Harvard Law Review, 116,* 1557–1657, p. 1557.

10. Gallagher, M. (n.d.). 1980 prison riot a black mark on state's history. Retrieved from http://vivelesmutins.freeservers.com/mexico.html

11. Ibid.

12. Morris, R. (1983). *Devil's butcher shop: The New Mexico prison uprising.* Albuquerque: University of New Mexico Press.

13. Moore, S. (2009). Hundreds hurt in California prison riot. *New York Times.* Retrieved from http://www.nytimes.com/2009/08/10/us/10prison.html

14. Boone, R. (2014). APNewsBreak: FBI investigates prison company. Retrieved from http://www.washingtontimes.com/news/2014/mar/7/apnewsbreak-fbi-investigates-prison-company-cca/

15. Gesch, C. B., Hamond, S. M., Hampson, S. E., Eves, A., & Crowder, M. J. (2002). Influence of supplementary vitamins, minerals and essential fatty acids on the antisocial behavior of young adult prisoners. *British Journal of Psychiatry: The Journal of Mental Science, 181*(1) 22–28.

16. Eves, S., & Gesch, B. (2003). Food provision and the nutritional implications of food choices made by young adult males in a young offenders' institution. *Journal of Human Nutrition and Dietetics, 16*(3), 167–179.

17. de Andrade, D. (2013). Research brief: The criminal careers of a prisoner cohort. *Queensland Corrective Services, 22,* 1–5.

18. Jiang, S., & Fisher-Giorlando, M. F. (2002). Inmate misconduct: A test of deprivation, importation, and situational models. *Prison Journal, 82,* 335–358.

19. Light, S. C. (1991). Assaults on prison officers: Interactional themes. *Justice Quarterly, 8*(2), 243–261.

20. Ibid, p. 258.

21. de Andrade, D. (2013). Research brief: The criminal careers of a prisoner cohort. *Queensland Corrective Services, 22,* 1–5.

22. Man, C. D., & Cronan, J. P. (2001). Forecasting sexual abuse in prison: The prison subculture of masculinity as a backdrop for "deliberate indifference." *Journal of Criminal Law and Criminology, 92*(1/2), 127–186, p. 128.

23. National Institute of Corrections. (n.d.). PREA resources. Retrieved from http://nicic.gov/library/prea/

24. Bates, S. (1936). *Prisons and beyond.* New York: MacMillan, p. 35.

25. *Newman v. Alabama,* 503 F.2d 1320 (5th Circuit) (1974).

26. *Estelle v. Gamble,* 429 U.S. 97 (1976).

27. McCarthy, B. (1981). *Exploratory study of corruption in corrections.* Doctoral dissertation, Florida State University.

28. Burton, D., Erdman, E., Hamilton, G., & Muse, K. (1999). *Women in prison: Sexual misconduct by correctional staff.* Washington, DC: U.S. Government Accountability Office.

29. Layman, E. P., McCampbell, S. W., & Moss, A. (2000). Sexual misconduct in corrections. *American Jails, 14*(5), 23–35.

30. Buell, M., Layman, E., McCampbell, S., & Smith, B. V. (2006). Addressing sexual misconduct in community corrections. *Perspectives, 27*(2), 26–37.

NOTES

31. Worley, R., Marquart, J. W., & Mullings, J. L. (2003). Prison guard perpetrators: An analysis of inmates who established inappropriate relationships with prison staff, 1995–1998. *Deviant Behavior, 24*(2), 175–194, p. 178.

32. Ibid, p. 189.

33. Burton, D., Erdman, E., Hamilton, G., & Muse, K. (1999). *Women in prison: Sexual misconduct by correctional staff.* Washington, DC: U.S. Government Accountability Office.

34. McCarthy, B. (1981). *Exploratory study of corruption in corrections.* Doctoral dissertation, Florida State University.

35. Souryal, S. S. (2009). Deterring corruption by prison personnel: A principle based approach. *Prison Journal, 89*(1), 21–45.

36. Worley, R. M., & Worley, V. B. (2011). Guards gone wild: A self-report study of correctional officer misconduct and the effect of institutional deviance on "care" within the Texas prison system. *Deviant Behavior, 32*(4), 293–319, p. 310.

37. Lambert, E. G., Hogan, N. L., & Barton, S. M. (2002). Satisfied correctional staff: A review of the literature on the correlates of correctional staff job satisfaction. *Criminal Justice and Behavior, 29*(2), 115–143.

38. Pitts, W. J. (2007). Educational competency as an indicator of occupational stress for probation and parole officers. *American Journal of Criminal Justice, 32*, 57–73.

39. Ibid.

40. Slate, R. N., Wells, T. L., & Johnson, W. W. (2003). Opening the manager's door: State probation officer stress and perceptions of participation in workplace decision making. *Crime & Delinquency, 49*(4), 519–541.

41. Holman, B., & Ziedenberg, J. (n.d.). *The dangers of detention: The impact of youth in detention and other secure facilities.* A Justice Policy Institute Report. Retrieved from http://www.justicepolicy.org/images/upload/06-11_rep_dangersofdetention_jj.pdf

42. Peterson-Badali, M., & Koegl, C. J. (2002). Juveniles' experiences of incarceration: The role of correctional staff in peer violence. *Journal of Criminal Justice, 30*, 41–49, p. 47.

43. Stephan, J. J. (2008). *Census of state and federal correctional facilities, 2005.* Washington, DC: Office of Justice Programs.

44. Pollock, S. (2009). You can't have it both ways: Punishment and treatment of imprisoned women. *Journal of Progressive Human Services, 20*(2), 112–128.

45. Griffin, M. L. (2006). Gender and stress: A comparative assessment of sources of stress among correctional officers. *Journal of Contemporary Criminal Justice, 22*(1), 5–25.

46. Gordon, J. A., Proulx, B., & Grant, P. H. (2013). Trepidation among the "keepers": Gendered perceptions of fear and risk of victimization among corrections officers. *American Journal of Criminal justice, 38*(2), 245–265.

47. Griffin, M. L. (2013). The influence of gender in the corrections work environment. In C. M. Renzetti, S. L. Miller, & A. R. Gover (Eds.), *Routledge international handbook of crime and gender studies* (p. 285). New York: Routledge.

48. Moyer, I. L. (1980). Leadership in a women's prison. *Journal of Criminal Justice, 8*(4), 233–241.

49. Moyer, I. L. (1984). Deceptions and realities of life in women's prisons. *Prison Journal, 64*(1), 45–56, p. 55.

50. Huggins, D. W., Capeheart, L., & Newman, E. (2006). Deviants or scapegoats: An examination of pseudofamily groups and dyads in two Texas prisons. *Prison Journal, 86*(1), 114–139.

51. Ibid.

52. Jiang, S., & Winfree, L. T. (2006). Social support, gender, and inmate adjustment to prison life: Insights from a national sample. *Prison Journal, 86*(1), 32–55.

53. Morash, M. (2010). *Women on probation and parole: A feminist critique of community programs & services.* Lebanon, NH: Northeastern University Press.

54. Payne, B. K., & Gainey, R. R. (1998). A qualitative assessment of the pains experienced on electronic monitoring. *International Journal of Offender Therapy and Comparative Criminology, 42*(2), 149–163.

55. Scroggins, K., & Malley, S. (2010). Reentry and the (unmet) needs of women. *Journal of Offender Rehabilitation, 49*, 146–163.

56. DeMichele, M. T., Payne, B. K., & Matz, A. K. (2011). *Community supervision workload considerations for public safety.* Washington, DC: Bureau of Justice Assistance.

57. Haffner, K., Ahmad, J., & Carmen, A. (2005). Probation officers and sex offenders: An examination of personality traits. *Criminal Justice Studies: A Critical Journal of Crime, Law and Society, 18*(2), 197–210.

58. Jenuwine, M. J., Simmons, R., & Swies, E. (2003). Community supervision of sex offenders-integrating probation and clinical treatment. *Federal Probation, 67*(3), 20–25.

59. Fitzgerald, S. (2013). Nation's prisons becoming modern-day asylums for mentally ill. Newsmax. Retrieved from http://www.newsmax.com/US/prison-mental-health-inmates/2013/09/26/id/527895/

NOTES

60. James, D. J., & Glaze, L. E. (2006). *Mental health problems of prison and jail inmates*. Washington, DC: Bureau of Justice Statistics.

61. Skeem, J., Emke-Francis, P., & Eno Louden, J. (2006). Probation, mental health, and mandated treatment: A national survey. *Criminal Justice and Behavior, 33*, 158–184.

62. Hartwell, S. W. (2004). Comparisons of offenders with mental illness only and offenders with dual diagnoses. *Psychiatric Services, 55*(2), 145–150.

63. Louden, J. E., Skeem, J. L., Camp, J., & Christensen, E. (2008). Supervising probationers with mental disorders: How do agencies respond to violations? *Criminal Justice and Behavior, 35*(7), 832–847; Skeem, J., Manchak, S., & Peterson, J. (2011). Correctional policy for offenders with mental illness: Creating a new paradigm for recidivism reduction. *Law and Human Behavior, 35*, 110–126.

64. Skeem, J., Manchak, S., & Peterson, J. (2011). Correctional policy for offenders with mental illness: Creating a new paradigm for recidivism reduction. *Law and Human Behavior, 35*, 110–126.

65. Ibid, p. 121.

66. *Furman v. Georgia*, 408, U.S., 238 (1972).

67. *Gregg v. Georgia*, 428, U.S., 153 (1976).

68. Death Penalty Information Center. (n.d.). *Methods of execution*. Retrieved from http://www.deathpenaltyinfo.org/methods-execution

69. Radelet, M. L., & Pierce, G. L. (2011). Race and death sentencing in North Carolina, 1980-2007. *North Carolina Law Review, 89*, 2119–2159, p. 2120.

70. Phillips, S. (2008). Racial disparities in capital punishment: Blind justice requires a blindfold. American Constitution Society for Law and Policy. Retrieved from https://www.acslaw.org/files/Phillips%20Issue%20Brief.pdf

71. Death Penalty Information Center. (n.d.). Retrieved from http://www.deathpenaltyinfo.org/

72. Van den Haag, E., & Conrad, J. P. (1983). *Death penalty—A debate*. New York: Plenum, p. 229.

73. Bowers, W. J., & Pierce, G. L. (1980). Deterrence or brutalization: What is the effect of executions? *Crime & Delinquency, 26*(4), 453–484.

74. Shepherd, J. M. (2005). Deterrence versus brutalization: Capital punishment's differing impacts among states. *Michigan Law Review, 104*, 203–256, p. 206.

75. Oleson, J. C. (2002). The punitive coma. *California Law Review, 90*(3), 829–901.

76. Pew Research Center for People & the Press (2012). Continued majority support for death penalty: More concern among opponents for wrongful convictions. Retrieved from http://www.people-press.org/2012/01/06/continued-majority-support-for-death-penalty/

77. Maggard, S. R., Payne, B. K., & Chappell, A. T. (2012). Attitudes toward capital punishment: Educational, demographic, and neighborhood crime influences. *Social Science Journal, 49*(2), 155–166.

78. Barkan, S. E., & Cohn, S. F. (2005). Why Whites favor spending more money to fight crime: The role of racial prejudice. *Social Problems, 52*(2), 300–314; Barkan, S. E., & Cohn, S. F. (2005). On reducing white support for the death penalty: A pessimistic appraisal. *Criminology & Public Policy, 4*, 39–44.

79. Bohm, R. M. (2003). American death penalty opinion: Past, present and future. In J. R. Acker, R. M. Bohm, & C. S. Lanier (Eds.), *America's experiment with capital punishment: Reflections on the past, present, and future of the ultimate sanction*. Durham, NC: Carolina Academic Press.

80. Maggard, S. R., Payne, B. K., & Chappell, A. T. (2012). Attitudes toward capital punishment: Educational, demographic, and neighborhood crime influences. *Social Science Journal, 49*(2), 155–166.

81. Cochran, J., & Chamlin, M. (2006). The enduring racial divide in death penalty support. *Journal of Criminal Justice, 34*(1), 85–99, p. 85.

82. Bohm, R. M., & Vogel, B. L. (2004). More than ten years after: The long-term stability of informed death penalty options. *Journal of Criminal Justice, 32*(4), 307–327.

83. Stack, S., Cao, L., & Adamzyck, A. (2007). Crime volume and law and order. *Justice Quarterly, 24*(2), 291–308.

84. Garland, D. W. (2012). You asked: Why does the U.S. have capital punishment? IIP Digital. Retrieved from http://iipdigital.usembassy.gov/st/english/pamphlet/2012/03/201203303047.html#axzz2yKUMSGm

85. Bureau of Justice Statistics. (2011). Prisoner recidivism analysis tool. Retrieved from http://www.bjs.gov/index.cfm?ty=pbdetail&tiid=2392

86. Bahr, S. J., Armstrong, A. H., Gibbs, B. G., Harris, P. E., & Fisher, J. K. (2005). The reentry process: How parolees adjust to release from prison. *Fathering: A Journal of Theory, Research, and Practice About Men as Fathers, 3*(3), 243–265.

87. Ibid.

88. Mellow, J., & Christian, J. (2008). Transitioning offenders to the community: A content analysis of reentry guides. *Journal of Offender Rehabilitation, 47*(4), 339–355.

NOTES

89. Hallett, M. (2012). Reentry to what? Theorizing prisoner reentry in the jobless future. *Critical Criminology, 20*, 213–228, p. 225.

90. Seveenson, M. E., Veeh, C., Burns, K., & Lee, J. (2012). Who goes back to prison; who does not: A multiyear view of reentry program participants. *Journal of Offender Rehabilitation, 51*(5), 295–315, p. 312.

91. Porporino, F. J., & Zamble, E. (1984). Coping with imprisonment. *Canadian Journal of Criminology, 26*, 403–422, p. 403.

92. Tyler, T. (1989). The psychology of procedural justice: A test of the group-value model. *Journal of Personality and Social Psychology, 57*(5), 830–838.

93. Alexander, M. (2010). *The new Jim Crow.* New York: New Press.

94. Urban Institute. (2014). *Returning home: Understanding the challenges of prisoner reentry.* Retrieved from http://www.urban.org/center/jpc/returning-home/

95. Martinson, R. (1974). What works: Questions and answers about prison reform. *Public Interest, 35*, 22–54.

96. Van Wormer, K., & Persson, L. E. (2010). Drug treatment within the U.S. federal prison system: Are treatment needs being met. *Journal of Offender Rehabilitation, 49*(5), 363–375.

97. Turner, S., & Petersilia, J. (1998). Work release: Recidivism and corrections costs in Washington state. *NIJ Brief: Alternatives to Incarceration*, 10–11.

98. Ibid, p. 11.

99. Menkel-Meadow, C. (2007). *Restorative justice: What is it and does it work?* Doctoral dissertation, Georgetown University. Retrieved from http://scholarship.law.georgetown.edu/cgi/viewcontent.cgi?article=1588&context=facpub, p. 104.

Chapter 15

1. Liptak, A. (2008). Inmate count in U.S. dwarfs other nations'. *The New York Times Online.* Retrieved April 9, 2014, from http://www.nytimes.com/2008/04/23/us/23prison.html?pagewanted=all&_r=0

2. Karlen, N. (1995). Greeting from minnesober. *New York Times.* Retrieved from http://www.nytimes.com/1995/05/28/magazine/greetings-from-minnesober.html

3. Lester, D., Motohashi, Y., & Yang, B. (1992). The impact of the economy on suicide and homicide rates in Japan and the United States. *International Journal of Psychiatry, 38*, 314–317, p. 314.

4. Cole, J. H., & Gramajo, A. M. (n.d.). *Female education and homicide rates across countries: Evidence and some explanations.* Retrieved from http://www.fadep.org/documentosfadep_archivos/E-14_female_educaction_and_homicides_rates.pdf

5. Van Dijk, J., van Kesteren, J., & Smit, P. (2007). Criminal victimization in international perspective: Key findings from the 2004-2005 ICVS and EU ICS. *WODC.* Retrieved from http://www.unicri.it/services/library_documentation/publications/icvs/publications/ICVS2004_05report.pdf

6. U.S. Department of State. (n.d.). *U.S. laws on trafficking in persons.* Retrieved from http://www.state.gov/j/tip/laws/

7. 22 U.S. C. § 2656(f)(d)(c).

8. U.S. Department of Justice. (n.d.). *Terrorism, 2002-2005.* Retrieved from http://www.fbi.gov/stats-services/publications/terrorism-2002-2005

9. Ibid.

10. Ibid.

11. Dyson, W. T. (2011). *Terrorism: An investigator's handbook.* Cincinnati, OH: Anderson.

12. Hegeman, R. (2010, February 2). Woman who shot KS abortion doc warns of violence. Retrieved from http://www.komonews.com/news/national/83402272.html

13. Michel, L., & Herbeck, D. (2001). *American terrorist: Timothy McVeigh & the Oklahoma City bombing.* New York: Harper Collins.

14. Leppard, B., & Wynick, A. (2013). *Waco siege 20 years on: Picture timeline of Texas massacre which killed 76 men, women and children.* Retrieved from http://www.mirror.co.uk/news/world-news/waco-siege-20-years-on-1838748

15. Hale, C. (2002). Cybercrime: Facts and figures concerning this global dilemma. *Crime & Justice International, 18*(65), 5, 6, 24–26; Sinrod, E. J., & Reilly, W. P. (2000). Cyber-crimes: A practical approach to the application of federal computer crime laws. *Santa Clara High Technology Law Journal, 16*(2), 178–229.

16. Hollinger, R. C., & Lanza-Kaduce, L. (1988). The process of criminalization: The case of computer crime laws. *Criminology, 26*(1), 114.

17. Richardson, R. (n.d.). *2008 CSI computer crime & security survey: The latest results from the longest-running project of its kind.* Retrieved from http://www.sis.pitt.edu/jjoshi/courses/IS2150/Fall11/CSIsurvey2008.pdf

18. Carter, D. L., & Katz, A, J. (1996). Computer crime: An emerging challenge for law enforcement. *FBI Law Enforcement Bulletin, 65*(12), 1.

19. Ibid.

20. Wiggins, L. M. (2002). Corporate computer crime: Collaborative power in numbers. *Federal Probation, 66(3)*, 19–29.

21. Collin, B. C. (2001). *The future of cyberterrorism: Where the physical and virtual worlds converge.* 11th Annual International Symposium on Criminal Justice Issues. Retrieved from http://afgen.com/terrorism1.html

22. Dorgan, B. (2013). Cyber terror is the new language of war. Retrieved from http://www.huffingtonpost.com/sen-byron-dorgan/cyber-terror-is-the-new-l_b_3612888.html

23. Federal Bureau of Investigation (n.d.). Cyber task force: Building alliances to improve the nation's cybersecurity. Retrieved from http://www.fbi.gov/about-us/investigate/cyber/cyber-task-forces-building-alliances-to-improve-the-nations-cybersecurity-1

24. McMullan, J., & Perreir, D. (2007). The security of gambling and gambling with security: Hacking law enforcement and public policy. *International Gambling Studies, 7*(1), 43–58.

25. Carter, D. L., & Katz, A., J. (1996). Computer crime: An emerging challenge for law enforcement. *FBI Law Enforcement Bulletin, 65*(12), 1; Speer, D. L. (2000). Redefining borders: The challenges of cybercrime. *Crime, Law, and Social Change, 34*(3), 259–273.

26. Payne, B. K. (2012). *White-collar crime: The essentials.* Thousand Oaks, CA: Sage Publication, p. 164.

27. Agingstats.gov (n.d.). *Number of older Americans.* Retrieved from http://www.agingstats.gov/Main_Site/Data/2010_Documents/docs/Population.pdf

28. Payne, B. K. (2011*). Crime & elder abuse: An integrated perspective.* Springfield, IL: Thomas.

29. Payne, B. K., & Gainey, R. R. (2009). *Family violence and criminal justice: A life-course approach* (3rd ed.). Cincinnati, OH: Anderson.

30. Planty, M., & Truman, J. (2013). *Firearm violence, 1993–2011.* Washington, DC: U.S. Department of Justice.

31. Ibid., p. 1.

32. www.handgunlaw.us. (2005). Virginia. Retrieved April 9, 2014 from http://www.handgunlaw.us/states/virginia.pdf

33. Monohan, B. A., & Burke, T. W. (2001). Project Exile: Combating gun violence in America. *FBI Law Enforcement Bulletin, 70*(10), 2–7.

34. Braga, A. A. (2002). *Gun violence among serious young offenders.* Problem Oriented Guides for Police, Problem Specific Guides Series 23. Washington, DC: U.S. Department of Justice.

35. Schilller, D. (1998). *Project Exile.* Retrieved from www.vahv.org/Exile/intro.htm.

36. Melton, R. H. (1998, June 18). Richmond gun project praised. *Washington Post.*

37. Monahan, B. A., & Burke, T. W. (2001). Project Exile: Combating gun violence in America. *FBI Law Enforcement Bulletin, 70*(10) 2–7.

38. Melton, R. H. (1998, June 18). Richmond gun project praised. *Washington Post.*

39. Conner, K. R., & Zhong, Y. (2003). State firearm laws and rates of suicide in men and women. *American Journal of Preventive Medicine, 25*(4), 320–324, p. 320.

40. Miller, M., Azreal, D., & Hemenway, D. (2001). Firearm availability and unintentional firearm deaths. *Accident Analysis and Prevention, 33*, 477–484.

41. Sherman, L. W. (2001). Reducing gun violence: What works, what doesn't, what's promising. In *Perspectives on crimes and justice.* Washington, DC: National Institute of Justice.

42. Ruddell, R., & Mays, G. L. (2005). State background checks and firearms homicides. *Journal of Criminal Justice, 33*(2), 127–136, p. 127.

43. White, H. R., & Gurman, D. M. (2000). Dynamics of the drug crime relationship. In Lafree, G. (Ed.), *Criminal justice 2000.* Washington, DC: U.S. Department of Justice.

44. Altschuler, D. M., & Brounstein, P. J. (1991). Patterns of drug use, drug trafficking, and other delinquency among inner-city adolescent males in Washington, D.C. *Criminology, 29*, 589–621.

45. Baumer, E., Lauritsen, J. L., Rosenfeld, R., & Wright, R. (1998). The influence of crack cocaine on robbery, burglary, and homicide rates: A cross-city, longitudinal analysis. *Journal of Research in Crime and Delinquency, 35*(3), 316–340.

46. Harocopos, A., & Hough, M. (2005). *Drug dealing in open-air markets.* Washington, DC: U.S. Department of Justice.

47. Ibid.

48. Shane, S. (2014). Why Colorado and Washington were wise to legalize pot. *Entrepreneur.* Retrieved from http://www.entrepreneur.com/article/230942#

49. Erb, K. P. (2014). It's no toke: Colorado pulls in millions in marijuana tax revenue. *Forbes.* Retrieved from http://www.forbes.com/sites/kellyphillipserb/2014/03/11/its-no-toke-colorado-pulls-in-millions-in-marijuana-tax-revenue/

NOTES

50. Bohm, R. M. (1993). On the state of criminal justice: 1993 presidential address to the national Academy of Criminal Justice Sciences. *Justice Quarterly, 10,* 529–540.

51. Vito, G. F. (1999). Research and relevance: Role of the Academy of Criminal Justice Sciences. *Justice Quarterly, 16*(1), 1–17, p. 14.

52. Clear, T. R. (2001). Has academic criminal justice come of age? *Justice Quarterly, 18*(4), 709–726, p. 725.

53. Clear, T. R. (2010). Policy and evidence: The challenge to the American Society of Criminology: 2009 presidential address to the American Society of Criminology. *Criminology, 48*(1), 1–25, p. 4.

54. Ibid., p. 2.

55. Petersilia, J. (1991). Policy relevance and the future of criminology. *Criminology, 29*(1), 1–15, p. 5.

56. DeMichele, M., & Payne, B. K. (2012). Measuring community corrections' officials' perceptions of goals, strategies, and workload from a systems perspective: Differences between directors and nondirectors. *Prison Journal, 92*(3), 388–410.

NOTES

INDEX

INDEX

INDEX

INDEX

INDEX

INDEX

INDEX

INDEX

INDEX

INDEX

INDEX